D0908486

THE ILLUSTRATED COLUMBIA ENCYCLOPEDIA

VOLUME 1

A-Apu

THE
ILLUSTRATED

COLUMBIA

This edition is published
and distributed by
Rockville House Publishers, Inc.
by arrangement with COLUMBIA
UNIVERSITY PRESS
NEW YORK & LONDON

ENCYCLOPEDIA

EDITED BY
WILLIAM BRIDGWATER
AND
SEYMOUR KURTZ

THIRD EDITION

Peasant on a mountain road
in Afghanistan.

Alexander the Great in the
Battle of Issus (detail from
a fresco).

COPYRIGHT © COLUMBIA UNIVERSITY PRESS 1963, 1964, 1967, 1969
FIRST EDITION 1935
SECOND EDITION 1950
THIRD EDITION 1963
COPYRIGHT COLUMBIA UNIVERSITY PRESS
1935, 1938, 1940, 1942, 1946, 1950, 1953, 1956
COPYRIGHT UNDER INTERNATIONAL COPYRIGHT UNION
ALL RIGHTS RESERVED

*Except for brief passages to be published in a
review or as citation of authority, no part of
this book may be reproduced in any form without the written permission of the publisher.*

LIBRARY OF CONGRESS CATALOG CARD NUMBER: 63-20205

MANUFACTURED IN THE UNITED STATES OF AMERICA

PREFACE

The Columbia Encyclopedia presents itself in a third edition, fresh as a new-minted penny. Yet it is at the same time old, burnished with tradition as a well-established and standard reference work. Like the two previous editions, this seeks to reach the goal set by Clarke Fisher Ansley, the editor of the first edition in 1935.

This is a general encyclopedia in compact form, ready for instant reference. It is intended to offer simple and accurate information to the ordinary reader on the topics—places, persons, and subjects —that can be condensed in usable form. In today's world it is not possible to condense all human knowledge in capsule size. Yet it is possible to present a small mirror that reflects that vast amount of thought and learning so that a person looking into it may find enough facts and gain enough information to advance upon the road without misgiving. He may also check the facts which he confidently knows. No makers of an encyclopedia can quite succeed in catching the whole sweep of knowledge in the reflection, but the makers of *The Columbia Encyclopedia* have, nevertheless, done their best.

This is an encyclopedia, and not a dictionary. It should be used with a dictionary at hand, for the exact word that must be used to make a statement clear cannot always be the simplest. We offer no definitions except where the article is unintelligible without an initial statement. If no further information can be offered, the heading is omitted.

The Columbia Encyclopedia is intended for the use of specialists but only in the fields outside their specialty. A nuclear physicist should not look up articles on nuclear physics in a general encyclopedia. We can tell him nothing that he does not know already. Yet what the specialist does find here in his own field is a rapid check on dates, bibliographies, and accepted spellings of names. Such data may for the uninformed open gateways to new worlds. We can, and do, offer to the general reader a guide to essential facts and enough information to help him to pursue further his search for knowledge.

The Third Edition brings information on important world events. We have here within the covers of these books accounts of the new space age with astronauts and satellites. The world now has automation and computers and color television. These things are reported in the new edition. The significance of the new edition, however, goes far beyond these obvious facts. The Third Edition is really new. Every article in the Second Edition has been reviewed and revised or replaced wherever the editors felt that change was necessary. By no means all the articles have been changed, for many have been weighed in the balance and found not wanting. They remain as they were in the Second Edition.

Man's activities that lead to knowledge and understanding are never stilled. The face of the universe is perpetually changing as the human mind and human machines explore it. Archaeologists dig and uncover lost cultures. *The Columbia Encyclopedia* must, then, have new articles on old civilizations and new information on ancient cities. Patient men use tape recorders to analyze exactly how a language is spoken. On the basis of these recordings the new scheme of the relationship of languages is established. *The Columbia Encyclopedia* in its full tables of languages presents in schematic form the present state of linguistic knowledge. Scientists discover methods of dating, and old geologic and historic dates must be discarded. A new play of Menander is discovered, and the record of ancient literature is revised. Nothing, no matter how long established, has been considered sacred.

This encyclopedia is intended for American readers, but American interest is not necessarily chauvinistic. Since the appearance of the Second

Edition, the focus of American interest has turned along with world interest. Today it is centered upon continents hitherto neglected. The Third Edition devotes much of its space to Africa and to Asia. Here the countries have emerged into prominence by shaking off colonialism. But even more, the ages lying behind them have grown in Western notice. American readers today must know about the civilizations that lie behind the present Ghana, the present Burma, the present Viet Nam. In the many pages of these books we have tried to present these insofar as Western knowledge of our time allows. Therefore, in the Third Edition, we give whatever facts we can verify about the old and the new cultures of continents that are, historically and prehistorically, more ancient than those of Europe and the Americas.

Yet *The Columbia Encyclopedia* persists in its preoccupation with American interests and American topics. We have listings for every town and city of the United States that has a population of 1,000 or more. Whatever material we could gather we have used. So far as is within our power, we have presented American local economy and history.

We also retain another feature that marked the First Edition and the Second Edition. We have an entry for every proper name in the Authorized Version (King James Version) of the Bible with alternate names and spellings of the revised versions wherever possible. In addition the place entries have been enriched by the discoveries of biblical archaeology, which has been making great strides forward.

Essentially *The Columbia Encyclopedia* offers first aid to all readers, specialist and nonspecialist alike. Such first aid and summaries of essential fact are all that a general encyclopedia can offer successfully in our era, and these are all that *The Columbia Encyclopedia* attempts to give. It does not contain technical treatises, but only ready reference. The substance of all articles is given in language intelligible to the ordinary reader.

The bibliographical suggestions are of this same first-aid nature. The ideal has been to name good books for reasonably elementary information. In some cases it has been impossible to list such books, and instead books in foreign languages and of a fairly technical nature have been given. These can easily be ignored by the reader who does not know the language or does not have the technical background to understand them. Enough suggestions are in most instances offered to enable any student to pursue the subject.

Since the encyclopedia is comprehensive there is necessarily a severe contest for space. To make as thorough use of space as possible, the system of inner cross reference is used. Information given under one heading is generally not repeated under another. Instead the reader is directed to the major heading that contains the information by printing the reference to that article in SMALL CAPITALS. The reader may benefit greatly by mastering this simple system at once.

The figures given in the separate articles are, so far as possible, taken from the most authoritative sources. For population figures, for example, the contributors and editors have had recourse to the most recent censuses or statistical publications. The best available official estimates have been utilized, but where for one reason or another the official estimates have proved unsatisfactory, unofficial estimates have been offered tentatively, though bitter experience has taught that both official and unofficial figures must be used with care. We have attempted to use that care. We do not give the very latest figures available on production, exports, imports, and the like. Such figures would be outdated by the time the book could be printed and offered on the market. We have, therefore, offered only such figures as would seem to be reasonably accurate and useful for the space of a few years.

The Columbia Encyclopedia is not the voice of opinion. Insofar as is humanly possible the editors give only generally accepted judgments. The ideal has been to summarize the general and accepted judgments rather than the individual interpretation, however brilliant. These books are intended to be a survey of prevailing views, as any worth-while general encyclopedia should and must be. When faced with a matter in great contention, the editors have tried to present the opposing views fairly, without bias or distortion. These books are essentially a repository of information, not of unestablished theory. The fundamental effort has been to collect the opinions of recognized authorities and to reproduce them without prejudice. Being human, the editors may have failed in their efforts to be objective, as all humans must. But we can only say that we have tried. Religious, political, and racial bigotry are given no voice in these books, and the prescription against them has been applied both to the "liberal" and the "conservative" views. As good editors of an encyclopedia, we present only the full spectrum of the opinions of others.

For this reason the articles are unsigned. They do not represent the expression of any one person. They have been sieved and filtered through many minds. In order to present unbiased articles we have had them reviewed by persons of many opinions. The result cannot help but be résumés of facts undeniable by any. These articles are not personal, they are anonymously objective.

To present the number of subjects that we offer in brief form for the general reader, special writing techniques must be employed. The actual final form of articles has, of course, been the responsibility of the editors themselves. They are trained in the methods of presenting factual material as simply and as briefly as possible. When they manage to present color and feeling also, so much the better. But the fundamental aim has been to present fact, not sentiment.

We have tried in these books to tell the reader how he may deal with foreign names. The pronunciations that we offer are not, of course, exact or linguistically scientific. They are simply signs that may be used to pronounce foreign names in polite society without disgrace.

This encyclopedia is neither an official nor an unofficial publication of Columbia University. Yet we must say in all humility that without Columbia University this book would have been impossible. We have been shameless in tapping the enormous sources of learning on Morningside Heights. It has been a never-ceasing pleasure to learn over again, day after day, that the men and women who have learning in their familiar possession are willing— even anxious—to share it. Since we are constrained by space, we cannot possibly list all the Columbia scholars who have given their time and their immense stores of knowledge to help us. Ungrudgingly they have given hours of their precious time. But it is not for the editors of *The Columbia Encyclopedia* to be grateful. They did not give their time to us; they gave to the many users of this book. We can only hope that those users will be at least a little aware of the immense debt they owe learned men and women of Morningside Heights.

We are, however, personally indebted to the almost overpatient members of the staff of the Columbia Libraries, who have helped and guided and informed all of us as we struggled to find out dates, facts, and controversial opinions. For their knowledge and their tact we are grateful.

We are grateful, too, to our readers. We have received thousands of letters, and our gratitude to the letter writers is beyond measure. It is for readers that we produce these books. An amazing number of those readers have knowledge that escapes even the pundits of Morningside Heights. For the letters of praise, censure, and correction, we can do nothing but say a weak, yet heartfelt *thank you.*

The editors of *The Columbia Encyclopedia* wish expressly to thank Frank D. Fackenthal, Chairman of the Board, Columbia University Press, for his unfaltering devotion to *The Columbia Encyclopedia,* for his staunch kindliness, for his true wisdom in viewing the troublesome problems of a major encyclopedia, and Charles G. Proffitt, President and Director, Columbia University Press, who has been from the very inception of the encyclopedia thirty-five years ago its guide and mentor and is the godparent of the Third Edition. Finally we wish to thank Eugenia Porter, Production Manager, who guided the book through the Second Edition and the Third Edition.

A special feature of this edition of The Illustrated Columbia Encyclopedia is the Supplementary Record of Events included in the last volume.

THE COLUMBIA ENCYCLOPEDIA

Editors: WILLIAM BRIDGWATER and SEYMOUR KURTZ

BEATRICE ALDRICH   EDITH P. HAZEN   ALICE R. STODDARD

Staff Editors

Edith Firoozi	Julio A. de la Torre	Stanley S. Amdurer
Barbara A. Goettel	Carla Greenhaus	Pamela Whittaker
David Syrett	Gwendolyn Jones	Beverlee Galli
Daniel J. Leab	Allan Knee	Lucie G. Nelson
Franklin N. Furness	Elizabeth M. Evanson	Trudy L. Hayden

Barry S. Augenbraun, Kenneth Bridenthal, Ariane Brunel, Nancy Caldwell, Alan Cary, Raymond J. Dixon, Jane S. Fix, Wilson R. Gathings, David Golding, Walter Hightower, Elva D. Hoover, Henry E. Isola, Ira Klein, Herbert Koenig, Jeanette Y. Kovalink, Katharine A. Peckham, Wassyl Znayenko, David Zucker

Editorial Assistants

Mary Jane Alexander, Helen Bajan, Cathleen N. Bingham, Dolores R. Bloesch, Donna Cameron, Lynn Chalmers, Carol A. Christie, Mark H. Dorfman, Joel Griffiths, David Hayden, Jane H. Hovde, Catherine L. Hoye, Barbara Hults, Susan D. Jones, Muriel Kotselas, William Labov, Euripides Lallos, Rosemary Latimore, H. P. Lee, Susan M. Leites, Diane L. Olsen, Esther I. Persson, Philomena Pileckas, Stephanie Prince, James Rivers, Sophie M. Rivers, Bernard E. Scott, Rose Marie Smith, H. McKim Steele, Jr., Mary F. Twombly, Carol C. Wagner, Barbara Wilcox, David Wray, Orestes Zervos, Dianne Zolotow

Associate Staff Members

Paul S. Adler	Norman A. Bailey	Ina S. Bohrer
Humayun Akhtar	Burton Baker	William Bouris
Henry Allison	Richard C. Bardot	Sarah H. Bowen
Julius Altman	Shirley R. Beresford	Barbara K. Boyriven
Peter G. Anderheggen	Peter Bergquist	Renate Bridenthal
Raymond J. Anderson	Lawrence Bernard	Charles C. Brown
Stanford Anderson	Roland Bertol	Dorothy J. Buckton
John R. Ano	Linda Bettman	Nancy S. Burrows
Isabel Aronin	Mario J. A. Bick	Walter Cahn
Hans J. Ashbourne	William R. Bishin	Kenneth Calkins
Mark W. Axelrod	Barbara J. Blasingame	Paul Carroll
Edward Babun	Ernest Boaten	Loren H. Carter

Eldon R. Clingan
John K. Cohen
Yvonne Cooperman
Mani Dharmgrongartama
Victoria di Zerega
John B. Duff
Noemi C. Emery
Jacob T. Evanson
Mary Ellen Fahs
David Fischer
William C. FitzGibbon
Isabel Ford
Lee Foster
Russell Freedman
Bruce H. Frisch
Judith J. Frisch
Karol N. Gess
Peter Glassgold
Gerta Goldner
Henry J. Grennon
Lowry Guibet

Carola L. Hamburger
Jonathan Harris
Vernon J. Harward
John F. Haskins
Jane Hayman
Thomas J. Hill
Robert P. Ho
Gertrude Hoffmann
James Holahan
Sherry Hyman
Hunter Ingalls
Neil D. Isaacs
Julie Jones
Arthur D. Kahn
Elizabeth Kaplan
Anne Kastenbaum
Rachel H. Kemper
Edward A. Kent
Bettina Knapp
Carol Kochman
Alice R. Koller

Stephen E. Koss
Carol H. Krinsky
Hans P. Krosby
Henry I. Kurtz
Robert H. Lafleur
Juliette Le Baron
Myra LeCompte
Vergene Leverenz
Carol Levine
Howard Levine
Richard A. Lewis
James E. Lewisohn
Peter J. Lippman
Daniel B. Lister

Robert K. MacDonald
Ronald C. Mace
Martin E. Mantell
Louis C. Marazita
Ethne K. Marenco
Eugene Marner
Edward H. Marshall
James R. Middleton
Robert N. Middleton
Hazel E. Mills
John J. Mitchell
Paul L. Montgomery
Thomas I. Moodie
Dorothea R. Mossman
Robert Muccigrosso
Miyeko Murase
Marian Nachman
G. T. Novobatzky
Dora Odarenko
Mohammed Osman
Frank S. Parker
Armand Patrucco
Stanley G. Payne
Joseph S. Peake
Luise E. Peake
Boneita L. Perskari
George W. Phillips
Nancy Pottishman

Robert A. Potts, Jr.
Wita Ravid
Barbara Rearden
Giovanna Ricoveri
Susan R. Ritner
Stanley Roth
Mignon Sauber

Homer D. Schaaf
Gisela Scott
Robert M. Sherwood
Elisabeth L. Shoemaker
Bruce D. Shoulson
Michael N. Shute
Allan M. Siegal
Mitchell Smith
Stuart A. Smith
Kenneth Sobol
Howard Sternberger
Jack M. Stuart
Judy Suratt
Joseph S. Szyliowicz
Melinda N. Talkington
Rene C. Taylor
Alfred W. Tesoro
Elizabeth K. Thornton
Myra Tomorug
Judith M. Treistman
Maurice S. Tuchman
Alfonso Vargas-Becerra
Mary Varney
Nahum Waxman
Robert E. Weiner
Dale A. Welke
Wayne A. Wilcox
Morrow Wilson
Suzanne Wilson
Robert Winick
Peter Wolfe
Kennerly M. Woody
Barbara Wyden
Rosemary R. Yardley
Nicholas J. Yonker

Picture Editors - Design and Layout

Donald D. Wolf

Margot L. Wolf

ACKNOWLEDGMENTS

Grateful Acknowledgment is made to *Armando Curcio Editore, Rome, Italy,* for providing the color illustrations used in this edition of the Illustrated Columbia Encyclopedia.

Illustrations courtesy of:
Key to picture position: t-top; c-center; b-bottom; r-right; l-left   Combinations: tr-top right; tl-top left; etc.

Alabama Bureau of Publicity - 113 t, 113 c
Alabama State C. of C. - 114 b
Alaska Airlines - 120 tr, 121 tr, 121 tl, 122
Alaska Steamship Co. - 119 t
Am. Mus. of Natl. History, N.Y. - 3, 52 c, 78, 79 bl, 91, 164 t, 279 b, 286 l
American Scandinavian Foundation - 236
Amherst College - 224
Australian News & Information Bureau - 28 r
Belgian Tourist Bureau - 294 t
Boston C. of C. - 206 t
British Information Service - 8, 18 b, 18 t, 55 t
B.O.A.C. - 75 c
California Mission Trails Assn. - 205 tl
Canadian Consulate General - 102 c, 129, 130 c, 207 br
Canadian Pacific Railway - 130 t, 130 b
Cape Cod C. of C. - 206 br
Cleveland Museum of Art - 209 br
Colonial Williamsburg, Va. - 205 br
Alfredo Curcio Editore, Rome - 14 l, 15, 17, 22 b, 24 b, 30 l, 35 t, 42, 45 tl, 53, 54 b, 55 b, 58, 67 t, 67 c, 69 tr, 86 l, 98, 99, 102 t, 109 t, 109 b, 124-125 t, 125 b, 128 t, 134, 140 l, 157 l, 159 t, 165, 166, 175 b, 177, 193, 202, 220 b, 222, 226, 227, 228, 233 t, 250 b, 252 tl, 253, 254 l, 257 t, 257 b, 260 tr, 268 t, 274, 276, 286 r, 292, 295, 296, 298, 301 b, 306 l, 306 r, 307, 308 t, 308 b
Florida State News Bureau - 204 r
Frankfort, Ky., Division of Publicity - 23
French Government Tourist Office - 180, 185 t, 265, 266
Ewing Galloway - 113 b, 114 tr, 152, 162 b, 247 t
German Information Office - 107 b
Goodyear Rubber Co. - 103 tr, 107 b
Government of India Tourist Office - 87 t, 285
Harvard University News Office - 210 tl
Irish Tourist Board - 7 t, 7 b
Italian State Tourist Office - 62 c
Kentucky State C. of C. - 205 bl
Lockheed Co. - 103 cr
Maeder Co. - 182 tl
Martin Co. - 103 bl
Mass. Dept. of Comm. - 205 tr
Federico Arborio Mella, Milano, Italy - 1, 6 br, 24 t, 25, 26 l, 26 r, 27, 28 l, 32, 35 b, 36, 40 t, 40 b, 45 tr, 48, 49 t, 52 t, 52 b, 59, 61 t, 61 b, 65 b, 66, 69 tl, 69 tc, 71 t, 82 tr, 85 t, 85 b, 86 r, 87 c, 93 b, 93 t, 109 c, 110, 115, 126 t, 126 b, 128 bl, 128 br, 131, 132, 136, 137 t, 141, 142, 143, 144 t, 145, 146 tl, 146 tc, 146 tr, 149 t, 149 b, 150, 151, 154, 156, 159 b, 161 c, 163 b, 164 b, 173, 175 t, 178 b, 187 b, 192, 198, 201 t, 201 b, 225, 229 t, 243, 247 b, 248, 250 t, 252 tr, 255, 256,

260 tl, 260 bl, 261 bl, 261 br, 264 bl, 264 br, 268 b, 269, 270, 272, 287 bl, 288 l, 288 r, 289, 290, 291, 293, 294 b, 299, 300, 301 t, 302, 305 tl
Met. Mus. of Art, N. Y. - 174, 208 tl, 209 bl, 210 tr, 219 t, 287 br
Mus. of Natl. History, Chicago - 2, 84, 178 t, 179, 237, 254 r, 258, 279 t
Mus. of Primitive Art, N. Y. - 79 t, 79 bl
Nat. Apple Institute - 305 tr
Natl. Archives, Washington, D. C. - 103 tl, 107 c, 206 bl, 208 b, 220 t, 221, 277 tr
Natl. Broadcasting Co. - 47 tl
Natl. Park Service - 283
New Mexico State Tourist Bureau - 135, 297
New Orleans News Bureau - 204 l
New York Botanical Garden - 106 t
New York Historical Soc. - 50
New York Public Library - 14 r, 16, 45 r, 46, 47 tr, 49 b, 54 t, 92 l, 104, 157 br, 170, 176
New York Soc. for Ethical Culture - 57
New York Zoological Soc. - 87 b, 127
North Carolina News Bureau - 105 tr, 303
Northrop Norair - 103 br
Nova Scotia Bureau of Information - 29
NYSPIX - 56, 207 bl, 211 tl
Pan Am World Airways - 119 c, 120 tl, 246
Pennsylvania Development Board - 169 t, 169 b
Perls Galleries - 212
Reynolds Metals Co. - 191
San Antonio C. of C. - 117
Schenley Laboratories, Inc. - 282 bl
Smithsonian Institution - 158, 208 tr
The Solomon R. Guggenheim Museum - 207 tr
South African Tourist Corporation - 75 t
South Dakota State Highway Commission - 211 tr
Spanish Tourist Office - 242 tr, 242 tl
Swiss Natl. Travel Bureau - 182 l, 183 b
Trans World Airways - 75 b, 106 b, 163 r
United Nations - 71 b, 72, 73 tl, 73 tr, 73 b, 161 t, 161 b, 162 t, 162 c, 199 tl, 199 tr
United Press International - 22 t, 62 b, 65 t, 82 l, 114 tl, 218, 219 b
U. S. Air Force - 103 cl
U. S. Coast Guard - 231
U. S. Dept. of Agri. - 92 tr, 273 t, 273 b, 282 br
U. S. Dept. of the Int. - 211 b
U. S. Navy - 100, 101 t, 101 c, 101 b, 103 tr, 107 t, 144 b, 267 l, 277 tl, 278
Virginia State C. of C. - 105 tl, 206 c
Margot Wolf - 168

KEY TO PRONUNCIATION

ā fate (fāt), fail (fāl), vacation (vākā'-shún)

â care (kâr), Mary (mâ'rē)

ă bat (băt), add (ăd), marry (mă'rē)

ä father (fä'dhùr), marble (mär'bùl)

ã French tant (tã), Rouen (rōōã'), and similar sounds in some other languages

b back (băk), cab (kăb)

ch chap (chăp)

d dock (dŏk), cod (kŏd)

dh father (fä'dhùr), then (dhĕn). Compare with th.

ē even (ē'vùn), clearing (klēr'ĭng), obvious (ŏb'vēùs)

ĕ end (ĕnd), met (mĕt), merry (mĕ'rē)

ẽ French vin (vẽ), bien (byẽ), and similar sounds in some other languages

f fat (făt), Philip (fĭl'ĭp)

g get (gĕt), tag (tăg)

h hat (hăt). See also ch, dh, kh, sh, th, zh, and hw

hw where (hwâr), what (hwŏt)

ī fine (fīn), buyer (bī'ùr)

ĭ pin (pĭn), pit (pĭt), spirit (spĭ'rĭt), fated (fā'tĭd)

j jam (jăm) edge (ĕj), ginger (jĭn'jùr)

k cook (kŏŏk), tackle (tă'kùl)

kh loch (lŏkh, German Aachen (ä'khùn), Licht (lĭkht), and similar sounds in some other languages

l peal (pēl), pull (pŏŏl)

ḷ crumple (krŭm'pḷ)

m hammer (hă'mùr)

m̦ fanaticism (fùnă'tĭsĭzm̦)

n dinner (dĭ'nùr)

ṇ dampen (dăm'pṇ)

ng singing (sĭng'ĭng), finger (fĭng'gùr), sang (săng), sank (săngk)

ō hope (hōp), potato (pùtā'tō)

ô orbit (ôr'bĭt), fall (fôl)

ŏ hot (hŏt), toddy (tŏ'dē), borrow (bŏ'rō)

õ French dont (dõ), chanson (shãsõ'), and similar sounds in some other languages

oi boil (boil), royal (roi'ùl)

ōō boot (bōōt), lose (lōōz)

ŏŏ foot (fŏŏt), purely (pyŏŏr'lē), manipulate (mùnĭ'pyŏŏlāt)

ou scout (skout), crowd (kroud)

p pipe (pīp), happy (hă'pē)

r road (rōd), appeared (ùpērd'), carpenter (kär'pùntùr)

s saw (sô), case (kās)

sh shall (shăl), nation (nā'shùn)

t tight (tīt), rating (rā'tĭng)

th thin (thĭn), myth (mĭth). Compare with dh.

ū fume (fūm), euphemism (ū'fùmĭzm̦)

û curl (kûrl), Hamburg (hăm'bûrg), French œuvre (û'vrù), peu (pû), German schön (shûn), Goethe (gû'tù), and similar sounds in some other languages

ŭ butter (bŭ'tùr), suds (sŭdz), hurry (hŭ'rē)

ù affair (ùfâr'), sofa (sō'fù), contravene (kŏntrùvēn'), monopoly (mùnŏ'pùlē), suburban (sùbûr'bùn), callous (kă'lùs), rather (ră'dhùr)

ü French Cluny (klünē'), German Lübeck (lü'bĕk), and similar sounds in some other languages

ū̠ French Melun (mùlū̠'), Chambrun (shäbrū̠'), and similar sounds in some other languages

v vest (vĕst), trivial (trĭ'vēùl)

w wax (wăks)

y you (yōō), bunion (bŭ'nyùn)

z zipper (zĭ'pùr), ease (ēz), treads (trĕdz)

zh pleasure (plĕ'zhùr), rouge (rōōzh)

' main accent, written after accented vowel or syllable: Nebraska (nùbră'-skù), James Buchanan (jāmz' būkă'-nùn)

" secondary accent: Mississippi (mĭ"-sùsĭ'pē)

— dash, replacing obvious portion of pronunciation: hegemony (hĭjĕ'mùnē, hē–, hĕ'jùmō"nē, hĕ'gù–)

- hyphen, to prevent ambiguity: Erlanger (ûr'lăng-ùr), dishearten (dĭs-här'tùn)

Cross References are indicated by SMALL CAPITALS

NOTES

The purpose of the pronunciation symbols is to give at least one serviceable way in which the word in question may be pronounced when used by careful speakers of English.

In this work a pronunciation is ordinarily indicated for words printed in boldface when this pronunciation is not obvious to the English-speaking reader. Of two or more words or names in succession spelled and pronounced alike, a pronunciation is frequently indicated for the first occurrence only.

For names and localities in English-speaking areas the local pronunciation is preferred, provided it is acceptable to careful speakers.

For foreign words and names the speaker of English desires to use a pronunciation that will be acceptable to other speakers of English (unless he is speaking in a foreign language). In many cases (e.g., Paris) there is a traditional pronunciation that resembles little the current native pronunciation, and attempts to introduce into English conversation an approximation of the native form (something like påre′) are regarded as an affectation. It is customary with foreign names that have no conventional English form to pronounce them with English sounds approximating the foreign ones. Such an approximation is indicated in this work, whenever there is no established usage to follow.

Actual good foreign-language pronunciations can be acquired only through imitation and study. Nevertheless, Englishmen and Americans have for many years made a practice of imitating roughly five French sounds: ã, ẽ, õ, ũ, and ü. A speaker of English can attain ã by saying äng without the closure at the back of the mouth necessary to make ng, breathing through nose and mouth as well; ẽ is similarly like the beginning of ăng, õ like that of ōng, and ũ like that of ûng. To approximate ü say o͞o with vigor, then, keeping the lips rounded, change the sound quickly to ē.

For Latin words the venerable English tradition is followed [e.g., Caesar (sē′zur)], except where some other pronunciation is well established, as in ecclesiastical names [e.g., Salve Regina (säl′vä rājē′nů)]. The so-called classical pronunciation, which approximates the pronunciation Caesar used [e.g., Caesar (kī′sår)], is not given, as being not usual in English conversation.

Cross References are indicated by SMALL CAPITALS

A, first letter of the ALPHABET. Its Greek correspondent is named alpha, as in the expression "Alpha and Omega" ("first and last"; see Ō), symbolizing God. It is a usual symbol for a low central vowel as in *father;* English ā is a diphthong of ĕ and y. In MUSICAL NOTATION it is the symbol of a note in the scale. In chemistry A was formerly the symbol for the element ARGON. The symbol now in use is Ar.

Aa (ä) [from a word for "water" of the same Indo-European root as Latin *aqua*], name of many small streams of N Europe and Switzerland. Aa, or a derivative of it, is a component part of hundreds of European place names.

Aabenraa (ô′bùnrô′), city (pop. 14,219), Denmark, SE Jutland, on the Aabenraa Fjord. It is a port and the commercial center of a rich agricultural region. As Apenrade it was part of Germany from 1864 to 1920.

Aachen (ä′khùn) or **Aix-la-Chapelle** (āks′-lä-shùpĕl′) or **Bad Aachen** (bät′ ä′khùn), city (pop. 153,288), Federal Republic of Germany, in North Rhine–Westphalia, W Germany, near the Belgian and Dutch borders. Formerly a center of Carolingian culture and one of the great historic cities of Europe, it is now chiefly important as an industrial center and railway junction. It is located in a hard-coal district and manufactures machinery, rubber goods, and textiles. Its hot mineral baths, frequented since Roman times, are still in use. CHARLEMAGNE, who was probably born here, made Aachen his northern capital. He built a splendid palace and founded the great cathedral, which contains his tomb. From Charlemagne's shrine Aachen derived its French name, Aix-la-Chapelle, which is also often used in English. The cathedral was rebuilt in the 10th cent. after a Norman invasion. It was little damaged in the Second World War, unlike most other historic buildings. From 813 to 1531 the German kings were crowned "kings of the Romans" at Aachen (see HOLY ROMAN EMPIRE). Though it declined in importance, Aachen remained a free imperial city until it was annexed (1801) by France. It passed to Prussia in 1814 and was placed in the Rhine Prov. From 1918 to 1930 it was occupied by the Allies, and in the Second World War it was the first important German city to fall (Oct., 1944) into Allied hands. Several important treaties were signed at Aachen (see AIX-LA-CHAPELLE, TREATY OF), and in 1818 a conference was held there, important to the development of the Holy Alliance.

Aagesen, Svend (svĕn′ ô′gùsùn), fl. 1185, Danish historian. He was a cleric in the service of Absalon, archbishop of Lund, who encouraged him to write a history of the early Danish kings. His brief account, written in rough Latin, is overshadowed by that of his contemporary, Saxo Grammaticus. Aagesen was probably the editor, and may have been the translator, of a Latin translation of the military laws of Canute the Great.

Aakjaer, Jeppe (yĕp′ù ôk′yär), 1866–1930, Danish poet and novelist. He wrote mostly of his native Jutland, and his concern for the poor is reflected in such novels as *The Peasant's Son* (1899) and *Children of Wrath* (1904). Aakjaer's finest work is his poetry; *Songs of the Rye* (1906) and *Heimdal's Wanderings* (1924) reveal his lyric gift.

Aaland Islands: see ALAND ISLANDS.

Aalborg, Dan. *Ålborg* or *Aalborg* (all: ôl′bôrg, ôl′bôr), city (pop. 85,800), Denmark, N Jutland, on the south side of the Lim Fjord. One of Denmark's leading industrial cities, it produces cement, liquor, ships, textiles, and tobacco. It is the chief transportation center in N Jutland and has an international airport. It was known in the 11th cent. and was chartered in 1342. It has a 14th-century church and is the see of a Lutheran bishop. There are two colleges.

Aalesund: see ALESUND.

Aalsmeer (äls′mär), town (estimated pop. 14,894), in North Holland prov., W Netherlands. It has one of the greatest flower nurseries in Europe.

Aalst: see ALOST.

Aalto, Alvar (ŏl′vär äl′tō), 1898–, Finnish architect and furniture designer. He is generally considered one of the foremost architects of the 20th cent. His work adapts Finnish building traditions to modern European techniques and to the specific

The great cathedral of Aachen.

Aalto's Canadian pavilion for the 1966 Venice Biennale.

instruments. It has a cantonal library, a 15th-century church, and an 18th-century town hall.

aardvark (ärd′värk) [Dutch,=ground pig], nocturnal mammal of the order Tubulidentata. There are two species of the genus *Orycteropus*, one in central Africa and the other in southern Africa. The aardvark, about 6 ft. long, has a long snout, large erect ears, an almost naked or sparsely haired body, and a long tail. Its forefeet are adapted for making burrows in the ground and for clawing open the nests of ants and termites in order to capture the insects with its long sticky tongue. Its cylindrical teeth are without enamel and roots. It is also called ant bear and earth pig.

Aardvark

function of the structure in boldly expressive style. The municipal library at Viipuri (1927–35; destroyed 1940) was notable for its lighting; the tuberculosis sanitarium at Paimio (1929–33) was specifically adapted to the patients' routine. He gained international fame by his remarkable designs for laminated-wood furniture and by his plans for the Finnish pavilions at the expositions in Paris (1937) and New York (1939). Appointed (1940) professor at Massachusetts Institute of Technology, he designed there the serpentine-shaped Baker House (1947–48). After the Second World War he was active in reconstruction in Finland. See study by Frederick Gutheim (1960).

Aandalsnes: see ANDALSNES.

Aanrud, Hans (häns′ ôn′rōōd), 1863–1953, Norwegian writer. He is best known for his children's books and short stories depicting preindustrial peasant life in his home valley, Gudbrandsdal. *Sidsel Sidsaerk* (1903) and *Solve Solfeng* (1910) have been translated in *Sidsel Longskirt and Solve Suntrap: Two Children of Norway* (1935).

Aar (är) or **Aare** (är′ŭ), river, c.183 mi. long, rising in the Bernese Alps; one of the longest rivers in Switzerland. It emerges from Grimsel Lake and flows N past Meiringen, then W through the Lake of Brienz, past Interlaken, and through the Lake of Thun (whence it is navigable). It passes Bern, Solothurn, Olten, and Aarau, and joins the Rhine opposite Waldshut, Germany. The river has several hydroelectric plants.

Aarau (ä′rou), town (estimated pop. 16,900), capital of Aargau canton, N Switzerland, at the foot of the Jura and on the Aar. A noted shoe-manufacturing center, it also produces bells and mathematical

Aare: see AAR.

Aargau (är′gou″), Fr. *Argovie* (ärgōvē′), canton (542 sq. mi.; pop. 360,940), N Switzerland. Aarau is the capital. It is traversed by the Aar and Reuss rivers, and there are wooded hills and fertile valleys. Cereals and fruit are raised, and textiles, paper, cement, and metal products are the main industrial manufactures. The canton has several hydroelectric plants. BADEN and RHEINFELDEN are noted health resorts. Originally a Celtic settlement, it was later occupied by the Romans. The territory was taken (1415) by BERN from the house of Hapsburg and governed by the Swiss

Bremgarten, a town in Aargau Canton.

cantons until 1798. In 1803 Aargau was admitted as a canton to the Swiss Confederation. Its population is mainly German-speaking and Protestant.

Aarhus, Dan. *Arhus* or *Aarhus* (all: ôr'hōōs), city (pop. 119,568), Denmark, E Jutland, on Aarhus Bay. It is the second largest city of Denmark and a commercial, industrial, and shipping center. It produces vegetable oils, locomotives, and tobacco. One of the oldest cities in Denmark, it developed rapidly after it became an episcopal see in the 13th cent. It declined after the Reformation but recovered its prosperity in the 18th cent. It is a cultural center with a university (opened 1928), a prominent theater, and a large library. Among its notable buildings are the 12th-century Cathedral of St. Clemens and the town hall (1942) made of Norwegian marble.

Aaron (â'rŭn), in the Bible, first high priest of the Hebrews, the brother of Moses and his spokesman in Egypt. His descendants were high priests and priests. The prestige of descent from him was emphasized especially after the Exile. He was the instrument of Jehovah in miracles, as in turning his rod into a serpent and in causing the rod to bud, blossom, and bear almonds. He made the golden calf and took part in the worship of it. Ex. 4.14–16; 6.20; 7.1–12; 28–32; Num. 12; 17; 18; 20; 33.38, 39; Deut. 10.6.

Aaron's-beard, name sometimes applied to several plants usually characterized by some beardlike aspect, as the St.-John's-wort because of its many stamens and the Kenilworth ivy because of its threadlike runners. Aaron's-beard cactus is *Opuntia leucotricha,* a true cactus.

Aaron's-rod, popular name for several tall-flowering, infrequently branching plants, such as goldenrod and mullein. The name is an allusion to the rod which Aaron placed before the ark and which miraculously blossomed and bore almonds (Num. 17.8).

Aas: see As, Norway.

Aasen, Ivar Andreas (ē'vär ändrā'äs ô'sŭn), 1813–96, Norwegian lexicographer. He enjoys the distinction of being perhaps the only man who, by standardizing the dialects of a people, created a speech (i.e., ⁄the *Landsmaal*) which became the national language. For this he was responsible largely through the publication of a grammar (1848) and a dictionary (1850).

abacá: see MANILA HEMP.

Abaco and Cays (ä'bŭkō, kēz', kāz'), island group, most northerly of the Bahama Islands. It includes Great Abaco (the largest), Little Abaco, and the surrounding islets. Great Abaco was settled by Loyalists from New York city in 1783.

abacus (ăb'ŭkŭs), in architecture, a flat slab forming the top member of a capital. In classic orders it varies, a square form having unmolded sides in the Greek Doric, thinner proportions and ovolo molding in the Greek Ionic, and sides incurving and corners cut in Roman Ionic and Corinthian examples. In Romanesque work the abacus is heavier in proportion projects less, and is generally molded and decorated. In Gothic work the form varies, appearing in square, circular, and octagonal forms with molded members.

abacus, in mathematics, simple calculating device. The type of abacus now best known is represented by frames with sliding counters used for scoring in billiards, for teaching children the elements of arithmetic, and for computing by the Chinese. An apparatus of pebbles or other movable counters was known in antiquity to the Egyptians, Greeks, Romans, and Chinese. An especial merit of the abacus was that it simplified the addition and subtraction of numbers written in Roman numerals. Another type of abacus includes a board covered with sand or wax to facilitate making and erasing marks. See D. E. Smith, *History of Mathematics* (1923–25; new ed., 1958).

Abadan (ăbŭdăn', äbädän'), city (pop. c.173,000), E Iran, on Abadan island, in the delta of the Shatt el-Arab at the head of the Persian Gulf. It was for centuries an unimportant village; it became prominent after the discovery (1908) of nearby oilfields. It is now the major oil port of Iran, the terminus of a pipeline (completed 1911), an industrial center, and the site of a huge oil refinery. In the modern section of the city, with its broad avenues, pleasant houses, clubs, and theaters, live the employees of the oil company, while the old section is native. The nationalization (1951) of the Anglo-Iranian oil company led to a temporary closing of the refinery and the withdrawal of foreign technicians.

Abaddon (ŭbăd'ŭn) [Heb.,=destruction], Hebrew name of APOLLYON. Rev. 9.11. In ancient Jewish tradition it was used for part of Sheol.

Abadeh (äbädä'), town (pop. c.8,200), S Iran, between Isfahan and Shiraz. It is the trade center for a grain and fruitgrowing region. Sesame oil, castor oil, and opium are also produced here.

Abagtha (ŭbăg'–), one of Ahasuerus' seven chamberlains. Esther 1.10.

Abakan (ŭbŭkän'), city (pop. 56,000), capital of the Khakass Autonomous Oblast, Krasnoyarsk Territory, RSFSR, in S central Siberia, on the Yenisei river. A commercial center on the South Siberian RR, it produces footwear, textiles, furniture, and metal products. Founded (1707) as a fortress, it was known as Ust-Abakanskoye until 1931. Bronze Age tumuli and Turkic inscriptions have been found here. It has a pedagogical institute.

abalone (ăbŭlō'nē) [Span.], popular name in America for a univalve mollusk of the genus *Haliotis,*

Abalone shell and jewelry.

3

Abbasid caliphate:
10th-century ceramic
vase and plates.

members of which are also called ear shells or sea ears. Off the California coast it is taken in vast numbers for food. The iridescent pearly shell is made into buttons and other articles. Before protective legislation was enacted much of the dried flesh and some shells were exported to the Orient.

Abana (úbā′nù), river of Damascus. 2 Kings 5.12. It is probably the Barada, flowing near Damascus. See also PHARPAR.

abandonment, in law, voluntary relinquishment of rights or property without conveying them to any other person. Abandonment also means willfully leaving one's spouse or children, intending not to return (see DESERTION). In many states the abandonment of a child is a criminal offense.

Abano, Pietro d' (pyā′trō dä′bänō), 1250?–1316?, Italian physician and philosopher, a professor of medicine in Padua. His famous work *Conciliator differentiarum* was an attempt to reconcile Arabian medicine and Greek speculative natural philosophy and was considered authoritative as late as the 16th cent. His efforts marked the rise of the Paduan school as a center for medical study. He was tried twice by the Inquisition on charges of heresy and practicing magic. Acquitted at the first trial, he was found guilty at the second, after his death.

Abarbanel, Isaac: see ABRAVANEL, ISAAC.

Abarim (ăb′ùrĭm) [Heb.,=districts beyond], general term for the country E of the Jordan. Num. 27.12; 33.47; Deut. 32.49. The same original term is translated in Jer. 22.20.

Abascal, José Fernando de (hōsā′ fĕrnän′dō dä äbäskäl′), 1743–1827, Spanish viceroy of Peru (1806–16). During the South American revolt against the colonial rule of Spain, he skillfully reconciled the Spanish and the creoles of Peru. He promoted educational reforms, abolished the Inquisition, reorganized the army, stamped out local rebellions, and opposed the revolutionists of Buenos Aires and Chile.

Abati, Niccolò dell': see ABBATE, NICCOLÒ DELL'.

A battery: see BATTERY, ELECTRIC.

abattoir (ăb″ùtwär′) [Fr.], a building for butchering. The abattoir houses the work of killing animals for food; dressing, cutting, and inspection of meats; and in some instances refrigeration, curing, and the manufacture of by-products. The largest abattoirs are those of the MEAT PACKING industry, highly developed especially in the United States. Plant construction, drainage, water supply, disposal of refuse, and all operations are under government regulation. Abattoirs are also called slaughterhouses.

Abbadides (ă′bùdĭdz), Arabian dynasty in Spain. It ruled SEVILLE from 1023 to 1091. Taking advantage of the disintegration of the caliphate of CÓRDOBA, the cadi (governor) of Seville seized power and became (1023) king of the newly founded state as Abbad I. His son, who succeeded him in 1042 as Abbad II, made Seville the most powerful kingdom in S Spain. He was noted for his cruelty. He was succeeded in 1069 by his son, Abbad III (Abbad al-Mutamid), a poet and a great patron of the arts, but an inept ruler. Seeking military support against ALFONSO VI of Leon and Castile, Abbad called in the ALMORAVIDES from Morocco. They defeated Alfonso in 1086, but deposed (1091) Abbad, who died in exile.

Abbas (ä′bùs, ä′băs″, äbäs′), d.653, uncle of Mo-

hammed the Prophet and of Ali the caliph. A wealthy merchant of Mecca, he was at first opposed to the religious movement initiated by his nephew Mohammed. In 629 he became a convert, however, and from then on he was a companion of Mohammed and the chief financial support of Islam. His descendants founded the Abbasid dynasty. The son of Abbas, Ibn Abbas (Abd Allah), was a celebrated authority on Islamic traditions and law.

Abbas I (Abbas the Great), 1557–1628, shah of Persia (1587–1628), of the Safavid dynasty. In 1597 he ended the raids of the Uzbeks, and subsequently (1603–23) he conquered extensive territories from the Turks. His reign was prosperous, and, holding a royal silk monopoly, he was interested in trade. With English aid he took (1622) Ormuz from the Portuguese and founded what is now the port of BANDAR ABBAS. He broke the power of the tribal chiefs and established a new tribe, the Shahsavan [friends of the Shah]. He erected the magnificent palace and mosque at ISFAHAN and had a palace and gardens (now in ruins) at Babol.

Abbas II (Abbas Hilmi), 1874–1944, khedive of Egypt (1892–1914). Nominally he ruled in subordination to the Ottoman Empire, but in fact Egypt was controlled by the British resident— at first Lord Cromer, and later Kitchener. In 1899 Abbas was forced to admit the British claim to rule jointly with Egypt over the Sudan. The British deposed him after Turkey joined the Central Powers in the First World War. He wrote *The Anglo-Egyptian Settlement* (1930). Lord Cromer wrote *Abbas II* (1915), a defense of British policy.

Abbasid (úbă′sĭd, ä′bùsĭd) or **Abbaside** (–sīd, –sĭd), Arabic family descended from ABBAS, the uncle of Mohammed. They held the caliphate from 749 to 1258, but they were recognized neither in Spain nor (after 787) west of Egypt. Under the Omayyad caliphs the Abbasids lived quietly until trouble began to gather early in the 8th cent. The family then joined with the Shiite faction in opposing the Omayyads, and in 747 the gifted ABU MUSLIM united most of the empire in revolt. The head of the Abbasid family became caliph as ABU-L-ABBAS AS-SAFFAH late in 749. The last Omayyad caliph, Marwan II, was defeated and killed and the Omayyad family nearly exterminated; one surviving member fled to Spain, which the Omayyads came to rule. Under the second Abbasid caliph, called MANSUR (d. 775), the capital was moved from Damascus to Baghdad, and Persian influence grew strong in the empire. The early years of Abbasid rule were brilliant, rising to true splendor under HARUN-AL-RASHID, the fifth caliph, and to intellectual brilliance under his son MAMUN, the seventh caliph. After less than a hundred years of rule, however, the slow decline of the Abbasids began. There were long periods of disorder control by Turkish soldiers, assassinations, depositions, and other trouble, and from the beginning there were rival caliphs (see CALIPHATE). In 836 the capital was transferred to SAMARRA, remaining there until 892. Under the later Abbasids, the power of the caliphate became chiefly spiritual. Many independent kingdoms sprang up, and the empire split into autonomous units. The Seljuk Turks came to hold the real power at Baghdad.

The conquests of Jenghiz Khan further lowered the prestige of the Abbasids, and in 1258 his grandson Hulagu Khan sacked Baghdad and overthrew the Abbasid caliphate. The 37th caliph died in the disaster, but a member of the family escaped to Cairo, where he was recognized as caliph (see MAMELUKES). The Cairo line of the Abbasid caliphate, completely subordinated to the Mamelukes, survived until after the Ottoman conquest (1517) of Egypt. See Sir William Muir, *The Caliphate* (rev. ed., 1924); Guy Le Strange, *Baghdad during the Abbasid Caliphate* (1925); Reuben Levy, *A Baghdad Chronicle* (1929); P. K. Hitti, *History of the Arabs* (7th ed., 1960).

Abbate or **Abati, Niccolò dell'** (nēk-kōlō' dĕl-läb-bä'tä, –bä'tē), 1512?–1571, Italian mannerist painter. From c.1552 he assisted Primaticcio in the decorations at Fontainebleau. He was one of the first in France to paint landscapes. Among them is the *Landscape with Orpheus and Eurydice* in the National Gallery, London.

Abbe, Cleveland (ăb'ē), 1838–1916, American meteorologist, b. New York city; brother of Robert Abbe. He studied astronomy at the Univ. of Michigan and under B. A. Gould at Cambridge, Mass. As director of the Cincinnati Observatory, he inaugurated daily weather forecasting based on telegraphic reports. This work prompted the establishment of the national weather service, under the Signal Corps (1870), which Abbe joined in 1871; from 1891 to 1916 he served in the U.S. Weather Bureau. See biography by Truman Abbe (1955).

Abbe, Ernst (ĕrnst' ä'bů), 1840–1905, German physicist. He was appointed professor in 1870 at the Univ. of Jena and director of its astronomical and meteorological observatories in 1878. From 1866 he was associated with the Carl-Zeiss optical works at Jena, of which he became sole owner in 1888. He subsequently reorganized the firm on a cooperative basis. He made his plant a laboratory for the development of model working conditions, created a noncontributory pension fund, a discharge compensation fund, and introduced other advanced ideas that have been influential in shaping thought on the conditions of labor. He invented the Abbe refractometer for determining the refractive index of substances and improved photographic and microscopic lenses.

Abbe, Robert (ăb'ē), 1851–1928, American surgeon, b. New York city, M.D. Columbia, 1874; brother of Cleveland Abbe. He was noted for his skill and resource, especially in plastic surgery. A friend of the Curies, Abbe was one of the first in the United States to use radium in treating cancer.

Abbeville (ăb'vĭl, ä'bēvĭl, Fr. äbvēl'), town (estimated pop. 19,502), Somme dept., N France, in Picardy, on the Somme river and near the English Channel. It manufactures linen and other textiles. Chartered in 1184, it was a prosperous town until the revocation of the Edict of Nantes (see NANTES, EDICT OF). Although heavily damaged in the Second World War, the town retains the late Gothic Church of St. Wolfram.

Abbeville (ăb'ēvĭl). **1** City (pop. 2,524), co. seat of Henry co., SE Ala., NNE of Dothan near the Chattahoochee, in a cotton and timber area. **2** Town (pop. 10,414), parish seat of Vermilion parish, S La., N of Vermilion Bay, in a rice-growing region. It grew around a Roman Catholic chapel built in 1845 by the French and preserves in its old buildings much of the early atmosphere. **3** City (pop. 5,436), co. seat of Abbeville co., NW S.C., near the Savannah and W of Greenwood, in a cattle and poultry region; inc. 1832. Cotton textiles and clothing are manufactured, and meat and poultry are processed.

Abbevillian: see PALEOLITHIC PERIOD.

Abbey, Edwin Austin, 1852–1911, American illustrator and painter, b. Philadelphia, studied at the Pennsylvania Academy of the Fine Arts. Employed by Harper & Brothers, he was sent to England, where he gathered materials for his illustration of Herrick's poems and other works. His illustration of Shakespeare is usually considered his best work. *The Quest of the Holy Grail* (a series of wall panels in the Boston Public Library) is perhaps his most famous painting. He was official painter of the coronation of Edward VII. See biography by E. V. Lucas (1921).

abbey, monastic house, especially among Benedictines and Cistercians, consisting of not less

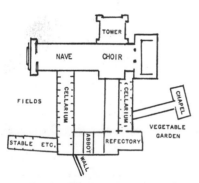

Benedictine abbey in Gall, Switzerland (right); (above) ground plan of an abbey.

than 12 monks or nuns ruled by an abbot or abbess. Many abbeys were originally self-supporting. In the Benedictine expansion after the 8th cent., abbeys were often important centers of learning and peaceful arts, and, like FULDA, sometimes the nuclei of future towns. The buildings surround a church and include a dormitory, refectory, and guest house, all surrounded by a wall. The courtyard, derived from the Roman ATRIUM, was a usual feature, as was the CLOISTER or arcade surrounding the court. The word cloister has come to be synonymous with monastic seclusion. Abbeys were constructed in the architectural style of the period, first Romanesque, later Gothic. Cluniac abbeys were always ornate, Cistercian ones notably bare. The design of the abbey has been radically altered in the modern Benedictine abbey built by Le Corbusier at La Tourette, France. The CARTHUSIANS with their special polity developed an altogether different structure called the charterhouse.

Abbey Theatre, Irish theatrical company devoted primarily to indigenous drama. W. B. Yeats was a leader in founding (1902) the Irish National Theatre Society with Lady Gregory, J. M. Synge, and A. E. (George Russell) contributing their talents as directors and dramatists. In 1904 Annie E. F. Horniman gave them a subsidy and the free use of the Abbey Theatre in Dublin. In 1910 the theater was bought for them by public subscription. Among dramatists whose works they first presented are Padraic Colum, Lennox Robinson, Sean O'Casey, and Paul Vincent Carroll. The acting company, which included such notable performers as William Fay and Frank Fay, Dudley Digges, Barry Fitzgerald, and Sara Allgood, several times toured the United States. See Lady Gregory *Our Irish Theatre* (1913), and her journals (ed. by Lennox Robinson, 1946); historical studies by Peter Kavanagh (1950), Lennox Robinson (1952), and Gerard Fay (1959).

Abbo of Fleury (äbō′, flûrē′), Fr. *Abbon de Fleury* (äbō′ dü), Latin *Abbo Floriacensis*, 945?–1004, French monk at the abbey of Fleury (at present Saint-Benoît-sur-Loire, near Orléans, France). Head of the monastery school, he later taught at the abbey in Ramsey, England, and in 988 became abbot at Fleury. He defended his monastery against domination by the high clergy and also served as a diplomat for King Robert II of France. Abbo wrote on grammar, astronomy, mathematics, and philosophy.

Abbot, Charles Greeley, 1872–, American astrophysicist, b. Wilton, N.H. He was acting director in 1896 and director in 1907 of the astrophysical observatory of the Smithsonian Institution; he was secretary of the institution from 1928 to 1944, when he became a research associate. Many of his research studies were initiated by S. P. Langley, his predecessor. He completed the mapping of the infrared solar spectrum and, over a long period of years, he carried out from stations at various altitudes in North and South America and in Africa systematic studies of variation in solar radiation, its relation to the sunspot cycle, and its effect upon weather variation. He also studied intensively the nature of atmospheric transmission and absorption. Abbot perfected various standardized instru-

The Abbey Theatre in Dublin, Ireland, before it was destroyed by fire in 1951 (above); and the new building.

ments now widely used for measuring the sun's heat, and he invented devices utilizing solar energy. In addition to scientific papers and reports he wrote *The Sun* (1911), *The Earth and the Stars* (1925; rev. ed., 1946), *The Sun and the Welfare of Man* (1929), and, with S. A. Mitchell, a standard textbook on astronomy (1927).

Abbot, George, 1562–1633, archbishop of Canterbury. He was one of the collaborators (from Oxford Univ.) on the Authorized Version of the Bible and was an authority on geography. He became archbishop in 1611. His firm Puritan views and antipathy toward the growing High Church party made him unpopular. His accidental killing of a gamekeeper while hunting (1621) was used against him. His steady opposition to William Laud, together with his refusal (1627) to countenance the elevation of the king's prerogative over law and Parliament, led Charles I to force him from active control.

Abbotsford (ăb′ŭtsfûrd), estate of Sir Walter Scott from 1812 to 1832, Roxburghshire, S Scotland, on the Tweed and near Melrose. The baronial mansion, built over a period of about 10 years, contains many relics of Scott.

Abbotsford, Scotland.

Abbotsford, village (pop. 1,171), central Wis., W of Wausau, in a dairy region; inc. 1894.

Abbott, Edith: see ABBOTT, GRACE.

Abbott, Edwin Abbott, 1838–1926, English clergyman and author, b. London. He wrote several theological works and a biography (1885) of Francis Bacon, but he is best known for his standard *Shakespearian Grammar* (1870).

Abbott, George, 1889–, American theatrical producer, b. Forestville, N.Y., grad. Univ. of Rochester, 1911. He gained repute as co-author and director of such plays as *The Fall Guy* and *Coquette,* and after the great success of *Three Men on a Horse* (1935) he was recognized as the master of crackling farce. He directed and produced many comedies and musicals, frequently writing dialogue and sometimes acting as producer. His later successes include *On Your Toes, The Boys from Syra-*

cuse, and *The Pajama Game.* He won (1960) a Pulitzer Prize for the musical *Fiorello!* (written in collaboration with Jerome Weidman).

Abbott, Grace, 1878–1939, American social worker, b. Grand Island, Nebr. She did notable work as director (1921–34) of the Child Labor Division of the U.S. Children's Bureau. *The Child and the State* (2 vols., 1938) is her most important publication. Her sister, **Edith Abbott,** 1876–1957, was made dean of the School of Social Service Administration, Univ. of Chicago, in 1924. Her publications include *Women in Industry* (1910) and *The Tenements of Chicago* (1936).

Abbott, Jacob, 1803–79, American writer of books for boys, b. Hallowell, Maine, grad. Bowdoin, 1820, and studied at Andover Theological Seminary. The *Rollo* series of 28 volumes and *The Young Christian* (1832) are perhaps the most famous of his 180 books, most of them reflecting the didacticism of a clergyman.

Abbott, Lyman, 1835–1922, American clergyman and editor, b. Roxbury, Mass., grad. New York Univ., 1853; son of Jacob Abbott. He was ordained a minister in 1860 and held various pastorates before succeeding Henry Ward Beecher at the Plymouth Congregational Church, Brooklyn, in 1888. With Beecher he had begun in 1876 to edit the *Christian Union,* the name of which he changed in 1893 to the *Outlook.* He championed a modern rational outlook in American Christianity. His works include *The Theology of an Evolutionist* (1897), *Henry Ward Beecher* (1903), and *Reminiscences* (new ed., 1923).

abbreviation, in writing, arbitrary shortening of a word, usually by cutting off letters from the end, e.g., U.S.A., Geo. (George). Contraction serves the same purpose but is understood strictly to be the shortening of a word by cutting out letters in the middle, the omission sometimes being indicated by an apostrophe. Many writers hold that a contraction (in which the last letter of the word appears) should not be followed by a period, though an abbreviation should. Usage, however, differs widely, and recently omission of periods has become common, as in NATO, UN. A period is never used when apostrophes appear. The forms in the following select list of abbreviations are those which are widely used in authoritative sources and are preferred by Columbia University Press.

LIST OF ABBREVIATIONS

A. = answer
a = are [100 sq. meters]
a. = acre, acres
A.A. = Alcoholics Anonymous
AAA = Agricultural Adjustment Agency
A.A.A. = American Automobile Association
A.B. = Able-bodied Seaman; *Artium Baccalaureus* [Bachelor of Arts]
abbr. (*or* abbrev.) = abbreviation, abbreviated
Abp. = Archbishop

abr. = abridged
AC = alternating current
Acad. = Academy
acct. = account
A.D. = *anno Domini* [in the year of the Lord] (often small capitals)
ad fin. = *ad finem* [to the end, at the end]
adj. = adjective
Adjt. = Adjutant
ad lib. = *ad libitum* [at pleasure]
Adm. = Admiral, Admiralty
adv. = adverb

ad val. (*or* adv.) = *ad valorem* [on the value]
advt. (*or* adv.) = advertisement
AEC = Atomic Energy Commission
A.E.F. = American Expeditionary Force
aet. (*or* aetat.) = *aetatis* [of age]
A.F. of L. (*or* A.F.L.) = American Federation of Labor
Afr. = Africa
agt. = agent
A.H. = *anno Hegirae* [in the year of the Hegira] (often small capitals)

A.I.A. = American Institute of Architects
A.L.A. = American Library Association
Ala. = Alabama
alt. = altitude
Alta. = Alberta
A.M. = *ante meridiem* [before noon] (often small capitals); *anno mundi* [in the year of the world] (often small capitals); *Artium Magister* [Master of Arts]
AM = amplitude modulation
A.M.A. = American Medical Association
A.M.D.G. = *ad majorem Dei gloriam* [to the greater glory of God]
Amer. (*or* Am.) = America, American
amp. = ampere, amperes
amt. = amount
anc. = ancient
ann. = annual, annals
anon. = anonymous
AP = Associated Press
APO = Army Post Office
app. = appendix, appointed
approx. = approximately, approximate
apt. = apartment
Arch. = Archipelago
Ariz. = Arizona
Ark. = Arkansas
art. = article
A.S. (*or* AS) = Anglo-Saxon
ASCAP = American Society of Composers, Authors, and Publishers
assn. = association
ASSR = Autonomous Soviet Socialist Republic
asst. = assistant
atty. = attorney
at. wt. = atomic weight
A.U.C. = *ab urbe condita* [from the founding of the city] *or anno urbis conditae* [in the year of the founding of the city] (often small capitals)
Aug. = August
AV = Authorized Version
Av. (*or* Ave.) = Avenue
av. = average, avoirdupois
AVC = American Veterans Committee
avdp. (*or* av.) = avoirdupois
Ave. (*or* Av.) = Avenue
AWOL = absent without leave
b. = born, born in
B.A. = Bachelor of Arts
bal. = balance
Bapt. = Baptist
B.Arch. = Bachelor of Architecture
Bart. = Baronet
B.B.C. = British Broadcasting Corporation
bbl. = barrel
B.C. = before Christ (often small capitals); British Columbia
B.D. = Bachelor of Divinity
bd. = board
bf = boldface
bibl. fn. = bibliographical footnote
Bl. = Blessed
Bldg. = Building
B. Lit. = Bachelor of Literature
Blvd. = Boulevard

B.Mus. = Bachelor of Music
bor. = borough
Bp. = Bishop
B.P.O.E. = Benevolent Protective Order of Elks
Br. (*or* Brit.) = British
Brig. Gen. = Brigadier General
Brit. (*or* Br.) = British
bro. = brother
B.S. = Bachelor of Science
B.Sc. = Bachelor of Science
B.T.U. = British thermal unit
bu. = bushel, bushels
bul. = bulletin
Bulg. = Bulgarian
bur. = bureau
B.V.M. = Blessed Virgin Mary
B.W.I. = British West Indies
C. = centigrade, Caius
c. = copyright
c. (*or* ca.) = *circa* [about]
ca = centare
cal. = calorie
Calif. = California
Can. = Canadian
can. = canon, canto
Cant. = Canticles (Song of Solomon)
Cantab. = *Cantabrigiensis* [of Cambridge]
cap. = capital letter, capitulum [chapter]
Capt. = Captain
car. (*or* k.) = carat
CARE = Cooperative for American Remittances to Everywhere
Cath. = Catholic
C.B. = Companion of the Order of the Bath
C.C. = Chamber of Commerce
c.c.(*or* cc.) = cubic centimeter, carbon copy
C.E. = Civil Engineer
cen. = central
cent. = century, centuries
CENTO = Central Treaty Organization
cf. = *confer* [compare]
cgs = centimeter-gram-second
chap. = chapter
Chem.E. = Chemical Engineer
Chron. = Chronicles
CIA = Central Intelligence Agency
Cia = *Compañia* [Company]
C.I.D. = Criminal Investigation Department
Cie = *Compagnie* [Company]
CINC = Commander in Chief
C.I.O. = Congress of Industrial Organizations
cm = centimeter, centimeters
Cn. = Cneius
Co. = Company
co. = county
c/o = care of
C.O.D. = cash (also collect) on delivery
Col. = Colonel, Colossians
col. = collector, column
Coll. = Collection
Colo. = Colorado
Comdr. = Commander
comp. = compiled, compiler
Cong. = Congressional, Congregational
conj. = conjunction

Conn. = Connecticut
cont. = continued
Cor. = Corinthians
cor. = corrected
corp. = corporation
CP = Communist party
c.p. = candle power
C.P.A. = Certified Public Accountant
Cpl. = Corporal
CPO = Chief Petty Officer
Cr. = credit, creditor
C.S. = Christian Science
C.S.A. = Confederate States of America
cu. = cubic
CVA = Columbia Valley Authority
cwt. = hundredweight
C.Z. = Canal Zone
D. = Don or Doña (Span. address), Dom or Dona (Port. address); Decimus
d. = daughter; *denarius* [penny], *denarii* [pence]; died, died in
D.A. = District Attorney
Dan. = Daniel, Danish
D.A.R. = Daughters of the American Revolution
DC = direct current
D.C. = District of Columbia
D.C.L. = Doctor of Civil Law
D.D. = Doctor of Divinity
D.D.S. = Doctor of Dental Surgery
DDT = Dichloro-diphenyl-trichloro-ethane
Dec. = December
deg. = degree, degrees
Del. = Delaware
Dem. = Democrat, Democratic
dept. = department
Deut. = Deuteronomy
dial. = dialect, dialectal
diam. = diameter
dict. = dictionary
dist. = district
div. = division
DM = Deutschemark
do. = ditto [the same]
doz. = dozen, dozens
DP = displaced person
Dr. = debtor, Doctor
dr. = dram, drams
D.S.C. = Distinguished Service Cross
D.Sc. = Doctor of Science
D.S.M. = Distinguished Service Medal
D.S.O. = Companion of the Distinguished Service Order
Du. = Dutch
D.V. = *Deo volente* [God willing]
dwt. = pennyweight
E = east
ECA = Economic Cooperation Administration
Eccles. = Ecclesiastes
Ecclus. = Ecclesiasticus
ECSC = European Coal and Steel Community
ed. = edited, edition, editor, educated
E.E. = Electrical Engineer
e.g. = *exempli gratia* [for example]
E.M. = Engineer of Mines
emf = electromotive force
ency. (*or* encyc.) = encyclopedia
ENE = east-northeast
Eng. = English

engr. = engraved
enl. = enlarged
Eph. = Ephesians
Epis. (*or* Episc.) = Episcopal
ERP = European Recovery Program
ESE = east-southeast
esp. = especially
Esq. = Esquire
est. = established, estimated
et al. = *et alibi* [and elsewhere]; *et alii* [and others]
etc. = *et cetera* [and others, and so forth]
et seq. = *et sequens* [and the following]
et sqq. = *et sequentes, et sequentia* [and those following]
Eur. = Europe
Ex. = Exodus
ex. = example, except
Ezek. = Ezekiel
F. = Fahrenheit, Fellow
F. (*or* Fri.) = Friday
f. = and the following page
f. (*or* fem.) = feminine
fac. = facsimile
F.A.G.S. = Fellow of the American Geographical Society
F. and A.M. = Free and Accepted Masons
FAO = Food and Agriculture Organization of the United Nations
FBI = Federal Bureau of Investigation
FCC = Federal Communications Commission
Feb. = February
fed. = federated, federation
fem. (*or* f.) = feminine
FEPC = Fair Employment Practices Committee
ff. = and the following pages
fig. = figure
fl. = *floruit* [flourished]
Fla. = Florida
fl. oz. = fluid ounce
FM = frequency modulation
fn. = footnote
fo. = folio
f.o.b. = free on board
FPO = Fleet Post Office
Fr. = French, Father, Friar
fr. = franc
F.R.A.S. = Fellow of the Royal Astronomical Society
F.R.C.P. = Fellow of the Royal College of Physicians
F.R.C.S. = Fellow of the Royal College of Surgeons
F.R.G.S. = Fellow of the Royal Geographical Society
Fri. (*or* F.) = Friday
front. = frontispiece
F.R.S. = Fellow of the Royal Society
ft. = foot, feet, fort
FTC = Federal Trade Commission
G. = specific gravity
g = gram, grams
Ga. = Georgia
Gal. = Galatians
gal. = galley, gallon, gallons
Gall. = Gallery
G.A.R. = Grand Army of the Republic
G.C. = Knight Grand Cross; Knight Grand Commander (of various British orders, when followed by abbreviation designating the order)
G.C.B. = Knight Grand Cross of the Order of the Bath
Gen. = General, Genesis
Ger. = German
GHQ = General Headquarters
gloss. = glossary
G.M.T. = Greenwich mean time
g.n.p. = gross national product
G.O.P. = Grand Old Party (Republican Party)
Gov. = Governor
govt. = government
Gr. = Greek
gr. = grain, grains
grad. = graduated, graduated at
ha = hectare
Hab. = Habakkuk
Hag. = Haggai
Heb. = Hebrew, Hebrews (NT)
hhd. = hogshead
H.M.S. = His (Her) Majesty's Ship; His (Her) Majesty's Service
Hon. = the Honorable
hp = horsepower
H.R. = House of Representatives
hr. = hour, hours
H.R.H. = His (Her) Royal Highness
ht. = height
Hung. = Hungarian
ib. (*or* ibid.) = *ibidem* [in the same place]
ICAO = International Civil Aviation Organization
ICBM = intercontinental ballistic missile
ICC = Interstate Commerce Commission
I.E. (*or* I-E *or* IE) = Indo-European
i.e. = *id est* [that is]
IGY = International Geophysical Year
IHS = *Iesus Hominum Salvator* [Jesus, the Savior of Men]; *in hoc signo* [in this sign] (originally three letters of the Greek for Jesus)
Ill. = Illinois
ill. (*or* illus.) = illustrated, illustration
ILO = International Labor Organization
in. = inch, inches
inc. = incorporated
incl. = including, inclusive
incog. = incognito [unknown, unrecognized]
Ind. = Indiana
ind. = index
inf. = infinitive, *infra* [below]
I.N.R.I. = *Iesus Nazarenus, Rex Iudaeorum* [Jesus of Nazareth, King of the Jews]
Inst. = Institute, Institution
inst. = instant [the present month]
int. = interest
introd. = introduction
I.O.O.F. = Independent Order of Odd Fellows
I O U = I owe you
I.Q. (*or* IQ) = intelligence quotient
Ir. = Irish
IRA = Irish Republican Army
IRBM = intermediate-range ballistic missile
Isa. = Isaiah
isl. = island
Ital. (*or* It.) = Italian
ital = italic type
I.W.W. = Industrial Workers of the World
JAG = Judge Advocate General
Jan. = January
Jap. = Japanese
J.D. = *Juris Doctor* [Doctor of Laws]
Jer. = Jeremiah
jg = junior grade (in U.S. Navy)
jour. = journal
J.P. = Justice of the Peace
Jr. = Junior
J.U.D. = *Juris Utriusque Doctor* [Doctor of Both Civil and Canon Laws]
K. = Kelvin
k. (*or* car.) = carat
K.C. = King's Counsel; Knight Commander (of various British orders, when followed by abbreviation designating the order)
K.C. (*or* K. of C.) = Knights of Columbus
kc = kilocycle, kilocycles
K.G. = Knight of the Order of the Garter
kg = kilogram, kilograms
KJV = King James Version
K.K.K. = Ku Klux Klan
kl = kiloliter, kiloliters
km = kilometer, kilometers
K. of C. (*or* K.C.) = Knights of Columbus
K.P. = Knights of Pythias
K.T. = Knight Templar
Kt. = Knight
kw = kilowatt, kilowatts
kwh = kilowatt hour, kilowatt hours
Ky. = Kentucky
L. = Left (in stage directions); Lucius; Lake
£ = *libra* [pound]
l = liter, liters
l. = line
La. = Louisiana
Lab. = Labrador
Lam. = Lamentations
Lat. = Latin
lat. = latitude
lb. = *libra* [pound], *librae* [pounds]
l.c. = lower case [not capitalized]
Lev. = Leviticus
L.H.D. = *Litterarum Humaniorum Doctor* [Doctor of Humane Letters]
L.I. = Long Island
Lieut. = Lieutenant
Litt.B. = *Litterarum Baccalaureus* [Bachelor of Literature]
Litt.D. = *Litterarum Doctor* [Doctor of Literature]
ll. = lines
LL.B. = *Legum Baccalaureus* [Bachelor of Laws]
LL.D. = *Legum Doctor* [Doctor of Laws]
loc. cit. = *loco citato* [in the place cited]
log. = logarithm
long. = longitude
Lt. = Lieutenant
Ltd. = Limited
Luth. = Lutheran
M. = mark [German coin]; *meridies* [noon] (often small capitals); Monsieur [Mr., Sir]; Marcus
m = meter, meters
m. = married

m. (or masc.) = masculine
M.A. = Master of Arts
Mac. = Maccabees
Maj. = Major
Mal. = Malachi
Man. = Manitoba
masc. (or m.) = masculine
Mass. = Massachusetts
Mat. = Matthew
M.D. = *Medicineae Doctor* [Doctor of Medicine]
Md. = Maryland
mdse. = merchandise
M.E. = Mechanical Engineer, Methodist Episcopal
M.E. (or ME or Mid. Eng.) = Middle English
memo. = memorandum
Messrs. = Messieurs [Gentlemen] (plural of Mr.)
Met. E. = Metallurgical Engineer
Meth. = Methodist
Mex. = Mexican
mfg. = manufacturing
M.F.H. = Master of Fox Hounds
mg = milligram, milligrams
Mgr = Monsignor
mgr. = manager
M.H.G. (or MHG) = Middle High German
mi. = mile, miles
Mich. = Michigan
Mid. Eng. (or M.E. or ME) = Middle English
min. = minute, minutes
Minn. = Minnesota
misc. = miscellaneous
Miss. = Mississippi
ml = milliliter, milliliters
Mlle = Mademoiselle [Miss]
MM. = Messieurs [Gentlemen] (plural of M.)
mm = millimeter, millimeters
Mme = Madame
Mo. = Missouri
mo. = month
Mon. = Monday
Mont. = Montana
M.P. = Member of Parliament
mph = miles per hour
Mr. = Mister (always abbreviated)
Mrs. = Mistress (always abbreviated)
MS = manuscript
M.S. (or M.Sc.) = Master of Science
Msgr = Monsignor
MSS = manuscripts
mt. = mount, mountain
mus. = museum, music
Mus.B. = *Musicae Baccalaureus* [Bachelor of Music]
Mus.D. = *Musicae Doctor* [Doctor of Music]
MVA = Missouri Valley Authority
N = north
n. = *natus* [born], neuter, noun
n. (or nom.) = nominative
N.A. = National Academy, North America
NAACP = National Association for the Advancement of Colored People
N.A.M. = National Association of Manufacturers
NASA = National Aeronautics and Space Administration

natl. = national
NATO = North Atlantic Treaty Organization
N.B. = New Brunswick; *nota bene* [note well]
N.C. = North Carolina
NCO = Noncommissioned Officer
n.d. = no date
N.Dak. = North Dakota
NE = northeast
N.E.A. = National Education Association
Nebr. = Nebraska
Neh. = Nehemiah
neut. (or n.) = neuter
Nev. = Nevada
N.F. = Newfoundland
N.H. = New Hampshire
N.J. = New Jersey
NLRB = National Labor Relations Board
N.Mex. = New Mexico
NNE = north-northeast
NNW = north-northwest
No. = *numero* [number]
Nor. = Norwegian
Nov. = November
N.P. = Notary Public
NRA = National Recovery Administration
NROTC = Naval Reserve Officers' Training Corps
N.S. = New Style; Nova Scotia; new series (of a periodical)
NT = New Testament
Num. = Numbers
NW = northwest
N.Y. = New York
NYA = National Youth Administration
OAS = Organization of American States
ob. = *obiit* [died]
Obad. = Obadiah
obs. = obsolete
Oct. = October
O.E. (or OE) = Old English
OECD = Organization for Economic Cooperation and Development
O.F.M. = *Ordo Fratrum Minorum* [Order of Friars Minor] (Franciscan)
O.Fr. (or O.F. or OF) = Old French
O.H.G. (or OHG) = Old High German
O.Ir. = Old Irish
O.K. (or OK) = correct
Okla. = Oklahoma
O.M. = Order of Merit
O.N. = Old Norse
Ont. = Ontario
O.P. = Order of Preachers (Dominicans)
op. = *opus* [work]
OPA = Office of Price Administration
op. cit. = *opere citato* [in the work cited]
opp. = opposite
O.S. = Old Style
O.S.B. = *Ordo Sancti Benedicti* [Order of St. Benedict] (Benedictines)
OSS = Office of Strategic Services
OT = Old Testament
Oxon. = *Oxoniensis* [of Oxford]
oz. = ounce, ounces

P. = Publius
p. = page
Pa. = Pennsylvania
Pat. Off. = Patent Office
p.c. = per cent
pd. = paid
Pd. D. = *Pedagogiae Doctor* [Doctor of Pedagogy]
P.E. = Protestant Episcopal
P.E.I. = Prince Edward Island
PFC (or Pfc) = Private First Class
Pg. (or Port.) = Portuguese
Ph.B. = *Philosophiae Baccalaureus* [Bachelor of Philosophy]
Ph.D. = *Philosophiae Doctor* [Doctor of Philosophy]
Philip. = Philippians
P.I. = Philippine Islands
pinx. = *pinxit* [he painted]
pk. = peck
pl. = plate
pl. (or plur.) = plural
plur. (or pl.) = plural
P.M. = Postmaster; *post meridiem* [afternoon] (often small capitals)
PO = Petty Officer
P.O. = post office
Pol. = Polish
pop. = population
Port. (or Pg.) = Portuguese
POW = prisoner of war
pp. = pages
P.R. = Puerto Rico
pref. = preface
prep. = preposition
Pres. = President
Presb. = Presbyterian
pron. = pronoun, pronounced
Prot. = Protestant
pro tem. = *pro tempore* [temporarily]
Prov. = Proverbs
prov. = province
prox. = *proximo* [of the next month]
P.S. = *post scriptum* [postscript]
Ps. = Psalm
pseud. = pseudonym
Pss. = Psalms
pt. = part, pint, pints, point
pub. = published, publisher
Pvt. = Private
PWA = Public Works Administration
Q. = Quintus, question
Q.C. = Queen's Counsel
Q.E.D. = *quod erat demonstrandum* [which was to be demonstrated]
Q.E.F. = *quod erat faciendum* [which was to be done]
QM = Quartermaster
qq.v. = *quae vide* [which see] (plural)
qt. = quart, quarts
Que. = Quebec
q.v. = *quod vide* [which see]
R. = Réaumur; *Rex* [King]; *Regina* [Queen]; Right (stage direction)
R.A. = Royal Academician
RAF = Royal Air Force
R.C. = Red Cross, Roman Catholic
Rd. = Road
recd. = received
rect. (or rept.) = receipt
Regt. = Regiment
Rep. = Republican, Representative
rept. = report
rept. (or rect.) = receipt
Ret. = Retired

Rev. = Revelations, the Reverend
rev. = revised
R.F.D. = rural free delivery
R.I. = Rhode Island
R.I.P. = *requiescat in pace* [may he rest in peace]
RM = Reichsmark
R.N. = Registered Nurse, Royal Navy
Rom. = Romans
rom = roman type
ROTC = Reserve Officers' Training Corps
rpm. = revolutions per minute
RR = railroad
RSFSR = Russian Soviet Federated Socialist Republic
RSV = Revised Standard Version
R.S.V.P. = *Répondez, s'il vous plaît* [An answer is requested]
Rt. Rev. = the Right Reverend
Rus. = Russian
RV = Revised Version
Ry. = railway
S = south
S. = *San, Santa, Santo,* or *São* [Saint]
S. (*or* Sun.) = Sunday
s. = *solidus* [shilling], *solidi* [shillings]
S.A. = Salvation Army; South America; *Sociedad Anónima, Société Anonyme* [Limited]
Sam. = Samuel
S.A.R. = Sons of the American Revolution
Sask. = Saskatchewan
Sat. = Saturday
S.C. = South Carolina
s.c. = small capitals
sc. = *scilicet* [namely]
Sc.D. = *Scientiae Doctor* [Doctor of Science]
S.Dak. = South Dakota
SE = southeast
SEATO = Southeast Asia Treaty Organization
SEC = Securities and Exchange Commission
sec. = second, seconds, section, sections
secy. = secretary
Sen. = Senator
Sept. = September
ser. = series
Sex. = Sextus
Sgt. = Sergeant
sing. = singular
S.J. = *Societas Jesu* [Society of Jesus]
Skt. = Sanskrit
Soc. = society
SOS = distress signal (not a true abbreviation)
Span. (*or* Sp.) = Spanish
S.P.C.A. = Society for the Preven-

tion of Cruelty to Animals
S.P.C.C. = Society for the Prevention of Cruelty to Children
sp. gr. = specific gravity
S.P.Q.R. = *Senatus Populusque Romanus* [the Senate and People of Rome]
sq. = *sequens* [the following]; square
sqq. = *sequentes, sequentia* [those following]
Sr. = Senior
SS. = Saints
S.S. = Steamship, Sunday School
SSE = south-southeast
SSR = Soviet Socialist Republic
SSW = south-southwest
St. = Saint, Street
S.T.D. = *Sacrae Theologiae Doctor* [Doctor of Sacred Theology]
Ste = *Sainte* [Saint, feminine]
Sun. (*or* S.) = Sunday
sup. = supplement, *supra* [above]
Supt. = Superintendent
s.v. = *sub verbo* (under the entry)
SW = southwest
Swed. (*or* Sw.) = Swedish
T. = Titus
Tenn. = Tennessee
T.H. = Territory of Hawaii
Th. (*or* Thurs.) = Thursday
Thess. = Thessalonians
Thurs. (*or* Th.) = Thursday
Ti. = Tiberius
Tim. = Timothy
T.N.T. (*or* TNT) = trinitrotoluene, trinitrotoluol
tp. = township
t.p. (*or* t.-p.) = title page
tr. = transitive, translated, translation, translator, transpose
treas. = treasurer
Tu. (*or* Tues.) = Tuesday
TVA = Tennessee Valley Authority
UAR = United Arab Republic
U.C.V. = United Confederate Veterans
U.D.C. = United Daughters of the Confederacy
UHF = ultra high frequency
UK = United Kingdom of Great Britain and Northern Ireland
ult. = *ultimo* [of the last month]
UN = United Nations
UNESCO = United Nations Educational, Scientific, and Cultural Organization
UNICEF = United Nations Children's Fund
uninc. = unincorporated
Unit. = Unitarian
Univ. = Universalist, University
UNRRA = United Nations Relief and Rehabilitation Administration

UPI = United Press International
U.S. = United States
USA = United States Army
U.S.A. = United States of America
USBGN = United States Board on Geographic Names
USCG = United States Coast Guard
USMC = United States Marine Corps
USN = United States Navy
USO = United Service Organizations
U.S.S. = United States Ship
USSR = Union of Soviet Socialist Republics
v. = *vide* [see]
v. (*or* vb.) = verb
v. (*or* vs.) = *versus* [against]
VA = Veterans' Administration
Va. = Virginia
V.C. = Victoria Cross
Ved. = Vedic
Ven. = the Venerable
VHF = very high frequency
V.I. = Virgin Islands
viz. = *videlicet* [namely]
vol. = volume, volunteer
vs. = verse, versus
Vt. = Vermont
W = west
W. (*or* Wed.) = Wednesday
WAC = Women's Army Corps
Wash. = Washington
WAVES = Women Accepted for Voluntary Emergency Service (United States Women's Naval Reserve)
W.C.T.U. = Woman's Christian Temperance Union
Wed. (*or* W.) = Wednesday
WHO = World Health Organization
W.I. = West Indies
Wis. = Wisconsin
wk. = week
WNW = west-northwest
WO = Warrant Officer
WPA = Work Projects Administration
WSW = west-southwest
wt. = weight
W.Va. = West Virginia
Wyo. = Wyoming
yd. = yard, yards
Y.M.C.A. = Young Men's Christian Association
Y.M.H.A. = Young Men's Hebrew Association
yr. = year
Y.W.C.A. = Young Women's Christian Association
Y.W.H.A. = Young Women's Hebrew Association
Zech. = Zechariah
Zeph. = Zephaniah

Abda [Heb.,=servant]. **1** Father of Solomon's officer Adoniram. 1 Kings 4.6. **2** Levite. Neh. 11.17. Obadiah: 1 Chron. 9.16.

Abd al-Rahman. For Moslem rulers thus named, see Abdu-r-Rahman.

Abdeel (ăb′dēĕl) [Heb.,=servant of God], father of

the Shelemiah sent to arrest Baruch and Jeremiah. Jer. 36.26.

Abd-el-Krim (ăb″dĕl-krĭm′, Arabic äb″dŏŏl-kŭrēm′), 1882?–1963, leader of the Riff tribes of Morocco, called in full Mohammed ben Abd-el-Krim. He was an important figure in the administration of

Abd-el-Krim

the Spanish Zone until 1920, when he took up arms against Spanish rule. In 1921 his small force wiped out a disorganized and ill-equipped Spanish army. In the next three years he strengthened his position and in 1924 drove the Spanish back to Tetuán. After capturing his only rival, Raisuli, he advanced into the French Zone in 1925. Defeated by combined Franco-Spanish forces, he surrendered in 1926 and was deported. He escaped (1947) into Egypt, was awarded (1958) the title national hero by King Mohammed V of Morocco, and in 1962 announced that he would return to Morocco.

Abdera (ăbdēr′ù), Gr. *Avdera* (ävdē′rä), town (pop. 1,222), in Thrace, NE Greece. It is a small agricultural settlement. Founded (c.650 B.C.) by colonists from Clazomenae, it was destroyed by the Thracians (c.550 B.C.) and rebuilt (c.500 B.C.) by refugees from Teos. Abdera lost its independence to Macedon in 352 B.C., and in 198 B.C. it became a free city under Roman rule. The Abderites were considered stupid by the ancient Greeks, and Abderite became a term of reproach. However, Protagoras and Democritus were born here.

Abdera: see ADRA.

Abderhalden, Emil (ā′mēl äp′dùrhäl′dùn), 1877–1950, Swiss physiologist and biochemist; pupil of Emil Fischer. From 1911 he was professor at Halle. He carried forward Fischer's work on enzymes, devised (1912) the Abderhalden pregnancy test, and investigated the metabolism of foods, especially of certain proteins. He wrote a textbook of physiological chemistry (1906) and edited a handbook of biochemic technique (9 vols., 1910–19) and a handbook of biological technique (106 vols. to 1939).

Abdi (ăb′dī) [Heb.,=my servant]. **1, 2** Merarite Levites. 1 Chron. 6.44; 2 Chron. 29.12. **3** Israelite married to a foreign wife. Ezra 10.26.

Abdias (ăbdī′ùs), Vulgate form of OBADIAH.

abdication, in a political sense, renunciation of high public office, usually by a monarch. Degrees of free will enter into the decision to abdicate; some abdications have reflected solely a personal desire and have been followed by undiminished prestige or even, as in the case of Philip V of Spain, by resumption of the throne. However, most abdications amount to a confession of failure of policy and loss of power; that of Emperor CHARLES V is unusual in that it was prompted by apparently sincere religious motives, and the emperor retained much prestige and actual power until his death. In China, forced abdication was frequent, the empire ending with the abdication of the boy ruler Hsüan T'ung in 1912 (see PU YI, HENRY). In Japan, however, voluntary abdication occurred more often; the retired ruler assumed a special title and led a life of religious contemplation, receiving many honors. Almost unique in political and constitutional history was the abdication of Edward VIII of England in 1936. Since 1688, when the English Parliament declared James II to have abdicated by reason of flight and subversion of the constitution, abdication by a British ruler without parliamentary consent has been forbidden. Though several written constitutions contain provisions for abdication, there are few uniformly accepted rules for dealing with it. Defeat and political chaos following the First and Second World Wars forced the abdication of many rulers, especially of Farouk of Egypt and Leopold III of Belgium.

Abdiel (ăb′dĭul) [Heb.,=servant of God], in the Bible, a Gadite. 1 Chron. 5.15.

abdomen, in man, portion of the trunk that lies below the diaphragm. The wall of the abdomen is a muscular structure covered by fascia, fat, and skin. The abdominal cavity, lined with a thin membrane, the peritoneum, contains the stomach, intestines, liver, pancreas, gall bladder, spleen, and kidneys, and in its lowermost portion (the pelvis) are the urinary bladder and the internal reproductive organs. The navel, or umbilicus, a circular scar on the abdominal wall, marks the point of attachment of the fetus to the maternal organism before birth.

Abdon [Heb.,=servile]. **1** Judge of Israel. Judges 12.13–15. **2** Officer under Josiah. 2 Chron. 34.20. Achbor: 2 Kings 22.12; Jer. 26.22; 36.12. **3, 4** Benjamites. 1 Chron. 8.23, 30; 9.36. **5** Unidentified boundary town, NW Palestine. Joshua 21.30; 1 Chron. 6.74. Hebron KJV and Ebron RSV. Joshua 19.28.

Abdu-l-Aziz IV (äb″dōōl-äzēz′), 1881?–1943, sultan of Morocco (1894–1908), son of Mulai-el-Hassan. His weak control was evident after the death (1900) of the regent Si Ahmed. His submissiveness to foreign influence, his indulgence in European novelties (which Moslems considered unbefitting his position as religious leader), and the higher taxes which he imposed to reorganize the army and to support his extravagances led to widespread unrest. A loan from France (1904) furnished a pretext for French demands which led in 1906 to the Conference of Algeciras. Moroccan disapproval of the settlement led to revolt; Abdu-l-Aziz was deposed (1908) by his brother Abdu-l-Hafid.

Abdu-l-Aziz, 1830–76, Ottoman sultan (1861–76), brother and successor of Abdu-l-Mejid. The reforms enacted under his rule could not outpace the decline of Turkey. In 1875 his bankrupt government repudiated the interest on the huge loans raised in Western Europe; this act led to foreign control over part of the Ottoman revenues. RUMANIA, SERBIA, and EGYPT gained virtual independence, and revolts broke out in Bosnia and Hercegovina and Bulgaria. Political decay was paralleled, however, by cultural rebirth. Many important schools were founded, and newspapers helped to educate the Turks politically. In 1876 MIDHAT PASHA, foremost among the liberals (the Young Turks), overthrew Abdu-l-Aziz, who died a few days later, probably by suicide. He was succeeded by his nephew, Murad V.

Abdu-l-Aziz ibn Saud: see IBN SAUD.

Abdu-l-Hafid (äb″dŏŏl-häfēd′), 1875?-1937, sultan of Morocco (1908-12). Put on the throne by the revolution which deposed his brother Abdu-l-Aziz IV, he was soon confronted with uprisings and the demands of European creditors. Besieged (1911) at Fez by rebels, he was relieved by a French army. On March 30, 1912, he accepted a French protectorate, and on Aug. 12 he abdicated.

Abdu-l-Hamid I (äb″dŏŏl-hämēd′), 1725-89, Ottoman sultan (1774-89), brother and successor of Mustafa III. His reign, one of decline, saw the end of the war of 1768-74 and the beginning of the war of 1787-91 with Catherine II of Russia (see RUSSO-TURKISH WARS). By the Treaty of Kuchuk Kainarji (1774) the Crimea became independent while Turkey lost Azov and granted Russia the position of protector of Moldavia and Walachia and of the Christians in general throughout the Ottoman Empire. The treaty, which established Russia as the foremost power in the Near East, had incalculable effects. In 1775 Austria, jealous of Russian expansion, forced the Porte to cede Bukovina. Abdu-l-Hamid was succeeded by his nephew, Selim III.

Abdu-l-Hamid II, 1842-1918, Ottoman sultan (1876-1909). His uncle, ABDU-L-AZIZ, was deposed by the Young Turks in 1876. Abdu-l-Hamid's brother, Murad V, succeeded, but was shortly declared insane, and Abdu-l-Hamid became sultan. He at first accepted (1876) the constitution of MIDHAT PASHA, but soon suspended it, dismissed Midhat, and eventually had him strangled. The war with Russia (see RUSSO-TURKISH WARS) led to the Treaty of SAN STEFANO, subsequently modified by the Congress of BERLIN. To save what remained of his empire, the sultan now pursued a policy of friendship with Germany. German officers reorganized the Turkish army, and German business interests obtained concessions, especially in the matter of the BAGHDAD RAILWAY. For his part in the Armenian massacres of 1894-96, he was called the Great Assassin and the Red Sultan. Ruling as an absolute monarch, he lived in virtual seclusion. In 1908 the Young Turks, who had penetrated the armed services, revolted and forced the sultan to adhere to the constitution of 1876. He was deposed (1909) when he tried to plot a counterrevolution and was succeeded by his brother, Mohammed V. See study by Joan Haslip (1958).

Abdu-l-Kadir (äb″dŏŏl-kädēr′), c.1807-83, Algerian leader claiming descent from Mohammed. Although of an anti-Turkish family, he was chosen emir of Mascara to fight the French invaders who had just defeated the Turks. From 1832 to 1839, by alternately fighting and coming to terms with the French, he extended his power over much of N Algeria, subduing hostile tribes and organizing the hinterland. A learned Moslem, he reformed his army along Western lines and finally proclaimed (1839) a holy war. In four years of fighting, Gen. Bugeaud drove him into Morocco, where he gained

Abdu-l-Aziz

Abdu-l-Kadir

the sultan's support. The Moroccan defeat at Isly (1844) soon forced the sultan to repudiate his ally. Abdu-l-Kadir surrendered in 1847 and was imprisoned in France until 1852. In 1860 he was awarded the Grand Cross of the Legion of Honor for assisting Christian victims of a riot in Damascus. See Wilfred Blunt, *Desert Hawk* (1947).

Abdullah (ăbdŭ′lŭ, äbdŏŏlä′), d. c.570, father of Mohammed.

Abdullah (Abdullah ibn Husein) (ăbdŭ′lŭ, äbdŏŏlä ĭ′bún hŏŏsīn′), 1882-1951, king of Jordan (1946-51), b. Mecca; son of HUSEIN IBN ALI. During the First World War, Abdullah led Arab revolts against Turkish rule and had British support. After the war he unsuccessfully fought against IBN SAUD for the control of the Hejaz. In 1921 Great Britain created Abdullah emir of Trans-Jordan. In the Second World War, Abdullah strongly opposed the Axis. Following the partition of Palestine (May, 1948) he led the troops of his British-trained force, the Arab Legion, against Israel. He annexed the portions of Palestine not assigned to Israel. His foreign policy was directed toward creation of an Arab federation, preferably under the rule of a member of his family. He was assassinated in Jerusalem in 1951. See his *Memoirs* (1951).

Abdullah ibn Yasin (ĭ′bún yäsēn′), d. 1059?, Mohammedan leader, founder of the ALMORAVIDES. A Berber leader in Morocco, he held sway by fiery zeal and strict observance of the Moslem law. He and his followers were marked by fanatic and puritanical intolerance.

Abdu-l-Malik (äb″dŏŏl-múlĭk′), c.646-705, 5th OMAYYAD caliph (685-705); son of Marwan I. At his accession, Islam was torn by dissension and hard pressed by the Byzantine Empire. With the help of his able general Hajjaj, Abdu-l-Malik overthrew the rival caliphs and united Islam. His battles with Byzantine forces were without final result. An able administrator, he introduced Arabic coins, improved postal facilities, made Arabic the official language, and reorganized the government.

Abdu-l-Mejid

Abdu-l-Mejid (äb″dŏŏl-mĕjēd′), 1823–61, Ottoman sultan (1839–61), son and successor of Mahmud II. The rebellion of MOHAMMED ALI was checked by the intervention (1840–41) of England, Russia, and Austria. Abdu-l-Mejid was influenced by the British ambassador, STRATFORD DE REDCLIFFE, who helped to bring on the CRIMEAN WAR (1853–56). The Congress of Paris (1856; see PARIS, CONGRESS OF) brought Turkey no advantage. Pressures from within and without Turkey persuaded Abdu-l-Mejid to introduce Western reforms. Two decrees (1839, 1856) led to many changes but did not have permanent effect. The sultan was succeeded by his brother, Abdu-l-Aziz.

Abdu-l-Mumin (äb″dŏŏl-mŏŏ′mĭn), d.1163, founder of the empire of the ALMOHADES. He was the favorite of the religious reformer Ibn Tumart and became (1130) his successor. Even before his rise to leadership, he had attacked the Almoravides. After long campaigns in Morocco and NW Algeria, he was able to destroy (1147) the Almoravide empire. In 1158 he invaded the Moslem states of Tunisia and NE Algeria which had been weakened by attacks by Arab nomads and Sicilian Normans. By 1160 his rule reached from the Atlantic to Tripoli. The last years of his life were spent fighting the Christians of Spain.

Abdu-r-Rahman (äb″dŏŏr-rä′män, –rämän′), 1778–1859, sultan of Morocco (1822–59). He sought, unsuccessfully, to take advantage of the overthrow of Turkish rule in Algeria in order to extend his territory. Later he allied himself with Abdu-l-Kadir, but after their defeat at Isly (1844) made peace with France and refused the emir further asylum in Morocco. Abdu-r-Rahman was at various times involved in difficulties with Austria, Spain, and England.

Abdu-r-Rahman I or **Abd· al-Rahman I** (äb″dŏŏl-), d. 788, first OMAYYAD emir of Córdoba (756–88). The only survivor when the Abbasids massacred· (750) his family, he fled from Damascus to Spain. There he defeated the emir of Córdoba at Alameda

and seized power. Despite the jealousy of the Arabian aristocracy and the turbulence of the Berbers, he reorganized and consolidated the state and tried to unite the various Moslem races. Though successful against the Franks, he did not recover all the territories taken by CHARLEMAGNE. The great mosque at Córdoba, which he started, was continued by his son and successor, Hisham I.

Abdu-r-Rahman III or **Abd al-Rahman III**, 891–961, OMAYYAD emir (912–29) and first caliph (929–61) of Córdoba. Under him Moslem Spain reached the height of its glory. He created internal peace and prosperity, consolidated the central government, and built up a strong army and navy. For a time (939–47) he controlled the Moslem northern part of Africa, and he successfully fought the Christian kings. He made CÓRDOBA one of the greatest cities in the West.

Abdu-r-Rahman or **Abd al-Rahman**, d. 732, Moslem governor of Spain (721–32). Invading (732) France, he won a victory at Toulouse but was defeated in the battle of Tours or Poitiers by CHARLES MARTEL.

Abdu-r-Rahman Khan (kän′, khän′), 1844?–1901, emir of Afghanistan (1880–1901); grandson of Dost Mohammed. He opposed his uncle, SHERE ALI, and had to go into exile in 1869. He was, however, recognized by the British as emir in 1880, and he supported British interests as against the Russians.

à Becket, Thomas: see THOMAS À BECKET, SAINT.

à Beckett, Gilbert Abbott (ŭbĕk′ĭt), 1811–56, English humorist and playwright. In 1831 he founded the humor magazine *Figaro in London;* he later became a regular contributor to *Punch.* Among his books are *The Comic History of England* (2 vols., 1847–48) and *The Comic History of Rome* (1852), both illustrated by John Leech.

Abed-nego (ŭbĕd′nēgō), one of the THREE HOLY CHILDREN.

Abel, son of Adam and Eve, a shepherd, killed by his older brother, Cain. Gen. 4.1–8. Mentioned as the first martyr. Mat. 23.35.

Abel, Sir Frederick Augustus, 1826–1902, English chemist, an authority on explosives. He was professor of chemistry at the Royal Military Academy (1851–55) and chemist to the War Dept. and government referee (1854–88). Among his achievements are improvements in the manufacture of guncotton; the invention, with Sir James Dewar, of cordite; a study, in collaboration with Sir Andrew Noble, Scottish physicist, of the behavior of black powder when fired; and the invention of an instrument used in the Abel test, named for him, to determine the flash point of petroleum. He wrote widely on explosives.

Abel, John Jacob, 1857–1938, American pharmacologist, b. Cleveland, grad. Univ. of Michigan, 1883, M.D. Univ. of Strasbourg, 1888. Professor of pharmacology (1893–1932) and director of the laboratory for endocrine research (from 1932) at Johns Hopkins, he is known for the isolation of epinephrine (adrenaline) in 1898 and later of insulin in crystalline form. Other contributions include the isolation of amino acids from the blood. He was a founder and editor (1909–32) of the *Journal of Pharmacology and Experimental Therapeutics.*

Abel, Thomas: see ABELL, THOMAS.

Abel. 1 Ostensibly a place name. 1 Sam. 6.18. The

RSV text does not give the name. **2** See ABEL-BETH-MAACHAH.

Abelard, Peter (ă'bŭlärd) Fr. *Pierre Abélard* (pyĕr' äbälär'), 1079–1142, French philosopher and teacher, b. Le Pallet, near Nantes. He went (c. 1100) to Paris to study under WILLIAM OF CHAMPEAUX at the school of Notre Dame and soon attacked the ultrarealist position of his master with such success that William was forced to modify his teaching. Abelard became master at Notre Dame but, when deprived of his place, set himself up (1112) at a school on Mont Ste Geneviève, just outside the city walls. Abelard's fame as a dialectician attracted great numbers of students to Paris; because of this fact Abelard is usually regarded as the founder of the Univ. of Paris. This part of his career was cut short by his romance with Heloise (d. c.1164), the learned and beautiful niece of Fulbert, canon of Notre Dame, who had hired Abelard as her tutor. After the birth of a son, a secret marriage was held to appease her uncle. Fulbert's ill-treatment of Heloise led Abelard to remove her secretly to the convent at Argenteuil. Fulbert, who thought that Abelard planned to abandon her, had ruffians attack and emasculate him. Abelard sought refuge at Saint-Denis, where he became a monk. In 1120 he left Saint-Denis to teach. At the instigation of his rivals, the Council of Soissons had his first theological work burnt as heretical (1121). After a short imprisonment, he returned to Saint-Denis but fell out with the monks and built a hermitage near Troyes. Students sought him out, and to house them he built a monastery, the Paraclete. When he became abbot at Saint-Gildas-en-Rhuys, Brittany, he gave the Paraclete to Heloise, who became an abbess of a sisterhood there. ST. BERNARD OF CLAIRVAUX thought Abelard's influence dangerous and secured his condemnation by the Council of Sens (1140). Abelard appealed to the pope, who upheld the council. Abelard submitted and retired to Cluny. He was buried at the Paraclete, as was Heloise; their bodies were later moved to Père-Lachaise in Paris. A Platonist in theology, Abelard emphasized the method of Aristotle's dialectic. His belief that the methods of logic could be applied to the truths of faith was in opposition to the mysticism of St. Bernard. He also opposed the extreme views of William of Champeaux and ROSCELIN on the problems of universals. His own solution, in which universals are considered as entities existent only in thought but with a basis in particulars, is called moderate realism and to some extent anticipates the conceptualism of St. Thomas Aquinas. His most influential work, the *Sic et non*, a collection of contradictory writings of the Fathers of the Church, formed the basis for the widely read *Sentences* of PETER LOMBARD, who may have been Abelard's pupil. Abelard was perhaps most important as a teacher; among his pupils were some of the celebrated men of the 12th cent., including John of Salisbury and Arnold of Brescia. Of Abelard's poetry only Latin hymns survive. He is chiefly remembered for the events of his life as chronicled in his autobiographical *Historia calamitatum* (Eng. tr. by J. T. Muckle, 1954) and revealed in the poignant letters of Heloise and Abelard (Eng. tr. by C. K. Scott Moncrieff, 1926).

Abelard installs Heloise as abbess of Paraclete.

See Joseph McCabe, *Life of Peter Abelard* (1901); J. G. Sikes, *Peter Abailard* (1932); E. H. Gilson, *Heloise and Abelard* (1938; Eng. tr., 1951).

Abel-beth-maachah (ā'bŭl-bĕth-mā'ŭkŭ) [Heb.,= meadow of the house of Maachah, perhaps the Syrian Maachah], town, Palestine, the modern Tel Abil (Israel), S of Metulla. It was attacked by Ben-hadad and taken by Tiglath-pileser. 1 Kings 15.20; 2 Kings 15.29. Abel and Beth-maachah: 2 Sam. 20.14. Abel of Beth-maachah: 2 Sam. 20.15. Abel-maim: 2 Chron. 16.4.

Abell, Kjeld (kyĕl' ä'bĕl), 1901–61, Danish playwright. His *Melody That Got Lost* (1935; Eng. tr., 1939) was an early success. Abell, trained as a stage designer, was an innovator in stage technique. He later turned to ethical and social drama; *Anna Sophie Hedvig* (1939; Eng. tr., 1944), *The Queen Walks Again* (1943), and *Silkeborg* (1946) are arresting and powerful problem plays concerned with justice, social protest, and the menace of National Socialism.

Abell or **Abel, Thomas** (both: ā'bŭl), d.1540, English Roman Catholic priest, chaplain to Katharine of Aragon. He vigorously opposed Henry VIII's divorce from Katharine both in his sermons and in a book, *Invicta veritas* [truth unconquered] (1532?).

Imprisoned on charges of concealing the treasons of Elizabeth Barton, the Maid of Kent, Abell spent six years in the Tower and was finally executed for upholding the validity of Henry's first marriage.

Abel-maim (–mā'ĭm) [Heb.,=meadow of the waters], the same as ABEL-BETH-MAACHAH.

Abel-meholah (–mĕhō'lù) [Heb.,=meadow of dancing], name of towns or districts mentioned in the Bible, probably not all different. **1** Near the Jordan; limit of the Midianites' flight. Judges 7.22. **2** In N central Palestine. 1 Kings 4.12. **3** Home of Adriel. 1 Sam. 18.19. **4** Elisha's home. 1 Kings 19.16. See MEHOLATHITE.

Abel-mizraim (–rā'ĭm) [Heb.,=meadow of the Egyptians], place "beyond Jordan" where Jacob was mourned. Gen. 50.11.

Abel-shittim: see SHITTIM.

Abenaki Indians: see ABNAKI INDIANS.

Aben Ezra, Abraham ben Meir: see IBN EZRA.

Abeokuta (ä″bēōkōō'tù, ä″–), city (pop. 84,451), SW Nigeria, founded c.1830. A fortified town, it was one of the YORUBA city-states which sprang up after the decline of the kingdom of Oyo. In the 19th cent. the town was constantly at war with slave raiders from Dahomey. Cotton cloth is dyed here.

Aberavon: see PORT TALBOT.

Aberbrothock: see ARBROATH.

Abercarn (ăbŭr'kärn'), urban district (pop. 19,221), Monmouthshire, W England. It is in a coal-mining district and has tin-plate works.

Aberconway: see CONWAY.

Abercrombie, Lascelles (lăs'ùlz ăb'ŭrkrŏmbĭ), 1881–1938, English poet and critic. His early books of poetry include *Interludes and Poems* (1908) and *Emblems of Love* (1912). He also wrote several influential works of criticism, notably *Thomas Hardy* (1912) and *The Theory of Poetry* (1924). A collected edition of his poems appeared in 1930.

Abercrombie, Sir Patrick, 1879–1957, British architect and town planner. Professor of civil design at the Univ. of Liverpool from 1915 to 1935 and of town planning at the Univ. of London after 1935, he acted as consultant in the rebuilding and planning of London, Edinburgh, Bath, and other British cities. He was knighted in 1945. His voluminous writing has been of considerable influence in the field of city and regional planning. He contributed numerous articles as well as founding (1910) and editing the *Town Planning Review*. His books include *The Preservation of Rural England* (1926) and *Town and Country Planning* (1933).

Abercrombie, Fort: See FORT ABERCROMBIE.

Abercromby, James, 1706–81, British general in the French and Indian Wars, b. Scotland. He arrived in America in 1756 and in 1758 replaced the earl of Loudoun as supreme British commander. After failing to take Ticonderoga from General Montcalm, Abercromby was replaced (1758) by Jeffrey AMHERST.

Abercromby, Sir Ralph, 1734–1801, British general. In his first period in the army (1756–83) he served on the Continent and retired chiefly because he had sympathized with the American colonists. Returning in 1793 for service against France, he won a major military reputation by his command of a brilliant retreat in Flanders in the winter of 1794–95. He was (1795–97) commander in chief in the West Indies, where he captured Grenada, St. Lucia, St. Vincent, and Trinidad. In 1800 Abercromby was sent to expel the French from Egypt and made a forced landing at Aboukir. In the first engagement, which was successful, he was mortally wounded. He is noted for having renewed the discipline and military reputation of the army.

Aberdare (ăbŭrdâr'), urban district (pop. 39,044), Glamorganshire, S Wales. It is in an anthracite and iron-ore region. Cables are made.

Aberdeen, George Gordon, 1st earl of (ăbŭrdēn'). 1637–1720, Scottish statesman. He exerted much influence on politics between 1680 and 1707. As lord chancellor of Scotland (1682–84), he enforced religious conformity, though not strictly enough to prevent his dismissal by the English commission. He refused to swear allegiance to the English revolutionary government that enthroned William III, was in retirement until 1703, and opposed the union of England and Scotland (1707) until he was assured that the Scots would not be treated as aliens.

Aberdeen, George Hamilton-Gordon, 4th earl of, 1784–1860, British statesman. Aberdeen negotiated, as ambassador to Austria, the Treaty of Töplitz (1813), which cemented Austria to the anti-Napoleonic coalition, and he helped arrange (1814) the peace terms at Paris. He was foreign secretary (1828–30) in the duke of Wellington's cabinet and colonial secretary (1834–35) under Sir Robert Peel. As foreign secretary (1841–46) in Peel's second government, he settled with the United States the Northeast Boundary Dispute by the Webster-Ashburton Treaty (1842) and ended the very threatening Oregon controversy by the treaty of 1846. He also improved relations with France. He supported Peel in abolishing the corn laws (1846) and resigned with him. As prime minister (1852–55), Aberdeen headed a brilliant coalition ministry, quite successful in home affairs. He was, however, unable to prevent Viscount Palmerston and others in his cabinet who wanted war from involving England on the side of Turkey in the Crimean War. Bad management of the campaigns and unpopularity of the war forced his resignation in 1855. See biography by Lady Frances Balfour (1922); study by W. D. Jones (1958).

George Hamilton-Gordon, 4th earl of Aberdeen.

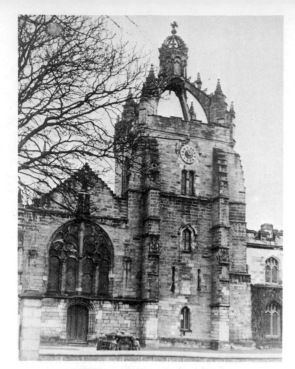

Crown Tower of King's College in Aberdeen.

Aberdeen Angus cow and calf.

England and the Low Countries as early as the 14th cent. It was a stronghold of royalist and episcopal sentiment in the religious wars of the 17th cent. Town records from 1398 are almost complete. Aberdeen is noted for its granite Cathedral of St. Machar. The Univ. of Aberdeen includes King's College (founded 1493) and Marischal College (founded 1593).

Aberdeen. 1 Village (pop. 1,484), SE Idaho, WNW of Pocatello, in a livestock, dairy, and irrigated farm region served by the Minidoka project. **2** Town (pop. 9,679), NE Md., NE of Baltimore, in a farm region; inc. 1892. The U.S. army's Aberdeen Proving Ground is nearby. **3** Cotton city (pop. 6,450), co. seat of Monroe co., NE Miss., on the Tombigbee and NNW of Columbus; inc. 1837. A number of ante-bellum houses remain. **4** Town (pop. 1,531), central N.C., WNW of Fayetteville; inc. 1893. It is a trade and shipping center for a tobacco and fruit area. **5** City (pop. 23,073), co. seat of Brown co., NE S.Dak., NW of Watertown; settled 1880, platted 1881, inc. 1882. The trade and distributing center for a wheat and livestock region, it has railroad shops, flour mills, and dairy-processing and meat-packing plants. Farm machinery and tools are made. A state teachers college is here. **6** City (pop. 18,741), W Wash., a port of entry on Grays Harbor, at the confluence of the Chehalis and the Wishkah rivers; settled 1867, platted 1884, inc. 1888. The lumber and fish-canning industries have been mainly responsible for the development of Aberdeen and its sister city, Hoquiam. Fishing is important, and there is also much shipping from both cities through the port on Grays Harbor. Aberdeen has a junior college.

Aberdeen Angus cattle, breed of black, hornless beef cattle originated in Scotland and introduced to the United States in 1873. They have low, compact bodies and are noted for the fine quality of their flesh. They are sometimes called Black Angus cattle.

Aberdeenshire (ăbŭrdēn′shĭr), county (1,971 sq. mi.; pop. 298,503), NE Scotland. ABERDEEN is the county town. The terrain varies from the GRAMPIANS in the southwest to the rolling farmlands of the Don valley and the treeless lowlands of BUCHAN. Oats, barley, turnips, and potatoes are grown.

Balmoral Castle in Aberdeenshire.

Aberdeen (ăbŭrdēn′), city (pop. 185,379), county town of Aberdeenshire, NE Scotland, on the North Sea at the mouth of the Dee. Part of the city lies in Kincardineshire. It is Scotland's third largest city and the only industrial center outside the midland belt. Famous as a herring and whitefish port, it is also known for its granite quarries. Other manufactures are paper, linen, and wool. There are engineering and chemical works and facilities for agricultural research. Aberdeen became a royal burgh in 1176 and was a leading port for trade with

Sheep and the famous Aberdeen Angus cattle are raised. Fishing is carried on from the North Sea ports of Aberdeen, FRASERBURGH, and PETERHEAD. The county was anciently inhabited by northern Picts. It was the headquarters of the Jacobite rising of 1715. BALMORAL CASTLE is the Scottish residence of the British kings and queens.

Aberhart, William (ā′bùrhärt), 1878–1943, premier of Alberta, Canada, b. near Seaforth, Ont., grad. Queen's Univ., 1906. He was a schoolteacher and a founder and dean of the Calgary Prophetic Bible Institute (opened 1927). About 1932 he became interested in SOCIAL CREDIT. He was an organizer of the Social Credit party of Alberta and was elected (1935) to the provincial legislature with enough supporters to control it. Thus Aberhart became premier (1935–43) of the first Social Credit government in the world. However, many of the legislative attempts to enact his principles were declared invalid by the courts.

Abernathy (ă′bùrnăthē), city (pop. 2,491), NW Texas, in the Llano Estacado N of Lubbock; platted 1909. It is a marketing and shipping point in a farm area.

aberration, in optics, a condition that causes a blurring and loss of clearness in the images produced by lenses or mirrors. Spherical aberration is caused by the failure of a lens or mirror to bring the rays of light from a point to a single focus. The effect results from the operation of the laws of optics, not from defects in construction. When there is a blurring of the image and fringes of color appear at its edges, the condition is called chromatic aberration. This results from the fact that some colors of light are bent more than others after passing through a lens. For example, violet is bent more than red, and violet light is brought to a focus nearer the lens than is red. See R. S. Longhurst, *Geometrical and Physical Optics* (1957).

Abersychan: see PONTYPOOL.

Abertawe: see SWANSEA.

Abertillery (ăbùrtĭlâr′ē), urban district (pop. 25,160), Monmouthshire, W England. It is in an area of coal and iron mines and produces tin plate.

Aberystwyth (-ĭst′wĭth), municipal borough (pop. 10,418), Cardiganshire, W Wales, on Cardigan Bay. It is a summer resort and a cultural center. It is the seat of a constituent college of the Univ. of Wales and of the National Library of Wales, which has an outstanding collection of Welsh manuscripts and which receives a copy of every book published in Great Britain.

Abez (ā′-), city of Issachar. Joshua 19.20.

Abgar, Epistles of: see PSEUDEPIGRAPHA.

Abi (ā′bĭ) [short for ABIJAH], King Hezekiah's mother. 2 Kings 18.2 Abijah: 2 Chron. 29.1.

Abia (ùbĭ′ù): see ABIJAH **2** and ABIJAH **6.**

Abiah (ùbĭ′ù), variant of ABIJAH. **1** Wife of Hezron. 1 Chron. 2.24. **2** Benjamite. 1 Chron. 7.8. **3** Second son of Samuel. 1 Sam. 8.2.

Abi-albon (ā″bĭ-ăl′-): see ABIEL **2.**

Abiasaph (ùbĭ′ùsăf) [Heb.,=my father has gathered], Levitical family. Ex. 6.24. Ebiasaph: 1 Chron. 6.23; 9.19. Asaph: 1 Chron. 26.1.

Abiathar (ùbĭ′ùthär) [Heb.,=father of plenty], priest, son of Ahimelech, the only one of his family who escaped massacre by Doeg. He fled to David, to whom he remained loyal. Later he sided with

Adonijah against Solomon, who took away from him the priesthood. 1 Sam. 22.9–23; 2 Sam. 15.17, 29; 1 Kings 1.7; 2.27; Mark 2.26. Name exchanged with his father's. 2 Sam. 8.17; 1 Chron. 18.16; 24.6.

Abida or **Abidah** (both: ùbĭ′–) [Heb.,=my father received knowledge], son of Midian. Gen. 25.4; 1 Chron. 1.33.

Abidan (ăb′ĭ–, ùbĭ′–) [Heb.,=my father is judge], Benjamite chief. Num. 1.11; 2.22; 7.60, 65; 10.24.

Abidjan (ăbĭjän′), city (pop. c.225,000), capital of the Republic of the Ivory Coast, S Ivory Coast, on the Ebrie Lagoon, off the Atlantic Ocean. It is the largest city of the Ivory Coast and a major rail terminus and port. Access to the ocean is by a canal through the lagoon bar. The city ships agricultural produce, notably coffee, cacao, and rubber. Built by the French in the early 1920s, it is one of Africa's most modern cities.

Abiel (ā′bēĕl, ùbĭ′ĕl, ăb′ēĕl) [Heb.,=my father is God]. **1** Grandfather of King Saul. 1 Sam. 9.1; 14.51. **2** One of David's mighty men. 1 Chron. 11.32. Probably erroneously Abi-albon. 2 Sam. 23.31.

Abiezer (ā″bĭē′zùr) [Heb.,=my father is help]. **1** Manassite. 1 Chron. 7.18. Jeezer. Num. 26.30. **2** One of David's chief men. 2 Sam. 23.27; 1 Chron. 27.12.

Abigail (ăb′ùgāl) [Heb.,=my father is joy]. **1** The wife of Nabal. She persuaded David not to take vengeance on her husband. When Nabal died, she married David. 1 Sam. 25; 2 Sam. 3.3; 1 Chron. 3.1. **2** David's stepsister, mother of Amasa. 2 Sam. 17.25; 1 Chron. 2.16, 17.

Abihail (ăbùhā′ùl) [Heb.,=my father is strength]. **1** Father of Queen Esther. Esther 2.15; 9.29. **2** Gadite. 1 Chron. 5.14. **3** Merarite woman. Num. 3.35. **4** Wife of Abishur. 1 Chron. 2.29. **5** Mother-in-law of Rehoboam. 2 Chron. 11.18.

Abihu (ùbĭ′hū) [Heb.,=he is father], son of Aaron, destroyed with his brother, Nadab, for offering "strange" fire. Ex. 6.23; 24.1,9; 28.1; Lev. 10.1; Num. 3.2,4; 26.60,61; 1 Chron. 6.3; 24.1,21.

Abihud (ùbĭ′hùd) [Heb.,=my father is majesty], grandson of Benjamin. 1 Chron. 8.3.

Abijah (ùbĭ′jù) [Heb.,=God is my father]. **1** See ABI. **2** Died c.911 B.C., king (c.914–c.911 B.C.) of Judah, the southern kingdom. He succeeded his father, Rehoboam, and King Jeroboam continued warfare against him. 2 Chron. 13. Abijam: 1 Kings 15.1–8. Abia: 1 Chron. 3.10; Mat. 1.7. **3** Son of Jeroboam, whose death was used by a prophet to foreshadow Jeroboam's. 1 Kings 14. **4,5** See ABIAH **2,3. 6** Priestly family. 1 Chron. 24.10. Abia: Luke 1.5. **7,8** Priests in the return to Jerusalem. Neh. 10.7; 12.4,17.

Abijam (ùbĭ′jùm): see ABIJAH **2.**

Abila (ăb′ĭlù), ancient town, W Syria. Its ruins lie between Damascus and Baalbek. It was the capital of Abilene, the tetrachy mentioned in Luke 3.1.

Abildgaard, Nikolaj Abraham (nē′kōlĭ ä′bĕlgôrd), 1743–1809, Danish painter of the neoclassical school. Among his pupils were Thorvaldsen and Eckersberg. Most of his work is in Copenhagen.

Abilene, Syria: see ABILA.

Abilene (ăb′ĭlēn). **1** City (pop. 6,746), co. seat of Dickinson co., central Kansas, on the Smoky Hill River and W of Topeka; laid out 1860, inc. 1869. It was (1867–71) a railhead for a large cattle-raising region extending SW into Texas. Under the promotion of J. G. McCoy, millions of head of cattle followed the Chisholm Trail into Abilene's stockyards, whence they were shipped. One of the wildest and toughest cowtowns of the old West, Abilene once had Wild Bill Hickok as its marshal. The city, now a shipping point for a wheat and farm region, has feed and flour mills. Greyhound racing dogs are bred here. Dwight D. Eisenhower lived in Abilene in his youth; the Eisenhower Center (completed 1961) includes his old family homestead, a museum, and the Eisenhower Library, containing documents of the former President's administration. Old Abilene Town is a replica of the old cattle town, with some of the original buildings restored. An annual state fair is held. See S. P. Verckler, *Cowtown Abilene* (1961). **2** City (pop. 90,368), co. seat of Taylor co., W central Texas, WSW of Fort Worth. Buffalo hunters first settled here, and the town was founded in 1881 with the coming of the railroad. It has grown as a shipping point for cattle ranches and is today the financial, commercial, and educational center of a large part of W Texas. The city manufactures oil-field equipment and is the headquarters of regional petroleum interests. Food and dairy products and cottonseed oil are made, and grain is handled. Abilene's colleges, all coeducational, are Hardin-Simmons Univ. (Baptist; 1891), Abilene Christian College (Church of Christ; 1906), and McMurry College (Methodist; 1920). Also here are a large state-owned hospital as well as Dyess Air Force Base and U.S. military installations. Abilene is proud of its planned neatness and of its interest in music. Within a radius of 25 mi. are the ruins of Fort Phantom Hill, an early army post and stagecoach stop; the ruins of the old frontier town of Buffalo Gap; and Lake Abilene, the city's reservoir, in a state park.

Abimael (ūbĭm′āĕl), descendant of Shem. Gen. 10.28; 1 Chron. 1.22.

Abimelech (ūbĭm′ulĕk) [Heb.,=my father is Melech, or king]. **1** Name or title of a king of Gerar, who had various dealings with Abraham and Isaac. Gen. 20; 21; 26. **2** See AHIMELECH 1. **3** Son of Gideon. He slew his 70 brothers, except Jotham, and became "king." Judges 9.1–57; 2 Sam. 11.21. **4** See ACHISH 1.

Abinadab (ūbĭn′udăb) [Heb.,=my father is liberal]. **1** Second son of Jesse. 1 Sam. 16.8; 17.13; 1 Chron. 2.13. **2** Son of King Saul, killed at the battle of Mt. Gilboa. 1 Sam. 31.2; 1 Chron. 10.2. **3** Man in whose house the ark remained 20 years. 1 Sam. 7.1,2; 2 Sam. 6.3,4; 1 Chron. 13.7. **4** Father of one of Solomon's chief officers. 1 Kings 4.11. The officer is called Ben-abinadab in RSV.

Abingdon (ăb′ĭngdŭn), municipal borough (pop. 14,283), Berkshire, S central England. It is a popular resort and an agricultural center. There are ruins of a Benedictine abbey dating from 675.

Abingdon. 1 City (pop. 3,469), W central Ill., S of Galesburg, in a farm area; inc. 1857. Plumbing supplies and pottery are made. **2** Town (pop. 4,758), co. seat of Washington co., extreme SW Va., NE of Bristol; settled c.1765, inc. 1778. Burley tobacco and livestock are auctioned here, and the town is noted for its handicrafts and the manufacture of lusterware. An annual festival of crafts and antiques is held. The Barter Theatre, opened in 1933, is here.

Abington, town (pop. 10,607), E Mass., NE of Brockton; settled 1668, inc. 1713. It has some manufacturing.

Abinoam (ûbĭn′ōŭm) [Heb.,=my father is loveliness], father of Barak. Judges 4.6,12; 5.12.

Abiram (ûbī′rŭm) [Heb.,=my father is the high one]. **1** Levite who died with his brother DATHAN. **2** Son of a rebuilder of Jericho, associated obscurely with its foundations. 1 Kings 16.34.

Abishag (ăb′−), Shunammite woman, David's attendant in his old age and the cause of Adonijah's murder. 1 Kings 1; 2.

Abishai (ûbĭsh′āī, ăb′ĭshī), nephew of David. 2 Sam. 2.18–24; 10; 18; 23.18; 1 Sam. 26.6–9.

Abishalom (ûbĭsh′ŭlŏm, ûbī′shŭ−) [Heb.,=my father is peace]: see ABSALOM.

Abishua (ûbĭsh′ūŭ). **1** Priest. 1 Chron. 6.4,5,50; Ezra 7.5. **2** Benjamite. 1 Chron. 8.4.

Abishur (ăb′ĭshŭr, ûbī′−) [Heb.,=my father is a wall], grandson of Jerahmeel. 1 Chron. 2.28.

Abital (ăb′ĭtăl) [Heb.,=my father is dew], mother of David's son Shephatiah. 2 Sam. 3.4; 1 Chron. 3.2.

Abitibi, Fort: see FORT ABITIBI.

Abitibi Lake (ăbûtĭb′ē), c.60 mi. long, on the Que.-Ont. boundary, Canada, NW of Rouyn, Que. It is drained by the Abitibi river, which flows c.200 mi. W and N to the Moose river near James Bay.

Abitub (ăb′ĭtŭb) [Heb.,=my father is good], Benjamite. 1 Chron. 8.11.

Abiud (ăb′ĭŭd) [Gr. for ABIHUD], son of Zerubbabel in Matthew's genealogy. Mat. 1.13.

Abkhaz Autonomous Soviet Socialist Republic (ăbkăz′, Rus. ŭpkhäs′) or **Abkhasia** (ăbkä′zhŭ, Rus. ŭpkhä′zĕŭ), autonomous state (3,300 sq. mi.; pop. c.400,000), NW Georgian SSR, between the Black Sea and the Greater Caucasus. Gagry and Sukhum, the capital, are the chief cities. Mainly a subtropical agricultural region, it also has coal mines and health resorts. Its inhabitants, mostly concentrated along the agricultural coastal strip, are Abkhasian (pop. c.74,000), Georgian, Russian, and Armenian. The Abkhasians, who call themselves Apsua, are an Orthodox Christian and Mohammedan people of the North Caucasian linguistic family. Originally colonized (c. 6th cent. B.C.) by the Greeks, Abkhasia was conquered by the Romans in 65 B.C. As part of W Georgia, Abkhasia came under Byzantine influence in the 6th cent. A.D. The Abkhasian kings united all of W Georgia in the 8th cent., and in the 10th cent. Abkhasia joined the Georgian state. In 1578, Abkhasia came under Turkish control, but it was annexed by Russia in 1810. It became an autonomous republic in 1922.

ablative (ă′blŭtĭv″) [Latin,=for carrying off], in Latin grammar, CASE used in a number of circumstances, particularly with certain prepositions and in locating place or time. The term is also used in the grammar of some languages (e.g., Sanskrit, Finnish) for a case of separation (e.g., translating "from the house").

ablaut (äp′lout) [Ger.,=off-sound], in INFLECTION, vowel variation (as in English *sing, sang, sung, song*) caused by former differences in syllabic accent. In a prehistoric period the corresponding forms of the language (known through scientific reconstruction) had differences in accent, not differences in vowel. A variation of vowel associated with variation of accent is seen in ǎ′tùm versus ùtǒ′mǐk, where ǎ′– alternates with ù– and –ǒ′– with –ù–. Such variation is often called gradation. See UMLAUT.

Abnaki Indians or **Abenaki Indians** (both: ăbnä′kē), North American Indians of ALGONQUIAN stock. The name is a vague one, applied by some of the Indians to all Atlantic seaboard tribes and used by early white visitors—notably Sébastien Rasles—to mean a more or less related group of tribes in present S New Brunswick and Maine, including the Malecite, the Passamaquoddy, and the Penobscot. After most of these Indians had removed to Canada, leaving only small remnants on the coast, the name referred more especially to the Penobscot. The Abnaki—under any definition of the term—were in settled villages, often stockaded, and lived by growing corn, fishing, and hunting. Their own name for their conical huts covered with bark or mats, *wigwam*, came to be generally used in English. See F. G. Speck, *Penobscot Man* (1940).

Abner [Heb.,=my father is Ner], relative of Saul and commander in chief of his army. Jealousy and revenge probably caused his death at Joab's hands. 1 Sam. 9.1; 14.50,51; 17.55; 2 Sam. 2; 3.

Abney, Sir William de Wiveleslie (wǐ′vŭlzlē), 1843–1920, British chemist and physicist. He experimented in photography and was the first to make plates that were sensitive to the red and infrared of the solar spectrum.

Abo: see TURKU.

abolitionists, in U.S. history, particularly in the three decades before the Civil War, those who agitated for the compulsory emancipation of Negro slaves. They are to be distinguished from those who opposed the further extension of slavery (the free-soilers), but the groups came to act together politically and otherwise in the antislavery cause. (For wider relations of the antislavery movement, see SLAVERY.) Although antislavery sentiment had existed during the American Revolution and Benjamin LUNDY began his work early in the 19th cent., the abolition movement did not reach crusading proportions until the 1830s. One of its mainsprings was a strong religious revival which, beginning in W New York in 1824, swept much of the North by 1830. The moving spirit in the revival was Charles G. FINNEY, who created among his converts a powerful impulse towards social reform—emancipation of the slaves, temperance, foreign missions, and woman's rights. Outstanding among Finney's converts were Theodore D. WELD and the brothers Arthur and Lewis TAPPAN. The Tappans and William Lloyd GARRISON, recently returned from Great Britain (which had just abolished slavery in the West Indies), were the principal organizers in Dec., 1833, at Philadelphia, of the American Anti-Slavery Society. The primary concern of the society was the denunciation of slavery as a moral evil. It flooded the slave states with literature until Southern Congressmen were provoked into seeking exclusion of abolitionist journals, pamphlets, and tracts from the mails. The society's agents, especially Weld and his disciples, journeyed throughout the North preaching the ambiguous doctrine of "immediate abolition, gradually accomplished," which confirmed most Northerners in their opinion that abolition-ists were impractical visionaries, dangerous to the security of society. However, many local branches of the society were founded; these, with women especially active, sent thousands of antislavery petitions to the House of Representatives. The congressional attempt to set aside these petitions (see GAG RULES) and the killing of the abolitionist editor Elijah P. LOVEJOY were ably exploited by abolitionists as flagrant violations of the constitutional guarantees of the right of petition and freedom of the press and won them increasing sympathy in the North. Abolitionists united in denouncing the African venture of the AMERICAN COLONIZATION SOCIETY, but disagreed among themselves as to how their goal might be best reached. Garrison believed moral suasion was the only weapon; he and his followers also tied other reforms, notably woman's rights, to their abolitionism, thus disturbing the less radical element. Direct political action was advocated by James G. BIRNEY, presidential candidate of the LIBERTY PARTY in 1840 and 1844. These differences caused the movement to dissolve into small factional groups in the early 1840s, although state and local societies continued and antislavery feeling expanded. Writers such as John G. WHITTIER and orators such as Wendell PHILLIPS gave their services to the cause, while Frederick DOUGLASS and other freed or escaped slaves also took to the lecture platform. An antislavery lobby was organized in 1842, and its influence grew under Weld's able direction. Abolitionists hoped to convert the South through the churches, until the withdrawal of Southern Methodists (1844) and Baptists (1845) from association with their Northern brethren. After the demise of the Liberty party, which, in its brief existence, had hastened the extinction of the WHIG PARTY, the political abolitionists supported the FREE-SOIL PARTY in 1848 and 1852, and in 1856 they voted with the Republican party. The passage of more stringent fugitive slave laws in 1850 increased abolitionist activity on the UNDERGROUND RAILROAD. *Uncle Tom's Cabin*, by Harriet Beecher STOWE, a most effective piece of abolitionist propaganda, and the KANSAS question further aroused both North and South, and the culminating act of extreme abolitionism occurred in the raid of John BROWN on Harpers Ferry. After the opening of the Civil War insistent abolitionist demands for immediate freeing of the slaves greatly embarrassed Lincoln in his struggle to keep the border states loyal (see EMANCIPATION PROCLAMATION). Though the movement was one of high moral purpose and courage, its uncompromising temper helped to prevent any other solution of the slavery question than that of war. See L. D. Turner, *Antislavery Sentiment in American Literature Prior to 1865* (1929); G. H. Barnes, *The Antislavery Impulse, 1830–1844* (1933, rev. ed., 1957); A. C. Cole, *The Irrepressible Conflict, 1850–1865* (1934); D. L. Dumond, *Antislavery Origins of the Civil War in the United States* (1939; rev. ed., 1959); A. Y. Lloyd, *The Slavery Controversy, 1831–1860* (1939); H. H. Simms, *A Decade of Sectional Controversy, 1851–1861* (1942); Lawrence Lader, *The Bold Brahmins: New England's War against Slavery* (1961).

abominable snowman or **yeti,** manlike creature so named because he is associated with the land of perpetual snow in Himalayan regions. A figure unknown except through tracks ascribed to him and through alleged meetings, he is described as 6 or 7 ft. tall, covered with long, dark hair. Attempts after the 1950s to verify these tracks (notably by Sir Edmund Hillary in 1960) have had no results. While many scholars dismiss existence of the snowman as a myth, others claim that he may be a form of hitherto unclassified ape.

abortion, expulsion of the product of conception before the fetus is viable. Any interruption of human pregnancy prior to the 28th week is known as abortion. Some authorities restrict the use of this term to the first 12 weeks and refer to the premature termination of pregnancy after the placenta is formed as a miscarriage. Popularly, miscarriage is used to signify accidental premature birth at any period, as opposed to purposely induced abortion. Spontaneous abortion may occur after the death of the fetus and hemorrhage in the uterus. Spontaneous expulsion during the last two thirds of pregnancy may be due to many causes, among them infectious disease (e.g., syphilis and toxemia), endocrine dysfunction (as in hypothyroidism and diabetes), and trauma. In certain cases, in order to save the life of the mother, the fetus is delivered within the first two thirds of pregnancy when it cannot survive. However, in any other case, to produce or to attempt to produce abortion in a pregnant woman is a legal offense in all states of the United States. Among animals a serious and fairly common disease is CONTAGIOUS ABORTION (see also UNDULANT FEVER).

Aboukir or **Abukir** (both: ă″bōōkēr′, ŭbōō′kŭr), village, Egypt, on Aboukir Bay, SW of the Rosetta mouth of the Nile and 13 mi. NE of Alexandria. The village is on a promontory where lay ancient CANOPUS. Horatio Nelson's victory here over the French fleet (sometimes called the battle of the Nile) on Aug. 1, 1798, restored British prestige in the Mediterranean and, with the land victory (1801) under Sir Ralph Abercromby, cut short Napoleon's venture.

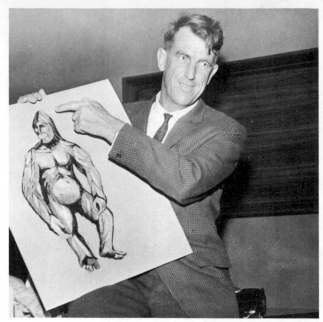

Sketch of the abominable snowman, displayed by Sir Edmund Hillary during a 1960 news conference in Chicago.

abracadabra (ăb′rŭkŭdăb′rŭ), magical formula used by the Gnostics of the 2d cent. to invoke the aid of benevolent spirits to ward off disease and affliction. It is supposed to be derived from, or similar in origin to, the abraxas, a word highly significant of the Supreme Power, which was engraved on gems and amulets or was variously worn as a protective charm. Handed down through the Middle Ages, the abracadabra gradually lost its occult significance, and its meaning was extended to cover any hocus-pocus.

Abraham [according to Gen. 17.5=father of many] or **Abram** [Heb.,=the father is high], progenitor of the Hebrews. He is the example of a man devoted to God, as in his journey to Canaan from Haran, his treatment of Lot, or his willingness to sacrifice his son. He is principally important as the founder of Judaism, the religion of a covenant. In this function he instituted circumcision and received the promise of Canaan for his people, who are descended from Isaac, the son of his old age. Gen. 11–25. Because of this dual role as founder of a race and its religion, the expression "Abraham's bosom," meaning the bliss awaiting his children, was current among later Jews and has become, for Christians, a synonym for heaven. Luke 16.19–31. His titles, Father of the Faithful and Friend of God (2 Chron. 20.7; Rom. 4.11), are used by Mohammedans, who deem him ancestor, through Ishmael, of the Arabs. The frequent use of his name among Christians and the numerous paintings depicting the story of the sacrifice of Isaac (e.g., by Andrea del Sarto) testify to the universal reverence in which worshipers of God have held this founder of their faith. Modern biblical research tends to accept his historicity. See Sir C. L. Woolley, *Abraham: Recent Discoveries and Hebrew Origins* (1936).

The battle of Aboukir.

Abraham, Plains of, comparatively level field adjoining the upper part of the city of Quebec, Canada. Here was fought in 1759 the famous battle between the English under Gen. James WOLFE and the French under MONTCALM which, by an English victory, decided the outcome of the last of the FRENCH AND INDIAN WARS and led to British supremacy in Canada. Part of the battle site is now occupied by suburban buildings, but a part is preserved as a national park. See C. P. Stacey, *Quebec, 1759: the Siege and the Battle* (1959).

Abraham ben Meir ibn Ezra: see IBN EZRA.

Abraham Lincoln Birthplace National Historic Site, 116.50 acres, central Ky., near Hodgenville; est. 1916. Abraham Lincoln was born in a log cabin in this area on Feb. 12, 1809. The exact location of the original cabin has not been conclusively established, but evidence seems to indicate that the cabin was situated on top of the knoll where the

Abraham Lincoln Birthplace National Historic Site, near Hodgenville, Ky.

memorial building now stands. Inside of the building is the log cabin traditionally accepted as Lincoln's birthplace.

Abram: see ABRAHAM.

Abramovich, Sholem (or Solomon) Yakob: see MENDELE MOCHER SFORIM.

Abramovitz, Max (ûbrăm′ŏvĭtz), 1908–, American architect, b. Chicago, grad. Univ. of Illinois (B.S., 1929), M.S. Columbia, 1931. He studied at the École des Beaux-Arts. In 1940 he and W. K. HARRISON became partners. In 1955 he became the supervising architect at Brandeis Univ., where his interfaith chapel group is most notable. He designed Philharmonic Hall at Lincoln Center and the law school at Columbia Univ., both completed in 1962.

Abrantès, Laure (Permon) Junot, duchesse d' (lôr′ pĕrmõ′ zhünō′, düshĕs′ däbrätĕs′), 1784–1838, French memoirist; wife of Gen. Andoche JUNOT. She was noted for her extravagance and frivolity. After her husband's death she joined in legitimist conspiracies, and under the Restoration her salon was a social and literary center. Her memoirs (1831–38), in many volumes, describe the scandals and personalities she knew.

Abrantes (ûbrän′tĭsh), town (pop. c.3,510), Santarém dist., central Portugal, in Ribatejo prov., on the Tagus river. It is the commercial center of a fruitgrowing region. Through the centuries it was a strategic point on the road to Lisbon. Alfonso I took it from the Moors in 1148. John I gathered his army here before the battle of Aljubarrota (1385). In the Napoleonic Wars, the French under Junot won the battle of Abrantes in 1807 but in 1810 were unable to take the town by siege.

abrasive, material used for grinding, smoothing, cutting, or polishing another substance. Among the important natural abrasives are DIAMOND (in the form of dust and small inferior stones), CORUNDUM, emery, SAND, ground quartz, PUMICE, kieselguhr, chalk, and TRIPOLI. Important artificial abrasives are alundum (see ALUMINA), carborundum (see SILICON CARBIDE), and boron carbide, all of which are very hard. Tripoli, chalk, and aluminum hydroxide, suspended in water, are efficient polishing agents. Silicon carbide, emery, and corundum are frequently mixed with cement and molded into wheels, blocks, and sticks. The finer powders are dusted on glue paper to produce emery paper, glass paper, and sandpaper. Pumice, finely powdered, is used to remove tartar from teeth. Sand is used to great advantage in sandblast machines. Automobile cylinders and valves are ground with emery or carborundum powder, mixed with oil, and tools are sharpened on emery wheels. Diamonds are cut by a thin disc of copper revolving at high speed and dipping into a small container of oil and diamond dust. Materials with abrasive qualities can do much damage to machinery, especially to bearings and sliding parts.

Abravanel or **Abarbanel, Isaac** (ûbrä′vŭnĕl, –bärbü′–), 1437–1508, Jewish theologian, biblical commentator, and financier, b. Lisbon. He served as treasurer to Alfonso V of Portugal until Alfonso's death and subsequently was employed by Ferdinand and Isabella and by the governments of Naples and Venice. His biblical commentaries are notable for their interpretation of the books of the Bible in terms of their various historical and social **backgrounds and for their liberal quotations from Christian commentaries.** Other sections of his work are devoted to the defense of miracles against the rationalistic explanations of Maimonides and to analyses of the Messianic prophecies. His son Judah, known as Leone Ebreo (1460–1521), was famous as the author of *Dialogues on Love,* which set forth that only through love could man reach a union with God.

Abruzzi, Luigi Amedeo, duca degli (lwē′jē ämädä′ŏ dōōkä dä′lyē abrōōt′tsē), 1873–1933, Italian explorer and mountain climber; cousin of Victor Emmanuel III. He led (1897) the first ascent of Mt. St. Elias in Alaska. His polar expedition (1899–1900) reached a point farther north than Nansen's record. He explored (1906) the

Absalom's death.

Ruwenzori range in Africa and unsuccessfully attempted (1909) to reach the peak of Mt. Godwin Austen. After 1919 he explored and tried to establish colonies in East Africa. A naval officer, he served in the Italo-Turkish war and the First World War. Records of his polar exploration and his Asiatic mountain climbing have been translated.

Abruzzi e Molise (äbrōōt′sē ā môlē′zĕ), region (5,881 sq. mi.; pop. 1,689,184), S central Italy, along the Adriatic Sea and in the Apennines, which culminate here in the GRAN SASSO D'ITALIA. The region is divided into five provinces named after their chief towns. Aquila, Chieti, Pescara, and Teramo, in the north, constitute the Abruzzi; Campobasso prov., in the south, is coextensive with Molise. Sheep are raised on the extensive pastures; vineyards and olive groves cover the lower mountain slopes; and cereals are produced along the coast and in the fertile area of reclaimed Lake Fucino. The region was conquered by the Romans in the 4th cent. B.C. It was part of the Lombard duchy of Spoleto (6th–11th cent.), the Norman kingdom of Sicily (12th–13th cent.), and the kingdom of Naples (13th–19th cent.).

Absalom (ăb′sŭlŏm) [Heb.,=father of peace], son of David. He murdered his brother Amnon for the rape of their sister Tamar and fled. After a time he returned, but no sooner was he reconciled with his father than he stirred up a rebellion ultimately fatal to himself. 2 Sam. 3.3; 13–19; 2 Chron. 11.20,21. The form Abishalom in 1 Kings 15.2,10 is probably a substitution from taboo.

Absalon (äp′sälôn) or **Axel** (äk′sŭl), c.1128–1201, Danish churchman, archbishop of Lund (1178–1201). He had great influence on political affairs under Waldemar I and Canute VI, warred against the pagan Wends, and in 1184 won a naval victory over Bogislav, duke of Pomerania. He attempted monastic reforms, introduced canon law into Denmark, and was patron of Svend Aagesen and Saxo Grammaticus. Absalon founded (1167) Copenhagen on the site of a village which had been granted to him by the king.

Absaroka Indians: see CROW INDIANS.

Absaroka Range (ăbsŭrō′kŭ), part of the Rocky Mts., c.150 mi. long, NW Wyo. and S Mont., partly in Yellowstone National Park and W of the Bighorns. Francs (or Franks) Peak is 13,140 ft. high. The Absarokas include Shoshone National Forest

Roman ruins dating from the 4th century B.C. in the Abruzzi e Molise region.

in Wyoming and part of Custer National Forest in Montana.

abscess, accumulation of pus in the tissues as a result of infection. Abscesses are characterized by inflammation and swelling, often painful. They occur in the skin, at the root of a tooth, in the middle ear (see MASTOID), on the eyelid (see STY), in the mammary glands, in the recto-anal area (see HEMORRHOIDS), and elsewhere in the body. In tuberculosis, abscesses (tubercles) may develop in lung tissue, in the lymph nodes, and in bone. A sinus abscess may result in a FISTULA, and abscess of the appendix in appendicitis. Unless an abscess discharges spontaneously, surgical incision and drainage is required. Many cases respond to treatment with antibiotics. See BOIL and CARBUNCLE.

Absecon (ăbsē′kún), city (pop. 4,320), SE N.J., NW of Atlantic City; settled c.1780, inc. 1902.

absentee ownership, system under which a person (or a corporation) controls and derives income from land in a region in which he does not live. Abuses existed in absenteeism in pre-Revolutionary France, in 19th-century Ireland, in E and SE Europe before the First World War, and in some oil-producing nations of the Middle East as late as the 1960s. Revolution and reform have abolished or greatly reduced the amount of absentee control in recent years. In the United States the term has been applied to the concentration of control of wealth through various corporate devices. Chain stores and branch banking are sometimes classified as types of absentee ownership.

absinthe (ăb′sĭnth), an emerald-green, toxic LIQUEUR distilled from wormwood and other aromatics, including angelica root, sweet-flag root, star anise, and dittany, which have been macerated and steeped in alcohol. Genuine absinthe is 70 to 80 percent alcohol. Excessive consumption of absinthe affects the digestive organs and nerve centers and may produce delirium and idiocy. Its manufacture and sale were prohibited by Switzerland (1908) and France (1915), formerly the chief producers. In 1912 the United States forbade the importation of absinthe.

absolute, in philosophy, the opposite of relative. The term has acquired numerous widely variant connotations in different philosophical systems. It means unlimited, unconditioned, or free of any relation; perfect, complete, or total; permanent, inherent, or ultimate; independent, or valid without reference to a perceiving subject. In logic, absolute means certain or indubitable as opposed to probable or hypothetical. As a substantive, the absolute is the ultimate basis of reality, the principle underlying the universe. Theologically, it is synonymous with, or characteristic of, God. Philosophically, it may be considered as the unknowable, the thing-in-itself; as that ultimate nonrelative which is the basis of all relation; as the ultimate, all-comprehensive principle in which all differences and distinctions are merged. The concept of the absolute was present in Greek philosophy. In modern days, both realists and idealists have used the term, but it is, perhaps, most intimately connected with the idealism of HEGEL.

absolute monarchy: see MONARCHY.

absolute music, term used for music dependent on its structure alone for comprehension. It is the antithesis of PROGRAM MUSIC. It is not associated with extramusical ideas or with a pictorial or narrative scheme of emotions, nor does it attempt to reproduce sounds in nature. Hence it is always instrumental, although not all instrumental music is absolute.

absolute pitch, the position of a tone in the musical scale determined according to the number of vibrations per second, irrespective of other tones. The term also denotes the capacity to identify any tone upon hearing it sounded alone or to sing any specified tone. Experiments have shown that this ability can be acquired through practice, but in some individuals it is inborn.

absolute zero: see TEMPERATURE.

absorption: see GAS; OSMOSIS; SPECTRUM.

abstinence: see FASTING; TEMPERANCE MOVEMENTS.

abstract art: see ABSTRACT EXPRESSIONISM and MODERN ART.

abstract expressionism, movement of abstract painting that emerged in New York city during the mid-1940s and attained singular prominence in American art in the following decade; also called action

Abstract expressionism: Jackson Pollock's **Night Dancer.**

painting and the New York school. It was the first important school in American painting to declare its independence from European styles and to influence the development of art abroad. Arshile Gorky gave signal impetus to the movement.

His paintings, first derived from the art of Picasso, Miró, and surrealism, became more personally expressive. Jackson Pollock's turbulent yet elegant abstract paintings were created by spattering paint on huge canvases placed on the floor. His paintings, with their radical method of execution, brought abstract expressionism before a hostile public. Willem de Kooning's first one-man show in 1948 established him as a highly influential artist. His intensely complicated abstract paintings of the 1940s were followed by images of *Woman*, grotesque versions of the movie-star ideal of womanhood, which were virtually unparalleled in the sustained savagery of their execution. Other important artists were Hans Hofmann and Robert Motherwell. Painters such as Philip Guston and Franz Kline turned to the abstract late in the 1940s and soon developed strikingly original styles—one, lyrical and evocative, the other, forceful and boldly dramatic. Abstract expressionism has presented a broad range of stylistic diversity within its largely, though not exclusively, nonrepresentational framework. For example, the impulsive stroking and charge in paintings by de Kooning or Pollock mark the op-

posite end of the pole from the simple, quiescent images of a Mark Rothko. Basic to most abstract expressionist painting are the attention paid to surface qualities, i.e., qualities of brushstroke and texture; the use of huge canvases; the adoption of an "all-over" space whereby all parts of the canvas play an equally vital role in the total work; the harnessing of "accidents" that occur during the process of painting; and the glorification of the act of painting itself as a means of visual communication.

abstract of title, in law, history of the title to a piece of land. A brief account is given of recorded documents, court proceedings, wills, mortgages, taxes, previous sales, and all other factors that at any time affected the ownership or use of the property. The old rule in England required that an abstract of title should cover the 60 years before the proposed sale. In 1874 this was changed to 40 years. No such rule exists in the United States, where the procedure is to trace the title, if possible, back to the original grant from the government.

Abubakar Tafawa Balewa, Alhaji Sir: see BALEWA, ALHAJI SIR ABUBAKAR TAFAWA.

Abu Bakr (ä′bōō bă′kŭr), 573–634, 1st caliph, friend, father-in-law, and successor of Mohammed. He was probably Mohammed's first convert outside the Prophet's family and certainly his most zealous believer. He alone accompanied Mohammed on the hegira. The marriage of his daughter Ayesha to Mohammed made the ties even stronger. On the Prophet's death in 632, Omar secured Abu Bakr's election over the tribal chiefs and Ali. The two years of his caliphate were critical for Islam. Though he was himself fervent rather than warlike, his party crushed opposition in Arabia and began the remarkable extension of Islam as a world religion. He was succeeded by OMAR.

Abubus (–bū′–), father of the Ptolemy who murdered Simon the Maccabee. 1 Mac. 16.11.

Abu Hanifa (ä′bōō hänē′fä), 699–767, Moslem

Mark Rothko's Composition No. 23.

Willem de Kooning's Marilyn Monroe.

Façade of the principal temple at Abu-Simbel, before its removal to higher ground above Lake Nasser.

jurist. He founded the Hanafite system of Islamic jurisprudence. This gives the judge considerable discretion when the Koran and the Sunna (traditions) are inapplicable (see ISLAM).

Abu Khasim: see ABULCASIS.

Abukir: see ABOUKIR.

Abu-l-Abbas as-Saffah (ä′bōol-äbäs′ äs-säfä′), d. 754, 1st ABBASID caliph (749–54). Raised to the caliphate by the armed might of ABU MUSLIM, he took the reign name as-Saffah [shedder of blood]. Most of the Omayyad family were exterminated, and the reign was one of massacre and force. He was succeeded by his brother MANSUR.

Abu-l-Ala al-Maarri (ä′bōol ä′lä äl-mä-är-rē′), 973–1057, Arabic freethinking poet. He was born and lived most of his life in Maarrah, S of Aleppo. He was blind from childhood. Brilliantly original, he became one of the literary reformers who discarded classicism for a modern intellectual urbanity. After 35 he lived a life of seclusion, and with his advocacy of an utterly ascetic purity, his poetry became more stereotyped. He believed in the ethical teachings of the monotheistic religions.

Abu-l-Atahiya (ä′bōolätä′hēyä), 748–828, Arabic poet. He lived in Kufa and Baghdad and was patronized by the caliphs Mahdi and Harun-al-Rashid.

Abulcasis (ä′bōolkä′sĭs) or **Abu Khasim** (ä′bōokä′sĭm), fl. 11th cent., Arabian physician. His chief work, a detailed account of medicine and surgery, was long a valued text. Known as the *Tasrif* [the collection], it consisted of three parts, dealing with cautery, with surgery, and with fractures and dislocations. It was translated many times into Latin and into other languages. His name also appears as Albucasis (ăl″būkä′sĭs).

Abu-l-Faraj: see BAR-HEBRAEUS.

Abu-l-Faraj Ali of Isfahan (ä′bōolfä′räj ä′lē, ēsfähän′), 897–967, Arabic scholar. He is mainly known for his invaluable KITAB AL-AGHANI (book of songs).

Abulfazl (ä′bōolfä′zúl, ū′bōolfŭz′úl), 1551–1602, minister of state and adviser to Akbar, Mogul emperor of India. His *Book of Akbar*, in Persian, recounts a history of the reign, describing the political and religious organization of the empire. He was in part responsible for the religious views adopted by Akbar.

Abu-l-Fida (ä′bōol-fē′dä, –fĭdä′), 1273–1331, Arab writer, b. Damascus. He fought against the Christians in the last period of the Crusades and later became (1310) governor of Hama in Syria. He was a patron of learning and wrote a universal history, a superior source for Arabic history from 700 to 1200, and a descriptive geography.

Abu-l-Walid Merwan ibn Janah: see JONAH, RABBI.

Abu Muslim (ä′bōo mōo′slĭm), c.728–755, Persian revolutionist. By political and religious agitation and by force of arms he started (747) a revolution against the Omayyads before he was 21, and in 749 he established the head of the Abbasid family in the caliphate as ABU-L-ABBAS AS-SAFFAH. Abu Muslim retired to Khurasan as governor, but the Abbasid caliphs feared him and Mansur treacherously murdered him.

Abu Nuwas (nōowäs′), d. c.810, Arabic poet. Born in Ahwaz, Persia, he spent most of his life in Baghdad. High in favor with the caliphs Harun-al-Rashid and Amin, he lived a courtier's life, the extravagance of which his highly talented poetry echoes with no reserve.

Abury: see AVEBURY, England.

Abu Said ibn Abi-l-Khair (ä′bōo sä′ĭd ĭb′ún ä′bēlkhĭr′), 967–1049, Persian poet, a Sufi and a dervish. He was the first to write rubaiyat in the Sufistic strain that Omar Khayyam made famous.

Abu-Simbel (ä′bōo-sĭm′búl) or **Ipsambul** (ĭp″-sämbōol′), village, S Egypt, 36 mi. N of Wadi

Halfa. It is the site of two rock-hewn temples constructed (c.1250 B.C.) in the reign of Ramses II. The façade of the principal temple bears four sitting statues (c.65 ft. high) of Ramses. As the most important of the Nubian archaeological sites to be flooded by the artificial lake behind the Aswan High Dam, the temples have been the objects of several conservation schemes. An Italian plan to cut the temples free from the cliff and raise them above water level was approved in 1961. UNESCO has undertaken studies of the temples and is to provide funds for saving them.

Abu Tammam Habib ibn Aus (täm-mäm′ häbēb′ ĭ′bǔn ous′), c.805–c.845, Arabic poet, compiler of the Hamasa. His poems, often describing historical events, are important sources.

abutilon: see Mallow.

Abydos (ȯbĭ′dǔs), ancient city of Egypt, c.50 mi. NW of Thebes. Associated in religion with Osiris, it became the most venerated place in Egypt. It was the favorite burial place for the kings of the earliest dynasties, and later kings such as Seti I and Ramses II continued to build temples and sanctuaries at Abydos. Its remains date from the I to the XXVI dynasty (3100–500 B.C.). A famous list of kings, found on the wall of the temple built by Seti I, has been valuable in determining the order of succession among the Egyptian kings from Menes to Seti.

Abydos, ancient town of Phrygia, Asia Minor, on the Asiatic side of the Hellespont opposite Sestos, in present Turkey. It was originally a Milesian

Bride of Abydos, *a painting by Ferdinand V. E. Delacroix.*

colony. Near here Xerxes built his bridge of boats in 480 B.C., and in 411 the Athenian fleet defeated the Spartans. A free city until it was taken by Philip V of Macedon in 200 B.C., it became a major city of Antiochus III. It was the scene of the story of Hero and Leander and of Byron's *Bride of Abydos.*

Abyssinia: see Ethiopia.

Ac, chemical symbol of the element actinium.

acacia (ȯkā′shȯ), any plant of the large genus *Acacia,* leguminous and often thorny shrubs and trees of the pulse family, chiefly of the tropics

Australian acacia in bloom.

and subtropics, where they are cultivated for decorative and economic purposes. Acacias are characteristic of savanna vegetation and are especially numerous in the South African bushveld. The foliage often appears feathery because of the many small leaflets, but in some species leaflike flattened stems contain chlorophyll and take the place of leaves. Various Old World species (especially *A. arabica* and *A. senegal*) yield *gum* arabic and senegal; others, chiefly *A. catechu,* yield the dye catechu. Blackwood (*A. melanoxylon*) is valued in Australia for its hardwood timber. Other members of the genus are valuable for lac, for perfume and essential oils, and for tannins; some are used as ornamentals. The Australian acacias are commonly called wattles; the pliable branches were woven into the structure of the early wattle houses and fences. *A. decurrens* is a major source of tannin, and many wattles are cultivated elsewhere, particularly in California, as ornamentals for their characteristic spherical, dense flowers. In Australia, Wattle Day celebrates the national flower at blossoming time. The Central American bullhorn acacias (e.g., *A. sphaerocephala*) have large hollow thorns inhabited by ants said to feed upon a sweet secretion of the plant and in turn to guard it against leaf-eating insects. The most common acacia indigenous to the United States is the cat's-claw (*A. gregii*) of the arid Southwest. The Biblical shittim wood is thought to have come from an acacia.

Various species of locust are sometimes called acacia, and acacias may be called mimosa; all are of the same family.

academic freedom, right of scholars to pursue their research, to teach, and to publish without control or restraint from the institutions which employ them. This is a civil right that is enjoyed, at least in statute, by the citizens of democratic countries. In the case of scholars whose occupation is involved with that right, the concept of academic freedom generally includes the property right of tenure of office. An essential to the acceptance of the concept is the notion that truth is best discovered through the open investigation of all data. A less clearly developed corollary of academic freedom is the obligation of all those who enjoy it to pursue the line of open and thorough inquiry regardless of personal considerations. Historically, academic freedom developed in the period of Enlightenment. Early cultures, where education was viewed as a system of absorbing a well-defined content of subject matter, offered little opportunity for speculation. The medieval universities also operated within a field of definite scope, primarily theological, and every teacher and scholar was in danger of the charge of heresy if he extended his inquiry beyond the approved limits. The Enlightenment initiated the scientific method of analyzing data and establishing hypotheses, much of the groundwork being laid by scholars outside university life, such as Thomas Hobbes, John Locke, and Voltaire. Germany was the first country to apply the new freedom within the university, and the tolerance of Frederick the Great aided this development. In England it was laymen like Jeremy Bentham, Ricardo, Herbert Spencer, Darwin, and Thomas Huxley who demonstrated the value of free investigation. The schools had to be secularized before there was general acceptance of this right within university walls. Not until 1828 was the first nonsectarian university established in London. In the United States the early colleges were religiously controlled, and there are still some denominational schools which define the areas of speculation. Another danger to academic freedom has been the control exerted by financial contributors whose endowments definitely stipulate the direction and extent of inquiry. The American Association of University Professors has been active in establishing standards of academic freedom and obligation and has investigated and passed judgment upon cases in question. See *Freedom: Its Meaning* (ed. by R. N. Anshen, 1940); C. L. Becker, *Freedom and Responsibility in the American Way of Life* (1945); Richard Hofstadter and W. P. Metzger, *The Development of Academic Freedom in the United States* (1955); R. M. MacIver, *Academic Freedom in Our Time* (1955). Jack Nelson and Gene Roberts, Jr., *Censors and the Schools* (1963).

Académie française: see FRENCH ACADEMY.

Academy, garden near Athens (named for the hero Academus) in which, beginning c.387 B.C., PLATO taught. The Academy was the first university of the Western world. Plato's followers met here for nine centuries until, along with other pagan schools, it was closed by Justinian in A.D. 529. The Academy has come to mean the entire school of Platonic philosophy, covering the period from Plato through Cicero. During this period Platonic philosophy was modified in various ways. These have been frequently divided into three phases: the Old Academy (until c.250 B.C.) of Plato, SPEUSIPPUS, and XENOCRATES; the Middle Academy (until c.150 B.C.) of ARCESILAUS and CARNEADES, who introduced and maintained skepticism as being more faithful to Plato and Socrates; and the New Academy (c.100 B.C.) of Philo of Larissa who, with subsequent leaders, returned to the dogmatism of the Old Academy. The term *academy* has in modern times designated an educational institution or a learned society.

Acadia (ŭkā′dēŭ), region and former French colony, E Canada, centered on Nova Scotia but including also Prince Edward Island and the mainland coast from the Gulf of St. Lawrence S into Maine. The first and chief town, Port Royal (now ANNAPOLIS ROYAL, N.S.), was founded by the sieur de Monts in 1605 (see SAINT CROIX **1**) and was soon involved in the imperial struggle that was to end in America with the FRENCH AND INDIAN WARS. Destroyed by the British under Samuel ARGALL in 1614, the town was later rebuilt, and as British claims temporarily lapsed (see NOVA SCOTIA), the colony grew to be fairly prosperous with farmers on their dike-protected fields, fishermen on the shore, and fur traders in the forests. Later, British attacks on Port Royal were resumed, and its capture in 1710 was confirmed as permanent in the Peace of Utrecht (1713). The British feared and distrusted their French-speaking, Roman Catholic neighbors,

Acadian relics are preserved in the Museum chapel in Grand Pré Memorial Park, Nova Scotia.

who were friendly with the Indians and, wishing only to remain neutral, refused to swear allegiance to Great Britain. In 1755 the British fell upon the peaceful Acadian farms and, seizing most of the Acadians, deported them to the more southerly

Acapulco, a Mexican resort on the Pacific Ocean.

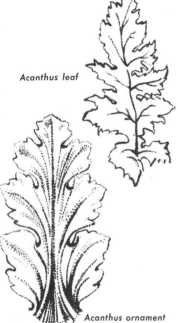

Acanthus leaf

Acanthus ornament

Acanthus flower

Acadian Exiles (1916); J. B. Brebner, *New England's Outpost* (1927) and *The Neutral Yankees of Nova Scotia* (1937).

Acadia National Park: see MOUNT DESERT ISLAND.

Acadia University: see WOLFVILLE, N.S., Canada.

Acajutla (äkähōōt′lä), town (pop. c.2,500) SW Salvador, a Pacific port. It is a railroad terminus and is in a resort area. Acajutla exports coffee.

acanthus (ŭkăn′–), common name for the Acanthaceae, a family of chiefly perennial herbs and shrubs, mostly native to the tropics. A few members of the family, many of which have decorative spiny leaves, are cultivated as ornamentals—especially the Mediterranean acanthus or bear's-breech (genus *Acanthus*), whose ornate leaves were the source of a stylized motif used in Greek and Roman art (see CORINTHIAN ORDER). In Christian art the acanthus symbolizes heaven. Some species of the genus *Ruellia* are native to and cultivated as ornamentals in North America, chiefly in the South.

Acapulco (äkäpōōl′kō), city (pop. c.28,500), Guerrero, SW Mexico. A fashionable resort, it has lavish hotels, deep sea fishing, and skin diving. Its fine natural harbor, surrounded by cliffs and promontories, served as a base for Spaniards exploring the Pacific. It also played an important role in the development of the Philippines. Acapulco has often been severely damaged by earthquakes and hurricanes.

Acarnania (ăkŭrnā′nēŭ), region of ancient Greece, between the Achelous river and the Ionian Sea. The inhabitants maintained their isolation, contributing little to Greek civilization. The chief city was Stratos. The Acarnanians generally sided with Athens, and Athens helped Acarnania to uphold its independence against Corinth and Sparta in the 5th cent. B.C. Later (390–375 B.C.) Sparta controlled the region. The persistent struggle with

British colonies, scattering them along the Atlantic coast from Maine to Georgia and sending some to the West Indies and Europe. The men were sent first, families were separated, farmhouses burned, and some lands abandoned to waste. In 1762 a new mass deportation was thwarted, the war ended in 1763, and hysteria subsided. The remaining Acadians and exiles who returned took the British oath, and after 1767 they rapidly became Nova Scotians. Today in Canada, Acadian (French *Acadien*) means a French-speaking inhabitant of the Maritime Provinces. Many exiles who did not return found havens elsewhere, the most celebrated being the region around St. Martinville in S Louisiana, where even yet the Cajuns—as they are popularly called—maintain a separate folk culture. The sufferings of the expulsion are pictured in Longfellow's *Evangeline*. See A. G. Doughty, *The*

the Aetolians cost Acarnania national existence for a time, but it was restored and the Acarnanians kept some autonomy under the Roman Empire until the Christian era. When the Byzantine Empire broke up (1204), Acarnania passed to Epirus and in 1480 to the Turks. In 1832 it became part of Greece.

Acarya: see BHASCARA.

Acastus (ŭkă'stŭs), in Greek mythology, son of Pelias, cousin of Jason. He accompanied Jason on the Argonaut expedition, but when Jason and Medea murdered Pelias, and usurped the throne of Iolcus, Acastus drove them away. Later his wife, rebuffed by Peleus, falsely accused Peleus of raping her. Acastus took revenge by leaving Peleus unprotected on Mt. Pelion. Rescued by the centaur Chiron, Peleus came back to kill Acastus and his wife.

Accad: see AKKAD.

Acca Larentia (–rĕn'shŭ) or **Acca Larentina**, in Roman mythology, wife of the shepherd Faustulus and foster mother of ROMULUS and Remus. Her 12 sons founded the priesthood of the Arval Brothers. According to one legend she was a wealthy courtesan who left all her money to the people of Rome.

Accaron: see EKRON.

Accault, Michel: see ACO, MICHEL.

accent, in language, emphasis given a particular sound. In English each independently spoken form has an accented vowel; often it is the first vowel. The English accent is phonemic (or significant), for there are words different from each other only in their accent, e.g., *contract*, verb and noun. In French the accent is entirely different, but the signs called accents have nothing to do with it. These so-called accents, acute (´), grave (`), and circumflex (^), are borrowed from Greek writing, where they probably showed differences in pitch. Some languages have significant variations of both pitch and loudness (or stress). Thus in English every utterance is marked as complete by having one of certain established pitch patterns (or intonations), meaning, for example, "complete definite declaration" in *He's a good boy*, "question" in *Is he there?* or "tentative statement" in *She'll probably come*. See ABLAUT and PHONETICS.

accessory (ăksĕ'sŭrē, ŭk–), in law, a person who, though not present at the commission of a crime, becomes a participator in the crime either before or after the fact of commission. An accessory before the fact is one whose counsel or instigation leads another to commit a crime. An accessory after the fact is one who, having knowledge that a crime has been committed, aids, or attempts to aid, the criminal to escape apprehension. In misdemeanors and in treason there is no distinction between principals and accessories. In some states the common law distinction between principal and accessory before the fact has been abolished, and the accessory before the fact is prosecuted as a principal. The penalties for being an accessory are usually much less severe than those meted out to the principal. Except where statutes provide differently, an accessory cannot be tried without his consent before the conviction of the principal, unless both are tried together. See STOLEN GOODS.

Accho (ăk'ō), Old Testament variant of ACRE.

accident, in law, an unusual or unexpected event producing physical injury or loss of property. The term includes events which happen without human agency (see ACT OF GOD) and those which are produced through human agency though without design. When not an act of God, an accident ordinarily involves NEGLIGENCE on the part of the perpetrator. Such terms as "mere accident" or "pure accident," however, connote absence of negligence. An inevitable accident is an act of God or an event produced through human agency which could not be foreseen or prevented. In equity, relief may be given from the effects of an accident that benefits a party; thus, if by accident the boundaries of property are confused, the party injured may seek a judicial determination of the true boundaries. In INSURANCE and in WORKMEN'S COMPENSATION statutes, the term accident has specifically defined meanings.

Accolti, Benedetto (bānādĕt'tō äk-kôl'tē), c.1415–1466?, Italian humanist and historian. From his history of the First Crusade, Tasso supposedly drew the idea for *Jerusalem Delivered*. His son **Bernardo Accolti** (bĕrnär'dō), 1465?–1535, was known in his day for extemporaneous poems. Another son, **Pietro Accolti** (pyā'trō), 1455–1532, was a cardinal and drew up (1520) the papal bull against Luther.

accordion, musical instrument consisting of a rectangular bellows expanded and contracted between the hands. Buttons or keys operated by the player open valves, allowing air to enter or to escape. The air sets in motion free reeds, frequently made of metal. The length, density, shape, and elasticity of the reeds determine the pitch. The first accordions were made (1822) by Friedrich Buschmann.

Accordion

Bouton added a keyboard (1852), thus producing a piano accordion. The accordion is frequently used in folk music.

accounting, classification, analysis, and interpretation of the BOOKKEEPING records of an enterprise. The accountant evaluates records drawn up by the bookkeeper and shows the results of his investigation as losses and gains, leakages, economies, or changes in value, so as to reveal the progress or failures of the business and also its limitations and possibilities. An accountant must also be able to draw up a set of books and prescribe the system of accounts that will most easily give the desired information; he must be capable of arriving at a comprehensive view of the economic and the legal aspects of a business, envisaging the effect of every sort of transaction both on the profit and loss statement and on the balance sheet; and he must recognize and classify all other factors that enter into the determination of the true condition of the business, e.g., statistics or memoranda relating to production and properties and financial records representing investment, expenditures, receipts, fiscal changes, and present standing. Cost accounting shows the actual cost in a certain period of each service rendered or of each article produced; by this system unprofitable ventures, services, departments, and methods may be discovered. While there were stewards, auditors, and bookkeepers in ancient times, the professional accountant who, instead of serving one employer, offers his services, for a fee, wherever they are needed is a 19th-century development. The profession was first recognized in Britain in 1854, when the Society of Accountants in Edinburgh was given a royal charter. Similar societies were later established in Glasgow, Aberdeen, and London. In the United States the first such professional society was the American Association of Public Accountants, chartered by the state of New York in 1887. All the states and also Puerto Rico and the District of Columbia now have laws under which the public accountant who complies with certain educational and experience requirements and passes the required examination may be granted the title Certified Public Accountant (C.P.A.). The holders of these certificates have organized into societies in most of the states. The bodies representing the accounting profession in this country are the American Institute of Accountants, which succeeded the American Association of Public Accountants in 1916, and the Ameri-

can Accounting Association, also organized in 1916. With the growth of corporate activity in the mid-20th cent., accounting has increased greatly in importance and has undergone many improvements in theory and techniques. The chief influences on modern accounting have been the need for keeping uniform accounts, so that a company's system of financial records is accessible to the government and to the public—and the increasingly complex income tax structure. Much of contemporary accounting has taken on managerial functions and is no longer primarily concerned with ascertaining financial condition but rather with how a company can act on this information. AUDITING is an important branch of accounting. See N. A. H. Stacey, *English Accountancy, 1800–1954* (1954); Morton Backer, ed., *Handbook of Modern Accounting Theory* (1955); Louis Goldberg and V. R. Hill, *The Elements of Accounting* (2d ed., 1958); James D. Edwards, *History of Public Accounting in the United States* (1960).

Accra (ŭkrä′, ă′krŭ), city (pop. 491,060), capital of the Republic of Ghana, a port on the Gulf of Guinea. Originally the village capital of a native kingdom, it developed into a sizable town around Danish, British, and Dutch forts built in the 17th cent. Accra supplanted Cape Coast as capital of the country in 1876. After the completion (1923) of a railroad to the mining and agricultural hinterland, it rapidly became the commercial center of the country. It has the characteristics of a modern city; older parts and slums contrast with the most up-to-date buildings and amenities. There are many small industries, such as brick and tile making, fruit and fish canning, and sawmilling. Accra has an international airport. The University College of Ghana is nearby.

Accra, capital of the Republic of Ghana.

Accrington, municipal borough (pop. 40,987), Lancashire, N England. The principal industry is the weaving of cotton. Accrington also engages in textile printing and dyeing and the manufacture of machinery and bricks.

acculturation: see CULTURE.

Accursius, Franciscus (frănsĭ'skŭs ŭkûr'shēŭs), c.1185–c.1260, Italian jurist. He was a professor of Roman law at the Univ. of Bologna. His great work on the Corpus Juris Civilis sums up the contributions of earlier Bolognese writers.

accusative (ŭkū'zŭtĭv″) [Latin,=for accusing], in Latin grammar, CASE typically meaning that the noun refers to the entity directly affected by an action. The term is used for similar, but often not identical, features in the grammar of other languages. Thus English *him,* usually called objective, is also called accusative.

Aceldama (ŭsĕl'dŭmŭ) [according to Acts 1.18,19= field of blood], potter's field bought with Judas' 30 pieces of silver; it is apparently the place where Judas died. The purchase of this field to bury strangers in is the origin of the term "potter's field" for the paupers' burying ground. Mat. 27.3–10; Acts 1.16–19.

acetaldehyde: see ALDEHYDE.

acetic acid (ŭsē'tĭk), weak organic acid, a colorless liquid with a characteristic pungent odor, boiling at 118.1° C. It is miscible with water in all proportions; heat is evolved. Glacial acetic acid is the concentrated acid of 99.5 percent purity which solidifies at 17° C. Acetic acid is the essential constituent of VINEGAR. Concentrated acetic acid for industrial uses is prepared either from acetylene by a reaction yielding acetaldehyde (see ALDEHYDE), which is oxidized to produce acetic acid, or from the distillate of hardwood which contains pyroligneous acid. Acetic acid reacts with other chemicals to form numerous compounds of commercial importance. Among them are cellulose acetate, used in making acetate rayon, noninflammable motion-picture film, lacquers, and plastics; lead acetate (see SUGAR OF LEAD) and potassium acetate, both of which are used in medicine; copper acetate (see VERDIGRIS); and amyl acetate (often called banana oil), butyl, and ethyl acetate, all of which are used as solvents, chiefly in certain quick-drying lacquers. Aluminum, chromium, and iron salts of acetic acid are used as mordants in dyeing textiles. Acetic acid is employed in the production of acetone and in organic syntheses.

acetone (ăs'ĭtōn) [from *acetic*], colorless, flammable liquid compound of carbon, hydrogen, and oxygen, with a characteristic minty taste and odor, boiling at 56.2°C. and solidifying at −94.8°C. It is the first member of the homologous series of aliphatic ketones. Acetone is used widely in industry as a solvent for numerous organic substances, in paint and varnish removers, and for dissolving and storing acetylene. It is used in the manufacture of celluloid, of smokeless powders (as cordite), of artificial silk, and of such substances as chloroform, iodoform, and sulphonal. It is produced commercially principally from propylene obtained from the cracking of petroleum.

acetylcholine (ăs'ŭtĭlkō'lēn), organic compound of carbon, hydrogen, oxygen, and nitrogen. It is believed that acetylcholine, liberated at the nerve endings, is a factor in the stimulation of muscles and organs. Acetylcholine is also an active principle in ERGOT.

acetylene (ŭsĕt'ĭlēn) [from *acetyl,* from *acetic*], colorless gas, boiling at −83.4°C., with an ethereal odor when pure. The offensive odor often noted in

Acetylene is used for cutting and welding metals.

the commercial product is caused by impurities. With air it forms an explosive mixture. It is soluble in acetone, alcohol, and water. When dissolved in acetone it is nonexplosive and is stored under pressure in cylinders for commercial use. It can be liquefied, but is explosive in this condition and is stored only in the smallest quantities. Acetylene is used as an illuminant, burning with a very luminous flame in special burners which mix it with air, and for cutting and welding metals (see OXYACETYLENE FLAME). Acetylene gas when subjected to high temperature undergoes polymerization and benzene is produced. Commercially the gas is usually prepared by the action of water on calcium carbide. It is used in the production of many organic compounds and of neoprene rubber, plastics, and resins. Acetylene is the first member of a series of unsaturated hydrocarbons, the **acetylene series.** The acetylene molecule consists of two hydrogen atoms and two carbon, the carbon atoms joined together by a triple bond and each holding one of the hydrogen atoms. In the acetylene series a definite relation exists between the number of hydrogen and carbon atoms; each member has two less hydrogen atoms than twice the number of carbon atoms. Thus, the second member of the series, allylene, has three carbon and four hydrogen.

Achaea (ùkē'ù), region of ancient Greece, in the northern part of the Peloponnesus on the Gulf of Corinth. It lay between Sicyon and Elis. Here the Achaeans supposedly remained when driven from other parts of Greece by the Dorian invasion. The small Achaean cities eventually banded together in the First ACHAEAN LEAGUE. In the late 8th cent. B.C. the Achaeans colonized part of S Italy but were at first of little significance in Greek politics. Later, however, the Second Achaean League became an important factor. After the downfall of the league, the name Achaea or Achaia (ùkā'ù, ùkī'ù) was given to a Roman province in the Peloponnesus.

Achaean League (ùkē'ùn), confederation of cities on the Gulf of Corinth. The little-known First Achaean League was formed presumably before the 5th cent. B.C. and lasted through the 4th cent. B.C., its purpose being mutual protection against pirates. The Achaeans remained aloof from the wars in Greece until they joined the opposition to Philip II of Macedon in 338 B.C. The confederation was dissolved soon after. The Second Achaean League was founded in 280 B.C. Sicyon was freed from the rule of its tyrant in 251 B.C., and it soon joined the confederation under the leadership of ARATUS. Other cities outside Achaea were incorporated on terms of equality, and in 247 B.C. the Macedonians were driven from Corinth. There was some promise of liberating all Greece, but unfortunately the interference of CLEOMENES III of Sparta threatened the Achaean League, and in 227 B.C. he began a war. The Achaean League then requested (224 B.C.) Macedonian aid against Sparta and the Aetolian League. The result was the eclipse of the confederation until the wars between Macedon and Rome. In 198 B.C. the Achaeans went over to Rome and with Roman aid won practically the whole Peloponnesus, forcing Sparta and Messene

to join. Later suspecting the Achaeans of again looking toward Macedon, the Romans deported (168 B.C.) many of them (including Polybius) to Italy. Anti-Roman feeling grew, and in 146 B.C. the Achaenas waged a suicidal war. Rome easily triumphed at Corinth, dissolved the confederation, and ended Greek liberty. A smaller Achaean League was formed, but it was powerless.

Achaeans, people of ancient Greece, of unknown origin. In Homer, the Achaeans are specifically a Greek-speaking people of S Thessaly. Historically, they seem to have appeared in the Peloponnesus during the 14th and 13th cent. B.C., and c.1250 B.C. they became the ruling class. There is no sharp line of separation between the earlier MYCENAEAN CIVILIZATION and the Achaean; the cultures seem to have intermingled. The invasions of the DORIANS supposedly forced some of the Achaeans out to Asia Minor; others were concentrated in the region known in classical times as Achaea.

Achaemenidae (ăkĭmē'nĭdē) or **Achaemenids** (ăkĭmē'nĭdz), dynasty of ancient Persia. They were descended presumably from one Achaemenes, a minor ruler in a mountainous district of SW Iran. His successors, when ELAM declined, spread their power westward. CYRUS THE GREAT established the Persian rule by his conquest of ASTYAGES of MEDIA. The Achaemenidae (c.550–330 B.C.) were important for their development of government administration, the appearance of literature written in CUNEIFORM, and the spread of ZOROASTRIANISM; during this period there was also a great flourishing of PERSIAN ART AND ARCHITECTURE. The Achaemenid rulers after Cyrus were Cambyses, the impostor Smerdis, Darius I, Xerxes I, Artaxerxes I, Xerxes II, Sogdianus, Darius II, Artaxerxes II (opposed by Cyrus the Younger), Artaxerxes III, Arses, and Darius III. The dynasty ended when Darius III died in his flight before Alexander the Great.

Achaeus: see CREUSA 1.

Achaicus (ùkā'ĭkùs) [Gr.,=Achaean], Christian. 1 Cor. 16.17,18.

Achai of Shabcha: see AHA OF SHABCHA.

Achan (ā'kăn) or **Achar** (ā'kär), Judahite who kept some of the spoil from the city of Jericho. For this he was stoned. Joshua 7; 1 Chron. 2.7.

Achard, Franz Karl (fränts' kärl' äkh'ärt), 1753–1821, German chemist. He made pioneer use of the discovery by MARGGRAF of sugar in beetroots. The government granted him an estate in Silesia where, in 1806, he succeeded in producing beet sugar. Among his other contributions is the discovery of a method for working platinum.

Acharius, Erik (ĕr'ēk äkä'rēōōs), 1757–1819, Swedish physician and botanist; pupil of LINNAEUS. He was long an authority on lichens and wrote *Lichenographia universalis* (1810).

Achaz (ā'kăz), variant of AHAZ. Mat. 1.9.

Achbor (ăk'bôr) [Heb.,=mouse], same as ABDON **2.**

Ache, Caran d': see CARAN D'ACHE.

Achelous (ăkēlō'ùs), in Greek mythology, river-god; son of Oceanus and Tethys. He possessed the power of appearing as a bull, a serpent, or a bullheaded man. Hercules defeated him and broke off one of his horns, which some say became the CORNU-

Achelous, depicted on an antique pendant.

COPIA. He is sometimes said to be the father of the Sirens.

Achelous, Gr. *Akheloos* (äkhĕlô′ôs), river, NW Greece. About 137 mi. long, it rises in the Pindus mts., flows generally southward, traversing many mountain gorges, and empties into the Ionian Sea opposite Cephalonia. It is used for floating logs and is an important source of hydroelectric power. It formed a part of the boundary between ancient Aetolia and Acarnania and was formerly called Aspropotamos.

Achenwall, Gottfried, (gôt′frĕt äkh′ŭnväl), 1719–72, German statistician and political scientist. He used the term *Statistik* for the first time in his *Staatsverfassung der heutigen vornehmsten europäischen Reiche und Völker im Grundrisse* [the political constitution of the present principal European countries and peoples] (1749). By the term he meant a comprehensive description of the social, political, and economic features of a state.

Acheron: see HADES.

Acheson, Dean Gooderham (ăch′ĭsŭn), 1893–, U.S. Secretary of State (1949–52), b. Middletown, Conn., grad. Yale, 1915, and Harvard Law School,

Dean Acheson

1918. He was (1919–21) private secretary to Louis D. Brandeis, became a successful lawyer, and served (1933) as Undersecretary of the Treasury until disagreement with President Roosevelt's fiscal policy caused his resignation. Assistant Secretary of State (1941–45) and Undersecretary of State (1945–47), he was appointed (Jan., 1949) Secretary of State. Under his direction the policy of containment of Communist expansion through foreign economic aid and military aid was developed. He played an important role in establishing the NORTH ATLANTIC TREATY ORGANIZATION and the security pact with Australia and New Zealand. His attempts to dissociate the United States from the Nationalist Chinese regime on Formosa drew the relentless attack of many Congressmen of his own party, as well as Republicans. His Korean policy similarly excited much criticism. His earlier friendly attitude toward Alger Hiss became the basis for personal abuse, and resulted in attacks of his handling of the loyalty and security policy of the Dept. of State. Returning to private practice in 1953, Acheson remained a spokesman for the Democratic party on foreign policy. He wrote *A Democrat Looks at His Party* (1955), *A Citizen Looks at Congress* (1957), and *Power and Diplomacy* (1958).

Acheson, Edward Goodrich, 1856–1931, American inventor, b. Washington, Pa. As an electric-furnace expert he specialized in carbon and silicon research. In 1891 he developed the abrasive product carborundum (see SILICON CARBIDE). He perfected several lubricating media and originated processes in silicon and aluminum production. He also invented a process important to industry for producing synthetic graphite of high purity.

Acheulian: see PALEOLITHIC PERIOD.

Achill (ăk′ĭl) [Irish,=eagle], island, 14 mi. long and 11 mi. wide, Co. Mayo, W Republic of Ireland. It is connected with the mainland by a bridge over Achill Sound. The land is barren, and the inhabitants subsist with great difficulty by fishing and farming. Many of the small villages are resorts. Achill is known for its magnificent cliff scenery; Slieve Mor at the north end rises to 2,204 ft.

Achilles (ŭkĭ′lēz), in Greek mythology, foremost Greek hero of the TROJAN WAR; son of Peleus and Thetis. He was a redoubtable warrior, possessed of a fierce and ungovernable anger. Thetis, knowing that Achilles was fated to die at Troy, disguised him as a girl and hid him among the women at the court of King Lycomedes (līkŏ′mŭdēz) of Skyros. He was discovered there by Odysseus, who persuaded him to go to Troy. One of Lycomedes' daughters, Deidamia (dēĭdā′mēŭ), bore to Achilles a son, Neoptolemus. According to Homer, Achilles came to Troy leading the 50 ships of the Myrmidons. In the last year of the siege, when Agamemnon stole Briseis from him, Achilles angrily withdrew and took his troops from the war. Later he allowed his intimate friend Patroclus (pŭtrō′klŭs) to borrow his armor and lead the Myrmidons in aid of the retreating Greeks. When Hector killed Patroclus, Achilles, possessed by grief and rage, returned to the battle, routed the Trojans, and killed Hector, viciously dragging his body around the walls of Troy. Achilles died of a wound inflicted by Paris.

*Achilles and Ajax at a playing table.
Sixth-century Greek vase painting.*

Some say that although Thetis attempted to make Achilles immortal by bathing him in the river Styx, the heel by which she held him remained vulnerable, and that Paris inflicted a fatal wound in that heel. Others say that Achilles was struck from behind and killed by Paris when he went to visit Priam's daughter Polyxena, with whom he had fallen in love. Achilles was the object of widespread hero worship.

Achim (ā'kĭm), name in the genealogy of Mat. 1.14.

Achish (ā'kĭsh). **1** King of Gath with whom David took refuge. 1 Sam. 27.2. Called Abimelech in the title of Ps. 34. **2** King of Gath in the time of Solomon. 1 Kings 2.39. Possibly a title; possibly only one person.

Achitophel (ākĭt'ûfĕl), variant of AHITHOPHEL.

Achmet. For Ottoman sultans thus named, see AHMED.

Achor (ā'kôr) [Heb.,=trouble], valley where Achan was stoned. Joshua 7.25,26; 1 Chron. 2.7.

Achsa or **Achsah** (both: ăk'sù) [Heb.,=anklet], Caleb's daughter, given as wife to Othniel. Judges 1.12–15; 1 Chron. 2.49.

Achshaph (ăk'shăf), town, N Palestine, taken by Joshua. Joshua 11.1; 12.20; 19.25.

Achurch, Janet (ùchûrch'), 1864–1916, English actress and manager, whose real name was Janet Achurch Sharp. She made her first appearance in 1883. In 1889, as manager of the Novelty Theatre, London, she produced *A Doll's House*, playing Nora, thus attaining the distinction of being the first English actress to play Ibsen. A favorite of Shaw, she was first to play his Candida.

Achzib (ăk'zĭb) [Heb.,=a lie]. **1** Seacoast Palestinian town, c.15 mi. S of Tyre. Joshua 19.29; Judges 1.31. **2** Unidentified city of Judah. Joshua 15.44; Micah 1.14. Chezib in Gen. 38.5 and Chozeba in 1 Chron. 4.22 may be the same.

acid, a compound that, according to the Arrhenius theory, yields hydrogen ions when dissolved in water. The Brönsted theory (for J. N. Brönsted, a Danish chemist), in considering the behavior of substances in nonaqueous solution, defines an acid as any substance that will release a PROTON. The Lewis theory (for G. N. LEWIS), based on the nature of the chemical bond (see VALENCE), defines an acid as a substance capable of accepting an electron pair. Certain properties of acids are characteristic and result from the presence in solution of the hydrogen ion. Acids in aqueous solution have a sour taste; they turn LITMUS red, react with bases and basic oxides (see NEUTRALIZATION) to form salts and water, and conduct electricity. When an electric current is passed through an acid, hydrogen is liberated. Acids are prepared in several ways. Commonly they are obtained either from the reaction of an acid anhydride and water, or from the action of an acid, such as sulfuric acid, on a SALT of the acid to be prepared. Under ordinary conditions and when pure, the majority of the more common acids are solids. A much smaller number are liquids; a few are gases. Such acids as hydrochloric, sulfuric, and especially nitric, which are largely ionized in solution, yielding many hydrogen ions, are called strong acids; those that are little ionized, e.g., acetic, boric, and carbonic, are called weak acids. An acid may be prepared in concentrated or dilute solution, depending upon the amount of acid dissolved. Acids are also classified according to the number of replaceable hydrogen atoms present in one molecule. For example, nitric acid is a monobasic acid since there is but one replaceable hydrogen atom in each molecule; sulfuric acid is dibasic, the molecule containing two atoms of replaceable hydrogen; phosphoric acid is tribasic. Acids which, like hydrochloric, are composed of two elements, hydrogen and some other, are binary acids. Organic acids are characterized in general by the presence in their molecule of a group of atoms (the carboxyl group or carboxyl radical) which comprises one atom of carbon, two of oxygen, and one of hydrogen, the radical being written in chemical symbols as –COOH. Such acids are formed naturally in plants and animals. Some of the more common organic acids are acetic, citric, formic, lactic, oxalic, and tartaric. Acids are widely used in many industrial chemical processes and also in medicine, agriculture, and the arts (e.g., etching).

acidophilus milk: see FERMENTED MILK.

acidosis, physiological condition brought about by an imbalance of the acid-alkali content of the body. The normal ratio is disturbed when the acid components exceed the normal amount, or when the alkali content is decreased. Such a metabolic disturbance can be engendered by a number of causes, e.g., starvation, severe dehydration, excessive ingestion of acid salts, diabetes, and liver and kidney disease. Acidosis may also be respiratory in origin, when severely diseased lungs retain too much carbon dioxide and take in too little oxygen. Acidosis is counteracted by the administration of alkaline solutions and by treatment of the original cause of the imbalance. In respiratory acidosis, measures must be taken to reduce the carbon dioxide content of the blood and to increase oxygenation. When the alkaline content of the body is in excess of normal, alkalosis results. It is usually brought on by ingestion of alkalies in quantities greater than the kidneys can handle or by hyperventilation (rapid breathing with increase in oxygen intake) in hysterical or emotional states. Here, too, treatment must be addressed to restoring the normal acid-alkaline balance and to removal of the original cause of the disturbance.

Acireale (ä″chērää′lā), town (estimated pop. 29,085), E Sicily, Italy. Beautifully situated on a volcanic plateau near the Ionian Sea, it has been frequented since Roman times for its warm sulphur springs. The town was injured by earthquakes (1169 and 1693) and was plundered in 1326.

Acis: see GALATEA **1.**

Ackerman, town (pop. 1,382), co. seat of Choctaw co., N central Miss., WSW of Columbus.

Ackia Battleground National Monument: see TUPELO, Miss.

Ackley, town (pop. 1,731), N central Iowa, W of Waterloo; inc. 1858. It is a farm trade center.

Acklins Island: see BAHAMA ISLANDS.

acknowledgment, in law, a formal declaration or admission that one executed an instrument (e.g., a will or a deed) which purports to be his. The acknowledgment is made before a court or a notary public or other authorized person. Acknowledgment permits the instrument to be given in evidence without further proof of its execution (e.g., witnesses).

Acmeists (ăk'mēĭsts), school of Russian poets started in 1912 by Gorodetsky and Gumilev as a reaction against the mysticism of the symbolists. They aspired to concreteness of image and clarity of expression. The leading Acmeists were Nikolai, Stepanovich Gumilev, Anna Akhmatova, and Osip Mandelstam. See Gleb Struve, *Soviet Russian Literature 1917–1950* (1951); Renato Poggioli, *The Poets of Russia, 1890–1930* (1960).

acne, inflammatory disease of the sebaceous (oil-producing) glands, characterized by blackheads and pustules and, in the more severe forms, by cysts and scarring. The lesions appear on the face, neck, back, chest, and arms. Acne is most prevalent among adolescents. Although its exact cause is not known, it is undoubtedly related to the increased hormonal activity that occurs at puberty. Cleanliness of the skin is essential when acne is present, and a mild soap and water should be used

Main street of Acireale, Sicily.

Acne as seen in a microphotograph of facial tissue.

several times a day. The contents of blackheads and pustular lesions should be evacuated by a physician under proper aseptic conditions to lessen the possibility of scarring. Astringent lotions may help to counteract the oiliness of the skin usually present in this condition. Foods rich in carbohydrate and fat, such as chocolate and nuts, should be eliminated from the diet. The more severe cases of acne may require antibiotic and hormonal treatment. It is now possible to improve the appearance of acne-scarred skin by a method of surgical planing known as dermabrasion.

Aco or **Accault, Michel** (mĕshĕl' äkō'), fl. 1680–1702, French explorer. He became La Salle's lieutenant, being favored by that explorer because of his courage, prudence, and wide acquaintance with Indian languages. When LA SALLE reached the mouth of the Illinois river on his famous voyage down the Mississippi, he sent Aco with two companions to explore the upper reaches of the Mississippi. One of the companions was Father Louis HENNEPIN, who in his *Nouvelle Decouverte* made himself the hero of the expedition. Near the Falls of St. Anthony, which they were the first to see, the three were captured by Sioux Indians and were released only through the energy and influence of Daniel Greysolon DULUTH. Little is known of Aco's subsequent life except that he was long a trader on the Illinois and that in 1693 he married the daughter of a Kaskaskia chief. His name also appears as Ako.

Acoma or **Acoma** (both: ă'kŭmŭ), pueblo (pop. 1,414), W central N.Mex., WSW of Albuquerque. This "sky city" is on top of a steep-sided sandstone mesa more than 350 ft. high and difficult of access. Below are cultivated fields that help support the inhabitants of the pueblo. There is also some grazing. The Acoma Indians are skilled pottery makers. They speak a Western Keresan language (see PUEBLO INDIANS). The location of the pueblo has astonished visitors from Coronado's men in 1540 to the tourists of today. Juan de Oñate was allowed to enter in 1598, but the Indians revolted fiercely in 1599 and were subdued only after severe fighting. The missionary Fray Juan Ramírez arrived in 1629. The Acoma people joined in the revolt of the Pueblo Indians in 1680, had to submit to Diego de Vargas in 1692, joined in the later rising of 1696, and were subdued again in 1699. They became thoroughly Christianized. Their chief festival is held on Sept. 2, the feast of their patron saint, Stephen. See Mrs. W. T. Sedgwick, *Acoma, the Sky City* (1926).

Acominatus, Michael (ŭkŏmĭnā'tŭs), or **Michael Choniates** (kōnēā'tēz), c.1140–1220, Byzantine writer and metropolitan of Athens. His speeches, poems, and letters give much information about medieval Athens, which he, a classicist, found barbarous and degenerate. After the capture (1204) of Athens by the army of the Fourth Crusade, he retired to the island of Keos, where he died.

Acominatus, Nicetas (nīsē'tŭs), or **Nicetas Choniates**, d.1216, Byzantine historian; younger brother of Michael Acominatus. He held high offices until the fall (1204) of Constantinople to the army of the Fourth Crusade, when he accompanied Theodore I to Nicaea. His vivid history, in 21 books, covers the period from 1118 to 1206. Largely based on personal observation and eyewitness accounts, it asserts the superiority of Byzantine to Latin civilization.

Aconcagua (äkōnkä'gwä), peak, 22,835 ft. high, Mendoza prov., Argentina, in the Andes N of Uspallata Pass and near the Chilean border; generally considered the highest peak of the Western Hemisphere. Aconcagua was first scaled in 1897. See also OJOS DE SALADO.

aconite (ăk'–) [Gr.], **monkshood**, or **wolfsbane**, any of several species of the genus *Aconitum* of the BUTTERCUP family, hardy perennial plants of the north temperate zone, growing wild or cultivated for ornamental or medicinal purposes. They contain violent poisons, recognized from early times and mentioned by Shakespeare (2 *King Henry IV*, iv:4), more recently used medicinally in a liniment, tincture, and drug and in India on spears and arrows, for hunting. The drug aconite, the active principle of which is the alkaloid aconitine, is used as a sedative, e.g., for neuralgia and rheumatism, and is obtained from *A. napellus*. Aconites are erect or trailing, with deeply cut leaves and, in late summer and fall, hooded showy flowers of blue, yellow, purple, or white. The name wolfsbane de-

Aconite (Aconitum napellus).

rives from an old superstition that the plant repelled werewolves. Winter aconite is a name for plants of the genus *Eranthis*, wild or garden perennials of the same family.

Acontius (ŭkŏn'shŭs), in Greek mythology, a young man who loved Cydippe (sēdĭ'pē). He met her at a festival of Artemis and threw before her an apple inscribed, "I swear by the temple of Artemis to marry Acontius." She read the inscription aloud. The goddess accepted her words as an oath and brought about the marriage of the lovers.

Açores: see AZORES.

acorn: see OAK.

Acosta, Joaquin (hwäkēn' äkō'stä), 1800–1852, Colombian historian and scientist. He served under Bolívar in the revolution. His scientific knowledge was broad, and he wrote about many aspects of Colombia, constituting himself a sort of intellectual publicity agent for his country.

Acosta, José de (hōsā' dā äkōs'tä), c. 1539–1600, Spanish Jesuit missionary to Peru. He wrote a well-known history of the Spanish colonial period, *The Natural and Moral History of the Indies* (1590; Eng. trs., 1604, 1880).

Acosta, Uriel (ōōr'yĕl), or **Uriel da Costa**, c.1585–1640, Jewish rationalist, b. Oporto, Portugal. His original name was Gabriel da Costa, and his family had been converted to Catholicism. When he reached manhood, he was restive in the Christian faith and persuaded his family to move to Amsterdam, where all of them returned to Judaism. In a work in 1624, he expressed rationalistic doctrines, criticized rabbinical Judaism, and demanded a return to the teachings of the Sadducees. He was tried, imprisoned, and excommunicated. In 1633 he recanted, but soon he offended again and was again excommunicated. After seven years, he once more recanted and was subjected to public humiliation. Rather than endure further trouble he committed suicide. He left an autobiographical sketch, *Exemplar humanae vitae* (1687; Eng. tr., *Specimen of Human Life*, 1695). Gutzkow wrote a tragedy about him, *Uriel Acosta*.

acoustics (ŭko͞o′stĭks, ŭkou–) [Gr.,=the facts about hearing], the science of SOUND, including its production, propagation, and effects. One important practical application of this science is in the designing of auditoriums, which requires a knowledge of the characteristics and behavior of sound waves. The most important factors to be considered are reverberation and INTERFERENCE. Reverberation is the persistence of sound in an enclosed space caused by repeated reflections of the sound waves back and forth by the walls. Reflection of sound sometimes causes an ECHO. Some reverberation in auditoriums is desirable, especially where music is performed, to avoid deadening of the sound to a degree that is unpleasant to the human ear. Depending on the location of the listener and the frequency of the sound, varying degrees of interference between the primary sound and its reflections will be produced. In a good auditorium these variations are minimized. Reflection can be reduced by the use of sound-absorbent materials, which are usually soft and porous, such as draperies, upholstery, carpets, acoustic tile, or plaster. In a room, reflection is decreased by the presence of people and open windows and doors.

acquired characteristics, modifications produced in an individual plant or animal as a result of mutilation, disease, use and disuse, or any distinctly environmental influence. Some examples are docking of tails, malformation due to disease, and muscle atrophy. Although belief in inheritability of acquired characteristics was accepted by Lamarck, it was later challenged by Darwin and Mendel. Modern geneticists have affirmed that inheritance is determined solely by the reproductive cells and is unaffected by somatic (body) cells. Belief in inheritance of acquired characteristics is therefore rejected, despite the efforts of some scientists, such as LYSENKO, to revive it.

Acre (ā′kŭr, ä′kŭr), Arabic *Acca*, Fr. *Saint-Jean d'Acre*, Heb. *Acco*, city (pop. c.18,000), N Israel,

a port on the Bay of Acre (part of the Mediterranean Sea) opposite Haifa. It is called Accho in the Old Testament (Judges 1.31) and Ptolemais in the New Testament (an early Christian center, Acts 21.7). An important port, it was a frequent military objective. Acre was taken by the Arabs in 638. In 1104 it was captured in the First Crusade and was held by Christians until 1187. In the Third Crusade it was won back (1191) by Guy of Lusignan, Richard I of England, and Philip II of France, who gave it to the Knights Hospitalers (the Knights of St. John, whence its French name). Its surrender (1291) to the Saracens after a century of prosperity marked the decline of the Latin Kingdom of Jerusalem and the Crusades. Acre was taken by Turkey in 1517. Turkish forces with the aid of Great Britain successfully withstood a 61-day siege by Napoleon in 1799. The city was taken in 1832 by Ibrahim Pasha for Mohammed Ali of Egypt, but European and Turkish forces won it back for Turkey in 1840. In the First World War

Acre: Fishermen in the harbor (below); interior of mosque built by Ahmad el-Jazzar (above); the Crusaders' Wall (right).

The Acropolis of Athens (above) and the Parthenon (opposite page).

British soldiers took it in 1918. The partition of Palestine (1948) assigned Acre to the Arabs, but in the course of military operations it was captured by Israeli forces. The name is also spelled Akka.

Acre (ä′krĭ), river rising at the border of Peru and Brazil. It flows northeast for c.220 mi. to join the Purus at Bôca do Acre. The ownership of the surrounding wild jungle territory was unsettled, but it was generally supposed to belong to Bolivia when in the late 1890s Brazilian wild-rubber traders took over the region. They declared an independent republic in 1899. Subsequent disorders, aggravated by an arrangement between Bolivia and a U.S. syndicate, led Bolivia and Brazil close to war. A settlement was reached by RIO BRANCO in the Treaty of Petrópolis (1903). Brazil received most of the area, but paid Bolivia a large indemnity and constructed a railroad on the Madeira river. The Brazilian area is a state (c.59,000 sq. mi.; pop. c.169,200) with its capital at Rio Branco.

acre [Indo-European,=field], measure of land used by the English-speaking peoples. The acre was originally the area a yoke of oxen could plow in a day and therefore differed in size from one locality to another. It is now fixed by statute as 10 square chains or 160 square rods, i.e., 4,840 sq. yd., 43,560 sq. ft., or 1/640 sq. mi. It is equal to about .4047 of a hectare or 4,046.873 square meters. Local customary acres survive in Scotland, Ireland, and several counties of England.

Acredale, uninc. village (pop. 1,022), extreme SE Va., a suburb SE of Norfolk.

Acrisius: see DANAË and PERSEUS.

Acroceraunia: see CERAUNIAN MOUNTAINS.

Acrocorinthus (ă″krōkûrĭn′thŭs), Gr. *Akrokorinthos* (ä″krôkô′rēnthôs), rock, 1,886 ft. high, central Greece, overlooking Old CORINTH; the site of the Acropolis of Corinth (of which some ruins

remain) and of a temple of Aphrodite. It was strongly fortified in the Middle Ages. Below gushed the fountain of Pirene, from which, in legend, PEGASUS drank when captured by Bellerophon.

Acrocorinthus with temple ruins in the foreground.

acropolis (ŭkrŏp′ŭlĭs) [Gr.,=high point of the city], elevated, fortified section of various ancient Greek cities. The Acropolis of Athens, a hill c.260 ft. high, with a flat oval top c.500 ft. wide and 1,150 ft. long, was walled before the 6th cent. B.C. by the Pelasgians. Devoted to religious rather than defensive purposes, the area was adorned during the time of Cimon and Pericles with some of the world's greatest architectural and sculptural

monuments. The top was reached by a winding processional path at the west end, where the impressive Propylaea stood. From here, the Sacred Way led past a colossal bronze statue of Athena (called Athena Promachus) and the site of the old temple of Athena to the PARTHENON. To the north was the Erechtheum and to the southwest the temple of Nike Apteros (Wingless Victory). On the southern slope were the Odeum of Herodes Atticus and the theater of Dionysus. The Acropolis was laid waste by the Persians in 480 B.C. Many of its treasures are in the national museum of Greece, in Athens. See W. B. Dinsmoor, *Architecture of Ancient Greece* (rev. 3d ed., 1950); A. W. Lawrence, *Greek Architecture* (1957).

Acropolita, George (ȧkrŏp″ŭlĭ′tu̇), 1217–82, Byzantine historian and statesman. He served as chancellor and general under John III and Theodore II of Nicaea, and after the Byzantine Empire was restored he represented (1274) Emperor Michael VIII at the Council of Lyons (see LYONS, SECOND COUNCIL OF). His valuable history of the period of the Latin Empire of Constantinople continues the work of Nicetas ACOMINATUS to 1261.

acrostic (u̇krŏ′stĭk, u̇krô′–), arrangement of words or lines wherein a series of initial, final, or other corresponding letters, when taken together, stand in a set order to form a word, a phrase, the alphabet, or the like. A famous acrostic was made on the Greek for Jesus Christ, God's Son, Savior: *Iesous Christos, Theou Uios, Soter* (*ch* and *th* being each one letter in Greek). The initials spell *ichthus*, Greek for fish; hence the frequent use of the fish by early Christians as a symbol for Jesus. There are several alphabetic acrostics in the Bible, e.g., in Ps. 119 and LAMENTATIONS. Acrostic verses are common, and very elaborate puzzles have been devised combining several schemes.

act, in law, anything done by a person, group, or body to which legal consequences attach. The term also refers to decrees, judgments, and awards handed down by an individual in an official position or by an official body (e.g., a judge or a legislature). In this sense it is often synonymous with statute, meaning a bill that has been enacted into law by the legislature. Public acts are those that relate to the entire community, whereas private acts operate only on particular persons or private concerns. A legislative act may be changed by amendment or abolished by repeal.

acta (ăk′tu̇), term for Roman official texts, whether written or carved on stone or metal. Usually acta were texts made public, although publication was sometimes restricted. Acta were first posted or carved for general reading c.131 B.C. These were accounts of general interest and were later called *Acta diurna*; they have been likened to modern newspapers. There were special acta of municipal, legal, or military content. The *Acta senatus*, according to a Roman administrative tradition, had long been kept secret, so that the public should have no knowledge of senatorial debate. In 59 B.C., Julius Caesar, as consul, ordered their publication along with the *Acta diurna*, but later the publication was censored. Acta was also the term used for laws enacted, primarily those promulgated by the emperors.

Actaeon (ăktē′ŭn), in Greek mythology, son of Aristaeus. Because he saw Artemis bathing naked, she changed him into a stag, and his own dogs killed him.

ACTH (adrenocorticotropic hormone), secretion of the anterior pituitary gland. Its chief function is to stimulate the cortex of the ADRENAL GLAND to elaborate adrenocortical substances, chiefly CORTISONE. When given intramuscularly or intravenously, ACTH produces the same pharmacologic and clinical effects as does cortisone, but since it is inactivated in the gastrointestinal tract and seems to have no value when used externally, it cannot be administered orally or externally as can cortisone. The action of ACTH also is contingent upon normally functioning adrenal glands; and ACTH is therefore useless in disorders caused by adrenal insufficiency, e.g., as replacement therapy where both adrenal glands have been removed.

acting, styles of: see THEATER.

actinic ray, light, especially in the green to ultraviolet end of the spectrum, having notable photochemical effect. See RAY; SPECTRUM; SUNLIGHT.

actinide series or **actinides** (from actinium), in chemistry, series of heavy radioactive metallic elements of atomic numbers 89 through 103, having chemical properties similar to actinium (atomic number 89). The actinides in order of increasing atomic number are ACTINIUM, THORIUM, PROTACTINIUM, URANIUM, NEPTUNIUM, PLUTONIUM, AMERICIUM, CURIUM, BERKELIUM, CALIFORNIUM, EINSTEINIUM, FERMIUM, MENDELEVIUM, NOBELIUM, and LAWRENCIUM. See PERIODIC TABLE.

actinium (ăktĭn′ēŭm) [Gr.,=like a ray], radioactive element of the ACTINIDE SERIES (symbol=Ac; in group III B of the PERIODIC TABLE; for physical constants, see ELEMENT, table). Actinium was first recognized in 1899 by André Debierne in uranium residues from pitchblende. It was found to be identical with an element discovered in 1902 by Fritz Giesel and called by him emanium. Actinium occurs in radioactive minerals containing uranium; the ratio of actinium to uranium is always the same. Actinium decays principally by beta emission. A number of isotopes, all radioactive, have been discovered. Actinium introduces the elements known as the actinides or actinide series, which is analogous to the LANTHANIDE SERIES.

action, in law: see PROCEDURE.

action painting: see ABSTRACT EXPRESSIONISM.

Actium (ăk′tēŭm, ăk′shēŭm), Gr. *Aktion*, promontory, NW Acarnania, Greece. There are vestiges of several temples and an ancient town. It is famous for the naval battle in which the forces of Octavian (later Augustus) under Agrippa defeated (31 B.C.) the fleet and land forces of Antony and Cleopatra and for the commemorative Actian games, held at Nicopolis every four years. The battle established Octavian as ruler of Rome.

active: see VOICE.

act of God, in law, an ACCIDENT caused by the operation of extraordinary natural force. The effect of ordinary natural causes (e.g., that rain will leak through a defective roof) may be foreseen and avoided by the exercise of human care; failure to take the necessary precautions constitutes NEGLIGENCE, and the party injured in the accident may be entitled to damages. An act of God, however, is so extraordinary and devoid of human agency that reasonable care would not avoid the consequences; hence, the injured party has no right to damages. Accidents caused by tornadoes, perils of the sea, extraordinary floods, and severe ice storms are usually considered acts of God, but fires are not so considered unless they are caused by lightning.

Acton, John Emerich Edward Dalberg Acton, 1st **Baron,** 1834–1902, English historian, b. Naples; grandson of Sir John Francis Edward Acton and of Emmerich Joseph, duc de Dalberg. He became (1859) a Liberal member of Parliament and editor of the *Rambler*, a Roman Catholic monthly. W. E. Gladstone, his close friend, nominated him to the peerage (1869), and in 1892 Acton was made lord in waiting. Acton's genuine and ardent liberalism gave frequent offense to some Catholic authorities. Though he opposed the Syllabus of Errors issued by PIUS IX and the promulgation of the dogma of papal infallibility, Lord Acton as a sincere Catholic accepted them after their pronouncement. In 1895 he was appointed professor of modern history at Cambridge and in the following years planned the cooperative *Cambridge Modern History*, of which only the first volume appeared before his death. Acton never completed a book; his influence was felt through his lectures, his writings for periodicals, and his personal contacts with the leading historians of his time. Many articles, essays, and lectures were brought together after his death in *Lectures on Modern History* (1906), *History of Freedom* (1907), and *Historical Essays and Studies* (1907). Some of these were reprinted in *Essays on Freedom and Power* (1948) and *Essays on Church and State* (1952). See F. A. Gasquest, ed., *Lord Acton and His Circle* (1906); studies by G. E. Fasnacht (1952) and Lionel Kochan (1954).

Acton, Sir John Francis Edward, 1736?–1811, Neapolitan statesman of British origin, b. Besançon,

Sir John Francis Edward Acton

France. He was minister of Ferdinand IV of Naples (later FERDINAND I of the Two Sicilies) from 1779 to 1804. The favorite of Queen MARIE CAROLINE, he overthrew Spanish influence on Naples and strengthened ties with Great Britain and with Austria; he was assisted by Lady Emma HAMILTON. After the fall of the PARTHENOPEAN REPUBLIC (1799), where he played a major role in the bloody reprisals, he consolidated absolutism, but Napoleon I forced his dismissal.

Acton, municipal borough (pop. 65,274), Middlesex, S central England, W of London, of which it is a residential suburb. Since 1920 engineering plants and light industry have moved into this district from London.

Acton, town (pop. 7,238), E Mass., NW of Boston; settled c.1680, inc. 1735. Electrical machinery and chemicals are produced. The town includes the village of South Acton (pop. 1,114).

Acts of the Apostles, book in the Bible between Gospels and Epistles, the only contemporary historical account of the expansion of Christianity in its earliest period. It was written in Greek between A.D. 60 and A.D. 80 as a sequel to the Gospel of St. Luke, and Luke is its traditional author. It falls into two divisions: the first 12 chapters, on the Palestinian church from Pentecost until Herod's death, having chiefly to do with St. Peter; the rest of the book, on the missionary work of St. Paul among the Gentiles (13–21.14) and his arrest, trial, and trip as prisoner to Rome (21.15–28). St. Luke was sometimes a companion of St. Paul, and the narrative is then in the first person plural (16.10–17; 20.5–21.18; 27.1–28.16). Three critical events are noteworthy—the descent of the Holy Ghost (Acts 2), the martyrdom of St. Stephen (Acts 6 and 7), and the conversion of St. Paul (Acts 9). See H. J. Cadbury, *The Book of Acts in History* (1955).

actuary, one who calculates the probabilities involved in any contingency for which INSURANCE is desired and establishes the premium necessary to cover such contingency. Originally, in England, the term was applied to a clerk or registrar appointed either to record court acts or to manage a joint stock company. Later it came to be used exclusively for managers of insurance companies. As insurance against loss of life is the most common type of policy, actuaries are particularly concerned with life tables based on age, health, and probable longevity. However, the contingencies involved in fire, accident, or group health policies are also important parts of the actuary's work. An actuary also calculates the probabilities upon which annuities are based and the amount of money, at compound interest, necessary to cover them.

Acuña, Cristóbal de (krěstō′bäl dä akōō′nyä), 1597–1676?, Spanish Jesuit missionary and explorer in South America, rector of the Jesuit college at Cuenca, Ecuador. In 1638 he was sent by the viceroy to accompany TEIXEIRA on his return journey down the Amazon. Acuña's *New Discovery of the Great River of the Amazons* (1639; modern Eng. tr. in C. R. Markham, *Expedition into the Valley of the Amazons,* 1859) was the earliest firsthand description of the Amazon to be printed.

Acuña, Juan de (hwän′ dä äkōō′nyä), 1658?–1734, Spanish-American administrator, viceroy of New

Spain (1722–34), marqués de Casa Fuerte, b. Lima, Peru. After a distinguished career in Spain he was sent to Mexico, where his creole origin and his wise government made him popular. He extinguished favoritism and corruption, extended and consolidated Spanish territorial claims, and ordered the construction of many public works. In his term the *Gaceta de México* and the *Mercurio de México* first appeared.

Acushnet (ŭkŏŏsh′nĭt), town (pop. 5,755), SE Mass., NE of New Bedford; settled c.1660, inc. 1860. The town was devastated in King Philip's War. In the Revolution it was the scene of a skirmish between British and American forces. Golf balls and wooden products are made here.

Acworth, city (pop. 2,359), NW Ga., NW of Atlanta, on Allatoona Reservoir; inc. 1860. Nearby is Kennesaw Mountain National Battlefield Park (see NATIONAL PARKS AND MONUMENTS, table).

Ada. 1 City (pop. 2,064), co. seat of Norman co., NW Minn., in the Red River valley, NNE of Moorhead; founded 1874, inc. 1881. It is a farm trade center. 2 Village (pop. 3,918), NW Ohio, E of Lima, in a farm area; laid out 1853 as Johnstown, inc. 1861 as Ada. Ohio Northern Univ. (Methodist; coeducational; 1871) is here. 3 City (pop. 14,347), co. seat of Pontotoc co., S central Okla., near the Canadian river SE of Oklahoma City; settled 1889. It is the center of an area producing chiefly cotton, grains, hay, livestock, and oil, with industries based on these. Cement and glass are also made. A state teachers college is here.

Adad: see HADAD.

Adadah (ăd′ŭdŭ), town of Judah in the southernmost part of Palestine. Joshua 15.22.

Adah (ā′dŭ) [Heb.,=ornament]. 1 Wife of Esau. Gen. 36.1–20. 2 Wife of Lamech. Gen. 4.19–24.

Adaiah (ŭdā′yŭ) [Heb.,=God has adorned]. 1 Josiah's mother's father. 2 Kings 22.1. 2 Gershomite Levite. 1 Chron. 6.41. Iddo: 1 Chron. 6.21. 3 Benjamite. 1 Chron. 8.21. Shema: 1 Chron. 8.13. 4 Priest. 1 Chron. 9.12; Neh. 11.12. 5,6 Men who had foreign wives. Ezra 10.29,39. 7 Father of MAASEIAH 2. 8 Ancestor of ASAIAH 4.

Adair, John, 1757–1840, American pioneer in Kentucky, b. North Carolina. He went into the Kentucky country in 1786 and gained note as an Indian fighter and as a political leader. In the War of 1812 he was a commander of Kentucky volunteers in the battle of New Orleans. As governor of the state (1820–24) he adopted a vigorous program of internal improvement to fight hard times. He was (1831–33) a member of the House of Representatives.

Adairsville (ŭdârz′vĭl), city (pop. 1,026), NW Ga., NW of Atlanta, in a farm area; inc. 1872. Textiles are produced.

Adak (ā′dăk, ä′dăk), off W Alaska, one of the ALEUTIAN ISLANDS. In the Second World War it was a U.S. military base.

Adalbert, Saint (ă′dŭlbûrt), d. 997, bishop of Prague. He was a missionary in Russia, Prussia, and Poland and was martyred in Danzig. He is patron of Bohemia and Poland. Feast: April 23.

Adalbert, d. 1072, archbishop of Hamburg-Bremen, a diocese which included Scandinavia. He was a favorite of Emperor Henry III, who even wanted (1046) to install him as pope, and was a guardian of Henry IV, but his relentless ambition to become ecclesiastical ruler of all N Europe defeated itself. The nobles envied his importance at court, the abbots hated him for his efforts to subordinate the abbeys, and the bishops feared his increasing ecclesiastical power. They accomplished his dismissal in 1066, but Henry IV recalled him in 1069. One of the ablest statesmen of his time, Adalbert, though working mainly for selfish aims, helped consolidate the imperial authority. See Adam of Bremen, *History of the Archbishops of Hamburg-Bremen* (Eng. tr., 1959).

Adalia (ădŭlĭ'ŭ), one of Haman's sons. Esther 9.8.

Adalia, Turkey: see ANTALYA.

Adam [Heb.,=man], in the Bible, the first man. For the account of his creation, of that of his wife EVE, of their life in the Garden of Eden (see EDEN, GARDEN OF), of their first disobedience, and of their expulsion, see Gen. 1.26–5.5. The opening chapters of Genesis are very interesting to believers of the three principal monotheistic religions; for conceptions derived therefrom, see SIN and GRACE; for examples of the mass of legends that Judaism and Islam have collected about the biblical account, see LILITH and PSEUDEPIGRAPHA. To St. Paul, Adam represented the earthy side of man, as in 1 Cor. 15.20–22, 42–58. The higher criticism has seen in Adam's story an attempt to harmonize Hebrew cosmogonic myths. They compare Babylonian myths of creation, which are similar to the biblical account in many features.

Adam, Adolphe Charles (ädōlf' shärl' ädä'), 1803–56, French composer of the popular *Cantique de Noël.* He composed more than 50 stage works.

Death of Adam, a fresco by Piero della Francesca.

Robert Adam

Adolphe Charles Adam

(1764). For decorative painting, Adam employed such artists as Angelica Kauffmann and Antonio Zucchi. The Adam manner gained great favor in his day, and designs in the Adam style have never ceased to appear. Especially interesting examples of Adam planning and decoration are Osterly Park, Middlesex (1761-80); Syon House, Middlesex (1762-69); and Luton Hoo, Beds. (1768-75). The brothers wrote *Works in Architecture of Robert and James Adam* (3 vols., 1778-1822). Robert was architect to the king from 1762 until 1768, when he was succeeded by James. Robert Adam was buried in Westminster Abbey. See James Lees-Milne, *The Age of Adam* (1948); John Fleming, *Robert Adam and His Circle* (1962).

Adam, town, on the upper Jordan. Joshua 3.16.
Adamah (ăd′ûmû), Naphtalite city. Joshua 19.36.
Adam de la Halle (ädä′ dù lä äl′) or **Adam le Bossu** (lù bōsü′), c.1240-1287, French dramatist and poet-musician, a great TROUVÈRE. Many of his songs and polyphonic motets are preserved, as is the pastoral comedy with music, *Le Jeu de Robin et Marion* (c.1283). Other important works are *Le Jeu de la feuillée* (1262) and an epic fragment, written in Naples, *Le Roi de Sezile.*
Adami (ăd′ûmī) or **Adami-nekeb** (-nē′-), border town of Naphtali. Adami-nekeb RSV. Two towns, Adami and Nekeb, in KJV. Joshua 19.33.
Adam le Bossu: see ADAM DE LA HALLE.
Adams, Abigail (**Smith**), 1744-1818, wife of President John ADAMS and mother of President John Quincy ADAMS, b. Weymouth, Mass. A lively,

He wrote comic operas such as *Le Postillon de Long-jumeau* (1836) and the ballet *Giselle* (1841).

Adam, Alexander, 1741-1809, Scottish educator and antiquary. As rector of Edinburgh High School from 1768, he aroused considerable opposition by introducing Greek into the curriculum. His *Rudiments of Latin and English Grammar* (1772), written in English instead of Latin, was also highly controversial, but his method was generally adopted by the time of his death. Sir Walter Scott, Brougham, and Jeffrey were among his pupils. His *Roman Antiquities* (1791) made him famous.

Adam, Lambert Sigisbert (läbĕr′ sēzhĕsbĕr′ ädä′), 1700-1759, French sculptor. He won the Prix de Rome at 23 and set to work copying and restoring antique statuary in Rome. When he returned to Paris, however, he emulated the baroque style. The influence of Bernini is apparent in his *Neptune Calming the Waves* (Louvre) and *Neptune and Amphitrite* (Versailles). The latter was done in collaboration with his brother **Nicolas Sébastien Adam** (nēkōlä′ sābästyĕ′), 1705-78, whose work reflects the more violent aspects of the baroque. Characteristic are his *Prometheus Bound* (Louvre) and the bas-relief *The Martyrdom of St. Victoire* (chapel, Versailles). Both brothers enjoyed the favor of Louis XV. A third brother, **François Balthasar Gaspard Adam** (fräswä′ bältäzär′ gäspär′), 1710-61, became sculptor to Frederick the Great. His work is to be seen at Potsdam.

Adam, Robert (ăd′ùm), 1728-92, and **James Adam,** 1730-94, Scottish architects, brothers. They designed important public and private buildings in England and Scotland and numberless interiors, pieces of furniture, and decorative objects. Robert possessed the great creative talents, his brother James serving chiefly as his assistant. Robert Adam designed his buildings to achieve the most harmonious relation between the exterior, the interior, and the furniture. His light and elegant, essentially decorative style was a free, personal reconstitution of antique motifs. He drew upon numerous sources including earlier English Palladian architecture, French and Italian Renaissance architecture, and the antique monuments themselves as he knew them through publications and personal investigation. Adam himself contributed an important study, *Ruins of the Palace of the Emperor Diocletian at Spalatro in Dalmatia*

Abigail Adams

intelligent woman, she was the chief figure in the social life of her husband's administration and one of the most distinguished and influential of the first ladies in the history of the United States. Her detailed letters are a vivid source of social history. The correspondence with her husband was edited in a number of volumes by Charles Francis Adams; her letters, as well as John's, are included in *The Adams-Jefferson Letters,* edited by Lester J. Cappon (1959); letters to her sister, Mary Smith Cranch, are in *New Letters of Abigail Adams, 1788-1801,* edited by Stewart Mitchell (1947). See biographies by Laura E. Richards (1917), Dorothie

Bobbe (1929), and Janet Whitney (1947). See also the bibliography under ADAMS, JOHN.

Adams, Brooks, 1848–1927, American historian, b. Quincy, Mass., grad. Harvard, 1870; son of Charles Francis ADAMS (1807–86). His theory that civilization rose and fell according to the growth and decline of commerce was first developed in *The Law of Civilization and Decay* (1895). Adams applied it to his own capitalistic age, of which he was a militant critic, but failed to find the universal law which he persistently sought. His ideas greatly influenced his brother Henry ADAMS, whose essays he edited in *The Degradation of the Democratic Dogma* (1919). In *America's Economic Supremacy* (1900) Brooks said that Western Europe had already begun to decline and that Russia and the United States were the only potential great powers left. His other chief works include *The Emancipation of Massachusetts* (1887), *The New Empire* (1902), and *Theory of Social Revolutions* (1913). See biography by A. F. Beringause (1955); J. T. Adams, *The Adams Family* (1930); T. P. Donovan, *Henry Adams and Brooks Adams* (1961).

Adams, Charles Francis, 1807–86, American statesman, minister to Great Britain (1861–68), b. Boston; son of John Quincy ADAMS. After a boyhood spent in various European capitals, he was graduated (1825) from Harvard and studied law under Daniel Webster. He practiced in Boston, looked after his father's business affairs, and wrote articles on American history for the *North American Review*. Adams served (1840–45) in both branches of the state legislature, founded and edited the Boston *Whig*, and became a leader of the Conscience Whigs. In 1848 he was the Free-Soil party candidate for the vice presidency. He represented (1858–61) his father's old district in Congress and assumed prominence as a Republican leader. On Seward's advice, Lincoln appointed him minister to Great Britain. In the face of English sympathy for the Confederacy, he maintained the Northern cause with wisdom and a bold dignity that won British respect, particularly in the serious *Trent* and *Alabama* incidents. He is credited with preventing British recognition of the Confederacy, thus contributing much to the Union victory. He later represented the United States in the settlement of the ALABAMA CLAIMS. He published many political pamphlets

Charles Francis Adams

and addresses and was an editor of the works (10 vols., 1850–56) of his grandfather, John Adams, and of the diary (12 vols., 1874–77) of his father. See biography by M. B. Duberman (1961); W. C. Ford, ed., *A Cycle of Adams Letters, 1861–1865* (1920); J. T. Adams, *The Adams Family* (1930).

Adams, Charles Francis, 1835–1915, American economist and historian, b. Boston, grad. Harvard, 1856; son of Charles Francis ADAMS (1807–86). In the Civil War he fought at Antietam and Gettysburg and was brevetted brigadier general of volunteers. Adams became a railroad expert after the war, writing *Chapters of Erie* (1871), which exposed the corrupt financing of the Erie RR, and *Railroads: Their Origin 'and Problems* (1878). In 1869 he became a member, and from 1872 to 1879 was chairman, of the Massachusetts Board of Railroad Commissioners, the first of its kind in the nation. Adams was made chairman of the government directors of the Union Pacific in 1878 and became president in 1884, but was ousted by the forces of Jay Gould in 1890. His reform of the public schools in the home town of the Adamses, Quincy, Mass., was described in *The New Departure in the Common Schools of Quincy* (1879), and the Quincy system was widely adopted. Adams served 24 years on the Harvard Board of Overseers and was president (1895–1915) of the Massachusetts Historical Society. He wrote *Three Episodes of Massachusetts History* (1892), *Studies: Military and Diplomatic, 1775–1865* (1911), *Trans-Atlantic Historical Solidarity* (1913), which was a collection of lectures he had given at Oxford, and biographies of his father (1900) and Richard Henry Dana (1890). See his autobiography (1916); W. C. Ford, ed., *A Cycle of Adams Letters, 1861–1865* (1920); J. T. Adams, *The Adams Family* (1930).

Adams, Charles Francis, 1866–1954, U.S. Secretary of the Navy (1929–1933), b. Quincy, Mass., grad. Harvard (B.A., 1888; LL.B., 1892); grandson of Charles Francis Adams (1807–86). He practiced law for a brief period in Boston but for most of his life was connected with a wide variety of business enterprises in that city and elsewhere. Adams served in the cabinet of Herbert Hoover.

Adams, Frank Dawson, 1859–1942, Canadian geologist, b. Montreal, educated at McGill Univ., Yale, Johns Hopkins, and Heidelberg (Ph.D., 1892). He was long associated with McGill Univ.—as Logan professor of geology, dean of the faculty of applied science, vice principal, and, for a time, acting principal. He was a fellow of the Royal Society of London as well as of Canada, and a fellow of the Geological Society of London (by whom he was awarded the Wollaston gold medal). His *Birth and Development of the Geological Sciences* (1938) is authoritative, as are his many pamphlets and papers on various aspects of geology.

Adams, Franklin Pierce, pseud. **F. P. A.,** 1881–1960, American columnist and author, b. Chicago, studied at Armour Scientific Academy and the Univ. of Michigan. He began (1903) work as a columnist on the Chicago *Journal* and continued it on the New York *Evening Mail*, the *Tribune*, the *World*, the *Herald Tribune*, and the *Post*. His column, "The Conning Tower," consisted of verse and humor by F. P. A. and his contributors. His Saturday column, an account of his week's activi-

Franklin Pierce Adams

Henry Adams

ties, imitated the style of Samuel Pepys and was republished as *The Diary of Our Own Samuel Pepys: 1911–1934* (1935).

Adams, Hannah, 1755–1831, American writer, b. Medfield, Mass. She was perhaps the first woman in the United States to make writing pay as a profession. Her most notable works are *An Alphabetical Compendium of the Various Sects* (1784) and *Summary History of New England* (1799), a pioneer history of the region.

Adams, Henry (Henry Brooks Adams), 1838–1918, American historian, b. Boston, grad. Harvard, 1858; son of Charles Francis ADAMS (1807–86). He was secretary (1861–68) to his father, then U.S. minister at the Court of St. James's. Upon his return to the United States, having already abandoned the law and seeing no opportunity in the traditional Adams calling, politics, he briefly tried journalism. He reluctantly accepted (1870) an offer to teach medieval history at Harvard, but stayed on seven years and also edited (1870–76) the *North American Review*. In 1877 Adams moved to Washington, D.C., his home thereafter. He wrote a good biography of Albert Gallatin (1879), a less satisfactory one of John Randolph (1882), and two novels (the first anonymously and the second under a pseudonym)—*Democracy* (1880), a cutting satire on politics, and *Esther* (1884). His exhaustive study of the administrations of Jefferson and Madison, *History of the United States of America* (9 vols., 1889–91; reprinted in 3 vols., 1929; condensed and ed. by Herbert Agar as *The Formative Years*, 2 vols., 1947), is one of the major achievements of American historical writing. Famous for its style, it is deficient, perhaps, in understanding the basic economic forces at work, but the first six chapters constitute one of the best social surveys of any period in U.S. history. Never of a sanguine temperament, Adams became even more pessimistic after the suicide (1885) of his adored wife. He abandoned American history and began a series of restless journeyings, physical and mental, in an effort to achieve a basic philosophy of history. Drawing upon the physical sciences for guidance and influenced by his brother, Brooks ADAMS, he found a satisfactory unifying principle in force or energy. He selected for intensive treatment two periods—1050–1250, pre-

sented in *Mont-Saint-Michel and Chartres* (privately printed 1904, pub. 1913), and his own era, presented in *The Education of Henry Adams* (privately printed 1906, pub. 1918). The first is a brilliant idealization of the Middle Ages, specifically of the 13th.-century unity brought about by the force of the Virgin, then dominant. The second, although written in the third person and reticent about much of his life, was classified by his publishers as an autobiography. Another *tour de force*, it describes his unsuccessful efforts to achieve intellectual peace in an age when the force of the dynamo is dominant. These two books, containing some of the most beautiful English ever written, rather than his monumental *History*, won Adams his lasting place as a major American writer. *The Degradation of the Democratic Dogma* (1919), edited and prefaced by a memoir of Henry Adams by his brother Brooks, contains three brilliant essays on his philosophy of history—"The Tendency of History," "A Letter to American Teachers of History" (pub. separately in 1910), and "The Rule of Phase Applied to History." Friendships, especially those with John HAY and Clarence KING, played a large part in Adams's life, and his personal letters reveal a warmer man, for an Adams, than one might suspect. See his letters, (ed. by W. C. Ford, 2 vols., 1930–38); J. T. Adams, *Henry Adams* (1933); Ward Thoron, ed., *The Letters of Mrs. Henry Adams, 1865–1883* (1936); H. D. Cater, ed., *Henry Adams and His Friends: a Collection of His Unpublished Letters* (1947); Ernest Samuels, *The Young Henry Adams* (1948) and *Henry Adams: the Middle Years* (1958); T. P. Donovan, *Henry Adams and Brooks Adams: the Education of Two Americans* (1961).

Adams, Henry Cullen, 1850–1906, American legislator and dairyman, b. Oneida co., N.Y., attended the Univ. of Wisconsin. As Congressman after 1902, he championed the Pure Food and Drugs Act, the Adams Act (for the support of state agricultural experiment stations), and the admission of Arizona and New Mexico as separate states.

Adams, Herbert Baxter, 1850–1901, American historian, b. Shutesbury, near Amherst, Mass., grad. Amherst, 1872. In 1876, the year he received his doctorate at Heidelberg, he became one of the original faculty of Johns Hopkins Univ. There, in 1880, he began his famous seminar in history, in which a large proportion of the next generation of American historians received their training. Adams founded the "Johns Hopkins Studies in Historical and Political Science," the first of such series, and brought about the organization in 1884 of the American Historical Association, of which he was secretary until 1900. He wrote *The Germanic Origin of New England Towns* (1882), *Life and Writings of Jared Sparks* (1893), and many articles and reports on the study of the social sciences which were very influential in their day. See W. S. Holt, ed., *Historical Scholarship in the United States, 1876–1901, as Revealed in the Correspondence of Herbert B. Adams* (1938).

Adams, Isaac, 1802–83, American printer and inventor, b. Rochester, N.H. In 1834 he invented the Adams press, a mechanical variation of the hand press, in which the platen remained stationary and the bed rose to meet it. The Adams press remained in general use until c.1875, when it was superseded by the cylinder press.

Adams, James Truslow (trŭ'slō), 1878–1949, American historian, b. Brooklyn, N.Y., grad. Polytechnic Institute of Brooklyn (B.A., 1898) and Yale (M.A., 1900). *The Founding of New England* (1921), which brought him the Pulitzer Prize in history for 1922, was followed by *Revolutionary New England, 1691–1776* (1923) and *New England in the Republic, 1776–1850* (1926). Among the best of his many books are *Provincial Society, 1690–1763* (Vol. III in the "History of American Life" series, 1927) and *The Epic of America* (1931), which was widely translated. *The March of Democracy* (2 vols., 1932–33) and *America's Tragedy* (1934) were also popular. *The Adams Family* (1930) and *Henry Adams* (1933) were books on the famous Massachusetts clan by an unrelated descendant of the Virginia Adamses. Adams, who spent much of his time in London as representative of his publishers, Charles Scribner's Sons, also wrote *Building the British Empire: to the End of the First Empire* (1938) and *Empire on the Seven Seas: the British Empire, 1784–1939* (1940). He was editor in chief of *Dictionary of American History* (6 vols., 1940; rev. ed., 1942), *Atlas of American History* (1943), and *Album of American History* (4 vols., 1944–48), three valuable reference works. Some of his later writings reflect his obvious distaste for the New Deal, of which he was a vigorous critic.

Adams, John, 1735–1826, 2d President of the United States (1797–1801), b. Quincy (then in Braintree), Mass., grad. Harvard, 1755. A lawyer, he emerged into politics as an opponent of the Stamp Act and, after moving to Boston, was a leader in the patriot group opposing the British measures that were leading to the American Revolution. Sent (1774) to the First Continental Congress, Adams distinguished himself, and in the Second Continental Congress he was a moderate but forceful revolutionary. He proposed George Washington as commander in chief of the Continental troops to bind Virginia more tightly to the patriot cause. He

President John Adams

favored the DECLARATION OF INDEPENDENCE, was a member of the drafting committee, and argued eloquently for it. As a diplomat seeking foreign aid for the just-born nation, he had a thorny career. Appointed (1777) to succeed Silas Deane as a commissioner to France, he accomplished little before returning home (1779) to be a major figure in the Massachusetts constitutional convention. Back he went (1779) to France, where he quarreled with Vergennes and was able to lend little assistance to Benjamin Franklin in his peace efforts. His attempts to negotiate a loan from the Netherlands were fruitless until 1782. Adams was one of the negotiators who drew up the momentous Treaty of Paris (1783; see PARIS, TREATY OF) to end the American Revolution. After this service he obtained another Dutch loan and then was envoy (1785–88) to Great Britain, where he met with British coldness and unwillingness to discuss the problems growing out of the treaty. He asked for his own recall and ended a significant but generally discouraging diplomatic career. In America once more, he was chosen Vice President and served throughout George Washington's administration (1789–97). Though he inclined to conservative policies, he acted somewhat as a balance wheel in the partisan contest between Alexander HAMILTON and Thomas JEFFERSON. In the 1796 election Adams was chosen to succeed Washington as President despite the surreptitious opposition of Hamilton. The Adams administration was one of crisis and conflict, in which the President showed an honest and stubborn integrity, and though allied with Hamilton and the conservative property-respecting Federalists, he was not dominated by them in their struggle against the vigorously rising, more broadly democratic forces led by Jefferson. Though the Federalists were pro-British and strongly opposed to post-Revolutionary France, Adams by conciliation prevented the near war of 1798 (see XYZ AFFAIR) from developing into a real war between France and the United States. Nor did the President wholeheartedly endorse the ALIEN AND SEDITION ACTS (1798), aimed at the Anti-Federalists. He was, however, detested by his Jeffersonian enemies, and in the election of 1800 he and Hamilton were both submerged in the tide of Jeffersonian democracy. After 1801 Adams lived in retirement at Quincy (in a mansion given in 1946 to the nation as a historic site), issuing sober and highly respected political statements and writing and receiving many letters, notably those to and from Jefferson. Their famous correspondence was edited by Lester J. Cappon in *The Adams-Jefferson Letters* (1959). By remarkable coincidence he and Jefferson died on the same day, Independence Day, July 4, 1826. John Adams and his wife, Abigail ADAMS, founded one of the most distinguished families of the United States; their son, John Quincy ADAMS, was also President. A definitive edition of the voluminous writings of the Adams family was begun with four volumes (1961) containing the diary and autobiography of John Adams. Until completion of the definitive edition, see Adams's *Works* (10 vols., ed. by J. Q. Adams and C. F. Adams, 1850–56; Vol. I is a biography by C. F. Adams); *The Selected Writings of John Adams and John Quincy Adams* (ed. by Adrienne Koch and William Peden,

1946). See also James Truslow Adams, *The Adams Family* (1930); Zoltán Haraszti, *John Adams and the Prophets of Progress* (1952); Manning J. Dauer, *The Adams Federalists* (1953); Stephen G. Kurtz, *The Presidency of John Adams* (1957); biographies by John T. Morse (1884), Gilbert Chinard (1933), and Page Smith (1962).

Adams, John Couch, 1819–92, English astronomer, grad. St. John's College, Cambridge, 1843. By mathematical calculation based on irregularities in the motion of Uranus, he predicted the position of the then unknown planet NEPTUNE. Because of delay in England in making a telescopic search for the planet, the credit for the discovery went to a Frenchman, LEVERRIER. In 1858 Adams became professor of mathematics at St. Andrews Univ., but he soon returned to Cambridge, to occupy the Lowndean chair of astronomy and geometry until his death. From 1861 he was also director of the university observatory, preferring this post to that of astronomer royal, which was offered to him in 1881. He made valuable studies of the moon's motions, of the Leonids in the great meteor shower of 1866, and of terrestrial magnetism. His collected papers, edited by his brother, were published at Cambridge in 1896 and 1901.

Adams, John Quincy, 1767–1848, 6th President of the United States (1825–29), b. Quincy (then in Braintree), Mass.; son of John and Abigail Adams and father of Charles Francis Adams (1807–86). He accompanied his father on missions to Europe and gained broad knowledge from study and travel —he even accompanied (1781–83) Francis Dana to Russia—before returning home to graduate (1787) from Harvard and to study law. Washington appointed (1794) him minister to the Netherlands, and in his father's administration he was minister to Prussia (1797–1801). In 1803 he became a U.S. Senator as a Federalist, but his independence of mind led him to approve Jeffersonian policies in the Louisiana Purchase and in the Embargo Act of 1807; the Federalists were outraged, and he resigned (1808). Sent as minister to Russia in 1809, he was well received at the tsarist court, but the wars of Napoleon eclipsed Russian-American relations. He then helped to draw up the Treaty of Ghent (1814), and his diplomatic training was completed as minister to Great Britain. As Secretary of State (1817–25) under President James Monroe, Adams gained an enduring fame. His best-known achievement was the MONROE DOCTRINE (1823). In 1824 Adams was a candidate for the U.S. presidency. Neither he, Andrew Jackson nor Henry Clay received an electoral majority, and the election was decided in the House of Representatives. There Clay supported Adams and made him President. Adams then appointed Clay Secretary of State, but the Jacksonians' cry that the appointment fulfilled a corrupt bargain was unfounded in fact. With little popular support and without a party, Adams had an unhappy, ineffective administration, despite his attempts to institute a broad program of internal improvements. After Jackson won the 1828 election, Adams retired to Quincy but returned to win new renown as U.S. Representative (1831–48); he was eloquent in attacking the gag rules and all measures that would extend slavery. His coldness and rather gloomy introspection

President
John Quincy Adams

still kept him from general popularity, but he was respected for his high-mindedness and his great knowledge. His interest in science led him to promote the Smithsonian Institution. His diary (selections ed. by C. F. Adams, 12 vols., 1874–77; abridged by Allan Nevins, 1928 and 1951) is a valuable document. Most of his writings were edited by W. C. Ford (7 vols., 1913–17), and some appear in *The Selected Writings of John and John Quincy Adams* (ed. by Adrienne Koch and William Peden, 1946). See biographies by John T. Morse (1883) and Bennett Champ Clark (1932); James Truslow Adams, *The Adams Family* (1930); Samuel Flagg Bemis, *John Quincy Adams and the Foundations of American Foreign Policy* (1949) and *John Quincy Adams and the Union* (1956); G. A. Lipsky, *John Quincy Adams, His Theory and Ideas* (1950).

Adams, Maude, 1872–1953, American actress, b. Salt Lake City, Utah. Her name was Kiskadden,

Maude Adams

but she used her mother's maiden name. She began acting at an early age and became leading lady to John Drew under the management of the Frohmans, an assignment that lasted for five years. She

49

made her first stellar appearance in Barrie's *Little Minister* (1897), the first of his plays in which she became famous. Others include *Quality Street* (1901), *Peter Pan* (1905), the play for which she was most loved, and *What Every Woman Knows* (1908). In her retirement after 1918, Miss Adams made valuable contributions to the development of stage lighting; in 1937 she became professor of drama at Stephens College. See biography by Phyllis Robbins (1956).

Adams, Roger, 1889–, American chemist, b. Boston, grad. Harvard (B.A., 1909; Ph.D., 1912) and studied in Berlin. After 1916 he taught at the Univ. of Illinois until 1957. He served in the First World War with the Chemical Warfare Service and in the Second World War on the Scientific Advisory Board and the National Defense Research Committee and as scientific adviser in the Occupation governments in Germany and Japan. Among his contributions to chemistry are the development of methods of identifying and preparing substances and of new methods of synthesis. He was among the first to synthesize the local anesthetics butyn and procaine. He has long been connected in various capacities with the annual publication of *Organic Syntheses* (editor in chief of Vols. I and VIII, 1921, 1927); with J. R. Johnson he wrote *Elementary Laboratory Experiments in Organic Chemistry* (1928).

Adams, Samuel, 1722–1803, American Revolutionary patriot, signer of the Declaration of Independence, b. Boston, Mass., grad. Harvard, 1740; second cousin of John Adams. A brewer, he undertook a political career and was a member (1764–74) and clerk (1766–74) of the lower house of the Massachusetts legislature. As colonial resistance to British laws stiffened, Adams spoke for the discontented and replaced James OTIS as leader of the extremists. He drafted a protest against the Stamp Act in 1765 and, as clerk, composed documents of historic significance. More important, he used his able pen in pamphleteering against the British and for the NATURAL RIGHTS of man. With the help of such men as John Hancock he organized the revolutionary Sons of Liberty and helped to foment revolt through the Committees of Correspondence. He was the moving spirit in the BOSTON TEA PARTY. Gen. Thomas Gage issued (1775) a warrant for the arrest of Adams and Hancock, but they escaped punishment and continued to stir up lethargic patriots. Samuel Adams was a member (1774–81) of the Continental Congress, but after independence was declared his influence declined; the "radical" was replaced by more conservative leaders, who tended to look upon Adams as an irresponsible agitator. He later (1794–97) served as governor of Massachusetts. See selection of his writings ed. by Elizabeth Lawson (1946); biographies by J. K. Hosmer (1885), R. V. Harlow (1923), and J. C. Miller (1936).

Adams, Samuel Hopkins, 1871–1958, American author, b. Dunkirk, N.Y., grad. Hamilton College, 1891. He was reporter for the New York *Sun* (1891–1900), then joined *McClure's Magazine*, where he gained a reputation as a muckraker for his articles on the conditions of public health in the United States. Adams also wrote a series of articles for *Collier's Weekly*, in which he exposed patent medicines; these were credited with influencing the passage of the first Pure Food and Drugs Act. Hopkins was a prolific writer producing both fiction and nonfiction. His best-known novel, *Revelry* (1926), based on the scandals of the Harding administration was later followed by *Incredible Era* (1939), a biography of Harding and his times. Among his other works are *The Great American Fraud* (1906), *Average Jones* (1911), *The Harvey Girls* (1942), and *Grandfather Stories* (1955).

Adams, William (Will Adams), 1564?–1620, first Englishman to visit Japan. As pilot of a Dutch ship, he reached there in 1600. He soon became a favorite of IEYASU. Adams's knowledge of shipbuilding, military science, navigation, mathematics, and Western affairs proved valuable. Many of the longer voyages which the Japanese made were in vessels constructed under his direction. Adams attempted to foster trade relations with England, and he himself made trading trips to the Ryukyu Islands, Siam, and Cochin China. He married a Japanese woman, acquired a Japanese name (Anjin Sama, or Mr. Pilot), and was given an estate at Yokosuka. He remained in Japan until his death. See his letters (ed. by Thomas Randall, 1850) and his logbook (ed. by C. J. Purnell, 1916); F. R. Dulles, *Eastward Ho! the First English Adventurers to the Orient* (1931); P. G. Rogers, *First Englishman in Japan* (1956).

Adams, William Taylor, pseud. **Oliver Optic,** 1822–97, American writer of children's stories, b. Medway, Mass. He edited *Oliver Optic's Magazine* (1867–75) and wrote 116 books, many of them related, such as the "Great Western" series. All combined exciting tales with wholesome, if elementary, instruction.

Adams. 1 Town (pop. 12,391), NW Mass., in the Berkshires, on the Hoosic river and S of North Adams; settled 1762, inc. 1778. It has textile and paper mills and calcium quarries. Susan B. Anthony was born here. **2** Village (pop. 1,914), N central N.Y., SSW of Watertown, in a dairy region; inc. 1851. **3** City (pop. 1,301), central Wis., S of Wisconsin Rapids; founded before 1860, inc. 1926.

Adams, Mount. 1 Peak in New Hampshire: see PRESIDENTIAL RANGE. **2** Peak, 12,307 ft. high, SW Wash., in the Cascade Range.

Samuel Adams

Adam's Bridge or **Rama's Bridge,** chain of shoals, c.20 mi. long, in the PALK STRAIT between India and Ceylon. A sort of natural bridge between India and Ceylon, it once formed an isthmus and according to legend was the site of a causeway built by Rama, hero of the Ramayana.

Adams National Historic Site: see NATIONAL PARKS AND MONUMENTS (table).

Adam's-needle: see YUCCA.

Adam's Peak, Singhalese *Sri Padastanaya* and *Samanaliya,* mountain, c.7,360 ft. high, S central Ceylon. It is a sacred mountain, famous as a goal of pilgrimage for Buddhists, Hindus, and Moslems. On its summit is a small plateau which bears the impression of a gigantic (c.10 sq. ft.) human foot. This stone footprint is regarded as Buddha's by Buddhists, Siva's by Hindus, and Adam's by Moslems (who believe this to be the site of Adam's fall from Paradise).

Adamstown, borough (pop. 1,190), SE Pa., SW of Reading; settled 1739, inc. 1850.

Adamsville. 1 Village (pop. 2,095), N central Ala., NW of Birmingham. **2** Town (pop. 1,046), SW Tenn., SE of Jackson, in a cotton area; inc. 1954.

Adana (ä′dänä), city (pop. 230,024), capital of Seyhan prov., S Turkey, on the Seyhan river. It is a commercial and industrial center and an agricultural market. An ancient town, it was colonized by the Romans, prospered and then declined, and was revived (c.782) by Harun al-Rashid. After changing hands many times it passed (16th cent.) to the Ottomans. Nearby is Karatepe, an ancient Hittite archaeological site.

Adanson, Michel (mēshĕl′ ädäsō′), 1727–1806, French botanist of Scottish descent. His *Familles des plantes* (1763) places him with the early systematists. The BAOBAB is named *Adansonia* in his honor.

Adapazari (ädäpäzä′rē), Turk. *Adapazari,* city (pop. 80,160), capital of Adapazari prov., NW Turkey, on the Sakarya river. At the heart of a rich agricultural region, it trades in tobacco, vegetables, and fruit. It is also a trading center for textiles and rugs.

adaptation, in biology, the adjustment of living matter to environmental conditions and to other living things. This ability is a fundamental property of protoplasm and constitutes a basic difference between living and nonliving matter. Most living things require free oxygen from the air or from water, but yeasts, many bacteria, and some other simple forms obtain the oxygen required for oxidation from molecules of substances which contain the element. Various animals and plants are adapted for securing their food and for surviving the extremes of temperature and of water supply in desert, tropical, and polar regions. For most organisms the optimum temperature is between about 20° C. (68° F.) and 40° C. (104° F.). Some algae and protozoa live in hot springs, and some bacteria can survive freezing. The CACTUS can survive heat and drought. Certain fish and other aquatic animals live in deep water and are so specialized to withstand the great pressure that they burst if lifted to sea level. Animals show anatomical adaptations—e.g., the body of the fish is suited to life in the water; the body of the BIRD is adapted for flight; the land mammals show wide variation in the structure of limbs and body which enables some to run swiftly, some to climb, some to swing from tree to tree, some to glide through the air, and others to jump. The whale, an aquatic mammal, can adjust to great pressure changes at different levels in the water. The beaks of birds which feed on different kinds of food—e.g., on seeds, on insects, on aquatic animals, and on small mammals—differ in shape and size. The feet and legs of birds also show modifications which fit them for perching, for wading, and for paddling through the water. Adaptive coloration is observed in many animals (see PROTECTIVE COLORATION). Among communal insects, such as ants and honeybees, the individuals are highly adapted to perform their functions in the community. It is believed by many scientists that life originated in the sea and that through gradual evolutionary changes some forms became adapted to life on land. Variations may arise as a result of MUTATION or of recombinations of the genes in the germ cells. Such variations are inherited (see GENETICS). Those which aid the individual to meet the conditions of a changing environment or help him in his competition with other living things enable him to survive and reproduce, the changes thus being passed on from one generation to another and in this way perhaps producing a new species. See also ECOLOGY; EVOLUTION; SELECTION.

Adar (ā–), in the Bible: see HAZAR-ADDAR.

Adare, Cape (ŭdâr′), northeastern projection of Victoria Land, Antarctica, located at the northwestern extremity of Ross Sea. Here C. E. Borchgrevink made (1894) the first landing in Antarctica.

Adasa (ăd′ŭsä), town, near Beth-horon, place of encampment of Judas Maccabaeus. 1 Mac. 7.40.

Adbeel (ăd′bēĕl), son of Ishmael. Gen. 25.13; 1 Chron. 1.29.

Adda (äd′dä), river, rising in the Alps of Lombardy, N Italy. Some 194 mi. long, it flows through Lake Como and at Lecco continues S into the Po. Its upper course furnishes much electric power. Many battles have been fought along its course, notably the Battle of LODI (1796).

Addams, Charles Samuel, 1912–, American cartoonist, b. Westfield, N.J. He studied at Colgate Univ., the Univ. of Pennsylvania, and the Grand Central School of Art, New York city. Since 1935 his work has appeared in the *New Yorker* magazine. Addams cartoons are famed for their display of wit, fantasy, and sense of the macabre. A ghoulish family emerges as one of his main themes. His cartoons are collected in *Drawn and Quartered* (1942), *Addams and Evil* (1947), *Monster Rally* (1950), and *Home Bodies* (1954).

Addams, Jane, 1860–1935, American social worker, b. Cedarville, Ill., grad. Rockford College, 1881. In 1889, with Ellen Gates Starr, she founded the famous Hull House in Chicago, one of the first social settlements in the United States. Based on the university settlements begun in England by Samuel Barnett, Hull House has had influence throughout the nation in the settlement movement. It has also been important in Chicago civic affairs, especially in its relations with foreign-born citizens. Jane Addams was a leader in the woman-suffrage and peace movements. She was the recipient (jointly with Nicholas Murray Butler) of the

Jane Addams

1931 Nobel Peace Prize. Her books on social questions include *The Spirit of Youth and the City Streets* (1909), *A New Conscience and an Ancient Evil* (1912), and *Peace and Bread in Time of War* (1922). See her autobiographical *Twenty Years at Hull-House* (1910) and *The Second Twenty Years at Hull-House* (1930); biographies by her nephew, J. W. Linn (1935), and Margaret Tims (1961).

Addan, unidentified Palestinian town. Ezra 2.59. Addon: Neh. 7.61.

Addar: see Ard.

adder, poisonous snake of the Viper family. In Great Britain the only venomous snake is the adder. Adults usually recover from the effects of its bite. In Africa are found the related puff adder and night adder. The names puff adder and spreading adder are sometimes applied to the harmless hog-nosed snake of North America. The death adder of Australia and the krait of India, which is often called the blue adder, are related to the Cobra.

Puff adder

adder's-tongue, name for several plants, among them Dogtooth Violet and a primitive fern genus (*Ophioglossum*).

Addi (ăd′ī), name in Luke's genealogy. Luke 3.28.

adding machine: see Calculating Machine.

Addington, Henry: see Sidmouth, Henry Addington, Viscount.

Addis Ababa (ă′dĭs ä′bŭbŭ) [Amharic, =new flower], city (pop. c.500,000), capital of Ethiopia. Situated on a hilly plateau in central Ethiopia, Addis Ababa is a large commercial center with exports of coffee, tobacco, grains, and hides. It was formerly a city of thatched huts with few modern buildings, but since 1958, when it became the seat of a UN commission, much new architecture was erected. Addis Ababa is the hub of a road network and the terminus of Ethiopia's only railroad, which extends to Djibouti in French Somaliland. Founded in 1887 by Menelik II, it became his capital in 1889. Here, in 1896, the Italians recognized Ethiopian independence. However, it was taken by Italy in 1936 and was the capital of Italian East Africa until 1941, when the Italians were driven from the country. Its notable buildings include the imperial palace, the parliament building, and a Coptic cathedral. There is a college.

Addison, Joseph, 1672–1719, English essayist, poet, and statesman. He was educated at Charterhouse (where he was a classmate of Richard Steele) and at Oxford, where he became a distinguished classical scholar. His travels on the Continent from 1699 to 1703 were recorded in *Remarks on Italy* (1705). Addison first achieved prominence with *The Campaign* (1704), an epic celebrating the victory of Marlborough at Blenheim. The poem was commissioned by Lord Halifax, and its great success resulted in Addison's appointment in 1705 as undersecretary of state and in 1709 as secretary to the lord lieutenant of Ireland. He also held a seat in Parliament from 1708 until his death. Addison's most enduring fame was achieved as an essayist. In 1710 he began his contributions to the *Tatler*, which Richard Steele had founded in 1709. He continued his efforts in its successors, the Spectator (1711–12), the *Guardian* (1713), and the new *Spectator* (1714). His contributions to these periodicals raised the English essay to a degree of technical perfection never before achieved and perhaps never since surpassed. In a prose style marked by simplicity, order, and precision, he sought to engage men's thoughts toward reason, moderation, and a harmonious corporate life. His authorship also included an opera libretto, *Rosamund* (1707); a prose comedy, *The Drummer* (1716); and a neoclassic tragedy, *Cato* (1713), which had an immense success in its own time, but has since been regarded as artificial and sententious. In his last years Addison received his greatest prominence, but the period (1714–19) was also marked by failing

Joseph Addison

A military parade in Addis Ababa.

health, a supposedly unhappy marriage, and the severing of his relations with his good friend Richard Steele. See biography by P. H. B. O. Smithers (1954).

Addison, Thomas, 1793–1860, English physician, b. near Newcastle, grad. Univ. of Edinburgh (M.D., 1815). In 1837 he became a physician at Guy's Hospital, London, where he conducted research on pneumonia, tuberculosis, and other diseases. He was first to recognize (1855) the disease of the suprarenal or adrenal glands, later known as Addison's disease.

Addison. 1 Village (pop. 6,741), NE Ill., WNW of Chicago; inc. 1884. Electronic equipment and metal products are among its manufactures. **2** Village (pop. 2,185), S central N.Y., on the Canisteo and WNW of Elmira, in a dairy region; inc. 1873. **3** Town, W.Va.: see WEBSTER SPRINGS.

Addison's disease [for Thomas Addison] or **chronic adrenal cortical insufficiency,** progressive disease brought about by atrophy of the adrenocortical (suprarenal) glands. The deterioration of these glands causes them to decrease their secretion of steroid hormones, which are important to the regulation of many metabolic functions. In about 50 percent of the cases of Addison's disease the cause of the wasting process is not known; in the other half the predominant cause is tuberculous destruction, while tumors and inflammatory disease account for the remainder. Symptoms are increasing weakness, abnormal pigmentation of the skin and mucous membranes, weight loss, low blood pressure, dehydration, and gastrointestinal upsets. Once considered inevitably fatal, Addison's disease can now be treated with cortisone injections that enable its victims to lead a near-normal life.

Addon, variant of ADDAN.

Addyston, village (pop. 1,376), extreme SW Ohio, on the Ohio river and W of Cincinnati; settled c.1789. Iron pipe and castings are made. The William Henry Harrison memorial park is near.

Ade, George, 1866–1944, American humorist and dramatist, b. Kentland, Ind., grad. Purdue Univ., 1887. His newspaper sketches and books attracted

George Ade

attention for their racy and slangy idiom and for the humor and shrewdness with which they delineated people of the Midwestern scene. He is best known for *Fables in Slang*, published in 1899. Other volumes include *People You Knew* (1903) and *Hand-made Fables* (1920). Ade also wrote several farcical plays and books for musicals, among them *The County Chairman* (1903) and *The College Widow* (1904). See *The America of George Ade* (selected writings ed. by Jean Shepherd, 1961); biography by F. C. Kelly (1947).

Adel. 1 (ă″dĕl′) City (pop. 4,321), co. seat of Cook co., S Ga., NE of Thomasville; inc. 1889. Settled nearby in 1860 as Puddleville, it was moved to its present site in 1888 to be on the railroad. It is a tobacco market and a trade center for a farm area. **2** (ŭdĕl′) Town (pop. 2,060), co. seat of Dallas co., S central Iowa, on the Raccoon river W of Des Moines, in a farm area; settled 1846 as Penoach, renamed 1849, inc. 1887.

Adelaide or **Adelheid** (ä′dŭlhīt), c.931–999, empress consort of Otto I, daughter of King Rudolf II of Arles. After the death of her first husband, King Lothair of Italy, she was about to be forced into a marriage with the son of BERENGAR II when she appealed to OTTO I, who rescued and married her in 951. She was sole regent for her grandson, Otto III, from 991 to 994. She was a great benefactress of religious houses.

Adelaide, city (pop. 562,500; metropolitan pop. 570,700), capital of South Australia, S Commonwealth of Australia, on the Torrens river. It has knitting mills. Named for the queen of William IV, it was founded in 1836 and is the oldest city in the state. Here are the Univ. of Adelaide (1874), a natural history museum (1895), the Waite Institute of Agricultural Research (1924), and Anglican and Roman Catholic cathedrals. GLENELG is one of its principal suburbs.

Adelard of Bath (ă′dŭlärd), fl. 12th cent., English scholastic philosopher, celebrated for his study of Arabian learning. He translated Euclid from Arabic into Latin. His major works were *Perdifficiles quaestiones naturales*, which embodied his scientific studies, and *De eodem et diverso*, his principal philosophical work, which attempts a solution to the problems of NOMINALISM and REALISM.

Adelheid: see ADELAIDE, empress.

Adélie Coast (ă′dŭlē, ädālē′), region, Antarctica, in the Australian quadrant, just W of George V Coast and E of Wilkes Land. It was discovered (1840) by DUMONT D'URVILLE, who named the area for his wife, and later explored by Douglas MAWSON. The region is heavily glaciated, and its continuous winds of 50 mi. per hour are stronger than those anywhere else on earth. France's claim to the area (formerly called Adélie Land) was the first polar claim made without benefit of administration or occupation. The claim was, however, supported when France established local meteorological stations in the area.

Adelphi College: see GARDEN CITY, N.Y.

Adelsberg: see POSTOJNA.

Ademar or **Adhemar** (both: ăd′ŭmär), Fr. *Adhémar de Monteil* (ädämär′ dù mõtä′), d. 1098, French prelate, bishop of Le Puy. At the Council of Clermont (1095), he energetically promoted the First Crusade (see CRUSADES) and was designated as papal legate on that expedition. He distinguished himself in the sieges of Nicaea and Antioch and carried the Holy Lance (with which Christ's side had been pierced by a Roman soldier) after its discovery, though he at first doubted its authenticity. He died at Antioch, but later was reported as appearing to his comrades in visions.

Aden (ä′dŭn, ä′-), British crown colony (80 sq. mi.; pop. c.140,000), SW Arabia, on the Gulf of Aden.

King William Street in Adelaide.

Aden is situated on the great trade route to the Orient.

It includes PERIM, the Kamaran Islands (off Yemen), and the Kuria Muria Islands (off the Dhofar coast of Oman). The colony proper is mostly comprised of two headlands (Aden town and Little Aden) of volcanic rock joined by a flat sandy foreshore. The bay behind the headlands is an excellent anchorage. The region was captured by Moslems in 632. Turkey occupied it almost continuously from 1538 to 1630 against Portuguese opposition. In 1839 it was occupied by Great Britain and was administered as part of India until 1937. The colony is ruled by an appointed governor, representing the British crown, and a cabinet which is responsible to a partly appointed and partly elected legislature. Aden is a free port which attracts much shipping on the trade route served by the Suez Canal. An oil refinery is located at Little Aden. The British protectorate of Aden or Aden protectorate (c.112,000 sq. mi.; pop. c.700,000) is bordered by Yemen and Saudi Arabia. It occupies a coast line c.740 mi. long. For the most part mountainous or desert, it has fertile valleys where grains are grown. The chief exports include coffee, cotton, hides, and skins. Aden protectorate is divided into an eastern and a western section—the eastern protectorate, which includes the HADRAMAUT and the island of Socotra, comprises six sultanates and sheikdoms; the western protectorate consists of 18 sultanates, emirates, and sheikdoms. The inhabitants, all Moslems, are governed by native rulers with the help of British advisers. In 1960 six of the 18 small states of the western Aden protectorate (the sultanates of Andhali, Fadhli, and Lower Yafa, the emirates of Beiban and Dhala, and the sheikdom of Anlaqi) formed the **Aden Federation.** Great Britain promised future independence to the federation and the eventual accession of the 12 remaining states of the western protectorate. Yemen, which claims Aden protectorate, strongly objected

to the formation of the federation. In early 1963 Aden colony and the Aden Federation were merged into the Federation of South Arabia. See Thomas Hickinbotham, *Aden* (1960); Bernard Reilly, *Aden and the Yemen* (1960).

Aden, Gulf of, western arm of the Arabian Sea, lying between Aden protectorate and Somaliland. It is connected with the Red Sea by the Bab el Mandeb. The gulf is on the great trade route from the Mediterranean Sea to the Indian Ocean via the Suez Canal. After the 16th cent. Portugal, Turkey, and Great Britain were the chief contenders for control of the gulf, but by the 19th cent. British power was dominant.

Adena (ụdē′nụ), village (pop. 1,317), E Ohio, SW of Steubenville, in a coal-mine area; inc. 1907.

Adenauer, Konrad (kôn′rät ä′dùnou″ùr), 1876–, German statesman. A lawyer and a member of the Catholic Center party, he was lord mayor of Cologne from 1917 until 1933, when he was dismissed by the National Socialist regime. He was twice imprisoned (1934, 1944) by the Nazis. Cofounder of the Christian Democratic Union (1945) and its president since 1946, he was elected chancellor of the German Federal Republic (West Germany) in 1949 and was reelected in 1953, 1957, and 1961. He also served (1951–55) as his own foreign minister, negotiating the West German peace contract (1952) with the Western Allies and obtaining recognition of West Germany's full sovereignty through the Paris Pacts and through an agreement with the USSR in 1955. Adenauer's strong will and political wisdom helped to give *Der Alte* [the old man] great authority in German public life. The political architect of the astounding West German recovery, he saw the solution of German problems in terms of European integration, and he helped secure West Germany's membership in the various organizations of the EUROPEAN COMMUNITY. In 1961 his party lost its absolute majority in the Bundestag, and he formed a coalition cabinet with the Free Democrats. In 1962 a cabinet crisis arose over the government's controversial police action against the magazine *Spiegel* [mirror], which had attacked the Adenauer regime. After agreeing to

Konrad Adenauer

exclude his defense minister, Franz Josef STRAUSS, from a new cabinet, Adenauer succeeded in re-forming a coalition, again with the Free Democrats. He was opposed by extreme nationalists, but his real opposition came from Social Democratic leaders, notably Willy Brandt. In Dec., 1962, it was announced that Adenauer would retire as chancellor in the fall of 1963. His writings include *World Indivisible* (Eng. tr., 1955). See Edgar Alexander, *Adenauer and the New Germany* (Eng. tr., 1957); Paul Weymar, *Adenauer* (Eng. tr., 1957); A. J. Heidenheimer, *Adenauer and the CDU* (1960).

adenoids, spongy masses of lymphoid tissue that occupy the nasopharynx, the space between the back of the nose and the throat. When these growths become enlarged they interfere with normal breathing and sometimes with hearing and normal dental development, resulting in an alteration of facial expression. Infection of the adenoids is common, the symptoms resembling those of tonsillitis, with which it is frequently associated. Surgical removal of the adenoids is advisable when enlargement and repeated infection interfere with development and health.

adenosine triphosphate: see ATP.

Ader (ā'–), Benjamite. 1 Chron. 8.15.

Adernò: see ADRANO.

Adeste Fideles (ạdĕs'tā fēdā'lĕs) [Latin,=come, ye faithful], Christmas hymn, of irregular meter. Although the Latin text is sometimes attributed to St. Bonaventure, it was perhaps written by a 17th- or 18th-century German or French (or, according to tradition, Portuguese) author. The most popular English translation is that of Frederick Oakeley (1802–80), beginning, "O come, all ye faithful." The melody occurs as early as 1746. It has been ascribed to several composers and has several names, the most popular of which is *Portuguese Hymn.*

Adhémar de Monteil: see ADEMAR.

adhesive, substance capable of adhering to surfaces and bonding them. Animal glue, a gelatin made from hides, hoofs, or bones, probably was known in prehistoric times and remained the leading adhesive until the 20th cent. Used now especially in cabinetmaking, glue is sold as a solid—either ground or in sheets to be melted in a water-jacketed gluepot and applied while hot—or as liquid glue (an acid solution). Since the 19th cent., adhesives from vegetable sources have become commercially important; these include natural gums and resins, mucilage, starch (used in flour-and-water pastes), and starch derivatives, e.g., dextrins. Such substances are commonly used as extenders and modifiers for synthetic adhesives, for sizing paper and textiles, and for labeling, sealing, and manufacturing paper goods. Other adhesives derived from animal and vegetable sources include protein glues such as casein, blood albumin, and soybean glues; rubber adhesives; and cellulose derivatives. From synthetic resins (see RESIN) are prepared adhesives having special properties for specific applications, becoming after setting flexible, rigid, heat-resistant, or thermoplastic as required. Adhesive tape has a coating of pressure-sensitive adhesive. Some synthetic adhesives, i.e., the epoxy resins, are strong enough to be used in place of welding or riveting in construction. The so-called "plastic steel" is a mixture of steel filings and an epoxy resin. See also CEMENT. See Irving Skeist, ed., *Handbook of Adhesives* (1962).

Adiel (ā'dĭl) [Heb.,=ornament of God]. **1** Father of David's treasurer. 1 Chron. 27.25. **2** Simeonite. 1 Chron. 4.36. **3** Priest. 1 Chron. 9.12.

Adige (ä'dējä), Ger. *Etsch* (ĕch), river, rising in the Tyrolean Alps, N Italy. It flows generally southeast for c.225 mi. near Bolzano and past Trent, and turns east to empty into the Adriatic north of the mouth of the Po.

Adighe: see ADYGE AUTONOMOUS OBLAST.

Adin (ā'–) [Heb.,=tender], family which returned from exile. Ezra 2.15; 8.6; Neh. 7.20; 10.16.

Adina (ăd'–, ụdī'–) [Heb.,=pliant], Reubenite captain. 1 Chron. 11.42.

Adino (ăd'–, ụdī'–), the EZNITE, one of David's men. 2 Sam. 23.8.

Adirondack Mountains (ădĭrŏn'dăk), NE N.Y., sometimes mistakenly included in the Appalachian

Adirondack Mountains: Wilmington Notch, Whiteface Mountain in background.

system. The group is bounded on the east by the west shore of Lake Champlain and the Lake George region and extends from foothills near the St. Lawrence on the north to the Mohawk valley on the south. Geologically the Adirondack region resembles the LAURENTIAN PLATEAU. Its pre-Cambrian metamorphic rock with intruded igneous rock (largely masses of granite) has been uplifted and eroded through countless years. Faulting has caused the eastern portion to be the most rugged. Layers of sedimentary rock (sandstone and limestone) containing marine fossils of Cambrian and Ordovician times are tilted against the mountains. Some of the oldest sedimentary rocks have metamorphosed to form marble, mica schist, and quartzite. A sheet of glacial till lies over the area, and there are lakes formed from streams backed up by moraines. The main range rises to 5,344 ft. in Mt. Marcy, highest peak in the state; among the other summits are Whiteface, MacIntyre, Haystack, Algonquin, and Skylight. Wild, rugged scenery, beautiful forests, and numerous lakes characterize the region, of which 2,273,378 acres have been set aside in the Adirondack Forest Preserve. Lake Placid and Lake George, Indian, Schroon, Long, Cranberry, Big and Little Tupper, Upper and Lower Saranac, and Raquette lakes, and the Fulton Chain have resorts on their shores. The Hudson, the Ausable, the Black, and several tributaries of the St. Lawrence have their sources in the Adirondacks. Important mineral products include iron ore, titanium, vanadium, and talc. See C. A. Sleicher, *The Adirondacks: American Playground* (1960).

Adithaim (ăd″ĭthā′ĭm), town of Judah, probably c.10 mi. from the coast. Joshua 15.36.

adjective, English PART OF SPEECH, one of the two which refer typically to attributes. The other is the adverb. These two classes overlap with the form class marked by *-er* and *-est* (or *more . . .* and *most . . .*). They are functionally distinct in that adjectives never occur far from nouns or pronouns, while adverbs are associated primarily with verbs. There is a small class of words (e.g., *very* and *too*) which typically precede adjectives and adverbs; these are also called adverbs. Many adverbs belong to a form class of words ending *-ly*. Adjective and adverb are typically Indo-European form classes, and probably most languages lack specialized classes with analogous functions. See Paul Roberts, *Understanding Grammar* (1954).

Adlai (ăd′lāī), father of SHAPHAT **4.** 1 Chron. 27.29.

Adler, Alfred (äd′lŭr), 1870–1937, Austrian psychiatrist, founder of the school of individual psychology. Although one of Freud's earlier associates, he soon rejected the Freudian emphasis upon sex. He maintained that all personality difficulties have their roots in a feeling of inferiority (see INFERIORITY COMPLEX) derived from physical handicaps or from conflict with the environment that restricts an individual's need for power and self-assertion. Thus he saw behavior disorders as overcompensation for deficiencies. In later life he lectured and practiced in the United States. Besides *The Practice and Theory of Individual Psychology* (1923), he wrote *The Neurotic Constitution* (1909) and *Understanding Human Nature* (1927). See biography by Phyllis Bottome (1939).

Adler, Cyrus, 1863–1940, American Jewish educator, grad. Univ. of Pennsylvania, 1883, Ph.D. Johns Hopkins, 1887. He taught Semitic languages at Johns Hopkins from 1884 to 1893. He was for a number of years librarian and then secretary of the Smithsonian Institution, was the founder of the American Jewish Historical Society, was one of the editors of the *Jewish Encyclopedia*, and edited the *American-Jewish Year-Book* after 1899. He was president of Dropsie College from 1908 to 1940 and of the Jewish Theological Seminary after 1924. He was a founder of the American Jewish Committee and of the Jewish Welfare Board. His writings include a number of articles on comparative religion, Assyriology, and Semitic philology; *Jews in the Diplomatic Correspondence of the United States* (1906), and, with Allan Ramsay, *Told in the Coffee House* (1898). See biography by A. A. Neuman (1942).

Adler, Felix, 1851–1933, American educator and leader in social welfare, founder of the ETHICAL CULTURE MOVEMENT, b. Germany. He was brought to the United States as a small child, was graduated

Felix Adler

from Columbia in 1870, and afterward studied in Germany. In 1876 he established the New York Society for Ethical Culture and, in connection with the Ethical Culture School, the first free kindergarten in New York city. Adler organized the Workingmen's Lyceum, helped to establish the Workingmen's School and the Manhattan Trade School for Girls, and founded (1883) the first child study society in the United States. He was a member (1885) of New York state's first tenement house commission and served for many years as chairman of the National Child Labor Committee. He became professor of political and social ethics at Columbia Univ. in 1902 and was Roosevelt professor (1908–9) at the Univ. of Berlin and Hibbert lecturer (1923) at Oxford Univ. Among his books are *Creed and Deed* (1877), *An Ethical Philosophy of Life* (1918), and *The Reconstruction of the Spiritual Ideal* (1924).

Adler, Viktor (vĭk′tôr), 1852–1918, Austrian politician and journalist, founder and leader of the Austrian Social Democratic party. A prominent figure in the Second International, he entered parliament in 1905. When the Austro-Hungarian empire was collapsing, he was made foreign secretary of German Austria, but he died on Nov. 11, one day before Austria proclaimed itself a republic.

Adlum, John, 1759–1836, American horticulturist, b. York, Pa. He originated the Catawba grape from a native variety and wrote two books on viticulture and wine making. The *Adlumia*, a climbing fumitory, is named for him.

Admah (ăd′mù), city destroyed with SODOM.

Admatha (ăd′–), counselor of Ahasuerus. Esther 1.14.

Admetus (ădmē′tùs), in Greek mythology, king of Pharae and husband of ALCESTIS. He was served by Apollo, whom Zeus had banished from Olympus for killing the Cyclopes. When Admetus was dying, Apollo persuaded the gods to spare him if someone consented to die in his place. Alcestis willingly gave her life but was later rescued from the dead.

administration, public: see ADMINISTRATIVE LAW.

administrative law, the law governing the powers and processes of administrative agencies. It deals with questions of the propriety of granting powers to agencies as well as with the judicial checks upon the activities of governmental agencies. Administrative agencies are part of the executive branch of government and are created either by statute, by executive order authorized by statute, or by constitutional provisions. The use of administrative agencies in the United States dates back to 1789 to the original legislative provisions made for the administration of customs laws, the regulation of oceangoing vessels and the coastal trade, and the payment of pensions to veterans. It was, however, with the growth of public utilities and public transportation that administrative agencies began to play a major role in American life. The passage of the Interstate Commerce Act and the establishment of the INTERSTATE COMMERCE COMMISSION in 1887 marked the start of administrative law in the United States as we know it today. The administrative process involves rule making, adjudication, investigating, supervising, prosecuting, and advising. Agencies have assumed legislative and judicial functions—the day-to-day supervision of details—for which neither Congress nor the courts are adapted. This has resulted in a blurring of the traditional notion of separation of powers that is said to characterize the Federal government. With the growing complexity of modern economic and social life, administrative agencies, having over-all knowledge of their fields, are therefore able to deal uniformly and quickly with the numerous complaints referred to them. The principle that Congress cannot delegate its legislative powers has been circumvented by having Congress set a primary standard and allowing the agency to fill in the gaps. As a result of the powers that have been granted the older agencies and the recent proliferation of agencies, administrative agencies have come to participate in nearly every aspect of American life. Administrative agencies affect activities ranging from collective bargaining to television programming. Because of the vast range of subjects dealt with by the agencies the Federal Administrative Procedure Act was enacted in 1946 to provide uniform standards of procedure that would be common to all agencies. The act guaranteed the right of judicial review to any person "suffering legal wrong because of any agency action." In general, administrative procedure would be set aside only for abuse of discretion. Under European legal codes, special administrative courts review the activities of administrative agencies. This is in contrast to common law, whereby the ordinary courts have complete jurisdiction over controversies involving the validity of acts of agencies. See FEDERAL COMMUNICATIONS COMMISSION; FEDERAL POWER COMMISSION; FEDERAL TRADE COMMISSION; NATIONAL LABOR RELATIONS BOARD; SECURITIES AND EXCHANGE COMMISSION. See M. M. Carrow, *The Background of Administrative Law* (1948); K. C. Davis, *Administrative Law and Government* (1960).

Admirable Crichton: see CRICHTON, JAMES.

Admiral's Men, theatrical company of players, officially designated the Admiral's Men in 1585. They were rivals of the CHAMBERLAIN'S MEN and performed at the theaters of Philip HENSLOWE. Their leading actor was Edward ALLEYN.

admiralty (ăd′mùrùltē), in British government, department in charge of the royal navy. It is headed by a board of five lords commissioners. The first lord of the admiralty is a member of the cabinet; he has charge of political matters, finances, and appointments. The operating staff has charge of supply and maintenance of the fighting forces. Admiralty jurisdiction, formerly under the high court of the admiralty, is now assigned to the high court of justice.

Admiralty Inlet, arm of the Pacific Ocean, NW Wash., entry and northernmost part of Puget Sound, between Whidbey Island and the mainland.

Admiralty Island, off SE Alaska, in the ALEXANDER ARCHIPELAGO and SW of Juneau. The large island (1,664 sq. mi.) is separated from the mainland by Stephens Passage. It is mountainous and heavily forested. Wildlife abounds.

Admiralty Islands, small volcanic group (area c.800 sq. mi.; estimated pop. 16,752), SW Pacific, W of New Ireland, in the BISMARCK ARCHIPELAGO and part of the Territory of New Guinea. A UN trust territory since 1947, the group is administered by Australia from Lorengau on Manus, the chief island. Copra and pearls are the principal products. Discovered in 1616 by Willem Schouten, the group passed to Germany in 1885 and was mandated to Australia in 1920.

Manus, the chief island of the Admiralty Islands.

admiralty law: see MARITIME LAW.

Admiralty Range, northern part of the great mountain range in Victoria Land W of the Ross Sea, Antarctica. It has peaks reaching 10,000 ft., and its heavy cover of snow gives it austere beauty.

Adna [Heb.,=pleasure], name of two Israelites of the returned community. Ezra 10.30; Neh. 12.15.

Adnah (–nú) [Heb.,=pleasure]. **1** Deserter from Saul. 1 Chron. 12.20. **2** Officer under Jehoshaphat. 2 Chron. 17.14.

adobe: see RAMMED EARTH.

adolescence (ă důlě'sůns) [from Latin,=youth], time of life from onset of puberty to full adulthood. The exact period of adolescence varies from person to person. It falls approximately between the ages 12 and 21. Adolescence is the period during which the individual in seeking emancipation from family ties, in finding a place in the vocational life of the community, and in making sex adjustments finds his life complicated by social pressures; hence psychologists tend to regard adolescence as a by-product of social pressures, not as a unique period of biological storm and stress.

Adolf of Nassau, d. 1298, German king (1292–98). He owed his election to the ecclesiastical electors' fear of the growing power and ambition of Albert of Austria (later King ALBERT I). Seeking to strengthen his kingship by establishing a territorial power of his own, Adolf seized Meissen and Thuringia. In the struggle between Edward I of England and Philip IV of France, he accepted subsidies from both sides. His independent actions and his failure to continue opposition to France led to his deposition (1298). Soon afterward he was defeated and killed by an army commanded by Albert.

Adonai: see GOD.

Adoni-bezek (ādō'nĭ-bē'zĕk,ăd'–) [Heb.,=lord of Bezek], king of Bezek captured and mutilated by the Judahites. Judges 1.5–7.

Adonijah (ăd″ůnĭ'jů, ůdŏn'ůjů) [Heb.,=God is my lord]. **1** Son of David. He wanted the throne which David gave to the younger son, Solomon. 2 Sam. 3.4; 1 Kings 1; 2.1–25. **2** Teacher of the law. 2 Chron. 17.7–9. **3** Sealer of the covenant after the return from the Exile. Neh. 10.16. Perhaps the same as **Adonikam** (–ĭ'kům, –dŏn'–) [Heb.,=my lord has risen], a name in the lists of families. Ezra 2.13; 8.13; Neh. 7.18.

Adoniram (ăd″ůnĭ'–) [Heb.,=my lord is on high], tax overseer. 1 Kings 4.6. Adoram: 2 Sam. 20.24; 1 Kings 12.18. Hadoram: 2 Chron. 10.18.

Adonis (ůdō'nĭs), in Greek mythology, beautiful youth beloved by Aphrodite and Persephone. He was born of the incestuous union of Myrrha (or Smyrna) and Cinyras, king of Cyprus. Aphrodite left him in the care of Persephone, who raised him and made him her lover. Aphrodite later demanded the youth for herself, but Persephone was unwilling to relinquish him. When Adonis was gored to death by a boar, both Persephone and Aphrodite claimed him. Zeus settled the dispute by arranging for Adonis to spend half the year (the summer months) above the ground with Aphrodite and the other half in the underworld with Persephone. Adonis' death and resurrection, symbolic of the yearly cycle of vegetation, were widely celebrated in the midsummer festival Adonia. As part of this worship, his image was surrounded by beds of plants

Adonis and Venus, a painting by Paolo Veronese.

(the gardens of Adonis) which quickly grew and withered. The worship of Adonis corresponds to the cults of the Phrygian ATTIS and the Babylonian TAMMUZ. See Sir J. G. Frazer, *Adonis, Attis, Osiris* (1907; new ed., 1961).

Adoni-zedec (ādō'nĭ-zē'dĕk, ăd'–) [Heb.,=lord of justice], chief at Jerusalem, leader of the allies routed at Gibeon. Joshua 10.1–27.

adoption, act by which the legal relation of PARENT AND CHILD is created between persons not naturally so related. Adoption is not known to the common law but was a familiar practice under Roman law. Its practice in the United States is regulated by statute and most states now allow it. Adoption is generally a judicial proceeding, requiring a hearing before a judge of a competent court in the jurisdiction. Adoption statutes usually provide that the consent of the parents or guardian of the child and that of the child, if above a certain age - must be obtained. An adopted child generally assumes the rights and duties of a natural legitimate child. Similarly, the rights and duties accompanying natural parenthood generally accompany adoptive parenthood (e.g., the right of custody and the obligation of support). The natural parents have no right to control an adopted child, nor have they any duties toward it, but in some states (e.g., New York) the child does not lose the right to inherit from them. See Carl Doss and H. G. Doss, *If You Adopt a Child* (1957).

adoptionism, heresy taught in Spain after 782 by Elipandus, archbishop of Toledo, and Felix, bishop of Urgel. They held that Christ at the time of his birth was purely human and only became the divine Son of God by adoption when he was baptized. Variations of this doctrine had been held as early as the 3d cent. by the THEODOTIANS, PAUL OF SAMOSATA, and by the Nestorians. It reappeared in the neo-adoptionist heresy among the followers of Abelard. Elipandus and Felix were condemned at Frankfurt (794). The vigorous refutation of ALCUIN had much to do with the sect's disappearance in the early 9th cent. See MONARCHIANISM.

Adoraim (ăd″ōrā′ĭm), town, near Hebron to the west. 2 Chron. 11.9. Adora: 1 Mac. 13.20.

Adoram (ùdō′–), the same as ADONIRAM.

Adoula, Cyrille (sērĭl′ -ädoō′lú), 1922–, African statesman in the Republic of the Congo. Educated in mission schools, he was a bank clerk during the Belgian administration of his country, became active in the trade-union movement, and helped Patrice Lumumba organize his political party, the Mouvement National Congolais. Elected to the senate when the Congo achieved independence (1960), he fell out with Lumumba. He held the ministries of the interior and defense under President Joseph Kasavubu and, in 1961, became premier of the Republic of the Congo. Working for the unification of his country, he fought the separatist activities of Antoine Gizenga and Moise Tshombe. He visited the United States in 1962.

Adour (ädoōr′), river, rising in SW France, in the Pyrenees of GASCONY. About 210 mi. long, it flows north and then describes a wide arc past Bagnères-de-Bigorre, Aire, and Dax and enters the Bay of BISCAY near Bayonne.

Adowa: see ADUWA.

Adra (ä′dhrä), town (pop. 14,766), Almería prov., S Spain, in Andalusia, on the Mediterranean. It is a port and the center of a fertile agricultural region. At the foot of a hill below the present town stood Abdera, founded by Phoenician traders. Adra was the last stronghold of the Moors under Boabdil.

Adrammelech (ùdrăm′ùlĕk). **1** God of a Samaritan cult. 2 Kings 17.31. **2** One of the two men named as murderers of their father, Sennacherib; Sharezer was the other. Babylonian sources mention one son. 2 Kings 19.37 (the same in Isa. 37.38).

Adramyttium (ăd″rùmĭt′ēùm), place, the modern Edremid, NW Turkey. Here St. Paul's ship was built. Acts 27.2.

Adrano (ädrä′nō), town (estimated pop. 29,064), in E Sicily, Italy, at the foot of Mt. Etna. It is a large agricultural center. Founded c.400 B.C. near a temple of the god Hadranus, it has ruins of ancient walls and an imposing 11th-century Norman castle. Fierce fighting took place here in the Second World War. It was formerly named Adernò.

Adrastus (ùdrăs′–), in Greek legend, king of Argos. He organized the ill-fated SEVEN AGAINST THEBES expedition and was the only survivor. Ten years later he successfully assisted the sons of the Seven, the EPIGONI, in their attack on Thebes.

adrenal gland (ădrē′nùl) [Latin,=at the kidney] or **suprarenal gland** (soōprùrē′nùl) [Latin,=over the kidney], glandular structure about 2 inches long atop each kidney. These glands are ductless; i.e., their secretions enter directly into the blood stream. The outer yellowish layer (cortex) of the adrenal gland secretes steroid hormones (mainly cortin and hydrocortisone) that are important in the regulation of many metabolic functions. These secretions control the output of ACTH (see ACTH) from the PITUITARY GLAND and thus control the water and chemical balance of the body, blood pressure, and the secondary sex characteristics. Steroid hormones also counteract inflammation and allergies. Synthesis of the steroid hormones has made it possible to treat many of the conditions related to underactivity of the adrenal cortex, e.g., ADDISON'S DISEASE. The inner reddish portion (medulla) of the adrenal gland secretes ADRENALINE.

adrenaline (ùdrĕn′ùlĭn) or **epinephrine** (ĕpĭnĕf′rĭn), an active agent in secretions of the medulla of the adrenal gland. Strong emotions such as fear and anger stimulate the flow of this hormone, causing acceleration of the heart beat, increase in blood pressure, and an increased flow of glucose from the liver. Adrenaline is a colorless crystalline substance composed of carbon, hydrogen, and nitrogen, soluble in alkalis and acids (with which it forms compounds) and in glycerin, but only slightly so in water. Adrenaline was first extracted from the glands of slaughtered animals by Jokichi Takamine in 1901; it was synthesized by Friedrich Stolz, a Bohemian chemist, in 1904 and by Henry D. DAKIN, an American research chemist, in 1905. It is used as a stimulant in stoppage of the heart and in shock, in the prevention of hemorrhage, and as an antispasmodic in bronchial asthma.

Adria (ā′drēù), ancient name of the Adriatic, extended to mean the central Mediterranean in Acts 27.27.

Adrian I, d. 795, pope (772–95), a Roman; successor of Stephen IV and predecessor of St. Leo III. At Adrian's urging, CHARLEMAGNE crossed the Alps and defeated the Lombard king, DESIDERIUS, who had annexed papal territory. This marks the end of the Lombard kingdom. Charlemagne, during the seige of Pavia, came to Rome (774) and there confirmed the Donation of Pepin and joined additional provinces to it. Adrian made Charlemagne Patrician of the Romans, acknowledging Charlemagne's protectorate over all Italy. Adrian supported Empress Irene in her struggle against iconoclasm, and he sent legates to the Second Council of Nicaea. The great Roman water systems were built during his rule.

Adrian IV, d. 1159, pope (1154–59), an Englishman (b. Langley, near St. Albans) named Nicholas Breakspear; successor of Anastasius IV and predecessor of Alexander III. At an early age he went to France. There he became an Austin canon and later an abbot. Pope Eugene III made him cardinal-bishop of Albano and sent him to Scandinavia to organize the church. After his election to the papacy, Adrian defeated (1155) opposition of ARNOLD OF BRESCIA. He crowned (1155) FREDERICK I but fell into conflict with Frederick when the latter, disregarding the Concordat of Worms, invested (1158 or 1159) imperial favorites in the archbishoprics of Cologne and Ravenna. To make peace (1156) with William of Sicily, who had invaded papal territory, Adrian acknowledged William's titles to Sicily, Apulia, and Capua. This angered Frederick, who had designs on the Two Sicilies, but it served to protect the Papal States against further imperial encroachments. Frederick's expressed intention to assume the government of Rome almost brought him excommunication.

Adrian, forced by imperial intrigues to leave Rome, died before he could pronounce sentence. He was the only English pope. The historicity of Adrian's donation of Ireland, as a papal fief, to Henry II of England has been the subject of scholarly dispute.

Adrian VI, 1459–1523, pope (1522–23), a Netherlander (b. Utrecht) named Adrian Florensz; successor of Leo X and predecessor of Clement VII.

Adrian VI.

He was the most recent non-Italian pope. He taught at Louvain and was tutor of the young prince, later Emperor CHARLES V. This was a time when Roman life was most extravagant, papal expenditures on worldly objects were at their height, and the Curia most needed drastic reform. Adrian, an ascetic and a pious man, did his best to curb the abuses he found, but he died after 20 months. The Italians rejoiced at his death.

Adrian, Roman emperor: see HADRIAN.

Adrian, Edgar Douglas Adrian, Baron, 1889–, English physiologist, M.D. Trinity College, Cambridge, 1915. He was research professor (1929–37) of the Royal Society and professor of physiology (1937–51) at Cambridge. In 1951 he became master of Trinity College. His research was chiefly on the physiology of the nervous system. He wrote *The Basis of Sensation* (1928), *The Mechanism of Nervous Action* (1932), and, with others, *Factors Determining Human Behavior* (1937). With Sir Charles S. Sherrington he shared the 1932 Nobel Prize in Physiology and Medicine for their work on the function of the neuron. He was awarded a barony in 1955.

Adrian. 1 City (pop. 20,347), co. seat of Lenawee co., S Mich., SW of Detroit; settled 1825, inc. as a village 1836, as a city 1853. It is a farm trade center and is known for its chrysanthemums. Automobile parts, aluminum products, and furniture are among its manufactures. Adrian College (Methodist; coeducational; 1845) and Siena Heights College (Roman Catholic; for women; 1919) are here. **2** Village (pop. 1,215), SW Minn., W of Worthington and near the Iowa line. It is a farm trade center. **3** City (pop. 1,082), W Mo., SSE of Kansas City, in a farm area; founded 1880, inc. 1883. It ships grain and poultry.

Adrianople (ā″drēŭnō′pŭl) or **Edirne** (ĕdēr′nĕ), Turk. *Edirne,* town (pop. 31,865), capital of Edirne prov., European Turkey, in Thrace. It is a commercial center with silk and cotton manufactures. It was named after Emperor Hadrian, who founded (A.D. c.125) it on the site of the older Uscudama; Byzantine writers also called it Orestia. Of great strategic importance and strongly fortified, the city had a turbulent history. The defeat (378) of Emperor VALENS by the Visigoths at Adrianople laid Greece open to the barbarians. Later conquered by the Avars, the Bulgarians, and

Adrianople, a city of mosques.

the Crusaders, the city passed to the Turks in 1361 and was the residence of the sultans until the conquest of Constantinople in 1453. In the 19th cent. the Russians captured Adrianople twice in the Russo-Turkish wars. In 1913 it fell to Bulgaria in the First Balkan War and was restored to Turkey after the Second Balkan War. It passed to Greece by the Treaty of Sèvres (1920) but was again restored to Turkey by the Treaty of Lausanne (1923). Among the landmarks of the town are several mosques, of which the great mosque of Selim I is the most impressive.

Adrianople, Treaty of, 1829, peace treaty between Russia and the Ottoman Empire (see RUSSO-TURKISH WARS). Turkey gave Russia the mouth of the Danube and additional territory on the Black Sea, opened the Dardanelles to all commercial vessels, granted autonomy to Serbia, promised autonomy for Greece, and allowed Russia to occupy Moldavia and Walachia until Turkey had paid a large indemnity.

Adriatic Sea (ădrē̆ă′tĭk), arm of the Mediterranean, between Italy and the Balkan Peninsula. It is c.500 mi. long and is 58 to 140 mi. wide, with a

Venice, one of the chief ports of the Adriatic Sea.

maximum depth of 4,100 ft. It extends from the Gulf of Venice, at its head, SE to the Strait of Otranto, which leads to the Ionian Sea. The Italian coast (west and north) is low; Venice, Ancona, Bari, and Brindisi are its chief ports. TRIESTE, once the chief Adriatic port, has declined as a port since its first annexation to Italy (1919). The eastern shore line belongs to Yugoslavia (north) and to Albania (south). The Yugoslav coast (see DALMATIA) is rugged; Rijeka (Fiume) and Dubrovnik are among its main ports.

Adriel (ā′−), husband of MERAB. 1 Sam. 18.17-20.

adsorption [Latin,=sucking toward], adhesion of the molecules of liquids, gases, and dissolved substances to the surfaces of solids. Certain solids

have the power to adsorb great quantities of gases. Charcoal, for example, which has a great surface area because of its porous nature, adsorbs large volumes of gases, including most of the poisonous ones, and is therefore used in gas masks. Certain finely divided solids have great adsorptive properties; for example, minute particles of platinum attract and hold multitudes of hydrogen molecules on their surfaces. Able to adsorb other gases, platinum is used in the production of sulfuric acid by the contact process and in the preparation of ammonia. Adsorption occurs also in solutions; colloidal particles suspended in a solution may adsorb much of the solvent (see COLLOID). Bone black and charcoal are used in industry to remove colors from solutions, since they absorb many coloring materials and carry these with them when separated from the solution. Liquid dye held to the surface of cloth by adsorption permeates the fibers so that when the liquid has evaporated the dye still remains. Adsorption is employed in the hydrogenation of oils, in gas analysis, and in chromatography, a method used in the chemical analysis of closely related substances.

Adua: see ADUWA.

Adullam (ŭdŭl′−), border town of Judah, SW of Jerusalem. Joshua 15.35; 2 Chron. 11.7; Neh. 11.30. David hid in the Cave of Adullam when he fled from Saul. From here three of his men went to get him water from the well at Bethlehem. 1 Sam. 22; 2 Sam. 23.13-17; 1 Chron. 11.15-19.

adult education, extension of educational opportunities to those adults, beyond the age of general public education, who feel a need for further training of any sort. The most common form of adult education today is the reading and discussion group, in which people meet informally to study and discuss a topic of common interest. Only in the past two centuries has the field of adult education acquired definite organization. Its relatively recent development results from various social trends—the general spread of public education, the intensification of economic competition with its premiums for skills,

Adult education: a lesson in writing.

the complexities of national and international politics demanding constant study, the stimulating effects of urbanization, and opportunity offered by increased leisure time. Modern and formal adult education probably orginated in Europe in political groups and after the Industrial Revolution as vocational classes for workers. Continuation schools for workers in Germany and Switzerland were common. The FOLK SCHOOL in Denmark, founded by Bishop Grundtvig, stressed intellectual studies, and the Adult Schools of the Society of Friends in England (1845) fostered the education of the unfortunates. Early American forms of adult education were the public lectures given in the LYCEUM (c.1826) and the Lowell Institute of Boston endowed by John Lowell (1836). In 1873 the CHAUTAUQUA MOVEMENT introduced the discussion group and modified lecture system. Free public lectures under the department of education of New York city were inaugurated in 1904. In 1926 the Carnegie Corp. of New York founded the American Association for Adult Education. This group, through its quarterly journal and its research, has worked to systematize the methods and philosophy of the field. The Fund for Adult Education, a unit of the Ford Foundation, has helped to increase interest in the area of adult education. It has financed the Center for the Study of Liberal Education for Adults, which sponsors evening college and extension programs in the nation's institutions of higher learning. Most important, public schools have been active in furnishing facilities and assistance to private adult education groups in many communities. Colleges have instituted evening programs, extension work, courses without credit, and correspondence courses; the adult enrollment in these programs continues to grow. Organizations designed to relieve ILLITERACY are instruments in adult education, as are the schools established for the education of the foreign-born in the English language and in the customs of the country. A large amount of adult education is carried on in the field of worker education by labor unions and in VOCATIONAL EDUCATION programs. Community centers, political and economic action associations, dramatic, musical, and artistic groups, are regarded by many as adult education activities. The "great books" groups, which read and discuss with trained leaders a specified list of about 70 books, began meeting in 1947; the movement grew out of great books seminars in Chicago and Columbia universities and St. John's College. In many places the public library sponsors the group. The Federal government in its Agricultural Extension Service and in the Works Progress Administration has been active in promoting adult education. See also PARENT EDUCATION. See *Handbook of Adult Education* and *Studies in the Social Significance of Adult Education* published by the American Association for Adult Education; William Sharlip and A. A. Owens, *Adult Immigrant Education* (1925); Lyman Bryson, *Adult Education* (1936); J. T. Adams, *Frontiers of American Culture* (1944); C. H. Grattan, *In Quest of Knowledge* (1955); M. S. Knowles, *The Adult Education Movement in the United States* (1962); P. E. Bergevin and others, *Adult Education Procedures* (1963).

adulteration of food: see FOOD ADULTERATION.

Adummim (ŭdŭm′) [Heb.,=red], ascent in the Jericho road. Joshua 15.7; 18.17.

Aduwa or **Adowa** (both: ä′dùwä), Ital. *Adua*, town (pop. c.10,000), N Ethiopia. The Ethiopian emperor, MENELIK II, destroyed in 1896 an Italian invasion force near the town. The defeat not only forced Italy to make peace with Ethiopia, but it helped create (1896–1901) a grave crisis in domestic Italian politics. The battle of Aduwa is often said to mark the beginning of the collapse of European colonialism. See G. F. Berkeley, *The Campaign of Adowa and the Rise of Menelik* (2d ed., 1935).

Advent [Latin,=coming, i.e., of Jesus], season of the Christian ecclesiastical year, lasting in the West from the Sunday nearest Nov. 30 (St. Andrew's) until Christmas. It is a season of penitence, to prepare for the holy day, and its liturgical color is purple. The first Sunday of Advent is the first day of the church calendar. In the Roman Catholic Church it is a period of fasting, but in the Anglican and the Lutheran Church its observance is primarily liturgical.

Advent Christian Church: see ADVENTISTS.

Adventists (ăd′vĕn″tĭsts) [advent, Latin,=coming], members of a group of related religious denominations whose distinctive doctrine centers in their belief concerning the second coming of Christ (see JUDGMENT DAY). The name Adventism is specifically applied to the teachings of William MILLER (1782–1849), who predicted the end of the world for 1843, then for 1844. When it did not occur, the Millerites, or Second Adventists, at a meeting at Albany in 1845 adopted a statement declaring their belief in the visible return of Christ at an indefinite time, when the resurrection of the dead would take place and the millennium would have its beginning. Later this body took the name Evangelical Adventists. Another and larger branch of the original Adventist group became known in 1861 as the Advent Christian Church. This branch was formed as a result of a controversy over the question of immortality. The largest Adventist body, the Seventh-Day Adventists, adopted in 1844 the observance of Saturday as the Sabbath. Formally organized in 1863, they are fundamentally evangelical, taking the Bible as the sole rule of faith and practice. Fundamental to their doctrine is their belief in the imminent, premillennial, personal, and visible return of Christ. The Seventh-Day Adventists carry on world-wide missionary work. The three other Adventist groups are the Church of God, which was organized as Churches of God in Christ Jesus in 1888 and then permanently organized as Church of God in 1921; the Life and Advent Union, which was organized in 1863; and the Primitive Advent Christian Church, a recent branch of the Advent Christian Church, which is organized only in West Virginia.

adverb: see PART OF SPEECH and ADJECTIVE.

advertising, in general, any openly sponsored offering of goods, services, or ideas through any medium of public communication. At its inception advertising was merely an announcement; for example, entrepreneurs in ancient Egypt used criers to announce ship and cargo arrivals. The newspaper classified advertisement is a present-day example of this concept. By 1758 Dr. Samuel Johnson was able to say: "Promise, large promise, is the soul of an advertisement." In the present century, with the rise of the specialized advertising profession, the most modern techniques of technology, psychology, and art have been used to make the "large promise" seem tenable. There is no question that advertising played a part in the economic growth of America. The invention of printing ushered in modern advertising. After the influence of salesmanship began to insert itself into public notice in the 18th cent., the present elaborate form of advertising began to evolve. The advertising agency has been chiefly responsible for this evolution. The advertising agent first came into prominence in the United States after the Civil War, beginning simply as an agent selling space for advertisements. Capitalizing on his special knowledge of the circulation and the reader interest of various publications, he bought space in those publications and resold it to advertisers, taking a commission of about 15 percent. After circulation and space rates in publications became standardized, the agent began to place more emphasis on planning, preparing and writing the advertisements for clients so that they could make profitable use of the space. Such work has come to be the chief function of the advertising agency, although payment of commissions by the advertising media is still the agency's accepted method of compensation. When the 15 percent commission is insufficient to provide a profit, the agency also charges clients a fee. Of the approximately 4,000 agencies in the United States in the 1960s, about 125 each place advertising worth $5,000,000 annually, and 25 of these each place advertising worth $50,000,000. Their gross is, of course, 15 percent of these sums. Advertisers may generally be classified into local (e.g., the corner grocery store) and national (the large manufacturers and retailers). Special interest groups, such as trade associations and political parties, are also large advertisers. In 1961 U.S. advertisers spent $11,845,000,000; the world total was $18,600,000,000. The largest group of advertisers are the food marketers, followed by marketers of drugs and cosmetics, soaps, automobiles, tobacco, appliances, and oil products. In 1961, national advertisers accounted for 61.2 percent of the total expenditure and local advertisers 38.8 percent. The major U.S. advertising media are newspapers, magazines, television and radio, business publications, billboards, and circulars sent through the mail. Most national media depend primarily on advertising revenue rather than circulation revenue. Since most large advertising agencies were once located on Madison Avenue in New York city, the term "Madison Avenue" is frequently used to symbolize the advertising business. The major criticisms of advertising are that it creates false values and impels people to buy things they neither need nor want. In reply, its defenders say that advertising is meant to sell products, not create values; that it can create a new market for products that fill a genuine, though latent, need; and that it furthers product improvement through free competition. The Association of National Advertisers and the American Association of Advertising Agencies, both founded in 1917, are the major associations. *Printers' Ink* and *Advertising Age* are the major trade publications. See Mar-

tin Mayer, *Madison Avenue, U.S.A.* (1958); O. A. Pease, *The Responsibilities of American Advertising* (1958); Poyntz Tyler, *Advertising in America* (1959); S. W. Dunn, *Advertising: Its Role in Modern Marketing* (1961); A. W. Frey, *Advertising* (3d ed., 1961).

advocate: see BAR, THE.

Ady, Andrew (ŏ′dē), Hung. *Ady Endre* (ĕn′drĕ), 1877–1919, Hungarian poet. He abandoned his studies in law for a career of journalism and literature. His first volume of poetry, *Versek*, appeared in 1899. After 1903 he spent most of his time in Paris, where he fell in love with Léda, who was to figure largely in his poems. He was influenced by the symbolists and became a leader of the radical Hungarian writers. His 12 volumes of published poetry, which employ myth and symbol, sing of the identity of the poet's destiny with that of his country. Ady also published seven volumes of prose. See René Bonnerjea, *Endre Ady: Poems* (1941) and Antal Nyerges, *A Selection of Poems* (1946).

Adyge Autonomous Oblast (ŭdĭgyĕ′), administrative division (1,700 sq. mi.; pop. c.286,000), KRASNODAR TERRITORY, SE European RSFSR, at the foot of the northwestern part of the Greater Caucasus and S of the Kuban river. Maikop is the capital. Livestock, wheat, and maize are raised, and there are oil and natural gas resources. The chief industries are lumbering, furniture making, food processing, and (in Maikop) the manufacture of machinery. The population is largely Moslem Adyge, a people related to the Circassians (see CIRCASSIA). They are known for their tapestries and other handicrafts. Gradually conquered (1830–64) by the Russians, the region became an autonomous oblast in 1922. The name also appears as Adyghe and Adighe.

Adzhar Autonomous Soviet Socialist Republic (ûjär′, ä′jär, Rus. ŭjär′) or **Adzharistan** (ûjä′rĭstän″, Rus. ŭjä″rēstän′), autonomous state (c.1,160 sq. mi.; pop. c.242,000), SW Georgian SSR, on the Black Sea, bordering on Turkey in the south. Batum, the capital, is the chief city. Its climate is subtropical, and there are many resorts. Tobacco, tea, and citrus fruits are grown, and copper is mined. The Adzhars, a largely Mohammedan people of the South Caucasian linguistic family, make up the majority of the population; the remainder is Georgian, Armenian, Russian, and Greek. One of the oldest regions of Georgia, Adzharistan was part of Colchis (6th–4th cent. B.C.) and was (until the middle of the 16th cent.) under Georgian domination. In 1878, it passed from Turkish control to Russia; it became an autonomous republic in 1921.

A. E.: see RUSSELL, GEORGE WILLIAM.

Aeacus (ē′ŭkŭs), in Greek mythology, son of Zeus and the nymph AEGINA. He was the father of Peleus and Telamon. After a plague had nearly wiped out the inhabitants of his land, Zeus rewarded the pious Aeacus by changing a swarm of ants to men (known as Myrmidons). According to one legend he and his people assisted Apollo and Poseidon in building the walls of Troy. After Aeacus' death Zeus made him one of the three judges of Hades.

Aëdon (āē′dŭn), in Greek legend, the wife of Zethus,

king of Thebes. She had only one son, while her sister-in-law, NIOBE, had many. Her jealousy increased until, in trying to murder Niobe's oldest son, she killed her own child. She was changed to a nightingale, and her song was a mournful call for her son, Itys or Itylus.

Aedui (ĕ′dūī) or **Haedui** (hĕ′dūī), Gallic people. occupying in the 1st cent. B.C. a part of later Burgundy. Defeated by ARIOVISTUS and at odds with their Gallic neighbors, they were allies of the Romans. The Aedui at first aided Julius Caesar in the GALLIC WARS and later were not wholehearted in their support of Vercingetorix's revolt against Caesar. Their early capital was BIBRACTE.

Aeëtes: see JASON.

AEF: see WORLD WAR, FIRST.

Aegadian Isles (ēgā′dēŭn), Ital. *Egadi* (ĕ′gädē), Latin *Aegates*, archipelago (c.15 sq. mi.; pop. 6,930) in the Mediterranean off W Sicily, Italy. The largest islands are Favignana, Marèttimo, and Levanzo. Here are the most important tuna fisheries of Sicily. A Roman naval victory over the Carthaginians near here in 241 B.C. ended the First Punic War.

Aegates: see AEGADIAN ISLES.

Aegean civilization (ējē′ŭn), general term for the cultures of pre-Hellenic Greece. The richness of these early civilizations was not suspected before the excavations of archaeologists in the late 19th cent. The most remarkable of the cultures was perhaps that of Crete which was flourishing by the beginning of the 3d millennium B.C.; this was the MINOAN CIVILIZATION. On the mainland of Greece excavations have showed the remains of MYCENAEAN CIVILIZATION. The exploration of the ruins of Troy gave knowledge of another culture, and ruins in the Cyclades have demonstrated remarkable early development there. The exact relationships of these different centers have not yet been worked out, and there are many subjects of conjecture such as the role of the Achaeans and the causes of the decline of Crete before 1100 B.C. New knowledge is, however, broadening the picture of these highly developed Aegean civilizations.

Aegean Sea, arm of the Mediterranean, c.400 mi. long and c.200 mi. wide, between Asia Minor and Greece. Irregular in outline, it is dotted with islands. Its ancient name, Archipelago, now applies to its islands, which include EUBOEA, the Northern and Southern SPORADES, the CYCLADES, SAMOS, CHIOS, LESBOS, SAMOTHRACE, THASOS, AEGINA, the DODECANESE, and many others. The strait of the Dardanelles connects the Aegean with the Sea of Marmara. The name Aegean has been variously derived from Aegae, a city of Euboea; from Aegeus, father of Theseus, who drowned himself in it believing his son had been slain by the Minotaur; and from Aegea, an Amazon queen, who drowned in it.

Aegeus: see THESEUS.

Aegina (ējī′nŭ), in Greek mythology, river nymph, daughter of the river-god Asopus. She was abducted by Zeus to the island Oenone, where she bore him a son, Aeacus. Aeacus later renamed the island in her honor.

Aegina, Gr. *Aigina* (ā′yĕnä), island (32 sq. mi.; pop. 8,958), off SE Greece, in the Gulf of Aegina or Saronic Gulf, an arm of the Aegean Sea. Sponge fishing and farming (figs, almonds, and peanuts)

are the most important occupations. The chief town is Aegina (pop. 4,989), on the northwest shore. The island, inhabited from late Neolithic times, was influenced in its culture by Minoan Crete. Conquered by Dorian Greeks, it grew rapidly as a commercial state and struck the first Greek coins. In 431 B.C. the Athenians, against whom Aegina sided in the Peloponnesian War, ex-

Aegean civilization: throne room of the legendary King Minos, excavated at Cnossus, Crete.

A windmill at Mykonos, on the Aegean Sea.

pelled the population of the island, and Aegina sank into insignificance. In the 12th cent. it served as a haven for pirates, and the Venetians, in suppressing the outlaws, conquered the island. Albanians settled here in the 16th cent., and during the Greek War of Independence the town of Aegina was for a brief period (1828–29) the capital of Greece. The AEGINETAN MARBLES were discovered in 1811 just east of the town.

Aegina, Gulf of (ējǐ′nù) or **Saronic Gulf** (sùrŏ′nǐk), inlet of the Aegean Sea, central Greece, bounded on the northeast by Attica, on the north by the Isthmus of Corinth, and on the southwest by the Argolis peninsula. The Isthmian Canal joins it to the Gulf of Corinth. Piraeus, Eleusis, and Megara are the main ports. The gulf contains many islands, notably Aegina and Salamis.

Aegineta, Paulus: see PAUL OF AEGINA.

Aeginetan marbles (ē″jǐnē′tùn), archaic Greek sculptures, c.500–480 B.C., from the temple of Aphaia at Aegina, discovered in 1811 and erroneously restored by Thorvaldsen. Now in the Glyptothek at Munich, they originally decorated the pediments of the temple. They represent scenes from the Trojan War.

aegis (ē′jǐs), in Greek mythology, weapon of Zeus and Athena. It possessed the power to terrify and disperse the enemy or to protect friends. The aegis was usually described as a garment made of goatskin, slung over the shoulder or as a piece of armor. The aegis of Athena bore the head of MEDUSA.

Aegisthus (ējǐs′thùs), in Greek mythology, according to most legends, the incestuous offspring of Thyestes and his daughter Pelopia. At Thyestes' behest he revenged the murder of his brothers by killing his uncle Atreus. Later he was known as

Aegisthus and Clytemnestra, *a mural from Herculaneum.*

the paramour of Clytemnestra and aided her in the murdering of her husband, Agamemnon. He was killed in revenge by Orestes.

Aegospotamos (ē″gùspŏ′tùmùs), river of ancient Thrace flowing into the Hellespont. At its mouth in 405 B.C. occurred the culminating battle of the PELOPONNESIAN WAR. Lysander and his Spartan fleet had come north to cut the grain supply of Athens. The Athenian fleet under CONON came to Aegospotamos and at first vainly tried to induce the Spartans to fight. Despite the warnings of ALCIBIADES, Conon and his men did not take proper precautions. Lysander fell upon them and completely destroyed the Athenian fleet.

Aegyptus: see DANAÜS.

Aehrenthal, Alois Lexa, Graf von (ä′lōēs lāk′sä gräf′ fŭn âr′ùntäl), 1854–1912, Austro-Hungarian foreign minister (1906–12). The chief event of his ministry was the Austrian annexation (1908) of BOSNIA AND HERCEGOVINA. The Russian foreign minister, IZVOLSKY, had given his formal agreement to the annexation in a secret meeting at Buchlau, Moravia; in return, Aehrenthal promised Austrian support for the opening of the Dardanelles to Russian warships. The annexation followed promptly, whereas Izvolsky was frustrated in his Dardanelles plan by English opposition. Serbian indignation at the annexation as well as belated Russian opposition almost led to a European war in 1909. Aehrenthal with difficulty restrained the Austrian war party led by Conrad von Hötzendorf. At last the Bosnian crisis was ended by German mediation. The signatory powers of the Congress of Berlin (1878), including Russia, ratified the annexation.

Aeken, Jerom van: see BOSCH, HIERONYMUS.

Ælfric (ăl′frĭk), c.955–1020, English writer and clergyman. He was the greatest English scholar during the revival of learning fostered by the Benedictine monasteries in the second half of the 10th cent. His aim was to educate the laity as well as the clergy. He wrote in English a series of saints' lives and homilies—designed for use as sermons by the preachers who were generally unable to read Latin. Ælfric was also the author of a grammar, a glossary, and a colloquy, which were long the standard texts for Latin study in English monasteries. Among his other writings are the *Heptateuch*, a free English version of the first seven books of the Bible. Ælfric is considered the chief prose stylist of the period. His later writings were strongly influenced by the balance, alliteration, and rhythm of Latin prose. See *Selected Homilies* (ed. by Henry Sweet, 1922) and the *Heptateuch and Other Writings* (ed. by Early English Text Society, 1922).

Aemilian Way: see ROMAN ROADS.

Aeneas (ē′nēùs, ĭnē′–), palsied man whom Peter cured. Acts 9.32–35.

Aeneas (ĭnē′ùs), in classical legend, a Trojan, son of ANCHISES and Venus. After the fall of Troy he escaped, bearing his aged father on his back. He tarried at Carthage with Queen Dido, then went to Italy, where his descendants founded Rome. The deeds of the "pious" Aeneas are the substance of the great Roman epic, the *Aeneid* of VERGIL.

Aeneas Sylvius Piccolomini: see PIUS II.

Aeneid (ĭnē′ĭd), epic written by VERGIL to glorify the origins of Rome. The hero Aeneas was first

Aeneas flees Troy, carrying his father on his shoulders and holding his son's hand. Relief on a Roman boundary stone.

geographic term but a collective term for the cities founded there by the Aeolians, a branch of the Hellenic peoples. The 12 southern cities were grouped in the Aeolian League; these were Temnos, Smyrna, Pitane, Neonteichos, Aegirusa, Notium, Cilla or Killa, Cyme, Gryneum, Larissa, Myrina, and Aegae.

Aeolus (ē′ŭlŭs), in Greek mythology. **1** The wind-god. He lived on the island of Aeolia, where he kept the winds in a cave. **2** Son of HELLEN and ancestor of the Aeolian branch of the Hellenic race.

aerial: see ANTENNA.

aerial photography, the art and science of taking still or moving-picture photographs from an aircraft in flight. It was tried before the advent of the airplane by using kites and balloons. The First World War demonstrated its tremendous military value and during the ensuing peacetime years methods were so far perfected for taking still pictures that photogrammetry, the science of measurement from photographs, became an important tool of agencies making any type of surface maps. During the Second World War, aerial photographs were a

Aerial photograph of Amsterdam, the Netherlands.

mentioned by Homer in the *Iliad*, but Vergil used the legends of later writers which told of Aeneas' wanderings after the fall of Troy. Out of these rather disconnected stories he created a true epic. He made Aeneas the paragon of the most revered Roman virtues—devotion to family, loyalty to the state, and piety. In 12 books, Vergil tells how Aeneas escaped from Troy to Carthage, where he became intimate with Dido and told her of his adventures. He then left Dido, went to Sicily, visited Hades, and landed in Italy. There he established the beginnings of the Roman state and waged successful war against the natives. The work ends with the death of Turnus at the hands of Aeneas. The verse in dactylic hexameters is strikingly regular, though Vergil's death left the epic incomplete and some of the lines unfinished. Other writers were forbidden by Augustus to complete or "improve" the work. The sonority of the words and the nobility of purpose make the *Aeneid* one of the greatest long poems in any literature. One of the many English translations is that of Rolfe Humphries (1951).

Aenon (ē′-) [Gr.,=spring], unidentified place, where John the Baptist baptized. John 3.21.

Aeolia: see AEOLIS.

Aeolian Islands: see LIPARI ISLANDS.

Aeolians: see GREECE.

Aeolis (ē′ŭlĭs) or **Aeolia** (ēō′lēŭ), ancient region of the west coast of Asia Minor. Aeolis was not a

most important source of intelligence. The aerial camera, because it is used at a distance high enough to be considered infinite, is of fixed focus. Below the focal plane, at the rear of the camera, is an opaque curtain which, upon release, carries a small slit across the plane, thus providing a small time exposure at any one point above the ground but a long exposure for the entire area. The pilot sets his aircraft on the correct speed and course before entering the area to be photographed to insure uniformity of speed and altitude. The camera is activated before entering the area and remains in operation until well past the area. This is done to insure longitudinal overlapping between this area and any adjacent area to be subsequently photographed so that the photographs may later be joined together. Aerial photographs may be high oblique (including the horizon), low oblique (below the horizon), or vertical (perpendicular to the earth). Only the vertical may be accurately scaled for map-making purposes. Often a multilens camera is used to photograph one section vertically and the adjacent areas obliquely. The individual oblique exposures are then corrected, scaled, and joined to the vertical section, and together form one continuous photograph. A photograph formed by fitting together several overlapping vertical photographs is called a mosaic. A reproduction of a photograph to which grid lines, place names and the like have been added is called a photomap. In addition to military uses, aerial photography has proved valuable in such fields as archaeology, geology, forestry, highway plotting and construction, map making, and land conservation. See H. T. U. Smith, *Aerial Photographs and Their Applications* (1943); Constance Babington-Smith, *Air Spy* (1957); D. R. Lueder, *Aerial Photographic Interpretation* (1959); W. H. Baker, *Elements of Photogrammetry* (1960).

aerodynamics, the study of the motion of gases, especially air. The principal application of aerodynamics is in the design of aircraft (see FLIGHT), in calculating both the forces (lift and drag) exerted on the aircraft by the air flowing around it and the speed and direction of the air flow. In practical aircraft design, the predictions of aerodynamics are tested by means of a WIND TUNNEL before actual flight is attempted.

aeroembolism, physiologic disorder caused by too rapid decrease in atmospheric pressure. It is also known as caisson disease, altitude sickness, and "the bends." This condition is encountered in persons who work under greatly increased atmospheric pressure below the surface of the earth (e.g., divers and other laborers who work under compressed air) when their return to normal atmospheric pressure is made too quickly. Airplane pilots who go rapidly from normal atmospheric pressure to high altitudes (low atmospheric pressure) in unpressurized aircraft or in aircraft with faulty pressurizing apparatus also encounter the disorder. The decrease in air pressure releases body nitrogen in the form of gas bubbles that block the small veins and arteries and collect in the tissues, cutting off the oxygen supply and causing nausea, vomiting, dizziness, pain in the joints and abdomen, paralysis, and other neurological symptoms. In severe cases there may be shock, total collapse and, if treatment is not prompt, death. Persons who work under increased atmospheric pressure must make the ascent to normal atmospheric pressure gradually, often through pressurized "locks." Inhalation of pure oxygen aids in clearing nitrogen from the body. Those who suffer symptoms of aeroembolism at high altitudes experience relief on returning to an atmospheric pressure normal to them; this and oxygen inhalation will usually effect recovery.

aeronautical engineering: see ENGINEERING.

aeronautics, the science and art of flight. For history and mechanics, see AERODYNAMICS; AIRPLANE; AIRSHIP; AIRWAY; AUTOGIRO; BALLOON; FLIGHT; GLIDER; HELICOPTER; JET PROPULSION; PARACHUTE; SEAPLANE. For notable flights, see AVIATION. For military and naval aeronautics, see AIRCRAFT CARRIER; AIR FORCES, and AIR POWER. See also AIR, LAW OF THE; MOTION SICKNESS; and articles on leading aviators and air pioneers. See also bibliography under AVIATION.

Aeschines (ĕ'skĭnēz), c.390–314? B.C., Athenian orator, rival of DEMOSTHENES. He rose from humble circumstances and became powerful in politics because of his oratorical gifts. At first he opposed Philip II of Macedon, then later changed sides, arguing that resistance to Macedonian power was useless. Both he and Demosthenes were members of the embassy to Philip in 348 B.C., and afterward Demosthenes bitterly and baselessly accused Aeschines of accepting Macedonian bribes. He was to have been joined in his action by Timarchus, but Aeschines prevented this by his oration *Against Timarchus* (345 B.C.). Aeschines defended himself well in his oration *On the False Legation* (342 B.C.)—a title also used by Demosthenes in his accusatory oration. The trouble between the orators grew and culminated in a dispute over a gold crown that the orator Ctesiphon proposed should be given Demosthenes in 330 B.C. Aeschines brought suit with *Against Ctesiphon*. Demosthenes replied with his sturdy defense *On the Crown*. Aeschines lost and was fined, and retired to Asia Minor where, Plutarch said, he lived as a professional sophist.

Aeschylus (ĕs'kĭlŭs, ēs'-), 525–456 B.C., Athenian tragic poet, b. Eleusis. The first of the three great Greek writers of tragedy, he was the predecessor of SOPHOCLES and EURIPIDES. He fought at Marathon and at Salamis. In 476 B.C. he went to Sicily to live at the court of Hiero I, and he died at Gela. He wrote perhaps 90 plays (seven survive in full) and won 13 first prizes. In each case four connected plays were submitted (a tragic trilogy and a lighter satyr play). It has been claimed that Aeschylus invented tragedy, as tragedy previously had been merely a dialogue between a chorus and one actor—a dramatically limited form. Aeschylus added an actor and increased the potentialities of his vehicle immeasurably. (Though only two actors and the chorus appeared on the stage at the same time, an actor often took more than one part.) Aeschylus introduced costumes, decorated his scene, and placed supernumeraries on the stage. By his supreme poetic ability and his piety he made Athenian tragedy more of an artistic and intellectual creation than it had been before. His choral lyrics are, at their best, rivals of the odes of Pindar. The choruses, more important in Aeschylus than in his successors, are both ethical commentaries on the action and the means for its presentation. Vivid in its character portrayal, majestic in its tone, and captivating in its lyricism, Aeschylus' tragic poetry is esteemed among the greatest of all time. He alone of Greek tragedians was honored at Athens by having his plays performed repeatedly after his death. His extant plays are hard to date. The earliest is probably *The Suppliants*, simple in plot (on the marriage of the 50 daughters of Danaüs) and with only one actor besides the chorus. *The Persians* (472? B.C.), glorifying the Athenian victory over Persia at Salamis, has two actors, but

Aeschines

Aeschylus

Aesop

the new form is still unpolished. *The Seven against Thebes* can be dated in 467. *Prometheus Bound* (see PROMETHEUS), of uncertain date, is striking for its bald attack on the vengefulness of the gods toward man, but the later two parts of its trilogy, which are lost, may have portrayed Zeus as just. The last three tragedies of Aeschylus compose the only extant ancient trilogy, called the *Oresteia*, with which the poet won first prize in 458. The three plays are *Agamemnon, The Choëphoroe,* and *The Eumenides;* in each play three actors are used —an innovation of Sophocles. *Agamemnon* is considered by many to be the greatest Attic tragedy. Browning's *Agamemnon* is a poetic translation, and Eugene O'Neill's *Mourning Becomes Electra* is an American version of the trilogy. The translation by David Grene and Richmond Lattimore in *The Complete Greek Tragedies* (1959) is one of many English translations of his plays. See studies by Gilbert Murray (1940) and G. D. Thomson (1941).

Aesculapius: see ASCLEPIUS.

Aesir: see GERMANIC RELIGION.

Aesop (ē'sŭp, ē'sŏp), Greek fabulist. About him little is known. An old legend makes him a slave of Samos in the 6th cent. B.C. and associates him with wild adventures. The fables called Aesop's fables were preserved principally through BABRIUS, PHAEDRUS, and PLANUDES MAXIMUS. See FABLE.

aesthetics (ĕsthĕt'ĭks), that branch of philosophy which is concerned with the nature of art and the criteria of artistic judgment. The classical conception of art as the imitation of nature was formulated by Plato and developed by Aristotle in his *Poetics*, while modern thinkers such as Kant, Schelling, Croce and Cassirer have emphasized the creative and symbolic aspects of art. The major problem in aesthetics concerns the nature of the beautiful. Generally speaking there are two basic approaches to the problem of beauty—the objective, which asserts that beauty inheres in the object and that judgments concerning it may have objective validity, and the subjective, which tends to identify the beautiful with that which pleases the observer. Outstanding defenders of the objec-

tive position were Plato, Aristotle, and Lessing and of the subjective position, Burke and Hume. In his *Critique of Judgment,* Kant mediated between the two tendencies by showing that aesthetic judgment has universal validity despite its subjective nature. Among the recent philosophers interested in aesthetics, the most important are Croce, Collingwood, Cassirer, Dewey, and Santayana. See Bernard Bosanquet, *A History of Aesthetic* (1892); George Santayana, *The Sense of Beauty* (1896); Irving Babbitt, *The New Laokoon* (1910); H. M. Kallen, *Art and Freedom* (2 vols., 1942); K. E. Gilbert and Helmut Kuhn, *A History of Esthetics* (1953 ed.).

aestivation: see HIBERNATION.

Aeta: see PYGMY.

Æthelbald (ĕ'thŭlbôld, ă'–), d. 757, king of Mercia (716–57), grandson of a brother of Penda. He spent many years in exile before he became king. A strong ruler, by 731 he controlled all England S of the Humber and led expeditions into Northumbria (740) and against the Welsh (743). He was murdered by his own bodyguard.

Æthelbald, d. 860, king of Wessex, son of ÆTHELWULF. During his father's pilgrimage to Rome (855–56), Æthelbald ruled, and in 856 he led a group who refused to receive Æthelwulf as king. Æthelwulf left Wessex to his son and resumed his reign over Kent, Surrey, Sussex, and Essex. After Æthelwulf's death, in 858, Æthelbald married his father's widow, Judith of France. At his death Æthelbald was succeeded by his brother Æthelbert.

Æthelbert (ĕ'thŭlbûrt, –bûrt, ă'–), d. 616, king of Kent (560?–616). Although defeated by the West Saxons in 568, he later reconstructed his broken power and became the strongest ruler in England S of the Humber. His wife, Bertha, daughter of a

Frankish king, was a Christian. Æthelbert received St. Augustine of Canterbury, who converted the king to Christianity—the first Christian king in Anglo-Saxon England—and made his capital, Canterbury, a great Christian center. The laws issued by him are the earliest extant body of laws in any Germanic language and in their list of payment for physical injuries reflect the social order of the time.

Æthelbert, d. 865, king of Wessex (860–65), son of Æthelwulf. In 858 at the death of his father he ruled Kent, Surrey, Sussex, and Essex, and he reunited them with Wessex when in 860 he succeeded his brother ÆTHELBALD in that kingdom. Throughout his reign the attacks of the Danes were severe, and they continued through the reign of his brother and successor, Æthelred.

Æthelflæd (ĕ′thŭlflĕd, ä′–) or **Ethelfleda** (ĕthŭl-flē′dù), d. 918, daughter of King Alfred the Great of Wessex and wife of Æthelred, ealdorman of Mercia. After her husband's death in 911 she reigned alone and was known as the Lady of the Mercians. Her energetic prosecution of resistance against the Danes and her wise government, both before and after her husband's death, won her the reputation as one of the most remarkable women in English history.

Æthelfrith (ĕ′thŭlfrĭth, ä–), d. 616, king of Northumbria. He was the first great leader to arise among the northern Angles, and he ruled over both Bernicia and Deira, uniting them into the kingdom of Northumbria, probably beginning in 593. He repulsed an attack by the Scottish Gaels under Aidan in 603 and about 10 years later defeated the Welsh at Chester. During Æthelfrith's lifetime (if not solely as a result of the battle of Chester) the West Welsh were separated from their northern brethren by the penetration of the English to the Irish Sea. Æthelfrith forced his brother-in-law EDWIN, who was heir to the throne in the Deiran line, into a long exile. Edwin found a protector in Rædwald of East Anglia, who made war on Æthelfrith and killed him in battle at the Idle river near present-day Nottingham.

Æthelmar of Valence: see AYMER OF VALENCE.

Æthelred (ĕ′thŭlrĕd, ä′–), d. 871, king of Wessex (865–71), son of Æthelwulf and brother of ALFRED. He succeeded his brother Æthelbert as king of Wessex and as overlord of Kent and possibly of East Anglia. Æthelred spent much of his short reign gathering forces to oppose the Danes, who had occupied York (866) and ravaged much of England. Alfred was his important second in command in a series of battles (870–71). Although Æthelred had young children, Alfred succeeded him in April, 871, as better fitted to defend the kingdom.

Æthelred, 965?–1016, king of England (978–1016), called Æthelred the Unready [from Old Eng. *unrœd* = without counsel]. He was the son of Edgar and the half brother of EDWARD THE MARTYR. The obscure circumstances of Edward's murder in 978 started Æthelred's reign under a cloud of suspicion. The catastrophes of the period occurred partly because Æthelred was a weak king, but his reign coincided with the height of Danish power, and his people were often treacherous. His first payment

of tribute to raiding Danes was in 991—a payment he raised by the DANEGELD then and frequently thereafter. In 997 the Danes came not only to raid but to stay and to plunder the rich realm until 1000. It is impossible to assign reasons or blame for the devastation of Strathclyde by the English in 1000 or the massacre of Danes in England in 1002, both of which may have been at the king's order. Æthelred tried to defend his kingdom; in 1002 he married Emma, sister of Richard II, duke of Normandy, perhaps in an attempt to gain an ally; in 1007 the army was placed under a single commander; by 1009 a navy had been built, but was rendered useless by the treason of many commanders, who took to piracy. A severe harrying (1009–12) by the Danes left England disorganized and hopeless, and when the Danish king SWEYN returned in 1013 to conquer, he was well received in the DANELAW, and London capitulated without much fighting. Æthelred fled to Normandy. Upon Sweyn's death in 1014, Æthelred's restoration was negotiated in the first recorded pact between an English king and his subjects. CANUTE, son of Sweyn, withdrew, but returned in 1015 and was opposed desperately by Æthelred and his son, EDMUND IRONSIDE. Æthelred died in April, 1016; Edmund was declared his successor and made a treaty with Canute, but died in November. Æthelred's heirs were restored only with EDWARD THE CONFESSOR.

Æthelstan: see ATHELSTAN.

Æthelwulf (ĕ′thŭlwŏŏlf, ä′–), d. 858, king of Wessex (839–56), son of Egbert and father of ÆTHELBALD, ÆTHELBERT, ÆTHELRED, and ALFRED. He had been lord of Kent, Surrey, Sussex, and Essex before his father's death in 839, and upon becoming king of Wessex he became overlord of Kent. He was compelled to defend his country against the invasion of the Danes, and with Æthelbald he won a notable victory over them at Aclea in 851. He also campaigned against the Welsh. A man of great piety, he sent his son Alfred to Rome and went there himself on a pilgrimage in 855. In 856 he took as his second wife Judith, daughter of Charles II (Charles the Bald) of France. Learning before his return to England that Æthelbald would resist his resumption of the kingship, Æthelwulf left his son as king of Wessex and himself ruled only in Kent and its dependencies, where Æthelbert succeeded him.

Aetius (āē′shĕŭs), d. 367, Syrian theologian. He became prominent (c.350) as an exponent of the extreme ARIANISM developed principally by his secretary EUNOMIUS. Members of his party were called Aetians and Anomoeans.

Aetius, c.396–454, Roman general. At first unfriendly to VALENTINIAN III, he later made his peace with Valentinian's mother, GALLA PLACIDIA, and was given a command in Gaul. An ambitious general, he was embroiled in difficulties with his rival BONIFACE, who defeated him near Rimini in 432. Aetius went briefly into exile among the Huns but returned in 433 and rose to be the chief ruler of the Western Empire. He defeated the Germans in Gaul, then crowned his career by commanding (451) Roman and Visigothic troops in the repulse of Attila and the Huns in the battle near the modern

Châlons-sur-Marne—a battle generally said to have saved the West. Valentinian, presumably jealous of Aetius' success, had him murdered.

Aetna: see ETNA.

Aetolia (ētōl'yù), region of ancient Greece, N of the Gulf of Corinth and the Gulf of Calydon, E of the Achelous river (separating it from Acarnania). Little is known of the early population of Aetolia, but later Aetolians, though they had coastal cities, were primarily an inland farming and pastoral people. They had famous shrines at Calydon (to Artemis) and at Thermum (to Apollo). Aetolia was of little significance in Greek history until the rise of the AETOLIAN LEAGUE. After the downfall of that confederation, Aetolia was absorbed by the Romans into Achaea.

Aetolian League, confederation centering in the cities of Aetolia. It was formed in the 4th cent. B.C. and began to gain power in the 3d cent. in opposing the ACHAEAN LEAGUE and the Macedonians. At its height, the league stretched across Greece from sea to sea, including Locris, Malis, Dolopes, part of Thessaly, Phocis, and Acarnania. In alliance with the Romans, the Aetolians helped to defeat Philip V of Macedon at Cynoscephalae in 197 B.C. The Aetolians, dissatisfied, turned against Rome and allied themselves with Antiochus III of Syria. His defeat (189) spelled the ruin of the league. Though formally it continued, its power had vanished.

Afanasyev, Aleksandr Nikolayevich (ŭlyĭksän'dùr nyĭkûlĭ'ùvĭch ûfûnä'syûf), 1826–71, Russian folklorist. His collections, published from 1866 on, were instrumental in introducing Russian popular tales to world literature. A selection was translated into English as *Russian Fairy Tales* (1945).

affenpinscher: see TOY DOG.

Afghan hound: see HOUND.

Afghanistan (ăfgă'nĭstan″, ăfgä″nistän'), kingdom (c.253,000 sq. mi.; pop. c.13,000,000), S central Asia. The capital is KABUL. Afghanistan is bordered by Iran on the west, by West Pakistan on the east and south, and by the USSR (Turkmen SSR, Uzbek SSR, and Tadzhik SSR) on the north. A narrow strip, the Wakhan, stretches in the northeast to touch Sinkiang prov., China, and Kashmir. The great mass of the country is steep-sloped with mountains, the ranges fanning out from the towering Hindu Kush (reaching a height of more than 24,000 ft.) across all the center of the country. There are, however, many fertile valleys and plains within the mountain ranges and on the edges.

Afghanistan's main link with Pakistan today is the "silk road" across the Khyber Pass that was for centuries a trade and invasion route from central Asia.

Afghanistan location map

Afghanistan's capital, Kabul, a contrast between old and new: an unveiled woman amid women wearing chuddars.

71

AFGHANISTAN

Afghan village children at school.

Here are cultivated fields of barley and wheat and orchards yielding fine fruits, such as the famous peaches and grapes of KANDAHAR. In the south and particularly in the southwest are great stretches of desert. To the north, between the north central mountain chains (notably the Koh-i-Baba, or Kuh-i-Baba, and the Paropamisus) and the Amu Darya river, which marks part of the boundary with the USSR, are the regions of Afghan Turkistan, the highlands of Badakshan (with the finest lapis lazuli in the world), the Amu Darya plain, and the rich valley of HERAT on the Hari Rud in the northwest corner of the country (the heart of ancient Ariana), connected with the Khurasan region. Farther east are the anciently splendid Balkh and the modern Mazar-i-Sharif. The regions thus vary greatly, though prevailingly the land is dry, and the rivers are mostly not navigable. The longest is the Helmand, which flows generally SW from the Hindu Kush to the Iranian border. Its water was used in the remote past for irrigation, and the waters of the Hari Rud and the Amu Darya have also been utilized. The Kabul river, on which the capital stands, is particularly famous because it leads to the KHYBER PASS and so south to the riches of India. This route has been much used by conquerors, and the incursions of various invaders from prehistoric days until relatively recent times helped to make the population of present Afghanistan almost as variegated as the regions. In the north there are the Tadzhiks about Herat and in the Wakhan, the nomadic Turkmen, and the Uzbeks. In the central mountains are the Hazararas, who are of Mongolian origin. In the east and the south are the Afghans and their almost, if not quite, indistinguishable kinsmen, the Pathans (a name used particularly for those in the North-West Frontier region, Pakistan); they speak Afghan, or Pushtu. This and Iranian are the principal languages of Afghanistan. A unifying factor among the people is religion, for almost all the inhabitants of Afghanistan are Moslem. The large majority are Sunnite, the minority (perhaps as many as 1,000,000) Shiite. Agriculture is the main occupation, but grazing is also of great importance in the economy, and the fat-tailed sheep is a staple of Afghan life, supplying skins and wool for clothing, meat and fat for food. Karakul is the largest single item of Afghanistan export. Fine horses are the pride of many tribesmen. Mineral wealth is being developed, and there are deposits of coal, copper, and sulfur; oil fields are found in the north. Formerly much silver and some gold came from Afghanistan. The region is also traditionally known for its native plants producing castor beans, madder, and asafetida. Industry was in the 1960s still only in the beginning stage, but hydroelectric power was increased by a modern dam on the Helmand river and another on the Kabul river. Communications are poor in this mountainous country, but motor roads are being improved and extended with international aid. Air transport promises to be a major carrier in modern Afghanistan,

History. The position of Afghanistan across the land road to India has enticed conquerors. The high mountain barriers, on the other hand, have helped the invaded. Thus, the very topography that kept Afghanistan disunited served at the same time to make the hill tribes independent. It is probable that there were well-developed civilizations in S Afghanistan in prehistoric times before the land had been reduced to utter desert, but the archaeological record has not yet been made clear. Certainly cultures had flourished in the north and the east before Darius I by conquest annexed those areas to the Persian Empire. Later Alexander the Great conquered them on his way to India, and after him came the independent kingdom of BACTRIA, which flourished with its capital at Balkh from the middle of the 3d cent. B.C. until the middle of the 2d cent. B.C. It fell to conquering Parthians and rebellious tribes (notably the Saka). The present Afghanistan remained divided as petty rulers rose and fell, struggling against conquerors from the west. Buddhism spread from the east, but it was wiped out, and the conquest by Moslems, which began in present W Afghanistan in the 7th cent. A.D., was to provide the stable religion. Small Moslem kingdoms were founded. The greatest of them was that with its capital at GHAZNI, and MAHMUD OF GHAZNI, who conquered the lands from Khurasan in Iran to the Punjab in India early in the 11th cent., was the greatest of the rulers. The state fell to conquering hordes from Ghor in 1152. Later Afghanistan was to succumb to the conquest of Jenghiz Khan and then to that of Tamerlane. BABER, a descendant of Tamerlane, used Kabul for his conquest of India and the establishment of the Mogul empire in the 16th cent. Meanwhile Islam had been accepted even by most of the remote hill tribes, and the new peoples who came in to take over the devastated land also took the new religion. Tribes and families continued at strife. In the 18th cent. Iranian conquest under Nadir Shah marked the real beginning of Afghanistan as a unit because after his death (1747) his

lieutenant, AHMED SHAH, established a unified state covering most of the present Afghanistan. His dynasty, the Durani, gave the Afghans the name (Durani) that they themselves frequently use. The Durani line ended when DOST MOHAMMED gained power in 1826. His rule saw the emergence of the 19th-century problem of Afghanistan. The struggle between Great Britain and Russia for central Asia and British desire to guard India led to the Afghan Wars. The first of these began in 1838, and though British soldiers took the major cities of the east and south, the war culminated in a massacre of the British in Kabul in 1842. The following decade saw the struggles that made Khyber Pass a famous name in British military annals. Dost Mohammed, ousted from his emirate, was restored with British help, but internal family and tribal strife continued. Dost Mohammed's successor, SHERE ALI, was opposed by his brothers and nephews. When he turned from British to Russian aid, the second of the full-scale Afghan Wars began (1878). Fortunes varied, but the upshot of the war was the ousting (1880) of Shere Ali and the establishment of the Anglophile ABDU-R-RAHMAN KHAN as emir until his death in 1901. He did much to institute order in his unruly land. The boundary between the then North-West Frontier Prov. and Afghanistan was established by Sir Mortimer Durand in 1893 as the Durand line, but the question of the exact status of some tribal lands was left unclear, and troubles continued with the Afridis, the Wazirs, and other border tribes. The Anglo-Russian agreement of 1907 guaranteed the independence of Afghanistan under British influence. That influence was resented, especially in the First World War, when the Afghans remained neutral but sympathized with the Moslem Turks; this feeling led in 1919 to a short war against the British, but the emir, AMANULLAH, soon negotiated the Treaty of Rawalpindi and then devoted himself to an earnest effort to modernize his country. The emirate was changed (1926) to a kingdom, and radical reforms were introduced. Westernization,

Agriculture is the main occupation of the people of Afghanistan (top left). Another source of income is the sale of skins of the fat-tailed sheep (top right). Recently, the government of Afghanistan has been working to improve and increase its industries. A knitting workshop (above) in Kabul.

however, provoked the wrath of his fanatical Moslem subjects, who rose in 1929 under a leader called the Water Boy. Amanullah had to resign, but Mohammed Nadir Shah, placed on the throne after the suppression of the revolt, continued moderate efforts to modernize Afghanistan until he was assassinated in 1933. His son and successor, Mohammed Zahir Shah (b. 1914), set out to strengthen the country and to build its economy. The king undertook social and economic reforms, and by the 1960s the aspect of Afghan life was a curious medley of anachronism and modernity. Afghan women were seen both veiled and unveiled, and the educational system, particularly the Univ. of Kabul (founded 1932), was being expanded. Afghanistan was deeply interested in the partition of India and Pakistan; in 1951 the Afghan government protested the incorporation of the tribal lands within the Durand line into Pakistan and urged the creation of an independent or autonomous state with a Pathan majority, to be made from the North-West Frontier region and to be called Pushtunistan. Pakistan has refused to yield the territory. The dispute is complicated by the fact that the nomadic Pathan tribes seasonally cross the Afghan-Pakistani border with flocks; relations grew increasingly bitter, and in 1961 the border between the two countries was closed. In modern international politics, Afghanistan has held a neutralist position, accepting large amounts of aid from the USSR and the United States. Afghanistan is a member of the United Nations. See Sir Percy Sykes, *A Short History of Afghanistan* (1940); Kerr Fraser-Tytler, *Afghanistan* (1950); D. N. Wilbur, *Afghanistan* (rev. ed., 1961); Christine Weston, *Afghanistan* (1962).

Afghan language (ăf′găn, –gŭn), occasional name for the Pushtu language.

Afghan Turkistan, wild region, N Afghanistan, between the Hindu Kush mts. and the Amu Darya river. Its chief city is Mazar-i-Sharif.

Afinogenov, Aleksandr Nikolayevich (ŭlyĭksän′dŭr nyĭkŭlī′ŭvĭch ŭfē″nŭgyĕ′nŭf), 1904–41, Russian playwright. He wrote the popular Soviet play *Fear* (1931; Eng. tr., 1934), in which a scientist's theory of the role of fear is refuted by a Bolshevik leader. Among his other melodramatic plays are *Dalyokoye* (1935; Eng. tr., *Remote*, 1936; *Distant Point*, 1941; *Far Taiga*, 1946) and *On the Eve* (1941; Eng. tr. in *Seven Soviet Plays*, 1946). Afinogenov was killed in a German air raid.

AFL: see American Federation of Labor and Congress of Industrial Organizations.

AFL-CIO: see American Federation of Labor and Congress of Industrial Organizations.

Afonso. For rulers thus named, see Alfonso.

Africa, continent (with adjacent islands c.11,684,000 sq. mi.; pop. c.261,000,000), lying across the equator, mainly in the Northern Hemisphere. Madagascar is the largest of the islands included. Africa is entirely surrounded by water, and makes up about 20 percent of the world's land area. At the points where it lies closest to Europe and Asia it is separated from them by the Straits of Gibraltar and the Suez Canal respectively. The continent is otherwise bounded by the Mediterranean Sea on the north, by the Red Sea, the Gulf of Aden, and the Indian Ocean (including the Mozambique Channel) on the east, and by the Atlantic Ocean (including the Gulf of Guinea) on the west. The unindented coast affords few natural harbors. Africa is mainly a plateau with an average height of 2,000 ft. above sea level. The lowest point on the continent is the Qattara Depression in Egypt, 440 ft. below sea level. Important mountain areas are confined to the northwest (Atlas Mts.), to the southwest tip (the Drakensberg), and to the east central region, split by the Great Rift Valley, where Mt. Kilimanjaro (19,565 ft.), the greatest continental elevation, is located. The high lakes of E central Africa, notably Lakes Rudolph, Nyasa, and Tanganyika and Victoria Nyanza and Albert Nyanza, are the continent's great reservoirs; they feed several of the large draining rivers, including the Nile (NE Africa), the Congo (equatorial Africa), and the Zambezi (SE Africa). The Niger drains W central Africa. Africa, although mainly in the tropics, displays many varieties of climate. Most of the north (which includes the Libyan Desert and the Sahara) and the Kalahari in the south are extremely arid. There are open savannas along the borders of the arid regions. Dense jungle covers W equatorial Africa, where rainfall is heavy throughout the year. Native Negro stocks, speaking a great variety of languages, inhabit most of the continent. Concentrations of non-Negro populations are in North Africa and in the Republic of South Africa.

Outline of History. In the civilization of Egypt, established before 3000 B.C., Africa can claim one of the most ancient settled cultures in the world. Ethiopia, the second oldest African country that survives in some form from antiquity, has been traced to the 3d cent. B.C. In ancient times the Mediterranean region of Africa was of great importance. Rome gradually acquired this area after defeating and destroying Phoenician Carthage in 149 B.C. With the dissolution of the West Roman Empire, the northern coastal regions were divided among barbarians. Later a degree of unity was restored by invading Arabs (7th–11th cent.), who propagated Islam effectively; today there are c.90,000,000 Moslems in Africa. After the 8th cent. the Moslems (chiefly Moors) from the northern lands of Africa invaded the Christian countries of S Europe and were not finally expelled until the 15th cent. Portugal, stimulated by the hope of establishing a safe trade route to India, began exploring the coasts of Africa; a Portuguese, Bartholomew Diaz, was the first European to round (1488) the Cape of Good Hope. He was followed by Vasco da Gama, who sailed to India in 1499. Portugal established many coastal stations to trade in the commodities for which Africa became famous—spices, ivory, gold, diamonds, and slaves. Dutch, English, and French competition restricted Portuguese activities in the 16th and 17th cent. In the 18th and 19th cent., exploration of the interior of Africa by, among others, James Bruce, Mungo Park, John Speke, David Livingstone, and Sir Henry Stanley exposed the continent's great natural wealth, which could be exploited by the founding of colonies. Though the Dutch had colonized the Cape of Good Hope area in the 17th cent. and the British had founded the colony of Sierra Leone in 1807, the really intense struggle for empire in Africa did not arise until the final disappearance of the slave trade in the mid-19th cent. By 1912 the major powers had partitioned Africa, and only Ethiopia and Liberia were independent. In the northwest, France ultimately acquired French

West Africa, French Equatorial Africa, and the French Cameroons and established protectorates in Algeria, Morocco, and Tunisia. Other French territories were French Somaliland, French Togoland, Madagascar, and Réunion. The main group of British possessions was in E and SE Africa; it included the Anglo-Egyptian Sudan, British Somaliland, Uganda, Kenya, Tanganyika, Zanzibar, Nyasaland, the Rhodesias, Bechuanaland, Basutoland, and Swaziland. The Union of South Africa was a dominion of the British Commonwealth of Nations. Gambia, Sierra Leone, the Gold Coast, and Nigeria were the British possessions on the west coast. Portugal's African empire was made up of Portuguese Guinea, Angola, and Mozambique, in addition to various enclaves and islands on the west coast. Belgium held the Belgian Congo and Ruanda-Urundi. The Spanish possessions in Africa were the smallest, being composed of Spanish Guinea, Spanish Sahara, Ifni, and the protectorate of Spanish Morocco. The extensive German holdings—Togoland, the Cameroons, German South-West Africa, and German East Africa—were lost after the First World War. Italy's empire included, before the conquest of Ethiopia (1936), Libya, Eritrea, and Italian Somaliland. Between the wars Egypt achieved (1922) a measure of sovereignty, and the Union of South Africa became virtually self-governing. Tangier, previously attached to Morocco, was made an international zone in 1925. In the Second World War there was a series of major campaigns in North Africa, culminating in the defeat of the Axis.

Independence in Africa. In 1945 Ethiopia, Egypt, Liberia, and the Union of South Africa were the only free states in Africa. Liberia alone had never been under European rule. By 1950, however, the groundswell of nationalism, which was to change the face of Africa, was surging forward. Libya gained independence in 1951. In 1952 Eritrea entered into a federation with Ethiopia; in 1962 Eritrea was merged into Ethiopia. The revolution that made (1953) Egypt a republic spurred the African nationalist movements. Morocco, Sudan, and Tunisia became free in 1956, Ghana in 1957, and Guinea in 1958. In 1957 the Tangier zone was absorbed by Morocco, as was Spanish Morocco in 1958. The high tide of African nationalism was reached in 1960. In that year the following republics were created from the former French colonies: Cameroon, the Central African Republic, Chad, the Congo Republic, Dahomey, Gabon, Ivory Coast, Malagasy, Mali (formerly the Sudanese Republic), Mauritania, Niger, Senegal, and Upper Volta. In addition 1960 saw the formation of the strife-torn Republic of the Congo, the Federation of Nigeria, Somalia, and Togo. In 1961 Sierra Leone and Tanganyika achieved sovereignty. The year also saw the seizure of the Portuguese enclave of São João Baptista de Ajudá by Dahomey, the division of the former British Cameroons between Nigeria and the Republic of Cameroon (now the Federal Republic of Cameroon), and the establishment of a republic in the former Union of South Africa. In 1962 Uganda, Algeria, the Republic of Rwanda, and the Kingdom of Burundi became separate free states. By early 1963 there were few European colonies left in Africa; only Portugal had

Victoria Falls in the upper Zambezi river.

Africa's greatest elevation, Mt. Kilimanjaro.

The Great Sphinx of Gizeh, Guardian of the Nile Valley.

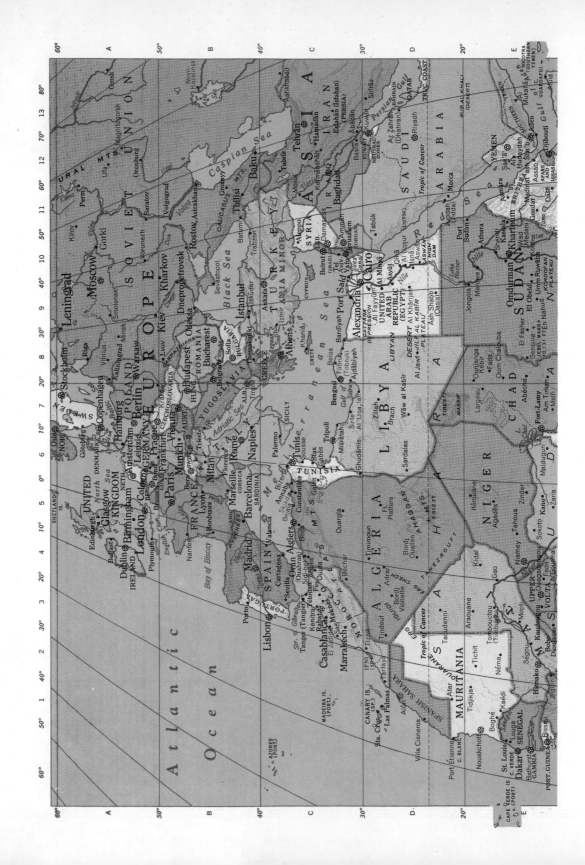

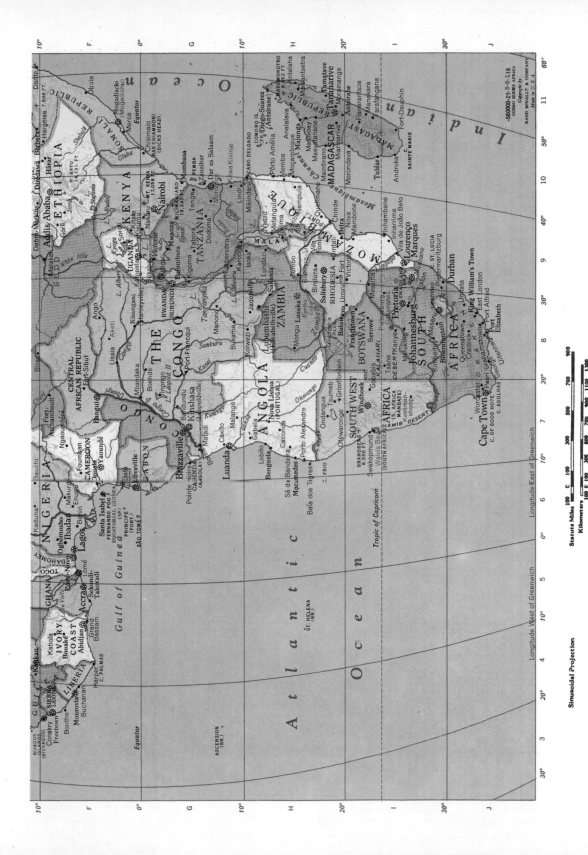

Simusoidal Projection

managed to retain extensive overseas territories. Portugal still held Angola, Cabinda, Mozambique, Portuguese Guinea, and São Tomé and Príncipe. Spain's possessions were Spanish Sahara, Ifni, the Canary Islands, and Spanish Guinea (made up of Río Muni and Fernando Po). Of the few remaining French colonies in Africa, French Somaliland and the Comoro Islands were overseas territories within the French Community and the island of Réunion was an overseas department of the French Republic. Britain still held the colony of Mauritius; the high commission territories of Basutoland, Bechuanaland, and Swaziland; the protectorates of Gambia, Zanzibar, Kenya, and the Seychelles; and the Federation of Rhodesia and Nyasaland, made up of the self-governing colony of Southern Rhodesia and the protectorates of Northern Rhodesia and Nyasaland. The Republic of South Africa held South-West Africa, mandated to it in 1921 by the League of Nations. Independence for the British protectorates and the French possessions seemed imminent; most of them already had constitutions and a measure of self-government. Spain and Portugal were not inclined to give up their colonies, and nationalist manifestations, notably the militant movement in Angola, were repressed. The UN was attempting to determine the future status of South-West Africa, which South Africa claimed for its own. The African states are a potent force in the UN, making up about one third of the membership. There were several attempts toward some sort of unity among the new states, but these so far have proved transient or ineffectual. The most pressing problem—the development of the continent's vast resources and the education of its people—was being solved with the help of aid from the UN, the West, and the Soviet bloc nations. See separate articles on the African countries. See also Malcolm Hailey, *An African Survey* (rev. ed., 1957); Heinrich Schiffers, *The Quest for Africa* (Eng. tr., 1958); John Hatch, *Africa, Today—And Tomorrow* (1960); G. H. T. Kimble, *Tropical Africa* (1960); Simon Ottenberg and Phoebe Ottenberg, *Cultures and Societies of Africa* (1960); Walter Fitzgerald, *Africa* (9th ed., 1961); Janheinz Jahn, *Muntu: an Outline of the New African Culture* (1961); Colin Legum, ed., *Africa: a Handbook* (1961); M. J. Herskovits, *The Human Factor in Changing Africa* (1962); G. W. Shepherd, *The Politics of African Nationalism* (1962).

African art, traditional art created by the peoples S of the Sahara. The predominant art forms are masks and figures, which were generally used in religious ceremonies. Established forms had evolved long before the arrival (late 15th cent.) of the Portuguese in Africa, but because of its perishable nature little work survives that is more than 150 years old. Wood—often embellished by clay, shells, beads, ivory, metal, feathers, and shredded raffia— was the dominant material. The discussion here is limited to the works of the peoples of W and Central Africa—the regions richest in indigenous art. *Western Sudan and Guinea Coast.* Here the style of wood carving is highly abstract. Distortion is often used to emphasize features of cultic significance. The figures of the Dogon tribe of central Mali stress the cylindrical shape of the torso. The Bambara of W Mali are famous for their striking wooden head-

Dahomey bronze casting showing tribal chief and entourage.

dresses in the form of stylized antelope heads. The art of the Baga of NW Guinea includes snake carvings, drums supported by small free-standing figures, and spectacular masks. The Poro society of Liberia made ceremonial masks notable for their massiveness, color, and vitality of expression. The Baulé of the Ivory Coast created figurines to house the spirits of the dead or to represent the gods. These have precise renderings in high relief of ornate hairdresses and scarification patterns (see BODY-MARKING). The art of the Guro of the Ivory Coast consists almost entirely of human masks and of weaving pulleys. Guro figures are characterized by slanting eyes and a carved zig-zag design just above the forehead. The southern groups of the Senufo of the Ivory Coast produced an art akin to that of the Baulé, but more simplified and geometric. Senufu masks represent human features with geometric projections and have legs jutting out from each side of the face. The ASHANTI kingdom of Ghana employed (18th and 19th cent.) a system of brass weights based on a unit that was used to weigh gold dust, the state currency. These weights are small figures, many less than 2 in. high, which were cast in the CIRE PERDUE process indigenous to many W African regions. They portray simplified human forms with a spontaneity unusual in African art. The sculptors of Dahomey also cast (16th–19th cent.) figures in brass by the cire-perdue process. Their work is notable for its naturalism and finely chased metal surfaces. Figures are shown in everyday activities. This art was purely aesthetic, and the statues were reserved for the enjoyment of royalty.

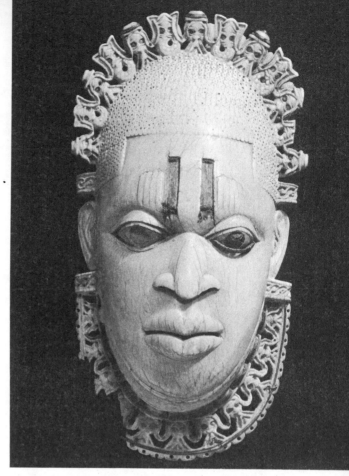

Headpiece, an example of Bambara art.

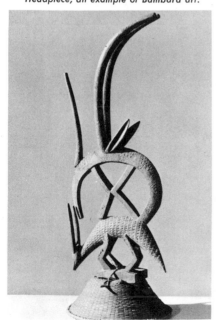

Pectoral ivory mask of the Benin peoples.

Bronze heads from Ife.

Nigeria. The art of southern Nigeria reveals considerable contrast. Yoruba work is often brilliantly polychromed. The world-famous Ife portrait heads in bronze and terra cotta are unique in Africa because of their naturalistic detail, perfection of modeling, and control over the cire perdue process. The art of BENIN arose from the needs of the royal household. It was largely commemorative, ritualistic, and ceremonial in function. Models of human heads were considered to be reincarnations of past kings, or Obas, and held to be divine. Abundant descriptive detail and sharp, precise lines are characteristic of Benin art. The Ibo, Ibibio, Ekoi, and Ijaw of SE Nigeria carved wooden masks for use in their rites and secret societies. Ibo masks were modeled after human skulls, with deep eye sockets, carved exposed teeth, and emaciated faces.

Cameroon. The small tribes of the Cameroon grasslands display a fairly homogenous style. Sculpture is bold in execution and vital in expression. Wood carvings include large house posts, masks, and other ritual objects.

Gabon. Among the Fang tribes, the decorative motif on stringed musical instruments, drums, and spoons emphasizes the human figure, often elongated with smooth surface planes. Some figures are said to act as guardian spirits over ancestors whose bones are kept in boxes. The art of the Bakota tribes consists almost entirely of highly stylized wood and metal figurines that were placed in reliquaries.

The Congo Region. The sculpture of the Bakongo kingdom is usually characterized by naturalism. Each of the ancestor figures seems to be a personalized portrait and reveals details of body decoration and dress. The best-known art works of the Bateke of the W Congo are small fetish figures. These asexual figures stand with arms close to the body in a stiff, frontal pose. The Bapende sculptors of the W Congo give a fluid surface to their ivory pendants, which represent human faces. In the Bushongo kingdom statues of royalty were carved (17th to 19th cent.). The king was shown in a pose of static aloofness, wearing a flat crown and often holding a ritual sword. The Basonge of the central Congo carved small, standing fetish figures and masks, bold in proportion and suggestive of cubism. The Baluba of the SE Congo produced bowls and stools supported by slender figures. Small ivory masks and neck rests were made in the E Congo. The art of the Badjokwe of S Congo and Angola consists of free-standing figures, ceremonial staff heads, masks, and carved stools. The dynamic and aggressive figures are particularly outstanding.

Influence. African art came to European notice c.1905, when artists began to recognize the aesthetic value of African sculpture. Such artists as Vlaminck, Derain, Picasso, and Modigliani were influenced by African art forms. In the United States, fine collections of African art can be found in the Museum of Primitive Art, New York; the Natural History Museum, Chicago; the Peabody Museum, Harvard Univ.; and the Univ. Museum at the Univ. of Pennsylvania. For a description of Africa, see AFRICA. See Robert Goldwater, *Primitivism in Modern Painting* (1938); Paul Wingert, *The Sculpture of Negro Africa* (1950); K. M. Trowell, *Classical African Sculpture* (1954); Eliot Elisofon and William Fagg, *Sculpture of Africa* (1958); *Traditional Art of the African Nations* (with introduction by Robert Goldwater, 1961).

African Methodist Episcopal Church, one of the leading Negro denominations of METHODISM. It was established in 1816 with Richard ALLEN as its first bishop. There are over 1,000,000 members.

African Methodist Episcopal Zion Church, Negro Protestant denomination. It was founded in 1796 by Negro members of the Methodist Episcopal church in New York city and was organized as a national body in 1821. The church operates in the United States, Africa, South America, and the West Indies and maintains Livingstone College in Salisbury, N.C. The membership of the church is c.710,000, making it the third largest Negro body in the United States. See D. H. Bradley, *A History of the A.M.E. Zion Church* (1956).

African Negro literature. The earliest examples of this literature are to be found perhaps in those ancient Moslem religious books written by African Negroes in Swahili and Arabic. A great oral tradition of literature exists in the seemingly inexhaustible folklore of the continent: myths, tales, riddles, and proverbs. Modern African Negro literature developed in areas long in contact with European civilization. It is written in native languages, French, or English. One of the first modern writers was Thomas Mofolo (c.1875–1948), who wrote *Chaka,* a novel in Sesuto (Eng. tr., 1931) about the Zulu chief. Negro writers from the French colonies in Africa made Paris their center. There the periodical *Présence Africaine* provided them with direction. Outstanding among them were the novelist René Maran (1887–), winner of the Goncourt Prize in 1921 for his novel *Batouala* about French Equatorial Africa; Léopold Sédar SENGHOR (1906–) of Senegal, a political and intellectual figure of note as well as poet and essayist; Paul Hazoumé, author of a novel about Dahomey (1937); Camara Laye (1928–), a novelist from Guinea; and Ferdinand Oyono (1928–), a novelist from the Cameroons. Outstanding among the many Africans writing in English are the novelist Peter Abrahams (1919–) of South Africa; Amos Tutuola (1920–), a Nigerian writer; and the South African critic Ezekiel Mphahlele, author of an autobiography entitled *Down Second Avenue* (1959). See Langston Hughes, ed., *An African Treasury* (1960). See also SOUTH AFRICAN LITERATURE.

African Negro music. The music of Africa south of the Sahara exhibits certain characteristics common to the different regions in spite of the great variations which justify the claim that there are as many kinds of music as there are languages. These common traits include the percussive, rhythmic quality of the music, with the distinctive use of two or more rhythms simultaneously; melody, rather than harmony, as the basis of song, as well as the overlapping of antiphonal call and response; improvisation of melody and text; and the production of tone color in song and instrumental music by the use of glissando, rising attack, and falling release. Scholars now define the African scale as diatonic, but this definition is not universally accepted.

Among the many African instruments are drums, rattles, whistles, bells, xylophones, wind instruments, and stringed instruments ranging from the one-stringed groundbow which uses a hole in the ground as resonator to many-stringed harps. The functional nature of the music is seen in the play songs, fishing songs, religious music, and the songs and dances for daily and seasonal activities as well as ceremonial occasions. The Negro is highly susceptible to the influence of other cultures, and European and Arabian elements have been assimilated to such an extent that it is sometimes difficult to determine what elements are native to African music. How much the spiritual of the American Negro is indebted to African music is still a subject of inquiry. See E. M. von Hornbostel, *African Negro Music* (1929); Percival Kirby, *Musical Instruments of the Native Races of South Africa* (1953); A. M. Jones, *Studies in African Music* (2 vols., 1959); Rose Brandel, *The Music of Central Africa* (1961).

Africanus, Sextus Julius (sĕk'stŭs jōōl'yŭs ăfrĭkā'nŭs), fl. 221, Christian historian, resident of Palestine. He wrote a history of the world from the creation to 221 (which was used by Eusebius of Caesarea), letters, and a sort of anthology, mostly of materials on magic.

African violet: see GESNERIA.

Afridis (ăfrē'dēz), Afghan tribe, North-West Frontier region, West Pakistan, near the Khyber Pass. The Afridis often raided trading caravans using the pass, and in the late 19th and early 20th cent. Great Britain dispatched numerous military expeditions to repress them.

Afrikaans (ă"frĭkäns', –känz'), standard language of the South African Boers. It is a Germanic language of the Indo-European family. See LANGUAGE (table).

Afro-Asian bloc, in modern international affairs. Common economic and political problems, as well as a desire for influence in world affairs, have given rise to a large degree of collaboration and joint consultation among the independent nations of Africa and Asia. Their number has greatly increased since the Second World War; between 1945 and 1962 some 40 African and Asian nations gained independence. Their cooperation has become particularly important in the United Nations. From 1950 informal discussions were held and agreements reached on matters of mutual interest by African and Asian members of the UN, but their first formal meeting took place in 1955 at the Bandung Conference. The 29 nations attending represented all the then independent states of Asia and Africa, except for South Africa, North Korea, South Korea, Israel, and Nationalist China, which were not invited. The group agreed to cooperate in opposing colonialism, and to make common cause in the UN. By 1962 the group numbered almost half the membership of the UN. Their influence was particularly important in urging the ending of "colonialism" in Africa and Asia. Thus, the 1960 General Assembly resolution calling for "immediate steps" for the granting of independence to the remaining trust territories and colonies was passed largely through their efforts. In 1961 they succeeded in having the General Assembly establish a Special Committee on Colonialism, to supervise the implementation of the 1960 resolution. In other respects, however, the group was by no means so closely knit. On foreign policy there was marked division between the Communist-aligned nations, the "neutralist" nations, who form the majority of the Afro-Asian bloc, and those nations linked to the Western powers through mutual defense treaties. Further division appeared in 1961, when a meeting of representatives of Ghana, Guinea, Mali, Morocco, and Egypt (UAR) resulted in the formation of the Casablanca group. These nations declared in the strongest terms their opposition to "imperialism," urged full recognition for Algeria, and condemned UN policy in the Republic of the CONGO. More pro-Western in its sympathies was the opposing Monrovia group, made up of Tunisia, Kenya, Liberia, Nigeria, Tanganyika, and most former French colonies of equatorial and W Africa (the latter are themselves known as the Brazzaville group). The nations of the Monrovia group also favored a loose alliance rather than the centralized UNION OF AFRICAN STATES favored by the Casablanca group and formed in 1961.

afterbirth: see PLACENTA.

afterdamp: see DAMP.

Afton (ăf'tŭn). **1** Town (pop. 1,111), extreme NE Okla., E of Bartlesville, in a farm region. The Grand River Dam is nearby. **2** Town (pop. 1,337; alt. c.6,100 ft.), W Wyo., near the Idaho line NNW of Jackson; settled 1895 by Mormons, inc. 1902. It is a trade center for the Star Valley, with flour and lumber mills and plants processing dairy goods. There is a Mormon tabernacle here, and nearby is a Univ. of Wyoming agricultural experiment station.

Afton, river of Ayrshire, SW Scotland. It is the "sweet Afton" of Burns's poem.

Afyonkarahisar (äfyōōn'kä"rähĭsär')[Turkish,=black castle of opium], town (pop. 38,392), capital of Afyon prov., NW Turkey. It is the center of a region growing opium poppies. It is also called Afyon.

Afzelius, Adam (ä'däm äfzä'lēōōs), 1750–1837, Swedish botanist and founder of the Linnaean Institute at Uppsala. He edited the autobiography of Linnaeus and wrote several books on the plants of the Guinea coast.

Afzelius, Arvid August (är'vēd ou'gŭst), 1785–1871, Swedish historian, mythologist, and song writer. He made a notable collection of folk material in *Swedish Folk Tunes from Olden Times* (3 vols., 1814–16). His autobiography was published in 1901.

Ag, chemical symbol of the element SILVER.

Agabus (ăg'ŭ–), prophet who foretold the famine in the time of Claudius Caesar and the imprisonment of Paul. Acts 11.27,28; 21.10,11.

Agade, ancient Mesopotamian city: see AKKAD.

Agadir (ägädēr', ägŭdēr'), city (pop. c.45,000), SW Morocco, port and seaside resort on the Atlantic Ocean. It was the scene of an international incident in 1911. When France was engaged in establishing a protectorate in Morocco, the German gunboat *Panther* appeared in Agadir with the announced intention of protecting German interests. For a time war seemed imminent, but the Germans agreed to drop their demands when France ceded to them a substantial part of the French Congo. In 1960 Agadir was almost completely destroyed by an earthquake.

Agag (ā′găg). **1** King of the Amalekites who was defeated and spared by Saul, but killed by Samuel. 1 Sam. 15. **2** The allusion is not understood in Num. 24.7.

Agagite (ā′gūgīt), a not necessarily ethnical term used of Haman because of his hatred of the Jews. Esther 3.1.

Aga Khan (Aga Sir Sultan Mahomed Shah) (ä′gä khän′), 1877–1957, Moslem leader, b. Bombay, India. Hereditary ruler of the Moslem Ismaili sect, with followers in India, Pakistan, East Africa, and Central Asia, the Aga Khan was born to great power and wealth. He tried to secure Moslem support for British rule in India, particularly by founding (1906) the All-India Moslem League, which he served as president (1909–1914). He was chairman of the British Indian delegation to the imperial conference in London in 1930–31. He also represented India at the Geneva disarmament conference (1932) and in the League of Nations (1932, 1934–37), where he was (1937) president of the general assembly. He was, however, perhaps best known for his fabulous wealth, for his liberal donations to Moslem causes, and for his interest in horse breeding and racing. He early took up residence in Europe, where he died. He named (1957) his

Aga Khan

grandson, Prince Karim (now Aga Khan IV) as his successor. See his memoirs (1954); biography by H. J. Greenwall (1952).

agalloch: see ALOES.

Agamedes: see TROPHONIUS.

Agamemnon (ă″gūmĕm′nŏn), in Greek mythology, leader of the Greek forces in the Trojan War; king of Mycenae (or Argos). He and Menelaus were sons of Atreus and suffered the curse laid upon PELOPS. Agamemnon married CLYTEMNESTRA, and their children were IPHIGENIA, ELECTRA, and ORESTES. To win favorable winds for the ships sailing against Troy, he sacrificed Iphigenia to Artemis and thus incurred the hatred of Clytemnestra. He went on to Troy and there had a quarrel with Achilles (recounted at length in the ILIAD). Agamemnon, deprived of the captive girl Chryseis, stole the captive princess Briseis from Achilles'

Agamemnon orders Iphigenia carried away to be sacrificed.

tent, but was finally compelled to assuage the wrath of Achilles by giving her back. On his return from Troy, Agamemnon was treacherously murdered by Clytemnestra and her lover, Aegisthus. Orestes and Electra to avenge his death were driven reluctantly to kill their mother.

Aga Mohamad Khan or **Agha Mohammed Khan** (both: ägä′ mōhä′mūd kän′), d. 1797, shah of Persia, founder of the Kajar (or Qajar) dynasty. Captured and emasculated by family enemies at the age of five, he grew up with hatred toward the world. He was vigorous and able, but his cruelty is proverbial. He captured and killed (1794) the last ruler of the Zand dynasty and ended his campaign with a wholesale massacre in Kerman. He made himself shah in 1796. Aga Mohamad resisted a Russian invasion and himself invaded (1795) Georgia. He was detested by his people and his murder was not regretted. His nephew Fath Ali succeeded him.

Agana (ägä′nyä), city (pop. 1,642), capital of Guam, on the west coast and ENE of Apra Harbor. It is the largest and most important city on the island. It was completely destroyed in the Second World War, but was rebuilt with U.S. appropriations made in 1946.

Aganippe (ăg″ŭnĭp′ē), in Greek mythology, nymph. Her spring on Mt. Helicon, sacred to the MUSES, gave poetic inspiration to all who drank from it.

Agapemone (ăgŭpĕm′ŭnē) [from Gr.,=abode of love], English religious community of men and women, holding all goods in common. It was founded (c.1850) at the village of Spaxton, Somerset, by Henry James Prince (1811–99), Samuel Starky, and others. Prince and Starky were clergymen who had left (c.1843) the Church of England after Prince claimed that the Holy Ghost had taken up residence in his body. The Agapemonites proclaimed the imminent second coming of Christ. Riotous conditions at the community caused scandal, and after Prince lost a lawsuit brought by two disenchanted followers in 1860 the community slipped from public notice. There was a period (c.1890) of renewed activity when J. H. Smyth-Pigott, who believed himself to be Jesus Christ reincarnated, conducted meetings at an Agapemonite branch establishment in Clapton, London. He succeeded Prince as leader of the sect, which soon vanished. See D. T. McCormick, *Temple of Love* (1962).

Agar (ā′gŭr), the same as HAGAR.

agar (ä′gär, ā′-, ăg′är) [Malay], product obtained from several species of red algae or SEAWEED, chiefly from the Ceylon or Jaffna moss (*Gracilaria lichenoides*) and species of *Gelidium*. Although most agar comes from the Far East, California also is a source of supply. Cooked in water and cooled, agar becomes gelatinous; its chief uses are as a culture medium (particularly for bacteria) and as a laxative, but it serves also as a thickening for soups and sauces, in jellies and ice cream, for clarifying beverages, and for sizing fabrics. It is conveniently marketed in the form of dried flakes.

Agasias (ăgā′shĕăs), 1st cent. B.C., Greek sculptor, commonly known as Agasias of Ephesus; son of Dositheus. His BORGHESE WARRIOR is in the Louvre.

Agassiz, Alexander (ăg′ŭsē), 1835–1910, American naturalist and industrialist, b. Neuchâtel, Switzerland; son of Louis Agassiz, stepson of Elizabeth Agassiz. He came to the United States in 1849 and studied at Harvard, receiving degrees in engineering (B.S., 1857) and natural history (B.S., 1862). Throughout his life he was connected in various capacities with Harvard. In 1871 he consolidated the Calumet and Hecla copper mines on Lake Superior and, as president, developed the combined interests with great success. He adopted safety and welfare measures. He spent his own wealth in the interests of science—chiefly in endowments to Harvard and to the Museum of Comparative Zoology founded there through his father's efforts. He also financed expeditions and publications of his own research. In 1877 he began his oceanographic explorations, including detailed observations of the Pacific and the Caribbean. Noting that the deep-sea animals of both are similar, he suggested that the Caribbean was a bay of the Pacific that had been cut off in the Cretaceous period by the rise of the Panama isthmus. He also developed a theory of the formation of coral atolls that differed from that of Darwin. His chief work is *Revision of the Echini* (2 vols., 1872–74). See study by his son G. R. Agassiz (1913).

Agassiz, Elizabeth Cabot Cary, 1822–1907, American author and educator, b. Boston. In 1850 she married Louis Agassiz. She went with him on expeditions to Brazil (1865–66) and along the Atlantic and Pacific coasts of the Americas (1871–72). She was influential in the founding of Radcliffe College, which she served until 1903 as its first president. Her writings include *A Journey in Brazil* (in collaboration with her husband, 1868); a biography of her husband (1885); and, with her stepson Alexander Agassiz, *Seaside Studies in Natural History* (1865). See study by L. A. Paton (1919); Louise Tharp, *Adventurous Alliance* (1959).

Agassiz, Louis (Jean Louis Rodolphe Agassiz) (zhä′ lwē′ rōdōlf′), 1807–73, Swiss-American zoologist and geologist, b. Fribourg, Switzerland. He studied at the universities of Zurich, Erlangen (Ph.D., 1829), Heidelberg, and Munich (M.D., 1830). Agassiz practiced medicine briefly, but his real interest lay in scientific research. In 1831 he went to Paris, where he became a close friend of Alexander von Humboldt and studied fossil fishes under the guidance of Cuvier. In 1832 he became professor of natural history at the Univ. of Neuchâtel, which he made a noted center for scientific study. Among his publications during this period were *Recherches sur les poissons fossiles* (5 vols. and atlas, 1833–44), a work of historic importance in the field (although his system of classification by scales has been discarded); studies of fossil echinoderms and mollusks; and *Étude sur les glaciers* (1840), one of the first expositions of glacial movements and deposits, based on his own observations and measurements. Agassiz came to the United States in 1846 and two years later accepted the professorship of zoology and geology at Harvard. His first wife died in Germany in 1848, and in 1850 in Cambridge he married Elizabeth Cabot Cary. In the United States he was primarily a teacher and very popular lecturer. Emphasizing advanced and original work, he gave major impetus to the study of science direct from nature and influenced a generation of American scientists. His extensive research expeditions included one along the Atlantic and Pacific coasts of the Americas from Boston to California (1871–72). His *Contributions to the Natural History of the United States* (4 vols., 1857–62) includes his famous "Essay on Classification," an extension of the theory of RECAPITULATION to geologic time. Despite his own evidences for evolution, Agassiz opposed Darwinism and believed that new species could arise only through the intervention of God. See biographies by Jules Marcou (including letters, 1896), J. D. Teller (1947), and Edward Lurie (1960); Lane Cooper, *Louis Agassiz as a Teacher* (1917).

Agassiz, Lake, c.700 mi. long and 250 mi. wide, of the Pleistocene epoch, formed by the melting of the continental ice sheet some 10,000 years ago over much of the present NW Minnesota, NE North Dakota, S Manitoba, and SW Ontario. It was named in 1879 in memory of Louis Agassiz for his contributions to the theory of the glacial epoch. Lake Traverse, Big Stone Lake, and the Minnesota river are in the channel of the original outlet (the prehistoric River Warren) to the south, but as the ice completely disappeared the water drained E into Lake Superior and then N into Hudson Bay, leaving Lakes Winnipeg, Manitoba, and Winnipegosis, Red Lake, Lake of the Woods, and many smaller lakes. The bed of the old lake, the Red River valley, has become an important wheat-growing region because of its rich, deep soil. See Warren Upham, *The Glacial Lake Agassiz* (1895; U.S. Geological Survey, Monographs, Vol. XXV).

agate, cryptocrystalline variety of QUARTZ banded in two or more different colors, extensively used as a semiprecious gem stone and in the manufacture of delicate balances. The banded appearance owes its origin to the fact that agates are built up by the slow deposition of silica from solution into cavities in older rock—often igneous rocks. The layers differ in porosity, and the stones can be artificially stained so as to produce combinations of color more vivid and pleasing than are found in the natural state. The cutting and staining of agates has

Agate

long had its center at Idar and Oberstein in Germany. Important sources of the stones are Brazil, Uruguay, India, and the United States (in the Lake Superior region and in some Western states). The moss agate or mocha stone is so called because it contains a dendritic inclusion resembling moss. See also CHALCEDONY; ONYX; SARD.

Agatha, Saint (ăg′ūthū), 3d cent., Sicilian virgin, martyred under Decius. She is mentioned in the Canon of the Mass and is invoked against outbreaks of fire. Symbols: palm and pincers. Feast: Feb. 5.

Agatharchus (ăg″ūthär′kūs), 5th cent. B.C., Greek painter of the Athenian school, b. Samos. He is credited with important discoveries in the application of shading and perspective and is said to have been the first painter of scenery for tragedies.

Agathocles (ūgă′thūklēz), 361?–289 B.C., Greek tyrant of Syracuse (317–289 B.C.). He warred with the other cities of Sicily and with Carthage. He undertook a campaign in Africa (310–307? B.C.) and threatened Carthage. Suffering ill fortune, Agathocles returned to Syracuse and reigned over E Sicily after assuming the title of king. He was known for his great cruelty.

Agathon (ăg′ūthŏn), c.450–c.400 B.C., Athenian tragedian. Plato's *Symposium* has as its scene the celebration of Agathon's first dramatic victory. Fragments of his work survive.

Agave: see PENTHEUS.

agave: see AMARYLLIS.

Agawam (ăg′ūwäm). **1** Town (pop. 15,718), SW Mass., on the Connecticut river below West Springfield; settled 1635, inc. 1855. Leather goods and machinery are produced. **2** Former name of IPSWICH, Mass.

Agdistis: see ATTIS and CYBELE.

age, in classical mythology, a period of the world's history, especially as systematized by Hesiod and Ovid. These ages were the Golden Age, ruled by CRONUS (Saturn), a period of serenity, peace, and eternal spring; the Silver Age, ruled by ZEUS (Jupiter), less happy than the preceding, with luxury prevailing; the Bronze Age, a period of strife; the Iron Age, the present, a time of travail, when

justice and piety are no more. Hesiod had also a Heroic Age before the Iron Age; in it the Trojan War was fought. See ERA.

Agee (ăg′ē-ē), father of Shammah, a mighty man. 2 Sam. 23.11.

Agee, James (ā′gē), 1909–55, American writer, educated at Harvard. He was a writer for *Fortune* magazine, a film critic for *Time* and for *The Nation*, and a script-writer. His works, many of which were published posthumously, include a prose commentary, *Let Us Now Praise Famous Men* (1941); a novel, *A Death in the Family* (1957), and a collection of his reviews, comments, and scripts, *Agee on Film* (2 vols., 1958–60). His anguish as a writer and as a man is poignantly expressed in the *Letters of James Agee to Father Flye* (1962).

Ageladas (ăj″ūlā′dūs), c.540–c.460 B.C., Greek sculptor of the Argive school, famous for his statues of gods and Olympian athletes. A popular tradition, discredited by many authorities, names him as the teacher of the great sculptors, Polycletus the elder, Phidias, and Myron.

Agen (äzhĕ′), town (estimated pop. 32,593), capital of Lot-et-Garonne dept., SW France, in Guienne, on the Garonne river. The center of a fruitgrowing region, it has several canneries. Originally a Gallic settlement, it became under the Carolingians the capital of the county of Agenois. It passed (1154) to England with the rest of Aquitaine. It was reconquered in the Hundred Years War and incorporated into the province of Guienne. Agen is noted for its numerous Gothic churches.

Agency for International Development, Federal agency created by Congress (Sept., 1961) to consolidate the foreign-aid programs of the United States. The agency incorporated the International Cooperation Administration, the Development Loan Fund, and related agencies such as the Office of Food for Peace. AID was organized into four divisions—one for each major underdeveloped area—the Far East, the Near East and South Asia, Latin America, and Africa and Europe. AID stressed long-run development goals financed through long-term loans and encouraged the investment of private capital through liberal investment guarantees. Countries applying for loans were required to show that they had made effective use of their human and material resources and had undertaken policies such as land reform so as to insure that AID benefits would reach the populace as rapidly as possible.

Agenor (ūjē′–), in Greek mythology. **1** King of Tyre, father of Cadmus and Europa. When Europa disappeared, he sent Cadmus and his other sons in search of her. **2** Trojan hero, son of Antenor.

agent-provocateur: see ESPIONAGE.

age of consent, the age at which the law provides that persons are bound by their words and acts. There are different ages at which one acquires legal capacity to consent to marriage, to choose a guardian, to conclude a contract, and the like. For marriage, the age is generally higher for males than for females. Age of consent also means the age below which consent of the female to sexual intercourse is not a defense to a charge of RAPE. Under common law this age was 10; state statutes in the United States generally set it between 13 and 18. See also CONSENT.

Ageratum (Ageratum houstonianum).

ageratum (ăj″ūrā′tŭm, ŭjĕr′ŭ–) [Gr.,=unaging], any plant of the genus *Ageratum*, tropical American annuals of the COMPOSITE family. The commonly cultivated species is the Mexican *A. houstonianum*, with thick terminal clusters of blue flowers. The similar mistflower, a *Eupatorium* (see BONESET), is a perennial sometimes called hardy ageratum.

Agesander: see LAOCOÖN.

Agesilaus II (ŭjĕ″sĭlā′ŭs), c.444–360 B.C., king of Sparta. After the death of Agis I (398? B.C.), he was brought to power by Lysander, whom he promptly ignored. After the Peloponnesian War the Greek cities in Asia Minor had not been ceded to Persia despite Sparta's promises, and in 396 Agesilaus went there to oppose the Persian satraps TISSAPHERNES and PHARNABAZUS by attacking them. He managed to rout Tissaphernes, but Persian naval power drove him back to Greece, where he won (394) a hollow victory over the Thebans and their allies at Coronea, but could not reestablish Spartan hegemony. By the King's Peace (or Peace of Antalcidas) in 386, the cities of Asia Minor were ceded to Persia. Thebes and Athens entered an alliance against Sparta, and war followed. When Agesilaus deliberately excluded Thebes from the peace talks, Thebes renewed the war and the Theban general Epaminondas won (371) a resounding victory at LEUCTRA. Sparta did not recover. Agesilaus took Spartan mercenaries to Asia Minor and Egypt and died on the way back. His rule had seen the ruin of Sparta, though he was lauded by his contemporaries, notably Xenophon.

Aggeus (ăgē′ŭs), Vulgate form of HAGGAI.

agglutination: see INFLECTION.

Agha Mohammed Khan: see AGA MOHAMAD KHAN.

Aghri Dagh: see ARARAT.

Aghrim: see AUGHRIM.

agilawood: see ALOES.

Agincourt (ă′jĭnkôrt, Fr. äzhĕkōōr′), modern Fr. *Azincourt* (äzĕkōōr′), village (pop. 275), Pas-de-Calais dept., N France, near Arras. Here, on Oct. 25, 1415, HENRY V of England defeated a much larger French army in the Hundred Years War. His success, which was due mainly to the superiority of the masses of English longbow men over the heavily armored French knights, demonstrated the obsolescence of the methods of warfare proper to

the age of chivalry. The battle is the central scene of Shakespeare's drama *Henry V*.

aging: see GERIATRICS.

Agis I (ā′jĭs), d. 398? B.C., king of Sparta. He was the Spartan general at MANTINEA (418 B.C.) during the PELOPONNESIAN WAR. Advised by ALCIBIADES, he quickly invaded Attica and established a post there. Later he quarreled with his adviser. Agis aided Lysander in the final Spartan victories of the war. He is sometimes called Agis II.

Agis II, d. 331 B.C., king of Sparta. He led a revolt of Peloponnesian cities against Alexander the Great, who was in Asia. The rebels were crushed, and Agis was killed at Megalopolis. His death ended Greek revolts against Alexander. He is sometimes called Agis III.

Agis III, d. c.240 B.C., king of Sparta. He sought by reform and by returning to the constitution of Lycurgus to revive dying Spartan power. He failed and was murdered. He is sometimes called Agis IV.

Aglaia: see GRACES.

Aglipay, Gregorio (grägō′rēō äglēpĭ′), 1860–1940, Philippine clergyman. A priest who joined the revolutionary forces of Emilio Aguinaldo, he was excommunicated (1902). He took his followers from the Roman Catholic Church to found the Philippine Independent Church. Bishop Aglipay

The Battle of Agincourt *(14th-century miniature painting).*

attracted many followers, said to number more than 1,000,000. His church, which retained many of the forms of the Roman Church, discarded celibacy and confession. Later it established friendly relations with the Unitarians. After Aglipay's death dissension shook the organization. In 1961, however, full communion was established between the Philippine Independent Church and the American Episcopal Church. Aglipay was defeated by Manuel Quezon in the presidential election of 1935.

Agnes, Saint, 4th cent., virgin martyr. A noble Roman girl, she was martyred at 13 after rejecting a

Saint Agnes, *painting by Andrea del Sarto.*

well-born suitor. She is commemorated in the Canon of the Mass. On her feast two lambs are blessed and from their wool are made the pallia sent by the pope to archbishops. Feast: Jan. 21.

Agnes Scott College: see DECATUR, Ga.

Agnew, David Hayes (ăg'nū), 1818–92, American surgeon, b. Lancaster co., Pa., M.D. Univ. of Pennsylvania, 1838. He practiced in Philadelphia and was professor of surgery at the Univ. of Pennsylvania. He attended President Garfield at the time of his assassination.

Agnew, Spiro Theodore, 1918–, Vice President of the United States (1969–), b. Baltimore, Md., grad. Univ. of Baltimore Law School, 1947. When Agnew's father, Theodore Spiro Anagnostopolous,. came to the United States from Greece in 1897, he shortened the family name. During the Second World War, Agnew served in the army for four years. In the 1950's he was active in local politics.

In 1962 he was elected to a four-year term as executive of Baltimore County. During this period, he secured passage of an ordinance barring discrimination in some public accommodations. Agnew was elected governor of Maryland in 1966. He was the fifth Republican governor of that state in 180 years. As governor, he signed the first statewide open-housing law below the Mason-Dixon Line. He was selected by Richard M. Nixon as his running mate in 1968 and was elected Vice President on the Republican ticket.

Agni: see HINDUISM.

agnosticism (ăgnŏs'tĭsĭzŭm), form of skepticism which holds that metaphysical positions cannot be logically proved or disproved. Among prominent agnostics have been Herbert Spencer, T. H. Huxley (who coined the word *agnostic*), and Auguste Comte. Kant was an agnostic who argued that belief in divinity can rest only on faith. Agnosticism is not to be confused with atheism, which asserts that there is no God.

Agnus Dei (ăg'nŭs dē'ī, än'yŏŏs dā'ē) [Latin], the Lamb of God, i.e., Jesus Christ. The lamb of the PASSOVER sacrifice is said to prefigure the crucifixion. Isaiah calls the expected Messiah the Lamb of God, and Jesus is met by John the Baptist with the words, "Behold, the Lamb of God, who takes away the sins of the world." In the MASS the Agnus Dei is the precommunion prayer. It is usually the final movement of sung masses. In Anglican worship it is sung during communion in English. In iconography a lamb with halo and cross is called an Agnus Dei.

agora (ă'gŭrŭ) [Gr.,=market], the public square or market place of a Greek city. It was usually in a readily accessible part of the city and served as a general meeting ground. It was often surrounded by the public buildings, such as the royal palace,

Madonna and Child *by Agostino di Duccio.*

the law courts, the assembly house, and the jail. A favorite architectural device was the colonnade surrounding the agora. The American School at Athens began to excavate the Athenian agora in 1931, and the stoa of Attalus has been restored as a museum. The agora was quite similar to the Roman FORUM.

Agoracritus (ăg"ōrăk'rĭtŭs), fl. 5th cent. B.C., Athenian sculptor born on the island of Paros, said to have been the favorite pupil of Phidias. His best-known work was the colossal *Nemesis* at Rhamnus in Attica, erroneously ascribed by some to Phidias himself. Fragments of this statue and its pedestal are in the British Museum and in the national museum in Athens.

Agostino di Duccio (ägōstē'nō dē dōō'chō), b. 1418, d. after 1481, Florentine sculptor who worked mainly in other parts of Italy. He carved marble narrative reliefs for the façade of the cathedral at Modena, decorated portions of the so-called Tempio Malatestiana at Rimini, and worked on the façade of San Bernardino at Perugia. Somewhat awkward in his rendering of anatomy, Agostino nevertheless developed a lively style. There are numerous charming reliefs by him of the *Madonna and Child* (Opera del Duomo, Florence; Louvre; National Gall. of Art, Washington, D.C.).

Agoult, Marie Catherine Sophie (de Flavigny), comtesse d' (märē' kätürēn' sōfē' dù flävēnyē' kōtĕs' dägōō'). pseud. **Daniel Stern**, 1805–76, French author, b. Frankfurt, Germany. She was the mistress of Liszt, by whom she had three children. A daughter, Cosima, became the wife of Hans von Bülow and later of Richard Wagner. Daniel Stern's works include autobiographical romances and social and political writings. She is the "Arabella" of George Sand's *Lettres d'un voyageur*. See the autobiographical *Mes Souvenirs, 1806–1833* (1877).

agouti (ùgōō'tē), name applied to rabbit-sized rodents of the family Dasyproctidae, found in Central and South America and in the West Indies. They have slender limbs with five front and three hind toes, rudimentary tails, and coarse rough hair which varies from reddish to dark brown with the species. Agoutis are nocturnal forest dwellers; they eat leaves, roots, nuts, fruits, and sugar cane. They are good swimmers. *Agouti* is occasionally used instead of *Cuniculus* as the generic name of the related paca or spotted CAVY.

Agra (ä'grù, ăg'rù), city (pop. 333,530), Uttar Pradesh state, N India, on the Jumna river. An important rail junction and commercial center, it is noted for its shoes, glass products, handicrafts, carpets, and above all for its historic architecture. The present city was established (1566) by AKBAR and was long a Mogul capital. In the reign of Shah Jehan (1628–58), the magnificent TAJ MAHAL was built. Other notable historic buildings are Akbar's fort, the Pearl Mosque, and the Great Mosque (within the fort). Agra's importance diminished after the Mogul court moved to Delhi in 1658. During the decline of the Mogul empire, the city frequently changed rulers until 1803 when it was annexed by the British. From 1835 to 1858 it was the capital of the Northwestern Provs. With Agra College (founded 1823) and a medical school, it is a major educational center of N India.

The Taj Mahal at Agra.

Agra and Oudh, United Provinces of, India: see UNITED PROVINCES.

Agram: see ZAGREB.

Agramonte, Arístides (ärē'stēdĕs ägrämōn'tā), 1869–1931, Cuban physician and pathologist, M.D. Columbia, 1892. A member of the medical corps of the U.S. army, he was appointed pathologist on the Commission on Yellow Fever in Havana, with Walter REED and James CARROLL, in 1900. He was professor of bacteriology and experimental pathology at the Univ. of Havana. Shortly before his death he undertook the organization of a department of tropical medicine at Louisiana State Univ.

Agramonte, Ignacio (ēgnä'syō), 1841–73, Cuban revolutionist. He played an important part in the Ten Years War. He became (1869) an official of the revolutionary government, but, disagreeing with Carlos Manuel de CÉSPEDES, resigned. For a time commander in chief of the revolutionary forces, he died in battle.

Agouti

87

Agrapha of Jesus (ăg′rū̇fû̇) [Gr.,=not written], sayings attributed to Jesus not found in the Gospels. There are quotations in the New Testament outside the Gospels (e.g., Acts 20.35), and in early Christian literature there are some Agrapha from oral tradition. Thus the papyri found at OXY-RHYNCHUS have given some new Agrapha. Many are probably PSEUDEPIGRAPHA, i.e., ascribed to Jesus with false intent.

agrarian laws, in ancient Rome, the laws regulating the disposition of public lands (*ager publicus*). It was the practice of Rome to confiscate part of the land of conquered cities and states, and this was made public land. So long as this remained public land, it was occupied by tenants who paid rent, usually in kind, to the state. From the earliest times the patricians gained the lion's share in the assignment of public lands for occupation, and the holding of public lands tended always in Italy to become the exclusive prerogative of the wealthy. There was also a tendency to consider land long occupied as real property of the occupier. The agrarian laws resulted from the continued efforts of the poorer classes to gain, by alienation or reallotment, some share in the public lands. Since these lands were occupied without lease, the strictly legal aspects were not difficult; but inasmuch as most agrarian legislation challenged the lucrative privilege of the powerful of retaining the lands they held, the agrarian laws were often flagrantly disobeyed or calmly ignored. In 486 B.C. Spurius CASSIUS VISCELLINUS tried to pass a law assigning some new lands in Gaul to the poor of Rome and Latium, but Roman jealousy prevented its passage. The most famous of early agrarian laws were the Licinian Rogations (367 B.C.) of C. LICINIUS CALVUS STOLO, which limited strictly the amount of land any citizen could hold and the number of sheep and cattle he could pasture on public land. These laws fell into desuetude. About 233 B.C., C. Flaminius succeeded in assigning some public lands to poor citizens. The next serious attempt to rectify an increasingly difficult situation was the Sempronian Law of 133 B.C. devised by Ti. Sempronius Gracchus (see GRACCHI). This reenacted the provisions of the Licinian Rogations and added to the maximum allowance an extra amount for each son. The occupants were to be reduced to the legal maximum and the surplus given to the poor. The occupants were to receive in compensation full title to the land they retained. A commission was set up to execute the law, but the senate by its obstructionist tactics weakened the commission, thus emasculating the law. In 123 B.C., Caius Gracchus revived the Sempronian Law, but this time the senate ruined the reform by allowing the new tenants to sell their new land, which the wealthy bought up. From time to time newly acquired lands would be assigned to the poor, but as a rule they simply passed into the hands of the wealthy landholders. In the 1st cent. B.C. there were several assignments of public lands to veterans in Italy as well as on the borders of the empire. The wholesale confiscation and reassignment of private lands by Sulla (82 B.C.) and Octavian and Antony (43 B.C.) were called agrarian laws. The first step in the final collapse of the democratic effort which had resulted in the agrarian laws was the edict of

Domitian (A.D. c.82) assigning the title of public lands in Italy to those who held them. The poorer classes were now confirmed in a dependency on the powerful which foreshadowed the greater dependency of FEUDALISM.

agrarian reform. In its narrowest and traditional conception agrarian or land reform is confined to the redistribution of property in land; in its widest and modern sense it includes other related changes in agricultural institutions, such as credit, taxation, rents, and cooperatives. Reform of the conditions for land tenure has been one of the recurring themes in history. The history of the Greek city-states is filled with struggles between landowners and the landless. The land reform issue erupted into violence several times in Rome's history and was a major part of the Gracchian AGRARIAN LAWS. The Middle Ages saw many peasant rebellions triggered by demands for land reform; among the more famous were the Peasants' Revolt in England led by John Ball and Wat Tyler in 1381, and the German PEASANTS' WAR of 1524–26. In the 20th cent. the advent of socialist and communist ideologies, and the seizure of power in Russia by the Communist leader, Lenin, added a new dimension to the concept of agrarian reform. The total socialization of agriculture (i.e., the ownership of all land by the state, partly through state farming, but mainly through collective farming under state control), is regarded by the Communists as vital to the completion of COMMUNISM. A major element in the success of the Russian Revolution was the great land hunger among the peasantry, who formed 80 percent of the population. A few hours after he seized power, Lenin published his decree (1917) declaring all land state property. The landed estates belonging to the nobility and gentry were seized by peasants, and until 1929 there were approximately 25,000,000 peasant holdings. Communist propaganda urging the collectivization of farms had little effect, and, under Stalin, collectivization had to be enforced at the cost of much bloodshed. After the Second World War most of the countries of Eastern Europe under Russian domination experienced similar agrarian reforms. Large landed estates, operated by laborers whose social and economic status was little better than that of serfs, were broken up and redistributed, with a maximum size of 20 to 30 hectares imposed. Following the pattern established in Russia, however, this step toward individual small holdings was only a prelude to the introduction of compulsory collectivization, the ultimate goal of Communist land reform. The same action was taken by the Chinese Communist regime after it acquired power in 1949. Following promises made to the peasantry during the civil wars, the regime expropriated and annihilated the landowning class and distributed land to the peasants, farm laborers, and tenants, as well as gradually developing cooperatives and marketing and distributing agencies. Again, this was only the first step toward collectivization. By 1959, the Chinese Communists had carried out the most thoroughgoing collectivization in history. Agriculture was completely communized or organized into large communes throughout the country; every aspect of the peasant's life was regulated. In the noncommunist world pressure for land reform is most powerful in the underdeveloped areas, particularly in Asia and Latin America. In Asia, especially in densely populated areas such as India, Pakistan, Ceylon, and Japan, agitation has been mainly for redistribution among landless laborers, for security of tenure, and for the elimination of middlemen rent receivers, oppressive rents, and usurious interest. A successful land reform program redressing such grievances was carried out in Japan during the post-war period, largely under the supervision of the Supreme Allied Command. In India and Pakistan similar programs of agrarian reform have been instituted. In Latin America land reform is a major problem. The agrarian structure in Latin America consists of enormous concentrations of land in relatively few units (*latifundios*) in few hands; roughly 90 percent of the land belongs to 10 percent of the population. Because of this degree of concentration, greater than that of any other world region of comparable size, there is a growing demand for expropriation and redistribution. Ownership is often of the absentee type and laborers are often in the position of being little more than serfs. Although the revolution in Mexico resulted in a land reform (1917), the program of redistribution of land to peasants is still only partially completed. A land reform law also followed the Bolivian revolution of 1952, but by the end of 1960 only 10 to 13 percent of the land had been redistributed. By 1963 one of the most complete agrarian reforms in Latin America was that of the Castro regime in Cuba, where land reform was one of the main platforms of the revolution. Nearly all the large holdings subject to expropriation were taken over by the powerful National Institute for Land Reform (INRA), which is responsible not only for administering land reform, but for planning and directing all agricultural policy. The great bulk of the land taken over by INRA has not been distributed to the peasants, but is being managed by the officials of INRA or by army personnel. See COLLECTIVE FARM. See United Nations, *Land Tenure, Land Reform: Defects in Agrarian Structure as Obstacles to Economic Development* (1951); Kenneth Parsons, ed., *Land Tenure* (1956); James Maddox, *Mexican Land Reform* (1957); Ronald Dore, *Land Reform in Japan* (1959); Clarence Senior, *Land Reform and Democracy* (1959); Kuo-chün Chao, *Economic Planning and Organization in Mainland China* (1960); Erich Jacoby, *Agrarian Unrest in South-East Asia* (2d ed., 1961).

Agricola (Cneius Julius Agricola) (ŭgrĭ′kŭlʉ), A.D. c.37–A.D. 93, Roman general, the conqueror of Britain. After a distinguished military and political career (partly in Britain), he was made consul (A.D. 77) and was governor (A.D. 78?–A.D. 85?) of Britain. He pacified most of the island, conquering North Wales and advancing far into Scotland. He also circumnavigated the island. An enlightened governor, he sought to Romanize Britain without harshness or oppression. As portrayed in the biography by his son-in-law, Tacitus, Agricola was the finest exemplar of the old Roman virtues in his day. See A. R. Burn, *Agricola and Roman Britain* (1953).

Agricola, Georg (gä′ôrk), Latinized from **Georg Bauer** (bou′ûr), 1494–1555, German physician and scientist, known as the father of mineralogy. He was a pioneer in physical geology and the first to classify minerals scientifically. His celebrated work *De re metallica* (1556) was a standard in metallurgy and mining for over a century and was translated into English (1912) by Herbert C. Hoover and Lou H. Hoover.

Agricola, Johann or **Johannes** (yō′hän, yōhä′nŭs), c.1494–1566, German Protestant minister, whose family name was Schnitter (originally Schneider). He was born at Eisleben and is sometimes called Magister Islebius. He was early associated with Martin Luther and was active in the founding of Protestantism. In 1536 he espoused antinomianism, thus breaking with Luther. He was court preacher in Brandenburg and helped draw up the Augsburg Interim. Agricola also made a collection of German proverbs.

Agricola, Rudolphus, 1443–85, Dutch humanist, whose real name was Roelof Huysman. He opposed scholasticism and spread the culture of the Renaissance throughout Germany.

Agricultural Adjustment Administration (AAA), U.S. government agency established (1933) in the Dept. of Agriculture under the Agricultural Adjustment Act of 1933 as part of F. D. Roosevelt's New Deal program. An administrator and six regional directors were appointed. Its purpose was to help farmers by reducing production of staple crops, thus raising farm prices and changing the agricultural pattern from overproduction of staples to more diversified farming. Farmers were offered contracts, by which they were given benefit payments in return for limiting acreage given to staple crops; in the case of cotton and tobacco coercive taxes forced (1934–35) farmers to cut the amounts that they marketed. The curtailment, along with severe droughts, helped to push farm prices up. In 1936 the Supreme Court declared important sections of the act invalid because they infringed upon the powers of the states. Congress promptly adopted (1936) the Soil Conservation and Domestic Allotment Act, which encouraged conservation by paying benefits for planting soil-building crops instead of staple crops, thus seeking to attain the chief end of the earlier act; other conservation practices were also encouraged. Business recession and bumper crops sent farm prices tumbling in 1937, and the Agricultural Adjustment Act of 1938 —declared valid by the Supreme Court in 1940— established the "ever-normal granary"; the AAA was empowered in years of good crops to make loans to farmers on staple-crop yields and store the surplus produce, to release it later in years of low yield, thus trying to establish stable prices. Soil conservation was continued and farmers could by two-thirds vote adopt compulsory marketing quotas (as they did for cotton and tobacco). In the Second World War, the AAA turned its attention to increasing food production for war needs. In 1942 it was renamed the Agricultural Adjustment Agency and was included in the Food Production Administration. In 1945 its functions were taken over by the Production and Marketing Administration. See E. G. Nourse and others, *Three Years of the Agricultural Adjustment Administration* (1937); G. S. Shepherd, *Agricultural Price Policy* (2d ed., 1947).

agricultural subsidies, financial assistance to farmers through government sponsored price-support programs. Since the 1930s most industrialized countries have developed active agricultural price-support policies to reduce the instability of farm prices and to raise farm income; the programs vary considerably from country to country. In food-importing countries, such as those of Great Britain and Europe, agricultural price-support programs are also aimed at encouraging home production to make the economies more self-sufficient. In food-exporting countries, such as the United States and Canada, agricultural subsidy programs are used primarily to increase farm income by raising the long-term level of prices above free-market levels. In the United States the Federal government first assisted agriculture directly in the 1920s. After the First World War, during which farmers had been encouraged to increase production, war-time levels of production were maintained, resulting in an over-supply which caused a disastrous collapse of prices. In Congress a nonpartisan farm bloc attempted to promote legislation favorable to farmers. The Agricultural Credits Act (1923) expanded Federal credit available to farmers for intermediate loans, but this did not solve the problem. Although President Coolidge vetoed the McNary-Haugen Bills (1927, 1928), which featured price fixing of products and direct subsidies, the situation of the farmers had so worsened by 1929, even before the onset of the depression, that President Hoover was forced to sign the Agricultural Marketing Act (1929), initiating a program of direct aid to agriculture. The act established a Federal Farm Board with a fund of $500 million to further farming co-operatives and to set up stabilization boards, which by their purchases on the open market were to fix the prices of grain and cotton. The purchases of the Farm Board, however, encouraged farmers to raise still larger crops in expectation of higher prices; the Farm Board failed and sold out its holdings at a loss of $200 million. The Agricultural Adjustment Act of 1933, one of the first pieces of legislation passed in the New Deal program, attempted to control farm prices, partly through the novel mechanism of reducing and controlling the supply of basic crops. Previous attempts to raise farm prices—such as the Farm Board had failed because of the difficulty in controlling supply. Through the AGRICULTURAL ADJUSTMENT ADMINISTRATION in the Department of Agriculture, the Secretary of Agriculture was empowered to fix marketing quotas for major farm products, to take surplus products off the market, and to cut the production of staple crops by offering producers payments for voluntarily reducing their acreage and the size of their crops. It was hoped that these measures would not only provide farmers with immediate relief in the form of cash payments but would increase the prices for their products by reducing their surpluses. The program was a success; acreages were reduced and prices steadily increased. Between 1932 and 1937 the prices for major farm products increased by approximately 85 percent. In 1936 the act was invalidated by the Supreme Court, which, however, upheld a new Agricultural Adjustment Act, passed in 1938. The new act, besides reenacting the old program, added Federal crop insurance against natural disaster. As in the earlier act, the goal was the establishment of the principle of parity, by which the level of price support is determined. Parity prices are computed by complex formulas prescribed by law which give to farm products the same buying power which they had enjoyed in a selected period (usually 1910–14), when prices received and paid by farmers were considered to be in good balance. From 1941 to 1948, during and just after the Second World War, price support increased in importance, supports being used as an incentive to increased farm production. By 1949 the agriculture of war-devastated Europe and Asia had recovered to a considerable extent, and demand for American farm products declined considerably. In the meantime, however, crop production in the United States had increased enormously, with the result that farm-commodity prices dropped, surpluses began to build up, and increased government activity became necessary. The Agricultural Act of 1948, which replaced war-time controls, maintained rigid support levels for the basic commodities. The Agricultural Act of 1949 went even further, retaining mandatory supports on basic products and providing mandatory support at flexible levels for a new list of nonbasic products. Since then surpluses have increased, largely through technical improvements which allow increased yields per acre. By 1960 the estimated value of government-held surplus farm products was over $9 billion. The estimated cost of handling and storage alone exceeds $1 billion annually. Support expended on crops in the 1961 fiscal year amounted to over $3 billion. Subsidies to maintain prices, once introduced, have proved extremely difficult to end. Representatives of the farm states have fought for their continuation despite the high prices for farm commodities and the growing surpluses. Until 1952 neither of the two major parties opposed subsidies and high parity prices, but after 1954, under pressure of mounting criticism, rigid price supports were partially relaxed. Serious questions continue to be raised about the price support program. Farm surpluses have been used as a form of foreign aid since the enactment of the Agricultural Trade Development Act of 1954. See O. B. Jesness, *Readings in Agricultural Policy* (1947); T. W. Shultz, *The Production and Welfare of Agriculture* (1949); Geoffrey Shepherd, *Agricultural Price and Income Policy* (3d ed., 1953); Karl Fox, *The Contribution of Farm Price-Support Programs to General Economic Stability* (1954); M. R. Benedict, *Agricultural Policy under Economic Development* (1956); Willard Cochrane, *Farm Prices, Myth and Reality* (1958); Wayne Dexter, *What Makes Farmer's Prices?* (1959); Charles Hardin, ed., *Agricultural Policy, Politics·and the Public Interest* (1960).

agriculture. In its narrowest sense, agriculture is the cultivation of fields; more broadly, it is the science of producing crops and livestock from the natural resources of the earth. The primary aim of agriculture is to cause the land to produce more abundantly and at the same time to protect it from deterioration and misuse. The diverse branches of modern agriculture include AGRONOMY, HORTICULTURE, entomology, animal husbandry, DAIRYING, agricultural engineering, soil chemistry, and agricultural economics. From his earliest days man

Early agriculture. Diorama of a European Neolithic village (about 2700 B.C.).

has depended for his life on hunting, fishing, and food gathering; to this day, some groups still pursue this simple way of life, and others have continued as roving herdsmen (see NOMAD). However, as various groups of men undertook deliberate cultivation of wild plants and domestication of wild animals, agriculture came into being. Needless to say, the transition was gradual, and precisely where and when it took place, thousands of years ago, is a matter of conjecture. Cultivation of crops—notably of grains such as wheat, rice, rye, barley, and millet—encouraged settlement of stable farm communities, some of which grew to be towns and city states in various parts of the world. Early agricultural implements—the digging stick, the HOE, the scythe, and the PLOW—developed slowly over the centuries, each innovation (e.g., the introduction of iron) causing profound changes in human life. From early times, too, men created ingenious systems of irrigation to control water supply, especially in semiarid areas and regions of periodic inundation—e.g., the Middle East, the American Southwest and Mexico, the Nile Valley, and S Asia. Farming was intimately associated with landholding (see TENURE) and therefore with political organization. Growth of large estates involved the use of slaves (see SLAVERY) and bound or semifree labor (see SERF). In the Western Middle Ages the MANORIAL SYSTEM was the typical organization of more or less isolated units and determined the nature of the agricultural VILLAGE. In the Orient large holdings by the nobles, partly arising from feudalism (especially in China and Japan), produced a similar pattern. As the Middle Ages waned, increasing communications, the commercial revolution, and the steady rise of cities in Western Europe tended to turn agriculture away from subsistence farming toward the growing of crops for sale outside the community (commercial agriculture). Especially in England, INCLOSURE converted farmland to grazing land and to the raising of staple crops. Everywhere recurrent plagues and famines contributed to the decay of the village and enlarged the army of homeless agricultural workers. In the 16th and 17th cent. horticulture was greatly developed, especially in the Low Countries, and contributed to the so-called agricultural revolution. The old, crude methods gave way with the development of horticultural knowledge of various crops, exchange of farming methods and products (e.g., the potato, which became almost as common in N Europe as rice is in SE Asia), the widespread application of scientific techniques to soil enrichment, and conscious efforts at selection and rotation of crops. The appearance of mechanical devices such as the sugar mill and Eli Whitney's cotton gin helped to support the system of large plantations based on a single crop. The Industrial Revolution after the late 18th cent. swelled the population of towns and cities and increasingly forced agriculture into greater integration with general economic and financial patterns. In the American colonies the independent, more or less self-sufficient farm worked by the farmer and his family became the norm in the North, while the plantation, using slave labor, was dominant (although not universal) in the South. The free farm pushed westward with the frontier, and the Civil War settled the competition through defeat of the South. The ensuing disappearance of Southern plantations demonstrated the dangers of dependence on a single crop (e.g., cotton), shown more dramatically in the decline of sugar production in the West Indies and NE Brazil. In the North and West of the United States the era of mechanized agriculture began with the invention of such farm machines as the reaper, the cultivator, the thresher, and the combine. Other revolutionary innovations (e.g., the tractor) continued to appear over the years, leading to a new type of large-scale agriculture. Modern science has also revolutionized food processing; refrigeration, for example, has made possible the large meat-packing plants (*frigorificos*) of South America, shipment of perishable foods, and packag-

Although mechanization of agriculture has made great strides, in many underdeveloped countries cultivation is still done with ox-drawn wooden plows.

A Mexican farmer (right) tills his soil. His method is not much different from that of the ancient Egyptians and Romans (left top and bottom).

ing of frozen foods. Urbanization has fostered the specialties of MARKET GARDENING and TRUCK FARMING. These changes have, of course, given new aspects to agriculture policies. Most of the governments of the world—including those under Communism—face their own type of "farm problem," and the attempted solutions vary as much as does agriculture itself: in a world where specialization and conservation have been highly refined in such countries as Denmark, farming in some forested areas, e.g., parts of Africa and N Brazil, still employs the "slash and burn" technique—i.e., cutting down and burning the trees, exhausting the ash-enriched soil, and then moving to a new area. In other areas (e.g., SE Asia) excessively small holdings and dense population necessitate intensive cultivation, using manpower and some animals but few machines; here the yield is low in relation to the expenditure of energy, and generally there is large seasonal unemployment of agricultural workers. In the United States and other leading food-producing nations agricultural colleges and government agencies attempt to increase output by disseminating knowledge of improved agricultural practices such as rotation of crops, irrigation, erosion control, reclamation of land, soil chemistry, and plant and animal breeding. In many countries extensive government programs control the planning, financing, and regulation of agriculture. See also DRY FARMING; GRANGER MOVEMENT; RANCH; RANGE.

Agriculture, United States Department of, division of the U.S. government. Specific agricultural aid from the Federal government began in 1839, when Congress appropriated $1,000 to the Patent Office for collecting and distributing seeds, making agricultural investigations, and procuring agricultural statistics. In 1862 the Dept. of Agriculture was created with a commissioner at its head. In 1889 the department was given cabinet status under a Secretary of Agriculture. The department is now one of the chief research, planning, service, and regulatory agencies of the government. Its principal duty is to serve farmers, by helping them to solve their problems of production, marketing, farm organization, land tenure, and land utilization. However, it also serves urban consumers, both directly and indirectly. The department is directed by the Secretary, an Undersecretary, and four Assistant Secretaries. Each Assistant Secretary is responsible for a separate area of the department's activities. One handles Federal-state relations, which include the Agricultural Research Service (controlling the experiment stations and the Agricultural Research Center at Beltsville, Md.), Forest Service, and Soil Conservation Service. Another secretary is responsible for agricultural stabilization, including the Commodity Credit Corporation and the Federal Farm Crop Insurance Corporation. A third secretary deals with marketing and foreign agriculture, and a fourth with administration. Other major departmental officers are the General Counsel, the Director of Agricultural Economics (whose agency is the main one for compiling and disseminating agricultural statistics), and the Director of Agricultural Credit Services (under whose jurisdiction are included the Farmers Home Administration and the Rural Electrification Administration). Of great value to farmers, horticulturists, and many others are the publications of the department. See *The Department of Agriculture* (U.S. Dept. of Agriculture, Miscellaneous Publication 532); J. M. Gaus and others, *Public Administration and the United States Department of Agriculture* (1940).

Agrigento (ägrējĕn′tō), Latin *Agrigentum*, city (estimated pop. 39,319), capital of Agrigento prov., S Sicily, Italy, on a height above the sea. Now an agricultural market and export center for sulphur, it was founded (c.580 B.C.) as Acragas or Akragas by Greek colonists of GELA and became one of the most prosperous cities of the Grecian world, as is shown by its imposing ruins. Destroyed c.406 B.C. by Carthage, it recovered but fell definitively to the Romans in 210 B.C. There are remains of several Doric temples (6th–5th cent. B.C.); the temple of Concord is very well preserved. There are also Roman remains, Christian catacombs, and an archaeological museum. Nearby Porto Empedocle is its port; it is named after Empedocles, who was born at Agrigento.

agrimony (ăg'rĭmō"nē), any plant of the genus *Agrimonia*, perennials of the ROSE family native to north temperate zones, to Brazil, and to Africa. They are found wild in the N and central United States. Agrimony is sometimes cultivated in herb gardens for its small yellow flowers and aromatic leaves, used for an astringent tea.

Agrippa, in Palestinian history: see HEROD.

Agrippa, Marcus Vipsanius (mär'kŭs vĭpsā'nēŭs ŭgrĭ'pŭ), c.63 B.C.–12 B.C., Roman general. A close friend of Octavian (later Emperor AUGUSTUS), he won a name in the wars in Gaul before becoming consul in 37 B.C. He organized Octavian's fleet and is generally given much credit for the defeat (36 B.C.) of Sextus Pompeius in the naval battles at Mylae and Naulochus (N Sicily). Agrippa took part in the war against Antony, and his naval operations were the basis of Octavian's decisive victory at Actium in 31 B.C. He was perhaps the most trusted of all Augustus' lieutenants and rendered many services, notably in putting down disorders in both East and West. His third wife was Augustus' daughter Julia. See biography by Meyer Reinhold (1933).

Agrippa von Nettesheim, Heinrich Cornelius (hĭn'rĭkh kôrnā'lyōōs ägrĭ'pä fŭn nĕ'tŭs-hĭm), 1486–1535, German physician and philosopher. His interest in magic involved him in trouble with the Church. His life under royal patrons in Germany, Italy, France, and the Netherlands was one of great storm and stress, and he died in poverty at Grenoble. His *De occulta philosophia*, a defense of magic, and his feminist *De nobilitate et praecellentia feminei sexus* are two of his chief works. See biography by Henry Morley (1856).

Agrippina I (ă"grĭpĭ'nŭ), d. A.D. 33, Roman matron; daughter of Agrippa and Julia and granddaughter

Agrippina I

The temple of Concord at Agrigento.

of Augustus. She was the wife of GERMANICUS CAESAR and accompanied him on his provincial duties. After her husband's death (A.D. 19), she accused TIBERIUS of having made Cn. Calpurnius Piso poison Germanicus, and thereafter she was consistently on bad terms with the emperor. Exiled to Pandateria Island in the Bay of Naples, she starved herself to death. She is also called Agrippina Major or Agrippina the Elder. Her son Caius became emperor (see CALIGULA).

Agrippina II, d. A.D. 59, Roman matron; daughter of Germanicus Caesar and Agrippina I. By her first husband, Cn. Domitius Ahenobarbus, she was the mother of NERO. After her brother Caligula became emperor, she had some power until she was discovered conspiring against him. She achieved her ambitions for her son after her uncle Emperor CLAUDIUS I took her as his third wife. She dominated the emperor and persuaded him to advance the interests of Nero at the expense of his own son, BRITANNICUS. She almost certainly poisoned Claudius, thus bringing Nero to power. She quarreled with Seneca, with Claudius' secretary Narcissus, and with the other ministers. Her son, weary of her intrigues, had her murdered. Colonia Agrippinensis (modern Cologne) was named for her.

agronomy, branch of agriculture dealing with crop production and field management. The science of agronomy applies to farming the principles of botany, biochemistry, soil conservation and enrichment, plant breeding, entomology, and plant pathology. Its aim is to increase the yield and quality of food, seed, forage, and fiber crops, using the land to its fullest capacity and with the greatest efficiency. The cropping or crop management plan for any farm must consider the entire design of the farm as an enterprise; crops should be selected after careful study of the soil, climatic conditions, market demands, and the plant diseases and insect pests of the given locality. The ground should be occupied for as many months of the year as possible, not only for economic reasons but also to prevent erosion and leaching. The long-prevalent belief that the land requires a resting period, i.e., should be kept fallow periodically, has been disproved; practices such as the ROTATION OF CROPS that have different nutritional requirements and the sowing of soil-improving plants (e.g., nitrogen-fixing legumes) as COVER CROPS actually return to the soil part of the nutrients removed with the harvest. See also AGRICULTURE and SOIL.

Agua (ä'wä, ä'gwä), inactive volcano, 12,310 ft. high, S Guatemala. In 1541, climaxing several days of unceasing rain and earthquakes, a wall of water, whose origin is not scientifically explained, swept down from its slopes, completely destroying CIUDAD VIEJA. Over 1,000 inhabitants were drowned, including the governor, Doña Beatriz de la CUEVA. The flood forced the founding of ANTIGUA.

Aguadilla (ä"gwädē'yä, ä"wä-), town (pop. 15,943), NW Puerto Rico, on Mona passage. It is a port and trade center for a rich agricultural region. Aguadilla was founded in 1775. Columbus is supposed to have landed in the vicinity in 1493.

Aguascalientes (ä"gwäskälyän'täs, ä"wäs-), state (2,499 sq. mi.; pop. 208,800), N central Mexico, on the Anáhuac plateau. A fertile agricultural region, it is bounded on the east, north, and west by Zacatecas. Cattle are raised on the wide plains and in the foothills, and there is some mining in the mountainous areas, though much of the mineral wealth, especially copper, remains unexploited. It is noted for the warm mineral springs, for which it is named, and for a fine climate. **Aguascalientes,** the capital (pop. c.130,000), is a pleasant health resort, noted for its mineral waters. It has a large smelter, textile mills, and other factories. The city is built over an ancient and intricate system of tunnels constructed by earlier inhabitants as yet unidentified. Founded in 1575, Aguascalientes was long a Spanish outpost against hostile Indians. Railroad development in the late 19th cent. made the city commercially important. Here, in 1914, took place the Convention of Aguascalientes, an unsuccessful attempt in the Mexican Revolution to end factional strife between Venustiano CARRANZA and Francisco VILLA.

ague: see MALARIA.

Aguesseau, Henri François d' (ärē' fräswä' dägĕsō'), 1668–1751, French orator and statesman. He became *procureur général* in the Parlement of Paris (1700) and chancellor of France (1717). Because of his opposition to John LAW he was briefly exiled to his estates. He served as chancellor again (1720–22, 1737–50) and devoted himself to judicial reform. The name also appears as Henri François Daguesseau.

Aguinaldo, Emilio (ägwĭnäl'dō; ämē'lyō ägēnäl'dō), 1869?–, Philippine leader. In the insurrection against Spain in 1896 he took command, and by terms of the peace that ended it he went into exile at Hong Kong. After the Spanish-American War broke out, he led a Philippine insurrection in concert with U.S. attacking forces. He set up a republic with its capital at Malolos and himself as president, and when Philippine independence was brushed aside in the peace treaty, he headed (1899–1901) a rebellion against U.S. occupying forces

until he was captured by Frederick FUNSTON. In 1935 he was defeated in the presidential election by Manuel Quezon. Aguinaldo was charged with cooperating with the Japanese occupying the Philippines in the Second World War and in 1945 was taken into custody but was not tried. In 1950 he declared open and active support of President Quirino. With V. A. Pacis he wrote *A Second Look at America* (1957).

Aguirre, Lope de (lō'pä dä agē'rä), c.1510–1561, Spanish rebel and adventurer in colonial South America. He was often involved in violence and sedition before joining (1560) the expedition of Pedro de URSÚA down the Marañón and the Amazon. He was one of the men who overthrew and killed Ursúa, then he killed Ursúa's successor, Fernando de Guzmán, and took command himself. He and his men reached the Atlantic—probably by the Orinoco—and on the way wantonly laid waste Indian villages. In 1561 he seized Margarita island and held it in a grip of terror. He was, however, foiled in his plan to take Panama secretly and crossed to the mainland, openly proclaiming rebellion against the Spanish crown. Surrounded at BARQUISIMETO, Aguirre in desperation crowned his infamous life by the murder of his own daughter. He surrendered and was shot. See A. F. Bandelier, *The Gilded Man* (1893); Walker Lowry, *Lope Aguirre, the Wanderer* (1952).

Agulhas, Cape (ŭgŭ'lŭs) [Port.,=needles], W Cape Prov., Republic of South Africa; the most southerly point of Africa. The name is derived from the saw-edged reefs and sunken rocks running out to sea; they have wrecked many vessels. A powerful lighthouse guards ships. The meridian of the cape (long. 20° E) is the dividing line between the Atlantic and the Indian oceans.

Agur (ā'-), unidentified author of Proverbs 30.

Agustini, Delmira (dĕlmē'rä ägōōstē'nē), c.1886–1914, Uruguayan poet. Her verse, although showing a disregard for traditional forms, is controlled and cadenced. Essentially a poet of ideas, she combined deep spiritual and erotic yearnings in bold and expressive imagery. Some critics consider her the greatest woman poet of Latin America. After a brief and unhappy marriage she was murdered by her estranged husband. *El Rosario de Eros* (1914) is one of her best-known collections; her complete works were published in 1924.

Ahab (ā'hăb) [Heb.,=father's brother], d. c.853 B.C., king of Israel (c.874–c.853 B.C.), son and successor of OMRI 1. Ahab was one of the greatest kings of the northern kingdom. He consolidated the good foreign relations his father had fostered, and he was at peace much of his reign. His marriage with JEZEBEL helped his friendship with Tyre, and the alliance of his daughter ATHALIAH 1 with the king's son in Jerusalem made Ahab sure of his less powerful neighbor. Ahab's prestige is seen in Assyrian inscriptions mentioning his alliance against SHALMANESER III, who won an indecisive victory (c.854 B.C.) at Karkar on the Orontes. After this campaign Ahab and BENHADAD 2 of Damascus went to war over the country E of the Jordan. Ahab was killed in battle. The biblical account of Ahab's reign (1 Kings 16.28–22.40) is most interested in its religious aspects. To the de-

vout, Ahab's foreign wife, with her Tyrian cults
and behavior, represented evil. Besides, she was a
willful woman and entertained exalted ideas of
royal prerogative. She met her match in ELIJAH,
the champion of Israel's God. He could not endure
compromise with national apostasy, and he must
have been an important factor in the discontent
which began to develop in Israel at this period.
Ahab was succeeded by his sons, first Ahaziah, then
Jehoram. The ruins of his palace have been excavated at SAMARIA. The Ahab of Jer. 29.21,22 is a
different person, a lying prophet.

Ahaggar: see SAHARA.

Aha of Shabcha (ä′hä, shäb′khä) or **Achai of Shabcha** (ä′khī), c.680–c.762, Babylonian rabbi. He
was the author of *Sheiltholh* (questions), a collection of legal and ethical sermons or treatises intended to be of use to laymen as well as to the
scholars for whom most of the learned Jews wrote.
Aha is the first scholar after the close of the compilation of the Talmud of whom there is record.
His work emphasizes the value of the basic virtues
and everyday morals.

Aharah (ähăr′ü), the same as AHIRAM.

Aharhel (ühär′–), Judahite family. 1 Chron. 4.8.

Ahasai (ähăs′āī, ähā′sī), priest. Ahzai RSV. Neh.
11.13. Jahzerah: 1 Chron. 9.12.

Ahasbai (ähăs′bāī, –bī), father of ELIPHELET 3.

Ahasuerus (ähăs″ūē′rŭs), Hebrew form of the name
Xerxes, as used in the Bible. The Ahasuerus of
Esther is probably Xerxes I. That of Tobit 14.15
may intend Cyaxares I, destroyer of Nineveh. The
name of the father of DARIUS THE MEDE is also
given as Ahasuerus.

Ahava (ähā′–), unidentified place, where Ezra collected one of his expeditions. Ezra 8.15,21,31.

Ahaz (ā′hăz) [Heb.,=he is possessor], d. c.727 B.C.,
king of Judah (c.731–727 B.C.), son of Jotham. His
reign marks the end of the real independence of
Judah. A coalition of Pekah of Israel and Rezin of
Syria attacked him and nearly took Jerusalem.
Ahaz appealed for help to Tiglath-pileser III of
Assyria, who defeated Ahaz's enemies, but demanded tribute of Judah. Ahaz sent some Temple
gold as payment. The greatest figure in this time
in Judah was the prophet Isaiah, who opposed the
Assyrian alliance. Ahaz is denounced in the Bible
for his heathen abominations and his sacrilege with
the Temple gold. In Ahaz's reign Judah lost Elath,
her Red Sea port, permanently. He was succeeded
by Hezekiah. 2 Kings 16; 2 Chron. 28; Isa. 7; 38.
Achaz: Mat. 1.9. A different Ahaz, otherwise unknown, is mentioned in 1 Chron. 8.35 and 9.42.

Ahaziah (ähŭzī′ŭ) [Heb.,=God has taken]. **1** Died
c.852 B.C., king of Israel (c.853–852 B.C.), son
of Ahab. He was a worthy successor of his father
only in that he followed Ahab's religious views.
He was succeeded by his brother JEHORAM **1**.
1 Kings 22.51–53; 2 Kings 1; 2 Chron. 20.35–37.
2 Died c.846 B.C., king of Judah (c.846 B.C.), son
of JEHORAM **2** and ATHALIAH **1**. He was considered a typical descendant of Ahab. He was
killed in Jehu's coup d'état while visiting at Jez-
reel. His mother succeeded him. 2 Kings 8.25–29;
9; 2 Chron. 22. He is called Azariah in 2 Chron.
22.6 and Jehoahaz in 2 Chron. 21.17 and 25.23.

Ahban (ä′băn), Jerahmeelite. 1 Chron. 2.29.

Aher (ā′–) [Heb.,=another], Benjamite. 1 Chron.
6.12. Perhaps the same as AHIRAM.

Ahi (ā′hī) [Heb.,=brother]. **1** Gadite. 1 Chron.
5.15. **2** Asherite. 1 Chron. 7.34.

Ahiah (ühī′ü), variant of AHIJAH.

Ahiam (ühī′ŭm) [Heb.,=mother's brother], one of
David's men. 2 Sam. 23.33; 1 Chron. 11.35.

Ahian (ühī′ŭn) [Heb.,=brotherly], Manassite. 1
Chron. 7.19.

Ahidjo, Ahmadou (ämä′dō ähhē′jō), 1922–, African
statesman in the Federal Republic of Cameroon.
The son of a Moslem Fulani chief, he was born in
the Northern Region of the French Cameroons. He
distinguished himself as a radio operator with
the French forces during the Second World War.
Rising to high position in the Jeunes Musulmans
movement, he strove for cooperation between the
northern and southern regions of the Cameroons
which had long been divided by tribal differences.
He was elected twice to the Territorial Assembly
(1947, 1952) of the French Cameroons and to the
Assembly of the French Union (1953). In 1956 he
became president of the Territorial Assembly of
Cameroon. He held various government posts in
the first administration of Cameroon until he succeeded (1958) André-Marie M'Bida as premier.
With the independence (1960) of the Cameroon
Republic, he was elected its first president. He
became president, also, of the Mouvement d'Union
Camerounaise, a political party affiliated with the
African Democratic Rally (R.D.A.), both of which
favored continued strong ties with France. As a
result of his continued efforts at reconciliation, the
Southern Cameroons voted overwhelmingly (1961)
to unite with the Cameroon Republic rather than
with Nigeria.

Ahiezer (ähīē′zŭr) [Heb.,=my brother is help]. **1**
Prince of Dan. Num. 1.12. **2** Chief of David's
bowmen. 1 Chron. 12.2.

Ahihud (ähī′hŭd) [Heb.,=my brother is majesty].
1 Prince of Asher. Num. 34.27. **2** Benjamite.
1 Chron. 8.7.

Ahijah (ühī′jü) [Heb.,=brother of God], common
name in the Bible, occasionally spelled Ahiah. **1**
Prophet from Shiloh. 1 Kings 11.29; 12.15; 14.1–18;
2 Chron. 10.15. **2** Priest in the time of Saul, perhaps the same as AHIMELECH **1**. 1 Sam. 14.3. **3**
One of David's mighty men. 1 Chron. 11.36. **4**
Scribe. 1 Kings 4.3. **5** Father of King BAASHA.
6 Jerahmeelite. 1 Chron. 2.25. **7** Benjamite.
1 Chron. 8.7. Ahoah: 1 Chron. 8.4. **8** Levite. 1
Chron. 26.20. **9** Sealer of the covenant. Neh. 10.26.

Ahikam (ühī′–) [Heb.,=my brother has gone up],
protector of Jeremiah and the father of Gedaliah.
2 Kings 22.12,14; 2 Chron. 34.20; Jer. 26.24; 40.5.

Ahilud (ühī′–). **1** Father of JEHOSHAPHAT **2**. **2**
Father of BAANA **3**.

Ahimaaz (ühĭm′āăz) [Heb.,=brother of anger].
1 Father of AHINOAM **1**. **2** One of the men set to spy
on Absalom. 2 Sam. 15.27; 17.17–21; 18.19–32. **3**
Husband of BASMATH and perhaps the same as **2**.

Ahiman (ühī′mŭn). **1** Son of ANAK. **2** Family of
porters. 1 Chron. 9.17.

Ahimelech (ühĭm′ŭlĕk) [Heb.,=my brother is king].
1 Priest at Nob, brother of, or perhaps the same as,
AHIJAH **2**. He befriended David, and Saul had
him killed. 1 Sam. 22.9–19. Abimelech: 1 Chron.

18.16. Name reversed with that of his son, Abiathar. 2 Sam. 8.17; 1 Chron. 18.16; 24.6. **2** Hittite in David's camp. 1 Sam. 26.6.

Ahimoth (ŭhī'mŏth) [Heb.,=brother of death]; Merarite Levite. 1 Chron. 6.25.

Ahinadab (ŭhĭn'–) [Heb.,=my brother is liberal], one of Solomon's stewards. 1 Kings 4.14.

Ahinoam (ŭhĭn'ōŭm) [Heb.,=my brother is loveliness]. **1** A wife of Saul. 1 Sam. 14.50. **2** One of David's early wives. 1 Sam. 25.43; 27.3; 30.5; 2 Sam. 2.2; 3.2.

Ahio (ŭhī'ō) [Heb.,=brotherly]. **1** One of those who drove the cart that carried the ark. 2 Sam. 6.3, 4; 1 Chron. 13.7. **2** Uncle of Saul. 1 Chron. 8.31; 9.37. **3** Benjamite. 1 Chron. 8.14.

Ahira (ŭhī'rŭ), prince of Naphtali. Num. 1.15.

Ahiram (ŭhī'–) [Heb.,=my brother is the high one], son of Benjamin. Num. 26.38. Ehi: Gen. 46.21. Aharah: 1 Chron. 8.1. AHER may be the same.

Ahisamach (ŭhĭs'ŭmăk) [Heb.,=my brother supports], father of AHOLIAB.

Ahishahar (ŭhĭsh'–, ŭhī'–), Benjamite. 1 Chron. 7.10.

Ahishar (ŭhī'–) [Heb.,=my brother sings], royal steward. 1 Kings 4.6.

Ahithophel (ŭhĭth'ŭfĕl), David's counselor who joined with Absalom against David. He killed himself when Absalom ignored his counsel. He may have been the grandfather of Bath-sheba. 2 Sam. 15.12; 16.20–17.23; 11.3; 23.34. The Vulgate form of the name is Achitophel.

Ahitub (ŭhī'–) [Heb.,=my brother is good]. **1** Father of AHIMELECH **1** and AHIJAH **2**. **2** Father, or grandfather, of ZADOK **1**. **3** Father of ZADOK **5**.

Ahlab (ä'lăb), town of Asher. Judges 1.31.

Ahlai (ä'lāī). **1** Jerahmeelitess. 1 Chron. 2.31,34. **2** Father of one of David's men, Zabad. 1 Chron. 11.41.

Ahlin, Lars (lärsh älēn'), 1915–, Swedish novelist. His writings are marked by great creative vitality, psychological realism, and a concern with spiritual values. Although often criticized for narrative meandering and excessive religious theorizing, as in *If* (1946), he displayed in *The Cinnamon Stick* (1953) a capacity for fine artistic discipline. His unremitting baring of human foibles and self-deceptions and his vision of life as seething and bizarre are reminiscent of Dostoyevsky.

Ahmadabad, India: see AHMEDABAD.

Ahmad Khan, Sir Sayyid (sä'yĕd ä'mäd kän'), 1817–98, Indian Moslem educator and leader. His family was long connected with the Mogul court, and he entered the civil service in 1841. He later won fame as an historian of Moslem rule in India. He inspired numerous changes in the moribund society and life of 19th-century Moslem India by organizing (1864) a society for the translation of English works into Urdu and another for the teaching of civics to the Indian public. In 1878 he established the Moslem university at Aligarh. Among his works are *Loyal Mohammedans of India* (1860–61) and *Causes of the Indian Revolt* (1873). See J. M. S. Balgon, *Reforms and Religious Ideas of Sir Sayyid Ahmad Khan* (1949).

Ahmadnagar or **Ahmednagar** (both: ämŭdnŭg'ŭr), city (pop. 145,000), Maharashtra state, W India.

It has textile manufacturing and some light industry. Founded in 1490 by Nizam Shah Bahri, it was the capital of a kingdom which lasted until 1600. Sivaji, leader of the Mahrattas, was born here.

Ahmad Shah: see AHMED SHAH.

Ahmed I (ä'mĕd), 1589–1617, Ottoman sultan (1603–17), son and successor of Mohammed III. The chief event of his reign was the Treaty of Szitvatorok (1606), which supplemented the Treaty of Vienna between Archduke (later Emperor) MATTHIAS and Prince Stephen BOCSKAY of Transylvania. By the treaty, the emperors, as kings of Hungary, ceased to pay tribute to the sultan, and Transylvania was recognized as independent. In the Asiatic provinces disorders were suppressed by Ahmed's vizier, the Croatian Murad Pasha, but after Murad's death (1611) they broke out again, allowing Shah Abbas I of Persia to retain Tabriz. On Ahmed's death, the law of succession was changed to favor the oldest male member of the house. Mustafa I, Ahmed's brother, succeeded.

Ahmed II, 1642–95, Ottoman sultan (1691–95), brother and successor of Suleiman II. Soon after his reign began, the Turkish defeat at SLANKAMEN (1691) heralded the conquest of Hungary by Austria. His nephew, Mustafa II, succeeded him.

Ahmed III, 1673–1736, Ottoman sultan (1703–30), brother and successor of Mustafa II. He gave asylum to CHARLES XII of Sweden and to MAZEPPA after Peter the Great had defeated (1709) them at Poltava. Charles's advice helped to bring about war between Turkey and Russia (1710–11). By the Treaty of the Pruth (1711) Turkey recovered Azov and the surrounding territory. Ahmed seized (1715) the Peloponnesus and the Ionian Isles (except Corfu) from Venice, but he was defeated by the Austrians under Prince EUGENE OF SAVOY in 1716–18. By the Treaty of Passarowitz (1718) the Banat, Lesser Walachia, and N Serbia, including Belgrade, were lost to the Hapsburg emperor. Ahmed's grand vizier after 1718 was Ibrahim, who encouraged learning by establishing several notable libraries and favored the rise of Greek PHANARIOTS to high offices. The sultan and his minister were overthrown by the Janizaries, who were jealous of the new aristocracy. Ahmed's nephew Mahmud I became sultan, and Ahmed died in prison.

Ahmed, 1898–1930, shah of Persia (1909–25), son of Mohammed Ali. The last of the Kajar (or Qajar) dynasty, he came to power through a coup d'état. He lost power in 1921 and was deposed in 1925. He was succeeded by REZA SHAH PAHLEVI.

Ahmedabad (ä"mŭdŭbăd'), city (pop. 1,400,000), Gujarat state, W India, on the left bank of the Sabarmati river. It is an industrial center, noted for its great cotton mills, and also a transportation hub and commercial center. Founded in 1412 by Ahmed Shah, it fell to Akbar in 1573; the city enjoyed great prosperity under the Moguls. The British opened (1619) a trading post here, and by the early 19th cent. they controlled the city. The cultural center of Gujarat, with many outstanding mosques and tombs, it is sacred to the Jains, who have over 100 temples here. The Jama Masjid, an ancient Hindu temple converted (15th cent.) to a mosque, is one of the most beautiful buildings. Gandhi lived here for a time and had very strong influence here. The city is the site of Gujarat Univ. (founded 1950). The name is also spelled Ahmadabad.

Ahmed al-Mansur (ä'mĕd äl mänsoõr') [al-Mansur =the victorious], d. 1603, emir of Morocco (1578–1603). Proclaimed ruler after his brother's death at the battle of ALCAZARQUIVIR, he gained great prestige from the victory over Portugal. The ransom of the Portuguese captives made him wealthy. He was able to give Morocco a quarter century of relative peace and prosperity. His conquest of Timbuktu (1590–91) marked the apogee of Morocco's extension into the lands south of the Sahara. The cost of maintaining an army at so great a distance prevented him from gaining any permanent benefit from the conquest. He engaged in a commercial correspondence with Queen Elizabeth I of England and encouraged foreign trade.

Ahmednagar, India: see AHMADNAGAR.

Ahmed Shah (ä'mĕd shä') or **Ahmad Shah** (ä'mŭd), c.1723–1773, Afghan ruler, founder of the Durani dynasty. His success in commanding Afghan forces in India for Nadir Shah of Iran won him the rule of Afghanistan on Nadir's death (1747). He invaded India several times and twice (1756, 1760) occupied and sacked Delhi, the capital of the Mogul empire. He conquered a vast territory, extending roughly from the Oxus to the Indus rivers and from Tibet to Khurasan, but he was unable to consolidate this empire and it soon disintegrated. He united and strengthened Afghanistan, however, and is therefore often considered its modern founder. His family retained power until the rise of Dost Mohammed.

Ahoah (ŭhō'ŭ), the same as AHIJAH 7. The patronymic **Ahohite** suggests this name; it occurs with the names of DODO 2 and ILAI.

Aholah (ŭhō'lŭ) [Heb.,=tent] and **Aholibah** (ŭhŏl'ĭbŭ [Heb.,=tent in her], the sisters in an allegory on Israel's idolatry. Ezek. 23.

Aholiab (ŭhō'lē–) [Heb.,=tent of the father], specially chosen worker on the tabernacle. Ex. 31.6; 35.34; 36.1,2; 38.23.

Aholibah (ŭhŏl'ĭbŭ): see AHOLAH.

Aholibamah (–hō″lĭbä'mŭ, ä″hŭlĭb'ŭ–) [Heb.,=my tent is raised]. **1** One of Esau's wives. Gen. 36.2. **2** Duke of Edom. Gen. 36.41.

Ahoskie (ŭhŏs'kē), town (pop. 4,583), NE N.C., W of Elizabeth City, in a farm and timber area.

Ahriman: see ZOROASTRIANISM.

Aht Confederacy: see NOOTKA INDIANS.

Ahumai (ŭhū'māĭ, –mĭ), Judahite. 1 Chron. 4.2.

Ahura Mazdah: see ZOROASTRIANISM.

Ahuzam (ŭhū'zŭm), Judahite. 1 Chron. 4.6.

Ahuzzath (ŭhŭz'ăth), friend of Abimelech of Gerar. Gen. 26.26.

Ahvaz, Iran: see AHWAZ.

Ahvenanmaa: see ALAND ISLANDS.

Ahwaz or **Ahvaz** (both: äwäz', ähwäz'), city (pop. c.100,000), SW Iran, on the Karun river. The capital of Khuzistan (the Sixth Prov.), it is an oil center, an industrial city, and a transportation hub on the Trans-Iranian RR. It has a petrochemical industry and manufactures chemical fertilizers and plastics. It was an old city, rebuilt by Ardashir I, who named it Hormuzd-Ardashir. In the 4th cent. A.D., Ahwaz became the seat of a bishopric, and a large church was built here. The discovery of important oil fields nearby in 1908 restored the town to its former importance. The new part of the town, the administrative and industrial center, is on the right bank of the Karun, but the population is still concentrated in the old section.

Ai (ā'ī) [Heb.,=heap of ruin]. **1** Canaanite royal city, E of Bethel. Here Abraham pitched his tent when he arrived in Canaan. It is probably the modern et-Tell, near Bethel (Jordan). Excavations have revealed a strongly fortified city, situated here c.3000 B.C. and destroyed in 2000 B.C. Ai was in ruins at the time of Joshua's conquest in the 12th cent. B.C. The account in Joshua 7 possibly refers instead to BETHEL 1, whose people may have used the nearby ruins of Ai as a bastion against the invading Israelites. Hai: Gen. 12.8; 13.3. Aiath: Isa. 10.28. Aija: Neh. 11.31. **2** City of the Ammorites, near Heshbon. Jer. 49.3.

Aiah (āī'ŭ). **1** Edomite. 1 Chron. 1.40. Ajah: Gen. 36.24. **2** Father of RIZPAH.

Aiath (āī'ŭth), the same as AI 1.

Aichi (ī'chē), prefecture (1,962 sq. mi.; pop. 4,206,313), central Honshu, Japan. NAGOYA is its capital. Bounded on the E by Ise Bay and on the S by the Philippine Sea, Aichi consists of a coastal plain and a mountainous, forested interior. It is drained by the Kiso river, an important source of hydroelectric power. The major industrial centers are Nagoya, Toyohashi, Okazaki, Ichinomiya, and Seto. Agriculture products and raw silk are produced, and lignite and quartz mined.

Aidan, Saint (ā'dŭn), d. 651, Irish bishop. He came at the request of Oswald of Northumbria to convert the English and founded the abbey on Lindisfarne. Symbols: torch and stag. Feast: Aug. 31.

aids, in FEUDALISM, type of feudal due paid by a vassal to his suzerain or lord. Aids varied with time and place, though in English-speaking countries it is traditional that aids were due on the knighting of the lord's eldest son, on the marriage of the lord's eldest daughter, and for ransom of the lord from captivity. These are the three aids specified in the MAGNA CARTA (1215), which forbade the king to levy aids from the barons on occasions other than these, except by the "common counsel" of the realm. It is difficult to distinguish aids from other feudal dues such as SCUTAGE and TALLAGE. The term had a much wider scope than was indicated in the Magna Carta. In general, aids fell into disuse with the decline of feudalism, though they continued nominally in most places. On the Continent, the aids often became land or justice taxes due the local lords. In France, the aids were converted later into a royal tax which continued until the Revolution.

Aiea (ä″ēä'ä), uninc. town (pop. 11,826), Hawaii, on S Oahu, NW of Honolulu, in a sugar-cane region. U.S. Fort Shafter is nearby.

Aiglon, L': see NAPOLEON II.

Aigues-Mortes (ĕg-môrt'), town (estimated pop. 3,746), Gard dept., S France, in Languedoc, in the Rhone river delta, near the Mediterranean. Developed as a port by Louis IX for his two crusades

Aigues-Mortes: 13th-century
ramparts and fortified towers.

(1248 and 1270), it gradually silted up and has long since lost its commercial prosperity. A well-preserved medieval town, its splendid 13th-century ramparts and fortified tower (Tour-de-Constance) remain intact.

Aija (ā'jū), the same as AI **1.**

Aijalon (ă'jū–, ī'jū–, ā'jū–) [Heb.,=place of harts]. **1** Town, on the border between Philistia and Israel, the modern Yalo (Israel), NW of Jerusalem. Judges 1.35; 2 Chron. 11.10. Ajalon: Joshua 19.42; 2 Chron. 28.18. In the Tel-el-Amarna letters it is called Aialuna. **2** Town in Zabulon. Judges 12.12. **3** Valley over which Joshua commanded the moon to stand still. Joshua 10.12.

Aijeleth Shahar (ăj'ŭlĕth shā'här) [Heb.,=hind, or help, of the morning], superscription of Ps. 22, probably the tune to which it was to be sung, named from the first words of some other verse set to it. Other superscriptions of similar explanation are: Al-taschith (ăl"tăs'kĭth) [Heb.,=destroy not]. Pss. 57; 58; 59; 75. Jonath-elem-rechokim (jō'nŭth-ē'lĕm-rēkō'kĭm) [Heb.,=dove of the distant terebinths or dove of the silence of distant places]. Ps. 56. Mahalath (mā'hŭlăth). Ps. 53. Mahalath Leannoth (lēăn'ŏth). Ps. 88. Shoshannim (shōshăn'ĭm) [Heb.,=lilies]. Pss. 45; 69. Shoshannim-Eduth (–ē'dŭth). Ps. 80. Shushan-eduth (shōō'shăn–). Ps. 60.

Aiken, Conrad (ā'kĭn), 1889–, American poet and novelist, b. Savannah, Ga., grad. Harvard, 1912. His writings reveal a persistent and ever-deepening concern for the workings of the mind, particularly for his own personal consciousness. Aiken wrote novels, short stories, literary criticism, and the autobiographical *Ushant* (1952), but he is best known as a poet. His poetry, noted for its preoccupation with the sound and structure of music, includes such collections as *The Charnel Rose* (1918), *Senlin, a Biography* (1925), *Brownstone Eclogues* (1942), and *A Letter from Li Po* (1956). His collected poems were published in 1953. Aiken's interest in psychopathology and in the stream-of-consciousness technique is revealed in such novels as *Blue Voyage* (1927) and *Great Circle* (1933).

His collected critical essays, *A Reviewer's ABC*, appeared in 1958, his collected short stories in 1961. See study by Jay Martin (1962).

Aiken, city (pop. 11,243), co. seat of Aiken co., W S.C., NE of Augusta, Ga.; laid out 1834, inc. 1835. With an excellent climate and located in the midst of sand hills and pine forests, Aiken still retains some of its popularity as a resort and polo center. It is also an industrial city, manufacturing textiles and wood and fiber-glass products and processing clay and granite. Nearby is the Atomic Energy Commission's Savannah River plant. Adjacent to the city are the unincorporated towns of Aiken South (pop. 2,980) and Aiken West (pop. 2,602).

ailanthus, any tree of the genus *Ailanthus,* native to the warm regions of Asia and Australia. Ailanthus wood is sometimes used for cabinet-making and for the manufacture of charcoal. The leaves are a source of food for a silkworm, and the bark and leaves are used medicinally. Females of a species called tree of heaven, native to China, are widely grown in European and American cities because of their attractive foliage and their resistance to smoke and soot; the male flowers, however, have a disagreeable odor.

aileron: see AIRFOIL.

Ailly, Pierre d' (pyĕr' dāyē'), 1350–1420, French theologian and writer, a cardinal of the Roman Church. He was the teacher of Gerson and his predecessor as chancellor at the Univ. of Paris (1385–95). Ailly figured prominently among the conciliarists working to end the Great Schism (see SCHISM, GREAT). He urged that in order to name a new pope a general council be called as the only means of settling the schism. He seems to have been more concerned with a practical solution than with the implications of the conciliar theory. He participated in both the Council of Pisa (see PISA, COUNCIL OF) and the Council of Constance (see CONSTANCE, COUNCIL OF). In the latter Ailly took part in the trial and condemnation of John Huss. His vast writings embrace theology, philosophy, cosmography, plans for ecclesiastical reform, and French religious verse.

His best-known work, the *Imago mundi*, an astronomical compendium, was studied by Columbus. See study by J. P. McGowan (1936).

Ailsa Craig (āl'sù), island, 2 mi. in circumference, Ayrshire, off SW Scotland, W of Girvan in the Firth of Clyde. It has granite quarries and a lighthouse and is a sanctuary for sea birds. It rises to 1,114 ft.

Ain (ĕ), department (2,249 sq. mi.; estimated pop. 311,941), E central France, in Burgundy, bordering on Switzerland. Bourg-en-Bresse is the capital. Bounded by the Rhone in the south and east and the Saône in the west, it is primarily an agricultural region. The Ain river, a tributary of the Rhone, divides the BRESSE and Dombes regions in the west, from the Bugey region in the east. The department is noted for poultry and cattle raising and the production of cheese and wine. Industry, chiefly the manufacture of plastics, chemicals, and metal goods, is concentrated in Oyonnax and Bellegarde. There are powerful hydroelectric plants on the Swiss border, notably the Genissiat Dam.

Ain (ā'ĭn). **1** Town, N Palestine. Num. 34.11. **2** See EN-RIMMON.

Ainsworth, trading city (pop. 1,982), co. seat of Brown co., N Nebr., SE of Valentine; settled 1877, inc. 1883. In a region of lakes and streams, it is a gateway to the cattle country.

Aintab: see GAZIANTEP.

Aintree, racecourse, Lancashire, N England near Liverpool. Started in 1836, it was one of the first regular steeplechase courses. The course, 4½ mi. long, with 30 jumps, is difficult and dangerous. The most important race run here is the Grand National, founded in 1839.

Ainu (ī'noō), aborigines of Japan. The more civilized Japanese invaders forced the Ainu to retreat to the northern islands, where today, in Hokkaido and in Sakhalin, fewer than 17,000 live as hunters and gatherers of sea food. Both native culture and population have markedly declined through intermarriage with the Japanese. Physically short and stocky, with abundant, slightly wavy hair, the Ainu lack Mongoloid traits and seem most closely akin to the races of Europe. Their language is unrelated to any other known speech. Once a warlike people, they have been thoroughly subdued for several centuries. Their religion is highly animistic and centers on a bear cult; a captive bear is sacrificed at an annual winter feast and his spirit, thus released, guards the Ainu settlements. See N. G. Munro, *Ainu, Creed and Cult* (1963).

air: see ATMOSPHERE; LIQUID AIR; RESPIRATION; VENTILATION.

air, law of the, in the broadest sense, all law connected with the use of the air, including radio and telegraph communications. More commonly, it refers to laws concerning civil aviation. The development of large-scale air transport after the First World War brought with it the need for regulation, both national and international. In 1919 a meeting of the nations victorious in the First World War resulted in the International Convention for Air Navigation, commonly called the Paris Convention. The convention was a compromise between two contradictory views: some nations held that a state had sovereignty over the air above it; others that there should be freedom of the air comparable to the freedom of the seas. The convention therefore recognized the sovereignty of each state over its own air space without prejudice to innocent passage by aircraft of another state. It further provided that each aircraft (like each ship) must have a registered nationality. Rules were adopted as to the airworthiness of aircraft, certification of pilots

Ainu family of Hokkaido, Japan.

as competent, and licensing of pilots. Among the 33 signatory nations were Great Britain, France, Italy, and Japan. The United States signed but did not ratify the convention. Nevertheless U.S. air laws were modeled on it. The Air Commerce Act of 1926 provided extensive Federal regulations as to licensing of pilots, airways, altitude of flying, scientific aids and equipment for flying, and the like. These regulatory powers were put in the charge of the Bureau of Air Commerce in the Dept. of Commerce. This was replaced in 1938 by the Civil Aeronautics Authority, an independent agency, whose functions were later transferred to the Civil Aeronautics Administration and the Civil Aeronautics Board in the Dept. of Commerce. The Civil Aeronautics Administration was superseded by the Federal Aviation Agency in 1958. Other countries also adopted legislation modeled on the Paris Convention. There were also many bilateral agreements among nations as well as general conventions—notably the Pan American Convention on Air Navigation (1925). The Second World War emphasized the need for sounder regulation of international air transport and for uniformity of equipment, laws, and regulations. Even before the war's end an international civil aviation conference met in Chicago in Nov., 1944. Representatives of 52 nations attended, but the USSR did not take part. Several agreements were drawn up. There was much discussion of the "five freedoms of the air"—freedom to fly across the territory of a state without landing; freedom to land for nontraffic purposes; the right to disembark in a foreign country traffic from the country of registry of the aircraft; the right to pick up in a foreign country traffic destined for the country of registry; and the right to carry traffic between two foreign countries. The first two were accepted, but the fifth was bitterly opposed; only the first two were included in the International Air Services Transit Agreement, which was generally signed. The conference, after considerable debate, set up the Provisional International Civil Aviation Organization (PICAO), which had its seat at Montreal. After ousting Spain, this organization became in 1947 the INTERNATIONAL CIVIL AVIATION ORGANIZATION (ICAO), affiliated with the United Nations. There have been several general conferences since the Chicago Convention to interpret its provisions, and many bilateral agreements have been concluded by parties to the convention. Although many problems of international civil aviation still remain unsolved, attention is rapidly turning to the creation of laws for the governing of space.

air brake: see BRAKE.

air conditioning, mechanical process for controlling the humidity, temperature, cleanliness, and circulation of air in buildings and rooms. Indoor air is conditioned and regulated to maintain the temperature-humidity ratio that is most comfortable and healthful. In the process, dust, soot, and pollen are filtered out, and the air may be sterilized, as is sometimes done in hospitals and public places. Most air-conditioning devices employ what is known as a vapor-compression cycle. This reverses, by mechanical means, the thermodynamic law that states that heat flows from higher to lower temperatures. By compression of gas in a closed circuit to the point at which it is warmer than the outside air, heat is made to flow from the gas to the cooler surrounding air, thus lowering the temperature of the gas. The gas is then expanded to a low pressure so that it is cooler than the air in the room. Heat now flows from the room to the gas and is expelled to the outside air. The cycle of compression and expansion is repeated continuously. At the same time a cooling coil containing liquid refrigerant cools outside air admitted by an intake fan, while a condenser collects and liquefies the refrigerant. In water-cooled air-conditioning units, water circulates through the condenser, extracting the heat from the air flowing to the compressor and eliminating it down a convenient drain. For recirculation in water-cooled units, a cooling tower is used. This apparatus maintains a constant level of water in the system and replaces water lost by evaporation. The development of small, self-contained systems has greatly expanded the use of air conditioning in homes. A portable or window-mounted unit using a 5 hp electric motor is usually adequate for one room. Often domestic heating systems are converted to provide complete air conditioning for a home. In the construction of office buildings in the United States, it is common to include air-conditioning systems as integral parts of the structure. First used c.1900 in the textile industry, air conditioning found little use outside of factories until the late 1920s. It is of great importance in chemical and pharmaceutical plants where air contamination, humidity, and temperature affect manufacturing processes. See R. C. Jordan and G. B. Priester, *Refrigeration and Air Conditioning* (rev. ed., 1958).

aircraft carrier, ship designed to carry aircraft and to permit take-off and landing of planes. The carrier's distinctive features are a flat upper deck (flight deck) which functions as a take-off and landing field, and a main deck (hangar deck) beneath the flight deck for storing and servicing the

The attack aircraft carrier U.S.S. John F. Kennedy was added to the U.S. fleet late in 1968.

A jet is catapulted (left) from the flight deck of the nuclear aircraft carrier U.S.S. Enterprise. Other planes await their turn.

Navy pilot (below), guided by a brilliant "meatball" of light reflected in the concave mirror at left, heads his jet plane for the deck of the aircraft carrier. The Navy has adopted the mirror landing system for installation on all carriers. The system, which replaces the wig-wagging method of landing aircraft, already is credited with saving many lives and millions of dollars. Landing accidents such as the one in the bottom photo are cut to a minimum.

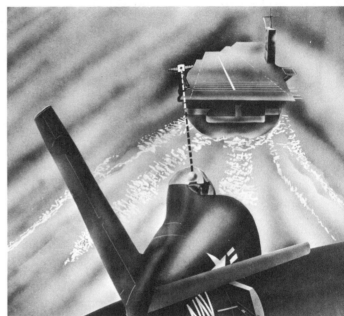

aircraft. Obstructions above the flight deck are minimized by localizing them along the starboard side amidships. The aircraft carrier emerged after the First World War as an experimentally modified cruiser. The first aircraft carrier built (1925) from the keel up as an aircraft carrier for the U.S. navy was the U.S.S. *Saratoga*. The aircraft carrier remained an experimental and untested war vessel until the Second World War, when the Japanese destroyed or drove out of the Far Eastern waters the British, American, and Dutch navies with carrier-borne aircraft. By 1942 the aircraft carrier had replaced the battleship as the major unit in a modern fleet, and in the Second World War it was indispensable in naval operations against sea- or land-based enemy. The battle of the Coral Sea (1942) was fought by naval aircraft, and the two opposing fleets never came within gunshot range of each other. After the Second World War aircraft carriers were enlarged and improved by the British and American navies, but except for the introduction of nuclear propulsion, they remained basically the same. See *Jane's Fighting Ships* (pub. annually).

air-cushion vehicle or ground-effect machine, device navigating at a height of not more than a few feet above ground or water. It is supported by a downward rush of air from a horizontal propeller or ducted fan beneath it. Forward thrust is usually provided by vertical propellers or by air jets. There are several kinds of air-cushion vehicles: the most common has a series of air jets directed downward and inward around its edge; another type has an apron around its edge that creates a plenum chamber underneath fed by a low-pressure fan; a third type has a lifting propeller like that of the helicopter. Still another air-cushion vehicle has three high-pressure pads a fraction of an inch above the ground. By 1961 there were at least 38 different designs, models, and actual air-cushion vehicles. Most early vehicles of this type came

Two types of air-cushion vehicles.

into existence in the late 1950s. In 1962 a British vehicle weighing 12½ tons became the first to go into active service on a 19-mile ferry run. It was powered by four gas turbines and attained a speed of 60 knots. Maximum size for air-cushion vehicles in 1962 was about 30 tons; machines up to 100 tons were planned and others up to 1,000 tons were discussed. The advantages expected from air-cushion vehicles include higher speeds than those of ships and most land vehicles and lower power requirements than for helicopters of the same weights. However, a relatively smooth land or water surface below is a necessity; most of these vehicles, for example, cannot clear more than 3- to 5½-foot waves.

Airdrie (âr′drē), burgh (pop. 33,620), Lanarkshire, S central Scotland. It produces chemicals and electrical and electronic equipment and has facilities for electronic research. Its free library was the first established in Scotland.

Airedale terrier: see TERRIER.

airfoil, surface designed to react in a particular way when exposed to a moving stream of air. For example, the wing surfaces of an airplane produce lift. Some airfoils are manipulated to produce variable reactions. Ailerons (surfaces hinged usually to the trailing edges of the wings) can be manipulated to produce banking and either clockwise or counterclockwise rotation of the plane; the propeller blades can be varied in pitch to change maximum thrust.

air forces. The history of air forces begins with the use of balloons by French forces in Italy in 1859 and by Union forces in the American Civil War. Balloons thereafter proved useful as a means of observation, but air forces in the modern sense date from the First World War, when the offensive capabilities of the airplane were first demonstrated. The airplane was first used for war purposes by Italy against the Turks in Tripoli in 1911, but until the First World War it had served mainly for reconnaissance. Germany, with a large number of airplanes and airships, established her superiority in the air at the beginning of the war. The German Fokker monoplane, with a fixed machine gun that could fire forward through the propeller blades, quickly assured Germany's superiority and inspired Allied efforts toward better aircraft. Indeed, throughout the First World War such development and counterdevelopment accounted for the rapid advance of military aeronautics. The initial use of aircraft for reconnaissance made control of the skies essential to military operations. As a result, aerial combat developed, which in turn led to formation flying, "dog fights," and the bombing of enemy lines of communication and munitions depots. Throughout most of the First World War the majority of the world's air forces were considered an extension of a nation's army and were mostly employed tactically in support of ground forces. As the effectiveness of aircraft as a tactical weapon increased, consideration was given to the establishment of air forces that would be independent of a nation's ground forces. Giulio DOUHET, an Italian, was the first to develop a full-scale theory of strategic air power and to suggest the primacy of an

American aviators' training school in France, 1917.

Observation balloons during the First World War.

Martin B-26 Marauders on Second World War bombing mission.

The F-80, first American jet fighter to enter the Korean war.

PILOT, a wingless rocket plane in experimental stage.

The U.S.A.F. Snark, an intercontinental guided missile.

independent air force. Also highly important in the development of the theory of strategic air power were England's Sir Hugh M. TRENCHARD and Gen. William MITCHELL of the United States. Theories of strategic air power called for the development of strong independent air forces to gain control of the air over an enemy's homeland and to destroy the enemy's means of resistance by intensive aerial bombardment of his industrial centers. This theory, together with rapid and extensive advance in aeronautical knowledge and technique which followed the First World War, brought about a much broader application of air power in the Second World War. During the 1930s Germany devoted great efforts to air armament and in the early years of the Second World War held a marked superiority over the Allies. The first great air battle in history was the BATTLE OF BRITAIN, in which the British Royal Air Force defeated the German Luftwaffe (1940) over Britain. In the Pacific Japan entered the war with a stunning air attack launched from aircraft carriers (see AIRCRAFT CARRIER) on PEARL HARBOR. In the Second World War the development of air power greatly altered the nature of warfare. The use of aircraft to control the air over both land and sea was decisive in nearly all major engagements. The many uses of aircraft during the war included strategic and tactical bombing; attacking of naval and merchant ships; transportation of personnel and cargo; mining of harbors and shipping lanes; antisubmarine patrols; photographic reconnaissance; and support of ground, naval, and amphibious operations. Throughout the war the British and United States air forces conducted strategical bombardment of Germany which led to the destruction of the Luftwaffe and the crippling of German industry, transportation, and communications. In the Pacific, American carrier-based aircraft by the end of 1944 had destroyed the Japanese fleet and air force. In the last months of the war Japan herself was subjected to massive strategical bombardment, ending with the dropping of two atomic bombs on Japan. Major developments of the Second World War included improved techniques of flying and aircraft design and an accumulation of geographical, aerological, and other knowledge essential to modern aviation. The development of the nuclear weapons, jet propulsion, and guided missiles have combined to alter the nature of air power and air forces, though the extent of this change is not yet certain. See H. B. Hinton, *Air Victory: the Men and the Machines* (1948); A. P. De Seversky, *Air Power: Key to Survival* (1950); Quentin Reynolds, *They Fought for the Sky* (1957); and *Jane's All the World's Aircraft* (pub. annually since 1911).

air gas: see FUEL.

airglow: see VAN ALLEN BELTS.

air lock, compartment connecting with the outer atmosphere that part of a CAISSON which contains compressed air. By its means access can be gained to the caisson without loss of pressure. It is also used at the head of tunnel excavations under water. It has a door at each end. When the outer door of the air lock is opened, men or material may be admitted into the compartment. The outer door is then closed. The pressure in the compartment is then raised by admitting compressed air to equal the pressure in the caisson, after which the inner door can be opened. The reverse of this procedure takes place on leaving the compressed-air region. Great care must be exercised in passing workmen through an air lock, so that the change of atmospheric pressure takes place gradually. Too sudden change of pressure may cause AEROEMBOLISM.

air mail. Demonstration flights which showed the feasibility of carrying mail by air were made in England and in the United States in 1911. In the United States, after money for experimentation was appropriated by Congress in 1918, the first regular air mail service for carrying civilian mail began on May 15, 1918. Army pilots and army equipment were used. The first flight was from New York city to Washington, D.C. The Post Office Dept. took over operation of the line in Aug., 1920, and in 1921 the line was discontinued. In May, 1920, the transcontinental route from New York city to San Francisco was completed. On July 1, 1924, coast to coast service all the way by air was scheduled for the first time (before then the mail had been transferred to trains at night). Transpacific air mail was introduced in 1935, and transatlantic air mail in 1939. The Civil Aeronautics Authority was established in 1938 to control all nonmilitary flying. It took over the work of the Bureau of Air Mail (created in the Interstate Commerce Commission in 1934). Air-mail service now extends to nearly all parts of the world.

Aïr Mountains: see SAHARA.

airplane, aeroplane, or **aircraft,** heavier-than-air craft, mechanically driven and fitted with fixed wings by means of which support is maintained through the dynamic action of the air. Early attempts were made to build flying machines according to the principle of bird FLIGHT, but it was not until the beginning of the 20th cent. that flight in heavier-than-air craft was achieved. On Dec. 17, 1903, Orville and Wilbur WRIGHT produced the first power-driven, full-sized, heavier-than-air flying machine near Kitty Hawk, N.C. The first flight lasted 12 seconds, but later flights on the same day were a little longer; a safe landing was made after

A 1678 suggestion for human flight.

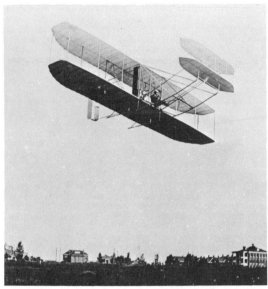

Orville Wright at the controls of his plane during his flight over Fort Meyers, Va., September 9, 1908.

Wright Memorial at the site of the first powered airplane flight in 1903 on Kill Devil Hill near Kitty Hawk, N.C.

each attempt. The machine was a biplane (an airplane with two main supporting surfaces, or wings) with two propellers chain-driven by a gasoline motor. Modern airplanes are monoplanes (airplanes with one main supporting surface, or wing) and may be high-wing, mid-wing, or low-wing. Airplanes may be further classified as propeller-, jet-, turbo-jet or rocket-driven. The airplane has six main parts—fuselage, wings, stabilizer (or tail plane), rudder, one or more engines, and landing gear. The fuselage is the main body of the machine, customarily streamlined in form. It usually contains control equipment, passengers, and cargo. The wings are the main supporting surfaces. The lift of an airplane, or its ability to fly, is basically the result of the direct action of the air against the lower surfaces of the wings and the vacuum thereby created on the upper side. The vacuum effect furnishes more than half the lift of the plane. The lift varies with the speed, there being a minimum speed at which flight can be obtained. At the trailing edge of the wings are auxiliary hinged surfaces known as ailerons which are used to gain lateral control and to turn the airplane. Directional stability is provided by the tail fin, a fixed vertical airfoil at the rear of the plane. The stabilizer, or tail plane, is a fixed horizontal airfoil at the rear of the airplane used to control the pitching motion. To the rear of the stabilizer are usually hinged the elevators, movable auxiliary surfaces. The rudder, generally at the rear of the tail fin, is a movable auxiliary airfoil which gives the craft a yawing movement when in normal flight. Until recently, most engines were of the internal-combustion type, which may be air- or liquid-cooled. During and after the Second World War, duct-type and gas-

turbine engines became increasingly important and since then JET PROPULSION has become the main form of power in most commercial and military aircraft. This has had a major effect upon airplane design, which is closely associated with the ratio between power load (horsepower) and weight. The Wright brothers' first engine weighed about 12 lb. per horsepower. The modern engine of conventional type weighs about 1 lb. or less per horsepower, and jet and gas-turbine engines are much lighter per horsepower. With jet engines the power load has increased to a point at which the airplane is less dependent for lift upon aerodynamic qualities in wing structures. As a result, these have been made shorter and swept back. In some cases they have been replaced by large finlike surfaces extending outward from front to rear in the shape of a triangle. Other surfaces such as the tail fin and stabilizer have been similarly altered. The landing gear is the understructure which supports the weight of the craft when on the ground or on the water and which reduces the shock on landing. There are five common types—the wheel, float, boat, skid, and ski types. Much has been done toward improving equilibrium, stability, control in flight, and other factors contributing to safety. See AVIATION; AUTOGIRO; HELICOPTER; GLIDER; ORNITHOPTER; SEAPLANE. See bibliography under AVIATION and also publications of the U.S. National Advisory Committee for Aeronautics.

air plant or **epiphyte,** any plant that does not normally root in the soil but grows upon another living plant while remaining independent of it except for support (thus differing from a PARASITE). An epiphyte manufactures its own food (see PHOTOSYNTHESIS) in the same way that other plants do,

Spanish moss (Tillandsia usneoides) *is a type of air plant.*

but obtains its moisture from the air or from moisture-laden pockets of the host plant, rather than from the soil. Some epiphytes are found in every group of the plant kingdom but particularly among the algae, lichens, mosses, and ferns. Of the flowering plants, the best-known epiphytes are orchids and Spanish moss. Epiphytes may grow upon the trunk, branches, or leaves of the host plant, sometimes so thickly as to damage the original plant by crowding out its leaves. They are most abundant in the moist tropics. Other plants not strictly epiphytes are popularly known as air plants. Such plants are usually capable of producing plantlets from the leaves without direct contact with the soil, as in *Bryophyllum.*

air pollution: see POLLUTION.

Airport, uninc. town (pop. 3,689), central Calif., SE of Modesto.

airport or **airfield,** place for landing and departure of aircraft, usually with facilities for shelter and main-

tenance of planes and for receiving and discharging passengers and cargo. The essential factors in airport construction are that the field be as level as possible; that the ground be firm and easily drained; that approaches to runways be free of trees, hills, buildings, and other obstructions; and that the site be reasonably free of smoke and fog. The runways of large airports vary from 2,500 to 7,000 ft. in length and 100 to 200 ft. in width. Besides the hangars (buildings for housing and servicing aircraft), airports are usually provided with office and terminal buildings which house administrative, traffic control, communication, and weather observation personnel. The rapid development of aircraft, especially after the introduction of jet propulsion, has created problems for all major airports. Greater speed and weight of aircraft have made longer and more durable runways necessary. The increasing number of high-speed jet aircraft has caused problems of traffic noise control. In England airports are sometimes called aerodromes. See H. K. Glidden, *Airports: Design, Construction and Management* (1946); C. A. Zweng, *Airport Operation and Management* (1947); J. W. Wood, *Airports and Air Traffic* (1949).

air power. The rapid development of aviation in the 20th cent. was reflected in the use of aircraft in war (see AIR FORCES) and gave rise to theories of the strategic value of air power. The rather tentative use of scout planes at the beginning of the First World War was followed by the creation of small forces of fighter planes, which engaged in aerial combat and some bombing. Yet the experience did little more than suggest the potential military use of aircraft. A few enthusiasts appreciated its significance, among them Gen. William MITCHELL, Air Chief Marshal Sir Hugh Montague TRENCHARD, and Gen. Giulio DOUHET. They fought for the intensive development of air power and pleaded for large air forces, arguing that future wars would be won by strategic bombardment of an enemy's industrial centers, thereby destroying the economic means of conducting a war. Although theories of air power were largely ignored, Great Britain, France, and Italy established separate departments

John F. Kennedy International Airport, New York. Passenger-loading platforms.

of government for air, headed by cabinet members. The first powers to devote themselves seriously to the development of air power were Hitler's Germany, Mussolini's Italy, and imperial Japan. The early days of the Second World War seemed to uphold Hitler's boasts of the power of the *Luftwaffe* under Hermann Goering. Aircraft were to a great extent responsible for German victories in Poland, Norway, the Low Countries, and France, and the first German setback was the failure of the *Luftwaffe* to destroy the Royal Air Force in the BATTLE OF BRITAIN. The capture of Crete (1941) by air-transported troops seemed to bear out some of the more extreme claims of air-power enthusiasts. The effect of air power in revolutionizing naval warfare was demonstrated by the attack of Japanese aircraft, launched from aircraft carriers, on PEARL HARBOR. Extensive use of the AIRCRAFT CARRIER was decisive in the battles of the CORAL SEA and MIDWAY, and thereafter aircraft were employed in all major naval battles. Throughout the war the Allies conducted an intensive campaign of strategic bombardment against Germany and wrought enormous destruction in German cities, but postwar studies have cast doubt on the effectiveness of this campaign. Aircraft also provided invaluable support to ground forces throughout the war by attacking enemy troops, transport, and supply bases. Air power played an incalculably large part for the Allies in winning the war. After the war the opponents of the extreme advocates of air power pointed out that no major battle had been won by air forces alone, but only by air forces combined with land or naval forces. The eminence of air power was, however, accepted by all. The introduction of nuclear weapons, jet propulsion, and guided missiles toward the end of the Second World War has altered the concept of air power and given rise to such theories as "massive retaliation," which means that a nation that is attacked will massively retaliate with nuclear weapons, destroying the attacking nation to such an extent that war between any two nations will be mutually self-destructive. See Giulio Douhet, *Command of the Air* (Eng. tr., 1942); *U.S. Strategic Bombing Survey*; W. F. Craven and J. L. Cate, ed., *The Army Air Forces in World War II* (9 vols., 1948–49); Charles Webster and Novle Franklin, *The Strategic Air Offensive against Germany, 1939–1945* (4 vols., 1961).

air pump: see PUMP.

airship, dirigible balloon, i.e., a balloon having a power plant and directional control. There are

One of the largest nonrigid airships, U.S. Navy's ZPG-3W.

The Shenandoah moored to mast on the U.S.S. Patoka.

The German airship Hindenburg on one of her Atlantic crossings.

three general types: nonrigid, in which the supporting structure is held in form by internal pressure in the gas bag; semirigid, in which the form is maintained in a similar manner with the addition of a rigid or jointed keel; and rigid, which has a completely rigid frame. The first successful power-driven airship was built by the Frenchman Henri Giffard (1825–1882) in 1852. Many experimenters followed his efforts; among them were Dupuy de Lome and the Tissandier brothers. In 1884 Charles Renard and Captain Krebs built and successfully operated an airship named *La France* with propulsion obtained from electric storage batteries. Other outstanding names in the development of the airship are Alberto SANTOS-DUMONT and Count Ferdinand von ZEPPELIN and Hugo ECKENER. Santos-Dumont was prominent in the early development of the nonrigid airship. This type, sometimes called blimp, simple in construction and very light, proved useful during the Second World War for coastal patrolling and antisubmarine warfare and before the war was used commercially in such activities as advertising, traffic control, and mail delivery. To Zeppelin and Eckener belongs the credit for successfully developing the rigid type of airship, which consists, in general, of a latticework structure of aluminum or duralumin, divided into separate compartments. All types of airships have accommodations for crew, passengers, and cargo. Lifting power is obtained by the use of hydrogen or helium; helium, although lesser in lifting power, has the decided advantage of being noninflammable. A number of means of propulsion were tried, but propellers proved best as suitable engines were developed. Except for the *Mayfly*, which met with disaster upon completion, the building of rigid airships was not undertaken in England until the First World War, when the *R33*, *R34*, and others were built. The *R34* was the first airship to cross (1919) the Atlantic, returning in 75 hr. Post-war airships constructed in England were the *R100* and *R101*, which were built as commercial vessels. The *Graf Zeppelin*, built in Germany in 1926–27, traveled 20,000 mi. around the world in 1929. The first rigid airship built in the United States, the *Shenandoah*, completed in 1923, was the first vessel to use helium as a lifting gas. She was wrecked by a violent storm in 1927. *The Los Angeles*, built by Germany as part of her reparations payment to the United States and completed in 1924, was successfully navigated across the Atlantic late in 1924 by Captain Eckener. The German airship *Hindenburg*, built in 1936, and those aboard burned at its mooring mast at Lakehurst, N.J., in 1937. No rigid airship survived the Second World War. See E. A. Lehmann and H. L. Mingos, *Zeppelins* (1927); C. E. Rosendahl, *What About the Airship?* (1938); Hugh Allen, *The Story of the Airship* (*Non-rigid*) (1942); John Toland, *Ships in the Sky* (1957).

airsickness: see MOTION SICKNESS.

airway, defined by the National Advisory Committee for Aeronautics as an air route between air traffic centers that is over terrain best suited for emergency landings, with landing fields at intervals equipped with aids to air navigation and with a communication system for the transmission of information pertinent to the operation of aircraft.

Airways do not always follow a straight line, since it is often advisable to detour in order to avoid mountains or certain localities where weather conditions are generally unfavorable. Definite flying rules have been established which require all aircraft to keep to the right of an airway and to observe regulations governing minimum altitudes, approaching and overtaking other aircraft, and acrobatic flying. See M. B. Baker, *Airlane Traffic and Operation* (1947); U.S. Dept. of Commerce, *Federal Airway Plan, Fiscal Years 1959–1963* (1958).

Aisha or **Aishah:** see AYESHA.

Aisne (ān, Fr. ĕn), department (2,868 sq. mi.; estimated pop. 487,068), NE France, in Île-de-France, Picardy, and Champagne, touching the Belgian border. Laon is the capital. Drained by the Oise, Aisne, Marne, and Somme rivers, it is primarily a fertile agricultural region. It has metallurgical industries in the Oise valley. Saint-Quentin and Bohain have noted textile industries; Saint-Gobain has a well-known mirror factory. Aisne gave its name to four battles in the First World War. There was especially severe fighting in the Château-Thierry sector.

Aitkin (ā′kǐn), village (pop. 1,829), co. seat of Aitkin co., central Minn., on the Mississippi and N of Mille Lacs Lake, WSW of Duluth; settled 1870. It is in a farm and resort region. A Federal wildlife refuge is nearby.

Aix-en-Provence (ĕks′-ä-prôvãs′, ĕk″sä-), city (estimated pop. 52,217), Bouches-du-Rhône dept., in Provence, SE France. A commercial center, it trades in olives, fruits, and wines. Founded (c.122 B.C.) by the Romans near the site of mineral springs, it was named Aquae Sextiae. Here, in 102 B.C., Marius defeated the Teutons. It was made an archiepiscopal see in the 5th cent. Since the 12th cent. Aix has been the capital of PROVENCE (except when replaced by Arles). Here, in 1486, the estates of Provence approved the union of Provence with the French crown. Aix was the seat (1501–1789) of a provincial PARLEMENT. A center of PROVENÇAL LITERATURE, Aix has a university (founded 1409), part of which is now at Marseilles. Among its chief historic structures are the Cathedral of Saint-Sauveur (13th–14th cent.) and a baroque town hall. A picturesque town, it has become a favorite sojourn for painters, and there is a music festival each summer. CÉZANNE was born here.

Aix-la-Chapelle: see AACHEN.

Aix-la-Chapelle, Treaty of. 1 Compact of May 2, 1668, which ended the French invasion of the Spanish Netherlands (see DEVOLUTION, WAR OF). France kept most of its conquests in Flanders; Cambrai, Aire, Saint-Omer, and the province of Franche-Comté were returned to Spain; and the remainder of Spain's possessions in the Low Countries were guaranteed by the TRIPLE ALLIANCE. **2** Treaty of 1748, ending the War of the AUSTRIAN SUCCESSION. In general, it restored the *status quo ante*, but awarded Silesia and Glatz to Prussia and conferred the duchies of Parma, Piacenza, and Guastalla on the Spanish infante, Philip. It confirmed the PRAGMATIC SANCTION of 1713, and it renewed Britain's privilege (acquired 1713) over transporting slaves to Spanish America, the trade agreements with Britain regarding the Spanish colonies, and the recognition of the Protestant succession in England.

Aix-les-Bains (āks′-lā-bĕ′, –băng′, Fr. ĕks′-lā-bĕ′), town (estimated pop. 15,680), Savoie dept., SE France, in Savoie, situated on Lake Bourget at the foot of the Alps. It is a popular resort and a picturesque old spa. Its alum and sulphur springs have been frequented since Roman times. There are ruins of Roman baths.

Aizu-Wakamatsu: see WAKAMATSU 1.

Ajaccio (ȯyȧ̆′chēo, ȯyȧ̆′sēō, Ital. ȧyät′chō) town (estimated pop. 32,997), capital of CORSICA, France, on the Gulf of Ajaccio, an inlet of the Mediterranean. A fortified seaport, it trades in wines, olives, and timber. Ajaccio also manufactures furniture and cork products. The birthplace of Napoleon I, Ajaccio still preserves the house where he was born.

Ajah (ā′jü), variant of AIAH 1.

Ajalon (ă′jü–, ā′–), variant of AIJALON.

Ajanta (ȯjŭn′tü), village, Maharashtra state, W central India, in the Ajanta Hills. It is the site of the famous Ajanta caves, which contain remarkable examples of Buddhist art. Excavated in the side of a steep ravine, the caves (some 29 in number) consist of monasteries and shrines and contain magnificent frescoes and sculpture depicting scenes from the life of the Buddha. Dating from early times to A.D. c.642, they provide a continuous narrative of Buddhist art.

Ajaccio, capital of Corsica, overlooking the Gulf of Ajaccio.

Ajax (ā′jăks), Gr. *Aias*, in Greek mythology. **1** Hero of the Trojan War, son of TELAMON, thus called the Telamonian Ajax, also called Ajax the Greater. In the *Iliad* he is represented as a gigantic man, slow of thought and speech, but quick in battle and always showing courage. He led the troops of Salamis against Troy and was one of the foremost Greek warriors, fighting both Hector and Odysseus to draws. He and Odysseus rescued the corpse of Achilles from the Trojans, but when the armor of Achilles was awarded to Odysseus the disappointment of Ajax was so great that he went mad and committed suicide. The *Ajax* of Sophocles deals with the madness and death of the great warrior. Ajax had hero cults at Salamis, Attica, and Troad. **2** Leader of the forces from Locris in the Trojan War, called the Locrian Ajax, Ajax of Oileus (after his father, Oileus), or Ajax the Lesser, because he was not the equal of the Telamonian Ajax. In the sack of Troy he violated Cassandra at the altar of Athena, and Athena caused him to be shipwrecked on the way home. Poseidon saved him, but Ajax, boasting of his own power, defied the lightning to strike him down and was instantly struck by it. Other versions of the story say that he stole the PALLADIUM and that later Poseidon destroyed him for blasphemy.

Frescoes in the Ajanta caves.

Ajax and Cassandra (Roman relief).

Ajivika (äjē′vĭkú), religious sect of medieval India, once of major importance. The Ajivikas were an ascetic, atheistic, anti-Brahmanical community whose pessimistic doctrines are related to those of JAINISM. Its founder, Gosala (d. c.484 B.C.), was, it is said, a friend of Mahavira, the founder of Jainism. Gosala denied that a man's actions could influence the process of transmigration, which proceeded according to a rigid pattern, controlled in the smallest detail by an impersonal cosmic principle, *Niyati*, or destiny. After a period of prosperity under Asoka, the sect rapidly declined and only retained local importance in SE India, where it survived until the 14th century. See A. L. Basham, *History and Doctrines of the Ajivikas* (1951).

Ajmer (ăjmēr′, ŭj–), former state, NW India. Now comprised in RAJASTHAN state, it formerly consisted of two detached areas surrounded by Rajasthan, and was identical with the former British province of Ajmer-Merwara. The city of **Ajmer** (pop. 196,633), the former capital, was founded in the 12th cent. It is a trade center and has cotton mills and large railroad shops. A Mogul military base, it was here that JEHANGIR received Sir Thomas Roe, ambassador of James I. A Jain temple (constructed 1153; now converted into a mosque); the tomb of the Moslem saint Muin-ud-din Chishti; and a palace of Akbar are the most notable historic buildings. Mayo Rajkumar College (opened 1875) is here.

Ajo (ä′hō), town (pop. 7,049), SW Ariz., SW of Gila; settled 1854. One of the oldest mining towns in the state, it still derives its income primarily from copper mining. Ajo is also a health resort. Nearby is Organ Pipe Cactus National Monument (328,691.01 acres; est. 1937), containing unique desert growth.

Ajodhya (ŭjōd′yú) or **Ayodhya** (ŭyōd′yú), town, Uttar Pradesh state, N India. It is a joint municipality with FYZABAD (total pop., 82,498). It was the capital of the kingdom of Kosala (7th cent. B.C.). Long associated with Hindu legend, the town is a center of pilgrimage. It is also called Oudh.

Akaba: see AQABA.

Akali Dal: see SIKHS.

Akan (ā′–), descendant of Esau. Gen. 36.27. Jakan: 1 Chron. 1.42.

Akbar (ăk′bär), 1542–1605, greatest Mogul emperor (1556–1605) of India; grandson of Baber. He succeeded his father, Humayun, under a regent. As a youth he learned the rigorous arts of war, and tiring of the regency, he asserted (1560) his full imperial authority. A magnetic personality, he inspired the Mogul armies and gradually enlarged his original domain in N central India to include Afghanistan, Baluchistan, and nearly all of the Indian peninsula N of the Godavari river. To unify this vast state he initiated administrative and fiscal reforms and held to a policy of religious toleration. He defeated the Rajputs, the most fearsome Hindu warriors, and then allied himself to them. Although he was himself illiterate, Akbar's courts at Delhi, Agra, and later FATHPUR SIKRI were centers of the arts, letters, and learning. He was much impressed with Persian culture, and because of him the later Mogul empire bears an indelible Persian stamp. At his sumptuous courts, where he reigned as a philosopher-king, Akbar surrounded himself with Moslem divines, Hindu Brahmans, and Jesuits. A passion for spiritual certainty and disillusionment with orthodox Islam led him to promulgate (1582) the Din-i-Ilahi [divine faith], an eclectic creed derived from Islam, Hinduism, Zoroastrianism, and Christianity. A simple, monotheistic cult, tolerant in outlook, it centered on Akbar as prophet. This religious revolution led to serious rebellions by outraged Moslems. The Din-i-Ilahi never took hold in India and disappeared soon after Akbar's death. See Vincent Smith, *Akbar the Great Moghul* (1917); Laurence Binyon, *Akbar* (1930); M. Roychondhuri, *The Din-i-Ilahi* (1941); E. S. Wellesz, *Akbar's Religious Thought, Reflected in Mogul Painting* (1953); R. Krishnamurti, *Akbar, the Religious Aspect* (1961).

Akeldama (úkĕl′dúmú), variant of ACELDAMA.

Akeley, Carl Ethan (āk′lē), 1864–1926, American naturalist, animal sculptor, and author, b. Orleans co., N.Y. He served (1887–95) at the Museum of Milwaukee, from 1895 to 1909 was at the Field Museum, Chicago (now the Chicago Natural History Museum), and from 1909 was affiliated

Mogul miniature depicting Akbar on a tiger hunt.

with the American Museum of Natural History, New York. His principal contribution was in the field of taxidermy; his system of mounting specimens by applying the skin to a finely modelled mannikin is still used by museums. His animal sculptures and paintings may be seen in Akeley Hall in the Museum of Natural History and in the Field Museum. The extraordinary realism of Akeley's displays derived from his wide field experience; he made numerous expeditions to Africa to collect specimens. He invented the cement gun for use in his own work, and the Akeley camera is widely used by naturalists. His influence led to the establishment in 1926 of the Albert National Park, an animal sanctuary in the Republic of the Congo. He wrote *In Brightest Africa* (1923). His first wife, Delia Denning Akeley (later Mrs. Warren D. Howe), aided him in field work and in mounting groups; in 1924 and 1928 she headed expeditions for the Brooklyn Museum. She wrote *J. T., Jr., the Biography of an African Monkey* (1928), *Jungle Portraits* (1930), and *All True* (1931). Akeley's second wife, Mary Jobe Akeley, before their marriage in 1924 had taught at Hunter College and had explored the Canadian Rockies (Mt. Jobe was named for her). She collaborated in Akeley's work and after his death in Africa assumed direction of the expedition on which they were then engaged. She made another expedition (1935–36) to the Transvaal and Southern Rhodesia. Her books include *Akeley's Africa* (1929), *Restless Jungle* (1936), *The Wilderness Lives Again* (1940), and, with Akeley, *Adventures in the African Jungle* (1930) and *Lions, Gorillas, and Their Neighbors* (1932).

Akenside, Mark (ă'kĭnsĭd), 1721–70, English poet and physician. He entered the Univ. of Edinburgh in 1739 to study theology, but soon changed to medicine, receiving a medical degree from Leiden in 1744. His chief literary work was the didactic poem, *The Pleasures of Imagination* (1744). Among his other works are the neoclassic *Odes on Various Subjects* (1745) and the *Epistle to Curio* (1744), a vigorous political satire. Akenside's conversion to Tory principles at the accession of George III earned him the appointment of physician to the queen. See biography by C. T. Houpt (1944).

Akershus (ä'kŭrs-hōōs"), province (1,895 sq. mi.; pop. 226,948), SE Norway, W and NW of the Oslo Fjord. It surrounds its capital, OSLO. The area has rich farms and considerable forests; its products include food, textiles, iron, metal, and wood manufactures.

Akhenaton: see IKHNATON.

Akhetaton: see TEL-EL-AMARNA.

Akhisar (äk"hĭsär'), town (pop. 40,013), Manisa prov., W Turkey. It is an agricultural market center and is noted for its rug production. It is the biblical THYATIRA.

Akhmatova, Anna (än'nŭ ŭkhmä'tŭvŭ), pseud. of **Anna Andreyevna Gorenko** (ŭndrä'ŭvnŭ gôryĕng'kô), 1888–, Russian poet of the Acmeist school. Her brief lyrics, simple yet rhythmic in the tradition of Pushkin, attained great popularity. Her themes were autobiographical, concerning love and tragedy. She divorced the poet Gumilev in 1918. After his execution as a counterrevolutionary in 1921, however, she wrote no new poetry until 1940.

During the Second World War her popularity revived, but in 1946 she was criticized for "bourgeois decadence." Her later poetry is considered inferior to her earlier work.

Akiba ben Joseph (ŭkē'bŭ), A.D. c.50–c.132, Palestinian rabbi. He was one of the first Jewish scholars to make a systematic compilation of the Hebrew oral laws. This compilation, known as the *Mishna of Rabbi Akiba*, exercised a profound influence upon the development of Mishnaic doctrines. Akiba believed in the Messianic mission of BAR KOKBA and sided with him in his revolt against Rome. He was an idol of the people; the facts of his life are obscured with legends. He was incarcerated and, it is said, tortured to death by the Romans; he is one of the martyrs mentioned in the Jewish penitential prayer. See biography by Louis Finkelstein (1936).

Akihito (äkē'hētō), 1933–, Japanese heir apparent, son of HIROHITO. In 1952 he was officially proclaimed heir to the throne. A popular figure, he represented the imperial family at Queen Elizabeth II's coronation in 1953, and on his journey he traveled in Canada and paid a visit to the United States. In April, 1959, he married Michiko Shoda, a commoner; it was the first time that an heir to the throne had wed outside of the court nobility. A son was born in 1960.

Akita (ä'kētä), city (pop. 203,661), capital of Akita prefecture, NW Honshu, Japan, on the Sea of Japan. An oil-refining center, it is also a large port which exports lumber and rice. It became an important feudal town in the 8th cent., and its castle-fort (733) still stands. **Akita** prefecture (4,503 sq. mi.; pop. 1,335,580) contains Japan's largest oil field and copper mine. Its mountains have extensive stands of quality timber, and its fertile lowlands yield crops of rice, tobacco, and fruit. Akita (the capital), Noshiro (the chief port), Tsushisoki, and Yokote are centers of population.

Akka: see PYGMY.

Akka, Israel: see ACRE.

Akkad (ă'kăd, ä'käd), region of Mesopotamia, occupying the northern part of later Babylonia. The southern part was SUMER. In both regions city-states had begun to appear in the 4th millennium B.C. In Akkad a Semitic language, Akkadian, was spoken. Akkad flourished after Sargon began (c.2340 B.C.) to spread wide his conquests, which ranged from his capital, Agade (ŭgä'dē, ŭgä'dē) (or the city of Akkad), to the Mediterranean shores. He united city-states into a vast organized empire. Furthermore, he was overlord of all the petty states of Sumer and Akkad, as were his successors, most notably Naram-sin. The merit of Sargonic art can be seen in the stele of Naram-sin. The naturalistic sculpture reflected a high achievement in glyptic art and depicted a wide range of mythological scenes. After more than a century the empire declined, and it was overrun by mountain tribes. When the Akkadian empire had fallen, Mesopotamia was in chaos. Peace was maintained only in the south in the city-state of Lagash under Gudea. Lagash was later absorbed by the 3d dynasty of Ur, which held sway over both Akkad and Sumer. Toward the end of the 3d millennium Elam took over most of the power as a new wave of Semitic-speaking peoples entered Mesopotamia. It was by defeating the Elamites that Hammurabi was able to create Babylonia. The name Akkad also appears as Accad.

Akkerman: see BELGOROD-DNESTROVSKY, Ukraine.

Akkub. 1 Descendant of David. 1 Chron. 3.24. **2** Levitical family. 1 Chron. 9.17; Ezra 2.42; Neh. 7.45; 11.19; 12.25. **3** One of the Nethinim. Ezra 2.45. **4** One who explained the law. Neh. 8.7.

Aklavik (äklä′vĭk), settlement, on the east channel of the Mackenzie river, Mackenzie dist., Northwest Territories, Canada, c.30 mi. from the Beaufort Sea, in a fur-trapping region. It was moved (1954–58) from the old site on the west channel. It is the administrative center for the western arctic. A service community for the Eskimos and Indians of the region, Aklavik has an airfield, a meteorological station, a radio station, and a hospital and schools.

Akmolinsk, Kazakh SSR: see TSELINOGRAD.

Ako, Michel: see ACO, MICHEL.

Akrabbim (ŭkrăb′ĭm): see MAALEH-ACRABBIM.

Akranes (ä′kränĕs″), town (pop. 3,822), SW Iceland, on a peninsula on Faxa Bay. It is a fishing port and industrial center with a huge cement plant.

Akron (ăk′rŭn). **1** Town (pop. 1,890), co. seat of Washington co., NE Colo., ENE of Denver, in a farm and oil-well area; founded 1882, inc. 1887. **2** Town (pop. 1,351), NW Iowa, on the Big Sioux (here marking the S.Dak. line) and NNW of Sioux City; platted 1871 as Portlandville, inc. 1882. It is a trade and processing point of a farm area. **3** Village (pop. 2,841), W N.Y., NE of Buffalo, in a farm and dairy region; inc. 1849. Metal products are made here. Nearby are the Tonawanda Indian Reservation (chiefly Seneca) and Akron Falls Park. **4** City (pop. 290,351), co. seat of Summit co., NE Ohio, on the Little Cuyahoga and S of Cleveland; settled 1807, inc. as a city 1865. It is an important industrial center, the hub of the country's rubber industry; automobile and aircraft parts, clay and metal products, chemicals, breakfast foods, and industrial machinery are also manufactured. The Ohio and Erie Canal and later the railroad spurred the city's commercial growth. It is a port of entry. Akron has a dirigible airdock and is the U.S. center for lighter-than-air craft; the dirigibles *Akron* and *Macon* were built here. The Portage Lakes are south. The first important application of the sit-down strike technique occurred in Akron in 1936; several thousand workers were involved. The Univ. of Akron (city supported; coeducational; 1870) is here. Its Institute of Rubber Research sponsors fundamental and applied research in natural and synthetic rubbers. **5** Borough (pop. 2,167), SE Pa., NE of Lancaster; inc. 1884. Shoes are made here.

Aksakov, Ivan Sergeyevich (ēvän′ sĕrgyä′ùvĭch ùksä′kùf), 1823–86, Russian publicist; son of Sergei Timofeyevich Aksakov. He was editor of various Slavophile journals, among them the weekly *Rus*. Aksakov exerted great political influence.

Aksakov, Konstantin Sergeyevich (kùnstùntyĕn′), 1817–60, Russian critic and writer, brother of Ivan Aksakov. Like his brother, he was an ardent Slavophile and strongly idealized the village community as a voluntary association. His literary criticism was devoted mainly to urging writers to seek closer ties with the peasantry.

Aksakov, Sergei Timofeyevich (syĭrgä′ tyĭmùfyä′ùvĭch), 1791–1859, Russian writer, known for his nostalgic descriptions of the Orenburg region. His chief work is *Family Chronicle* (1856; Eng. tr., 1924), a picture of country life in the days of serfdom. His *Years of Childhood* (1858; Eng. tr., 1960) describes his happy youth. Though influenced by Gogol, his work is devoid of social criticism.

Aksu: see AQSU.

Aksum or **Axum** (both: äksoom′), town (pop. c.10,000), N Ethiopia. It was the capital of a line of emperors who ruled (1st–6th cent.) what is now N Ethiopia and N Eritrea. Here, they erected gigantic, carved obelisks. Aksum is a major center of Ethiopian Christianity, and the emperors of Ethiopia traditionally have been crowned here in the Cathedral of Mary of Zion.

Akte: see ATHOS.

Aktyubinsk (ŭktyoo′bĭnsk), city (pop. c.97,000), capital of Aktyubinsk oblast, NW Kazakh SSR, on the Ilek river. On the Trans-Caspian RR, it has metallurgical, machine, and food-processing plants. Founded in 1869, it grew rapidly as an industrial center after the opening (1905) of the railroad.

Akureyri (ä′kùrä″rē), city (pop. 8,835), N Iceland, at the head of the Eyja Fjord. The second largest city of Iceland, it is a fishing, commercial, and industrial center. It has clothing and footwear factories, machine shops, and shipyards. It was chartered in 1862.

Akyab (äkyăb′, äkyäb′), city (pop. 42,329), capital of the Arakan regional division and of Akyab prov., W Burma, on the Bay of Bengal. It is an important Burmese port and rice-milling center. Originally a small fishing village, it became a large center for exporting rice after the British occupation in 1826. Akyab was held (1942–45) by the Japanese in the Second World War.

Al, chemical symbol for the element ALUMINUM.

Alabama (ălùbă′mù), state (51,609 sq. mi.; 1960 pop. 3,266,740), SE United States, admitted 1819 as the 22d state (a slaveholding state). The capital is MONTGOMERY, the largest city is BIRMINGHAM, and the seaport is MOBILE. Alabama is bounded on the north by Tennessee, on the east by Georgia, on the south by Florida and the Gulf of Mexico,

Alabama location map

State Seal of Alabama

The Capitol in Mont-
gomery, Alabama.

and on the west by Mississippi. Except for the mountainous section in the northeast (the southern end of the CUMBERLAND PLATEAU), the state is a rolling plain with a mean elevation of c.500 ft. in two geologic regions—the Appalachian piedmont above the fall line and the coastal plain below. These plains, drained by the ALABAMA and the TOMBIGBEE rivers and their tributaries, are primarily given over to agriculture. The central BLACK BELT yields cotton (which has declined in importance), corn, peanuts, hay, sweet potatoes, oats, Irish potatoes, and peaches; beef and dairy cattle are also raised here. Where the Tennessee river loops across the north, hydroelectric power from the TENNESSEE VALLEY AUTHORITY has been increasingly turning an agricultural land into an industrial section. The mineral riches of coal, iron, and limestone have also contributed to the state's industries, and Birmingham is a leading U.S. iron and steel center. Lumbering, stock-raising, and Gulf fishing also add to the wealth of Alabama, which is still largely devoted to farming. Agriculture was known to the four great Indian groups of the region (Creek and Cherokee in the east, Choctaw and Chickasaw in the west) when the Spanish explorers arrived. Pánfilo de Narváez may have visited Alabama in 1528, Cabeza de Vaca certainly did, and Hernando DE SOTO spent some time in the region in 1540. White settlement was begun, however, not by the Spanish but in 1702 by the French under the sieur de BIENVILLE in the Mobile area. French and British contended for the furs gathered by the Indians, and the region went (1763) to the British, who were victorious over France and Spain in the French and Indian Wars. At the close of the American Revolution, Great Britain ceded (1783) to the United States all lands east of the Mississippi except the Floridas (see WEST FLORIDA CONTROVERSY). The Territory of Mississippi was set up in 1798, but the land was still largely wilderness with a considerable fur trade, centered at SAINT STEPHENS, and with only the beginnings of cotton cultivation. Both were interrupted in the War of 1812, when part of the

The first White House of the Confederacy, in Montgomery.

Wilson Dam, at Muscle Shoals, Alabama, a link in the great TVA chain of hydroelectric power plants.

Most of Alabama's iron and steel mills are situated in or near Birmingham.

The Black Belt of Alabama is rich cotton country.

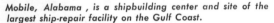
Mobile, Alabama , is a shipbuilding center and site of the largest ship-repair facility on the Gulf Coast.

Creek Confederacy took the warpath under William WEATHERFORD. Andrew JACKSON decisively defeated the Indians at HORSESHOE BEND on March 27, 1814. This victory, coupled with the need of England for cotton, ushered in the period of heavy settlement. New settlers poured into the Alabama region, especially from Georgia and Tennessee. The wealthy newcomers took up land in the fertile bottom lands and established great slave-worked plantations that produced cotton for the markets of the great southern ports. Poorer newcomers took over less fertile uplands, where they scrabbled a living as best they could. So many came that the

Territory of Alabama was set up in 1817 with William W. BIBB as governor; two years later it became a state. In cotton-prosperous Alabama the slave-owning planters were dominant, and as the Civil War loomed closer the support of Southern rights and secession sentiment grew under the urging of "fire-eaters" such as William L. YANCEY. Alabama broke away from the Union on Jan. 11, 1861, when its second constitutional convention passed the ordinance of secession. The government of the Confederacy was organized at Montgomery on Feb. 4, 1861. Federal troops held the Tennessee valley after 1862. One of the great naval battles of the war was won by Admiral D. G. FARRAGUT in Mobile Bay in 1864, but most of the state was not occupied in force until 1865. In the RECONSTRUCTION era, Alabama's ruined agricultural economy supported a corrupt regime of scalawags and carpetbaggers. Few reforms emerged, but the mining of coal and iron was expanded by Daniel PRATT and his successor H. F. De Bardeleben to mark the rise of Alabama industry. Farming was still dominant, and the fortunes of the state still rose and fell with the market price of cotton, but constant use and erosion began to exhaust the land. Diversification of crops, much advocated in the 20th cent., was sped when the boll weevil invaded the cotton fields and the great demand in the First World War brought high prices for food crops. The depression and the agricultural program of F. D. Roosevelt's New Deal caused more farmers to produce subsistence crops and took more land away from the wasting cotton culture. The social and economic problems of Alabama were brought to national attention in the quarrels concerning the SCOTTSBORO CASE and the operations of TVA. The state contributed such figures of importance to the national scene as Hugo L. BLACK. Industrialization was greatly increased in the Second World War with the appearance of factories producing machines, munitions, powder, and war supplies, and many varied industries arose. HUNTSVILLE became a center for rocket research, and its population jumped from 16,437 in 1950 to 72,365 in 1960. Industrialization and commerce increased throughout the state. Adding impetus to this growth was an ambitious development program of Alabama's inland waterways. This program provided cheap water transportation, more hydroelectric power, and flood-control measures. In 1954 the U.S. Supreme Court passed a decision ruling racial segregation in public elementary and secondary schools unconstitutional, and the decision was followed by a severe rise in racial tension (see INTEGRATION). Alabama, like much of the Deep South, is passing through a difficult period of transition. Among Alabama's educational institutions are the Univ. of Alabama, at Tuscaloosa (see ALABAMA, UNIVERSITY OF); AUBURN UNIVERSITY, at Auburn; BIRMINGHAM-SOUTHERN COLLEGE and Howard College, at BIRMINGHAM; Huntingdon College, at MONTGOMERY; Alabama College at MONTEVALLO; and TUSKEGEE INSTITUTE, at Tuskegee. See A. J. Pickett, *History of Alabama* (1900); W. L. Fleming, *Civil War and Reconstruction in Alabama* (1905); T. P. Abernathy, *The Formative Period in Alabama, 1815–1828* (1922); A. B. Moore, *History of Alabama* (1935); C. S. Davis, *The Cotton Kingdom in Alabama* (1939); Federal Writers' Project, *Alabama: a Guide to the Deep South* (1941); W. T. Jordan, *Ante-bellum Alabama, Town and Country* (1957).

Alabama, river formed in central Alabama by the confluence of the Coosa and the Tallapoosa rivers just above Montgomery. It flows c.315 mi. W, SW, then S to the Tombigbee, with which it forms the Mobile river N of Mobile. It is navigable.

Alabama, ship: see CONFEDERATE CRUISERS.

Alabama, University of, mainly at University, near Tuscaloosa; state supported, coeducational; chartered 1820, opened 1831. An experimental station of the U.S. Bureau of Mines, the state natural history museum, the state geological survey, and a business research bureau are here. See also INTEGRATION.

Alabama claims. In the Civil War the *Alabama* and other CONFEDERATE CRUISERS inflicted great damage on Northern merchant marine. Since these were built, fitted out, and otherwise aided by British interests, the United States claimed damages. These claims came to be the sore point in British-American relations, already aggravated by other disputes. W. H. Seward failed to reach a settlement while he was Secretary of State. However, his successor, Hamilton Fish, brought about the Treaty of Washington (1871), which provided for arbitration. Charles Francis Adams for the United States, Alexander J. E. Cockburn for Great Britain, and three members from neutral countries constituted the tribunal, which met at Geneva in 1871–72. The arbitrators threw out American claims for indirect losses, but they awarded the United States $15,500,000 for all the direct damage done by the *Alabama* and the *Florida* and for most of the damage caused by the *Shenandoah*. The British were absolved of blame in the cases of several less important cruisers.

Alabama College: see MONTEVALLO.

Alabama Polytechnic Institute: see AUBURN UNIVERSITY.

alabamine: see ASTATINE.

Alabaster, village (pop. 1,623), central Ala., S of Birmingham.

alabaster (ăl′ūbăs″tûr), fine-grained, massive, translucent variety of GYPSUM, pure white or streaked with reddish brown, used in statuary and for other decorative purposes. It is soft enough to be scratched with the fingernail and hence is easily carved, but also easily broken, soiled, and weathered. It is quarried in England and also in Italy. Vases and statuettes of Italian alabaster are sold as "Florentine marbles." The alabaster of the ancients, called Oriental alabaster and onyx marble, to distinguish it from true alabaster, is MARBLE, a calcium carbonate, whereas gypsum is a calcium sulphate. The calcium carbonate form occurs both in underground masses (TRAVERTINE) and in cave formations (see STALACTITE AND STALAGMITE). Important sources of supply are Algeria, Egypt, Iran,

Alabaster chessmen

and Mexico (from which it is exported under the name Mexican onyx); in the United States there are important sources in Utah and Arizona. Oriental alabaster was extensively used by the Egyptians in sarcophagi, in the linings of tombs, in the walls and ceilings of temples, and in vases and sacrificial vessels. The Romans worked the Algerian and Egyptian quarries and used the stone for similar purposes. In modern times it was used by Mohammed Ali for his mosque in Cairo. The French make extensive use of alabaster in interior decoration. See G. P. Merrill, *Stones for Building and Decoration* (3d ed., 1903); John Watson, *British and Foreign Marbles* (1916).

Alachua (ŭlăch′ōō), city (pop. 1,974), N central Fla., NW of Gainesville; founded 1884. Meat products are made.

Alacoque, Margaret Mary: see MARGARET MARY, SAINT.

Alagez, Mount: see ARAGATS, MOUNT.

Alagoas (älägō′ŭs) [Port.,=lagoons], state (c.10,700 sq. mi.; pop. c.1,271,100), NE Brazil, on the Atlantic Ocean. MACEIÓ is the capital. Its southwestern boundary is formed by the São Francisco river, and the spectacular Paulo Afonso falls are in the extreme western part of the state. Cacao and sugar are grown in the forested coastal belt, where oil has recently been found. Cotton growing and cattle breeding are the chief occupations of the semiarid interior (the *sertão*). The area was occupied by the Dutch in the mid-17th cent.

Alai or **Alay** (both: älī′), mountain range, SW Kirghiz SSR, in Soviet central Asia. A western branch of the Tien Shan system, it extends c.200 mi. west from the border of China and rises to c.19,280 ft. in its western portion. The Alai valley, south of the range, is a fertile elevated (c.9,800 ft.) pasture area, with irrigated grain cultivation in the west.

Alain de Lille (älē′ dù lēl′), c.1128–c.1202, French scholastic philosopher, a Cistercian, called The Universal Doctor. He was born in Lille; he taught at Paris and Montpellier before retiring to Cîteaux. In his writings he attempted to give rational support to the tenets of faith. He held that the mind unaided by revelation can know the universe, but by faith alone can man know God. Though his thought was largely Neoplatonic, he made use of numerous Aristotelian and neo-Pythagorean elements. The mathematical and deductive method had an important place in the working out of his theology. One of his chief works, *De fide catholica contra haereticos*, was written in order to refute heretics and unbelievers. Alain de Lille was also one of the foremost didactic poets of his day; his chief poem *Anticlaudian* (Eng. tr., 1935) is a complicated allegory. He is also called Alanus de Insulis.

Alain-Fournier (älē′-fōōrnyä′), 1886–1914, French novelist, whose real name was Henri Alban Fournier. He was killed in the First World War. His single full-length work is his poetic novel of a youthful search for the ideal, *Le Grand Meaulnes* (1913; Eng. tr., *The Wanderer*, 1928). Set in an imaginary locale called "the domain," it is based partly on Alain-Fournier's own mystical experiences and ideas. His published correspondence reveals the novel's evolution from symbolism to realism.

Alais: see ALÈS.

Alajuela (älähwä′lä), city (pop. c.18,000), capital of Alajuela prov., central Costa Rica. One of the four principal cities of the central plateau, it is a commercial center with sugar and coffee processing industries. A cathedral is here.

Alamán, Lucas (lōō′käs älämän′), 1792–1853, Mexican historian and statesman. As deputy to the Spanish Cortes, he failed to win a hearing for the insurgents in Mexico. Returning to Mexico, he was twice minister of foreign affairs in the government after the fall of ITURBIDE. Alamán founded the Archivo General and the National Museum, in Mexico city. He is chiefly remembered for his magnificent history of Mexico, *Historia de Méjico* (5 vols., 1849–52).

Alamanni or **Alemanni, Luigi** (lwē′jē älämän′ē), 1495–1556, Italian poet and patriot. He was a friend of Macchiavelli, who may have encouraged his conspiracy (1522) against Cardinal Giulio de' Medici (later Pope Clement VII). Its failure forced him to flee to the French court. He returned (1527) to Florence to fight the Medici, but after their restoration (1532) he was declared a rebel. Alamanni was versatile and prolific. He wrote plays (*Flora*, a comedy and *Antigone*, a tragedy) and lively letters to his friends and introduced the epigram into modern Italian poetry.

Alameda. **1** (ălùmē′dù, –mä′dù) City (pop. 63,855), W central Calif., on an island just off the eastern shore of San Francisco Bay, S of Oakland; settled 1850, inc. as a town 1854, as a city 1884. It has excellent beaches and parks and is a manufacturing and shipping center. Shipbuilding is its chief industry. Large U.S. naval installations are here. The city is connected with the mainland by bridges and a tunnel. **2** (ălùmē′dù), City (pop. 10,660), SE Idaho, a suburb NNE of Pocatello; laid out 1912, inc. 1924.

Alamein (ălùmān′, ä–) or **El Alamein** (ĕl), town, N Egypt, on the Mediterranean coast 70 mi. W of Alexandria. It was the site of a decisive British victory in the North African campaigns of the Second World War (see NORTH AFRICA, CAMPAIGNS IN). In preparation for Marshal Rommel's attack from Libya (begun May 26, 1942) the British forces retreated into Egypt and by June 30 had set up a defense line extending 35 mi. from Alamein S to the Qattara Depression, a badland which could neither be crossed nor flanked. If this position had fallen, the British might have lost Alexandria and might have been forced to withdraw from North Africa. In August, Gen. Bernard L. Montgomery took command of the 8th Army, newly supplied and with its ranks filled. The British offensive opened on Oct. 23 with tremendous air and artillery bombardments. Montgomery's forces cleared the German mine fields and on Nov. 1 and 2 burst through the German lines near the sea and forced a swift Axis retreat out of Egypt, across Libya, and into E Tunisia. Egypt was definitely saved, and with the landing on Nov. 7 and 8 of American troops in Algeria the Axis soon suffered total defeat in North Africa. For his victory Montgomery was made a viscount with the title Montgomery of Alamein. See Michael Carver, *El Alamein* (1962).

Alameth (ăl′–), Benjamite. 1 Chron. 7.8.

Alamgir: see AURANGZEB.

Alammelech (ùlăm′ùlĕk), village of Asher, NW Palestine. Joshua 19.26. The modern Wadi el-Melek near Mt. Carmel perhaps echoes the name.

Alamo (ăl′ùmō). **1** Uninc. village (pop. 1,791), W Calif., ENE of San Francisco, in a farm area; settled 1852. **2** Town (pop. 1,665), co. seat of Crockett co., W Tenn., NW of Jackson, in a farm area; inc. 1911. **3** City (pop. 4,121), extreme S Texas, NW of Brownsville, in the irrigated district of the lower Rio Grande valley; inc. 1924. Fruits and vegetables are canned.

Alamo, the [Spanish,=cottonwood], building in San Antonio, Texas, "the cradle of Texas liberty." Built as a chapel after 1744, it is all that remains of the mission of San Antonio de Valero, which was founded in 1718 by the Franciscans and later converted into a fortress. In the Texas Revolution, San Antonio was taken by Texas revolutionaries in Dec., 1835, and was lightly garrisoned. When Santa Anna approached with an army of several thousand in Feb., 1836, only some 150 men held the Alamo, and confusion, indifference, and bickering among the insurgents throughout Texas prevented any help going to them, except for 32 volunteers from Gonzales who slipped through the Mexican lines after the siege had already begun. Defying Santa Anna's demands for surrender, the

The Alamo, San Antonio, Texas.

Texans in the fort determined to fight against the hopeless odds. The siege, which began Feb. 24, ended with hand-to-hand fighting within the walls on March 6. William B. TRAVIS, James Bowie, David Crockett, and some 180 other defenders were dead, but the heroic resistance roused fighting anger among Texans, who six weeks later defeated the Mexicans at San Jacinto, crying, "Remember the Alamo!" The chapel-fort was bought by the state in 1883, the surrounding area was added in 1905, and the whole was restored and improved in 1936–39. See Lon Tinkle, *13 Days to Glory* (1958); Walter Lord, *A Time to Stand* (1961).

Alamogordo (ăl″ùmùgôr′dō, –dù), city (pop. 21,723), co. seat of Otero co., S N.Mex., near the Sacramento Mts. and NNE of El Paso, Texas; settled 1898. The home of Holloman Air Force Base, Alamogordo is a center for weapons research and testing; in an uninhabited desert area nearby (see WHITE SANDS) the first atomic bomb was exploded on July 16, 1945. The city is also a trade center of a livestock, timber, and recreation area. Near Alamogordo are White Sands National Monument (140,247.04 acres; est. 1933); the Mescalero Apache Indian Reservation; Lincoln National Forest; and several military reservations.

Alamo Heights, city (pop. 7,552), S central Texas, a suburb ENE of San Antonio; inc. 1926.

Alamosa (ălùmō′sù), city (pop. 6,205; alt. 7,500 ft.), co. seat of Alamosa co., S Colo., SW of Pueblo and on the Rio Grande; founded and inc. 1878. It is in an irrigated farm region of the San Luis Valley. Lettuce and potatoes are among its crops. Adams State College of Colorado (coeducational; 1921) is here. Nearby is the Great Sand Dunes National Monument (34,979.88 acres; est. 1932).

Alamoth (ăl′–), Hebrew musical term, unknown in meaning, although some have guessed "soprano,"

connecting it with a word for "maidens." It occurs in 1 Chron. 15.20 and in the title of Ps. 46. The term *Sheminith* (shĕm′ĭ–) [Heb.,=eighth], in the titles of Pss. 6 and 12, has been explained as "bass," complementary to Alamoth.

Aland Islands (ä′lùnd, ̥ô′–), Finnish *Ahvenanmaa* (ä′vĕnänmä′), Swed. *Ålandsöerna* (ō′läntsû′ùrnä), archipelago (572 sq. mi.; pop. c.29,000), in the Baltic Sea, between Sweden and Finland, at the entrance of the Gulf of Bothnia. It belongs to Finland. The chief town is MARIEHAMN, a port on Aland, the largest of the islands. Shipping, farming, and tourism are the chief occupations. The islands, colonized by Swedes, are of strategic importance. With Finland, they were ceded by Sweden to Russia in 1809. In the Crimean War the Russian fortifications were destroyed (1854), and remilitarization was forbidden by the Treaty of Paris (1856). At the end of the First World War, the islanders sought to join Sweden. The League of Nations in 1921, however, recognized Finland's sovereignty, but guaranteed the autonomous status of the islands and confirmed their demilitarization. After the Finnish-Russian War (1939–40) Finland and Russia signed a demilitarization agreement which was renewed after the Second World War. Under pressure from Russia, Finland's Parliament renounced the League guarantee of autonomy in 1951 but at the same time accorded the islanders additional rights of self-government. Pro-Swedish sentiment continues, however, and emigration to Sweden has caused a population decline in recent years. Aaland is another spelling.

Alans or **Alani:** see SARMATIA.

Alarcón, Hernando de (ĕrnän′dō dä älärkōn′), fl. 1540, Spanish explorer in the Southwest. He was given command of a fleet that was supposed to support the land expedition of Francisco Vásquez de

CORONADO. In the summer of 1540 he sailed up the Gulf of California, proved definitely that Lower California was a peninsula, not an island, and discovered the Colorado river. He failed, however, to make contact with Coronado's expedition. He explored the river a few months before García López de CÁRDENAS discovered the Grand Canyon.

Alarcón, Pedro Antonio de (päd'rō äntō'nyō), 1833–91, Spanish writer and diplomat. He was active in politics during his youth and became editor of a revolutionary journal in Madrid; later he was ambassador to several countries of Europe. In 1875 he was admitted to the Spanish Academy. His first important literary work was the very successful report on the war in Africa (1860). This was followed by books on travel and such lighter works as *El sombrero de tres picos* (1874; Eng. tr., *The Three-cornered Hat*, 1891), on which Manuel de Falla based his popular ballet, and *El capitán Veneno* (1881; Eng. tr., *Captain Venom*, 1914). In these works the author shows a keen power of observation, an extraordinary ability to describe with color and plasticity, and a subtle humor. Two of his longer novels are *El escandalo* (1875; Eng. tr., *The Scandal*, 1945) and *El niño de la bola* (1880).

Alarcón y Mendoza, Juan Ruiz de (hwän' rōōēth' dä älärkōn' ē mändō'thä), 1581?–1639, Spanish dramatic poet, one of the great literary figures of the Golden Age, b. Mexico. After studying law in Spain (1600–1608) and Mexico, he returned (1613) to Spain, where he later obtained a minor post in the Council of the Indies. Like Molière, Alarcón was a comedic moralist; his comedies (2 vols., 1628–34) are notable for brilliant characterization and lively dialogue. His plays are more carefully wrought than those of his more prolific contemporaries. Best known is *La verdad sospechosa* [the suspicious truth], which was the model for Corneille's *Le Menteur*. Among the others are *Las paredes oyen* [the walls have ears] and *El anticristo*.

Alaric I (ă'lŭrĭk), c.370–410, Visigothic king. He headed the Visigothic troops serving Emperor Theodosius I, after whose death (395) they rebelled and chose Alaric as their leader (see VISIGOTHS). Alaric devastated Thrace, Macedonia, and Greece. Stopped, but not defeated, by STILICHO, he retired northward, and by an agreement with the Eastern emperor, ARCADIUS, occupied Epirus. About 400 he invaded Italy, where after some indecisive warfare he agreed with Stilicho on a joint attack against the Eastern Empire. This attack failed to materialize, and in 408 Alaric again left Epirus and invaded Italy. Stilicho persuaded the Romans to buy Alaric's alliance through a huge payment, but shortly afterward Emperor HONORIUS had Stilicho executed for treason. Alaric again turned on Rome (409) and forced the city to accept a puppet emperor, Attalus, whom he himself deposed, the next year, for disregarding his advice. After the failure of renewed negotiations with Honorius (who all the while held out at Ravenna) Alaric stormed and sacked Rome (410) and then marched south to attack Sicily and Africa. A storm destroyed his fleet, and Alaric, having turned back, died of an illness. His brother Ataulf was elected his successor. It is said that Alaric was buried with his treasures near Cosenza in the bed of the Busento river, which was temporarily diverted from its course. That the secret might be kept, the slaves employed in the labor were killed.

Alaric II, d. 507, Visigothic king of Spain and of S Gaul (c.484–507), son and successor of Euric. He issued (506) at Toulouse the BREVIARY OF ALARIC for his Roman subjects. Alaric's adherence to Arianism gave CLOVIS I, king of the Franks, an easy pretext for attacking him in the name of orthodoxy. Alaric was defeated and slain at Vouillé (507), and the Visigoths lost all their possessions in Gaul save Septimania.

Alasco or **à Lasco, Johannes:** see LASKI, JOHN.

Alasehir (ä″läshĕ'hēr), Turk. *Alasehir*, town (pop. 13,923), Manisa prov., W Turkey, at the foot of Mt. Tmolus. It is a trading center. A picturesque town, it has narrow winding streets and an ancient Byzantine wall. Nearby is the site of ancient PHILADELPHIA.

Alaska, state (571,065 sq. mi.; with water surface 586,400 sq. mi.; 1960 pop. 226,167), NW North America, admitted 1959 as the 49th state. More

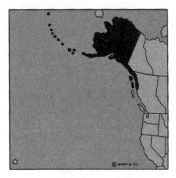

Alaska location map

than twice the size of Texas, it is the largest state in the Union, but it is also the least populous. JUNEAU is the capital, ANCHORAGE the largest city. Alaska is a huge block of land at the northwest extremity of the continent between the Arctic Ocean on the north and the Pacific Ocean on the south. The tip of the Seward Peninsula is separated by only a few miles from Asiatic USSR by the narrow BERING STRAIT. The strait widens in the north to the Chukchi Sea, which cuts into Alaska with Kotzebue Sound, N of the Seward Peninsula; in the south the strait widens to the Bering Sea, which cuts into Alaska with NORTON SOUND, S of the Seward Peninsula, and Bristol Bay, N of the Alaska Peninsula. Alaska extends toward the USSR again in the Alaska Peninsula, which is continued by the ALEUTIAN ISLANDS, reaching out toward the Russian KOMANDORSKI ISLANDS; together they divide the Bering Sea from the Pacific. The south shore of Alaska is deeply indented by two inlets of the wide Gulf of Alaska, Cook Inlet and Prince William Sound; the Kenai Peninsula between them extends southwest toward KODIAK ISLAND. Where the coast runs SE from the Gulf of Alaska lies the narrow Panhandle of Alaska, cutting into the Canadian province of British Columbia. Except for the Panhandle, the eastern boundary of Alaska is the Yukon territory.

State Seal of Alaska

Juneau, Alaska, the town of
Douglas in the background.

Fairbanks, Alaska

The rough coast and the high mountain ranges of
Alaska cut the state into isolated regions. The
difficulties of communication are one of the most
troublesome problems of Alaska; air transport is
answering it in part, and all Alaskan cities have
airports, but even so the cities are still fundamentally isolated, self-contained units. This is true even in
the Panhandle, the most populous of the regions,
with the capital and others of the best-known
cities—KETCHIKAN, old SITKA, and SKAGWAY.
This region is one of a narrow coast, rising steeply
to the mountains of the Coast Range and the St.
Elias Mts., and of islands of the ALEXANDER
ARCHIPELAGO. Its connection with Seattle is by
steamships plying the Inside Passage. The Panhandle is more "civilized" than the other sections
of Alaska, although tourists find the abrupt
mountains, the dense forests, and the Indian

villages exotic and remote. Winters in the Panhandle are generally mild, with heavy rainfall and,
except on the upper slopes of the mountains, comparatively little snow. The scenic wonders of the
mountains and the rugged fjord-indented coast are
augmented by glaciers such as the MALASPINA
Glacier at the entrance to the Panhandle and the
acres of blue ice in GLACIER BAY NATIONAL MONU-
MENT. The chief economic reliance of the people
here is upon fishing (especially salmon and halibut),
lumbering, and tourism. Production of gold in the
Panhandle has almost entirely ceased, but uranium
and beryllium deposits are being exploited. Much
of the land is generally too steep for agriculture.
This is not true, however, of S central Alaska,
where, between the mountains of the coast and the
wide curve of the Alaska Range, there are wide
valleys that can support farms. Here is the
MATANUSKA VALLEY, with much of the best agricultural land in Alaska. The KENAI PENINSULA
also has farmlands. Kodiak Island is a center for
salmon fishing, fox breeding, and whaling. The
highest point in North America, Mt. McKinley
(in MOUNT MCKINLEY NATIONAL PARK), is located in the Alaska Range of S central Alaska.
Anchorage is the metropolis of the region and,
more important, the center for the Alaska RR, for
airways, and for U.S. defense installations; it is
also connected with the Alaska Highway. This
region of Alaska developed rapidly with the Second
World War, and continuing defense activity here
has brought a large increase in population. The
port of SEWARD, having lost its commanding
position as terminus of the Alaska RR to Whittier,
fell back upon the development of a highway.
Valdez on Prince William Sound is connected by a
highway to FAIRBANKS (linked with the Alaska
Highway). CORDOVA, injured by the closing
(1938) of the railroad to the big Kennecott copper
mine, took recourse to sea communications; the
products of its fish canneries are now taken away
by steamer. Kodiak also depends upon the ocean

Eskimo family carving ivory and sewing mukluks, shoes made from reindeer hide, near Nome, Alaska.

Totem poles in Sitka, Alaska.

lanes. Extreme SW Alaska is dominated by the ALEUTIAN RANGE, which is the spine of the Alaska Peninsula (c.500 mi. long) and is continued in the grass-covered, treeless Aleutian Islands. The climate here is unremittingly bad—foggy and, in the winter, disagreeably damp and cold and subject to violent winds (the williwaws). The native Aleuts were the first to feel the pressure of white civilization when Russian fur traders came in the 18th cent. When the hunting of the sea otter declined in the 19th cent. so did the importance of the islands, only to be reawakened when the Japanese attack in the Second World War showed the strategic significance of the islands. Bloody fighting took place there (notably on ATTU), and Dutch Harbor became a major key of the U.S. defense system. On the Alaska Peninsula volcanic action has attracted much interest, particularly in the Valley of Ten Thousand Smokes in 1912 (the area is now in KATMAI NATIONAL MONUMENT). North of the Alaska Peninsula is Bristol Bay, where much salmon fishing goes on in summer. The PRIBILOF ISLANDS in the Bering Sea, also belonging to the region of W Alaska, are noted principally as the source of sealskins and the pelts of the Pribilof blue fox. Farther to the north is the Seward Peninsula, with the fabulous NOME, where gold was gathered on the beaches after 1899. Except for the gold, however, the Seward Peninsula—mostly tundra covered—remained unexploited. The Eskimo lives his simple and efficient life on the peninsula and the islands off the coast and gets his food from the surrounding waters. The interior of Alaska, between the Alaska Range in the south and the

Brooks Range in the north, was also opened to settlement by the discovery of gold, and gold is still mined in Fairbanks, the metropolis of the interior. Agriculture has been slowly developing around Fairbanks, in the valley of the Tanana river (a tributary of the Yukon). The climate of the interior of Alaska is marked by short but very hot summers and long and very cold winters. Arctic Alaska, N of the Brooks Range, is mostly barren grounds, cut by numerous short rivers and one long river (the Colville). The ground is permanently frozen, and the temperature in winter reaches 10 to 40 degrees below zero. The entire coast here is ice-bound in the winter, and all shipping comes to a halt. The northernmost reach of Alaska is POINT BARROW. Alaska, which still seems a remote land to most of the people of the United States, was first reached by white men not from the United States or Canada, but from Russia. The adventurous and disastrous voyage of Vitus BERING and Aleksey CHIRIKOV in 1741 capped the march of Russian traders across Siberia. The survivors who returned with fine sea-otter skins started a rush of fur traders (the *promyshlenniki*) to the Aleutian Islands. Rough, resourceful men, they survived great hardships to take away fortunes in fur. Their hardships were, however, mild in comparison with the harsh treatment they gave the unfortunate natives. The trade was later organized by merchants on a more systematic basis during the reign of Catherine II. Grigori SHELEKHOV in 1784 founded the first permanent settlement in Alaska on Kodiak Island and sent (1790) to Alaska the man who was to dominate Russian

Drilling rigs (above left) bring oil from beneath the waters of Cook Inlet near Anchorage, Alaska. The petroleum industry has become one of the state's most promising economic developments. Mt. McKinley, (above right) 20,300 feet, highest peak on the North American continent, viewed from highway near Wonder Lake.

days there, Aleksandr BARANOV. A monopoly was granted to the Russian American Company in 1799, and it was Baranov who directed its activities in Alaska. Sitka was founded in 1799 as his capital and was rebuilt after destruction by the Indians in 1802. From a "castle" at Sitka, Baranov ruled, extending the Russian trade far down the coast and even, after several unsuccessful attempts, founded (1812) a farming settlement at Fort Ross in Alta California (N of San Francisco near the mouth of the present Russian river). Rivalry for the Northwest coast was strong. Explorations by Capt. James COOK, George VANCOUVER, Sir Alexander MACKENZIE, and the Lewis and Clark expedition had stimulated both British and American interests, and competition between British and American trading vessels began to cause the Russians alarm regarding the safety of their monopoly. In 1821 the tsar issued a ukase which warned foreign vessels not to come within 100 Italian mi. of Alaska and extended its southern boundary to the 51st parallel. British and American protests, the promulgation of the Monroe Doctrine, and Russian embroilments elsewhere resulted (1824) in a negotiated settlement of the boundary question at lat. 54° 40′ (the present southern boundary of Alaska). Russian interests in Alaska gradually receded, and after the Crimean War Russia sought to dispose of the territory altogether. In 1867 the territory was bought by the United States for $7,200,000. The purchase was made solely through the determined efforts of Secretary of State William H. SEWARD, and for many years afterward the land was derisively called Seward's Folly or Seward's Ice-

box because of its supposed barrenness. Since there was no immediate financial return, Alaska was neglected. The Alaska Commercial Company inherited the Russian commercial rights but was not active. The U.S. army officially had Alaska in charge until 1876, when scandals caused the soldiers to be withdrawn. After a small lapse when government resided only in customs men, the U.S. navy was given charge in 1879. Most of the territory was not even known, although the British (notably Sir John FRANKLIN and Capt. F. W. BEECHEY) had early explored the coast of the Arctic Ocean, and Hudson's Bay Company men had explored the Yukon. It was not until the discovery of gold in the Juneau region in 1880 that Alaska was given a governor and a feeble local administration by the Organic Act of 1884. Missionaries, who had come to the region in the late '70s, exercised considerable influence. Most influential of them all was Sheldon JACKSON, best known for his introduction of reindeer to help the Alaskan Eskimo, beggared by the wanton destruction of the fur seals. The sealing was the subject of a long international controversy (the BERING SEA FUR-SEAL CONTROVERSY), which was not ended until after gold had changed Alaska permanently. Paradoxically, the first finds that had tremendous influence on Alaska were not in Alaska at all, but in Canada. The development at Fortymile Creek and in the upper Yukon area prepared the way for the great KLONDIKE strike of 1896, which brought a stampede. Most of the miners were from the United States, and most of them came through Alaska. The big discoveries in

Alaska itself followed—Nome in 1899, Fairbanks in 1902. The miners and prospectors—the sourdoughs—took over Alaska, and the era of the rough mining camps reached its height; this was the Alaska of Jack London. It was lawless, and a criminal code was belatedly applied in 1899. Not until 1906 did Alaska get a territorial representative in Congress. The longstanding controversy concerning the boundary between the Panhandle of Alaska and British Columbia was aggravated by the stampede of miners traveling the Inside Passage to reach the gold fields. The matter was finally settled in 1903 by a six-man tribunal. The American representatives secured from the representatives of Canada and Great Britain a decision generally favorable to the United States, and a period of rapid building and development began. Mining, requiring heavy financing, passed into the hands of Eastern capitalists, notably the monopolistic Alaska Syndicate. Opposition to the "interests" became the burning issue in Alaska and was catapulted into national U.S. politics in the charges and countercharges about the giving of Alaskan coal lands to the large companies and their cohorts; Gifford PINCHOT and R. A. BALLINGER were the chief antagonists, and this was a major issue on which Theodore Roosevelt split with President W. H. Taft. A new era began for Alaska when local government was established in 1912 and it became a U.S. territory (Juneau had officially replaced Sitka as capital in 1900 although it did not begin to function as such until 1906). The building of the Alaska RR from Seward to Fairbanks was commenced with government funds in 1915. Already, however, the flush of gold fever had begun to die, and Alaska receded into one of its periods of lull. The fishing industry, quietly going forward in the noise of gold rushes, became the major Alaskan industry. Mining was revived by use of the deep-dredging process in the 1920s, and a rise in the price of gold also aided the mines. Alaska enjoyed its greatest boom on the approach of the Second World War. The ALASKA HIGHWAY was built, supplying a still-weak but much-needed link in communication with the United States, and with the growth of air travel after the war, a more modern air transport system was created. The permanent defense bases (which play a vital role in the nation's defense system), the establishment of the Univ. of Alaska (see ALASKA, UNIVERSITY OF), and the success of arctic farming in Siberia—all brightened the hopes for further development of farming and the growth of stable settlements. Between 1950 and 1960 the population of Alaska was nearly doubled. On July 7, 1958, President Eisenhower signed a bill making Alaska the 49th state of the Union; in a special election held on Aug. 26 Alaskans approved statehood by a 5 to 1 margin. In the November elections, held under Alaska's traditional "honor system" (whoever swears that he is eligible to vote can vote), the Democrats won all the major political offices. On Jan. 3, 1959, the President officially proclaimed Alaska a state, the first to be admitted since Arizona in 1912. See W. W. Woollen, *The Inside Passage to Alaska, 1792-1920* (1924); Jeanette P. Nichols, *Alaska: a History* (1924); S. R. Tompkins, *Alaska: Promyshlennik and Sour-*

Campus of the University of Alaska.

dough (1945); Ernest Gruening, *The State of Alaska* (1954); C. C. Hulley, *Alaska, Past and Present* (1959); Herbert and Miriam Hilscher, *Alaska, U.S.A.* (1959); Ben Adams, *The Last Frontier; a Short History of Alaska* (1961).

Alaska, University of, at College, near Fairbanks; land grant and state supported; coeducational; chartered 1917, opened 1922 as Alaska Agricultural College and School of Mines. In 1935 it became a university.

Alaska Highway, 1,523 mi. long, from Dawson Creek, British Columbia, to Fairbanks, Alaska. Built (March-Sept., 1942) in the Second World War by U.S. troops to supply the forces in Alaska, it was a significant engineering feat because of the difficulties of terrain and weather. A Canadian road already connected Dawson Creek with Edmonton, Alta. The Haines Cutoff connects the Alaska Highway with the Panhandle of Alaska. In the last stretch to Fairbanks the road used the previously built Richardson Highway. In 1946 the Canadian part of the road was transferred to Canadian control. In 1947 the highway was opened to unrestricted travel. It was formerly known as the Alaska Military Highway, the Alaskan International Highway, and the Alcan Highway. See G. R. Stewart, *N.A.1: the North-South Continental Highway Looking North* (1957).

Alaskan Malamute dog: see WORKING DOG.

Alaska Range, S central Alaska, rising to the highest mountain in North America, Mt. McKinley (20,320 ft.). The range divides S central Alaska from the great plateau of the interior.

Alastor (ŭlă'stŭr), in Greek mythology, the spirit of vengeance. It is an epithet applied to Zeus or any other god in his aspect as avenger and is also sometimes applied to the evildoer who is subject to vengeance.

Ala-Tau (ä'lä-tou') [Turki,=snowy mountains], several ranges of the Tien Shan system in central Asia, near Lake Issyk Kul. All are economically unproductive and are chiefly inhabited by Turki-speaking pastoral tribes. The **Dzungarian Ala-Tau** (zŏŏngă'rēŭn) is for c.130 mi. the border between the Kazakh SSR and Sinkiang prov., China, and rises to c.16,550 ft. This, the northernmost branch of the Tien Shan, extends from southwest to northeast c.250 mi. There are silver and lead mines here. The **Kungei Ala-Tau** (kŏŏng-gä'), a branch of the Tien Shan, rises to c.16,300 ft. and lies north of the lake. It extends from east to west c.130 mi. and forms part of the boundary between the Kirghiz SSR and the Kazakh SSR. The **Kuznetsk Ala-Tau** (kŏŏznĕtsk'), SW Siberia, Russian SFSR, rises to c.6,890 ft. It extends generally from north to south c.250 mi. The **Talass Ala-Tau** (täläs'), a range of the Tien Shan in NW Kirghiz SSR, forms the southern watershed of the upper Talas river valley, rises to c.13,200 ft., and extends from east to west c.150 mi. The **Terskei Ala-Tau** (tĕr'skā), in the Kirghiz SSR, extends from east to west c.225 mi. and rises to c.16,440 ft. The **Trans-Ili Ala-Tau** (trăns'-ēlē'), a range of the Tien Shan in Kazakh SSR, on the Kirghiz SSR border, rises to c.16,460 ft. and extends from east to west c.250 mi. It is intensively cultivated and irrigated on the north slope, site of Alma-Ata.

Alatyr (ŭlŭtĭr'), city (pop. c.35,500), Chuvash Autonomous SSR, SE European RSFSR, at the confluence of the Sura and Alatyr rivers. Founded in 1552, it is a river port and railroad junction with locomotive and food-processing plants.

Álava: see BASQUE PROVINCES.

Alay: see ALAI.

Alba or **Alva, Fernando Álvarez de Toledo, duque de** (äl'bù, al'vù, Span. both: fĕrnän'dŏ äl'väräth dä tōlā'dhŏ dōō'kä dä äl'vä), 1508–82, Spanish general and administrator. After a distinguished military career in Germany and Italy, Alba returned to Spain as adviser to King Philip II. Advocating a stern policy toward the rebels against Spain in the NETHERLANDS, he was appointed (1567) captain general there, with full civil and military powers. The regent, MARGARET OF PARMA, opposed him and resigned, and Alba became regent and governor general. A religious fanatic and ruthless absolutist, he set out to crush the Netherlanders' attempts to gain religious toleration and political self-government. The special court he set up at Brussels, popularly known as the Court of Blood, spread terror throughout the provinces, where Alba's name is still remembered with loathing. Some 18,000 persons were executed (among them the popular EGMONT and HOORN), and their properties were confiscated. Increased taxation also fanned popular resentment. Several cities rebelled, but were punished with much bloodshed, and the forces of WILLIAM THE SILENT, who had invaded the Netherlands, were defeated. Nevertheless, after six years of rule, Alba found the Netherlands more resolutely opposed to Spanish rule than ever, while at the court of Philip II he was accused of having compromised the royalist cause. His resignation (1573) was accepted, and Requesens was appointed in his stead. In 1580 Philip again resorted to him for the conquest of Portugal. After seizing Lisbon, Alba permitted a massacre of the citizens.

Albacete (älbäthā'tä), city (pop. 72,456), capital of Albacete prov., SE Spain, in Murcia, at the south-

east end of La Mancha plateau. Under the Moors, Albacete was a part of the Kingdom of MURCIA, with which it was incorporated (1269) into Castile. The city now has a modern aspect and is mainly an agricultural center. It is noted for the manufacture of fine knives and daggers.

albacore: see TUNA.

Alba-Iulia (äl'bä-yōō'lyä), Hung. *Gyulafehérvár*, Ger. *Karlsburg*, town (pop. c.15,000), central Rumania, in Transylvania. It is the center of a wine-producing region. Founded by the Romans in the 2d cent. A.D., it was destroyed by the Tatars in 1241 and later by the Turks. It was the seat (16th–17th cent.) of the princes of Transylvania, of a Roman Catholic bishop, and of an Eastern Orthodox metropolis. From 1599 to 1601 it was the capital of the united principalities of Walachia, Transylvania, and Moldavia. The town has an 18th-century fortress (built by Emperor Charles VI), a 13th-century Roman Catholic cathedral, and an Orthodox cathedral.

Alba Longa (äl'bù lông'gù), city of ancient Latium, in the Alban Hills near Lake Albano, c.12 mi. SE of Rome. It was a city before 1100 B.C. and apparently the most powerful in Latium. Legend says that it was founded by Ascanius, son of Aeneas, that Romulus and Remus were born here, and that it was thus the mother city of Rome. Tradition also said that Tullus Hostilius, king of Rome, razed it in 665 B.C. Possibly Rome was founded from Alba Longa, and certainly the Romans destroyed it (c.600?). The modern Castel Gandolfo occupies the site.

Alban, Saint, 3d or 4th cent., traditionally the first British martyr. He lived and died at Verulamium, now St. Albans. Feast: Roman Catholic Church, June 22; Church of England, June 17.

Albanel, Charles (shärl älbänĕl'), 1616–96, French missionary explorer in Canada, a Jesuit priest. After arrival in Canada (1649), he was stationed many years at Tadoussac and explored the surrounding wilderness. At the time when the British Hudson's Bay Company was beginning operations, he was a leader of a French party that went (1671–72) by the Saguenay river, Mistassini Lake, and the Rupert river to Hudson Bay. The region was claimed for France. On another journey there he was captured (1674) by the British and taken to England. After returning (1676) to Canada, he served at missions in the West and died at Sault Ste Marie.

Albanese, Licia (lē'chēä älbänä'sä), 1913–, Italian-American soprano, b. Bari. She made her debut (1935) in *Madame Butterfly* in Parma. She first sang at the Metropolitan Opera House in 1940. During the Second World War she lived in Italy, returning to the United States in 1945. She appeared with Arturo Toscanini and the NBC Symphony Orchestra and continued to sing lyric soprano roles at the Metropolitan Opera House.

Albania (älbā'nyù), Albanian *Shqipnija* or *Shqiperia*, republic (11,097 sq. mi.; estimated pop. 1,665,000), SE Europe, on the Adriatic coast of the Balkan Peninsula between Yugoslavia on the north and east and Greece on the south. Tirana is the capital. Save for a fertile coastal strip Albania is rugged and mountainous, rising in the north to more than 8,000 ft. The climate, typically Med-

Albania
location map

iterranean along the Adriatic coast, is moderate in the inland regions. Albania shares two lakes (Scutari and Ohrida) with Yugoslavia and one (Prespa) with Yugoslavia and Greece. The Drin, the Mat, the Shkumbi, and the Vijose are the chief rivers. More than half of the land is covered by forests and swamps, about a third is under pasture, and only about 10 percent is cultivated. Albania is rich in mineral resources, notably oil, lignite, copper, chrome, and bitumen. Before the Second World War Albania had few industries and no railroads. In the postwar period the Communist regime speeded up industrialization and promoted mining and manufacturing. Two hydroelectric plants were completed (1952, 1957) and two railroads were built linking the port of Durazzo with Tirana and Elbasan. However, communications are still poor and the roads linking the chief inland cities (Tirana, Scutari, Elbasan, Koritsa, and Argyrokastron) and the main ports (Durazzo, Valona, and Sarande) continue to be the principal means of transportation. Agriculture remains the chief occupation of the Albanians. Wheat, corn, cotton, tobacco, and sugar beets are the main crops. Olives and grapes are grown, and sheep raising is important. Albania exports chrome and copper ores, petroleum products, bitumen, and tobacco and imports machinery, industrial equipment, and metal products. The Shkumbi river, which cuts Albania approximately into halves, separates speakers of the northern dialect (Gheg) of Albanian from speakers of the southern dialect (Tosk). Albanian is one of the Indo-European languages (see LANGUAGE, table). Some Greek is spoken in the south. The great majority of the population are Moslem, and there are minorities belonging to the Orthodox and Roman Catholic churches. There is a university at Tirana. As a region, Albania is often understood to extend deeply into SW Yugoslavia and, to a lesser extent, into NW Greece.

Historic Albania. The Albanians are considered to be descendants of Illyrian and Thracian tribes who settled the region in ancient times. It then comprised parts of ILLYRIA and EPIRUS and was known to the ancient Greeks for its mines. The coastal towns, Epidamnus (see DURAZZO) and APOLLONIA, were colonies of Corcyra (Corfu) and Corinth, but the interior formed an independent kingdom, which reached its height in the 3d cent. B.C. Fought over by Macedon and Rome, the region was under nominal Roman rule by the 1st cent. A.D. In fact, the Albanian mountain tribes were never fully subdued by any of their many conquerors; throughout the centuries the chieftains of their clans retained much authority. After the division (395) of the Roman Empire, Albania passed to the Byzantine Empire. Overrun (4th–5th cent.) by the Ostrogoths, it was reconquered (535) by Justinian I. While nominally (until 1347) under Byzantine rule, northern Albania was invaded (7th cent.) by the Serbs, and southern Albania was annexed (9th cent.) to Bulgaria. In 1014 Emperor Basil II reconquered southern Albania, which remained in the Byzantine Empire until it passed (1204) to the despotate of Epirus. In the 11th cent. Venice established coastal colonies at SCUTARI and Alessio, and the Normans under ROBERT GUISCARD began (1081) to dispute Albania with Byzantium. The Norman efforts were continued by the Neapolitan Angevins, and in 1272 Charles I of Naples was proclaimed king of Albania. However, in the 14th cent. the Serbs under STEPHEN DUSHAN conquered most of the country. After his death (1355) Albania was ruled by native chieftains until the Turks began (15th cent.) their conquests. The stout resistance to the Turks, led by the Albanian national hero, SCANDERBEG, and supported by Venice and Naples, collapsed in 1478, and Albania passed under Ottoman rule. Durazzo, acquired by Venice in 1392, held out against the Turks till 1501. Ottoman domination lasted longer and influenced Albania more deeply than that of any other foreign power. Islam became the majority religion. Numerous local revolts were suppressed. Early in the 19th cent. ALI PASHA ruled Albania like a sovereign, but was at last brought to ruin by the Porte.

National Independence. The first of the BALKAN WARS gave the Albanians the opportunity to proclaim (1912) their independence. An international control commission traced the borders of Albania in 1913 and destroyed the dream of a Greater Albania by assigning large tracts to Montenegro, Serbia, and Greece. In the Second Balkan War (1913) Albania was occupied by the Serbs. In 1914 WILLIAM, PRINCE OF WIED, became king of Albania, but he was soon expelled by his premier, ESSAD PASHA. In the First World War Albania was occupied by Serbs, Montenegrins, Greeks, and Italians; these, though allied, had conflicting interests. In 1916 the Bulgarians and Austrians en-

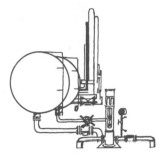

University, archaeological, ethnographical museum, and library of Tirana, Albania.

Oil refining is an important industry in Albania.

Market at Lesh, at the mouth of the Drin river, Albania.

tered Albania, which remained a battleground till the end of the war. The Congress of Lushnje (1920) reasserted Albania's independence, elected a new government, and moved the capital to Tirana. In 1925 Albania was proclaimed a republic under the presidency of Ahmed Zogu, who in 1928 made Albania a monarchy and became King Zog. In April, 1939, Italy, which had come to exert a virtual protectorate over the country, occupied Albania and united it with the Italian crown. The chronic dispute between Albania and Greece regarding their respective minorities furnished a pretext for the Italian attack (1940) on Greece in the Second World War; S Albania again became the scene of heavy fighting. The Albanian puppet government declared war on the Allies in 1940, but resistance forces later fought guerrilla warfare against the Axis Powers. The strongest of these groups, led by Enver Hoxha, was radically leftist. After Allied forces landed late in 1944, Hoxha's partisans seized most of Albania and formed (1945) a provisional government. A Communist-dominated legislature proclaimed (1946) Albania a republic with Hoxha as premier. In 1946 the United Kingdom and the United States broke diplomatic relations with Albania. After the expulsion (1948) of Yugoslavia from the Cominform, Albania sided with the USSR. The death of Stalin (1953) and the easing of relations between Yugoslavia and the Soviet bloc led to the resumption (1953) of diplomatic relations with Yugoslavia. Albania joined the Council for Economic Mutual Assistance (1949) and the Warsaw Treaty Organization (1955), and was admitted (1955) into the United Nations. In 1960, in an ideological dispute between the Soviet and Chinese Communists, Albania sided with China; a complete break with the USSR came in Dec., 1961, when the Soviet government severed diplomatic relations with Albania. See Ferdinand Schevill, *History of the Balkan Peninsula* (1922); E. P. Stickney, *Southern Albania or Northern Epirus in European International Affairs, 1912–1923* (1926); Stavro Skendi, ed., *Albania* (1956); Harry Hamm, *Rebellen gegen Moskau: Albanien-Pekings Brückenkopf in Europa* (1962, in German).

Albania (ălbā′nēŭ), ancient name of a mountainous region in E Transcaucasia, bordering on the Caspian Sea. It is now within the Azerbaijan SSR and the Dagestan ASSR. The Albanian or Caspian Gates (Latin *Albaniae Pylae*) are probably identical with the Iron Gates at Derbent, RSFSR.

Albano, Lake (älbä′nō), crater lake, central Italy, in the Alban hills. It is c.6 mi. in circumference. An underground tunnel built in the 4th cent. B.C. is still its only outlet. Alba Longa was located near the lake. South of the lake is Albano Laziale, a small town on the Appian Way, noted for the beautiful villas built here by the ancient Romans. There are also several Roman tombs.

Albany, Alexander Stuart or **Stewart, duke of:** see Stuart or Stewart, Alexander.

Albany, Louisa, countess of (ôl′bṹnē), 1752–1824, wife of Charles Edward Stuart (the Young Pretender), self-styled count of Albany; daughter of a German noble, the prince of Stolberg-Gedern.

*Countess Louisa
of Albany*

Married in 1772, she was made unhappy by her dissolute husband, left him after eight years, and became the mistress of the poet Vittorio Alfieri until his death in 1803. After that she was mistress of a French artist, François Fabre. Secret marriages with both men were rumored, but not well attested. See biography by Margaret Mitchiner (1937).

Albany, Robert Stuart or **Stewart, 1st duke of:** see STUART OR STEWART, ROBERT, 1ST DUKE OF ALBANY.

Albany, ancient and literary name of Scotland. Variants are Alban and Albin. ALBION usually refers to England.

Albany, town (pop. 9,672), Western Australia, SW Commonwealth of Australia, a port on Princess Royal Harbour of King George Sound. It is a rail terminus. Fruit is the chief export. Founded in 1826 as a penal colony, Albany is the oldest settlement in the state.

Albany. 1 Residential city (pop. 14,804), W Calif., on San Francisco Bay adjoining Berkeley on the north; inc. 1908. A U.S. Dept. of Agriculture research laboratory and a Univ. of California agricultural experiment station are here. **2** City (pop. 55,890), co. seat of Dougherty co., SW Ga., on the Flint river; founded 1836, inc. 1841. It is an industrial city in a productive pecan and peanut area of the coastal plain. Meat is packed, and hosiery is produced. Albany is also a tourist center; nearby Radium Springs is a popular resort, and Chehaw State Park is just east. Albany State College (coeducational; 1903) is here. Turner Air Force Base and a U.S. Marine Corps supply center are in the vicinity. **3** Town (pop. 2,132), E central Ind., NE of Muncie, in a farm area. **4** Town (pop. 1,887), co. seat of Clinton co., S central Ky., SSW of Danville, in the Cumberland foothills near the Tenn. line; settled c.1800. The area yields timber, coal, oil, and farm produce. **5** Village (pop. 1,375), central Minn., WNW of St. Cloud. Milk products are made. **6** City (pop. 1,662), co. seat of Gentry co., NW Mo., on the East Fork of the Grand and NE of St. Joseph, in a farm region; laid out 1845, inc. 1851. **7** City (pop. 129,726), state capital, and co. seat of Albany co., E N.Y., on the west bank of the Hudson and SE of Schenectady. In 1609 Henry Hudson visited the site, and four years later the Dutch built a fur-trading post, called Fort Nassau, on Castle Island. In 1624 several Walloon families began permanent settlement at the Dutch post Fort Orange, which was renamed Albany (1664) when the English took control. Chartered as a city in 1686, Albany was long important as a fur-trading center and was involved in the French and Indian Wars. In 1754 the ALBANY CONGRESS met here, and after the Revolution the state capital was moved (1797) to Albany. The city's trade grew with the development of the state, particularly after the opening of the Champlain and Erie canals in the 1820s. A port of entry, Albany handles much shipping and is a major transshipment point. The city has grain elevators, railroad shops, and oil refineries. Among its products are chemicals, paper, textiles, and woodwork. Albany is the seat of the New York State College for Teachers, the schools of pharmacy, law, and medicine of UNION UNIVERSITY, and the Albany Institute of History and Art. Among the many old buildings is the Schuyler mansion (1762), where Gen. Philip Schuyler's daughter, Elizabeth, was married to Alexander Hamilton. Dominating the city is the capitol (built 1867–98). Bret Harte was born in Albany. **8** City (pop. 12,926), co. seat of Linn co., NW Oregon, on the Willamette river and S of Salem; founded 1848, inc. 1864. It is an important lumbering center and processing point in a fertile area of farms and orchards. Titanium and zirconium are mined, and a U.S. Bureau of Mines experimental station is here. **9** City (pop. 2,174), co. seat of Shackelford co., N Texas, NE of Abilene. A state park has been established at the nearby site of the frontier army post Fort Griffin (occupied from 1867 to 1881). Albany, earlier a ranching and salt-working town, is still noted for its Hereford cattle. It is also a farm market and an oil-refining center.

State Street in Albany, N.Y., Hudson Building in background.

Albany, river rising in W central Ont., Canada, and flowing east and northeast to the west side of James Bay. It is c.600 mi. long. The Kenogami, Little Current, and Ogoki rivers are its chief tributaries. The river was named for the duke of York and Albany, later James II.

Albany, Fort: see FORT ALBANY.

Albany Congress, 1754, meeting at Albany, N.Y., of commissioners representing seven British colonies in North America to treat with the Iroquois, chiefly because war with France impended. A treaty was concluded, but the Indians of Pennsylvania were resentful of a land purchase made by that colony here and allied themselves with the French in the ensuing French and Indian War. The meeting was notable as an example of cooperation among the colonies, but Benjamin Franklin's Plan of Union for the colonies, though voted upon favorably at Albany, was refused by the colonial legislatures and by the crown as demanding too great a surrender of their powers. See Robert Newbold, *Albany Congress and the Plan of Union of 1754* (1955).

Albany Regency, name given, after 1820, to the leaders of the political machine developed in New York state by Martin VAN BUREN. The name derived from the charge that Van Buren's principal supporters, residing in Albany, managed the machine for him while he served in the U.S. Senate. During the Jacksonian period the Regency controlled the Democratic party in New York. It was one of the first effective political machines, using the SPOILS SYSTEM and rigid party discipline to maintain its control. Notable figures in the Regency were William L. MARCY, Silas WRIGHT, Azariah C. FLAGG, and the elder Benjamin F. BUTLER. After 1842 it split into factions (BARNBURNERS and HUNKERS) over issues of internal improvements and slavery and so lost its power.

albatross (ăl′bŭtrôs), sea bird of the order of tube-nosed swimmers, which includes petrels, shearwaters, and fulmars. The wandering albatross, made famous by Coleridge's *Rime of the Ancient Mariner*, has a wingspread of from 10 to 12 ft., although the wings are only about 9 in. wide. Albatrosses eat mainly fish, floating carrion, and refuse. Most albatrosses are found in the S Pacific region, e.g., the wandering and the sooty species; a few, the black-footed, the short-tailed, and the Laysan albatrosses, regularly frequent the N Pacific.

Albay: see LEGASPI.

Albee, Edward (ăl′bē), 1928–, American dramatist, b. Washington, D.C. His plays—clever, satiric, often vindictive commentaries on the American way of life—include the one-acters *The Zoo Story* (1960) and *The American Dream* (1961) and the full-length *Who's Afraid of Virginia Woolf?* (1962).

Albemarle, Arnold Joost van Keppel, 1st earl of (ăl′bŭmärl), 1669–1718, Dutch adherent and constant companion of William III of England. He accompanied the king to England (1688), was made an earl in 1696, and served William throughout his reign, then returned to Dutch service. He fought in the War of the Spanish Succession.

Albemarle, George Monck or **Monk, 1st duke of:** see MONCK OR MONK, GEORGE.

Albemarle, town (pop. 12,261), co. seat of Stanly co., central N.C., ENE of Charlotte; est. 1842, inc. 1857. A marketing center in a timber, dairy, and grain region, Albemarle manufactures aluminum products and textiles.

Albemarle: see GALÁPAGOS ISLANDS.

Albemarle Point, site on the Ashley river, S.C. Here the English colonists of CHARLESTON made their first settlement in 1670.

Albemarle Sound, arm of the Atlantic Ocean, NE N.C., extending inland c.60 mi. The Chowan and the Roanoke rivers empty into the sound; it is bridged near Edenton.

Albéniz, Isaac (ēsäk′ älbä′nĕth), 1860–1909, Spanish pianist and composer. He made his debut as a pianist at the age of four. When still young, he ran away from home and traveled in North and South America and Spain, supporting himself by playing the piano. As a composer, he was influenced by Liszt and later by Debussy, and studied with D'Indy and Dukas, among others. Filipe Pedrell interested him in Spanish music. Although he wrote operas, songs, and many short piano pieces, he is best remembered for his later piano works (especially *Iberia*, 1906–9), which combine stylized use of Spanish folk material with a brilliant pianistic idiom. See Gilbert Chase, *The Music of Spain* (1941).

Alberdi, Juan Bautista (hwän′ boutē′stä älbĕr′dē), 1810–84, Argentine political philosopher, patriot, and diplomat. With other young intellectuals he opposed Juan Manuel de ROSAS, and after 1838 he spent years of exile in Uruguay, in Chile, and in Europe writing against Rosas. After the overthrow of Rosas by URQUIZA (1852), Alberdi was employed on diplomatic missions. Many of the suggestions made in his *Bases y puntos de partida para la organización política de la república argentina,* a masterpiece of political science published in 1852, were incorporated into the Argentine constitution of 1853.

Galapagos albatross (Diomedea irrorata)

After Urquiza was defeated (1861), Alberdi settled in Paris and wrote political tracts against MITRE and SARMIENTO, sociological works, and essays.

Alberni (ălbûr′nē), city (pop. 4,616), on Vancouver Island, British Columbia, Canada. PORT ALBERNI (pop. 11,560), which adjoins it, is at the head of Alberni Canal, a 22-mile inlet allowing passage to the largest ocean vessels. The cities' industries are based on forest products.

Alberoni, Giulio (jōō′lyō älbärō′nē), 1664–1752, Italian statesman in Spanish service, cardinal of the Roman Church. As representative after 1713

Giulio Alberoni

of the duke of Parma at the court of PHILIP V of Spain, Alberoni gained influence and ultimately became prime minister. With the princesse des URSINS he arranged the marriage of the king with ELIZABETH FARNESE. His aim was to strengthen Spain, nullify the Peace of Utrecht (see UTRECHT, PEACE OF), and crush Austrian hegemony in Italy. The expeditions by which he recovered Sardinia from Austria (1717) and Sicily from Savoy (1718) precipitated the QUADRUPLE ALLIANCE of Britain, the Netherlands, France, and Austria. Spain had to yield, and Philip was forced to dismiss and banish (1719) Alberoni, who retired to Rome. He later became papal legate in the Romagna and in Bologna.

Albert I, 1875–1934, king of the Belgians (1909–34), nephew and successor of Leopold II. He married

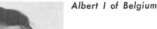

Albert I of Belgium

Prince Albert

(1900) ELIZABETH, a Bavarian princess. In the First World War his heroic resistance (1914) to the German invasion of Belgium greatly helped the Allied cause. Albert spent the entire war at the head of his army, and in 1918 he led the Allied offensive which recovered the Belgian coast. The king and his queen did much to improve social conditions in Belgium and in the Belgian Congo. Albert's democratic and affable ways won him great regard at home and abroad. He died in a rock-climbing accident and was succeeded by his son, Leopold III. His daughter, Marie José, married the crown prince (later King Humbert II) of Italy. See biography by Emile Cammaerts (1935).

Albert I, c.1250–1308, German king (1298–1308), son of RUDOLF I. Albert was invested with Austria and Styria in 1282. His ambitious disposition and his power caused the electors to reject (1292) his candidacy for the crown and to choose ADOLF OF NASSAU. In 1298 Albert led an army to the diet of Frankfurt, which deposed Adolf; he was subsequently chosen as Adolf's successor. Albert's alliance (1299) with Philip IV of France, his support of the Rhine towns, and his unsuccessful attempt (1300) to add Holland and Zeeland to the Hapsburg domains brought an ill-fated revolt (1300–1302) of the Rhenish electors, who were backed by Pope BONIFACE VIII. Albert's title was not recognized by Boniface till 1303. Albert interfered to keep Hungary out of the hands of WENCESLAUS II of Bohemia, but his campaign was unsuccessful until Wenceslaus's death (1305). Albert's son Rudolf succeeded Wenceslaus III (1306), but Bohemia was lost to the Hapsburgs at Ruldolf's death (1307). Albert was assassinated by a band of conspirators, one of them his nephew. He was succeeded by Emperor Henry VII.

Albert II, 1397–1439, German king, king of Hungary and Bohemia (1438–39), duke of Austria (1404–38). He was the son-in-law of Emperor Sigismund, whom he aided against the Hussites. He was unable to suppress the revolt of the Bohemians and died on a disastrous campaign against the Turks. With Albert began the lasting HAPSBURG rule over the Holy Roman Empire.

Albert (Prince Albert), 1819–61, royal consort of Victoria of Great Britain, whom he married in 1840. He was of WETTIN lineage, the son of Ernest I, duke of Saxe-Coburg-Gotha. His unpopularity as an alien prince in England was not diminished by his great deference to advice offered by Baron STOCKMAR. The English came in time to admire him for his irreproachable character, his devotion to the queen and their children, and his responsible and studious concern with public affairs. His influence was particularly strong in diplomacy, and his insistence on a moderate approach to the TRENT AFFAIR (1861) may have averted war with the United States. See biographies by Hector Bolitho (1932), Roger Fulford (1949), and Frank Eyck (1959).

Albert, 1490–1545, German churchman, a cardinal of the Roman Church. A member of the house of Brandenburg, he became (1514) archbishop-elector of Mainz. It was on his authorization that Johann TETZEL began in 1517 to preach an indulgence in Albert's diocese—occasioning Martin Luther's first attack on the Church. A patron of Ulrich von HUTTEN, Albert was expected to join the Reformers, but after 1525 he actively opposed them. Later he invited the Jesuits to preach in his diocese. He was a friend of Erasmus.

Albert, Lake: see ALBERT NYANZA.

Alberta (ălbûr′tù), province (c.248,800 sq. mi., with water surface 255,285 sq. mi.; pop. 1,331,944), W

*Alberta
location map*

Canada. The capital is EDMONTON; other important cities are CALGARY, LETHBRIDGE, and MEDICINE HAT. Alberta is bounded on the east by Saskatchewan, on the north by Mackenzie dist., Northwest Territories, on the west by British Columbia, and on the south by Montana. Westernmost of the Prairie Provs., it lies on a high plateau, rising in the west to the Continental Divide at the British Columbia border. There are the foothills of the Rocky Mts. and the mountains themselves, with three noted national parks—Jasper, Banff, and Waterton Lakes (the Canadian section of Waterton-Glacier International Peace Park). Although it is known as a prairie province, only about one quarter of its area is actually treeless—the undulating prairie of S Alberta. Central Alberta has parklike, partly wooded country, and the northern stretches bear thousands of acres of virgin timberland. Endowed with many lakes, streams, and rivers, the province is drained by the Peace, the Athabaska, the north and south branches of the Saskatchewan, the Red Deer, the St. Mary, the Milk, and many other rivers. The population is concentrated in S and central Alberta; except for farm centers in the fertile valley of the Peace, the northern portion is sparsely settled and still knows the presence of the fur trapper. Agriculture is the basic industry of the economy; grain, especially wheat, is a dominant crop, but diversified farming is increasingly important. In the south, large irrigation developments, such as the St. Mary-Milk development and those around Calgary, have placed thousands of additional acres under cultivation. In this area is grown a variety of crops, such as vegetables and sugar beets. The province is noted as well for the quality of its livestock, which ranks after grains in importance to the economy. Alberta is rich in mineral resources. Vast coal beds contain about one half of Canada's minable reserves. Oil has been commercially important since it was discovered in 1914 in quantity at Turner Valley, near Calgary, and rich new deposits, such as the Leduc oil field in central Alberta, have been developed in recent years. The sands along the Athabaska river in N Alberta, as yet untapped, contain some of the world's greatest oil reserves. Alberta produces about 90 percent of Canada's oil. The province also has extensive deposits of natural gas. Among Alberta's chief industries are meat packing, flour milling, food processing, oil refining (including petrochemicals), dairying, lumbering, textile milling, and the manufacture of iron, steel, and clay products. Alberta's early history was dominated by the fur trade. Traders arrived from the upper Great Lakes before Sir Alexander Mackenzie crossed the region on his way to the Pacific. The area remained under the control of the Hudson's Bay Company, with the most important post at Fort Chipewyan. In 1870 the region became part of Canada. Ranching began soon afterward and is still important. The Canadian Pacific Railway, completed in 1885, brought the homesteader. Alberta received its name when it was separated (1882) from the Northwest Territories and was created a district. It became a province in 1905. In 1935 the Social Credit party captured the provincial legislature and William ABERHART became premier of the first SOCIAL CREDIT government. Social Credit administrations have been elected since Aberhart's death in 1943, but most attempts

The skyline of Edmonton, Alberta, the Legislative Buildings seen in the center.

Trail riders near Banff National Park, Alberta.

Maligne Lake Narrows, Jasper National Park, Alberta.

Ploughing with oxen among the apple blossoms near Calgary, Alberta.

to reform banking and money control have been declared unconstitutional by the courts. The Univ. of Alberta is at Edmonton. See W. A. McIntosh, *Prairie Settlement: the Geographical Setting* (1934); P. F. Sharp, *The Agrarian Revolt in Western Canada* (1948); C. B. Macpherson, *Democracy in Alberta* (1954); E. J. Hanson, *Dynamic Decade* (1958).

Alberta, University of, at Edmonton; provincially supported, coeducational; chartered 1906, opened 1908. It has faculties of agriculture, engineering, arts and science, dentistry, education, law, and medicine and schools of commerce, household economics, nursing, and pharmacy. Affiliated are two men's colleges, St. Joseph's (Roman Catholic) and St. Stephen's (United Church). It has as one of its extensions the Banff School of Fine Arts, at Banff.

Albert Achilles, 1414–86, elector of Brandenburg (1470–86); third son of Elector FREDERICK I. He succeeded his brother in 1470 and in 1473 issued the *Dispositio Achillea*, which established the indivisibility of Brandenburg and subjected it to the law of primogeniture. The *Dispositio* remained in force until 1918.

Albert Canal, waterway, N Belgium, from the Meuse at Liège to the Scheldt at Antwerp. Some 81 mi. long, it was inaugurated in 1939 and named for King Albert I, who started it in 1930. Connecting the vital industrial area of Liège with the chief port of Belgium, the canal was also intended as a defense barrier. However, its fortifications were quickly overrun by the Germans in the Second World War.

Alberti, Domenico (dōmā′nēkō älbĕr′tē) c.1710–c.1740, Venetian singer, player on the harpsichord, and composer. The Alberti bass (which he probably did not invent) is a broken-chord accompaniment used frequently in the 18th cent.

Alberti, Leone Battista (lāō′nä bät-tēs′tä), 1404–72, Italian architect, musician, painter, and humanist, active at the papal court, Florence, Rimini, and Mantua. His treatise *De re aedificatoria* was written c.1450. Though largely dependent upon Vitruvius, it was the first modern work on architecture and influenced the development of Renaissance architectural style. Buildings erected from his designs from c.1450 until his death are among the most dignified and classical of the 15th cent. They include the exteriors of the churches of San Francesco, Rimini, and San Andrea and San Sebastiano in Mantua; part of the façade of Santa Maria Novella, Florence; and the Palazzo Rucellai, Florence, where superimposed orders of architecture articulate the façade for the first time since antiquity. His treatise on painting (1436), the first book in this field to treat theory as well as technique, exercised a great influence on the Renaissance painters and sculptors; in it appear discussions of the imitation of nature, beauty, perspective, and ancient art. His treatise on sculpture, written c.1464, another first work in its field, dealt, in addition, with human proportions. Other writings include mathematical studies, a treatise on St. Potitus, one on the family, and works on ethics, jurisprudence, and other subjects.

Alberti, Rafael (räfäĕl' älbĕr'tē), 1902–, Spanish poet. After starting as a painter, he turned to poetry. His first book, *Marinero en tierra* (1925), was widely applauded. His poems show the influence of Juan Ramón Jiménez and of the Spanish classics, especially of Góngora. *Sobre los ángeles* (1929), a collection of lyrics bold in conception, reveals his genius. It also has a tinge of surrealism. A Loyalist in the Spanish civil war, Alberti sought exile in Buenos Aires after Franco triumphed. His later poetry tends to intimate, spiritual lyricism. Translations of some of his verse appeared as *Selected Poems* (1944). See Eleanor Turnbull, ed. and tr., *Contemporary Spanish Poetry* (1945).

Albert Lea (lē), city (pop. 17,108), co. seat of Freeborn co., S Minn., near the Iowa line S of Minneapolis; settled 1835, platted 1856, inc. 1878. It is a trade and manufacturing center in a farm area. Its products include meat, heating equipment, and fertilizer. A state park is nearby.

Albert Nile: see BAHR-EL-JEBEL.

Albert Nyanza (nĭăn'zŭ, nyăn'zŭ), lake, area 2,064 sq. mi., E central Africa, on the border of the Republic of the Congo and Uganda. It is also called Lake Albert. The lake, almost enclosed by cliffs and wooded slopes, is c.100 mi. long, c.25 mi. wide, and has an average depth of 2,200 ft.; it is part of the Great Rift Valley. Albert Nyanza receives the Semliki river and the Victoria Nile and is drained by the Albert Nile, which becomes the BAHR-EL-JEBEL at the northern border of Uganda. There is steamer service reaching to Murchison Falls on the Victoria Nile and Nimule on the Albert Nile. Discovered by Samuel Baker in 1864, the lake was named for the consort of Queen Victoria.

Albert of Brandenburg, 1490–1568, grand master of the TEUTONIC KNIGHTS (1511–25), first duke of Prussia (1525–68); grandson of Elector Albert Achilles. In 1525 he became a Protestant, secularized, on Luther's advice, the dominions of the order which had elected him, and transformed them into the hereditary duchy of PRUSSIA, for which he did homage to King Sigismund I of Poland. On the extinction of his line (1618), Prussia passed to the senior line of Brandenburg, and in 1701 it was made a kingdom.

Albert the Bear, c.1100–1170, first margrave of Brandenburg (1150–70). He was a loyal vassal of Emperor Lothair II, who, as duke of Saxony, helped him take (1123) Lower Lusatia and the eastern march of Saxony. Albert lost these lands in 1131. He was rewarded (1134) for his share in Lothair's first Italian campaign with the North March. Calling himself margrave of Brandenburg as early as 1136 or 1142, he used the North March as a base for campaigns against the Wends. Invested (1138) with Saxony by Conrad III, he relinquished it to HENRY THE PROUD and in 1142 made peace with HENRY THE LION. He took part in the Wendish Crusade of 1147, but preferred more conciliatory methods of dealing with his pagan neighbors. As a result he inherited (1150) Brandenburg from its last Wendish prince. Albert's

The façade of the church of San Andrea in Mantua, built after Leone Battista Alberti's design.

achievements in Christianizing and Germanizing NE Germany were important.

Albertus Magnus, Saint (ălbûr'tŭs măg'nŭs), or **Saint Albert the Great,** b. 1193 or 1206, d. 1280, scholastic philosopher, called the Universal Doctor. A nobleman of Bollstädt in Swabia, he joined (1223) the Dominicans and taught at Hildesheim, Freiburg, Regensburg, Strasbourg, and Cologne before the Univ. of Paris made him doctor of theology in 1245. Later he taught again at Cologne, and he was also briefly (1260–62) bishop of Regensburg. He was a thorough student of Aristotle, and he not only followed Robert Grosseteste in his approach to Aristotelian thought but also did much to introduce Aristotle's scientific treatises and scientific method to Europe. Like Roger Bacon, he had a scientific interest in nature. He made notable botanical observations (recorded in such works as *De vegetabilibus*), was the first to produce arsenic in a free form, and studied the combinations of metals. In philosophy he set out in his *Summa theologiae* to controvert AVERROËS and others and to reconcile the apparent contradictions of Aristotelianism and Christian thought. He wrote many treatises, and many more have been ascribed to him; the problem of determining which are

Saint Albertus Magnus

genuinely of his authorship is difficult. He was a strong influence on his favorite pupil, St. Thomas Aquinas. Albertus was canonized in 1931. Feast: Nov. 15.

Albertville (älbĕrvēl'), town (pop. c.30,000), E Republic of the Congo, on Lake Tanganyika. It is a commercial center and a rail-steamer transfer point, handling the Congolese trade moving to Dar-es-Salaam and Kigoma in Tanganyika. There are textile factories and cement works. It was founded in 1891 as a military outpost against Arab slave traders.

Albertville, city (pop. 8,250), NE Ala., NNW of Gadsden, in a cotton, truck-farm, and poultry area; inc. 1890. It has textile mills.

Albi (älbē'), town (estimated pop. 34,693), capital of Tarn dept., S France, in Languedoc, on the Tarn river. A commercial and industrial center of a coal mining region, it manufactures textiles, glass, and metals. An episcopal see since the 5th cent., it was ruled by its bishops from the late 12th cent. until the French Revolution. It was the center of the heresy to which it gave its name (see ALBIGENSES). The council finally ending the heresy was held here in 1254. Built of red bricks, Albi is a marvel of medieval architecture. The huge Gothic Cathedral of Sainte-Cécile (13th–14th cent.) resembles a fortress rather than a church. Other structures include the episcopal palace (13th–15th cent.) and an 11th-century bridge. The birthplace of Toulouse-Lautrec, Albi has a museum containing much of his work.

Albia (ăl'bēủ), city (pop. 4,582), co. seat of Monroe co., S central Iowa, W of Ottumwa, in a coal area; founded 1848 as Princeton, inc. 1859. Aluminum millwork is produced here.

Albigenses (ălbĭjĕn'sēz) [Latin,=people of Albi, one of their centers], religious sect of S France in the Middle Ages. They were officially heretics, but actually they were CATHARI, i.e., not Christians at all, but Provencal adherents of the great Manichaean dualistic system that was endemically popular in the Mediterranean basin for centuries (see MANICHAEISM and BOGOMILS). They held the coexistence of two principles, good and evil, represented by God and the Evil One, light and dark, the soul and the body, the next life and this life, peace and war, and the like. They believed that Jesus lived only in semblance (a typically Gnostic idea). They were extremely ascetic, bound to absolute chastity, and abstaining from flesh in all its forms, including milk and cheese. They were in two classes, believers and Perfect, the former much more numerous, making up a catechumenate not bound by the stricter rules such as the Perfect observed. The Perfect were those who had received the sacrament of *consolamentum,* a kind of laying on of hands. The Albigenses held their clergy in high regard. One of the most curious practices of the sect was the custom of suicide, preferably by starvation; for if this life is essentially evil, its end is to be hastened. They had proselyting enthusiasm and preached vigorously. This fact partly accounted for their success, for at that time preaching was unknown in ordinary parish life. In the field of asceticism also the contrast between local clergy and the Albigenses was helpful to the new sect. Albigensianism appeared in the 11th cent. and soon had powerful protectors. Local bishops were ineffectual in dealing with the problem, and the pope sent St. Bernard of Clairvaux and other Cistercians to preach in Languedoc, the center of the movement. In 1167 the Albigenses held a council of their own at Toulouse. Innocent III attacked the problem anew, and his action in sending (1205) St. Dominic to lead a band of poor preaching friars into the Albigensian cities was decisive. These missionaries were hampered by the war that soon broke out. In 1208 the papal legate, a Cistercian, Peter de Castelnau, was murdered, probably by an aid of RAYMOND VI of Toulouse, one of the chief Albigensian nobles. The pope proclaimed (1208) the **Albigensian Crusade.** From the first, political interests in the war overshadowed others; behind Simon de MONTFORT, the Catholic leader, was France, and behind Raymond was Peter II of Aragon, irreproachably Catholic. Innocent attempted to make peace, but the prize of S France was tempting, and the crusaders continued to harry the whole region. In 1213, at Muret, Montfort was victor and Peter was killed. The war went on, with the son of Philip II (later Louis VIII) as one of the leaders. Simon's death in 1218 robbed him of victory and left his less competent son to continue the fight. Raymond's son, Raymond VII, joined the war, which was finally terminated with an honorable capitulation by Raymond. By the Peace of Paris (1229) Louis IX acquired the county of Toulouse. The religious result of the crusade was negligible. In 1233 Pope Gregory IX established a system of legal investigation in Albigensian centers and put it into the hands of the Dominicans; this was the birth of the medieval INQUISITION. After 100 years of the Inquisition, of tireless preaching by the friars, and of careful reform of the clergy, Albigensianism was dead. See Steven Runciman, *The Medieval Manichee* (1947).

albino (ălbī′nō) [Portuguese,=white], animal or plant lacking normal pigmentation. The absence of pigment is observed in the body covering (skin, hair, and feathers) and in the iris of the eye. The blood vessels of the iris show through, giving it a pink or reddish color, and the eyes are highly sensitive to light. Albinism is inherited as a Mendelian recessive character in humans and other animals. Through experimental breeding, races of albinos have been established among some domestic animals, e.g., mice, rabbits, pigeons, and chickens. Albino animals are sometimes held sacred, e.g., white elephants in Siam and white cattle in India. The presence of an excess of black pigment is called melanism.

Albion (ăl′bēŭn), ancient and literary name of Britain. It is usually restricted to England and is perhaps derived from the chalk cliffs [Latin *albus*= white]. ALBANY generally designates Scotland.

Albion (ăl′bēŭn). **1** City (pop. 2,025), co. seat of Edwards co., SE Ill., E of Belleville; founded 1818 by Englishmen led by Morris BIRKBECK and George FLOWER, inc. 1869. **2** Town (pop. 1,325), co. seat of Noble co., NE Ind., NNW of Fort Wayne; laid out 1847. Lake resorts are nearby. **3** Industrial city (pop. 12,749), S Mich., on the Kalamazoo river S of Lansing; settled 1833, inc. as a village 1855, as a city 1885. Among its manufactures are television tubes, iron and wire products, and heating and cooling equipment. The city is the seat of Albion College (Methodist; coeducational; 1835). **4** City (pop. 1,982), co. seat of Boone co., E central Nebr., SW of Norfolk; settled 1871, inc. 1873. Feed and electronic equipment are among its products. **5** Village (pop. 5,182), co. seat of Orleans co., W N.Y., on the Barge Canal W of Rochester; inc. 1828. Food is processed here. **6** Manufacturing borough (pop. 1,630), NW Pa., SW of Erie; settled 1815, inc. 1861.

Albizu Campos, Pedro (pād′rō älbē′sōō käm′pōs), 1891–, Puerto Rican political leader, grad. Harvard (B.A., 1916; LL.B., 1921). After service in the First World War, during which time he was assigned to a Negro unit, he developed a lasting enmity for the United States and became the fiery champion of Puerto Rican independence. His Nationalist party, however, failed to receive popular support in the Puerto Rican elections of 1932, and Albizu Campos turned increasingly to violent action. Convicted of seeking to overthrow the U.S. government, he was imprisoned (1937–43) at Atlanta, then hospitalized in New York before returning to Puerto Rico in 1947. His party made a poor showing in the 1948 election, and in 1950 Nationalists attacked the governor's mansion in Puerto Rico and Blair House in Washington. Charged with inciting to murder, Albizu Campos was again imprisoned. He was pardoned (1953) by Gov. Luis Muñoz Marín because of failing health, but the next year he was implicated in the armed attack by a group of Nationalists on the U.S. House of Representatives in Washington. His pardon revoked, he was sentenced to life imprisonment.

Alboin (ăl′boin), d. 572?, first Lombard king in Italy (569–572?). With the Avars he defeated the Gepidae. He then led (568) a mixed host across the Alps into Italy, took (569) Milan, and after a three-year siege reduced Pavia, which became his capital. He conquered most of N and central Italy from the Byzantines (see LOMBARDS). According to a legend probably based on fact, he was murdered at the instigation of his wife, ROSAMOND.

Alborg: see AALBORG.

Albornoz, Gil Álvarez Carrillo de (hēl′ äl′värāth kärē′lyō dä älbōrnōth′), 1310?–1367, Spanish and papal statesman and general, cardinal of the Roman Church. He was archbishop of Toledo before he received (1350) the red hat. Under Alfonso XI of Castile he distinguished himself fighting the Moors at Tarifa and Algeciras and was chancellor of Castile, but at the accession (1350) of Peter I (Peter the Cruel) he left Spain and entered the service of the pope, then at Avignon. Put in charge of the papal armies, he was sent (1353) to the Papal States as cardinal legate. Using the prestige of Cola di RIENZI, Albornoz entered Rome with him. By skillful diplomacy and force of arms, he restored papal authority in the Romagna and the Marches, where the communes and petty local tyrants had enjoyed practical autonomy. He compiled the law code of the Marches, known as the Constitutions of Aegidius (1357), which was in use until 1816. He died soon after becoming papal legate at Bologna, where the college he founded for Spanish students still exists. His work prepared the way for the return (1378) of the popes from Avignon to Rome.

Albrecht. For rulers thus named, see ALBERT.

Albrechtsberger, Johann Georg (yō′hän gā′ôrg äl′brĕkhtsbĕr″gŭr), 1736–1809, Austrian musical theorist, teacher, and composer. He became (1772) court organist in Vienna and later was chief organist, conductor, and choirmaster of St. Stephen's cathedral, Vienna. He composed more than 240 works and wrote one of the most important books on counterpoint in the 18th cent. Considered the best teacher of composition in Vienna in his time, he taught Beethoven.

Albret, Jeanne d': see JEANNE D'ALBRET.

Albret (älbrā′), former duchy, SW France, in the LANDES of Gascony. The powerful lords of Albret became kings of NAVARRE by the marriage (1494) of Jean d'Albret with Catherine de Foix, queen of Navarre, who also brought him FOIX and BÉARN. Their son, Henri d'Albret, married (1527) Margaret of Angoulême, who thus became MARGARET OF NAVARRE. The marriage added ARMAGNAC to his territories, which now included nearly all of Gascony. In 1556 Albret was raised to a duchy. Henri's daughter and heir, JEANNE D'ALBRET, married Antoine de BOURBON, and their combined territories were inherited by Henry of Navarre, who in 1589 became king of France as Henry IV.

Henry added Albret to the royal domain in 1607 as part of the province of Gascony.

Albright, Jacob (ôl'brīt), 1759–1808, American religious leader, founder of the Evangelical Association (later the Evangelical Church), b. near Pottstown, Pa. A Pennsylvania German and a Lutheran, he was converted c.1790 to Methodism. Preaching and forming classes among his converts in the German settlements, he was ordained a minister (1803) by representatives from these classes and was elected bishop at the first annual conference held by his followers in 1807. The movement, unrecognized by the Methodists, did not take the name Evangelical Association until after Albright's death. A college in Reading, Pa., bears his name. The Evangelical Church united in 1946 with the United Brethren in Christ to form the EVANGELICAL UNITED BRETHREN CHURCH.

Albright College: see READING, Pa.

Albumazar (ăl″bōomä′zŭr), 805?–885, Arabian astronomer, more fully Abu-Mashar Jafar ibn Mohammed. Something of his achievement is known through manuscripts in the Escorial library in Spain and other libraries of Europe. In his *De magnis conjunctionibus* he claimed that fhe world had been created when the seven planets were in conjunction in the first degree of Aries and that its end would come when they should be in conjunction again in the last degree of Pisces. In his astronomical tables he used the Persian calculations of the years and pointed out that they did not follow the Jews' reckoning of time. The name of Albumazar was given to the chief character in a play, *L'astrologo* (1606), by G. B. della Porta, and an adaptation in English, called *Albumazar*, by Thomas Tomkis was performed in 1614.

albumin (ălbū′mĭn) [from Latin,=white of egg], member of a class of PROTEINS that are soluble in water, coagulated by heat, and usually deficient in the AMINO ACID glycine. They are distributed widely in plant and animal tissues, e.g., ovalbumin of egg, muscle myogen, serum albumin of the blood, lactalbumin of milk, legumelin of peas, and leucosin of wheat. Some albumins contain CARBOHYDRATE as well as protein. Albumin of blood serum can be separated from other types of blood proteins by electrical means and by chemical means (fractionation by ammonium sulfate precipitation), although the latter method usually produces mixtures of globulins and albumins. Albumins constitute about 55 percent of the total protein content of blood plasma. Albumin adheres chemically to many types of substances in the blood, e.g., amino acids, fatty acids, drugs, and thus plays a significant role in the transport of substances in the circulatory system. In human and animal bodies the albumin and other proteins of the blood plasma play an important role in regulating the distribution of water in the body. In conditions of shock the circulating blood volume may become very low and cause impairment of heart action. Intravenous albumin solution may then be used to restore fluid volume. Albumins are also used in textile printing, in the fixation of dyes, in refining sugar, and in other processes.

Albuquerque, Afonso de (äfō′zō dù ăl″bùkĕr′kù), 1453–1515, Portuguese admiral, the real founder of the Portuguese Empire in the East. He first went to India in 1503, and in 1506 he set out with Tristão da CUNHA, carrying secret instructions to supersede Francisco de ALMEIDA in command. After they had gone along the coasts of Madagascar and E Africa and captured the island of Socotra, Albuquerque left Tristão da Cunha and with his own fleet ravaged the Oman coast and took (1507) Hormuz; he attempted to build a fort at Hormuz, but had to retire to Socotra when some of his men deserted. Almeida disavowed the conquest and, after Albuquerque had arrived in India, refused to yield command and imprisoned

Afonso de Albuquerque

him. When a Portuguese fleet arrived with confirmation of Albuquerque's appointment, Almeida gave way (1509). Albuquerque captured Goa (1510), making it the mainstay of Portuguese power in India; Malacca (1511), extending Portuguese domination to SE Asia; and Hormuz (1515), thus cutting off the Arab spice trade. While returning from Hormuz to India, Albuquerque learned that he had been replaced. He died at the entrance to Goa harbor. Albuquerque had built forts at Goa, Calicut, Malacca, and Hormuz; reconstructed those of Cannanore and Cochin; began shipbuilding and other industries in Portuguese India; and established relations with the rulers of SE Asia. The main goals of his policy—control over the sources of spices and of the trade routes—were nearly attained during his brief tenure of power. See K. G. Jayne, *Vasco da Gama and His Successors* (1910).

Albuquerque (ăl′bùkûr″kē), city (pop. 201,189), co. seat of Bernalillo co., W central N.Mex., on the upper Rio Grande and SW of Santa Fe; inc. 1890. The largest city in the state, it is an important commercial, industrial, and transportation center serving a rich timber, livestock, and farm area. The city has railroad shops, lumber mills, and food-processing plants; manufactures include bricks and tiles, wood products, and Indian jewelry and curios. Kirtland Air Force Base and an Atomic Energy Commission installation are in the area. Albuquerque is divided into the old town and the new town. The old town was founded in 1706 and named San Felipe de Alburquerque in honor of Philip V of Spain and the duke of Alburquerque

Albuquerque, N.M., Sandia Mountains in the background.

(the first *r* was later dropped from the name of the city). New Albuquerque was platted in 1880 in connection with the railroad. In a mountain region, it is a noted health resort with many sanatoriums and hospitals (including a U.S. veterans' hospital and a U.S. Indian hospital). The Univ. of New Mexico (see NEW MEXICO, UNIVERSITY OF) and a U.S. school for Indians are at Albuquerque. Points of interest in and about the city include the Church of San Felipe de Neri (1706), the old-town plaza, and nearby Indian pueblos. See Erna Fergusson, *Albuquerque* (1947).

Alburg (ôl'bûrg), town (pop. 2,927), NW Vt., on a peninsula extending into N Lake Champlain, crossed by the Canadian line. It is a port of entry. Settlement, attempted by the French in 1735, was accomplished in 1782.

Alburtis (ălbûr'tĭs), borough (pop. 1,086), SE Pa., SW of Allentown; inc. 1913. Clothing and machinery are made.

Albury (ăl'bûrē), town (pop. 16,726), New South Wales, Commonwealth of Australia, and on the Murray. It is a gold-mining and wool-trading center. The HUME RESERVOIR is nearby.

Alcaeus (ălsē'ûs), d. c.580 B.C., Greek poet of Lesbos, a noted early writer of personal lyrics. The extant fragments are mostly convivial and light, but his political poetry is sterner. An aristocrat, he was often embroiled in political battles with the ruling tyrants. He was, according to tradition, a close associate of SAPPHO. The Alcaic strophe (ălkā'ĭk), said to have been his invention, was much used by Greek lyrists. It was greatly admired by Horace who employed it with slight modification. See C. M. Bowra, *Greek Lyric Poetry* (1936); Denys Page, *Sappho and Alcaeus* (1955).

Alcalá de Henares (älkälä' dā änä'räs), town (pop. 18,004), Madrid prov., central Spain, in New Castile. Leather, soap and china are made here; the surrounding agricultural district yields wheat. It is triply famous as the former seat of a great university founded in 1508 and transferred in 1836 to Madrid, as the birthplace of Cervantes, and as the scene of the Cortes in which ALFONSO XI promulgated the *Ordenamiento de Alcalá*. The town was severely damaged in the Spanish civil war. Among the landmarks are a Gothic collegiate church and the former archiepiscopal palace.

Alcalá la Real (lä rääl'), town (pop. 30,062), Jaén prov., S Spain, in Andalusia. It has well-known mineral springs. Here, in 1810, the French defeated the Spanish in the Peninsular War.

Alcalá Zamora, Niceto (nēthä'tō älkälä' thämō'rä), 1877–1949, Spanish statesman and president of Spain (1931–36). After holding several cabinet posts under the monarchy, he turned republican and was jailed for his political activity in 1930. He helped lead the successful revolution of 1931 and became first provisional and then constitutional president of the Spanish republic. A middle-of-the-road liberal, he was deposed by the Cortes on a Socialist motion (April, 1936) and was succeeded as president by Manuel Azaña. He went into exile first to France and then (1942) to Argentina.

alcalde (ălkăl'dē, Span. älkäl'dä) [Span., from Arabic,=the judge], Spanish official title, in existence at least since the 11th cent. Originally it designated a judge with certain administrative functions. The office was deprived of most of its purely judicial powers in 1812; since 1877 the alcalde has been the chief of the municipal government and at the same time the local representative of the central government. The office was also instituted in the Spanish colonies. There, the *alcalde mayor* was the administrator of a provincial division usually smaller than that of a corregidor; he might even be the assistant of a corregidor. The alcalde proper became the *alcalde ordinario*, an elected municipal officer, who frequently exercised the powers of mayor and sheriff and was in some villages the sole representative of the law. A Spanish title of the same derivation, *alcaide* or *alcayde*, is used to designate the governor of a castle or fortress.

Alcamenes (ălkŭmē'nēz), 5th cent. B.C., Athenian sculptor, said to have been a pupil and rival of Phidias. He worked in gold, ivory, and bronze. His *Aphrodite of the Gardens* at Athens is one of the great masterpieces of antiquity. Pausanias erroneously attributed to him the sculptures of the west pediment of the temple of Zeus at Olympia. He was also well known for his *Hermes of the Gateway* (Hermes Propylaios) at the entrance of the Athenian Acropolis. A Roman copy found at Pergamum is in the Turkish Museum of Antiquities in Istanbul.

Alcamo (äl'kämō), city (estimated pop. 43,443), NW Sicily, Italy. A large agricultural center, it is noted for its white wine. The ruins of ancient SEGESTA are nearby.

Alcántara (älkän'tärä), town (pop. 4,150), Cáceres prov., W Spain, in Estremadura, near the Tagus. There are a fine Roman bridge built in honor of Emperor Trajan and ruins of the convent and church of the Knights of Alcántara. The **Order of Alcántara**, one of the great military religious orders of Spain, established its seat here in the 13th cent. after the expulsion of the Moors and enjoyed a period of great splendor (13th–14th cent.). The dignity of grand master passed to the Castilian crown in the 15th cent.

Alcatraz (ăl'kŭtrăz"), rocky island in San Francisco Bay, W Calif. Fortified by the Spanish and used after 1859 as a U.S. military prison, it was made in 1933 a Federal prison for dangerous criminals.

Nicknamed "The Rock," it came to be a symbol of the impregnable fortress prison, with maximum security and extraordinarily strict discipline. It was closed in 1963.

Alcazarquivir (älkä″thärkēvēr′), city (pop. 35,922), N Morocco. Near here on Aug. 4, 1578, the Moroccans signally defeated the Portuguese. SEBASTIAN of Portugal had invaded Morocco in support of a pretender to the Moroccan throne. The three leaders present at the engagement, the ruler of Morocco, Sebastian, and the Moroccan pretender all died that day. As a result of this battle, Portugal soon passed to Philip II of Spain and the new Moroccan ruler, AHMED AL-MANSUR, began his reign with tremendous prestige. The name of the city also appears as Al Qasr al Kabir and Ksar el Kebir.

Alcestis (ălsĕ′stĭs), in Greek mythology, daughter of Pelias. She was won in marriage by ADMETUS, who fulfilled her father's condition that her suitor come for her in a chariot pulled by a wild boar and a lion. So great was her wifely devotion that when Admetus was granted life by the gods if someone would die in his place, she willingly gave her life. In some myths Hercules rescued her from the dead; in others Persephone was so touched by her devotion that she reunited husband and wife. The legend was dramatized by Euripides in his play *Alcestis.*

alchemy (ăl′kŭmē), ancient art of obscure origin in which chemistry had its roots. Some scholars hold that it was first practiced in early Egypt and others that it arose in China (in the 5th or in the 3d cent. B.C.) and was from there carried westward. Alchemy centered chiefly around experiments with metals and with other chemical materials. Alchemical apparatus included the alembic (or *ambix*) for distillation and the *kerotakis* for sublimation. A chief goal of alchemy was to transmute the base metals into gold. In its beginnings alchemy was chiefly a craft and it embraced many kinds of metalwork, including the use of alloys resembling gold and silver. Alexandria is generally considered a center of early alchemy, and the art was influenced by the philosophy of the Hellenistic Greeks; the conversion of base metals into gold (considered the most perfect of metals) was a part of a general striving of all things toward perfection. Alchemy was early associated with astrology. It is believed that the concept of the philosophers' stone (called also by many other names including the elixir and the grand magistery) may have originated in Alexandria; this was an imaginary substance capable of transmuting the less noble metals into gold and also of restoring youth to man. Alchemy, strongly tinged with magic, reached the Arabs (perhaps in the 8th cent.) and remained for several centuries under the Moslem influence; in the 12th cent. it reached parts of Europe through translations of writings of the Arabs (the early Greek treatises were not known in Europe in the Middle Ages). Arabian alchemy was preserved especially in the works of GEBER, and the earlier Greek alchemy in that of Zosimus and others. The alchemical writings of the Middle Ages were couched in symbolic and cryptic language. The alchemists became obsessed with their quest for the secret of transmutation; some adopted deceptive methods of experimentation, and many gained a livelihood from hopeful patrons. This pseudo-alchemy fell into disrepute. However, in the searching experimental quests of the alchemists chemistry had its beginnings; indeed, the line between alchemy and chemistry is impossible to draw. TRANSMUTATION OF ELEMENTS has been accomplished in modern chemistry. See Lynn Thorndike, *A History of Magic and Experimental Science* (8 vols., 1923–58); A. J. Hopkins, *Alchemy: Child of Greek Philosophy* (1943); Mark Graubard, *Astrology and Alchemy* (1953); E. J. Holmyard, *Alchemy* (1957); John Read, *Through Alchemy to Chemistry* (1957).

Eighteenth-century engraving of alchemist in his laboratory.

Alcibiades (ălsĭbĭ'ǔdēz), c.450–404 B.C., Athenian statesman and general. Of the family of Alcmaeonidae, he was a ward of Pericles and was for years a devoted attendant of Socrates. He turned to politics after the Peace of Nicias (421 B.C.), and

Alcibiades

during the PELOPONNESIAN WAR he was the leader in agitating against Sparta. He was so successful that Athens joined an alliance against Sparta. When Sparta attacked (418 B.C.) Argos, Alcibiades led an Athenian force to help the Argives, but Athens and the allies were beaten at Mantinea. He was (415 B.C.) the chief promoter of the Sicilian campaign and was one of the three leaders (with Nicias and Lamachus) of the Athenian forces. On the night before the expedition sailed, all the statues of Hermes (the hermae) in Athens were mutilated, a sacrilege that caused fear and commotion in the city. Alcibiades was accused—almost certainly falsely—of the crime and was not allowed to have an immediate trial before sailing. When the forces reached Sicily, he proposed an attempt to win allies rather than attacking the hostile cities of Selinus and Syracuse at once. NICIAS carried out this policy to ultimate disaster. Alcibiades had meanwhile been summoned home to stand trial. Instead he fled to Sparta, where he gave advice to King AGIS I, who was successful against Athens. Alcibiades later fell into trouble with the Spartan king, and c.413 he fled to the protection of the Persian satrap TISSAPHERNES and then sought to return to Athens. After the oligarchy of the Four Hundred fell (411), he was recalled at the instance of Thrasybulus. Athens had a short era of greatness as Alcibiades directed brilliantly the Athenian fleet in the Aegean and in 410 won a victory over the Peloponnesian fleet off Cyzicus. In command of Athenian forces, he recovered (408) Byzantium and was acclaimed in Athens. A new Spartan commander, however, appeared in Lysander, who defeated the Athenian fleet at NOTIUM in c.406 B.C. Though Alcibiades was absent on another expedition at the time, he was, nevertheless, blamed and exiled. He went to a castle he owned on the western shore of the Hellespont. There in 405 B.C. he attempted to warn the Athenian fleet at AEGOSPOTAMOS against a surprise attack by the Spartans, but his advice was ignored. In 404 at the behest of Lysander, the Persian satrap PHARNABAZUS had Alcibiades murdered. Historians have disagreed in their estimate of Alcibiades from his own day to the present; some have viewed him as a highly competent and unappreciated leader, but most have considered him to be largely responsible for the decline of Athens.

Alcimus (ăl'sĭ–) [Gr.,=brave], Hellenizing Jew, appointed to the high priesthood, but opposed by the Maccabees. 1 Mac. 7; 9.1,54–57; 2 Mac. 14.3,13,26.

Alcinoüs (ălsĭ'nōŭs), in Greek mythology, king of Phaeacia; father of Nausicaä. He aided Odysseus in his journey back to Ithaca. In the story of Jason, he protects Jason and Medea from the Colchians.

Alciphron (ăl'sĭfrŏn, –frŭn), fl. A.D. c.200?, Greek satirist. His extant work (in fine Attic style) consists of 122 imaginary letters by common people living in Athens in the 4th cent. B.C. They tell much about domestic life of the times.

Alcmaeon (ălkmē'ŭn), in Greek legend, son of Amphiaraüs and Eriphyle, a leader of the expedition of the EPIGONI against Thebes. He murdered his mother in revenge for his father's death and for this matricide was haunted by the Erinyes until he found haven on Achelous' island. There he married Callirrhoë (kŭlĭr'ōē), daughter of Achelous, and lived in peace until his wife demanded the robe and necklace of Harmonia. When he tried to regain these from his former wife, Arsinoë, her brothers killed him.

Alcmaeonidae (ălk″mēŏ'nĭdē), Athenian family powerful in the 7th, the 6th, and the 5th cent. B.C. Blamed for the murder of the followers of Cylon, the would-be tyrant (c.632 B.C.), they were considered attainted and were exiled. They were again in Athens in the 6th cent. The most prominent members of the family later were CLEISTHENES, PERICLES (whose mother was an Alcmaeonid), and ALCIBIADES.

Alcman (ălk'mŭn), fl. before 600 B.C., Greek poet of Sparta, founder of the Dorian school of choral lyric poetry. Short choral fragments and a longer one (part of a *parthenion* or choir song for girls) survive. His verse, simple, clear, and musical, was often sung at festivals. See his *Partheneion* (ed. by Denys L. Page, 1951).

Alcmene (ălkmē'nē), in Greek mythology, wife of AMPHITRYON. Zeus, in love with her, visited her in the form of Amphitryon. She bore twin sons, Hercules to Zeus and Iphicles to Amphitryon.

Alcoa (ălkō'ŭ), industrial city (pop. 6,395), E Tenn., S of Knoxville; inc. 1919. It was founded in 1913 by the Aluminum Company of America, which has established large reduction plants here.

Alcobaça (ălkōōbä'sŭ), town (pop. c.5,000), Leiria dist., W central Portugal, in Estremadura. It became a center of the Cistercians in the reign of Alfonso I, and the abbey (building begun 1152) was the greatest of medieval Portugal. It exercised enormous influence on education, social conditions, finance, and politics. The early kings of Portugal are buried here.

alcohol [from Arabic *al kuhul*,=powdered antimony, with which it is mixed to make a cosmetic], any of a class of organic compounds having the general chemical formula R–OH, in which R is a RADICAL comprising carbon and hydrogen in various proportions and OH represents one or more hydroxyl (see HYDROXIDE) radicals. In common usage, the term *alcohol* is applied to ethyl alcohol. The class includes methyl alcohol; the amyl, butyl, and propyl alcohols; glycol, a colorless liquid with a sweetish taste used sometimes as a substitute for glycerin in explosives; and glycerin, or glycerol. Alcohols are generally classified according to the number of hydroxyl groups in the molecule. Those that have one hydroxyl group are called monohydric, or monatomic, alcohols. These include methyl, ethyl, propyl, butyl, and amyl alcohol. Glycol, with two hydroxyl groups, is a dihydric alcohol, and glycerol, with three hydroxyl groups, is trihydric. The monohydric alcohols are further classified as primary, secondary, or tertiary according to the number of carbon atoms attached to the carbon atom that is bound to the hydroxyl group. Chemical reactions involving the hydroxyl (oxygen-hydrogen) group of atoms present in an alcohol molecule are of two types: that in which the hydroxyl group as a whole is replaced, and that in which the hydrogen only is involved in the reaction. Alcohols differ in boiling and melting points, densities, and other physical properties; at ordinary temperatures they range from volatile liquids to paraffinlike solids.

alcoholism, condition resulting from the ingestion of relatively large amounts of ethyl alcohol. Alcohol is absorbed through the gastrointestinal tract; the rate of absorption is dependent chiefly upon the concentration of the alcohol—the presence of food in the stomach decreases the rate. Ingestion of adulterated alcoholic beverages containing methyl (wood) alcohol results in a condition known as methyl-alcohol poisoning. One of the disastrous effects of such poisoning is optic neuritis, which may lead to complete blindness within a few days. Washing out the stomach is the treatment. Consumption of alcohol in small amounts may have no obvious effects. Taken in larger quantities it usually causes muscular incoordination; the reflexes are less rapid; the face becomes flushed, occasionally pallid; and nausea and vomiting may occur. A state of partial consciousness may be followed by coma. The condition known as acute alcoholism results from the action of alcohol on the central nervous system. The term alcoholism, however, more usually means chronic alcoholism, caused by the cumulative effect upon the organs and tissues of the body following the frequent ingestion of large amounts of alcohol. Physiological and structural changes may ensue, e.g., chronic gastritis, which leads to loss of appetite and malnutrition. Neuritis and DELIRIUM TREMENS are among related disorders. Chronic alcoholism is now considered a symptom of psychic instability, and the problem is being studied by various educational institutions. At Yale Univ. scientific studies of alcoholism were undertaken at the laboratory of applied physiology in 1930, and a school of alcoholic studies was established there in 1943. The first free clinics in the United States for diagnosis, treatment, and guidance of inebriates were established (1944) in New Haven and Hartford, Conn. The organization known as Alcoholics Anonymous was founded in 1934 for aiding those who desire help, chiefly through association with and encouragement from others who have been alcoholics. In 1937 the Research Council on Problems of Alcohol was organized, and in 1938 it became affiliated with the American Association for the Advancement of Science. See E. M. Jellinek, ed., *Alcohol Addiction and Chronic Alcoholism* (1942); S. B. Wortis and A. Z. Peffer, *The Management of Alcoholism* (1950); Mrs. Marty Mann, *New Primer on Alcoholism* (1958).

Alcott, Bronson (Amos Bronson Alcott) (ôl′kŭt), 1799–1888, American advocate of educational and social reform, b. near Wolcott, Conn. His meager formal education was supplemented by omnivorous reading, while he gained a living from farming, working in a clock factory, and as a peddler in the South. He taught in several places before he opened (1834) his Temple School in Boston. His own records, as well as those made by Elizabeth Palmer Peabody, his assistant, show his concern with the integrated mental, physical, and spiritual development of the child. Yet unfavorable reactions to his advanced and liberal theories forced him to close his school. His disappointment was lessened when he heard of Alcott House, a school founded by his disciples in England. He wrote for the transcendental periodical *Dial* (the "Orphic Sayings" being his most famous contribution) and was a nonresident member of Brook Farm. He was one of the founders (1843) of a cooperative vegetarian community, "Fruitlands," near Harvard, Mass., but it was abandoned in 1844. Poverty continually plagued the life of the Alcotts until the writings of Louisa May Alcott relieved the family of financial worry. He became superintendent of the Concord public schools, whose reformation he described in his *Reports*. From 1879 he was dean of the Concord School of Philosophy, which annually gathered disciples to hear him and many other speakers. Among his writings are *Observations on the Principles and Methods of Infant Instruction* (1830), *Record of a School* (1835), and *Ralph Waldo Emerson* (1882). See his journals (ed. by Odell Shepard, 1938); Odell Shepard, *Pedlar's Progress* (1937).

Alcott, Louisa May, 1832–88, American novelist and writer of children's books, b. Germantown, Pa.; daughter of Bronson Alcott. She is chiefly remembered for one of the most popular girls' books ever written, *Little Women*, in which the character Jo March is largely autobiographical. She knew Emerson and Thoreau well, and her first book, *Flower Fables* (1854), was a collection of tales originally created to amuse Emerson's daughter. Louisa Alcott was determined to contribute to the small family income and worked as a servant and a seamstress before she made her fortune as a writer. By 1860 her poems and short stories were appearing in the *Atlantic Monthly*. Her letters written to her family when she was a Civil War nurse and published as *Hospital Sketches* (1863) were received with enthusiasm, and her first novel, *Moods*, followed in 1864. In 1867 she became editor of a children's magazine, *Merry's Museum*. Then came *Little Women*, published in two volumes in 1868–69. This beloved book, its sequels, *Little Men* (1871) and *Jo's Boys* (1886), and her other novels for children, notably *Eight Cousins* (1875) with its sequel *Rose in Bloom* (1876) and *Under the Lilacs* (1879), picture family life in Victorian America with warmth and perception. Another novel, *Work* (1873), draws on her early experiences. Her letters and journal were edited by E. D. Cheney

(1889). See biographies by M. B. Stern (1950) and M. M. Worthington (1958).

Alcoy (älkoi'), city (pop. 51,007), Alicante prov., E Spain, in Valencia, on the Alcoy river. An important industrial center manufacturing paper (especially cigarette paper), matches, and textiles, it also has trade in grain, wine, and oil from the surrounding region.

Alcuin (ăl'kwĭn), 735?-804, English churchman and educator. He was educated at the cathedral school of York by a disciple of Bede; he became principal in 766. CHARLEMAGNE invited him (781?) to court to set up a school. For 15 years Alcuin was the moving spirit of the Carolingian renaissance. He combated illiteracy with a system of elementary education. On a higher level he established the study of the seven liberal arts, the trivium and quadrivium, which became the curriculum for medieval Western Europe. He encouraged the study and preservation of ancient texts. His dialogue textbook of rhetoric, called *Compendia*, was much used. He wrote verse, and his letters were preserved. Alcuin's treatise against Felix of Urgel did much to defeat the heresy of ADOPTIONISM. He died as head of the abbey of St. Martin of Tours, where he had one of his most famous schools. See studies by E. J. B. Gaskoin (1904), Eleanor Duckett (1951), and Gerald Ellard (1956).

Alcyone: see HALCYONE.

Aldan (ŭldän'), city (pop. c.12,100), Yakut Autonomous SSR, E Asiatic RSFSR, on the Aldan Plateau. A gold-mining center since 1923, it also has mica mines. Until 1939 it was called Nezametny.

Aldan (ôl'dŭn), borough (pop. 4,324), SE Pa., a suburb SW of Philadelphia; inc. 1893.

Aldan (ŭldän'), river, Yakut ASSR, E Asiatic RSFSR, in E Siberia. It rises in the Stanovoi Range and flows c.1,400 mi. N and E around the Aldan Plateau, then turns northward and finally westward to enter the Lena c.100 mi. N of Yakutsk. It is navigable for c.1,100 mi. The Amga (left) and the Uchur and Maya (right) are its main tributaries.

Aldanov, Mark (märk' ŭldä'nŭf), pseud. of **Mark Aleksandrovich Landau** (ŭlyĭksän'drŭvĭch län'dou), 1886-1957, Russian writer. He emigrated to France after the October Revolution and won fame abroad with *The Thinker*, a tetralogy on the revolutionary era 1793-1821 comprising *The Ninth Thermidor* (1923; Eng. tr., 1926), *The Devil's Bridge* (1925; Eng. tr., 1928), *The Conspiracy* (1927), and *St. Helena: Little Island* (1921; Eng. tr., 1924). *The Tenth Symphony* (1931; Eng. tr., 1948) is based on the life of Beethoven. The Bolshevik Revolution is the background for *The Key* (1930; Eng. tr., 1931) and *The Flight* (1930), published together in English as *The Escape* (1950). *The Fifth Seal* (1939; Eng. tr., 1943) portrays the decay of revolutionary idealism during the Spanish civil war. The clash between Soviet and American ideologies is described in *Nightmare and Dawn* (Eng. tr., 1957). *A Night at the Airport* (Eng. tr., 1949) is a collection of short stories. He came to the United States in 1941 but returned to France shortly before his death.

aldehyde (ăl'dĭhīd) [quasi-abbreviation of *alcohol* and New Latin *dehydrogenatus*=deprived of hydrogen], any member of a class of organic compounds characterized by having in their molecules a carbon-hydrogen-oxygen (CHO) group of atoms. The aldehydes result from partial oxidation of primary alcohols (when some hydrogen is removed) and are named for the acids which they produce when they in turn are oxidized. For example, by the oxidation of ethyl alcohol, acetaldehyde, a typical aldehyde, is formed, which upon oxidation yields acetic acid. The aldehydes are important in industry in the manufacture of synthetic resins (e.g., bakelite) and of dyestuffs, and also as disinfectants. Many aldehydes occur in essential OILS of certain plants. The term *aldehyde* is commonly used to indicate acetaldehyde, called also acetic aldehyde or ethanal, a colorless liquid, boiling at 20.8° C. and melting at −123° C. It is used in silvering mirrors and in the manufacture of dyes and of the hypnotic drug paraldehyde. Benzaldehyde, called also benzoic aldehyde or, commercially, oil of bitter almonds, is a colorless liquid with a characteristic almond odor, boiling at 180° C., soluble in alcohol, but insoluble in water. It is formed by the oxidation of benzyl alcohol and is oxidized to benzoic acid. It is prepared in various ways: from bitter almonds crushed and boiled in water, when a glucoside called amygdalin is hydrolyzed; from toluene; or directly from benzal chloride by treatment with an alkali or from benzyl chloride by oxidation. Benzaldehyde is used in the preparation of certain aniline dyes and of other products, such as perfumes and flavorings. FORMALDEHYDE is the first member of the aldehyde series. See also FURFURAL.

Alden, Henry Mills (ôl'-), 1836-1919, American editor, b. Mt. Tabor, Vt., grad. Williams, 1857, and Andover Theological Seminary, 1860. He was editor of *Harper's Magazine* from 1869 until his death. A highly religious and fastidious man, he directed his efforts toward making *Harper's* a family magazine.

Alden, John, c.1599-1687, Puritan settler in Plymouth Colony. He came to America on the *Mayflower* and was prominent as assistant to the governor of the colony. He moved (c.1627) to Duxbury and there was neighbor and friend of Miles STANDISH. Alden's marriage to Priscilla Mullens gave rise to the romantic legend made familiar by Longfellow's poem, *The Courtship of Miles Standish.*

Alden (ôl'dŭn), resort village (pop. 2,042), W central N.Y., E of Buffalo; inc. 1869.

Alder, Kurt (äl'dŭr), 1902-58, German chemist, educated at Berlin and at Kiel. He was on the research staff of the Beyer Dye Works (1936-40) before becoming (1940) professor of chemistry and director of the chemical institute of the Univ. of Cologne. He shared with Otto Diels the 1950 Nobel Prize in Chemistry for discovering a process for the synthesis of complex organic compounds.

alder, name for deciduous trees and shrubs of the genus *Alnus* of the BIRCH family, widely distributed, especially in mountainous and moist areas of the north temperate zone and in the Andes. The black alder (*A. glutinosa*) is an Old World species now naturalized in E North America. Its bark, still used for dyes and tanning, was formerly considered medicinal; its wood is useful chiefly as charcoal. *A. rugosa*, the speckled alder, forms extensive swamp thickets in Eurasia and North

America. The red alder (*A. rubra*), the largest tree of the genus, is the most important hardwood timber tree in its native region, the Pacific coast of North America.

Alderney (ôl'dûrnē), Fr. *Aurigny* (ōrēnyē'), anc. *Riduna*, island (pop. 1,449), area c.3 sq. mi., in the English Channel, northernmost of the larger CHANNEL ISLANDS. It is separated from the French coast and from other islands by swift tidal races. The soil is fertile and well cultivated about St. Anne, the principal town; the main crops are potatoes and grains. Cattle breeding is important.

Aldershot (ôl'dûrshŏt), municipal borough (pop. 31,260), Hampshire, S England. It is the site of the largest and most complete military training center (est. 1854) in the United Kingdom.

Alderson, residential town (pop. 1,225), S W.Va., on the Greenbrier river and NE of Bluefield; settled 1777, inc. 1871.

Aldhelm, Saint (ôld'hĕlm), 639?–709, English churchman and scholar. He was abbot of Malmesbury (from 675) and became the first bishop of Sherborne (705). A distinguished student of the classics, whose own Latin prose style was widely imitated, he was also a skilled musician and wrote hymns, popular songs, and ballads for the people. He founded several monasteries, built several churches, one still standing at Bradford-on-Avon, and promoted the Latin reckoning of EASTER. His name also occurs as Ealdhelm. Feast: May 25.

Aldington, Richard (ôl'–), 1892–1962, English poet and novelist. Fascinated by the imagery and unrhymed cadence of Greek poetry, he launched, while still in his teens, a creative attack upon the prevailing romantic poetic tradition. He became the leading exponent of the imagist school of poetry and was an editor of the *Egoist*, the principal imagist organ. His early poems were published under the title *Images* (1915). *Images of War* and *Images of Desire* followed in 1919; the latter marked a departure from pure imagism. His first novel, *Death of a Hero* (1929), was a bitter indictment of war. It was followed by *The Colonel's Daughter* (1931), equally biting in its satiric intent. Aldington is at his best when in an angry state of artistic and intellectual rebellion; experiments with milder satire proved less effective. After the Second World War he published little poetry; his most important work was in biography—*Portrait of a Rebel: the Life and Work of Robert Louis Stevenson* (1957). See his autobiographical *Life for Life's Sake* (1941).

Aldrich, Nelson Wilmarth, 1841–1915, U.S. Senator from Rhode Island, b. Foster, R.I. He rose in local politics as state assemblyman (1875–76) and U.S. Representative (1879–81) before he served as Senator (1881–1911). Aldrich, after the death of Henry B. Anthony, dominated Rhode Island politics, and because of his wide interests in banking, manufacturing, and public utilities he was popularly considered the spokesman of big business in the Republican party and the nation. After the controversy of 1888 he was the great proponent of protective tariffs and was successful in saving the Payne-Aldrich Tariff Act of 1909 even against the combined opposition of the Democrats and the Progressives. He took charge of Republican administrative legislation after 1897 and helped force

the Silver Republicans out of the party, the Gold Standard Act of 1900 completing the work. As Theodore Roosevelt's sympathies grew increasingly progressive Aldrich led the Senate opposition to him. Aldrich was deeply concerned with monetary problems, helped shape the Aldrich-Vreeland Currency Act of 1908, and headed the National Monetary Commission to study bank reform. He visited Europe in the course of this study, which he continued after leaving the Senate. The "Aldrich plan," published in 1911, was not made into law but it did offer information used by the Democrats in setting up the Federal Reserve System. See biography by N. W. Stephenson (1930).

Aldrich, Thomas Bailey, 1836–1907, American author and editor, b. Portsmouth, N.H. *The Story of a Bad Boy* (1870), a vigorous narrative based on his own boyhood, remains his most widely read work. His short stories, especially those in *Marjorie Daw and Other People* (1873), are noted for their naturalness and craftsmanship. Aldrich also excelled in the writing of light verse. In 1881 he succeeded W. D. Howells as editor of the *Atlantic Monthly*, a position he held until 1890. See biography by Ferris Greenslet (1908); Mrs. T. B. Aldrich, *Crowding Memories* (1920).

Thomas Bailey Aldrich

Ulisse Aldrovandi

Aldrovandi, Ulisse (ōōlēs'sä äldrōvän'dē), 1522–1605, Italian naturalist, professor at the Univ. of Bologna. He instigated the establishment (1567) of the Bologna Botanical Garden and wrote an early pharmacopoeia. His chief work was the *Natural History* (14 vols.), of which four volumes (some sources say five) were published before his death; the rest were prepared for publication from his manuscripts.

Aldus Manutius (ăl'dŭs mÿnū'shŭs), 1450–1515, Venetian printer. He was educated as a humanistic scholar and became tutor to several of the great ducal families. One of them, the Pio family, provided him with money to establish a printery in Venice. Aldus was at this time almost 45 years old.

Aldus Manutius

He devoted himself to publishing the Greek and Roman classics, in editions noted for their scrupulous accuracy; a five-volume set of the works of Aristotle, completed in 1498, is the most famous of his editions. He was especially interested in producing books of small format for scholars at low cost. To this end he designed and cut the first complete font of the Greek alphabet, adding a series of ligatures or tied letters, similar to the conventional signs used by scribes, which represented in the width of one character two to five letters. To save space in Latin texts he had a type designed after the Italian cursive script; it is said to be the script of Petrarch. This was the first *italic* type used in books (1501). Books produced by him are called Aldine and bear his mark, which was a dolphin and an anchor. Aldus employed competent scholars as editors, compositors, and proofreaders to insure accuracy in his books. Much of his type was designed by Francesco Griffi, called Francesco da Bologna. The Aldine Press was later managed by other members of his family, including a son, Paulus Manutius (1512–74), and a grandson, Aldus Manutius (1547–97).

ale: see BEER.

Aleandro, Girolamo (jĕrō′lämō älään′drō), 1480–1542, Italian scholar, cardinal of the Roman Church, called Hieronymus Aleander. A principal actor in the Lutheran crisis, he obtained the condemnation of Luther at the Diet of Worms (1521), and he made an outline of policy for the Catholic Reformation. His grandnephew **Girolamo Aleandro,** the younger, 1574–1649, was a humanist. He is known for his antiquarian studies.

Alecsandri, Vasile (väsē′lē ălĕksän′drē), 1821–90, Rumanian poet and statesman. He was (1858) provisional foreign minister and subsequently served in various diplomatic posts. Besides writing lyric poetry he collected Rumanian folk songs.

Alecto: see FURIES.

Aledo (ŭlē′dō), city (pop. 3,080), co. seat of Mercer co., NW Ill., SSW of Rock Island, in a farm area; inc. 1885. Roosevelt Military Academy is here.

Alegría, Ciro (sē′rō älägrē′ä), 1909–, Peruvian novelist. Imprisoned several times for his political activities as a member of the APRA party, he finally went as an exile to Chile in 1934. In 1941 he won the Latin American Novel Prize for *El mundo es*

ancho y ajeno (Eng. tr., *Broad and Alien Is the World,* 1941), in which he depicted the exploitation of the Indian by the white man. The novel is primarily a strong social document. Alegría was already well known in South America for an earlier prize-winning novel, *La serpiente de oro* (1935; Eng. tr., *The Golden Serpent,* 1943).

Aleichem, Sholom (shō′lŭm älä′khŭm) [Heb.= Peace be upon you!] (a very common form of greeting in Yiddish), 1859–1916, Yiddish author, b. Russia. His real name was Solomon, or Shalom, Rabinowitz. The first part of his pseudonym is also written Sholem or Shalom. His five novels, many plays, and some 300 short stories, all written in Yiddish, have been translated into Russian, German, and other European languages, but he is perhaps best known for his humorous tales of life among the poverty-ridden and oppressed Russian Jews of the late 19th and early 20th cent.; English translations of some of these include *The Old Country* (1946) and *Tevye's Daughters* (1949). In the last years of his life Sholom Aleichem lived in the United States; he died in New York city. His autobiographical writings include *Adventures of Mottel* (Eng. tr., 1953) and *The Great Fair* (Eng. tr., 1955). See Maurice Samuel, *The World of Sholom Aleichem* (1943); Melech Grafstein, ed., *Sholom Aleichem Panorama* (1949).

Aleijadinho (äläzhädē′nyō) [Port.,=little cripple], 1730–1814, Brazilian sculptor, a native of Minas Gerais. His real name was Antônio Francisco Lisboa. In spite of being maimed in hands and feet, he is known for the brilliance of his church sculpture. His most famous works are the carvings in the Church of São Francisco at OURO PRÊTO and the statues of the Twelve Prophets at Congonhas do Campo. The distinctive baroque style of his own works, carved in wood and native soapstone, has caused much church sculpture in Minas Gerais to be attributed to him.

Aleixandre, Vicente (vēthĕn′tä älähän′drä), 1900?–, Spanish lyric poet. He won the national prize for literature for *La destrucción o el amor* (1935). His verse, often free in form, is pessimistic and surrealistic; it expresses the anguish and hope of man. Among his works are *Sombra del paraíso* (1944) and *Historia del corazón* (1954).

Alekhine, Alexander A. (ŭlyĕkh′ēn), 1892–1946, Russian-French chess player, b. Moscow. He became a naturalized French citizen after the Russian Revolution. At the age of 16 he gained the rank of master and in 1927, by a surprising defeat of Capablanca at Buenos Aires, became world champion. In 1930 at San Remo, Italy, he won without losing a single game in a tournament that included all of the major European players. In 1935 he lost the championship to Max Euwe but regained it in 1937 and kept it until his death. His clear and realistic style and the brilliance of his middle-game and end-game combinations are found in his book, *My Best Games of Chess, 1924–1937* (1939).

Aleks-. For some Russian names beginning thus, see ALEX–; e.g., for Aleksandr, see ALEXANDER.

Aleksandropol, Armenia: see LENINAKAN.

Aleksandrov (ŭlyĭksän′drŭf), city (pop. c.36,600), W central European RSFSR. It has radio, textile, and food industries. It came under the control of the Muscovite princes in 1302. IVAN IV resided here (1564–81) and here organized his political police, the Oprichnina. It is the site of the first printing establishment in Russia, founded during the reign of Ivan IV, and of the famous Uspenski convent (late 17th cent.).

Aleksandrov-Grushevski: see SHAKHTY.

Aleksandrovsk, Ukraine: see ZAPOROZHE.

Aleksandrovsk-Sakhalinski (ŭlyĭksän′drŭfsk-sŭkhŭlyĕn′skē), city (pop. c.23,000), on N Sakhalin, SE Asiatic RSFSR. A port on the Tatar Strait, it is a coal-mining center with lumber and fish industries. It was founded in 1881 as a place of exile.

Alekseyev, Mikhail Vasilyevich (mēkhŭyēl′ vŭsē′lyŭvĭch ŭlyĭksyä′ŭf), 1857–1918, Russian general, chief of staff (1915–17) of Nicholas II. With other officers he urged the tsar to abdicate in favor of the tsarevich in order to save the dynasty. Alekseyev was briefly chief of staff under the Kerensky government. After its overthrow, he and General KORNILOV organized an anti-Bolshevik movement in the south.

Alema (ăl′–), unidentified town, E of the Jordan. 1 Mac. 5.26.

Alemán, Mateo (mätä′ō älämän′), 1547–1614?, Spanish novelist. He studied medicine, was chief accountant at Madrid, led an exciting and adventurous life, was sent to jail twice for his debts, and at the age of 60 found a refuge in Mexico. He owes his fame to the fine picaresque novel, *Guzmán de Alfarache*. The first part was published in 1599 and the second part in 1604. It was translated into many languages; Le Sage adapted it in French, and James Mabbe translated it into English as *The Rogue; or, The Life of Guzmán de Alfarache* (1922).

Alemán, Miguel (mēgĕl′ älämän′), 1902–, president of Mexico (1946–52). Son of a revolutionary general, Alemán became a highly successful lawyer and a champion of Mexican labor. He was governor of Veracruz from 1936 to 1940 but resigned to manage the presidential campaign of Manuel Ávila Camacho, under whom Alemán held (1940–45) the ministry of the interior. After defeating Ezequiel Padilla in the presidential election of 1946, Alemán became the first civilian president of Mexico since Francisco I. MADERO. He changed the name of the official government party from National Revolutionary party to Party of the Institutionalized Revolution (PRI), to indicate the permanent status of the revolution. Alemán's administration was characterized by a vigorous program of modernizing the nation. He encouraged foreign investment, developed reclamation and power projects, improved communication and education, and generally raised the standard of living.

Alemanni (ălĭmă′nĭ), Germanic tribe, a splinter group of the Suebi (see GERMANS). The Alemanni may have been a confederation of smaller tribes. First mentioned (A.D. 213) as unsuccessfully assaulting the Roman wall between the Elbe and the Danube, they later settled (3d cent.) in upper Italy. By the 5th cent. they occupied territories on both sides of the Rhine south of its junction with the Main (present Alsace, Baden, and NE Switzerland). Their westward expansion brought them into conflict with the Franks, whose king CLOVIS I defeated them in 496. In 505 he forced them to retire into Rhaetia, and in 536 they passed under Frankish rule. By the 7th cent. they had accepted

Christianity. SWABIA is also known as Alamannia, and the High German dialects of SW Germany and Switzerland are called Alemannic. In French speech the name *Allemands* came to signify all Germans.

Alemanni, Luigi: see ALAMANNI, LUIGI.

Alembert, Jean le Rond d' (zhä′ lŭ rō′ dälăbĕr′), 1717–83, French mathematician and philosopher. The illegitimate son of the chevalier Destouches, he

Jean Le Rond d'Alembert

was named for the St. Jean le Rond church, on whose steps he was found. His father had him educated. Diderot made him coeditor of the ENCYCLOPÉDIE, for which he wrote the "preliminary discourse" (1751) and mathematical, philosophical, and literary articles. Discouraged by attacks on his unorthodox views, he withdrew (1758) from the *Encyclopédie*. A member of the Academy of Sciences (1741) and the French Academy (1754; appointed secretary, 1772), he was a leading representative of the ENLIGHTENMENT. His writings include a treatise on dynamics (1743), in which he enunciated a principle of mechanics known as D'ALEMBERT'S PRINCIPLE; a work on the theoretical and practical elements of music (1759); and a valuable history of the members of the French Academy (1787).

Alembert's principle: see D'ALEMBERT'S PRINCIPLE.

Alemeth (ăl′ŭ–). **1** Descendant of Saul. 1 Chron. 8.36; 9.42. **2** Town, NE of Jerusalem, the modern Khirbet Almit (Jordan). 1 Chron. 6.60. Almon: Joshua 21.18.

Alemtejo: see ALENTEJO.

Alencar, José de (zhōō″zĕ′ dē älĕnkär′), 1829–77, Brazilian writer. He produced a monumental body of work, but his fame rests chiefly on two Indian novels, *O Guarani* [the Guarani] and *Iracema*, noted for their poetic style. The first of these was made into an opera by Antônio Carlos GOMES.

Alençon, François, duc d': see FRANCIS, duke of Alençon and Anjou.

Alençon (äläsō′), town (estimated pop. 21,893), capital of Orne dept., N France, in Normandy, on the Sarthe. A commercial center in a fertile agricultural region, it is particularly noted for its fine lace work. It was the capital of the county, and later duchy (after 1414), of Alençon, and passed to the French crown in 1525. It was heavily damaged in the Second World War.

Alentejo (ălăntă′zhŏ), historic province, SE Portugal, now divided into Upper Alentejo (Port. *Alto Alentejo;* 4,888 sq. mi.; pop. c.225,510) and Lower Alentejo (Port. *Baixo Alentejo;* 5,318 sq. mi.; pop. c.283,152). The capital of Upper Alentejo is Évora, and the capital of Lower Alentejo is Beja. Estremoz and Vila Viçosa are also in the province. Alentejo, "the granary of Portugal," is drained by the Guadiana and tributaries of the Sado. The climate varies greatly with the seasons. Sheep, horses, cattle, and hogs are bred, and grains, olives, cork trees, and fruits are grown. It was from the time of Portugal's beginning involved in the many wars with Castile (see PORTUGAL). The name formerly was spelled Alemtejo.

Alep (ùlĕp′) or **Aleppo** (ùlĕ′pō), Arabic *Haleb*, city (pop. 407,613), NW Syria. It was the Greek and biblical Beroea or Berea (as in 2 Mac. 13.4). An ancient city, it was the center of a Hittite kingdom before 1000 B.C. and was taken by the various conquerors of Syria. Its importance was enhanced after the fall of Palmyra in A.D. 272. It became a key point on the main caravan route across Syria to Baghdad. A flourishing city of the Byzantine Empire, it was taken by the Arabs in the 7th cent., recovered by the Byzantines in the 10th cent., and taken by the Seljuk Turks late in the 11th cent. The Crusaders besieged it, but without success, in 1124. Saladin took it in 1183 and made it his stronghold. It was conquered by the Mongols under Hulagu Khan in 1260 and again by Tamerlane in 1401, but was not long held. In 1517 the Ottoman Turks made it a part of their empire, and it was a great commercial center. Ibrahim Pasha took it (1832) for Mohammed Ali of Egypt, who was forced to give it up in 1840. Its importance declined with the establishment of new trade routes, but it revived after Syria was established as a French mandate and then recovered its independence. It has silk and cotton textile industries and much trade in wool, hides, and fruit. It has often been severely damaged by earthquake.

Alep, city in northwest Syria.

Ales, Alexander: see ALESIUS, ALEXANDER.

Alès (äles′), formerly **Alais** (älä′, äles′), city (estimated pop. 36,893), Gard dept., S France, in Languedoc, at the foot of the Cévennes. A center of an industrial and coal-mining region, it has blast furnaces, steel mills, and glass and metal works. The Peace of Alais (1629) stripped French Protestants (see HUGUENOTS) of their political power.

Alesia (ùlē′zhù), hilltop town of Celtic and Roman Gaul, on the site of Alise-Sainte-Reine, near Dijon. It was held by VERCINGETORIX and his men (52 B.C.) when Caesar besieged it. Caesar prevented Vercingetorix' allies from raising the siege and starved out the town. Gallic resistance to Rome ended.

Alesius, Ales, or **Aless, Alexander** (ùlē′shùs; both: ùles′), 1500–1565, Scottish Protestant theologian. As canon of the collegiate church at St. Andrews he tried to reclaim Patrick Hamilton, abbot of Fern, from his heretical Lutheran views but was himself persuaded to accept the reformed teachings. In 1532 he escaped to the Continent, where he gained the confidence of Luther and Melanchthon, and joined in signing the Augsburg Confession. By them he was commended to Henry VIII, and arriving in England in 1535, he enjoyed friendly association with Cranmer, Thomas Cromwell, and others. He lectured on divinity at Cambridge and afterward practiced medicine in London. After Cromwell's fall in 1540, Alesius returned to Germany, where he was professor of theology, first at Frankfurt-an-der-Oder and later at Leipzig.

Alessandri, Arturo (ärtōō′rō älĕsän′drē), 1868–1950, president of Chile (1920–25, 1932–38). Presidential candidate of the Liberal Alliance in 1920, a conglomerate group made up of all the enemies of the conservatives, Alessandri was elected on a reform platform. During his first administration, the conservatives were able to block most of his program, and when his cabinet refused to support him, Alessandri went (1924) into voluntary exile. Returning in 1925, he supervised the writing of a new constitution which guaranteed universal male suffrage, granted greater provincial powers, and effectively ended the power of the conservative-clerical oligarchy. During these years, Chile underwent a political reformation which was supported essentially by the middle class and the labor unions. His second term was likewise stormy, but marked by continued political and social reforms.

Alessandria (älĭsăn′drèù, Ital. äläs-sän′drēä), city (estimated pop. 85,964), capital of Alessandria prov., in Piedmont, N Italy, on the plain between the Po and the Ligurian Alps. An industrial city, it is also an agricultural market. Alessandria was built (1164–67) as a stronghold of the LOMBARD LEAGUE and was named for Pope Alexander III. At first a free commune, it passed in 1348 to the duchy of Milan and, in 1707, to the duke of Savoy. It was the scene of a pro-Mazzini conspiracy in 1833. There are two 13th-century churches and several interesting modern buildings.

Alesund or **Aalesund,** Nor. *Ålesund* (all: ô′lùsōōn), city (pop. 18,957), Møre og Romsdal prov., W Norway. An Atlantic seaport, it has the largest fishing fleet in Norway. There are clothing factories and large dairies. An early-13th-century stone church is nearby.

Aletsch (ä'lĕch), glacier (66 sq. mi.), S central Switzerland, largest in the Swiss Alps. It lies between the Jungfrau and the Aletschhorn (ä'lĕch-hôrn), one of the highest (13,721 ft.) peaks in the Bernese Alps.

Aleut (ăl'ē<del></del>ōōt), native inhabitant of the Aleutian Islands. Of the same stock as the ESKIMO, the Aleuts have become, through long contact with Indians and whites, chiefly a mixed breed. In their semicivilized mode of life they more closely resemble their North American Indian neighbors than they do the Eskimos. Their language is a member of the Eskimo-Aleut family. When they were first noted by Bering in 1741, their estimated population was between 20,000 and 25,000. Because of their skill in hunting sea mammals, the Aleuts were dispersed by Russian fur traders throughout the coastal waters of the Gulf of Alaska, some as far south as California. The ruthless policies of their masters and conflict with the fierce mainland natives reduced their population by the end of the 18th cent. to one tenth its former size. They now number less than 1,000. The strategic importance of their islands in the Second World War focused the attention of the U.S. government on their condition, and measures were instituted for their economic betterment. They continue to live in relative isolation. Converts of the Russian Orthodox Church, they yet retain a few of their earlier superstitious beliefs. See H. B. Collins, Jr., *The Aleutian Islands: Their People and Natural History* (1945).

Aleutian Islands (ûlōō'shŭn), chain of islands curving southwest from the tip of the Alaska Peninsula and approaching the Russian Komandorski Islands. Actually a partially submerged continuation of the Aleutian Range, they divide the Bering Sea from the Pacific Ocean. They fall into four main groups. The Fox Islands nearest Alaska include among the larger islands Unimak, Unalaska

Aletsch glacier, seen from the Jungfrau.

(with Dutch Harbor on small Amaknak island), Umnak, and Akutan. The Andreanof Islands are many; some of the larger ones are Amlia, Atka, Adak, Kanaga, and Tanaga. Among the Rat Islands the most important are Amchitka and Kiska. The Near Islands are farthest west and the smallest group of all; the two larger islands are Agattu and Attu. Within their general area are Shemya and the other Semichi Islands. The islands are generally rugged and show the traces of volcanic action. There are few good harbors, and the many reefs make navigation treacherous. Temperatures are relatively moderate, but constant fog makes the climate dreary. The islands, almost completely treeless, have a luxuriant growth of grass, bushes, and sedges. Sheep have been grown on some of them. Vitus BERING discovered them in 1741, and the native Aleuts were exploited for fur hunting by Russian traders. Fishing and fur hunting are now government controlled. Dutch Harbor, one of the few good harbors, became a transshipping point for Nome in 1900, after the discovery of gold turned Nome into a boom town. In 1940 a U.S. naval base was established at Dutch Harbor, and the Aleutian Islands were important in the Second World War. On June 3, 1942, the Japanese bombed Dutch Harbor and in the following two weeks occupied Attu and Kiska. From bases established on Adak and Amchitka, the United States launched a counterattack. In 1943, after bitter fighting, U.S. forces took Attu, and the Japanese withdrew from Kiska. U.S. bases were also built on Shemya, Umnak, and Atka. See Murray Morgan, *Bridge to Russia* (1947).

Aleutian Range, mountain chain, SW Alaska, extending along the entire Alaska Peninsula and continuing, partly submerged, in the Aleutian Islands. The range has shown recent volcanic activity, notably at Katmai (see KATMAI NATIONAL MONUMENT).

alewife: see HERRING.

Alex-. For some Russian names beginning thus, see ALEKS-; e.g., for Alexandrov, see ALEKSANDROV.

Massacre Bay, Attu, Aleutian Islands.

Alexander III, d. 1181, pope (1159–81), a Sienese named Orlando Bandinelli; successor of Adrian IV and predecessor of Lucius III. He was a learned canonist who had studied law under Gratian and had taught at Bologna. He came to Rome under Eugene III, was made a cardinal, and became a trusted adviser of Adrian IV. Alexander's election to the papacy was opposed by a few cardinals, who elected an antipope, Victor IV. Although the antipope was supported only by Germany and some Lombards, the schism thus begun continued until 1178 with antipopes Paschal III and Calixtus III. Alexander was forced (1162) by Emperor FREDER-ICK I into exile in France. In the long struggle with the emperor, the pope was aided by the LOMBARD LEAGUE, which named the town of Alessandria for him. After the battle of Legnano (1176), the emperor was forced to submit. Alexander had already (1174) received the penance of Henry II of England for the murder of St. Thomas à Becket, whom Alexander canonized (1173). He convened and presided at the Third LATERAN COUNCIL. One of the great medieval popes, he issued many decretals, established the procedure for canonizing saints, inaugurated the two-thirds rule for papal elections, protected the universities, and was one of the most distinguished champions of ecclesiastical independence in the Middle Ages.

Alexander VI, 1431?–1503, pope (1492–1503), a Spaniard (b. Játiva) named Rodrigo de Borja or, in Italian, Rodrigo Borgia; successor of Innocent

Alexander VI

VIII and predecessor of Pius III. He took Borja as his surname from his mother's brother Alfonso, who was Pope Calixtus III. Rodrigo became cardinal (1456), vice chancellor of the Roman Church (1457), and dean of the sacred college (1476). Cardinal Borgia had four children by a Roman woman, Vannozza; among them were Cesare and **Lucrezia Borgia**. The conclave that elected Alexander was corrupt. The foreign relations of the papacy in his time were dominated by the increasing influence of France in Italy, culminating in the invasion of Charles VIII in 1494. Alexander prevented Charles from taking the church property

in Rome, but he turned over to the French the valuable Ottoman hostage Djem, brother of BAJAZET II. Alexander's son, Cesare Borgia, was the principal leader in papal affairs, and papal resources were spent lavishly in building up Cesare's power. For his daughter Lucrezia, Alexander arranged suitable marriages. The favoritism shown his children and the lax moral tone of Renaissance Rome as well as the unscrupulous methods employed by Cesare and other papal officials have made Alexander's name the symbol of the worldly irreligion of Renaissance popes. Alexander faced an outspoken opponent and critic in Savonarola. Recent studies tend to minimize the pope's immorality and stress his solid achievements as political strategist and church administrator. It was Alexander who proclaimed the line of demarcation which awarded part of the new discoveries in the world to Spain, part to Portugal (see TORDESILLAS). Alexander was a munificent patron of the arts. See Orestes Ferrara, *The Borgia Pope: Alexander VI* (1940); Michael de La Bedoyère, *The Meddlesome Friar and the Wayward Pope* (1958).

Alexander I, 1777–1825, emperor and tsar of Russia (1801–25), son of PAUL I (in whose murder he may have taken an indirect part). In the first years of his reign the liberalism of his Swiss tutor, Frédéric César de LA HARPE, seemed to influence Alexander. He suppressed the secret police, lifted the ban on foreign travel and books, made (1803) attempts to improve the position of the serfs, and began to reform the backward educational system. In 1805 Alexander joined the coalition against NAPOLEON I, but after the defeats of Austerlitz and Friedland he formed an alliance with Napoleon by the Treaty of Tilsit (1807) and joined Napoleon's CONTINENTAL SYSTEM. Alexander requested M. M. SPERANSKI to draw up proposals for a constitution, but adopted only one aspect of Speranski's scheme, an advisory state council, and dismissed him in 1812 to placate the nobility. During this period Russia gained control of Georgia and parts of Transcaucasia as a result of prolonged war with Persia (1804–13) and annexed (1812) Bessarabia after a war with Turkey (1806–12). Relations with France deteriorated, and Napoleon invaded Russia in 1812. His defeat of the French made Alexander one of the most powerful rulers in Europe. At first his foreign policy was liberal. He insisted on a constitutional charter and mild treaty terms for France at the Congress of Vienna, and he gave autonomy to Finland (annexed in 1809) and a constitution to Poland, of which he became king in 1815. From 1812 Alexander was preoccupied by a vague, mystical Christianity. Under the influence of the pietistic Julie de Krüdener and others, he created the HOLY ALLIANCE to put his religious theories into practice. Alexander then became increasingly conservative. The notorious "military colonies," which were agricultural communities run by peasant soldiers, were introduced. Alexander's powerful favorite, A. A. ARAKCHEYEV, administered the colonies. The tsar now supported METTERNICH in suppressing all national and liberal movements. Alexander's policies caused the formation of secret political societies, and when Alexander's brother NICHOLAS I succeeded him the societies led an abortive revolt (the

Alexander II
of Russia

Alexander III
of Russia

Alexander I
of Russia

DECEMBRIST CONSPIRACY). After Alexander's death, rumors persisted that he escaped to Siberia and became a hermit. His tomb was opened (1926) by the Soviet government and was found empty; the mystery remains unsolved. In Alexander's reign St. Petersburg became a social and artistic center of Europe. KRYLOV and PUSHKIN dominated the literary scene. An excellent picture of Alexander's period is found in Tolstoy's *War and Peace.* See biography by C. Joyneville (3 vols., 1875).

Alexander II, 1818–81, emperor and tsar of Russia (1855–81), son and successor of Nicholas I. Influenced by Russia's defeat in the Crimean War and by peasant disorders, Alexander II embarked on a series of reforms which helped to modernize Russia. The most important reform was the emancipation of the serfs (1861; see EMANCIPATION, EDICT OF). This failed to meet the needs of the major groups involved, but it prompted further reforms. In 1864 a system of limited local self-government was introduced (see ZEMSTVO). A new judicial system (1864) brought some Western practices and standards into the Russian courts. Municipal government was changed (1870), and the introduction (1874) of universal military training accompanied modernization of the army. Alexander temporarily relaxed censorship and controls over education. The incomplete nature of his reforms failed to satisfy either the liberals or the radicals and socialists. Such radicals as CHERNYSHEVSKY, HERZEN, and BAKUNIN favored a reconstruction of Russian society, but they disagreed on the means to this end. Some favored propaganda and education; others terror and insurrection. The failure of the agrarian Populist (or "to the people") movement led to the formation of terrorist groups, such as People's Will. A member of this organization assassinated Alexander on the very day that he had approved the plan of LORIS-MELIKOV to grant the zemstvos a legislative role. In his foreign policy Alexander attempted a moderate policy toward Poland, but after the Polish revolution of 1863–64 he enforced severe Russification on the country. In 1867 Rus-

sia ceded Alaska to the United States. From 1865 to 1876 Russia extended her control into Central Asia, conquering the khanates of Kokand and Khiva and the emirate of Bokhara. In 1872–73 the THREE EMPERORS' LEAGUE of Russia, Germany, and Austria was formed, and in 1877–78 Russia was again at war with Turkey. During the reigns of Alexander II and his son and successor, Alexander III, Russian literature and music reached great heights in the achievements of Turgenev, Dostoyevsky, Leo Tolstoy, Moussourgsky, and Tchaikovsky. See studies by W. E. Mosse (1958) and E. M. Almedingen (1962).

Alexander III, 1845–94, emperor and tsar of Russia (1881–94), son and successor of Alexander II. His father's assassination, his limited intelligence and education, his military background, and the influence of such advisers as Konstantin P. POBYEDONOSTZEV and Mikhail N. KATKOV all contributed to his reactionary policies. On his accession he discarded Loris-Melikov's modest proposals for reform. Alexander increased the repressive powers of the police and tightened censorship and control of education. He limited the power of the zemstvos and the judiciary, increased controls over the peasantry, subjected the national minorities to forcible Russification, and persecuted all religious minorities, especially the Jews. His energetic minister of finance, Count WITTE, used governmental pressure and investments to stimulate industrial development and to begin construction of the TRANS-SIBERIAN RAILROAD. The tsar and his foreign minister, Nikolai K. GIERS, worked for peace in Europe, although Russian expansion in Central Asia almost led to conflict with Great Britain. In the Balkans, Russia's attempts to make Bulgaria a satellite proved unsuccessful. The Three Emperors' League of Russia, Austria, and Germany was replaced (1887) with a Russo-German alliance. This was not renewed in 1890, and a Franco-Russian entente grew after 1891 (see TRIPLE ALLIANCE AND TRIPLE ENTENTE). Alexander was succeeded by his son Nicholas II.

Alexander, 1893–1920, king of the Hellenes (1917–20), second son of CONSTANTINE. After his father's abdication, he succeeded to the throne with the support of the Allies, who distrusted the sympathies of his elder brother George (later King George II). Alexander died of a monkey bite. He was succeeded by Constantine.

Alexander III, king of Macedon: see ALEXANDER THE GREAT.

Alexander I, 1078?–1124, king of Scotland (1107–24), son of Malcolm III and St. Margaret of Scotland. He succeeded his brother Edgar, who had divided the kingdom so that Alexander ruled only N of the Forth and the Clyde. Early in his reign he decisively quelled an uprising in N Scotland. Alexander encouraged, as his mother had, ecclesiastical conformity with English ways and established several monasteries, including the abbeys at Inchcolm and Scone. He opposed, however, the efforts of the English hierarchy to rule the Church in Scotland.

Alexander II, 1198–1249, king of Scotland (1214–49), son and successor of William the Lion. When the English king John became embroiled with his barons, Alexander, who held land in England, joined them (1215). With Henry III, John's successor, Alexander agreed to give up his claims as overlord in old Northumbria and to exchange lands he held in central England for lands in the north. Later Henry and he nearly went to war over the homage Alexander owed for these northern lands. Alexander was assiduous at home in quelling disorder. His reign saw a notable growth in religious houses and ecclesiastical architecture.

Alexander III, 1241–86, king of Scotland (1249–86), son and successor of Alexander II. He married a daughter of Henry III of England and disputed with him over the old English claims to overlordship in Scotland. The great achievement of Alexander was his final acquisition for Scotland of the Western Islands and of the Isle of Man, which his father had already claimed from Norway. To drive the Scots from the islands King Haakon IV of Norway sailed with a great fleet in 1263, but a storm battered his ships, and he fought the inconclusive battle of Largs in the River Clyde (1263). Alexander signed a treaty with Haakon's successor, Magnus VI, assigning the Western Isles and the Isle of Man to Scotland. This was followed by an arrangement with Norway providing for the marriage of Magnus's son Eric with Alexander's daughter Margaret. Alexander survived his children, and when he died his only near relative was his little granddaughter MARGARET MAID OF NORWAY. See biography by James Fergusson (1937).

Alexander (Alexander Obrenovich) (ŏbrĕ′nŭvĭch) 1876–1903, king of Serbia (1889–1903), son of King MILAN. He succeeded on his father's abdication. Proclaiming himself of age (1893), he took over the government, abolished (1894) the relatively liberal constitution of 1889, and restored the conservative one of 1869. He recalled his father, gave him command of the army, and permitted him to undertake a campaign against the pro-Russian Radical party. In 1900 he married Draga Mashin (see DRAGA). The scandal of the marriage exasperated his opposition. In 1903, after Alexander had suspended and restored the constitution, he and his queen were assassinated by a clique of officers. Peter Karageorgevich was recalled as King Peter I, and the Obrenovich dynasty came to an end.

Alexander, 1888–1934, king of Yugoslavia (1921–34), son and successor of Peter I. Of the Karageorgevich family, he was educated in Russia and became crown prince of Serbia upon the renunciation (1909) of the succession by his brother George. He led the Serbian army in the Balkan War of 1912, became regent in June, 1914, led the Serbian army in the First World War, and became (Nov., 1918) regent of the kingdom of the Serbs, Croats, and Slovenes. In 1922 he married Princess Marie of Rumania. After his accession increasing disorder arose from the Croatian autonomy movement. After the assassination (1928) of Stefan RADICH, Alexander in 1929 dismissed the parliament, abolished the constitution and the parties, and became absolute ruler. To emphasize the unity he hoped to give the country he changed (Oct., 1929) its official name to Yugoslavia. Though he announced the end of the dictatorship in 1931 and proclaimed a new constitution, he kept power in his own hands. His authoritarian and centralizing policy brought him the hatred of the separatist minorities, particularly the Croats and Macedonians, as well as the opposition of Serbian liberals. In foreign policy he was loyal to the French alliance and to the LITTLE ENTENTE. In 1934 he debarked at Marseilles on a state visit to France. A member of a Croatian terrorist organization fired on his car, killing the king and fatally wounding the French foreign minister, Louis Barthou. Alexander was succeeded by his young son, Peter II. See Stephen Graham, *Alexander of Yugoslavia* (1939).

Alexander (Alexander of Battenberg), 1857–93, prince of Bulgaria (1879–86); second son of Prince Alexander of Hesse-Darmstadt by his morganatic wife, Countess Julia von Hauke. He served in the Russian army against the Turks (1877–78) and, backed by the tsar, was elected hereditary prince of Bulgaria under Turkish suzerainty. In 1885 the revolutionaries in Eastern RUMELIA proclaimed the union of that province with Bulgaria. Alexander accepted the union, thus incurring the wrath of the Russian tsar and of Serbia, which declared war. Alexander was victorious and by an agreement with Turkey became governor of Eastern Rumelia, but he was forced to abdicate by a group of officers. Ferdinand was elected to succeed him. See biography by E. C. Corti (1920; Eng. tr., 1955).

Alexander (Alexander Karageorgevich) (kărŭjôr′jŭvĭch), 1806–85, prince of Serbia (1842–58), son of KARAGEORGE. He was elected to succeed the deposed MICHAEL of Serbia. Weak and vacillating, he did not send troops to aid the Slavic minorities in Hungary during the revolution of 1848–49. He later submitted to Turkish and Austrian pressure in withholding his support from Russia in the Crimean War. Discontent with his ineffective government finally led his subjects to depose him and to recall MILOSH as king. In 1868 Alexander was condemned to death *in absentia* by a Serbian court for his alleged part in the assassination of Michael, who had succeeded Milosh. Alexander was the father of Peter I of Yugoslavia.

Alexander, in the Bible. **1** Kinsman of Annas. Acts 4.6. **2** Son of Simon of Cyrene, probably a Christian. Mark 15.21. **3** Heretic condemned by Paul. 1 Tim. 1.20. **4** Coppersmith who did Paul harm. 2 Tim. 4.14. **5** Jew who tried to speak during a riot at Ephesus. The last three may be the same man. The Alexanders in the books of the Maccabees are Alexander the Great and ALEXANDER BALAS.

Alexander, in Greek mythology: see PARIS.

Alexander, Grover Cleveland, 1887–1950, American baseball player, b. St. Paul, Nebr. One of the great right-hand pitchers of the National League, Alexander pitched 696 games, won 373 of them, and compiled a .642 winner percentage. He played for the Philadelphia Phillies (1911–17 and again in 1930), the Chicago Cubs (1918–26), and the St. Louis Cardinals (1926–29). Alexander was elected to the National Baseball Hall of Fame in 1938.

Alexander, Harold Rupert Leofric George, 1st Earl Alexander of Tunis, 1891–, British field marshal, b. Ireland, son of a nobleman. He was educated at Harrow and Sandhurst. His long military career was highlighted by service in the First World War and in the North-West Frontier Prov., India (1934–38). In the Second World War he directed the retreats at Dunkirk (1940) and in Burma (1942) and then became (Aug., 1942) head of the Middle Eastern Command (see NORTH AFRICA, CAMPAIGNS IN). He commanded the conquest of Sicily (1943) and the bitter fighting in Italy. In 1944 Alexander was made field marshal and Allied commander in chief in the Mediterranean; in 1946 he was appointed governor general of Canada (holding the post until 1952) and created viscount. He became minister of defense under Sir Winston Churchill and was raised (1952) to the rank of earl.

Alexander, Samuel, 1859–1938, British philosopher, b. Australia. From 1893 to 1924 he was professor of philosophy at Victoria Univ., Manchester. Strongly influenced by the theory of evolution, Alexander conceived of the world as a single cosmic process in which there periodically emerge higher forms of being. The basic principle of this process is space-time, and the result is God. He has written *Space, Time, and Deity* (1920), *Spinoza and Time* (1921), *Art and the Material* (1925), and *Beauty and Other Forms of Value* (1933). See studies by M. R. Konvitz (1946), J. W. McCarthy (1948), and A. P. Stiernotte (1954).

Alexander, Sir William, d. 1640: see STIRLING, WILLIAM ALEXANDER, EARL OF.

Alexander, William, known as **Lord Stirling,** 1726–83, American Revolutionary general, b. New York city. Although the House of Lords rejected his claim to succeed as the 6th earl of Stirling, he was, nevertheless, in America generally considered a nobleman. He served in the French and Indian Wars and joined the Continental army early in the Revolution. He fought well at the battle of Long Island (1776) and was captured by the British but was soon exchanged and later saw action at Trenton, Brandywine, Germantown, and Monmouth. In 1778 he helped to expose the CONWAY CABAL.

Alexander Archipelago, just off SE Alaska. It and the mountainous coast make up the Panhandle of Alaska. A submerged mountain system, the islands rise steeply from the sea. Deep fjordlike channels separate them and cut them off from the mainland, and the INSIDE PASSAGE from Seattle to Alaska threads its way among them. Some of the islands are CHICHAGOF ISLAND, ADMIRALTY ISLAND, BARANOF ISLAND (with Sitka), WRANGELL ISLAND (with Wrangell), REVILLAGIGEDO ISLAND (with

Ketchikan), Kupreanof Island, Mitkoff Island, and PRINCE OF WALES ISLAND.

Alexander Balas (bā′–), d. 145 B.C., ruler of Syria, putative son of Antiochus IV. He seized power from his uncle Demetrius I (c.152 B.C.); Jonathan the Maccabee supported him. Eventually he was defeated by Ptolemy Philometor. 1 Mac. 10–11.

Alexander Bay, town (pop. c.900), NW Cape Prov., Republic of South Africa, at the mouth of the Orange River. It has some of the richest alluvial diamond deposits in the world.

Alexander City, city (pop. 13,140), E central Ala., SE of Birmingham, in a farm area; founded in the mid-19th cent. on the site of an Indian village, inc. 1873. Textile, metal, and lumber products are made. Lake Martin is nearby.

Alexander John I, prince of Rumania: see CUZA, ALEXANDER JOHN.

Alexander Karageorgevich: see ALEXANDER, prince of Serbia, and ALEXANDER, king of Yugoslavia.

Alexander Nevsky (nĕv′skē) [Rus.,=of the Neva], 1220–1263, grand duke of Vladimir-Suzdal. As prince of Novgorod (1236–52) he earned his surname by his victory (1240) over the Swedes on the Neva river. He successfully defended N Russia against its western neighbors by defeating the Livonian Knights (1242) and the Lithuanians (1245). In domestic affairs Alexander followed the orders of the Golden Horde, and he was appointed (1252) grand duke by the khan. His submissive attitude toward the Tatars and his suppression of the anti-Tatar movements in Novgorod and other cities provoked much resentment among the local princes and the common people. Russian popular tradition, however, made him a national hero, and he was canonized by the Russian Orthodox Church. An order instituted (1725) in his name by Peter I of Russia, though abolished in 1917, was revived by the Soviet government in 1942.

Alexander of Aphrodisias (ăfrōdĭsh′ēŭs) fl. 200, Greek Peripatetic philosopher. A celebrated ancient commentator on Aristotle, he was often called the Exegete. During the Renaissance, his interpretations of Aristotle were used to counter those of the Church. Two original treatises are extant.

Alexander of Hales (hālz), d. 1245, English scholastic philosopher, called the Unanswerable Doctor. He was a Franciscan and a lecturer at the Univ. of Paris. His *Summa universae theologiae* was the first systematic exposition of Christian doctrine to introduce Aristotle as a prime authority. His eclectic work also contains elements of Neoplatonism and Augustinian and Arabic ideas; these are not always harmonized. Alexander held that all created things, spiritual as well as corporeal, are made up of matter and form. This teaching became the central feature of Franciscan scholasticism. Alexander was one of the important influences on St. Thomas Aquinas.

Alexander of Pherae (fēr′ē), d. 358 B.C., tyrant of the city of Pherae in Thessaly after 369 B.C. He was opposed by other Thessalian cities and by the Thebans. PELOPIDAS failed (368) in one expedition against him and was briefly imprisoned. Returning in 364 Pelopidas destroyed Alexander's power in the battle of Cynoscephalae, though he himself was killed. Alexander was murdered by members of his own family.

Alexander Severus

Alexander Severus (Marcus Aurelius Alexander Severus) (sĭvēr'ŭs), d. 235, Roman emperor (222–35), b. Syria. His name was changed (221) from Alexius Bassianus when he was adopted as the successor to HELIOGABALUS. He was of a virtuous and studious character, and during his reign Christians enjoyed a brief immunity from the persecutions of his century. Although he won a triumph in a campaign (232) against Ardashir I of Persia, he could not maintain discipline among his own troops and had to retire from battle. In a mutiny on the Rhine, he and his mother, Julia Mamaea, were murdered by the supporters of MAXIMIN (d. 238).

Alexanderson, Ernst Frederik Werner, 1878–, American engineer and inventor, b. Uppsala, Sweden, grad. Royal Institute of Technology, Stockholm, 1900. He came to the United States in 1901 and joined (1902) the General Electric Company at Schenectady, later becoming a consulting engineer there. He was also chief engineer (1920–24) of the Radio Corporation of America. Alexanderson did pioneer work in television, electric ship propulsion, and railroad electrification. His inventions include the Alexanderson high-frequency alternator and a multiple-tuned antenna.

Alexander the Great or **Alexander III,** 356–323 B.C., king of Macedon, conqueror of much of Asia, one of the greatest leaders of all time. The son of PHILIP II of Macedon and OLYMPIAS, he had Aristotle as his tutor and was given the education of a model prince. Alexander had no part in the murder of his father, though he may have resented him because he neglected Olympias for another wife. He succeeded to the throne in 336 B.C. and immediately showed his brilliance by quieting the restive cities of Greece, then putting down uprisings in Thrace and Illyria. Thebes revolted on a false rumor that Alexander was dead. The young king rushed south and sacked the city, sparing only the temples and Pindar's house. Greece and the Balkan Peninsula secured, he then crossed the Hellespont (334) and undertook the war on Persia that his father had been planning. The march he had begun was to be one of the greatest in history. At the Granicus river (near the Hellespont) he met and defeated a Persian force and moved on to take Sardis, Miletus, and Halicarnassus. None could stand up against his military skill. For the first time in history Persia faced a united Greece, and Alexander saw himself as the spreader of Pan-Hellenic ideals. Having taken most of Asia Minor, he entered (333) N Syria and there in the battle of Issus met and routed the hosts of DARIUS III of Persia, who fled before him. Alexander, triumphant, now envisioned conquest of the whole of the Persian Empire. It took him nearly a year to reduce Tyre and Gaza, and in 332, in full command of Syria, he entered Egypt. There he met no resistance. When he went to the oasis of Amon he was acknowledged as the son of Amon-Ra, and from that time forward he seems to have had a conviction of his own divinity. In the winter he founded Alexandria, perhaps the greatest monument to his name, and in the spring of 331 he returned to Syria, then went to Mesopotamia where he met Darius again in the battle of Guagamela (also called the battle of Arbela after the town 60 mi. away). The battle was hard, but Alexander was victorious. He marched S to Babylon, then went to Susa and on to Persepolis. He was now the visible ruler of the Persian Empire, pursuing the fugitive Darius to Ecbatana, which submitted in 330, and on to Bactria. There the satrap Bessus, a cousin of Darius, had the Persian king murdered and declared himself king. Alexander went on through Bactria and captured and executed Bessus. He was now in the regions beyond the Oxus (the modern Amu Darya), and his men were beginning to show dissatisfaction. In 330 a conspiracy against Alexander was said to implicate the son of one of his generals, PARMENION; Alexander not only executed the son but also put the innocent Parmenion to death. This act, and his harshness further alienated the soldiers, who had murmured against Alexander's use of Persian dress and his manners of an Oriental despot. Nevertheless Alexander conquered all of Bactria and Sogdiana after hard fighting and then went on from what is today Afghanistan into N India. Some of the princes there received him favorably, but at the

Alexander the Great (antique bronze statuette).

Alexander the Great at the battle of Issus (mosaic from Pompeii, Italy).

Hydaspes (the modern Jhelum) he met and defeated an army under Porus. He overran the Punjab, but here his men would go no farther. He had built a fleet, and after going down the Indus to its delta, he sent Nearchus with the fleet to take it across the unknown route to the head of the Persian Gulf, a daring undertaking. He himself led his men through the desert regions of modern Baluchistan, S Afghanistan, and S Iran. The march was accomplished only with great suffering but finally ended at Susa in 324. Here he found that many of the officials he had chosen to govern the conquered lands had indulged in corruption and misrule. After leaving Susa, Alexander spent four months in Persepolis, and toward the end of his visit the city was almost completely burned. The classical writers say that Alexander burned the city, but this seems unlikely since Alexander's policy was never to destroy a conquered city, and furthermore the region had already completely succumbed to his forces. Meanwhile certain antagonisms were developing against Alexander; in Greece, for instance, many decried his execution of Aristotle's nephew, the historian CALLISTHENES, and the Greek cities resented his request that they treat him as a god. Alexander's Macedonian officers disliked his attempt to force them to mingle and even intermarry with the Persians (he had himself married ROXANA, a Bactrian princess, as one of his several wives), and they resisted his Orientalizing ways and his vision of the equality of peoples. There was a mutiny, but it was put down. In 323 Alexander was planning a voyage by sea around Arabia when he caught a fever and died at 33. Whether or not he had plans for a world empire cannot be determined. He had accomplished greater conquests than any before him, but he did not have time to mold the government of the lands

he had taken, and after his death his generals fell to quarreling about dividing the rule (see DIADOCHI). His only son was Alexander Aegus, born to Roxana after Alexander's death and destined for a short and pitiful life. Incontestably, Alexander was one of the greatest generals of all time and one of the most powerful personalities of antiquity. He influenced the spread of HELLENISM and instigated profound changes in the history of the world. There are many legends about him, e.g., his feats on his horse Bucephalus and his cutting of the Gordian knot. The famous Greek sculptor Lysippus did several studies of Alexander. Arrian and Plutarch wrote biographies of him in ancient times, and the literature of the Middle Ages romanticized his life. See modern biographies by Ulrich Wilcken (Eng. tr., 1932), F. A. Wright (1934), L. V. Cummings (1940), W. W. Tarn (1948), C. A. Robinson, Jr. (1952), and J. F. C. Fuller (1960).

Alexandra, 1844–1925, queen consort of Edward VII of Great Britain, whom she married in 1863. She was the daughter of Christian IX of Denmark.

Alexandra, Mount: see RUWENZORI.

Alexandra Feodorovna (fĕô″dúrŏv′nú, Rus. fyô′-dúrŭvnú), 1872–1918, Russian empress, consort of NICHOLAS II; she was a Hessian princess and a granddaughter of Queen Victoria. Neurotic and superstitious, she was easily dominated by RASPUTIN, who was able to check the hemophilia of her son. When Nicholas took command (Sept., 1915) of the forces at the front, she assumed control in St. Petersburg and prevailed upon her weak husband to replace independent and liberal ministers with those favored by Rasputin. Her great unpopularity was increased by widespread suspicions that she was pro-German. With her husband and children, she was shot by the Bolsheviks.

Alexandrescu, Grigore (grēgô′rĕ úlĕksúndrĕ′skŏŏ),

1812 85, Rumanian poet. Of a noble family, he was active in secret revolutionary societies. In his fables he commented ironically on contemporary events and tried to encourage pride in the national heritage.

Alexandretta: see ISKENDERUN.

Alexandretta, sanjak of (sän″jăk′, ă″lĭgzăndrĕ′tů), former name of Hatay prov. (2,141 sq. mi.; pop. 441,198), S Turkey, comprising the cities of Antioch (now Antakya) and its port, Alexandretta (now Iskenderun). It has a mixed population, with a high percentage of Syrian Christians. Awarded to Syria in 1920, it became in 1936 the subject of a complaint to the League of Nations by Turkey, which claimed that Turkish minority privileges in the sanjak were being infringed. An agreement between France (then mandatory power in Syria) and Turkey was effected (1937) by the League, and Alexandretta was given autonomous status. Riots between Turks and Arabs resulted (1938) in the establishment of joint French and Turkish military control. Finally, in 1939, France transferred the district to Turkey.

Alexandria, Arabic *Al Iskandariya,* city (pop. 1,513,000), N Egypt, a port on the Mediterranean Sea. It is at the western extremity of the Nile delta on a narrow isthmus between the sea and Mareotis lake. The city was founded late in 332 B.C. by Alexander the Great. It was the capital (304 B.C.– 30 B.C.) of the Ptolemies, and much of the Mediterranean trade passed through its sheltered port. Alexandria soon outgrew Carthage and became the largest city in the West. It was the great center of

Cosmopolitan shopping district in Alexandria, Egypt.

Hellenistic and Jewish culture (the Septuagint was prepared here). The city contained two celebrated royal libraries, to which Antony added a vast collection of rolls from PERGAMUM. One library was kept in a temple of Zeus and the other in the museum. The collections at their maximum were said to contain about 490,000 different rolls or, counting duplicates, a total of about 700,000 rolls. Around the museum a great university arose and attracted many scholars, including Aristarchus of Samothrace, the collator of Homeric texts; Euclid, the mathematician; and Herophilus, the anatomist, who founded a medical school. Alexandria formally became part of the Roman empire in 30 B.C. It was the greatest of the provincial capitals, with a population of c.300,000 free persons and an even larger number of slaves. Julius Caesar had occupied (47 B.C.) the city while in pursuit of Pompey, and Octavian (later Augustus) entered it (30 B.C.) after the suicide of Antony and Cleopatra. In the late centuries of rule under the Roman and Byzantine empires Alexandria was a center of Christian learning rivaling Rome and Constantinople, and a patriarchate was established here. The famous libraries were destroyed—possibly in part in Julius Caesar's invasion, certainly more under Aurelian and still more in the razing of pagan temples and structures under Theodosius I in A.D. 391. Although a decline in shipping had severely hurt Alexandria's prosperity, it still had c.300,000 inhabitants when it fell in 642 to the Arabs. They moved the capital of Egypt to what is now Cairo, and Alexandria's decline continued, becoming especially rapid in the 14th cent., when the canal to the Nile silted up. On his campaign in Egypt, Napoleon took the city in 1798 but lost it to the British in 1801. In the 19th cent. Alexandria (sunk to 12,000 persons) gradually regained importance when the canal was reopened and the harbor improved. Today there is a modern harbor (lying to the west of the ancient disused harbor) which handles most of Egypt's foreign trade. There are rail connections with Cairo and most of the Nile valley in Egypt. The city is noted for its extensive parks and its fine beaches on the Mediterranean. Much of the ancient city is covered by modern buildings or is under water. Only a few landmarks are readily accessible; these include ruins of the emporium and the Serapeum and a granite shaft called Pompey's Pillar. Nothing remains of the lighthouse on the PHAROS. The spacious Greco-Roman museum houses a vast collection of antiquities. See Harold T. Davis, *Alexandria, The Golden City* (2 vols., 1957) and E. M. Forster, *Alexandria: a History and a Guide* (3d ed., 1961).

Alexandria. 1 City (pop. 5,582), E central Ind., N of Anderson, settled c.1821. Rockwool insulation is made. **2** Town (pop. 1,318), a co. seat of Campbell co., N Ky., SSE of Cincinnati, Ohio. **3** City (pop. 40,279), parish seat of Rapides parish, central La., on the Red River and SW of Shreveport; laid out 1810, inc. 1818. Its industries are based on the materials produced in the area—cotton, sugar cane, farm products, and timber. The city is the headquarters of Kisatchie National Forest. England Air Force Base is nearby. The unincorporated town of Alexandria Southwest (pop. 2,782) is adjacent. **4** City (pop. 6,713), co. seat of Douglas

George Washington Masonic National Memorial Temple on Shootor's Hill in Alexandria, Va., rises 200 feet.

co., W Minn., SE of Fergus Falls, in a resort region with many lakes; settled 1857, laid out 1865. It is the trade center of a rich farm area. Knute Nelson lived here after 1871. The KENSINGTON RUNE STONE has been exhibited at the Chamber of Commerce here. **5** City (pop. 91,023), N Va., just S of Washington, D.C., a port of entry on the Potomac; patented 1657, permanently settled in the early 18th cent., laid out 1749, inc. as a town 1779, as a city 1852. Primarily a residential suburb of Washington, D.C., it also has extensive railroad yards and repair ships and manufactures metal and lumber products. Many of its historic buildings (often associated with George Washington) have been restored; among them are Gadsby's Tavern (1752), Carlyle House (1752; Washington received his commission as major from General Braddock here), Christ Church (1767–73), and Ramsay House (1749–51). The George Washington Masonic National Memorial Temple (1923–32) houses Washington mementos. One of the Washington family estates, Woodlawn, was made a national shrine in 1949. Alexandria was part of the District of Columbia from 1789 to 1847. Nearby are an Episcopal seminary (1823) and Mt. Vernon.

Alexandria Bay, resort village (pop. 1,583), N N.Y., on the St. Lawrence and N of Watertown; inc. 1878. It is a port of entry and a gateway to the Thousand Islands. Sturgeon fisheries and dairy farms are here. The Thousand Islands Bridge spans the St. Lawrence to Canada from Collins Landing near here.

Alexandria Southwest, La.: see ALEXANDRIA.

Alexandria Troas (trō′ăs) or **Troas,** ancient Greek seaport city, Mysia, NW Asia Minor. It was important under the Greeks and Romans. Acts 16.8, 11; 20.5,6; 2 Cor. 2.12; 2 Tim. 4.13.

alexandrine, in prosody, a line of 12 syllables (or 13 if the last syllable is unstressed). It derives its name probably from a 12th-century romance of Alexander the Great. In English an iambic HEXAMETER line is often called an alexandrine. The most notable example is found in the Spenserian stanza, which contains eight iambic pentameters and an alexandrine rhyming with the last PENTAMETER. In French, rhyming couplets of two alexandrines of equal length, usually containing four accents, have been the classic poetic form since the time of Ronsard, e.g., in the dramas of Racine and Corneille.

Alexandroupolis (ălĕksändrōō′pôlēs), city (pop. 16,-632), W Thrace, Greece, on the Gulf of Ainos, an inlet of the Aegean Sea. It is near the Turkish frontier. It is a commercial center with rail connections to Salonica and Adrianople; wheat, cotton, rice, tobacco, salt, and dairy products are traded. Originally called Dedeagach, it developed from a small village after 1871. It supplanted the older port of Enos upon the completion (1896) of the Salonica-Istanbul RR. It suffered greatly at the hands of the Bulgarians in both world wars. It was ceded to Greece in 1919, when it was renamed for King Alexander of Greece.

Alexis (ûlĕk′sĭs) (Aleksey Mikhailovich) (ûlyĭksyä′mĕkhī′lйvĭch), 1629–76, tsar of Russia (1645–76), son and successor of Michael. His reign, marked by numerous popular outbreaks, was crucial for the later development of Russia. A new code of laws was promulgated in 1648 and remained in effect until the early 19th cent.; it favored the middle classes and the landowners, but tied the peasants to the soil. The reforms of Patriarch NIKON resulted in a dangerous schism in the Russian Church, and Nikon's deposition (1666) was a prelude to the abolition of the Moscow patriarchate in 1717. In 1654 the Cossacks of Ukraine, led in revolt against Poland by Bohdan CHMIELNICKI, voted the union of Ukraine with Russia. War with Poland ensued and ended in 1667 with Russia retaining most of Ukraine. A serious revolt (1670) among the Don Cossacks under Stenka RAZIN was quelled by 1671. Alexis was succeeded by his son Feodor III. A younger son, by a second marriage, became Peter the Great (Peter I).

Alexis (Aleksey Petrovich) (ûlyĭksyä′ pĕtrô′vĭch), 1690–1718, Russian tsarevich; son of Peter I (Peter the Great) by his first wife and father of Peter II. Opposing his father's anticlerical policy, Alexis renounced his right of succession and fled (1716) to Vienna. Peter, who feared that Alexis might win foreign backing, enticed him to return; he then had him arrested and tried for treason. Sentenced to death, Alexis died from the effects of torture shortly before his scheduled execution.

Alexishafen (ûlĕk′sĭs-hä″fûn), small harbor of N Astrolabe Bay, E New Guinea, in the Territory of New Guinea. It is sometimes called Sek Harbour.

Alexius I (Alexius Comnenus) (ûlĕk′sēŭs, kйmnē′nús), 1048–1118, Byzantine emperor (1081–1118). Under the successors of his uncle, ISAAC I, the empire had fallen prey to anarchy and foreign invasions. In 1081 Alexius, who had become popular as a general, overthrew Nicephorus III and was proclaimed emperor. Among the dangers besetting the empire, that of the Norman invasions (1081–85) under ROBERT GUISCARD and his son BOHE-

MOND I was the most immediate. Alexius obtained Venetian help at the price of valuable commercial privileges. This and a truce with the Seljuk Turks enabled him to defend the Balkan Peninsula until the death of Robert Guiscard, when the Normans temporarily withdrew (1085). Next, Alexius secured the alliance of the CUMANS and with their help defeated (1091) the PETCHENEGS, who had besieged Constantinople. He then repulsed the Cumans, who had turned against him, regained territory from the Turks, and suppressed insurrections in Crete and Cyprus. Alexius continued to seek help from the West, but the First Crusade (see CRUSADES) did not come in direct response to his request. Faced with the presence of an unruly and pillaging host near his capital, Alexius sought both to rid himself of the Crusaders and to employ them for his own purposes. Thus he furnished them with money, supplies, and speedy transportation to Asia Minor after he had persuaded the leaders to swear him fealty and to agree to surrender to him all conquests of former Byzantine territories. In return, he promised to join the Crusaders, who at first complied. Bohemond, however, seized Antioch for himself, and in 1099 Alexius began operations against him. In 1108 Bohemond was forced to acknowledge Alexius as his suzerain. The last years of Alexius' reign were consumed by fresh struggles with the Turks and by the intrigues of his daughter ANNA COMNENA against his son and heir, John II. Alexius' reign restored Byzantine military and naval power and political prestige, but brought onerous taxation, the depreciation of currency, and the extension of feudalism by grants of estates, draining imperial strength. See biography by F. M. Chalandon (1900, in French).

Alexius II (Alexius Comnenus), c.1168–1183, Byzantine emperor (1180–83), son and successor of Manuel I. His mother, Mary of Antioch, who was regent for him, alienated the population by favoring the Latin element in Constantinople. In 1183 Alexius' cousin Andronicus, after instigating a massacre of the Latins, stormed the city, had Alexius sign the death sentence of his mother, and, as Andronicus I, became coemperor. One month later he strangled Alexius and married his widow.

Alexius III (Alexius Angelus) (ăn'jŭlŭs), d. after 1210, Byzantine emperor (1195–1203). He acceded to power by deposing and blinding his brother Isaac II. This act served as pretext for the leaders of the Fourth Crusade (see CRUSADES) to attack Constantinople (1203). The Crusaders made Isaac II and his son Alexius IV coemperors, Alexius III having fled. In 1204 Alexius III's son-in-law was briefly emperor as Alexius V. Another son-in-law, Theodore I, became emperor of Nicaea. Alexius died in obscurity.

Alexius IV (Alexius Angelus), d. 1204, Byzantine emperor (1203–4), son of ISAAC II. When his father was deposed, Alexius fled to Italy and then went to Germany. Encouraged by his brother-in-law, Philip of Swabia, he obtained (1202) from the leaders of the Fourth Crusade (see CRUSADES) the promise of help in deposing his uncle, Alexius III. Made joint emperor with Isaac II after the Crusaders entered Constantinople, he was overthrown for his subservience to his allies and was strangled by order of Alexius V.

Alexius V (Alexius Ducas Mourtzouphlos), (dōō'kŭs mōōrt'sōōflŏs), d. 1204, Byzantine emperor (1204), son-in-law of Alexius III. The head of the Byzantine national party, he overthrew Emperors Isaac II and Alexius IV (who had been installed by the Crusaders), thus precipitating the conquest and sack of Constantinople (1204) by the army of the Fourth Crusade (see CRUSADES). He was deposed and executed, and Baldwin I was elected by the Crusaders as Latin emperor of Constantinople.

Aleyn, Simon: see BRAY, England.

alfalfa (ălfăl'fù) or **lucern**, perennial plant (*Medicago sativa*) of the PULSE family, the most important pasture and hay plant in North America, also grown extensively in Argentina, S Europe, and Asia. Probably native to Persia, it was introduced to the United States by Spanish colonists. Of high yield, high protein content, and such prolific growth that it acts as an effective weed control, alfalfa is also valued in crop rotation and for soil improvement because of the nitrogen-fixing bacteria it harbors in its leguminous roots. The several varieties of the species grow well in most temperate regions except those with acid soil or poor drainage. The alfalfa belt of the United States centers chiefly in the northern and western parts of the country. Young alfalfa shoots have been used as food for humans and have antiscorbutic properties. Carotene and chlorophyll for commercial use are extracted from the plant. Alfalfa is also called medic, the name for any plant of the genus *Medicago*, all Old World herbs with blue or yellow flowers similar to those of the related clovers. Black medic (*M. lupulina*) and the bur clovers (*M. arabica* and *M. hispida*) are among the annual species naturalized as weeds in North America and sometimes also grown for hay and pasture.

Al-Farabi (äl-färä'bē) or **Alfarabius** (ăl'fùrā'bēùs), d. 950, Arabian philosopher of Damascus. Author of an encyclopedic work which draws largely from Aristotle, he was one of the earlier Moslem philosophers to develop a philosophical method reconciling Aristotle and Islam. Neoplatonism also is clearly influential in Al-Farabi. See Nicholas Rescher, *Al-Farabi: an Annotated Bibliography* (1962).

Alfaro, Flavio Eloy (flä'vyō āloi' älfä'rō), 1867–1912, president of Ecuador (1897–1901, 1907–11). Regarded as a champion of liberalism, he introduced legal and material reforms that largely undid the clerical privileges granted by Gabriel García Moreno. Exiled by the opposition, he returned to lead a revolt but was defeated, imprisoned, and murdered by an angry mob.

Al-Fasi, Isaac ben Jacob ha-Kohen (äl-fä'sē), 1013–1103, Jewish Talmudic scholar, b. near Fez, North Africa. His *Halachoth*, a codification of the Talmud, is his greatest work; it contains a simplified exposition of complicated Talmudic passages. It has been reprinted many times, and the edition of 1881 is appended to the regular editions of the Talmud. He is also known for his collection of *Responsa*, a great deal of which was written in Arabic and later translated into Hebrew.

Alfieri, Vittorio, Conte (vēt-tō'rēō kōn'tä älfyĕ'rē), 1749–1803, Italian tragic poet. A Piedmontese, born to wealth and social position, he spent his youth in dissipation and adventure. From 1767 to

1772 he traveled over much of Europe but returned to Italy fired by a sense of the greatness of his own country. He saw himself as a prophet called to revive the national spirit of Italy and chose tragic drama as his means. The first of his plays, *Cleopatra*, written in a vigorous, harsh, and individual style, was staged in Turin in 1775. From 1776 to 1786 he wrote 19 tragedies, among them *Philip*

Conte Vittorio Alfieri

the Second, Saul, Antigone, Agamemnon, Orestes, Sophonisba, and Maria Stuart—all belonging in the tradition of French classical tragedy. He also wrote comedies; a bitter satire against France, the *Misogallo*; and a revealing autobiography (1804; Eng. tr. by W. D. Howells, 1877). Alfieri's most productive period coincided with the beginning of his friendship with the countess of Albany, wife of Charles Edward Stuart, the Young Pretender. The remainder of his life was spent with her; they may have married secretly after her husband's death. Alfieri's complete works, which figured in the rise of Italian nationalism, were posthumously edited and published (1805–15) by the countess. His tragedies were translated into English in 1815 and 1876. *Della tirannia* appeared as *Of Tyranny* (1961). See biographies by Gaudense Megaro (1930) and C. R. D. Miller (1936).

Alfold: see HUNGARY.

Alfonsine tables or **Alphonsine tables** (ălfŏn'sĭn), improved planetary tables. They were a revision of the Ptolemaic tables and were made at Toledo by about 50 astronomers, assembled for the purpose by Alfonso X of Castile. The tables, completed c.1252, were printed in Venice in 1483.

Alfonso I, d. 1134, king of Aragon and of Navarre (1104–34), brother and successor of Peter I. He was the husband of URRACA, queen of Castile. His life was spent in continuous warfare. He was obliged to abandon his efforts to extend his authority over Castile in order to fight the Moors, from whom he captured Saragossa (1118), Calatayud (1120), and many other towns. His raid into Andalusia had a great moral, if not practical, effect. Alfonso encouraged Christians in Moslem lands to settle in his domain. He was succeeded by his brother Ramiro II in Aragon (see ARAGON, HOUSE OF) and by García IV in NAVARRE.

Alfonso II, 1152–96, king of Aragon (1162–96) and, as Raymond Berengar V, count of Barcelona (1162–96), son and successor of Raymond Berengar IV of Barcelona and Petronilla of Aragon. He inherited Provence (1166) and Roussillon (1172) and successfully defended against the counts of Toulouse the claims to the French fiefs of his house. He conquered (1171) Teruel from the Moors and resettled it, and he released himself from homage to Castile, but followed a varying policy toward the Castilian king, Alfonso VIII. A patron of troubadours, he wrote Provençal verse. His son Peter II succeeded him.

Alfonso III, 1265–91, king of Aragon and count of Barcelona (1285–91), son and successor of Peter III. He was forced to grant wide privileges to the cortes of the Aragonese nobles. At first he supported the claim to Sicily of his brother James (later JAMES II of Aragon) against CHARLES II of Naples. Later, however, he recognized papal suzerainty over Sicily and pressed James to abandon his claim. He also made war on Castile and on his uncle, JAMES I of Majorca. James II succeeded him.

Alfonso IV, 1299–1336, king of Aragon and count of Barcelona (1327–36), son and successor of James II. Before his accession he conquered (1323–24) SARDINIA, where later a revolt involved him in a war with Genoa and Pisa. He was succeeded by his son, Peter IV.

Alfonso V (Alfonso the Magnanimous), 1396–1458, king of Aragon and Sicily (1416–58) and of Naples (1443–58), count of Barcelona. He was the natural son of Ferdinand I, whom he succeeded in Aragon and Sicily. In 1420 Queen JOANNA II of Naples sought his aid against LOUIS III, rival king of Naples, and adopted him as her heir. They quarreled in 1423, and at her death (1435) Joanna left her throne to RENÉ of Anjou. Attempting to conquer Naples, Alfonso was captured by the Genoese, but he was released through the agency of the duke of Milan. In 1442 he defeated René, took Naples, and was recognized (1443) as king by the pope. Leaving his Spanish possessions under the rule of his wife and his brother, Alfonso spent the rest of his life in Naples, where he accorded great privileges to Spanish nobles and tried to introduce Spanish institutions. A patron of arts and letters, he held a splendid court and beautified the city. Alfonso took part in Italian politics and tried through diplomacy to stem the advance of the Turks. He left Naples to his son Ferdinand I and the rest of his kingdom to his brother John II.

Alfonso I, Port. *Afonso Henriques*, 1111?–1185, first king of Portugal, son of Henry of Burgundy. After his father's death (1112), his mother, Countess Teresa, ruled the county of Portugal with the help of her Spanish favorite, Fernando Pérez, until in 1128 young Alfonso, allying himself with discontented nobles, took power and drove her into Leon with Pérez (Alfonso did not, despite the popular legend, put her in chains at Guimarãis). Beginning as little more than a quasi-independent guerrilla chief, Alfonso spent his life in almost ceaseless fighting against the kings of Leon and Castile and against the Moors to increase his prestige and his territories. In 1139 he defeated the Moors in the battle of Ourique (fought not at Ourique, but at some undetermined place). In 1147 he took Santarém by surprise attack and, with the help of the English, Flemish, and German crusaders, captured Lisbon. Styling himself king after 1139, he put (1143) his lands under papal protection, and Alfonso VII of Castile recognized the title, which was confirmed (1179) by Pope Alexander III. Alfonso's son SANCHO I ascended an established throne.

Alfonso II (Alfonso the Fat), 1185–1223, king of Portugal (1211–23). His reign was spent in struggles with the Church and his brothers and sisters, to whom his father, Sancho I, had left many of his estates. Alfonso's measures against the Church holdings and the bishops led to his excommunication (1219). Though he was himself unwarlike, Portuguese soldiers took part in the battle of Navas de Tolosa and pushed conquests against the Moors. He was succeeded by his son Sancho II (reigned 1223–48).

Alfonso III, Port. *Afonso o Bolonhez* [Alfonso of Boulogne], 1210–79, king of Portugal (1248–79), son of Alfonso II; successor of his brother Sancho II. By his marriage with Matilda, countess of Boulogne, he became count of Boulogne. He succeeded in attaining the throne of Portugal through intrigues which were capped by an agreement reached (1245) in Paris with the archbishop of Braga and the bishop of Coimbra to depose Sancho II. Alfonso's reign saw the completion of the reconquest of Portugal from the Moors with the taking (1249) of the rest of the Algarve. This involved him in a long quarrel with Alfonso X of Castile, who had been receiving revenues from Algarve, but the two kings reached an agreement by which Alfonso III married the illegitimate daughter of Alfonso X, and Alfonso X was to relinquish all rights to the Algarve when the heir born of this union (the later King DINIZ) should reach the age of seven. Alfonso's second marriage brought the Portuguese king into disfavor with the Church because Matilda was still living, but her death ended the conflict. Despite the promises he had made in Paris, Alfonso seized lands that had been alienated to the Church. This caused a long break with the Church, healed shortly before his death. He called the Cortes of Leiria (1254), the first Portuguese Cortes to include commoners. He also instituted administrative and financial reforms, encouraged the cities and commerce, and commuted many feudal dues into money payments. French and Provençal culture was imported to the court, and the period was one of great intellectual activity.

Alfonso IV, 1291–1357, king of Portugal (1325–57), son and successor of DINIZ. Disgruntled by the favoritism his father showed toward Alfonso's illegitimate half brothers, Alfonso rose in revolt in 1320, and though peace was patched up twice by his mother, St. Elizabeth (or St. Isabel) of Portugal, he was estranged from Diniz most of the five years before his father's death. He was then involved in a fruitless war with Alfonso XI of Castile until 1340. The two kings immediately thereafter campaigned together against the Moors and won the notable battle of Tarifa. Alfonso is, however, best remembered for countenancing the murder of his son's mistress (or wife), the most romantic figure in Portuguese history, Inés de CASTRO, in 1355. His son (later PETER I) promptly led a rebel-

lion, but peace between father and son was restored before Alfonso's death.

Alfonso V (Alfonso the African), 1432–81, king of Portugal (1438–81), son of Duarte and Queen Leonor. In his minority there was a struggle for the regency between the queen mother and the duke of Coimbra (Dom Pedro, uncle of Alfonso). The duke was triumphant and retained power after Alfonso was declared of age (1446) until, influenced by the illegitimate half brother of Dom Pedro (see BRAGANZA, family), the young king took unjust measures against Dom Pedro and brought on a civil war. The king's troops killed (1449) his uncle at Alfarrobeira. Alfonso undertook ventures in Morocco and by capturing Alcacer-Seguer (1458) and Tangier (1471) won the name Alfonso the African, but these campaigns were ultimately not fruitful. Even less rewarding was his long attempt to win the throne of Castile after his marriage—never sanctioned by the Church—in 1475 to JUANA LA BELTRANEJA, officially the daughter and heiress of Henry IV of Castile though generally thought to be the child of Beltrán de la Cueva. This claim brought Alfonso into war with ISABELLA I of Castile and her husband, FERDINAND V of Aragon. Alfonso, badly beaten, capitulated in 1479. During his reign Prince HENRY THE NAVIGATOR was active. Alfonso's son, the later John II, exercised control in Portugal before Alfonso's death.

Alfonso VI (Alfonso the Victorious), 1643–83, king of Portugal (1656–67), son and successor of John IV. Slightly paralyzed and mentally defective, he distinguished himself under the regency of his mother by associating with rowdy youths. After their ringleader was dismissed, Alfonso, directed by the count of Castelo Melhor, ousted his mother in 1662. The count of Castelo Melhor then ruled ably, and he organized the army to repulse (1663) the Spanish under John of Austria, thus earning for the king the ironic title "the Victorious." After the marriage (1666) of Alfonso to Marie Françoise of Savoy, daughter of the duke of Nemours, the young queen took a hand in government. She and the king's younger brother (later PETER II) fell in love, forced Castelo Melhor from power, and made Alfonso abdicate in favor of Peter, who became prince regent. A quick annulment of her marriage to Alfonso enabled his queen to wed the new regent. Alfonso was confined in the Azores until 1674 and at Sintra thereafter.

Alfonso I (Alfonso the Catholic), 693?–757, Spanish king of Asturias (739–57). He was the son-in-law of PELAYO. A Berber rebellion against the Moors facilitated his conquests in parts of Galicia, Leon, and Santander.

Alfonso II (Alfonso the Chaste), 759?–842, Spanish king of Asturias (791–842), grandson of Alfonso I. He continued the struggle against the Moors and established his residence at Oviedo, which his father, Fruela I, had founded. His alliance with Charlemagne and Emperor Louis I met opposition among his nobles. Alfonso II built the first church on the site of SANTIAGO DE COMPOSTELA.

Alfonso III (Alfonso the Great), 838?–911?, Spanish king of Asturias (866–911?). He conquered Leon. The kingdom was consolidated in his reign, though after his forced abdication it was divided among his sons.

Alfonso V (Alfonso the Noble), 994?–1027, Spanish king of Asturias and Leon (999–1027). While he was still a minor, the Moorish ruler Al-Mansur died, and the Spanish court recovered the city of Leon. Alfonso gave (1020) Leon its *fuero* [charter] and was killed in the siege of Viseu.

Alfonso VI, 1030–1109, Spanish king of Leon (1065–1109) and Castile (1072–1109). He inherited Leon from his father, Ferdinand I. Defeated by his brother Sancho II of Castile, he fled to the court of Al-Mamun, Moorish ruler of Toledo. After Sancho's assassination (1072) he succeeded to the throne of Castile and took Galicia from his brother García (1073), thus becoming the most powerful Christian ruler in Spain. He encouraged Christians in Moslem lands to migrate north. He raided Moslem territory and penetrated as far as Tarifa. After the conquest of strategic Toledo (1085), he took many other cities and reached the line of the Tagus. Aroused by his advance, Abbad III (see Abbadides) and his Moslem allies called to their aid the Almoravide Yusuf ibn Tashufin, who defeated Alfonso in 1086. Again the Spanish lost in 1108; Alfonso's only son died in the battle. Alfonso's reign gave a great crusading impulse to the reconquest of Spain and was also notable for the exploits of the Cid. His court at Toledo became the center of cultural relations between Moslem and Christian Spain, while French influence also grew strong through his many French followers. At this time the Cluniac reform was introduced into Spain. Alfonso was succeeded by his daughter Urraca.

Alfonso VII (Alfonso the Emperor), 1104–57, Spanish king of Castile and Leon (1126–57), son and successor of Urraca. He recovered the places in Castile which his stepfather, Alfonso I of Aragon, had occupied. Soon he gained supremacy over the other Christian states in Spain. In 1135 he had himself crowned emperor in Leon. His many victories over the Moors had no permanent results; the most famous were the conquests of Córdoba (1146) and Almería (1147). Alfonso left Castile to his son Sancho III (reigned 1157–58) and Leon to his son Ferdinand II.

Alfonso VIII (Alfonso the Noble), 1155–1214, Spanish king of Castile (1158–1214), son and successor of Sancho III. Chaos prevailed during his minority, but he quickly restored order after assuming the government. He married Eleanor, daughter of Henry II of England, and their daughter, Blanche of Castile, married Louis VIII of France. Alfonso took Cuenca (1177) and incorporated the provinces of Álava and Guipúzcoa into Castile (1200). Attacked simultaneously by a coalition of Navarre, Aragon, and Leon and by the Moors, he was defeated (1195) by the Moors. He later made peace with his former Christian enemies and led them to the great victory over the Almohades at Navas de Tolosa (1212). At Palencia he founded the first university in Spain (1212 or 1214). He was succeeded by his son, Henry I (1214–17), who was succeeded by Ferdinand III.

Alfonso IX, 1171–1230, Spanish king of Leon (1188–1230), son and successor of Ferdinand II. He conquered from the Moors several cities in Estremadura and was frequently at war with Alfonso VIII of Castile. His marriages with Teresa of Portugal and Berenguela of Castile were both annulled by the pope. He defeated (1230) the Moors at Mérida. His son by Berenguela, Ferdinand III, reunited (1230) Leon and Castile.

Alfonso X (Alfonso the Wise), 1221–84, Spanish king of Castile and Leon (1252–84), son and successor of Ferdinand III, whose conquests of the

Fifteenth-century illustrations for Songs to the Virgin, attributed to Alfonso X.

Moors he continued, notably by taking Cádiz (1262). His mother, Beatriz, was a daughter of Emperor Philip of Swabia and a granddaughter of Isaac II, the Byzantine emperor. On the death (1256) of Conrad IV and of William, count of Holland, Alfonso was elected by a faction of German princes as antiking to Richard, earl of Cornwall, and (after 1272) to Rudolf of Hapsburg. Because of papal opposition and Spanish antagonism, he did not go to Germany, however, and in 1275 he renounced his claim. In his domestic policy, his assertion of authority led to a rebellion of the nobles. He debased the coinage, thus adding to the general discontent. After the death (1275) of his eldest son, Ferdinand, while fighting the Moors, civil war for the succession broke out between Ferdinand's children and Alfonso's second son, who eventually succeeded him as Sancho IV. Sancho's partisans in the cortes at Valladolid even declared Alfonso deposed (1282). The king died while the dynastic dispute was still unsettled. Alfonso stimulated the cultural life of his time. Under his patronage the schools of Seville, Murcia, and Salamanca were furthered, and Moslem and Jewish culture flowed into Western Europe. He was largely responsible for the *Siete Partidas*, a compilation of the legal knowledge of his time; for the ALFONSINE TABLES in astronomy; and for other scientific and historical works. A collection of poems, *Songs to the Virgin*, in Galician, is attributed to him. See study by E. E. S. Procter (1951).

Alfonso XI, 1311–50, Spanish king of Castile and Leon (1312–50), son and successor of Ferdinand IV. His vigorous campaign against Granada led to an invasion by the Moors from Morocco; they took Gibraltar in 1333. In 1340, having formed alliances with Portugal, Navarre, and Aragon, Alfonso won the great victory of Tarifa (also called the battle of Salado); in 1344, aided by many foreign soldiers, he took Algeciras. He died while besieging Gibraltar. Alfonso was succeeded by his son Peter the Cruel. By the *Ordenamiento de Alcalá*, issued at Alcalá de Henares in 1348, he enforced the *Siete Partidas* of Alfonso X.

Alfonso XII, 1857–85, king of Spain (1870–85), son of ISABELLA II. He went into exile with his parents at the time of the revolt of the CARLISTS in 1868 and was educated in Austria and England. In 1870 his mother abdicated in his favor, and in 1874 he was proclaimed king. He entered Madrid in triumph early in 1875 and soon won great popularity. Supported by MARTÍNEZ DE CAMPOS and CÁNOVAS DEL CASTILLO, he consolidated the monarchy, suppressed republican agitation, and restored order. His wife, MARIA CHRISTINA (1858–1929), was regent during the minority of his posthumous son, Alfonso XIII.

Alfonso XIII, 1886–1941, king of Spain (1886–1931), posthumous son and successor of Alfonso XII. His mother, MARIA CHRISTINA (1858–1929), was regent until 1902. In 1906 Alfonso married Princess Victoria Eugenie of Battenberg. In spite of his personal popularity, the monarchy was threatened by social unrest in the newly industrialized areas, by Catalan agitation for autonomy, by dissatisfaction with the Moroccan situation, and by the rise of socialism and republicanism. After keeping Spain out of the First World War, Alfonso, dissatisfied with the functioning of parliamentary government, supported (1923) PRIMO DE RIVERA in establishing a military dictatorship. At the fall (1930) of Primo de Rivera, popular discontent was running high. After the municipal elections of 1931 showed an overwhelming republican majority, Alfonso "suspended the exercise of royal power" and went into exile (April 14, 1931). A few weeks before his death in Rome he renounced his claim to the throne in favor of his third son, Juan (see BOURBON, family).

Alfred [Old Eng. Ælfred], 849–899, king of Wessex (871–99), sometimes called Alfred the Great, b. Wantage, Berkshire. Youngest of the four sons of King Æthelwulf, he was sent in 853 and again in 855 to Rome, where the pope invested him with the honorary dignity of a Roman consul. He lacked adequate instruction and learned to read English only after he was 12. His adolescence was marked by ill-health and deep religious devotion, both of which persisted for the rest of his life. Little is known of him during the end of his father's reign and the reigns of his older brothers, Æthelbald and Æthelbert, but when ÆTHELRED took the throne (865), Alfred became his *secundarius* (viceroy?) and aided his brother in subsequent battles against the Danes, who now threatened to overrun all England. When the Danes turned from the east and north regions late in 870 to Wessex, Æthelred and Alfred resisted with varying fortunes in a victory at Ashdown, Berkshire, a defeat at Basing, and several indecisive engagements. Upon his brother's death after Easter in 871, Alfred became king of the West Saxons and overlord of Kent, Surrey, Sussex, and Essex. Faced by an enemy too powerful to defeat decisively, Alfred cleared the Danes from Wessex by a heavy payment of tribute (see

Alfonso XII

Alfred the Great

157

DANEGELD) in 871. In 876 and 877 the Danes returned to ravage for several months and finally, halted by Alfred's army, swore to leave Wessex forever. However, in a surprise invasion early in 878 the Danes crushed Alfred's forces, and he fled to Athelney in the fens of Somerset, from which he continued to wage guerrilla war. The famous legend of Alfred and the cakes, in which he appears as an unrecognized king, exposed to the scolding of a peasant woman, probably reflects this period of his life. Alfred rallied his army to win a complete victory at Edington. He then dictated the Peace of Chippenham (or Wedmore) by which Guthrum, the Danish leader, accepted baptism and probably agreed to separate England into English and Danish "spheres of influence." The Danes moved into East Anglia and E Mercia, and Alfred established his overlordship in W Mercia. In later campaigns, scantily recorded, Alfred captured London and again defeated the Danes. Another treaty with Guthrum in 886 marked off the DANELAW E and N of the Thames, the Lea, the Ouse, and Watling Street, leaving the south and west of England to Alfred; established the relative indemnities of Englishmen and Danes in law; and attempted to prevent border raids.

Alfred's Achievements. Security gave Alfred his chance. He instituted reforms. Against further probable attacks by the Danes, he reorganized the militia or *fyrd* about numerous garrisoned forts throughout Wessex and commanded the construction of a fleet. Drawing from the old codes of ÆTHELBERT of Kent, INE of Wessex, and Offa of Mercia, he issued his own code of laws, marked at once by Christian doctrine and measures for a stronger centralized monarchy. He reformed the administration of justice and energetically participated in it. He came eventually to be considered the overlord of all England, although this title was not realized in concrete political administration. His greatest achievements were the revival of learning and the establishment of Old English literary prose. Alfred gathered together a group of eminent scholars, including the Welshman Asser. They strengthened the Church by reviving learning among the clergy and organized a court school like that of Charlemagne, in which not only youths and clerics but also mature nobles were taught. Alfred himself between 887 and 892 learned Latin and translated several Latin works into English— Gregory the Great's *Pastoral Care*, Bede's *Ecclesiastical History*, Orosius's universal history, Boethius's *Consolation of Philosophy*, and St. Augustine's *Soliloquies*. The adaptation of Boethius is most remarkable for the liberal interpolation of his own thoughts. The Orosius is interesting for the addition of accounts of voyages made by the Norse explorers, OHTHERE and Wulfstan. Although he did not write it, Alfred greatly influenced the extant form of the ANGLO-SAXON CHRONICLE. All these pursuits were interrupted, but not ended, by new Danish invasions between 892 and 896. The struggle was severe because Alfred's military reforms had not been completed and because the invading forces were joined by settlers from the Danelaw. He received strong support from his son EDWARD THE ELDER, his daughter Æthelflæd, and her husband, Æthelred of Mercia, and in the critical year of 893 the great Danish fort at Benfleet was successfully stormed. One Danish expedition attempting conquest by way of the Thames and Severn was defeated at Buttington; another occupying Chester was besieged and forced back to Essex. In 896 the Danes slowly dispersed to the Danelaw or overseas, and Alfred's new long ships fought with varying success against pirate raids on the south coast. Alfred's career was later embroidered by many heroic legends, but history alone justifies the inscription on the statue at his birthplace: "Alfred found learning dead, and he restored it; the laws powerless, and he gave them force; the Church debased, and he raised it; the land ravaged by a fearful enemy, from which he delivered it. Alfred's name shall live as long as mankind shall respect the past." Our knowledge of Alfred's life depends upon the biography by Asser, the *Anglo-Saxon Chronicle*, the royal charters, and Alfred's own writings. See the various editions of Alfred's works; R. H. Hodgkin, *A History of the Anglo-Saxons*, Vol. II (1935); biography by E. S. Duckett (1956).

Alfred. 1 Town (pop. 1,201), co. seat of York co., SW Maine, W of Biddeford; settled 1764, inc. 1794. **2** Village (pop. 2,807), SW N.Y., SW of Hornell; inc. 1881. Alfred Univ. is here.

Alfred University, at Alfred, N.Y.; state and private support; coeducational; opened as a school 1836, chartered 1857 as Alfred University. It is especially known for the state college of ceramics.

Alfreton (ôl′frŭtŭn), urban district (pop. 22,998), Derbyshire, central England. Its products include clothing, cosmetics, and agricultural machinery.

Alfsborg: see ALVSBORG.

algae (ăl′jē) [plural of Latin *alga*=seaweed], group of plants belonging to the most primitive phylum

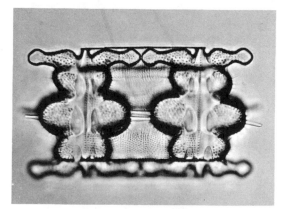

Photomicrograph of a diatom.

of the plant kingdom, the thallophytes, plants that lack true roots, stems, leaves, and flowers. Unlike the fungi, the other large group of thallophytes, the algae have chlorophyll. They are of world-wide distribution and form the chief aquatic plant life both in the sea and in fresh water. Practically all seaweeds are marine algae. The simplest algae are

Enteromorpha, the common green alga.

percent of available solar energy for photosynthesis and carbohydrate production, as compared to 0.1 percent for land plants in general. Algae have also been suggested as a source of oxygen and food for prolonged space travel. Seaweeds (e.g., AGAR) have long been used as a limited source of food, especially in the Orient (see SEAWEED). Algae are also much used as fertilizer.

Algardi, Alessandro (äls-sän′drō älgär′dē), 1595–1654, Italian sculptor and designer, b. Bologna, studied under Lodovico Carracci. In Rome, his friend Domenichino obtained his first commissions for him, the *Magdalene* and *St. John* statues for San Silvestro al Quirinale. When Bernini temporarily fell from favor, Algardi replaced him c.1644 as the most important sculptor in Rome under Pope Innocent X and received numerous commissions even from Spain. Although greatly influenced by Bernini, he retained the classic inclination of the Bolognese in his work, lacking Bernini's emotional vitality. An example of Algardi's work in relief is *The Meeting of Leo and Attila* (St. Peter's). A few prints in the style of Agostino Carracci are attributed to Algardi.

Algarve (älgär′vù), province (1,958 sq. mi.; pop. c.328,230), extreme S Portugal, coextensive with Faro dist. The capital is Faro, and other important cities are Silves, Portimão, and Lagos. Al-

The Meeting of Leo and Attila *by Alessandro Algardi.*

single cells, e.g., the diatoms; the more complex forms consist of many cells grouped in a spherical colony (e.g., *Volvox*), in a ribbonlike filament (e.g., *Spirogyra*), or in a branching thallus form (e.g., *Fucus*). The cells of the colonies are generally similar, but some are differentiated for reproduction and for other functions. Many algae are microscopic, though the marine thalloid forms may attain a length of more than 100 ft. *Euglena* and similar genera are one-celled forms that contain chlorophyll but are also free swimming; they are therefore classified either as protozoan animals or as a unique group separate from both plant and animal phyla. The blue-green algae and green algae include most of the fresh-water forms. The POND SCUM, a green slime found in stagnant water, is an alga, as is the green film found on the bark of trees. The more complex brown algae and red algae are chiefly salt-water forms; the green color of the chlorophyll is masked by the presence of other pigments. Algae, the major food of fish (and thus indirectly of many other animals), are a keystone in the food chain of life. They are also important to aquatic life in their capacity to supply oxygen through photosynthesis; hence algae are a necessary component of a healthy aquarium. Research has investigated the possibility of sea gardening with algae (especially the diatoms, the most numerous of marine plants) as a solution to the problem of insufficient output of land agriculture to meet the needs of the growing world population. In experimental cultivation, algae utilize about 2

garve grows much fruit (almonds, citrus, grapes, olives, figs, pomegranates) and has offshore tuna and sardine fisheries. Settled by the Phoenicians, the region later prospered under the Moors, who made it their last stronghold in Portugal. Alfonso III completed its reconquest in 1249.

Al-Gazel (ăl-gŭzĕl'), or **Al-Ghazali** (gäzä'lē), c.1058–1111, Arabian philosopher, native of Khurasan. He was a professor at Baghdad for some years but abandoned his career and became a mystical ascetic. His *Destruction of the Philosophers* shows a profound distrust of speculation and philosophic method in approaching the mysteries of religion. He was one of the opponents of Moslem rationalism, and his teaching undoubtedly was influential in causing the suppression of rationalism in Baghdad in the 13th cent. He is also the author of ethical treatises and other works on religion and philosophy. See W. Montgomery Watt, *The Faith and Practice of Al-Ghazali* (1953).

algebra: see MATHEMATICS.

Algeciras (ăljŭsēr'ús, Sp. älhäthē'räs), city (pop. 69,343), Cádiz prov., S Spain, in Andalusia, on the Bay of Algeciras opposite Gibraltar. A Mediterranean seaport, it has fishing and varied industries (notably the processing of cork). It was taken from the Moors in 1344. In the naval engagements of July, 1801, near Algeciras, the British defeated the French and Spanish fleets.

Algeciras Conference: see MOROCCO.

Alger, Horatio (ăl'jŭr), 1834–99, American writer of boys' stories, b. Revere, Mass. He wrote over 100 books for boys, the first, *Ragged Dick*, being published in 1867. By leading exemplary lives, struggling valiantly against poverty and adversity, Alger's heroes gain wealth and honor. His works were amazingly popular and left a strong mark upon the character of a generation of American youth. See H. R. Mayes, *Alger: a Biography without a Hero* (1928).

Alger, Russell Alexander, 1836–1907, U.S. Secretary of War (1897–99), b. near Medina, Ohio. After moving to Michigan he engaged in the lumber business, in which he later made a fortune. In the Civil War he rose from the ranks to be a brevet major general. He was (1885–86) a popular governor of Michigan and was prominent in national affairs of the Republican party. He was made Secretary of War by President McKinley, but the inefficiency of his department—in bad condition when he took charge—and his appointment of William R. SHAFTER as leader of the Cuban expedition were bitterly criticized, and he resigned. He was later (1902–7) Senator from Michigan.

Alger (ăl'jŭr), village (pop. 1,068), W central Ohio, E of Lima, in a farm area; inc. 1896.

Algeria (ăljēr'ēú), Fr. *Algérie* (älzhärē'), republic (846,124 sq. mi.; pop. c.11,000,000), NW Africa. Algiers is the capital; a new capital at Rocher Noire was under construction in 1963. Other important cities are ORAN, BÔNE, PHILIPPEVILLE, and CONSTANTINE. Algeria fronts on the Mediterranean in the north, with c.650 mi. of coast between Tunisia and Libya on the east and Morocco and Spanish Sahara on the west. In the south it has a desert frontier with Mauritania, Mali, and Niger. The northern coastal strip is narrow and broken, with poor natural harbors. From it the

mountains of the Tell Atlas (or Maritime Atlas) rise abruptly. Between the fertile Tell and the fastnesses of the Saharan Atlas lies a corridor of semiarid plateaus which since time immemorial formed part of the best land route across N Africa. These plateaus are suitable for grazing and for the cultivation of alfa (esparto); they are dotted with salt marshes and shallow salt lakes called shotts. Beyond lies the great harshness of the Sahara itself, interrupted only by a few date-bearing oases, such as those of Touggourt, Tuat, and Biskra. In the southeast is the Hoggar, a center of the nomadic Tuareg culture. The remote Tuareg represent only one of the many variations in the native peoples usually called Berbers.

History. The tribesmen in early days had little or no unity, and indeed Algeria has no natural boundaries and was not a political entity until after the French occupation. Native groups contended for regional power over parts of the land before the Romans knew the coastal and subsidiary area. Carthaginian power extended over the present Algerian coast. The richness of the Tell attracted the Roman conquerors to take part in the wars of NUMIDIA and MAURETANIA, and after 146 B.C., Rome gradually took control of the hills and some of the plateau country beyond. Grain ships went from the little ports with precious food for Rome, and the cities came to be Latinized. However, the countryside and the more inaccessible mountain regions remained steadfastly Berber. In the Christian days of the empire, coastal N Africa was an integral part of the great whole, and St. Augustine was bishop at Hippo (now Bône). This civilization was worn away not only by the incursions of desert tribes and Berber hillmen but also by revolts and dissensions in the Roman colonies themselves. The drastic conquests of the Vandals in 430–31 only marked the culmination of a long process. Though the Byzantines regained part of old Roman Africa in 534, their hold was insecure and Roman culture did not revive. The next conquerors had a far more profound effect, for when the Arabs arrived in the 7th cent. they brought with them Islam, and gradually all of the peoples of present Algeria took over the religion. Many of the Berbers adopted the Arabic language, and Arabs were mingled with the older population, except in such remote areas as the Hoggar and Kabylia (the region of the Kabyles in the northeast). Little dynasties rose and fell with their capitals at Tiaret,

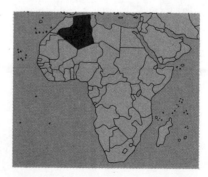

Algeria location map

Bedouins from the south of Algeria graze their camels and sheep on the road between Sétif and Constantine.

Bougie, and Tlemcen, and sometimes the region or part of it was molded into a greater whole, usually with religious as well as political power. The ALMORAVIDES and the ALMOHADES, for instance, united much of the present Algeria with Morocco and Spain in a great Moorish empire. The local control was, however, lax, and local potentates were always able to establish themselves, even if nominal power resided in a larger unit. In 1518 Algiers was seized and brought under Turkish rule (see BARBAROSSA), but the Turkish power never extended much beyond the Tell, and its strength was concentrated on the coast, which became a stronghold for pirates preying on the Mediterranean commerce (see Barbary States). A number of punitive expeditions were sent against the city of Algiers, but to little effect. The ruler in the city, the dey, became virtually independent of Turkish rule altogether at the beginning of the 18th cent., and he maintained himself as ruler of much of present Algeria partly from the proceeds of piracy. The so-called Algerine War in the second decade of the 19th cent. did have the effect of forcing a halt in holding European and American captives for ransom. The dey, however, maintained his hostile attitude toward foreigners until he was engulfed in the imperial ventures of the French. France took Algeria in 1830, conquered (1830–47) the northern belt against opposition led by ABDU-L-KADIR, and took upland Kabylia after 1850. The Sahara region in the south was not brought under effective control until the period 1900–1909. France undertook to develop the resources of the land. Modern ports were built at Algiers, Oran, Bône, and Philippeville; a railroad with branch lines was constructed through the Tell; and a road system was stretched out through the Sahara. Irrigation increased cultivable areas, and new products became important, notably wine and tobacco. Mineral resources, such as the phosphates near Tebessa, and iron ore were exploited. The country was enormously enriched when, in the 1950s, vast deposits of oil and natural gas were discovered in the Saharan region. Education and health services were begun and expanded. Many colonists came to the northern area, though only a little more than 10 percent of the population was of European

Municipal theater in Algiers, Algeria.

Ruins of the ancient Roman town of Timgad, Algeria.

The port of Oran, Algeria.

Market at El Harrach, Algeria.

El Oued, Algeria, an oasis village in the Sahara.

descent. Algeria played a part in the Second World War, notably in the attack of British vessels on the French vessels at Oran in 1940 and after the Allied landing for the conquest of North Africa in 1942. Algiers became the Allied headquarters and was also the seat of Charles de Gaulle's provisional French government. The war also had the effect of fanning the desire of the Moslem natives for independence.

Independence. Spurred on by the example of the struggle of Morocco and Tunisia for independence, the Algerian nationalists demanded civil rights and an equitable electoral system for the Moslem population. The denial of these requests by France resulted in the emergence (1954) of the aggressive National Liberation Front (FLN) as the leading nationalist group. The FLN's use of terrorism, both against the French and rival Moslem groups, and the resulting French countermeasures soon grew into a bloody, open war that by 1955 had engulfed almost all of Algeria. The political impasse arising from the insistence on independence by the FLN, and the implacable opposition to any Algerian autonomy by the European settlers caused a French military junta to seize power (1958). The Moslem rebels then proclaimed the Algerian Republic and established headquarters of their provisional government in Tunis (1959). It was only after Charles de Gaulle assumed power in 1958 that negotiations took place between France and the FLN at Évian-les-Bains (May–July, 1961) which ended the eight-year war and gave Algeria independence. The agreement reached there gave France strategic and economic rights in Algeria, especially over the exploitation of Saharan oil. While the French people in a referendum gave overwhelming support (April, 1962) to the agreement, the Organization of the Secret Army (OAS), an organization of right-wing settlers, formed to fight Algerian independence, and led by the French general Raoul Salan, unleashed a wave of terror against Moslem civilians. The OAS collapsed soon after Salan's capture (April, 1962); a mass exodus of Europeans began from Algeria. Independence brought new troubles to Algeria. The leaders of the FLN engaged in a struggle for power over control of the government. The contest was essentially between Ben Youssef Ben Khedda, who had succeeded Ferhat Abbas as premier of the provisional government, and Ahmed Ben Bella, vice president of the provisional government. The struggle between the two factions almost developed into a civil war after Algeria, in a referendum, voted (July, 1962) overwhelmingly for independence. The conflict was resolved when Ben Bella took power (Aug., 1962). Ben Bella consolidated his power by arranging elections (Sept., 1962) to the National Assembly from a single list of his own candidates. Ben Bella was chosen premier and Ferhat Abbas president of the provisional government. The new Algeria, defining its internal policy as socialist and its foreign policy as neutralist, became a member of the Arab League (Aug., 1962) and joined the UN (Oct., 1962). See Stéphane Gsell, Georges Marçaise, and Georges Yver, *Histoire d'Algérie* (1929); Pierre Bourdieu, *Sociologie de l'Algérie* (1956); Michael K. Clark, *Algeria in Turmoil* (1959); Richard Brace and Joan Brace, *Ordeal in Algeria* (1960); Joan Gillespie, *Algeria, Rebellion and Revolution* (1960); W. G. Andrews, *French Politics and Algeria* (1962).

Algerine War. The TRIPOLITAN WAR (1801–5) had brought a temporary halt to the pirate activities of the Barbary States. However, during the later Napoleonic Wars and the War of 1812 the Barbary pirates renewed their predatory raids on American Mediterranean commerce, and Algiers actually declared war on the United States. In 1815 Stephen DECATUR was sent to Algiers at the head of a squadron of 10 ships. After two minor engagements he sailed into the harbor of Algiers and forced (June 30) the dey of Algiers to sign a treaty renouncing U.S. tribute and agreeing to release all U.S. prisoners without ransom. Decatur then exacted similar guarantees from Tunisia (July 26) and Tripoli (Aug. 5), and the so-called Algerine War was ended.

Al-Ghazali: see AL-GAZEL.

Algiers (ăljērz′) Fr. *Alger* (älzhā′), city (pop. c.588,-000), N Algeria, capital of Algeria, a chief port of N Africa. Founded by the Phoenicians and called Icosium by the Romans, the city disappeared after the fall of the Roman Empire. It was refounded in the late 10th cent. by the Moslems. In 1511 the Spanish occupied an island in its harbor, but they were driven out (1518) when BARBAROSSA captured the city for the Turks. A mole was then built to protect the anchorage, and Algiers became a base for the Moslem fleet that preyed upon Christian commerce in the Mediterranean (see BARBARY STATES). Under the Turks the city grew to 100,000 inhabitants. The ruling Turkish official in Algeria, the dey of Algiers, made himself virtually independent of Constantinople in the 18th and 19th cent. As European navies grew stronger they repeatedly attacked Algiers, and the prosperity of the city, which was based on piracy, declined. When the French captured the port in 1830 there were fewer than 40,000 inhabitants. During their occupation the French built a modern port, and extensive European sections grew up. The small Moslem town remains, surmounted by the 16th-century Casbah [fortress] which now lends its name to this older quarter. The modern city has an observatory, botanical gardens, and a Pasteur Institute. The Univ. of Algiers was established in 1909. In the Second World War Allied forces captured the city on Nov. 8, 1942. For a time thereafter it was the headquarters of the Allied forces and of Charles de Gaulle's provisional French government. In May, 1958, Algiers was the principal scene of a revolt which ended the Fourth French Republic and brought General de Gaulle to power a second time. In 1959 and 1962 revolts by French generals in the city failed to overthrow de Gaulle. In the last months before Algeria gained independence (1962) there were frequent bombings by the Organization of the Secret Army (OAS), French terrorists, and many of the city's industrial and communications facilities were damaged. The city is to continue as headquarters of the new republic until the administrative center at Rocher Noir is completed. The principal exports of Algiers are wine, citrus fruit, and iron ore. The city has chemical and light metallurgical industries.

Algoa Bay (ălgō′ů), arm of the Indian Ocean, indenting SE Cape Prov., Republic of South Africa.

Street in the Casbah of Algiers.

Modern section of the city of Algiers near the harbor.

Discovered by the Portuguese in the late 15th cent., it was used as an anchorage. Port Elizabeth is on the shore of the bay.

Algoma (ălgō′mŭ), city (pop. 3,855), NE Wis., S of Sturgeon Bay; settled 1851, inc. 1879. Wood products and hammocks are made. A teachers college is here.

Algona (ălgō′nŭ). **1** City (pop. 5,702), co. seat of Kossuth co., N Iowa, on the Des Moines river and N of Fort Dodge, in a farm area; settled 1854, inc. 1872. A local building was designed by Louis Sullivan. Varied products are manufactured in Algona. A state park is nearby. **2** City (pop. 1,311), W central Wash., E of Tacoma.

Algonac (ăl′gŭnăk), resort village (pop. 3,190), SE Mich., on the St. Clair and NE of Detroit; inc. 1867. It has long been a shipbuilding center and makes speedboats and marine hardware. A state park is nearby.

Algonquian (ălgŏng′kwĕŭn, –kĕŭn), linguistic family of North America. It was one of the most widespread of Indian linguistic stocks; in historical times tribes speaking the languages extended from coast to coast. The culture of the various peoples of the Algonquian family varied with their location; some were hunters, some were fishermen, and others were food gatherers. Generalizations about them are usually based on the tribes of the Atlantic

Blackfoot Indians, members of the Algonquian family.

seaboard and Canada which have been longest known to the whites. Some of the peoples of the Algonquian family may be listed as Algonquin (from whom the name Algonquian is taken), Abnaki, Montagnais, Massachuset, Mahican, Micmac, Narragansett, Pennacook, Penobscot, Wampanoag, Wappinger, Delaware, Chickahominy, Powhatan, Shawnee, Potawatami, Menominee, Cree, Ojibwa, Ottawa, Arapaho, Blackfoot, and Cheyenne (see also LANGUAGE, table). The name also appears as Algonkian.

Algonquin, village (pop. 2,014), NE Ill., on the Fox river and N of Elgin, in a dairy and resort region; inc. 1890. It has some industry.

Algonquin Indians (ălgŏng′kwĭn, –kĭn), North American Indian tribe. The name of the ALGONQUIAN linguistic stock (to which they belong) is derived from their name. A small tribe of Canada, they were among the first Indians with whom the French formed alliances, and their name was used to designate other tribes in the area. Despite French aid, they were dispersed in the 17th cent. by the Iroquois, and the remnants of the tribe found refuge chiefly near white settlements in Quebec and Ontario. Little remains of Algonquin culture. The name is also spelled Algonkin.

Algonquin Provincial Park, 2,741 sq. mi., S Ont., Canada, set aside in 1893 as a game preserve and public recreation area. It is on the watershed between the Ottawa river and Georgian Bay and is a region of fine forests, innumerable lakes, and many clear streams.

Algren, Nelson, 1909–, American novelist, b. Detroit, educated at the Univ. of Illinois. He grew up in Chicago, and much of his fiction is laid in the slums. His novels— *Never Come Morning* (1942), *The Man with the Golden Arm* (1949), and *A Walk on the Wild Side* (1956)—and short stories in *The Neon Wilderness* (1948) are brutally realistic.

algum: see ALMUG.

Alhambra (ălhăm′brŭ), city (pop. 54,807), S Calif., ENE of Los Angeles; founded 1881, inc. 1903. Its manufactures include aircraft parts, electronic equipment, and plastics.

Alhambra [Arabic,=the red], extensive group of buildings on a hill overlooking Granada, Spain.

The Court of Lions of the Alhambra.

They were built chiefly between 1230 and 1354 and they formed a great citadel of the Moorish kings of Spain. After the expulsion of the Moors in 1492, the structures suffered mutilation, but were extensively restored after 1828. The Alhambra is a true expression of the once flourishing Moorish civilization and is the finest example of its architecture in Spain. It comprises citadel-remains, the so-called palace of the kings, and the quarters once used by officials. The halls and chambers surround a series of open courts, which include the Court of Lions containing arcades resting on 124 white marble columns. The interior of the building is adorned sumptuously with magnificent examples of the so-called honeycomb and stalactite vaulting; its walls and ceilings are decorated with geometric ornament of great minuteness and intricacy, executed with surpassing skill in marble, alabaster, glazed tile, and carved plaster. See Washington Irving, *Legends of the Alhambra* (1832); A. F. Calvert, *The Alhambra* (1907).

Ali (ä'lē, älē'), 600?–661, fourth caliph (656–61). He was the son of Abu Talib, Mohammed's uncle, but was more closely related to the Prophet as the husband of FATIMA. One of the Prophet's most faithful followers, he was expected to become caliph on Mohammed's death, but Abu Bakr was chosen. Ali succeeded only on Othman's death. He was strongly opposed by AYESHA, who fomented a revolt in Iraq. This Ali put down, but he was never able to suppress MUAWIYA. Ali was murdered at Kufa by fanatics (the Kharijites), and his son HASAN abdicated in favor of Muawiya. The division in Islam between SUNNITES and SHIITES comes from the time of Ali. He and his son Husein are the great saints of the Shiites.

Aliah (älī'ù): see ALVAH.

Alian (älī'ùn): see ALVAN.

Alibamu Indians (ălĭbă'mōō), North American Indian tribe of the Uto-Aztecan linguistic stock. They lived in S Alabama in the early 18th cent. and were members of the Creek confederacy. During the 19th cent. they moved to W Louisiana. Alabama takes its name from them.

Ali Bey: see BADIA Y LEBLICH, DOMINGO.

Alicante (älēkän'tä), city (pop. 105,525), capital of Alicante prov., SE Spain, in Valencia. A Mediterranean port and resort, it exports wine, oil, cereals, fruit, and esparto from the fertile surrounding region. After reconquest (c.1250) from the Moors, the city was contested between Castile and Aragon until it went to Aragon in 1309.

Alice, city (pop. 20,861), co. seat of Jim Wells co., S Texas, W of Corpus Christi; inc. 1910. Long a cow town at a railroad junction, Alice still ships cattle. Oil wells and farms are in the vicinity. The unincorporated village of Alice Southwest (pop. 1,813) is adjacent.

Alice Springs, town (pop. 4,000), Northern Territory, central Commonwealth of Australia, in a pastoral area nearly in the center of the continent and at the terminus of the Central Australian RR. Formerly called Stuart, it was (1926–31) the capital of Central Australia, a former subdivision of the Northern Territory. There is opal mining.

Aliceville, town (pop. 3,194), W Ala., WSW of Tuscaloosa and near the Tombigbee, in a farm area; inc. 1907. It has textile mills.

alien, person not belonging to the sociological or political group with which he is in physical association. The attitude of the group toward aliens is a matter of custom, usage, and law. All modern governments have laws covering the rights and privileges of aliens, and there is a large body of international law on the subject. A state has the right to exclude undesirable aliens, and most states, including the United States, forbid the admission of criminals, paupers, and the diseased. A state may exclude completely certain groups and nationalities, but such discrimination is likely to cause unfriendly feelings. From the right to exclude aliens proceeds the right to establish the conditions upon which they will be admitted and to make special laws concerning them. An alien, while he resides in a country, is subject to the laws of that country and not to those of his own country, except in the case of EXTERRITORIALITY jurisdiction. A state distinguishes between aliens who are merely traveling or living there temporarily and those who have come to stay or to earn their livelihood, and wider powers are assumed over the second class. Such aliens are subject to taxation and may even be drafted to serve in the national defense. An alien, though he be under the laws of the country in which he resides, still owes ALLEGIANCE to his own country and as a citizen may call upon it to intercede if he feels that the country in which he lives has failed properly to protect his person or property. The home state usually points out or protests injustice, but it may threaten reprisals. Such situations have frequently caused international dispute, and there is controversy as to how far a nation is justified in interfering in behalf of its nationals abroad. On the other hand, an alien may find ASYLUM in the country to which he has fled unless treaties of EXTRADITION provide for the DEPORTATION of such refugees. A state also

Alicante

has the right to expel an alien who was once admitted. As population in a state increases and the competition for livelihood becomes more intense, hospitality towards the alien tends to change to hostility. This process was seen in the United States in more restrictive IMMIGRATION laws and more stringent deportation laws. In time of war the laws governing aliens are stricter, and special restrictions usually govern enemy aliens. Treaties between most of the important governments of the world provide that in case of war a reasonable period should be given enemy citizens in either country to withdraw under supervision. After this time the remaining enemy aliens may be expelled or may be permitted to remain under whatever conditions the government chooses to impose. Thus, in the Second World War, enemy aliens in the United States were required to register, were excluded from certain areas, and in some cases confined to camps. Aliens are required to register each year under the Immigration and Nationality Act of 1952.

Alien and Sedition Acts, 1798, four laws enacted by the Federalist-controlled U.S. Congress, allegedly in response to the hostile actions of the French Revolutionary government on the seas and in the councils of diplomacy (see XYZ AFFAIR). The legislation was actually designed to destroy Thomas Jefferson's Republican party, which had openly expressed its Francophile sympathies. Depending on recent arrivals from Europe for much of their voting strength, the Republicans were adversely affected by the Naturalization Act, which postponed citizenship, and thus voting privileges, until the completion of 14 (rather than 5) years of residence, and by the Alien Act and the Alien Enemies Act, which provided, among other things, for strict supervision of new immigrants and gave the President complete control over all aliens who, in his opinion, posed a danger to the national government. President John Adams made no use of the alien acts. Most controversial, however, was the Sedition Act, devised to silence Republican criticism of the Federalists. Its broad proscription of spoken or written criticism of the government, the Congress, or the President virtually nullified the First Amendment freedoms of speech and the press. Prominent Jeffersonians, most of them journalists, such as John Daly Burk, James T. Callender, Thomas COOPER, William DUANE (1760–1835), and Matthew LYON were tried, and some were convicted, in sedition proceedings. The Alien and Sedition Acts provoked the KENTUCKY AND VIRGINIA RESOLUTIONS and did much to foster Republican victory in the election of 1800. See John C. Miller, *Crisis in Freedom* (1951); James Morton Smith, *Freedom's Fetters* (1956).

Aligarh (ŭlēgŭr′), city (pop. 141,618), Uttar Pradesh state, N India. An important agricultural trade center, it also has cotton mills. Aligarh is chiefly famous for its university, opened in 1875 as Anglo-Oriental College, which is the leading school of Indian Moslems. There are ancient Buddhist remains and numerous Moslem buildings. The native name is Koil.

alimentary canal, the gastrointestinal tract, about 30 ft. long in the human adult, through which the swallowing, DIGESTION, assimilation, and elimina-

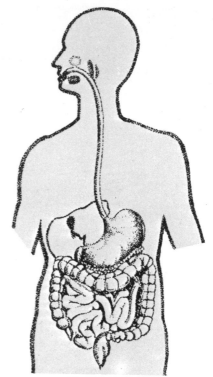

Alimentary canal

tion of food are accomplished. Beginning at the MOUTH, all food must pass through the pharynx, esophagus, STOMACH, and INTESTINES (small and large) before it reaches the rectum as waste matter to be eliminated. The outer walls of the alimentary canal are comprised of layers of muscle and tissue which by contraction (peristalsis) push the food along the gastrointestinal path. The inner lining contains glands that secrete the acids and enzymes necessary for the breakdown of food before it can be utilized by the body.

alimony, in law, allowance for support which by order of a court a husband pays to his wife who is not living with him. Temporary alimony is allowed pending the outcome of a suit for DIVORCE, for SEPARATION, or for a decree of NULLITY OF MARRIAGE, whether the wife be plaintiff or defendant. Permanent alimony is the allowance to the wife after the action has been tried and the decree rendered. Laws concerning the award of alimony vary greatly in the states of the United States. Usually it is not allowed in annulments. It is allowed after separation by judicial decree, but in some states only if the wife is not the guilty party and in others at the discretion of the court. Alimony originally was not granted after a divorce, but the contrary practice is now general in the United States. Alimony ceases on the death of the husband, because it is not payable out of his estate unless there are arrears. Although remarriage does not necessarily terminate alimony, the amount may be reduced or cut off at the court's discretion if the second husband is able to support the wife. In all cases the amount of, and the continuing need for, alimony are questions which can always be reopened in a court having jurisdiction over the parties. The rule that the husband cannot obtain alimony from the wife has been changed in a few states but for the most part holds, since the wife generally has no duty to support the husband. A decree awarding alimony is a court order issued to the husband personally, and failure to pay constitutes CONTEMPT OF COURT.

Alingsas, Swed. *Alingsås* (ä″lĭngsōs), city (pop. 17,763), Alvsborg prov., SW Sweden. It is an industrial center, with leather and textile factories, breweries, foundries, and electrical works. It was chartered in 1619.

Ali Pasha (ä′lē päshä′), 1744?–1822, Turkish military governor, the pasha of Yannina (now Ioannina), called the Lion [Turkish *Arslan*] of Yannina. His father, governor at Tepelene in S Albania, was murdered, and Ali went to live with the mountaineer brigands who infested the country. He soon rose to leadership among them, came to the attention of the Turkish government, and as its agent put down the rebellion of a governor at Scutari in Albania. About 1787 he became governor of Yannina, where his power grew until he ruled as a quasi-independent despot over most of Albania and Epirus. He made war on the French along the Adriatic coast and entered an alliance (1814) with Great Britain. Valuing Ali's services, the Porte let him do as he wished, until in 1820 Ali ordered the assassination of an opponent in Constantinople. Mahmud II ordered him deposed. Ali refused to comply, thus keeping Turkish troops engaged against him while they were needed against the Greeks, who had begun their fight for independence. Ali was assassinated by an agent of the Porte; his head was exhibited at Constantinople. The rugged court of Ali was described by French and English visitors, notably by Byron in *Childe Harold*.

Aliquippa (ălĭkwĭp′ù), borough (pop. 26,369), W Pa., on the Ohio river, in an industrial region NW of Pittsburgh; inc. 1894. Aliquippa grew after the expansion of steel mills in 1909. A large Jones & Laughlin Steel Corp. plant is here.

Alisal, Calif.: see SALINAS.

alizarin (ùlĭz′ùrĭn) [from Arabic, =juice], mordant vegetable dye, a compound of carbon, hydrogen, and oxygen obtained originally from the root of the madder plant (*Rubia tinctorum*). The term also includes a group of synthetic dyestuffs prepared from coal-tar derivatives. A method for the synthesis of alizarin was first discovered (1868) by Karl Graebe and Karl LIEBERMANN, German chemists. With salts of metals the compound forms brilliant lakes (see LAKE), although by itself it is a poor dye. Turkey red is produced with an aluminum mordant, other shades of red with calcium and tin salts, dark violet with iron mordants, and brownish red with chromium. Purpurin, also used in dyeing, occurs with alizarin in madder and is produced synthetically.

Aljubarrota (älzhōōbùrô′tù), village (pop. c.500), Leiria dist., W central Portugal, S of Leiria. Here was fought on Aug. 14, 1385, the momentous battle in which the Portuguese, aided by English archers, defeated the forces of the Spanish King John I of Castile, thus assuring Portuguese independence and making possible the vigorous administration of John I of Portugal. Nun'Álvares Pereira was the Portuguese hero of the battle.

alkali (ăl′kùlĭ) [ultimately from Arabic, *al gili=* ashes of saltwort, which contain much soda], a water-soluble, highly ionized, metallic hydroxide (see BASE). Alkalies exhibit marked basic properties, having a characteristically acrid taste; they neutralize acids to form salts and water. Strong alkalies, e.g., sodium hydroxide and potassium hydroxide, are commonly called caustic alkalies. They are used commercially in the manufacture of SOAP, cotton goods, and paper. Sodium hydroxide for household use is sold under the name LYE. The **alkali metals,** a group so called because the members all react violently with water to form strong bases, include the univalent (see VALENCE) elements CESIUM, RUBIDIUM, POTASSIUM, SODIUM, and LITHIUM. These all belong to group I A of the PERIODIC TABLE. They are soft and have low melting points; their reactivity accounts for the fact that they occur naturally only in the compounds. The **alkaline earths,** which are a group of oxides resembling the alkalies in character, include the oxides of barium, strontium, and calcium (see LIME) and also sometimes that of magnesium. Each of these oxides reacts with water to form the hydroxide of its constituent metal. The active, divalent metals themselves are termed the metals of the alkaline earths. **Alkali soils** contain an excess of the soluble salts natural to all soils (see SOIL).

alkaloid (–loid), any of a class of organic compounds composed of carbon, hydrogen, nitrogen, and usually oxygen and derived from plants. Although the name means alkalilike, some alkaloids, i.e., ricinine, do not exhibit alkaline properties. Many alkaloids, though poisons, have physiological effects that render them valuable as medicines. For example, curarine, found in the deadly extract CURARE, is a powerful muscle relaxant; ATROPINE is used to dilate the pupils of the eyes; and physostigmine is a specific for certain muscular diseases. Narcotic alkaloids used in medicine include MORPHINE and CODEINE for the relief of pain and COCAINE as a local anesthetic. Other common alkaloids include QUININE, CAFFEINE, NICOTINE, and STRYCHNINE. Aconitine is the alkaloid of ACONITE. Cinchonine and quinine are derived from CINCHONA, coniine is found in poison HEMLOCK, and reserpine is an extract of rauwolfia roots. Emetine is an alkaloid of IPECAC.

alkalosis: see ACIDOSIS.

Al-Khowarizmi (äl-khōwärēz′mē), fl. 820, Arabian mathematician of the court of Mamun in Baghdad. His treatises on Hindu arithmetic and on algebra made him famous. He is said to have given algebra its name, and the word *algorism* is said to have been derived from his name. Much of the mathematical knowledge of medieval Europe was derived from Latin translations of his works.

Al-Kindi: see KINDI.

Alkmaar (älk′mär), town (estimated pop. 43,208), in North Holland prov., NW Netherlands. An important market center, it has varied industries. The cheese market of Alkmaar, held weekly in

The cheese market in Alkmaar.

front of the ancient weighhouse, is world famous. Chartered in 1254, it was besieged by the Spanish under Alba in 1573.

alkyl: see RADICAL.

Allah (ă′lŭ, ä′lŭ), Arabic name of GOD. It is used not only in ISLAM but also among Arabic-speaking Christians. The name Allah was well known in pre-Islamic Arabia, when religion there was polytheistic. It was the Prophet MOHAMMED who emphasized the uniqueness of the god Allah and introduced the idea of monotheism to Arabia. See S. M. Zwemer, *The Moslem Doctrine of God* (1905); F. M. Fitch, *Allah, the God of Islam* (1950); Daud Rahbar, *God of Justice* (1960).

Allahabad (ăl″ŭhŭbăd′, –băd′), city (pop. c.431,-000), Uttar Pradesh state, India. On the site of Prayag, an ancient Indo-Aryan holy city, Allahabad is at the junction of two sacred rivers, the Jumna and the Ganges, and is visited by many Hindu pilgrims. The oldest monument is a pillar (c.242 B.C.) with inscriptions from the reign of Asoka. The city was the scene of much fighting in the Sepoy Rebellion (1857). Allahabad was the capital of the United Provs. from 1901 to 1949. It is a trading center and has a university.

All-American Canal, SE Calif.; built 1934–40. A part of the Federal irrigation system of the Hoover Dam, it taps the Colorado river at Imperial Dam c.20 mi. above Yuma, Ariz., and runs 80 mi. west to a point beyond Calexico, Calif. Three main canals, diverting from the All-American Canal, supply water to the IMPERIAL VALLEY. The Coachella Canal, completed in 1948, diverts from the All-American 36 mi. from its head and carries water 123 mi. N and E to the Coachella Valley.

Allan, Sir Hugh, 1810–82, Canadian financier and shipowner, b. Scotland. He emigrated to Canada in 1826, was employed by a large shipbuilding company in Montreal, and later founded the Allan line of steamships. He was given the contract to build the Canadian Pacific Railway, but the PACIFIC SCANDAL (1873) led to its cancellation.

Allegan (ăl′ĭgăn), city (pop. 4,822), co. seat of Allegan co., SW Mich., on the Kalamazoo river SSW of Grand Rapids, in a farm region; settled 1834, inc. as a village 1838, as a city 1907. Automobile parts are made. A state forest is near.

Allegany (ăl′ŭgă″nē, ăl″ŭgă′nē), village (pop. 2,064), SW N.Y., on the Allegheny river and W of Olean, in an oil region; inc. 1906. St. Bonaventure Univ. (Roman Catholic; coeducational; 1855) is nearby, as are a state park and the Allegany Indian Reservation.

Alleghany, variant spelling: see ALLEGHENY.

Allegheny (ăl′ŭgă″nē, ăl″ŭgā′nē), river rising in N central Pennsylvania and flowing NW into New York, thence generally southwest c.325 mi. to the Monongahela, forming the Ohio, at Pittsburgh. Before the advent of railroads, the river was an important channel of commerce and is still used to some extent in the transport of bulky freight. Dams on the river's tributaries include the Crooked Creek (165 ft. high; 1,450 ft. long; completed 1940) on Crooked Creek and the Mahoning (completed 1941) on Mahoning Creek. Work was begun in 1960 on the Allegheny River Dam. See Frederick Way, Jr., *The Allegheny* (1942).

Allegheny College: see MEADVILLE, Pa.

Allegheny Mountains, a western part of the Appalachian Mts., extending SW from N Pennsylvania through Maryland, West Virginia, and Virginia. The heights vary from c.2,000 ft. in the north to over 4,000 ft. in the south. The eastern portion of the range, with a steep escarpment often called the Allegheny Front (c.1500–1600 ft. high), is generally more rugged than the western portion, which is a plateau reaching into E Ohio and Kentucky. The Allegheny upland, like the Cumberland upland into which it extends on the south, was largely formed by the folding of sedimentary rocks. There

Allegheny Mountains

by birth within the bounds of a political society; express allegiance arises from an oath or promise to support a political society and usually results from NATURALIZATION; local allegiance is the temporary allegiance one may owe a government when residing under its protection as an alien; and legal allegiance arises from an oath taken in certain cases to support a government temporarily, as when a foreign soldier joints its armed forces or when areas are taken by an enemy and such an oath is administered to the remaining inhabitants. Under the customary law of Europe a subject did not have the right to change his allegiance without the consent of his government, but in the 19th cent., under the lead of the United States, this conception was challenged, and the right of all persons to choose the government to which they wished to give allegiance was partly established. Great Britain in 1870 gave British citizens the right to expatriate themselves, and Sweden, Denmark, Germany, and other European states followed, but the right of EXPATRIATION is by no means universally allowed.

allegory, in literature, symbolic story that serves as a disguised representation for other meanings than those indicated on the surface. The characters of an allegory often have no individual personality, but are embodiments of moral qualities and other abstractions. Allegory is closely related to the parable, fable, and metaphor, differing from them largely in intricacy and length. A great variety of literary forms have been used for the allegory. The medieval morality play *Everyman*, personifying such abstractions as Fellowship and Good Deeds, recounts the death journey of Everyman. John Bunyan's *Pilgrim's Progress*, a prose narrative, is an allegory of man's spiritual salvation. Spenser's poem *The Faerie Queene*, besides being a chivalric romance, is a commentary on morals and manners

has been much subsequent erosion and leveling. The Alleghenies are rich in coal and contain iron, petroleum, and natural gas.

allegiance, formal tie which binds one to a superior, whether a person or an institution. The term usually refers to allegiance to governments, but it may have reference to any institution which one is bound to support. Allegiance in strict usage is a legal tie, but as used in ordinary speech the term includes also those emotional ties which supplement the legal one, and thus it is synonymous with loyalty. Allegiance to the government is due from both CITIZENS and subjects, and may be of four kinds: natural allegiance arises from membership

The confluence of the Allegheny and Monongahela rivers at the Golden Triangle at Pittsburgh, Pa.

in 16th-century England as well as a national epic. Although allegory is still used by some authors, its popularity as a literary form has declined in recent times in favor of a more personal form of symbolic expression (see SYMBOLISTS).

Alleluia, Latin form of the expression HALLELUJAH.

Allemands (äl'mŭnz), uninc. village (pop. 1,167), SE La., on Bayou des Allemands and WSW of New Orleans.

Allen, Ethan, 1738–89, hero of the American Revolution, leader of the Green Mountain Boys, and promoter of the independence and statehood of Vermont, b. Litchfield (?), Conn. He had some schooling and was proud of his deist opinions, with which he annoyed orthodox Congregational ministers. He later incorporated his ideas in *Reason the Only Oracle of Man* (1784). A man of Gargantuan strength with a taste for showy clothes and manners and great volubility of speech, he was a born leader. After fighting briefly in the French and Indian Wars, he interested himself in land speculation, and in 1770 he appeared as one of the proprietors in the NEW HAMPSHIRE GRANTS. He and his brothers, notably Ira ALLEN, became the leaders of the New England settlers and speculators in the disputed lands—inveterate enemies of the Yorkers (settlers under New York patents) and violent opponents of all attempts of New York to exert control in the area. He was active in forming the GREEN MOUNTAIN BOYS and became their leader in defying the New York government and harrying the Yorkers. Governor Tryon of New York put a price on the heads of Allen and two of his followers, but Ethan was not captured. After the outbreak of the American Revolution, he made the Green Mountain Boys into an independent patriot organization. Joined by Benedict ARNOLD (with a commission from Massachusetts) and some Connecticut militia, Ethan Allen and his men captured Fort Ticonderoga from the British on May 10, 1775. Legend says that when the British officer asked him under what authority he acted, Ethan Allen roared, "In the name of the Great Jehovah and the Continental Congress!" The story is, however, almost certainly apocryphal. Allen then urged an expedition against Canada, and the Green Mountain Boys were attached to Gen. P. J. Schuyler's invasion force, but the men chose not Allen, but his cousin Seth WARNER, as leader. Allen went on the expedition and in a rash plan to capture Montreal before the main patriot army arrived was captured (Sept., 1775) by the British. He told his own story of this in the popular *Narrative of Colonel Ethan Allen's Captivity*, which appeared in 1779, a year after he had been exchanged. He returned to VERMONT, which had declared its independence but was unrecognized by the Continental Congress. Ethan and his brother Ira then devoted themselves to insuring the new political unit in one way or another. The region remained in danger of British attack, and the British late in 1779 opened negotiations with Ethan Allen in an attempt to attach Vermont to Canada. Ethan and his brother entered into devious negotiations with the British agents and Tories either with the serious intent of annexation to Canada or with the aim of protecting Vermont and enhancing its value to the United States. No conclusion was reached, and the victory at Yorktown ending the American Revolution also ended the talks. Ethan Allen withdrew from politics in 1784, and Vermont was still independent and still dickering with Congress and dealing with internal struggles between the Allen party and their opponents when he died at Burlington. He is remembered as a salty, colorful leader, a strong adherent to the principles of individual liberty, and the fiery defender of the men of the Vermont country. See Matt B. Jones, *Vermont in the Making* (1939); biography by Stewart Holbrook (1940).

Allen, Frederick Lewis, 1890–1954, American social historian and editor, b. Boston, grad. Harvard (B.A., 1912; M.A., 1913). After teaching English at Harvard, he was an assistant editor of the *Atlantic Monthly* (1914–16), then managing editor of *The Century* (1916–17). After wartime service with the Council of National Defense, Allen returned to editorial work with *Harper's Magazine*, where he remained until 1953, becoming chief editor in 1941. His historical writing has been criticized as journalistic but is nonetheless penetrating social history. His works include *Only Yesterday* (1932), *The Lords of Creation* (1935), *Since Yesterday* (1940), *The Great Pierpont Morgan* (1949) and *The Big Change* (1952).

Allen, Hervey, 1889–1949, American novelist and poet, b. Pittsburgh, grad. Univ. of Pittsburgh, 1915, and studied at Harvard, 1920–22. After service in the First World War he taught English

Ethan Allen in prison.

in Charleston, S.C., where in collaboration with DuBose Heyward he wrote *Carolina Chansons* (1922). He wrote other volumes of poetry, but is best known for his biography of Poe, *Israfel* (1926), and the picaresque novel *Anthony Adverse* (1933), which achieved enormous popular success. Later he undertook but did not live to complete a series of novels about the early American frontier.

Allen, Horatio, 1802–89, American civil and mechanical engineer, b. Schenectady, N.Y., grad. Columbia, 1823. In Aug., 1829 he operated the first steam locomotive in the United States to run on rails. This was the *Stourbridge Lion,* built by the English engineer George STEPHENSON and brought to America after being purchased by the Delaware & Hudson Company. Later he specialized in marine engines, becoming one of the foremost designers of steamboats. He served as chief engineer and as president of the Erie RR and as consulting engineer for the Panama RR and for the Brooklyn Bridge.

Allen, Ira, 1751–1814, political leader in early Vermont, b. Cornwall, Conn. He was the younger brother and the assistant of Ethan ALLEN. Though he was a member of the GREEN MOUNTAIN BOYS, he took little part in their activities. His cool shrewdness, his adeptness in business matters, and his brilliant planning complemented the colorful vigor and rash violence of his brother. He organized the Onion River Land Company and secured the lands about the Winooski and Lake Champlain that the Allens worked hard to protect. He took part in the conventions at Dorset and Westminster that brought about the independence of VERMONT, and he was a leading figure in its political life in the years following, holding many offices. He was involved in the long negotiations with the British and was accused of treason. After Vermont became a state he was forced out of politics. He helped to establish the Univ. of Vermont. In 1798 Allen published his *Natural and Political History of the State of Vermont.* See biography by J. B. Wilbur (1928).

Allen, James Lane, 1849–1925, American novelist, b. Lexington Kentucky, grad. Transylvania College, 1872. Among his "genteel" novels are *A Kentucky Cardinal* (1894), *Aftermath* (1895), and *The Choir Invisible* (1897). See study by G. C. Knight (1935).

Allen, Richard, 1760–1831, founder of the African Methodist Episcopal Church. He was born a slave in Philadelphia. He became pastor of a Negro group, which had seceded from the Methodist Episcopal Church in Philadelphia. When the African Methodist Episcopal Church was organized nationally (1816), Allen was consecrated its first bishop.

Allen, William, 1704–80, American jurist, b. Philadelphia. He and his father-in-law, Andrew Hamilton, decided the choice of Philadelphia instead of Chester as provincial capital, and he helped finance the building of Independence Hall. Allen was (1750–74) chief justice of Pennsylvania, secured (1763) postponement of the sugar duties, and helped (1765) Franklin's efforts to have the Stamp Act repealed. He wrote *The American Crisis* (1774), containing a plan for colonial reconciliation with England. When it was not accepted, he made

his home in England. Allentown, Pa., was named for him.

Allen, Zachariah, 1795–1882, American inventor, b. Providence, R.I., grad. Brown, 1813. He devised belt drives to be used instead of cogwheels for transmitting power and invented an automatic cutoff valve for steam engines. He is credited with developing, in 1821, the first hot-air system for the central heating of homes and buildings.

Allen, town (pop. 1,005), S central Okla., near the Canadian river and SE of Oklahoma City.

Allen, Bog of, area of morass and peat bog with patches of cultivable land, near the center of Ireland, in Counties Offaly, Laois, and Kildare.

Allen, Lough (lŏkh, lŏk), lake, 8 mi. long and 3 mi. wide, Co. Leitrim and Co. Roscommon, N Republic of Ireland, near the headwaters of the Shannon.

Allenby, Edmund Henry Hynman Allenby, 1st **Viscount,** (ă'lŭnbē), 1861–1936, British field marshal, educated at Sandhurst. After active service in Bechuanaland (1884–85) and Zululand (1888) and in the South African War (1899–1902) he commanded the cavalry in France on the outbreak of the First World War (1914) and then the 3d Army (1915–17). As commander of the Egyptian Expeditionary Force (1917–19), he waged the last of the great cavalry campaigns by invading Palestine, capturing Jerusalem, and ending Turkish resistance after the battle of Samaria (Sept. 18–21, 1918). He served as British high commissioner for Egypt and the Sudan (1919–25). He was made viscount in 1919. See A. P. Wavell, *Allenby* (1941) and *Allenby in Egypt* (1945).

Allendale. 1 Borough (pop. 4,092), NE N.J., NNE of Paterson; settled 1740, inc. 1894. **2** Town (pop. 3,114), co. seat of Allendale co., SW S.C., near the Savannah SW of Orangeburg, in a hunting and fishing area; inc. 1873. Textile and lumber products are made.

Allende, Ignacio (ēgnä'syō äyän'dä), 1779–1811, Mexican revolutionist. He was a captain in the army when he entered into the movement against Spanish control. He played a prominent part in the revolution and after the great defeat at Calderón Bridge (Jan. 17, 1811) took chief command of the forces, leaving Miguel HIDALGO Y COSTILLA, with whom he had quarreled, only nominal power. The revolutionists went northward, hoping to reach the United States, but the treachery of one of their leaders led to capture by the royalists. Allende was shot at Chihuahua.

Allen Park, city (pop. 37,494), SE Mich., a suburb SW of Detroit; settled c.1819, inc. as a village 1927, as a city 1957. Tubing, alloys, and metal products are among its manufactures.

Allenstein (ä'lŭnshtīn) or **Olsztyn** (ôl'shtĭn), city (estimated pop. 64,300), N Poland (since 1945), formerly in East Prussia. It is a trade, manufacturing, and railroad center. Founded (1348) by the Teutonic Knights, who built its impressive castle, it was ceded to Poland in 1466 and to Prussia in 1772. Allenstein was retained by Germany after a plebiscite in 1920. The city, which suffered heavy damage in the Second World War, was entirely resettled by Poles after 1945 and was made the capital of Olsztyn prov.

Allenstown, town (pop. 1,789), S N.H., on the Suncook river and SE of Concord; granted 1722, settled c.1748, inc. 1831. Timber for the U.S.S. *Constitution* was cut here. The town includes the unincorporated village of Blodgett (pop. 1,489).

Allentown. 1 Borough (pop. 1,393), E central N.J., SSE of Princeton. **2** Industrial city (pop. 108,347), co. seat of Lehigh co., E Pa., on the Lehigh river and N of Philadelphia; laid out 1762 as Northampton, inc. as a borough 1811, renamed Allentown c. 1836, inc. as a city 1867. In the Pennsylvania Dutch region, it is a trading center for farmers. Machinery, clothing, truck and bus bodies, textiles, and cement are made. One of the largest county fairs in the country is held here each September. Allentown is the seat of Cedar Crest College (United Church of Christ; for women; 1867) and Muhlenberg College (Lutheran; coeducational; 1848). A flourishing town before 1790, it was settled by representatives of various German religious groups. The Liberty Bell was brought here (1777) for safekeeping, and the city became a munitions center for the Continental army. Civil War recruits from the city were so numerous that they became known as "the First Defenders."

Alleppey (ŭlĕp'ē), town, Kerala state, India, a port on the Arabian Sea. Copra and jute are its chief exports.

allergy, altered reaction of the body tissues of certain individuals to exposure to certain substances which, in similar amounts and circumstances, are innocuous to other persons. These substances (antigens or allergens) stimulate the production of antibodies in the sensitive individual, who may show allergic sensitivity to one substance or to several. Allergens can be air-borne substances (e.g., pollens, dust, smoke), infectious agents (bacteria, fungi, parasites), foods (strawberries, chocolate, eggs), contactants (poison ivy, chemicals, dyes), or physical agents (light, heat, cold). Inhalants as a rule affect the respiratory system, the reaction manifesting itself as asthma or hay fever. Contactants involve the skin, causing wheals and rashes. Foods and other allergens may also affect the skin, or may act on the gastrointestinal tract, causing nausea and vomiting. The best treatment of allergic reactions is prevention, i.e., elimination of the offending substances from the sensitive person's environment. If this is not possible, desensitization (i.e., deliberate production of the allergic reaction by injecting the allergen, after which the sufferer is no longer susceptible) is sometimes helpful. Antihistamine drugs may give temporary relief. See ANTIBODY and HISTAMINES.

Allerton, Isaac (ăl'ŭrtŭn), c.1586–1659, Pilgrim settler in Plymouth Colony. Possibly a London tailor, he had been a merchant in Leiden before coming to America on the *Mayflower*. From 1626 to 1631 he was often in England, acting as the agent of the colony, and there he bought up the rights of merchants in the enterprise and in 1630 secured a new patent (see PLYMOUTH COLONY)— but not the sort of grant William Bradford and others wanted. Allerton was at best incompetent and ran up the debt, even if he was not—as his neighbors accused him of being—dishonest. He probably left Plymouth Colony in 1631 and was later at Marblehead, at New Amsterdam, and in the New Haven colony.

Alleyn, Edward (ăl'ĭn), 1566–1626, English actor.

He was the foremost member of the ADMIRAL'S MEN, joining the group c.1587, and was the only rival of Richard Burbage. He gained fame for his portrayals in Marlowe's *Tamburlaine, Jew of Malta,* and *Faustus.* He married the stepdaughter of Philip Henslowe and with him owned the Rose and Fortune Theatres. His popularity brought him wealth, which he employed in the founding (1613) of Dulwich College and in aiding contemporary writers. After his wife's death, he married a daughter of John Donne.

Allia (ă'lēŭ), small river, in Latium, central Italy. Near its confluence with the Tiber, N of Rome, the Gauls defeated the Romans in 390 B.C.

Alliance. 1 City (pop. 7,845), co. seat of Box Butte co., NW Nebr., in the Great Plains region, NE of Scottsbluff; founded 1887 as the terminus of the Chicago, Burlington, & Quincy RR. A shipping and trade center for a large grain and livestock area, it has railroad repair shops and a seed-potato testing ground Farm machinery, electronic equipment and dairy goods are among its products. **2** City (pop. 28,362), NE Ohio, SE of Akron and on the Mahoning; laid out 1838 as Freedom, inc. as a village 1854, as a city 1889. It is an industrial, distributing, and rail center, with manufactures of steel, aircraft, heavy mill machinery, and other industrial equipment. It is the seat of Mount Union College (Methodist; coeducational; 1846), with Clarke Observatory.

Alliance for Progress (Alianza para Progreso), a program of economic assistance announced by President J. F. Kennedy in March, 1961, which is administered through a regional bureau of the U.S. Agency for International Development. The program was created in order to help solve the economic and social problems of Latin America. The Charter of the Alliance, formulated at the Inter-American Economic and Social Council conference at PUNTA DEL ESTE in August, 1961, envisioned a minimum annual increase of 2.5 percent in per capita income. To achieve this a capital investment of $80 billion over a period of ten years was pledged by the Latin American countries (excluding Cuba) who in turn agreed to carry out tax and land reforms. The United States agreed to supply or guarantee 60 percent of an additional $20 billion in outside financing. Private capital was asked to supply a yearly average of $300 million of this amount. A committee of experts nominated by the International Bank for Reconstruction and Development and the Economic and Social Council of the OAS was set up to coordinate requests for aid. See J. C. Dreier, ed., *The Alliance for Progress* (1962).

Allier (älyä'), department (2,850 sq. mi.; estimated pop. 372,689), central France, in BOURBONNAIS. Moulins (the capital), Montluçon, and VICHY are the chief towns. Drained by the Allier and Loire rivers, it is mainly a fertile agricultural plain. Industry is concentrated in the MONTLUÇON area.

Allier, river, rising in central France, Lozère dept., in the Cévennes. It flows c.255 mi. NW past Vichy and Moulins to join the Loire below Nevers.

alligator [Span.,=the lizard], large reptile similar to the CROCODILE; both animals belong to the order Crocodilia. The American alligator, which is about 12 to 14 ft. long, is found from North Carolina to

American alligator

iting later Dauphiné and Savoy. They were conquered (121 B.C.) by Quintus Fabius Maximus, who was called Allobrogicus. In the time of Julius Caesar they sided with Rome.

Allon [Heb.,=oak]. **1** Simeonite. 1 Chron. 4.37. **2** Naphtalite city. Joshua 19.33.

Allon-bachuth (–băk'ŭth) [Heb.,=oak of weeping], spot close to Bethel, where they buried Rebecca's nurse. Gen. 35.8.

allopathy (ŭlŏp'ŭthē) [Gr.,=other disease], term introduced by Samuel HAHNEMANN in the early 19th cent. to designate the regular, or established, school of medicine, as opposed to his own system of HOMEOPATHY.

allotropy (ŭlŏt'rŭpē) [Gr.,=other form], term indicating the occurrence of a chemical element in two or more forms. Allotropes differ in physical properties such as color and hardness. They may also differ in the number or arrangement of atoms in the molecule and in chemical activity, but they are alike in most other chemical properties. Diamond and graphite are two of the allotropic forms of CARBON. Among other elements that exhibit striking allotropism are OXYGEN, PHOSPHORUS, and SULFUR. An analogous phenomenon in the case of compounds is called POLYMORPHISM.

Allouez, Claude Jean (klōd' zhä' älwä'), 1622–89, French missionary in Canada and the Old Northwest, a Jesuit priest. After arriving (1658) in Canada he served at posts in the St. Lawrence region until 1665, when he went to Lake Superior and founded the Chequamegon Bay mission (near present Ashland, Wis.). A canoe trip around Lake Superior in 1667 supplied material for the well-known Jesuit map of the lake. Later he founded several missions, including that at De Pere, made his headquarters at Green Bay, and spent his last years as missionary to the Illinois and Miami Indians. His accurate and informed reports made the Great Lakes country known.

Alloway (ăl'–), village, Ayrshire, SW Scotland; it has been part of Ayr since 1935. The birthplace of Robert Burns and the scene of "Tam o' Shanter," it has a Burns museum and monument.

alloy (ăl'oi, ŭloi') [O. Fr.,=combine], substance having metallic properties and consisting of metal fused with one or more metals or nonmetals or with both. Upon cooling, the resultant alloy may be either a homogeneous solid solution, a heterogeneous mixture of tiny crystals, a compound, or any combination of these. Alloys have properties different from those of their constituent elements; e.g., they are poorer conductors of heat and electricity, often harder, and, with the exception of aluminum alloys, more resistant to corrosion. Because of these and other properties, alloys are used more extensively than pure metals. An alloy containing mercury is called an AMALGAM. Because gold is very soft it is usually alloyed with copper or silver. The proportion of gold is indicated in terms of carats; pure gold is 24 carats. Coin silver is 90 percent silver and 10 percent copper; sterling silver is 92.5 percent silver and 7.5 percent copper. Two important alloys of copper are BRASS and BRONZE. Nickel coins are made of an alloy of about 75 percent copper and 25 percent nickel. MONEL METAL is a nickel alloy. Iron is alloyed with carbon to form steel, the proportions being varied to suit the pur-

Florida and in the Gulf states. When young, it is dark brown or black with yellow transverse bands. These fade as the animal grows older, and the adult is black. Alligators eat fish and other water life; they are not known to attack man except in self defense. From 20 to 50 eggs are laid in a mound of vegetation. The demand for alligator leather has reduced the number of wild specimens. The Chinese species is smaller than the American. Closely related to the alligator is the cayman, or caiman, of Central and South America.

alligator pear: see AVOCADO.

Allingham, William (ăl'ĭngŭm), 1824–89, English poet, b. Donegal, Ireland. He is best known for his short lyrics, most notably "The Fairies," beginning "Up the airy mountain, Down the rushy glen."

Allison, William Boyd, 1829–1908, U.S. Senator from Iowa (1873–1908), b. Ashland co., Ohio, grad. Western Reserve College, 1849. He served (1863–71) in the House of Representatives and entered the Senate in 1873. One of the most influential Republican members of Congress, he spoke for the farmers of the Midwest and was considered a "moderate." Allison opposed high tariffs on goods needed in quantity by the farmers and helped to build compromise tariff bills. He changed the bill for "free and unlimited coinage" of silver to allow specified limited coinage and thus gave his name to the BLAND-ALLISON ACT. See biography by Leland Sage (1956).

Allison, uninc. village (pop. 1,285), SW Pa., S of Pittsburgh.

Alloa (ăl'lŏŭ), burgh (pop. 13,895), Clackmannanshire, central Scotland, on the river Forth. Mining, brewing, and bottle making are the principal industries. A 15th-century tower on Mar's Hill marks the seat of the Erskine earls of Mar.

Allobroges (ŭlŏ'brŭjēz), Celtic tribe in Gaul, inhab-

pose. Among the metals added to steel to form special purpose alloys are chromium, tungsten, and manganese.

All Saints, Nov. 1, feast of the Roman Catholic and Anglican churches, the day on which the church glorifies God for all his saints, known and unknown. Old names are Allhallows and Hallowmass. It is one of the principal feasts of the year in the Roman Catholic Church: all are obliged to hear Mass on it, and it has an octave and a vigil of fasting and abstinence. Its origin probably lies in the common commemoration of martyrs who died in groups or whose names were unknown. In the 7th cent. the Pantheon at Rome was dedicated to Our Lady and all martyrs, and before 900 All Saints was generally celebrated on Nov. 1. The vigil (Oct. 31), Halloween, is associated, in countries where Celtic influence is strong, with age-old customs peculiar to that night. In certain parts of the British Isles bonfires and fortunetelling like those of midsummer night continue. Elsewhere, especially in America, mumming and masquerading are popular, and jack-o'-lanterns are displayed. Tales of witches and ghosts are told, and in remote communities old superstitions are kept. One of the special games, bobbing for apples, is known to date from the Middle Ages. These pagan survivals of Halloween probably represent old Celtic practices associated with Nov. 1, the beginning of winter.

Probably All Saints rose apart from Celtic influence, and the customs of Halloween have survived independently of the Christian feast. ALL SOULS' DAY has no connection with Halloween.

All Saints Bay: see TODOS OS SANTOS BAY.

All Souls College: see OXFORD UNIVERSITY.

All Souls' Day, Nov. 2 (exceptionally, Nov. 3), feast of the Roman Catholic Church on which the church on earth prays for the souls of all the faithful departed still suffering in PURGATORY. The proper office is of the dead, and the Mass is a REQUIEM. All Souls' Day and Christmas are the only days of the year on which a priest may say three Masses. General suffrages for the departed, e.g., for those of a parish, a city, or a regiment, are very ancient (2 Mac. 12.43–45); but the modern feast was probably first established by an 11th-century abbot of Cluny for his community and later extended throughout the Church. In Catholic countries there are many customs peculiar to All Souls' Day, e.g., leaving lights in the cemeteries on the night before. These vary from region to region. For the customs of Halloween (Oct. 31), apparently an independent development, see ALL SAINTS.

allspice: see PIMENTO.

Allston, Washington, 1779–1843, American painter and author, b. Georgetown co., S.C. After graduation from Harvard (1801) he went to London, where he studied painting under Benjamin West. A result of four years in Rome was his lifelong friendships with Coleridge and Washington Irving. The peak of his fame as a painter was reached in England, 1810–18; an important work of this period was a portrait of Coleridge. After his return to America (1818) his career declined, most of his efforts being expended on the colossal but never completed *Belshazzar's Feast* (now in the Boston Athenaeum). His paintings, usually biblical or classical in subject, show the influence of the Venetian school. Despite his preference for monumental figure compositions in the neoclassic style, his most successful paintings were his romantic landscapes or seascapes such as *The Deluge* (Metropolitan Mus.), *Moonlight Landscape* (Mus. of Fine Arts, Boston) and the magnificent chalk drawing *Ship in a Squall* (Fogg Mus., Cambridge). One of his numerous pupils was Samuel F. B. Morse. Allston began to write verse as a student at Harvard; the only published collection of his poetry is *The Sylphs of the Seasons* (1813). *Monaldi,* a romance, was published in 1841. Allston's first wife was William Ellery Channing's sister, Ann; after her early death he married Martha Dana, sister of Richard Henry Dana. See biographies by J. B. Flagg (1892) and E. P. Richardson (1948).

Allward, Walter Seymour, 1876–1955, Canadian sculptor, b. Toronto. He created the Vimy Ridge Memorial in France, commemorating the Canadian troops of the First World War, and many monuments in Canada.

Alma (älmä′, ăl′mù), city (pop. 13,309), S Que., Canada, on the Saguenay near Lake St. John and NW of Chicoutimi. In 1954 its name was shortened from St. Joseph d'Alma. There are granite quarries in the region, and the town's industries include lumbering, wool carding, and the manufacture of paper products and bricks.

Washington Allston's A Spanish Girl.

Battle of Alma, in the Crimean War.

Alma (ăl′mṳ). **1** Town (pop. 1,370), W Ark., near the Arkansas river and NE of Fort Smith. It has a cannery. **2** City (pop. 3,515), co. seat of Bacon co., SE Ga., N of Waycross, in the coastal-plain farm area; inc. 1906. Tobacco, cotton, peanuts, pulpwood, and naval stores are produced. **3** City (pop. 8,978), S Mich., N of Lansing; settled 1853, inc. as a village 1872, as a city 1905. It has oil refineries, sugar-processing plants, and factories producing trailers and automobile parts. The city is the seat of Alma College (Presbyterian; coeducational; 1886). Several Indian mounds are in the vicinity. **4** City (pop. 1,342), co. seat of Harlan co., S Nebr., SW of Grand Island, on the Republican river near the Kansas line, in a farm area; founded 1871. Harlan County Dam (107 ft. high; 11,828 ft. long; completed 1952) is nearby. **5** City (pop. 1,008), co. seat of Buffalo co., W Wis., on the Mississippi and SW of Eau Claire; settled c.1852, inc. 1885. A Federal lock and dam is here.

Alma (äl′mṳ), river, S Crimean oblast, Ukrainian SSR. It is c.45 mi. long and enters the Black Sea 16 mi. N of Sevastopol. It was the scene (Sept., 1854) of an allied victory over the Russians in the Crimean War.

Alma-Ata (ăl′mṳ-ä′tä, Rus. ŭlmä′-ŭtä′), city (pop. c.456,000), capital of Kazakh SSR and Alma-Ata

Alma-Ata, U.S.S.R.

oblast, SE Kazakh SSR, in the northern foothills of the Trans-Ili Ala-Tau. It has metallurgical, machine, and food-processing plants. Alma-Ata is the center of a motion picture industry. Founded in 1854 as a fortress called Verny, it was destroyed by earthquakes in 1887 and 1910. It grew rapidly after the construction of the Turkistan-Siberia Railroad and was renamed in 1921. Alma-Ata has a university (founded 1928), an academy of sciences (1945), and an observatory.

Almadén (älmädhän′), town (pop. 14,125), Ciudad Real prov., central Spain, in New Castile. It is the center of one of the richest mercury-mining regions in the world. The mines have been exploited since Roman times.

Almagest (ăl′mṳjĕst) [Arabic distortion of Gr.,= the greatest composition], name derived from the Arabian translation of the less well-known Greek title of the *Syntaxis*, the famous astronomical work of Claudius Ptolemy. The original Greek version was translated, some centuries after it was written, into Arabic and then into Latin. It was highly influential in Europe in the Middle Ages. Chiefly an abstract of the astronomical science of the Alexandrian Greeks, it preserved the work of Hipparchus.

Almagro, Diego de (dyä′gō dä älmä′grō), c.1475–1538, Spanish conquistador, a leader in the conquest of Peru. A partner of Francisco PIZARRO, he took part in the first (1524) and second (1526–28) expeditions and in the bloody subjugation of the Inca after 1532. He aided (1534) BENALCÁZAR in thwarting Pedro de ALVARADO in the conquest of Ecuador. No match for the Pizarro brothers, he lost out in the division of spoils, but was granted the lands S of CUZCO. In 1535 Almagro set out on a march incredible in its hardships—south through the freezing cordillera of the Andes, probably as far as Coquimbo in present Chile, and then, after finding no gold, back north through the desert wastes of ATACAMA. He believed Cuzco was within his jurisdiction and so seized (1537) the city from Hernando PIZARRO, whom he injudiciously set free. Civil War ensued, and Almagro's forces were de-

175

feated. Begging for his life, he was promised it; then he was garroted by orders of Hernando Pizarro. His half-Indian son, Diego de Almagro, inherited his rights. Later the youth nominally headed the revolt which began with the assassination of Francisco Pizarro, but in 1542 he was captured and executed by the new governor, VACA DE CASTRO.

Al-Mamun: see MAMUN.

almanac, calendar with notations of astronomical and other data. In simple form almanacs have been known almost since the invention of writing, for they served to record religious feasts, seasonal changes, and the like. The Roman *fasti,* originally a list of *dies fasti* (days when legal business might be transacted) and *dies nefasti* (days when legal business should not be transacted), were later elaborated into various lists, some of them resembling modern almanacs. The almanac did not become a really prominent type of reading matter until the introduction of printing in Western Europe in the 15th cent. Regiomontanus produced one of the famous early almanacs (his *Ephemerides*), incorporating his astronomical knowledge. Most early almanacs were devoted primarily to astrology and predictions of the future. Prediction of the weather has persisted in many modern almanacs, but the crude and sensational magic began to disappear early, to be replaced by more or less scientific information. There appeared late in the 18th cent. truly scientific almanacs—notably the British NAUTICAL ALMANAC (founded 1767), which was the inspiration for the *American Ephemeris and Nautical Almanac* (founded 1855). The popular almanac, however, developed in the 17th and 18th cent. into a full-blown form of folk literature, with notations of anniversaries and interesting facts, home medical advice, statistics of all sorts, jokes, and even fiction and poetry. The first production (except for a broadside) of printing in British North America was an almanac for the year 1639. One of the best colonial almanacs was the *Astronomical Diary and Almanack* begun by Nathaniel Ames in 1725, and this was the forerunner of the most famous of them all, Benjamin Franklin's *Poor Richard's Almanack* (pub. by him 1732–57), which in its title recalled one of the most popular and long-lasting of English almanacs, that of "Poor Robin" (founded c.1662). The most enduring of all American almanacs was first published in 1793 by Robert Baily Thomas; it came later to be called *The Old Farmer's Almanack.* The best types of present-day almanacs are handy and dependable compendiums of large amounts of statistical information. Noteworthy are *The World Almanac and Book of Facts* (first pub. as a booklet in 1868; discontinued 1884; revived 1885), *Information Please Almanac* (first pub. 1947), and the regional *Texas Almanac* (first pub. 1857). The name almanac has also been applied to many other types of literature not properly considered almanacs, such as the *Almanach de Gotha,* a periodical record of the royal, princely, and noble houses of Europe.

Al-Mansur: see MANSUR.

Alma-Tadema, Sir Lawrence (ăl'mu̇-tăd'ĭmu̇), 1836–1912, English painter, b. Friesland. He studied in Belgium, where he lived until 1869. In that year he went to England; there he became a citizen

A page from the Rhode-Island Almanack of 1729.

and enjoyed a long popularity and many honors. He is best known for his scholarly and meticulous paintings of intimate classical subjects.

Almeida, Antonio José de (äntô'nyō zhōōzā' dú älmä'dù), 1866–1929, Portuguese statesman. A republican, he was minister of the interior in the provisional government after the revolution of 1910. As leader of the moderate Evolutionist party, he was premier of a coalition cabinet in the First World War and later (1919–23) was president of the republic.

Almeida, Francisco de (fränsĕsh'kō), c.1450–1510, Portuguese admiral, first viceroy of Portuguese India. He arrived in India in 1503 as captain major of a fleet and helped Portuguese forces defeat the ruler of Calicut. In 1505 he was back as viceroy, instructed to develop Portuguese commerce by building fortifications on the east coast of Africa, securing the allegiance of the Indian rulers, and taking control of the spice trade from the Arabs.

In Africa he built a fort at Kilwa and burned Mombasa, and in India he worked diligently to become master of all sea trade. The Egyptians, seeing their commerce threatened, built a fleet (with the help of Venice) and defeated (1508) Almeida's son, who was killed in the action. Off Diu in 1509 Almeida won a great naval battle against them and their Indian allies. Almeida at first refused to yield his power to Afonso de ALBUQUERQUE and had Albuquerque imprisoned (1509), but later gave him command. On his way home Almeida was killed by Hottentots near the Cape of Good Hope. See K. G. Jayne, *Vasco da Gama and His Successors* (1910).

Almeida Garrett, João Batista de (zhwã̌o' bútĕsh'tú dú älmä'dú gúrĕt'), 1799–1854, Portuguese dramatist and poet, leader of the romantic movement in Portugal. The family fled to the Azores during the French occupation, and there he spent some years before returning to graduate from the Univ. of Coimbra. An ardent democrat, he supported the revolution of 1820. The reactions of politics forced him twice into exile (1823–26, 1828–32). Upon his return he abandoned classicism for a romanticism which he expressed most effectively in the plays *Alfagome de Santarém* and *Frei Luis de Sousa* and the long poems *Camões* and *Dona Branca*. Generally considered the greatest of Portuguese dramatists, he was a great poet and folklorist as well. A supporter of Dom Pedro in the war (1832–33) with Dom Miguel, he later held many political offices and did much to forward the democratic cause. His works include collections of poetry, *Flores sem fruto* [flowers without fruit] (1844), *Fôlhas caídas* [fallen leaves] (1853); a book of folklore, *Romanceiro* (1843); and the prose *Viagens na minha terra* [journeys in my native land] (1846).

Almelo (äl'múlō), city (estimated pop. 50,548), in Overijssel prov., E Netherlands. An industrial center, it has a large textile industry.

Almería (älmärē'ä), city (pop. 79,332), capital of Almería prov., S Spain, in Andalusia. A busy port of the Gulf of Almería, it ships the celebrated grapes of the region, other fruits, esparto, as well as iron and other minerals mined nearby. Probably founded by Phoenicians, Almería flourished from the 13th to the 15th cent. as the outlet of the Moorish kingdom of Granada. It fell to the Christians in 1489. There is a Moorish fort, now in ruins, and a Gothic cathedral. In 1937, during the civil war, the city was shelled by German warships, but it has since been restored.

Almodad (–mō'–), descendant of Shem. Gen. 10.26; 1 Chron. 1.20.

Almohades (äl'múhädz, –hädz) or **Almohads** (–hädz), Berber Moslem dynasty that ruled Morocco and Spain in the 12th and 13th cent. It had its origins in the puritanical sect founded by Mohammed ibn Tumart, who (c.1120) stirred up the tribes of the Atlas Mts. area to purify Islam and oust the Almoravides. His successors, ABDUL-MUMIN, Yusuf II, and YAKUB I, succeeded in conquering Morocco and Moslem Spain, and by 1174 the Almohades had completely displaced the Almoravides. With time the Almohades lost some of their fierce purifying zeal; Yakub had a rich court and was the patron of Averroës. Yakub defeated (1195) ALFONSO VIII of Castile in the battle of Alarcos, but in 1212 the Almohade army was defeated and Almohade power in Spain was destroyed by the victory of the Spanish and Portuguese at Navas de Tolosa. In Morocco they lost power to the Merenide dynasty, which took Marrakesh in 1269.

Almon: see ALEMETH **2.**

almond, name for a small tree (*Prunus amygdalus*) of the ROSE family and for the nutlike edible seed of its drupe fruit. The "nuts" of sweet almond varieties are eaten raw or roasted and are pressed to obtain almond oil. Bitter almond varieties also yield oil, from which the poisonous prussic acid is removed in the extraction process. Almond oil is used for flavoring, in soaps and cosmetics, and medicinally as a demulcent. The tree, native to central Asia and perhaps the Mediterranean, is now cultivated principally in the Orient, Italy, Spain, and (chiefly the sweet varieties) California. It closely resembles the peach, of which it may be an ancestor, except that the fruit is fleshless. The pink-blossomed almond and the similar and closely related flowering almonds (e.g., *P. triloba*), pink-to white-blossomed shrubs also native to central Asia, are widely cultivated as ornamentals. Several Asian types are known as myrobalan, a name applied also to the cherry plum, with which flowering almonds are sometimes hybridized. The beauty of the almond in bud, blossom, and fruit gave

North façade of the cathedral of Almería.

Almond
branch
with fruit

motif to sacred and ornamental carving. In Syria and Palestine, where the tree breaks into sudden bloom in January, it came to symbolize beauty and revival. The rod of Aaron in the Bible (see AARON'S-ROD) bore almonds.

Almon-diblathaim (–lùthā'ĭm), camping place of the Israelites. Num. 33.46,47. Called Beth-diblathaim in a denunciation of Moab. Jer. 48.22.

Almont (ăl'mŏnt), village (pop. 1,279), SE Mich., N of Detroit; inc. 1855. Locks and automobile parts are made.

Almoravides (ălmô'rùvīdz, –vĭdz) or **Almoravids** (–vĭdz), Berber Moslem dynasty that ruled Morocco and Moslem Spain in the 11th and 12th cent. The Almoravides may have originated in what is now the Islamic Republic of Mauritania. Its real founder was ABDULLAH IBN YASIN, who by force of arms converted some Saharan tribes to his own reformed religion and then advanced on Morocco. After his death (c.1059), YUSUF IBN TASHUFIN and his brother Abu Bakr came to power. MARRAKESH was founded in 1062 and was the center of a powerful empire. Called by the Moors in Spain to help stem Christian reconquest, Yusuf entered Andalusia and defeated (1086) Alfonso VI of Castile. Later he subdued the local Moslem rulers and governed Moslem Spain and N Morocco (Abu Bakr having sway over S Morocco). The dynasty also pushed south, destroying the ancient state of GHANA. The Almoravides were rough and puritanical, contemptuous of the luxurious Moslem courts in Spain. Their rule was never entirely

stable and in the 12th cent. was attacked by the ALMOHADES, who finally (by 1174) won both Morocco and Moslem Spain.

Almquist, Carl Jonas Love (kärl' yōō'näs lōō'vù älm'kvĭst), 1793–1866, Swedish writer. He has been called the only Swedish novelist of genius in the period 1830–50. At first a somewhat bizarre romanticist, inclined toward anarchy, he later became more concerned with realism and democracy. This transition is seen in *The Book of the Thorn Rose* (14 vols., 1832–51), which contains most of his novels, stories, plays, and poems. His novel *Sara Videbecke* (1839) appeared in English in 1919. In his varied career he was civil servant, teacher, clergyman, and socialist. Accused of forgery and suspected of murder, he fled first to America and after 1865 lived in Bremen as Professor Westermann. See Axel Hemming-Sjoberg, *A Poet's Tragedy* (Eng. tr., 1932).

almug or **algum**, precious wood mentioned in the Bible (2 Chron. 2.8; 9.10,11), used in the Temple of Solomon and in his palace, brought from Ophir and Lebanon. It is perhaps a red SANDALWOOD.

Aloadae (ùlō'ùdē) or **Aloidae** (ălōī'dē), in Greek mythology, two giants who warred on the Olympian gods. Their names were Otus and Ephialtes (ĕfēăl'tēz), and they were the sons of Aloeus' wife by Poseidon. They tried to reach heaven to overthrow the gods by piling Mt. Ossa on Mt. Olympus and Mt. Pelion on Mt. Ossa. Some said they were killed by Apollo; others that they killed each other while shooting at a hind sent by Apollo. For their wickedness they were condemned to eternal torture in Tartarus. To pile Pelion on Ossa is thus to attempt an enormous but fruitless task.

alod (ă'lŏd). In feudal tenure lands held without obligation to any suzerain were termed held in alod. Alodial lands existed in England and on the Continent. Their number early decreased as landowners sought protection by turning their lands over to more powerful lords and receiving the holdings back as fiefs. In modern times the distinction between fee simple and alod has vanished.

aloe (ăl'ō) [Gr.], any species of the genus *Aloe* (ăl'-ōē), succulent perennials of the LILY family, native

Aloe

chiefly to the warm dry areas of the African Cape region and also to the tropics, but cultivated elsewhere for their rugged aspect. The juice of aloe leaves contains the purgative aloin. Today the various drug-yielding species, e.g., *A. barbadensis* and *A. chinensis*, are still used for their traditional medicinal properties as well as for X-ray-burn treatment, insect repellent, and a transparent pigment used in miniature painting; from the leaf fibers are made cords and nets. In ancient times the juice was used in embalming. A Mohammedan, returned from his pilgrimage to Mecca, hangs an aloe above his door. The American and false aloes are agaves, an AMARYLLIS family group that is the American counterpart in habit and general appearance to the true aloes. There is evolutionary evidence that the aloes and the agaves should be considered a single separate family, the Agavaceae. The Scriptural ALOES is unrelated.

aloes (ăl′ōz), drug obtained from the ALOE; also a biblical name for an aromatic substance of various uses, mentioned in connection with myrrh and spices (Ps. 45.8; Prov. 7.17; Cant. 4.14; John 19.39) and thought to be the fragrant wood of the modern aloeswood, also called eaglewood, agalloch (ŭgăl′-ŭk), or agilawood (ăg′ĭlŭ–), an *Aquilaria* native to Asia. In the East the aloeswood has been valued for medicinal purposes, as an incense, and for the beautiful grain of its wood which takes a high polish and was used for setting precious stones. The tree lignaloes (līnăl′ōz, lĭgnăl′ōz) of Num. 24.6, sometimes thought to be the aloeswood, may have been a different plant. The aloe and the American aloe or agave (see AMARYLLIS) are not to be confused with the aloes of the Scriptures.

Aloidae: see ALOADAE.

Alor Star (ä′lôr stär′), town (pop. 32,424), capital of Kedah, NW Malaya, on the Kedah river. It is a major center for trade in rice and rubber. The residence of the Sultan of Kedah is here.

Alorton (ăl′ŭrtĭn), village (pop. 3,282), SW Ill., a suburb SSE of East St. Louis; inc. 1944.

Alost (älôst′), Flemish *Aalst* (älst), town (estimated pop. 44,965), East Flanders prov., N Belgium. It is a market center and manufactures textiles, leather, and shoes. Known since the 9th cent., it was the capital of Austrian Flanders in the 18th cent. The Church of St. Martin (15th cent.) has a Rubens painting.

Aloth (ā′lŏth): see BEALOTH.

Aloysius, Saint (ălŏĭ′shŭs), 1568–91, Italian Jesuit, of the Gonzaga family. He died of the plague, which he caught from people he had tended. He is the patron of youth. St. Aloysius has been especially extolled for his purity. Feast: June 21.

alpaca (ălpăk′ủ), partially domesticated South American hoofed mammal of the camel family. It belongs to the same genus (*Lama*) as the wild guanaco and the vicuña and, like the llama, is probably a descendant of the guanaco. Although the flesh is sometimes used for food, the animal is bred chiefly for its long, lustrous wool, which varies from black, through shades of brown, to white. Flocks of alpaca are kept by Indians in the highlands of Bolivia, Chile, and Peru. They feed on grasses which grow close to the snow line, and they require a pure water supply. The Incas had domesticated the alpaca and utilized its wool before the Spanish

Conquest. Exporting of alpaca wool to Europe began after Sir Titus Salt discovered (1836) a way of manufacturing alpaca cloth. The name alpaca is sometimes used for materials such as mohair which do not contain alpaca wool.

Alpaca

Alp Arslan (älp ärslän′), 1029–72, Seljuk sultan of Persia (1063–72). In 1065 he led the Seljuks in an invasion of Armenia and Georgia and in 1066 attacked the Byzantine Empire. The success of his campaign was crowned (1071) by his brilliant victory over Romanus IV at MANZIKERT. After defeating the Byzantines, he wrested Syria from the Fatimites. In Dec. 1072, while campaigning beyond the Oxus river, he was murdered by one of his captives. He was succeeded by his son Malik Shah, who consolidated the victories his father had won.

Alpena (ălpē′nủ), resort city (pop. 14,682), co. seat of Alpena co., N Mich., on Thunder Bay of Lake Huron and NNE of Bay City; laid out 1856 as Fremont, renamed 1859, inc. 1871. Limestone quarries are here. Cement, paper, automobile parts, machinery, and insulating materials are made. The city's harbor handles about 3,000,000 tons of cement, coal, and limestone per year. Alpena is the seat of a junior college.

alpenhorn: see ALPHORN.

Alpes-Maritimes (älp′-märētēm′), department (1,-644 sq. mi.; estimated pop. 515,484), SE France, bounded by Italy in the east and surrounding the independent principality of Monaco. Nice is the capital. It is largely mountainous with some ski resorts. Near the coastline the cliffs drop abruptly to the beaches and to the resorts of the French RIVIERA, notably Cannes, Nice, Antibes, and Menton. Grasse manufactures much of the perfume produced in France. In 1947 the Alpes-Maritimes acquired a frontier strip which included the districts of BRIGUE AND TENDE.

Villefranche, harbor in the department of Alpes-Maritimes.

Alpha, borough (pop. 2,406), NW N.J., near the Delaware and SSE of Phillipsburg; inc. 1911.

alphabet [Gr. *alpha-beta*, like Eng. ABC], system of WRITING, theoretically having a one-for-one relation between character (or letter) and phoneme (see PHONETICS). Few alphabets have achieved the ideal exactness. A system of writing is called a syllabary when one character represents a syllable rather than a phoneme; such is the kana, used in Japanese to supplement the originally Chinese characters normally used. The alphabet of modern Western Europe is the Roman alphabet, the base of most alphabets used for newly written languages of Africa and America, as well as for scientific alphabets. Russian, Serbian, Bulgarian, and many languages of the USSR are written in the Cyrillic alphabet, an augmented Greek alphabet. Greek, Hebrew, and Arabic all have their own alphabets. The great writing of India is the Devanagari, an alphabet with syllabic features; this, invented probably for Sanskrit, is the source of a number of Asiatic scripts. The Roman is derived from the Greek, perhaps by way of Etruria, and the Greeks had imitated the Phoenician alphabet. The exact steps are unknown, but the Phoenician, Hebrew, Arabic, and Devanagari systems are based ultimately on signs of the Egyptian HIEROGLYPHIC writing. This was not alphabetic, but in the phonogram it bore the germ of phonemic writing; thus the sign "bear" might (to use an English analogy) mean also the sound *b*, and "dog" *d*. A similar development created the Persian CUNEIFORM syllabary. Two European alphabets of the late Roman era were the RUNES and the OGHAM. An exotic modern system is the Cherokee syllabary of SEQUOYAH, suggested by, but not based on, the Roman alphabet. Another was the Mormon Deseret alphabet, which quickly fell into disuse. See David Diringer, *Story of the Aleph Beth* (1958); Samuel Mercer, *The Origin of Writing and Our Alphabet* (1959); Oscar Ogg, *The 26 Letters* (2d ed., 1961).

Alpha Boötis: see ARCTURUS.

Alphaeus (ălfē′ŭs). **1** See CLEOPHAS. **2** Father of the evangelist Matthew. Mark 2.14.

alpha particle and **alpha ray:** see RADIOACTIVITY; RADIUM; RAY.

Alpharetta (ălfŭrĕ′tŭ), city (pop. 1,349), W central Ga., NNW of Atlanta.

Alphege, Saint (ăl′fēj), d. 1012, English churchman, archbishop of Canterbury after having been bishop of Winchester. The Danes captured him and held him for ransom, but St. Alphege would not ask his people to buy him back. The Danes murdered him.

Alpheus, river-god: see ARETHUSA.

Alpheus (ălfē′ŭs), Gr. *Alpheios* (ălfēôs′), river, rising in the Taygetus mts., S Greece. The longest river in the Peloponnesus, it flows c.70 mi. NW through the Peloponnesus, past Olympia, and into the Ionian Sea. In Greek mythology, its waters were said to pass under the sea and to emerge at Syracuse in the fountain of ARETHUSA. Hercules, to clean the stables of AUGEAS, turned the Alpheus through them. It is the river Alph of Coleridge's poem, *Kubla Khan*. The lower Alpheus was formerly known as Rouphia.

Alphonse (ălfôs′), 1220–71, count of Poitiers and of Toulouse, brother of Louis IX of France. By his marriage to the daughter of RAYMOND VII, count of Toulouse, he inherited Raymond's lands in 1249. An able administrator, he did much to heal the wounds of the crusade against the Albigenses. During the absence of Louis in the Holy Land, Alphonse was coregent (1250–52) with Blanche of Castile and regent (1252–54). He left no heir, and at his death his lands were incorporated (1271) into the holdings of Philip III, king of France.

Alphonsine tables: see ALFONSINE TABLES.

Alphonso. For rulers thus named, see ALFONSO.

Alphonsus Liguori, Saint (ălfŏn′sŭs lĭgwō′rē), 1696–1787, Italian churchman, doctor of the Church. He was named Alfonso Maria de' Liguori. In 1732 he founded the Congregation of the Most Holy Redeemer (the Redemptorists) for religious work among the poor, especially in the country. He refused the archiepiscopal see of Palermo but accepted (1762) a miserable country diocese near Capua. He labored incessantly until 1775, when sickness forced him to resign. He worked for his order under great difficulties, caused by an anticlerical government and overzealous monks. Goatherds of the mountains were his especial care. St. Alphonsus was an accomplished musician and wrote many hymns and instrumental pieces. His point of view in casuistry, which has become standard, is called equiprobabilism: in deciding whether a course of conduct is morally permissible, the opinions of good theologians are to be followed; when they differ, a course is allowable which a substantial number allow; in general the less austere point of view is preferable. St. Alphonsus

Egyptian hieroglyphics.

Alphabet (12th-century illuminated French miniature).

Detail of an Etruscan inscription at Tarquinia, Italy.

was unusual, even among Catholics, for his great devotion to the Virgin. Feast: Aug. 2. See biography by D. F. Miller and L. X. Aubin (1940).

alphorn or **alpenhorn** [Ger.,=Alps horn], wooden horn from 3 to 12 ft. long, sometimes curved slightly, with conical bore and a cup-shaped mouthpiece. It produces only the natural harmonics of the tube, slightly modified, however, by the material of the horn and its somewhat irregular shape. In Switzerland it is used to call cattle and to entertain tourists. The RANZ DES VACHES is played upon it.

The playing of the alphorn requires special skill and "lung-power."

Alpine (ăl'pīn). **1** Uninc. village (pop. 1,044), S Calif., NE of San Diego, in an area of poultry, fruit, and truck farms; founded in the 1880s. **2** Town (pop. 4,740), co. seat of Brewster co., W Texas, in the mountains N of the Big Bend of the Rio Grande. Founded in 1882 with the coming of the railroad, it is today a railroad junction and a shipping point for cattle and sheep. Sul Ross State College (coeducational; 1917) is here. The mountain scenery attracts many visitors; BIG BEND NATIONAL PARK is nearby.

alpine plants, high-altitude representatives of various flowering plants (chiefly perennials) that because of their dwarfed form, profuse blooming, and the preference of many for shady places are cultivated for use in alpine and ROCK GARDENS. Some species require specially constructed gardens duplicating mountain terrain, including systems for supplying cool water underground, comparable to the melting snows of their natural habitat. Others thrive without special care in favorable conditions (e.g., cool climate, short growing season, and sweet, rocky soil). Alpine species of gentians, saxifrages, and stonecrops are among those most commonly planted. Many garden plants (e.g., roses, iris, and primroses) have alpine representatives. The EDELWEISS is a popular alpine.

Alps, great mountain system, S central Europe. It is c.680 mi. long and swings north, east, and southeast in a great arc from the Mediterranean coast between France and Italy to the Adriatic coast of Yugoslavia, with its northernmost point in S Bavaria. The Alps thus form a barrier separating the great plain of the Po in N Italy from France (west), Germany (north), and the Danubian plain (east). The larger parts of Switzerland and Austria, between Germany and Italy, are covered by

Two common alpine plants: calamint (left), yellow gentian (right).

Mont Blanc, highest point in the French Alps, rises 15,781 feet.

The snowcapped Bernina Alps, on the Swiss-Italian border.

the Alps and their foothills. Cut by numerous gaps and saddles (passes), the Alps do not form a complete climatic or strategic barrier. However, the cisalpine (i.e., of N Italy) climate is noticeably milder than that of the transalpine slopes; moreover, though the Alps have often been crossed by invaders, they are easily defensible. Alpine waters drain, through three rivers rising there, to the North Sea (the Rhine), to the W Mediterranean (the Rhone), and to the Adriatic (the Po); they also feed the Danube, which flows to the Black Sea. The Alpine chain represents the western culmination of a vaster mountain system, stretching SE to the Caucasus and the Himalayas. It is more immediately connected with the Jura, from which it is separated by the Rhone; the Carpathians, from which it is separated by the Danube; the DINARIC ALPS, which continue the main chain along the Yugoslav coast and link it with the Balkans; and the APENNINES. The Alps are the result of extensive folding and overthrusting of the earth's crust due to pressure exerted from the south. Movements of the crust probably began in the Mesozoic; the uplift of the mountain mass probably culminated in the Pleistocene epoch of the Cenozoic. Where the sedimentary layers have been worn away, the older crystalline rocks are exposed, forming the angular peaks. Among the

Country church in the Carnic Alps.

Bolzano, Italy, on the Isarco river, is a center of the alpine tourist region in the Dolomites.

Alpine peoples the word *Alp* or *Alm* designates not the snow-capped peaks, but the high pastures above the timber line, where the cattle (cows, goats, and sheep) are taken to graze in summer. In the high Alps, dairying is the chief industry and cheese the staple food. Agriculture is confined to the valleys and foothills; viticulture and fruitgrowing are important on the southern slopes. New industries, especially chemical, metallurgical, and textile industries, have been introduced through increasing exploitation of the vast hydroelectric potential and have radically altered the traditional Alpine economy. The tourist trade, especially in the Western and the Central Alps, has contributed to the prosperity of the frugal and hard-working Alpine population and has received great impetus from the growing popularity of MOUNTAINEERING. The relatively low base level (3,000–4,000 ft.) of the magnificent Alpine peaks stresses the majesty of their height and allows a great diversity of climate and vegetation on various levels. Many valleys contain large and beautiful lakes, notably those of Geneva, Lucerne, Zurich, Constance, Como, and Garda, and the Lago Maggiore. Alpine resorts are world famous. Above the timber line there is a wealth of characteristic ALPINE PLANTS, and, still higher, vast glaciers (see GLACIER) and a perpetual mantle of snow. The alpine fauna is sparse; the CHAMOIS and the MARMOT are its only distinctive members. The subdivisions of the Alps are generally arbitrary. The Western Alps, stretching from the Riviera to the SIMPLON, comprise, from south to north, the Maritime Alps in Provence and Liguria; the Cottian and Graian Alps in DAU-PHINÉ and Piedmont; and the MONT BLANC group and the Pennine Alps in SAVOY, the Val d'AOSTA, and the VALAIS. Mont Blanc (15,781 ft.) is the highest peak of the entire Alpine system; Monte VISO, the MATTERHORN, the GRAN PARADISO, and Monte ROSA are among the other chief peaks of the Western Alps; the Mont CENIS and Simplon tunnels and the Great and Little SAINT BERNARD passes are the main thoroughfares. The Central Alps include the Bernese Oberland (see BERN); the Lepontine Alps, centered around the SAINT GOTTHARD group; and the Rhaetian Alps (E Switzerland, including the ENGADINE). The JUNGFRAU, the FINSTERAARHORN, and Piz BERNINA are among the loftiest of all Alpine peaks; the St. Gotthard and LÖTSCHBERG tunnels and the FURKA, SPLÜGEN, MALOJA, and STELVIO passes are vital links. The Eastern Alps comprise the Alps of VORARLBERG; the Austrian and Italian Tyrol (including the ÖTZTAL ALPS, the ZILLERTAL ALPS, the ORTLES group and the DOLOMITES); the HOHE TAUERN, with the GROSSGLOCKNER; the Alps of BAVARIA and Salzburg; the SALZKAMMERGUT; the Alps of Styria; and, farther south, the Carnic Alps (between Carinthia and Italy), the Karawanken (between Carinthia and Yugoslavia), and the Julian Alps (between Yugoslavia and Italy). The ARLBERG, BRENNER, and Semmering passes and tunnels are the main through routes. See A. E. H. Tutton, *High Alps* (1931); R. L. G. Irving, *The Alps* (1940); J. H. Walker, *Walking in the Alps* (1951); J. H. Green, *The Swiss Alps* (1962).

Alps, Australian: see AUSTRALIAN ALPS.

Als (äls), Ger. *Alsen* (äl′zùn), island (121 sq. mi.;

pop. c.50,000), Denmark. It lies in the Little Belt and is separated from S Jutland by the narrow Als Sound. Sonderborg, the chief city, is on both sides of the sound. Agriculture, fruitgrowing, and light industry are the main occupations. After being ceded to Prussia in 1864, the island was restored to Denmark as a part of N Schleswig after the plebiscite of 1920.

Alsace (ăl'sás, ăl'săs, Fr. älzäs'), Ger. *Elsass* (ĕl'zäs), region and former province, E France. It is separated in the east from Germany by a part of the Rhine river. It comprises three departments, Bas-Rhin, Haut-Rhin, and the Territory of Belfort. There is a fertile agricultural plain between the Rhine river and the Vosges mts. In addition to part of the Vosges in the west, it includes small portions of the Jura mts. in the south. Strasbourg is the ancient capital of the province and the leading industrial center of the region. Other important cities are Mulhouse, Colmar, and Belfort. There are textile industries in the Mulhouse-Colmar area. Wines, notably Riesling, are produced here. Hydroelectric plants are at Kembs and Ottmarscheim. Virtually the whole population speaks French, but a very large majority have also retained their Alemannic dialect. About 75 percent of the population is Roman Catholic. A part of the Roman province of Upper Germany (see GAUL), Alsace fell to the Alemanni (5th cent.) and to the Franks (496). The Treaty of Verdun (843; see VERDUN, TREATY OF), included it in Lotharingia; the Treaty of MERSEN (870) put it in the kingdom of the East Franks (later Germany). The 10 chief cities of Alsace gained (13th cent.) virtual independence as free imperial cities. The remainder of the region was divided into petty feudal and ecclesiastic fiefs with the exception of Upper Alsace (S Alsace), where the HAPSBURG family consolidated its original holdings. In alliance with the Swiss, the Alsatian towns successfully resisted (1476–77) the pretensions of Charles the Bold of Burgundy. They accepted the Reformation, but the rural areas remained generally Catholic. The Peace of Westphalia (1648) transferred all Hapsburg lands in Alsace to France; it also transferred all imperial rights throughout the "landgraviate of Alsace" to the French crown. The vagueness of this clause

helped Louis XIV when, on various pretexts, he forcibly took control (1680–97) of virtually all Alsace, including Strasbourg. The Treaty of Ryswick (1697) confirmed France in its new possessions. Mulhouse, being allied to Switzerland, and a few other isolated holdings were not annexed to France until the French Revolution. The province, with its own PARLEMENT at Colmar, retained a favored fiscal and religious status until 1790. The Edict of Nantes, promulgated before the annexation of Alsace, could not be revoked here; therefore religious worship remained free. In 1871, on debatable historical grounds, all Alsace except Belfort was incorporated into Germany, as a result of the FRANCO-PRUSSIAN WAR. Until its recovery (1918) by France, Alsace and part of Lorraine formed the "imperial land" (*Reichsland*) of Alsace-Lorraine, held in common by all the German states that formed the empire. Many Alsatians emigrated to France rather than submit to a policy of thorough

Old part of the city of Strasbourg in Alsace.

Fertile plain of Alsace between the Rhine River and the Vosges mountains.

"Germanization." Clamor for the return of Alsace-Lorraine became the chief rallying force for French nationalism and was a major cause of the armaments race that led to the First World War. After the decline of early enthusiasm over the reunion with France, confirmed by the Treaty of Versailles (1919), a strong particularist movement gained ground, demanding cultural and even political autonomy. The movement received considerable impetus from recurrent efforts by the French government to end the CONCORDAT OF 1801, which had remained valid in Alsace-Lorraine though it had been ended in the rest of France in 1905. These efforts met the determined resistance of Catholic conservatives. In 1940 German forces occupied Alsace; a large part of the population had already been evacuated to central France. Alsace was treated as a part of Germany. French and American troops recovered (Jan., 1945) Alsace for France and were generally hailed as liberators. Alsace retains many old customs such as the wine and harvest festivals.

Alsen: see ALS.

alsike: see CLOVER.

Alsip, village (pop. 3,770), NE Ill., a suburb SSW of Chicago; inc. 1927.

Alsop, Richard (ôl'sŭp), 1761–1815, American author, b. Middletown, Conn. Best remembered as one of the CONNECTICUT WITS, he collaborated with Theodore Dwight and others in writing light satiric verse for the *Political Greenhouse* and the *Echo.* See biography by K. P. Harrington (1939).

Alta (ăl'tù), town (pop. 1,393), NW Iowa, ENE of Sioux City, in a farm area; inc. 1878.

Alta California, term used by the Spanish to refer to that area of their possessions along the entire Pacific coast north of what is now the Mexican state of Baja California. Till the middle 18th cent., California was frequently represented on maps as an island some 3,000 mi. long. Early in the 18th cent. the Jesuit Father Eusebio KINO by actual exploration proved anew that the southern part of the area was a peninsula and the rest of it mainland. Thereafter the peninsula came to be called Baja (Lower) and the mainland Alta (Upper) California.

Altadena (ăltùdē'nù), uninc. residential city (pop. 40,568), S Calif., N of Pasadena, in an orange and avocado area; founded 1887.

Alta Hill, uninc. village (pop. 1,078), N central Calif., NNE of Sacramento, in a farm area; founded 1866.

Altai or **Sharasume** (shäräsōōmä'), town (pop. c.30,000), northernmost Sinkiang prov., China, on the northern slopes of the Altai mts. It is a trade center near the Mongolian border and was part of Mongolia until 1907. Gold is mined nearby. Since 1955 Altai has been under the jurisdiction of the Ili Kazakh Autonomous Region. Altai is called Chenghwa in Chinese.

Altai or **Altay** (both: ăltī', ăl'tī, ältī', Rus. ŭltī') mountain system, largely in the MOUNTAIN-ALTAI Autonomous Oblast, RSFSR, and in the Kazakh SSR. In the northeast the Kuznetsk Ala-Tau and the Salair Ridge adjoin the Altai and enclose the KUZNETSK BASIN. The Soviet Altai are bounded by the Sayan range in the west, the Mongolian Altai in the south, and the Tannu-Ola range in the

east. The highest sections of the Soviet Altai are the Kaun, the Chuya, and the Sailyugem ranges. The rest of the Altai are in Mongolia, where they are known as the Mongolian and Gobi Altai. The highest peak, Belukha (15,157 ft.), is in the Katun range (RSFSR). In the Soviet Altai are the headwaters of the Ob and the Irtysh. There are rich deposits of gold, silver, mercury, iron, lead, zinc, and copper. Timberlands cover the slopes, and farmlands lie in the foothills. Russians entered the area early in the 17th cent. The mining centers are Ust-Kamenogorsk, Glubokoye, Leninogorsk, and Zyryanovsk. Leninogorsk and Ust-Kamenogorsk are also industrial centers.

Altaic (ăltā'ĭk), family of languages which includes Turkish, Mongolian, and Manchu. See LANGUAGE (table.)

Altai Territory, administrative division (c.101,000 sq. mi.; pop. c.2,685,000), SW Asiatic RSFSR. Drained by the upper Ob river, it includes the MOUNTAIN-ALTAI Autonomous Oblast and the Kulunda steppe. It is crossed by the Turksib and South Siberian railroads. Bisk, Chesnokovka and Barnaul, the capital, are major industrial centers. Rubtsovsk is the principal producer of farm machinery for W Siberia. A rich agricultural area, the Altai Territory was intensively cultivated during the Virgin Land Campaign (1953).

Alta Loma (ăl'tù lō'mù), uninc. village (pop. 1,020), S Texas, NW of Galveston; est. c.1893.

Altamira: see PALEOLITHIC ART.

Altamirano, Ignacio Manuel (ēgnä'syō mänwěl' ältämērä'nō), 1834–93, Mexican novelist and poet. An unlettered Indian boy of pure blood, he became after formal education an advocate of learning and freedom. He joined Benito JUÁREZ in the struggle against Maximilian and afterward was a key figure in the reconstruction of the republic. He edited the *Correo de Mexico* and as a poet interpreted the Mexican landscape. He is best known for two novels—*Clemencia* and a story sketching Mexican customs, *La Navidad en las Montañas* [Christmas in the mountains].

Altamira y Crevea, Rafaél (räfäěl' ältämē'rä ē krävä'ä), 1866–1951, Spanish jurist and historian. He was appointed professor of the history of the law in the universities at Oviedo (1897), Madrid (1914), and Mexico city (1945), and he served (1921–45) as a judge of the Permanent Court of International Justice (the World Court). Among his numerous works on education, social science, literature, law, and history, his *Historia de España y de la civilización española* (5 vols., 1913–29; Eng. tr., *A History of Spanish Civilization*, 1930) is the best known; an English adaptation is C. E. Chapman, *A History of Spain* (1931).

Altamont (ăl'tùmŏnt). **1** City (pop. 1,656), S central Ill., SE of Springfield; inc. as a village 1872, as a city 1901. It is a railroad junction and a shipping point in a farm area. **2** Village (pop. 1,365), E central N.Y., WNW of Albany, in a farm area; inc. 1890. **3** Uninc. town (pop. 10,811), S Oregon, a suburb SE of Klamath Falls.

Altamonte Springs, town (pop. 1,212), E central Fla., N of Orlando.

Altamura (äl"tämōō'rä), city (estimated pop. 43,178), in Apulia, S Italy. It is an agricultural center. The imposing cathedral, with twin cam-

Altar in the church of St. Joseph in Tepoztlán, Mexico (gilded and painted wood; 17th century).

paniles, was begun by Emperor Frederick II in 1232.

altar, table or platform for the performance of sacrifice. In its simplest form the altar is a small pile, with a square or circular surface, made of stone or wood. Its features vary according to its purpose; the altar of libation usually has a drain for the liquid, and so does the altar of bloody sacrifice. The altar of burnt offering (including incense) often has a depressed hollow for a fire. Altars in Egypt, in Mesopotamia, in Greece, and in Rome and among the Aztec and the Maya were highly adorned with friezes, cornices, elaborate platforms, and canopies. At Pergamum there was a huge monumental altar 40 ft. high. Altars as a

Pergamum altar

rule were out of doors in the ancient world and in Central America. The Christian altar is the place to celebrate the EUCHARIST, a sacrifice in the traditional view. In the Western Church the altar is a long narrow table of stone, often reminiscent of a tomb; at its back is a REREDOS, which often bears a canopy. In the Roman rite there are in the middle of the altar a crucifix and a tabernacle to contain the reserved Host. There is a recess in each altar stone containing bones of martyrs; this is even true of tiny portable altars carried by chaplains. In Eastern rites the altar is square and has no backing or reredos; it is away from the wall. Most Protestant denominations have no altar; instead, a typical practice is to have a **permanent communion table below and in front of the pulpit.**

Al-taschith: see AIJELETH SHAHAR.

Altavista (ăltŭvĭs'tù), industrial town (pop. 3,299), S central Va., on the Roanoke and SSW of Lynchburg; inc. 1910, rechartered 1936. The town has cedar-chest, rayon, and cotton industries.

Altay: see ALTAI, mountain system.

Altdorf (ält'dôrf), town (estimated pop. 7,100), capital of Uri canton, central Switzerland. It manufactures cables and rubber goods. Altdorf is the scene of the traditional exploits of William Tell, commemorated by a monument (1895) and the William Tell theater.

Main square of Altdorf, Switzerland, with Tell monument.

Altdorfer, Albrecht (äl'brĕkht ältdôr'fûr), 1480–1538, German painter and engraver. He served as city architect of Regensburg, where much of his life was spent. Although influenced by Dürer, Altdorfer's works are less severe in mood. The forms and lines in his works seem to vibrate with intense movement. These qualities may be seen

St. Florian's Departure, painting by Albrecht Altdorfer.

especially clearly in his white-ink drawings of figures and landscapes. Landscape was among his major interests, and he was probably the first German to paint a pure landscape. His choice of subject matter was wide, ranging from *Susanna Bathing* and pairs of lovers to *St. George and the Dragon* and the *Virgin and Child*. Other subjects include the *Battle between Alexander and Darius, Pride, Pyramus and Thisbe, The Synagogue at Regensburg* and saints. Equally skilled at painting, woodcutting, and engraving, he executed these subjects in one or sometimes a variety of media.

Altenburg (äl'tùnbōōrk), city (estimated pop. 47,476), German Democratic Republic, in the former state of Thuringia, S central Germany, on the Pleisse river. There are manufactures of sewing machines, textiles, and playing cards. Lignite is mined nearby. The city was known in 976 and became (12th cent.) an imperial city. It passed (1329) to the house of Wettin and later was the capital of the duchy of SAXE-ALTENBURG. It was burned by the Hussites in 1430. The tower of the monastery, founded (1172) by Emperor Frederick I, still stands.

alternating current: see ELECTRICITY; GENERATOR.

Altgeld, John Peter (ält'gĕlt), 1847–1902, governor of Illinois (1892–96), b. Germany. He was taken by his immigrant parents to Ohio, where he grew up with little formal schooling. After service in the Union army he spent some years as an itinerant worker on farms, read law, and became county attorney of Savannah, Mo. In 1875 he moved to Chicago, where he wrote *Our Penal Machinery and Its Victims* (1884), arguing that American judicial methods were weighted against the poor. In 1886 he was elected to the Cook co. superior court, and in 1892 he was elected governor. In office he established himself as a champion of labor, reform, and liberal thought. Charging a miscarriage of justice, he pardoned three anarchists imprisoned as parties to the Haymarket riot of 1886. During the PULLMAN strike of 1894, when President Cleveland sent Federal troops into Chicago, Governor Altgeld publicly termed the act unconstitutional. His extreme liberalism, coupled with his espousal of free silver, lost him reelection in 1896. Denounced as a radical in his own day, he is now venerated as a defender of the freedom of the individual against entrenched power. See his writings and speeches, ed. by H. M. Christman (1960); biographies by W. R. Browne (1924) and Harry Barnard (1938).

althea, shrubby: see MALLOW.

Althing (äl'thǐng) [Icelandic,=general diet], parliament of Iceland. This assembly, the oldest in Europe, was convened at Thingvellir, SW Iceland, in 930. It was dissolved in 1800, was revived as an advisory body in 1843, and in 1874, when Iceland was granted a constitution, became again a legislative body. The members serve for four years. Its upper house (one third of the members) and lower house (two thirds) sometimes work together in a United Althing. The Althing in 1944 voted the independence of Iceland from Denmark,

a decision ratified by popular vote. In 1959 the Althing adopted proportional representation.

Altichiero da Zevio (ältēkyä'rō dä tsäv'yō), c.1330–c.1395, early Italian painter, follower of Giotto. He worked in Verona and then Padua. His frescoes in the churches of Sant' Antonio and San Giorgio are notable as early examples of the use of rational proportions in the treatment of figures and space.

altimeter (ăltǐm'ǐtŭr, ăl'tǐmē″tŭr), device for measuring altitude. The most common type is an aneroid BAROMETER calibrated to show the drop in atmospheric pressure in terms of linear elevation as an airplane, balloon, or mountain climber rises. Corrections for temperature, local atmospheric pressure, and elevation of the landing field adjust the altimeter to show altitude above sea level or above the landing field. Another instrument, the terrain-clearance indicator, measures altitude above the ground below by bouncing radio waves off the surface and measuring the time elapsed between sending and receiving the echo.

altitude, in astronomy, the angular distance of a heavenly body above the astronomical horizon. The angle used in measuring is that which a line drawn from the eye of the observer to the heavenly body makes with the plane of the horizon. The reading of the apparent altitude, as determined by a telescope attached to a graduated circle, must be corrected for refraction and certain other errors to ascertain the true altitude. In navigation, observations are made with a sextant.

altitude, in physical geography, the elevation of a physical feature of the earth above the mean sea

Virgin and Child Worshipped by Members of the Cavalli Family, fresco by Altichiero da Zevio in the Cavalli Chapel of Sant' Anastasia, Verona, Italy.

level. Mean sea level, the average of the heights of the surface of the sea over a long period of time, is determined by a recording apparatus called a tide gauge. The altitude of any feature is calculated by trigonometric triangulation or (less accurately) by photographic surveying or barometric readings. On topographical maps altitude is represented usually by contour lines and sometimes by hachures or by differential coloring.

altitude sickness: see AEROEMBOLISM.

Alto Adige: see TRENTINO–ALTO ADIGE.

Alton (ôl'tŭn). **1** City (pop. 43,047), SW Ill., on bluffs above the Mississippi and N of St. Louis; laid out 1815 in a region visited by Jolliet and Marquette in 1673, inc. as a town 1833, as a city 1837. A shipping and industrial center, it has numerous manufactures, including glass, steel, metal products, ammunition and firearms, petroleum, paperboard, and explosives. It is the seat of a boys' military academy and a junior college for girls. There is a monument to Elijah P. Lovejoy. A tablet marks the scene of a Lincoln-Douglas debate (1858). The PRINCIPIA (at Elsah) and Pere Marquette State Park are nearby. **2** Town (pop. 1,048), NW Iowa, on the Floyd river and NE of Sioux City; inc. 1883. **3** Town (pop. 1,241), S N.H., on the Merrymeeting river and NE of Concord, in a resort area; settled 1770, inc. 1796. Clothing is made. The town includes the villages near the southern end of Lake Winnipesaukee.

Altona (äl'tōnä), river port of Hamburg, Federal Republic of Germany, N Germany, on the Elbe. It was incorporated into the city of Hamburg in 1938. Fishing and chemical manufactures are the leading industries. Chartered in 1664, it became one of the first free ports of N Europe.

Alton North, uninc. village (pop. 1,505), SW Ill., N of Alton.

Altoona (ăltōō'nŭ). **1** Town (pop. 1,458), central Iowa, NE of Des Moines. **2** Industrial city (pop. 69,407), central Pa., near the source of the Juniata and E of Pittsburgh; settled c.1769, laid out 1849, inc. as a borough 1854, as a city 1868. Bituminous coal is mined nearby. Machinery, electrical equipment, shoes, textiles, and food and paper products are made. A railroad center with shops, the city is east of the famous scenic Horseshoe Curve of the Pennsylvania R.R. Governor Curtin called a conference of governors in 1862 at Altoona to pledge support to Lincoln's administration. The nearby historic hotel, Fountain Inn, was mentioned by Dickens in his *American Notes.* **3** City (pop. 2,114), W central Wis., SE of Eau Claire; settled 1882, inc. 1887.

Alto Park, uninc. town (pop. 2,526), NW Ga., just NW of Rome.

alto-relievo: see RELIEF.

Altrincham (ôl'trĭng-ŭm), municipal borough (pop. 41,104), Cheshire, W England, near Manchester. It has a textile-printing industry and engineering works.

Altschuler, Modest (mŭdyĕst' ält'schōō"lŭr), 1873–, Russian-American conductor, studied at the Moscow Conservatory. In 1903 he organized the Russian Symphony Orchestra, which before 1919 introduced to American audiences works of Rachmaninov, Scriabin, and other Russian composers.

Alturas (ăltōōr'ŭs), city (pop. 2,819), co. seat of Modoc co., NE Calif., NE of Redding; inc. 1901. A trade center in a timber, grain, and livestock area, it is the headquarters for Modoc National Forest.

Altus (ăl'tŭs), city (pop. 21,225), co. seat of Jackson co., SW Okla., W of Lawton, in a cotton and cattle area; founded c.1892, inc. 1901. A junior college is here, and Altus Air Force Base is nearby Lake Altus, chief unit of the W. C. Austin reclamation project, and a state park are north of the city.

alum (ăl'ŭm), any of a series of double sulfate salts. They are hydrated sulfates of a univalent (see VALENCE) cation (a positively charged atom or radical), e.g., sodium, potassium, lithium, ammonium, or thallium, combined with a trivalent cation, e.g., aluminum, iron, chromium, or manganese. Generally the terms *alum* and *common alum* are applied to potassium alum, or potash alum—the double sulfate of potassium and aluminum—used in the purification of water, in tanning hides, as a mordant in dyeing, and as an astringent. Sodium aluminum sulfate, also known as alum, is used in some baking powders. Chromium potassium sulfate, or chrome alum, is used in the textile industry as a mordant, in tanning, and in the fixing bath to harden the gelatin on photographic films and plates.

alumina (ŭlōō'mĭnŭ) [from Latin,=alum] or **aluminum oxide.** chemical compound occurring almost pure in nature as corundum, e.g., ruby and sapphire. It is combined with silica in many minerals, including clays, feldspars, and micas, and with iron and water as bauxite. The crystalline forms are extremely hard. Corundum, the natural substance closest to the diamond in hardness, and emery (an impure form of corundum) are used as abrasives. Alundum, or aloxite, an artificial form of the oxide, is a hard white or gray crystalline powder prepared from bauxite and extensively used as an abrasive. It is used also in making crucibles and other laboratory apparatus. When precipitated from solutions containing coloring matter, alumina absorbs these dyes and insoluble pigments are formed. Such a precipitate is called a lake, and the process employing lakes is mordant dyeing. Alumina is insoluble in water and in most acids but reacts with sodium hydroxide. Alumina prepared from bauxite is used in the preparation of metallic aluminum.

aluminum [from Latin,=alum], called in British countries **aluminium** (ăl"ŭmĭn'ŭm), metallic element (symbol=Al; in group III A of the PERIODIC TABLE; for physical constants, see ELEMENT, table). Its lightness, fairly high strength, and toughness, especially in alloys, account for its use in aircraft and other transportation industries. Although chemically active, it resists corrosion by the formation of a self-protecting oxide coat. Since it keeps its brightness and is an excellent conductor of heat, it is used extensively in the manufacture of cooking utensils and kitchenware. Ductile and a conductor of electricity, it is often employed in place of copper for high-tension wires. It is highly malleable and, in the form of aluminum foil, is used extensively as a wrapping material. Aluminum powder is used in paints. Since it is a powerful reducing agent, the metal is mixed in very small quantities

Open-pit mining of bauxite, source of aluminum ore.

metallurgist. Hall's process consists essentially of the electrolysis of alumina prepared from bauxite and dissolved in fused cryolite. In the electric furnace an iron tank lined with carbon serves as the cathode and large blocks of carbon as the anode; the electric current generates sufficient heat to keep the cryolite melted. The molten aluminum collects on the walls and bottom of the tank and oxygen is liberated at the anode. The development of methods for coloring aluminum has led to its use in jewelry, on wall surfaces, and in colored kitchenware. Important among the alloys of aluminum are DURALUMIN, aluminum bronze, and MAGNALIUM. The development of cheap hydroelectric power greatly aided the expansion of the aluminum industry.

aluminum oxide: see ALUMINA.

Alum Rock, uninc. town (pop. 18,942), W central Calif., a suburb NE of San Jose. The town has a large park with many mineral springs.

alundum: see ALUMINA.

Alush (ā′lŭsh), wilderness camping ground of the Israelites. Num. 33.13,14.

Alva, Fernando Álvarez de Toledo, duque de: see ALBA, FERNANDO ÁLVAREZ DE TOLEDO, DUQUE DE.

Alva (ăl′vū), city (pop. 6,258), co. seat of Woods co., NW Okla., on the Salt Fork of the Arkansas river NW of Enid; settled 1893. It is the center of a large wheat and ranch area. Northwestern State College (coeducational; 1897) is here.

Alvah (–vū), duke of Edom. Gen. 36.40. Aliah: 1 Chron. 1.51.

Alvan, Horite. Gen. 36.23. Alian: 1 Chron. 1.40.

Alvarado, Juan Bautista (hwän′ boutēs′tä älvärä′-dhō), 1809–82, governor of Alta California (1836–42), b. Monterey, Calif. Out of the chaotic times in the neglected Mexican province of Alta California, he emerged as a brilliant politician. After a small but successful revolt in 1836, he declared California an independent state with himself as governor. He pacified his opponents in San Diego and Los Angeles, but the southern faction continued to view the northern upstart with suspicion until he secured (1838) regular appointment as Mexican governor. He and his uncle, Mariano Guadalupe Vallejo, who acted as military commander, could not accomplish much, and after they disagreed both men were removed in 1842. Alvarado was one of the leaders of a new and successful revolt in 1844–45, but the new government was shortly faced with the Bear Flag revolt and the Mexican War, and Alvarado's public career, typical of the turbulence of California in his day, ended.

Alvarado, Pedro de (pä′dhrō dä), 1486–1541, Spanish conquistador. He went to Hispaniola (1510), sailed in the expedition (1518) of Juan de Grijalva, and was the chief lieutenant of Hernán CORTÉS in the conquest of Mexico. He commanded at Tenochtitlán in the absence of Cortés, and his brutality provoked a brief Indian rebellion. Sent out by Cortés in 1523, he conquered Guatemala and Salvador. He was governor of Guatemala until his death. He met with much opposition from the *audiencia* in Mexico, but strengthening his power on two voyages to Spain (1527–28, 1536–39), he exercised absolute control. He founded many cities and developed the colony. An expedition to Ecuador (1534–35), made in an attempt to share

with molten iron and steel to assure sound castings (i.e., without holes); the aluminum combines with the gaseous impurities. This reducing power is also employed in obtaining certain elements, such as manganese and chromium, from their oxides. When a mixture of powdered aluminum and iron oxide called THERMITE is ignited, much heat is generated and the reaction is utilized in welding. Although it is the most abundant metal in the earth's crust, aluminum does not occur free in nature. It is an important constituent of many minerals, including CLAY, BAUXITE, MICA, FELDSPAR, ALUM, CRYOLITE, and the several forms of aluminum oxide (ALUMINA), such as emery, CORUNDUM, SAPPHIRE, and RUBY. Although the metal was not isolated until the 19th cent., compounds of aluminum have long been used. Various astringent compounds used by the Romans were called alum by them. Sir Humphry DAVY and other chemists in the early 19th cent. recognized aluminum as the metal and alumina as its oxide. H. C. OERSTED succeeded (1825) in obtaining the impure metal, but Friedrich WÖHLER had greater success and is usually credited with its first isolation (1827). H. E. SAINTE-CLAIRE DEVILLE first prepared the pure metal in 1854 and set about perfecting a process for its commercial production. However, it was not until 1886 that the method by which aluminum is produced today was discovered independently—in the United States by C. M. HALL, a student at Oberlin College, and in France by Paul Héroult, a

in the booty Francisco PIZARRO was taking from the Inca empire, ended in defeat. In 1540, Alvarado, sailing for the Moluccas, stopped in Mexico where he was diverted to a search for the fabled Cibola by the viceroy, Antonio de MENDOZA, and by the tales of MARCOS DE NIZA. When the Indians of Nueva Galicia unexpectedly revolted in 1541, Alvarado took part against them in the Mixtón War. He led a foolhardy attack and was accidentally killed in the subsequent retreat. Juan Rodríguez CABRILLO took command of the maritime expedition. Alvarado's wife, Doña Beatriz de la CUEVA, succeeded him as governor of Guatemala. His letters concerning the conquest of Guatemala have been published. See J. E. Kelly, *Pedro de Alvarado* (1932).

Alvarado (ălvŭrä'dŭ), city (pop. 1,907), N Texas, SSE of Fort Worth. It is a trade center in a blackland farming area.

Álvarez, José (José Álvarez de Pereira y Cubero) (hōsā' äl'väreth dā pĕrä'rä ē kōōbä'rō), 1768–1827, Spanish classicist sculptor; follower of Canova. He was employed on the decoration of the Quirinal Palace in Rome. On returning to Madrid he became director of the Academy of San Fernando and sculptor to Ferdinand VII. He is best known for his portrait statues of Spanish royalty and for his mythological figures in marble.

Álvarez, Juan (hwän' äl'väräs), 1780–1867, Mexican general, president of Mexico (1855). An Indian, he fought well under Morelos y Pavón and was later the first governor of Guerrero. In 1854 he led the liberal Revolution of Ayutla, which overthrew (1855) SANTA ANNA. After two months he yielded the presidency to Ignacio COMONFORT. Alvarez later fought against Maximilian and the French invaders.

Álvarez Quintero, Serafín (sāräfēn' äl'väräth kĕntä'rō), 1871–1938, and **Joaquín Alvarez Quintero** (hwäkēn'), 1873–1944, Spanish dramatists. They wrote in collaboration a large number of highly successful plays, the most popular being genre comedies of Andalusian middle-class life, which are racy, brilliant, and witty. The brothers were admitted to the Spanish Academy in 1922. Among their best-known plays are *Los galeotes* (1900), *Mañana de sol* (1905; Eng. tr., *A Bright Morning*,

Joaquín Alvarez Quintero

1916), *El genio alegre* (1906), *Las de Caín* (1908), *Doña Clarines* (1909), and *Malvaloca* (1912).

Alvear, Carlos María de (kär'lōs märē'ä dā älväär'), 1789–1852, Argentine general and statesman. After distinguished service with the Spanish army in Europe he returned with his friend San Martín and became a leader in the domestic revolution of 1812 and a member of the constituent assembly of 1813. He was in command of the patriot army when the Spanish royalists at Montevideo capitulated (1814). In 1815 Alvear was named supreme director of the United Provs. of the Río de la Plata, but was deposed when he attempted to become a dictator. In the war with Brazil he won the decisive battle of Ituazingó (Feb. 20, 1827). From 1838 until his death he was minister to the United States.

Alvear, Marcelo Torcuato de (märsä'lō tōrkwä'tō), 1868–1942, Argentine statesman and diplomat, president of the republic (1922–28). A Radical, he became minister to France after a victory of the Radical party in 1916 placed IRIGOYEN in the presidency. Succeeding Irigoyen in 1922, he secured enactment of some reforms, especially agricultural measures, but largely because of a split with Irigoyen his administration was, on the whole, fruitless. Later the breach was healed, and Alvear became the leader of the Radical party. In 1931 he was barred from the presidential race, and in 1937 he was defeated by Roberto M. Ortiz.

Alverstone, Richard Everard Webster, 1st Viscount (ôl'vûrstŭn), 1842–1915, lord chief justice of England (1900–1913). He served on various international arbitration commissions, including those dealing with the Bering Sea Fur-Seal Controversy and the Venezuela Boundary Dispute (1898–99). In the Alaska Boundary Dispute, he gave the deciding vote against the Canadian claims. He wrote *Recollections of Bar and Bench* (1914).

Alves, Antônio de Castro: see CASTRO ALVES, ANTÔNIO DE.

Alvin, city (pop. 5,643), S Texas, SSE of Houston. It is in a region of the Gulf Coast plain which produces truck crops and flowers. Oil and natural gas are also found in the vicinity. A junior college is here.

Alviso (ălvē'sō), city (pop. 1,174), W central Calif., NNW of San Jose; founded 1849, inc. 1852.

Alvord, Clarence Walworth (ăl'vŭrd), 1868–1928, American historian, b. Greenfield, Mass. Educated at Williams (B.A., 1891), Friedrich Wilhelm Univ. in Berlin, and the Univ. of Chicago, he became (1901) an instructor in history at the Univ. of Illinois (Ph.D., 1908) and was full professor there (1913–20) and at the Univ. of Minnesota (1920–23). He was general editor (1906–20) of the *Illinois Historical Collections*, edited the *Centennial History of Illinois* (6 vols., 1918–24) and wrote its first volume, and was the principal founder of *The Mississippi Valley Historical Review* and its managing editor (1914–23). He also wrote *The Mississippi Valley in British Politics* (1917).

Alvord, Henry Elijah, 1844–1904, American agriculturist, educator, and specialist in dairy husbandry, b. Greenfield, Mass. He pioneered in developing the cooperative creamery system and served (1886–93) as professor and president of various state agricultural colleges. In 1895 he became first chief of the dairy division of the

Bureau of Animal Industry, U.S. Dept. of Agriculture.

Alvsborg, Swed. *Älvsborgs län* (ĕlfs'bôr"yŭs lĕn'), province (4,919 sq. mi.; pop. 375,037), SW Sweden. The capital is Vanersborg. Its northern section, the historic province of Dalsland, W of Vanern lake, is an agricultural and lumbering district; the rest of the province consists of the western part of the historic Vastergotland prov., with important textile plants and large power stations at TROLLHATTAN. Alvsborg was formerly also spelled Alfsborg or Elfsborg.

Alyattes (ălĕă'tēz), d. 560 B.C., king of Lydia. He built up the kingdom. While he was warring with Cyaxares of Media, an eclipse of the sun occurred (585 B.C.). The two kings then made peace. Alyattes continued Lydian conquest of the Ionian cities of Asia Minor. The remains of his tomb can still be seen N of Sardis. He was the father of CROESUS.

Alypius or **Alypios** (both: ŭlĭp'ēŭs), fl. c.360, Greek author of *Introduction to Music*, chief source of modern knowledge of Greek musical notation.

alyssum (–lĭs'–), any species of the genus *Alyssum* of the MUSTARD family, chiefly annual and perennial herbs native to the Mediterranean area. A few species, notably the perennial golden tuft (*A. saxatile*), are cultivated as rock-garden or border ornamentals for their masses of yellow or white flowers. The annual sweet alyssum (popularly called *A. maritima* but separated by most botanists as *Lobularia maritima*) is a similar plant with fragrant white or lilac blossoms. The alyssums have been called madwort or heal-bite because of an old belief that they cured hydrophobia.

Am, chemical symbol of the element AMERICIUM.

Amad (ā'măd), unidentified city of Asher, NW Palestine. Joshua 19.26.

Amadas or **Amidas, Philip** (both: ăm'ŭdăs), 1550–1618, English navigator. With Arthur Barlowe he was sent by Sir Walter Raleigh in 1584 to explore the North American coast. Their favorable report on Roanoke Island, N.C., led to the colonizing expedition (1585) under Sir Richard Grenville and Sir Ralph LANE.

Amadeus VIII (ămùdē'ùs), 1383–1451, count (1391–1416) and duke (from 1416) of Savoy, antipope

Amadeus VIII

(1439–49) with the name Felix V. In 1434 he appointed his son regent of Savoy and retired to the hermitage of Ripaille, on Lake Geneva, which he had founded. In 1439 the Council of Basel (see BASEL, COUNCIL OF) declared EUGENE IV deposed and elected Amadeus, much respected for his probity, to the papacy. Although a layman, Amadeus reluctantly accepted, believing that he could bring peace to the Church. As Felix V, he received only scattered recognition from the secular powers. When Nicholas V became pope, Felix yielded his claim. He was subsequently made a cardinal. He was the last of the antipopes.

Amadeus, 1845–90, king of Spain (1870–73), duke of Aosta, son of Victor Emmanuel II of Italy. Juan PRIM urged his election as king by a constituent assembly after the expulsion (1868) of Queen ISABELLA II. Amadeus accepted the crown reluctantly. Just before the new king arrived in Spain, Prim was assassinated. The upper classes were opposed to Amadeus, who belonged to the anticlerical house of Savoy, and repeated attempts were made on his life. When a new rebellion by the CARLISTS began, Amadeus abdicated and returned to Italy. A year later Alfonso XII was proclaimed king.

Amadis of Gaul (ă'mŭdĭs), Fr. *Amadis de Gaule* (ämädēs' dù gōl'), famous romance of chivalry, first composed in Spain or Portugal and probably based on French sources. It dates from the 13th or 14th cent., but the first extant version in Spanish, a revision by García de Rodríguez de Montalvo, was published in 1508. It was translated into French in 1540 and appeared in English in 1619. It was immensely popular in France and Spain until superseded by *Don Quixote*, and it was, indeed, a sign of inelegance not to be acquainted with its code of honor and knightly perfection. Numerous sequels were written. Its influence is apparent in Sir Philip Sidney's *Arcadia*. The story became the subject of a lyric tragedy by Philippe Quinault (1684), with music by Lully, and it inspired the opera *Amadigi* (1715) by Handel.

Amado, Jorge (zhôr'zhĭ ämä'dŏŏ), 1912–, Brazilian novelist. His works deal largely with the sufferings of the common man and have a strong leftist viewpoint. They are marked by grim and violent realism with a fluently poetic appreciation of Brazilian life and land and compassion for the oppressed. Typical are *Cacau* [cacao] (1933), *Suor* [sweat] (1934), *Terras do sem fim* (1942; Eng. tr., *The Violent Land*, 1945), and *Gabriela, cravo e canela* (1958; Eng. tr., *Gabriela, Clove and Cinnamon*, 1962).

Amagansett (ă"mùgăn'sĭt), uninc. fishing village (pop. 1,095), SE N.Y., on the south shore of Long Island, ENE of Southampton; settled 1650. It is a resort noted for its Colonial houses and giant shade trees.

Amagasaki (ä'mägäsä'kē), city (pop. 405,955), Hyogo prefecture, S Honshu, Japan, a port on Osaka Bay. An important industrial center, with iron and steel factories, chemical plants, and textile mills, it lies on the banks of the Yodo river. It has a 16th-century castle.

Amager (ä'mägùr), island (25 sq. mi.; pop. 178,184), Denmark, in the Oresund. Its northern end is occupied by part of Copenhagen.

Amakusa Islands (ämäkōō'sä), archipelago (341 sq.

mi.), Kumamoto and Kagoshima prefectures, in the East China Sea, W of Kyushu, Japan. There are some 67 islands in the group; Hondo is the chief town. Mountainous and fertile, the archipelago produces rice and camellia oil and markets porcelain. Amakusa clansmen made the islands a major center of Christianity in the 16th cent. In 1637, when Christianity was banned in Japan, the islanders, suffering economic hardship, joined in the rebellion at Shimabara. After the revolt was mercilessly suppressed (1638), the islands passed under the control of the Tokugawa shogunate.

Amal (ā'mŭl), Asherite. 1 Chron. 7.35.

Amal, Swed. *Åmål* (ō'mōl), city (pop. 9,299), Alvsborg prov., SW Sweden, on Vanern lake. It has sawmills, railroad workshops, and electrical plants. Chartered in 1643, it is the only city in the historic prov. of Dalsland.

Amalasuntha (ă"mŭlŭsŭn'thŭ), d. 535, Ostrogothic queen in Italy (534–35), daughter of Theodoric the Great. After her father's death (526) she was regent for her son Athalaric. He died in 534, and she and her husband, Theodahad, became joint rulers of Italy. Her good relations with the Byzantine emperor, Justinian I, alienated her people. In 535 the Goths revolted; Amalasuntha was imprisoned and murdered by order of her husband. Justinian used her murder as his pretext for attacking and reconquering Italy.

Amalekites (ăm'ŭlŭkīts), aboriginal people of Canaan and the Sinai peninsula. They waged constant warfare against the Hebrews until dispersed by Saul. Their eponymous ancestor, Amalek, was a duke of Edom and Esau's descendant. Gen. 14.7; 36.12,16; Ex. 17.8–16; Num. 13.29; 14.25,45; 24.20; Judges 3.13; 6.3,33; 7.12; 1 Sam. 15.5–8; 30.1–20; 1 Chron. 1.36; 4.43.

Amalfi (ŭmăl'fē, Ital. ämäl'fē), town (estimated pop. 6,663), in Campania, S Italy. It is a small fishing port on the N shore of the Gulf of Salerno. Legend says it was founded by Romans; it became (9th cent.) an early Italian maritime republic, rivaling Pisa, Venice, and Genoa in wealth and power. Its maritime code, the *Tavole Amalfitane*, had wide influence. After capture (1131) by the Normans, the city was sacked (1135, 1137) by the Pisans, and its decline was rapid, particularly after a destructive storm in 1343. The cathedral in Sicilian-Arabic style (10th cent.; repeatedly restored) has an imposing façade; its fine bronze doors were cast (11th cent.) in Constantinople; it has a picturesque cloister (*chiostro del Paradiso*).

amalgam, alloy of mercury with any of the well-known metals except iron and platinum; also a rare mineral occurring in nature comprised of a solid solution of silver in mercury. Amalgams, prepared by bringing the metals into contact with mercury, are liquid or solid, depending upon their proportion of mercury. These alloys are widely used—e.g., zinc amalgam to prevent the polarization of the zinc plates in batteries; tin amalgam in the manufacture of mirrors; and silver, gold, and copper amalgams in dentistry. In the **amalgamation process** for the extraction of gold and silver from their ores the ore is crushed and treated with mercury, in which the metal dissolves. The amalgam thus formed is heated, the mercury vaporizes at a comparatively low temperature, and the metal remains.

Amalia, duchess of Saxe-Weimar: see ANNA AMALIA.

Amalric I (ŭmăl'rĭk, ă'mŭlrĭk) or **Amaury I** (ŭmô'rē, Fr. ämōrē'), c.1137–1174, king of Jerusalem (1162–74); brother and successor of Baldwin III. He spent his reign in attempts to gain and hold the suzerainty of Egypt, but was balked by the Turkish sultan NUREDDIN, one of whose lieutenants finally obtained control of the country and left it at his death to SALADIN. During Amalric's frequent absences in Egypt, Nureddin repeatedly raided the increasingly weak Latin states of the East. Amalric was succeeded by his son, Baldwin IV.

Amalric II or **Amaury II**, c.1155–1205, king of Jerusalem (1197–1205) and king of Cyprus (1194–1205); brother and successor (in Cyprus) of GUY OF LUSIGNAN. His title to Jerusalem was established through his marriage with Isabella, eldest daughter of Amalric I (see JERUSALEM, LATIN KINGDOM OF).

Amalric of Bena (bē'nŭ), d. 1207?, French professor of philosophy. He taught heretical precepts concerning God, a pantheistic universe, and a progressive Trinity. Before he died, he publicly retracted, but his followers in Champagne formed a heretical sect, the Amalricians. They were condemned by Pope Innocent III and by councils held at Paris (1210) and the Lateran (1215). The heresy resulted in a temporary ban on Aristotle and the Arabic philosophers at the Univ. of Paris and later led to condemnation of some of the works of John Scotus ERIGENA.

Amalthaea (ămŭlthē'ŭ), in Greek mythology, she-goat or nymph who nursed the infant Zeus. It was said that Zeus made one of her magnificent horns into the CORNUCOPIA and set her image among the stars as the constellation Capricorn.

Amam (ā'măm), city of Judah. Joshua 15.26.

Aman (ā'–), the same as HAMAN.

Amana (ŭmā'nŭ), unidentified mountains. Cant. 4.8.

Amana Society (ŭmăn'ŭ), corporate name of a group of seven small villages (total pop. c.1,500), E central Iowa, clustered around the Iowa river WNW of Iowa City; settled 1855 by members of the Ebenezer Society. The society originated in one of the Pietist religious sects of 17th-century Germany. Led by Christian Metz (1794–1867), members came to America in 1843 to escape persecution at home. Settling first near Buffalo, N.Y., they developed a communal way of life which reached its flowering in Iowa. Amana became one of the most successful of such communities in America. In 1932 it was made a cooperative corporation, with separation of religious and economic administration. The church is now officially called the Amana Church Society. Long famous for the products of their woolen mills (especially blankets) and fertile farms, the quaint villages also attract many visitors. See B. M. Shambaugh, *Amana That Was and Amana That Is* (1932); Barbara Yambura, *A Change and a Parting: My Story of Amana* (1960).

amanita: see MUSHROOM.

Ama-no-hashidate: see MIYAZU.

Amanullah (ämŭnoo'lŭ), 1892–1960, emir (1919–26) and king (1926–29) of Afghanistan. To win pop-

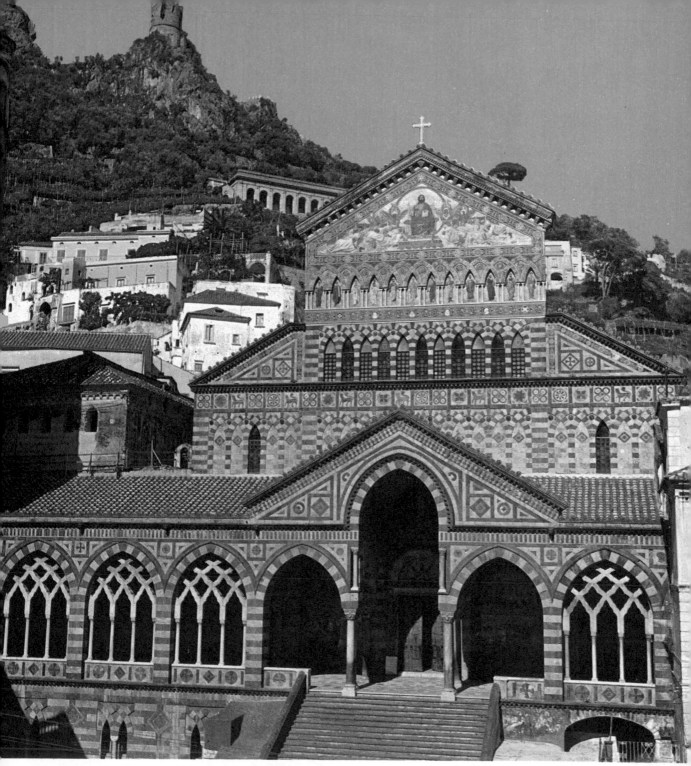

The majestic façade of the cathedral at Amalfi, Italy.

ular support for his rule he invaded India, but no really serious fighting occurred before the Treaty of Rawalpindi was signed (1919). After a tour of Europe, the emir attempted to introduce a number of Western reforms, but his subjects rebelled against his program, and he fled the country in 1929. He remained in exile in Switzerland until his death.

Amapá (ämäp′ä), federal territory (c.53,700 sq. mi.; pop. c.68,900), extreme N Brazil. Macapá (pop. c.46,900) is the capital. Bounded by French Guiana on the north, it is heavily forested, with a coastal band of swamp and savanna. It has important manganese mines. Its northern half, long disputed by France and Brazil, was given to Brazil by arbitration in 1900.

Amapala (ämäpä′lä), town (pop. c.5,300), S Honduras, on Tigre Island, in the Gulf of Fonseca. It is the chief Pacific port of Honduras. Products are transshipped between the mainland and Amapala by launch.

amaranth (ăm′–) [Gr.,=unfading], common name for the Amaranthaceae, a family of herbs, trees, and vines of warm regions, especially in the Americas and Africa. The genus *Amaranthus* includes several widely distributed species called amaranths, which are characterized by a lasting red pigment in the stems and leaves. They have been a poetic symbol of immortality from the time of ancient Greece. *Amaranthus* also includes species called TUMBLEWEED and PIGWEED, as well as several cultivated plants—e.g., love-lies-bleeding, or tassel flower, and Joseph's coat. Other ornamentals in the family are the globe amaranth (genus *Gomphrenia*), sometimes called bachelor's button, and the cockscomb (*Celosia*), both originally tropical annuals. They can be preserved and are used in EVERLASTING bouquets.

Amarapura (ù″mùräpōō′rä), town (pop. 10,519), Mandalay prov., N central Burma, near the Irrawaddy river. A silk-weaving center, it also has varied handicraft manufactures. It was twice (1783–1823, 1837–60) the capital of Burma, but in

Amaryllis longifolia

1860 it was replaced by Mandalay. Its royal palace, great temples, and fortifications are now in ruins.

Amaravati (ŭ″mùrävŭ′tē), ancient ruined city, Andhra Pradesh state, SE India, near the mouth of the Kistna river. The former capital of the Buddhist Andhra kingdom, it is a well-known archaeological site with a beautiful Buddhist stupa (1st cent. A.D.).

Amariah (ăm″ùrī′ù) [Heb.,=whom God promised]. **1** High priest, son of Meraioth. 1 Chron 6.7,52. Perhaps he is the same as **2** and **3**. **2** High priest, son of Azariah. 1 Chron. 6.11. Perhaps he is the same as **1**, **3**, and **4**. **3** Ancestor of Ezra. Ezra 7.3. Perhaps he is the same as **1** and **2**. **4** High priest under Jehoshaphat. 2 Chron. 19.11. Perhaps he is the same as **2**. **5** Levite. 1 Chron. 23.19; 24.23. **6**, **7** Contemporaries of Ezra, perhaps the same person. Ezra 10.42; Neh. 11.4. **8** A priestly family. 2 Chron. 31.15; Neh. 10.3; 12.2,13. See IMMER **1** and IMRI **1**. **9** Ancestor of the prophet Zephaniah. Zeph. 1.1.

Amarillo (ămùrĭl′ō, –rĭl′ù), city (pop. 137,969), co. seat of Potter co., extreme N Texas, N of Lubbock. The metropolis of the Panhandle, it is a prosperous city with tall buildings and tree-lined streets in the midst of treeless plains that are swept by summer dust storms and winter blizzards. The spot was known to Indians, buffalo hunters, and cowboys before the coming of the railroad in 1887. The first huddle of buffalo-hide shelters was succeeded by a noisy cow town, which in the 20th cent. became a market for wheat farms. After the discovery of natural gas and oil, it mushroomed into an industrial city. Amarillo packs meat, mills flour, smelts zinc, refines oil, makes synthetic rubber, and processes farm and dairy products. It is also the banking and commercial nucleus of a highly industrialized region. In nearby communities are numerous industrial and military establishments, including a U.S. government helium plant, a U.S. air force base, and an atomic energy project. There is a junior college and a veterans' hospital. A symphony orchestra is maintained.

Amarna: see TEL-EL-AMARNA.

amaryllis (ăm″ùrĭl′ĭs), common name for the Amaryllidaceae, a family of mostly perennial, lilylike

Amaryllis (Agave americana)

plants with narrow, flat leaves and with flowers borne on separate, leafless stalks. They are widely distributed throughout the world, especially in flatlands of the tropics and subtropics. Many ornamental plants of this family are mistakenly called lilies; they can be distinguished from members of the lily family by the anatomical placement of the ovary (see FLOWER) and are considered more advanced than the lilies in evolution. Several fragrant, showy-blossomed species are commonly called amaryllis: the true amaryllis (*Amaryllis belladonna*), or belladonna lily, of S Africa and the more frequently cultivated tropical American species of *sprekelia*, *lycoris*, and especially *hippeastrum* (e.g., the Barbados lily). The large *Narcissus* genus, including jonquils and daffodils, is native chiefly to the Mediterranean and the Orient, but has been naturalized and is now widespread in the United States. Although the common names are sometimes used interchangeably, strictly the daffodil is the yellow *N. pseudo-narcissus*, with a long, trumpet-shaped central corona; the jonquil is the yellow *N. jonquilla*, with a short corona; and the narcissus is any of several usually white species, e.g., the poet's narcissus (*N. poetica*) with a red rim on the corona. The Biblical ROSE OF SHARON may have been a narcissus. Among many others that have become naturalized and are cultivated in Europe and America are the snowdrops (any species of *Galanthus*), small early-blooming plants of the Old World whose flowers are symbolic of consolation and of promise, and the tuberose (*Polianthes tuberosa*), a waxy-flowered Mexican plant. Economically, the most important plants of the family are of the nonbulbous genus *Agave* (ŭgā'vē, –gā'–), the tropical American counterpart of the African *Aloe* genus of the lily family. Different agaves provide soap (e.g., those called amoles—see SOAP PLANT), food and beverages, and hard fiber. Henequen and SISAL HEMP are among the fibers obtained from agaves; fique and Cuban hemp come from other similar genera. *Maguey* (mŭgā') is the Mexican name for various species (chiefly *A. americana*) called American aloe or century plant that contain the sugar agavose, sometimes used medicinally but better known as the source of the popular alcoholic beverages PULQUE and MESCAL. The name "century plant" arises from the long intervals between bloomings—from 5 to 100 years. After blooming, the century plant dies back and is replaced by new shoots. The agave cactus (*Leuchtenbergia principis*) is a true CACTUS that resembles the agave.

Amasa (ăm'ŭsŭ, ŭmā'sŭ) [Heb.,=burden]. **1** Cousin of Absalom, with whom he revolted. Later he became David's commander in chief; he was murdered by Joab. 2 Sam. 17.25; 19.13; 20.4–13; 1 Kings 2.5. **2** Ephraimite chief. 2 Chron. 28.12.

Amasai (ămăs'āī, āmā'–) [Heb.,=burdensome]. **1** Chief of the deserters from Saul to David. 1 Chron. 12.18. **2** Priest. 1 Chron. 15.24. **3** Levite. 1 Chron. 6.25,35. **4** Levite contemporary with Hezekiah. 2 Chron. 29.12.

Amashai (ŭmā'shāī), priest contemporary with Nehemiah. Neh. 11.13. He is perhaps the same as MAASIAI.

Amasiah (ăm″ŭsī'ŭ) [Heb.,=whom God bears], captain in Jehoshaphat's army. 2 Chron. 17.16.

Amasis I (ŭmā'sĭs), d. c.1545 B.C., king of ancient Egypt (c.1570–1545 B.C.). The founder of the XVIII dynasty, he drove the Hyksos out of the Nile delta and pursued them into Palestine. His name also appears as Ahmose.

Amasis II, d. 525 B.C., king of ancient Egypt (569–525 B.C.), of the XXVI dynasty. In a military revolt he dethroned APRIES. He erected temples and other buildings at Memphis and Saïs and encouraged Greek merchants and artisans to settle at Naucratis. He also had alliances with Greek leaders and maintained himself partly with the aid of Greek mercenaries. His revision of the laws is said to have influenced the laws of Solon. Amasis II died just before the Persian invasion (525 B.C.) under CAMBYSES. The name also appears as Ahmose II.

Amateis, Louis (ämätä'ēs), 1855–1913, Italian-American sculptor, b. Turin, Italy, studied at the Turin Royal Academy. He moved to the United States in 1884, was naturalized, and later opened a studio in Washington, D.C., where he also established the School of Architecture and Fine Arts of George Washington Univ. His best-known works are the bronze doors for the Capitol, the Alamo monument in Austin, Texas, and the military memorial in Galveston, Texas. His son Edmond Amateis, 1897–, b. Rome, Italy, has also executed sculpture for many public buildings and monuments throughout the United States.

amateur. The Amateur Athletic Union of the United States declares that "an amateur sportsman is one who engages in sports solely for the pleasure and physical, mental, or moral benefits he derives therefrom." A professional athlete, on the other hand, is paid. Definitions and rules governing amateurs differ from sport to sport and from country to country. Baseball, football, rowing, tennis, and golf are outside the jurisdiction of the Amateur Athletic Union of the United States, each of these sports having a governing body of its own. Intercollegiate sports are theoretically open only to amateurs, and present-day "athletic scholarships" and other forms of athletic subsidies are considered by many educators and students a violation of the amateur spirit. For international athletic meets, such as the Olympic games, each contestant must be certified as an amateur by the authorized athletic organization of his country.

Amati (ämä'tē), family of violinmakers of Cremona, Italy. The founder of the Cremona school was Andrea Amati (ändrā'ä) (c.1535–c.1578), whose earliest violins date from c.1564. His labels bore the name Amadus, and he deserves credit for the design of the modern violin. His sons were Antonio Amati (äntō'nyō) and Girolamo or Geronimo Amati (jērō'lämō, järō'nēmō), who worked together and followed in general the patterns of their father in making small violins of graceful shape and sweet but not very powerful tone. Niccolò Amati (nĕkkōlō') (1596–1684), son of Girolamo, brought the Amati violin to its height after c.1645. Although he still used the family's designs, he made some larger instruments of more powerful tone. Antonio STRADIVARI and Andrea Guarneri were pupils of Niccolò. Niccolò's son, Girolamo (1649–1740), was the last of his line to achieve distinction. The Latin forms of the first names, Andreas, Antonius,

Hieronymus, and Nicolaus, were generally used on the labels, and the family name was sometimes Latinized as Amatus.

Amato, Giovanni Antonio d' (jōvän'nē äntō'nyō dämä'tō), 1475–1555, Neapolitan painter, called Il Vecchio [the elder]. He imitated the style of Pietro Perugino. Paintings by him are in many churches in Naples, among them the *Holy Family* in a chapel of San Domenico Maggiore.

Amaury. For persons thus named, see AMALRIC.

Amaziah (ăm"ŭzī'ŭ) [Heb.,=strength of God]. **1** Died c.775 B.C., king of Judah (c.802–c.775 B.C.), son and successor of Jehoash of Judah. The two incidents of his reign were the conquest of Edom, including the capture of Petra, and an unprovoked attack by Amaziah on King Jehoash of Israel. Jehoash took Amaziah prisoner, entered Jerusalem, and sacked the Temple. Amaziah died at Lachish, assassinated, and his son Uzziah succeeded. 2 Kings 14; 2 Chron. 25. **2** Simeonite. 1 Chron. 4.34. **3** Levite. 1 Chron. 6.45. **4** Priest at Bethel, Amos's enemy. Amos 7.10–15.

Amazon (ă'mŭzŏn), in Greek mythology, one of a tribe of warlike women who lived in Asia Minor. The Amazons had a matriarchal society, in which women fought and governed while men performed the household tasks. Each Amazon had to kill a man before she could marry, and all male children were either killed or maimed at birth. It was believed that the Amazons cut off one breast in order to shoot and throw spears more effectively. They were celebrated warriors, believed to have been the first to use cavalry, and their conquests were said to have included many parts of Asia Minor, Phrygia, Thrace, and Syria. Several of the finest Greek heroes proved their mettle against the Amazons: Hercules took the golden girdle of Ares from their queen HIPPOLYTE; THESEUS abducted Hippolyte's sister Antiope and then defeated a

Battle of Amazons (relief on Hellenistic sarcophagus).

vengeful army of Amazons at Athens. A contingent of Amazons fought with the Trojans under PENTHESILEA.

Amazon, Port. *Amazonas* (ämäzō'nùs), river formed by the junction in Peru of two major headstreams, the UCAYALI and the shorter MARAÑÓN. With the Ucayali, it flows c.3,700 mi., traversing N Brazil before entering the Atlantic. The Amazon is one of the greatest rivers of the world, and carries more water than any other. The gradient of the river is very low: Manaus, c.1,000 mi. upstream, is only c.100 ft. higher than Belém near the mouth and is an ocean port; ships with a draft of 14 ft. can reach IQUITOS, Peru, more than 2,000 mi. from the sea. The drainage basin is enormous (c.2,500,000 sq. mi.), gathering waters from both hemispheres and covering not only most of N Brazil—the states of AMAZONAS and PARÁ and the territories of ACRE, AMAPÁ, Rio BRANCO, and RONDÔNIA—but also parts of Bolivia, Peru, Ecuador, Colombia, and Venezuela. In the lowlands stretching E from the Andes is the largest rain forest in the world—a wet, green land, rich in both animal and vegetable life. The tropical climate is tempered by its heavy rainfall (exceeding 100 in. annually in spots of the upper and lower regions); the average temperature at Santarém, 400 mi. upriver, is 78°. For much of its course, the Amazon wanders in a maze of brownish channels amid countless islands; its banks shift with constant erosion. Its headstreams, however, arise cold and clear in the heights of the Andes not far from the Pacific Ocean. They descend northward before turning east and joining to form the Amazon proper (which is, however, occasionally called the Solimões from the Brazilian border to the junction with the Rio NEGRO). The NAPO comes in from the north before the Amazon flows eastward out of the rain forests of Peru into the rain forests of Brazil. Before it reaches the mouth of the Negro, the Amazon receives the PUTUMAYO or Içá and the Caquetá or JAPURÁ from the north and the JURUÁ and the PURUS from the south. On the large Negro just before its junction with the Amazon is MANAUS, and below that the Madeira pours in the waters collected over the large Madeira-Mamoré drainage basin to the south. The TAPAJÓS enters the river from the south near Santarém, and the XINGU (also a southern tributary) joins the Amazon farther east. Below the Xingu the river reaches its delta, with many islands formed by alluvial deposit and submergence of the land. Around the largest of these, MARAJÓ, the river splits into two large streams. The northern stream threads its way around many islands; the southern, called the Pará river, receives the TOCANTINS and has the important port of BELÉM. The awesome bore of the Amazon is called *pororoca*, and the river's immense discharge is visible far out to sea. It was probably first seen in 1500 by Vicente Yáñez Pinzón, who explored the lower Amazon. Real exploration of the river came with the voyage of Francisco de ORELLANA down from the Napo in 1540–41; his fanciful stories of female warriors gave the river its name. Not long afterward (1559) Pedro de Ursúa began the expedition that ended with the baleful melodramatics of Lope de AGUIRRE. Nearly a century later Pedro TEIXEIRA led the voyage upstream (1637–38) that really opened

Small craft unloading cargo at Amazonian port of Manaus.

River workers cutting jute along the banks of the Amazon.

the Amazon to world knowledge. The river continued to be of enormous importance to explorers and naturalists, among them Charles Darwin and Louis Agassiz. The valley was largely left to its sparse Indian inhabitants (mostly groups of the Guarani-Tupi linguistic stock and meager material culture) until the mid 19th cent., when steamship service was regularly established on the river and when some settlements were made (such as that of Confederate veterans from the United States at Santarém). In the late 19th and early 20th cent., the brief wild-rubber boom on the upper Amazon attracted settlers from Brazil's northeastern states, and since the 1930s Japanese immigrants have developed jute and pepper plantations. But the area still remains largely unpopulated and undeveloped, yielding small quantities of forest products (rubber, timber, vegetable oils, and medicinal plants) and cacao. The establishment of a health service (chiefly by launch) in the Second World War was followed by the creation of a UNESCO research institute in 1948, and several developmental programs, both governmental and private, have been set up in Brazil in recent years to foster the valley's development. Oil and manganese resources (recently discovered) are now exploited near Manaus and in Amapá. See W. L. Herndon, *Exploration of the Valley of the Amazon* (1854; reprinted 1952); C. R. Markham, ed., *Expeditions into the Valley of the Amazon* (1859); H. W. Bates, *The Naturalist on the River Amazon* (1910); H. M. Tomlinson, *The Sea and the Jungle* (1928); Charles Wagley, *Amazon Town* (1953); Alain Gheerbrant, *Journey to the Far Amazon* (Eng. tr., 1954); Peter Matthiessen, *The Cloud Forest* (1961).

Amazonas (ämäzō'nủs), state (c.602,000 sq. mi.; pop. c.721,215), NW Brazil. It is bounded on the north and west by Venezuela, Colombia, and Peru. The capital is MANAUS. It covers a major part of the Amazon basin and is the largest but least populated of Brazilian states.

Ambarvalia (ămbũrvăl'yủ), in Roman religion, yearly agricultural rite held at the end of May. To insure fertility and disperse evil, each farmer led members of his household and a sacrificial beast in a procession around the boundaries of his fields.

ambassador: see DIPLOMATIC SERVICE.

Ambato (ämbä'tō), city (pop. c.39,000), central Ecuador, in a high Andean valley. A major commercial and transportation hub, Ambato is also noted for the variety of fruit grown in its outskirts. Sugar cane, grains, and cotton are also grown and hides are processed. A picturesque garden city, it is a favorite resort of the rich. Among its fine buildings is an old cathedral. Near Ambato in 1821 the patriot Antonio José de Sucre, at first defeated by Spanish royalists, later won over them after receiving help from José de San Martín. This victory led to the decisive battle of Pichincha. The city has been frequently damaged by volcanic eruptions and earthquakes, most recently in 1949.

amber [Arabic], yellow to brown fossil resin exuded by coniferous trees now extinct. Capable of being highly polished, it is used in the manufacture of beads, amulets, mouthpieces, cigar and cigarette holders, pipes, and other small ornamental objects. Its chief chemical constituents are carbon, hydrogen, and oxygen, in varying proportions. Baltic amber also contains succinic acid and is often called succinite. An essential oil (amber oil) is obtained from amber. When rubbed with a cloth, amber becomes charged with static electricity. The chief source of the world's amber is the Baltic coast of Germany, Lithuania, and Latvia; millions of pounds have been taken from the mine at Palmicken in former East Prussia. Some is found off the coasts of Sicily and England. The best amber is transparent, but some varieties are cloudy. Bubbles of air, leaves, bits of wood, and insects are frequent inclusions, the insects sometimes being of extinct species. Amber was known in the Bronze Age and to the Greeks and Romans, who used it extensively in jewelry. Thales was familiar with its electrical properties, and Pliny recounts several instances of its artistic uses. It is connected with many superstitions and is believed to be a preventive against disease and bad luck.

Amberg (äm'běrk), city (pop. 41,574), Federal Republic of Germany, N central Bavaria, on the Vils river. Precision instruments, textiles, and porcelain are manufactured. Nearby there are large iron mines known since the Middle Ages. A Gothic church and a 15th-century town hall are its outstanding buildings. Here, in 1796, Archduke Charles of Austria defeated the French under Jourdan. Until 1810 Amberg was the capital of the Upper Palatinate.

Amberger, Christoph (krĭs'tôf äm'běrgùr), fl. 1530–61, German painter. Working in Augsburg, he was influenced by earlier Augsburg portrait painters and by the Venetian artist Bordone. Portraits of Emperor Charles V (1532) and Sebastian Münster (1552), representative works, are in Berlin.

ambergris (ăm'bùrgrēs), waxlike substance originating in the intestine of the sperm whale as a morbid concretion. Lighter than water, it is found floating on tropical seas or cast up on the shore in yellow, gray, black, or variegated masses, usually a few ounces in weight, though pieces weighing several hundred pounds have been found. Ambergris was greatly valued from earliest times, chiefly for its supposed medicinal properties. Soluble in alcohol, it is now used as a fixative in perfumes. Its active principle is ambrain.

Amberley, village (pop. 2,951), SW Ohio, a suburb NE of Cincinnati; inc. 1940.

Ambers, Lou, 1913–, American boxer, b. Herkimer, N.Y. He was originally named Louis D'Ambrosio. Ambers won the world lightweight championship from Tony Canzoneri in 1936. Henry Armstrong beat him in 1938, but Ambers regained the title in a return bout in 1939. During his professional career (1932–41), the Herkimer Kid, as he was called, had 102 matches. He won 87 fights, including 29 by knockout; lost 9; and drew in 6. He lost the title to Lew Jenkins in 1940.

Ambiorix (ămbī'ùrĭks), fl. 54 B.C., Gallic chieftain of the Eburones (in what is now central Belgium). He had been favorably treated by the Romans, but he joined another tribe in attacking Julius Caesar's legates. When he heard of Caesar's approach, he fled across the Rhine.

Ambler, Eric, 1909–, English novelist. A successful businessman, he turned exclusively to writing after his novels—realistic suspense stories—became popular. His heroes are usually ordinary men who become accidentally or innocently involved in international intrigues. Included among his "thrillers" are *A Coffin for Dimitrios* (1939), *Journey into Fear* (1940), and *Passage of Arms* (1959).

Ambler, suburban borough (pop. 6,765), SE Pa., N of Philadelphia; inc. 1888. Asbestos, metal products, and chemicals are manufactured. A school of horticulture for women is here.

Ambleside, village, Westmorland, N England, near the head of Lake Windermere. It is a tourist center for the Lake District. The parish church, built by Sir George Gilbert Scott in 1854, contains a stained-glass window contributed by English and American admirers of William Wordsworth. Nearby is a Roman camp with two forts, one of which is excavated and preserved. Harriet Martineau lived here for nearly 30 years.

Amboina (ămboi'nù), Malay **Ambon**, island (c.314 sq. mi.; pop. 56,037), E Indonesia, one of the Moluccas, in the Banda Sea, SW of Ceram. A mountainous island, it is well watered and fertile and produces cloves, sago, rice, sugar, and copra. The population is generally Christian in the south and Moslem in the north. Discovered by the Portuguese in 1512, it was captured by the Dutch in 1605. A British settlement here was destroyed in 1623 by the Dutch during the so-called massacre of Amboina. Amboina was temporarily under British rule from 1796 to 1802 and again from 1810 to 1817. The chief town, also called Amboina, is a port (exporting copra and spices) and has an airport. In 1950, during the short-lived South Moluccan Republic, Amboina was the scene of a revolt against the Indonesian government. The name is sometimes spelled Amboyna.

Amboise, Georges d' (zhôrzh' däbwäz'), 1460–1510, French statesman, cardinal of the Roman Church. He became archbishop of Rouen in 1493. In 1498, as the most intimate friend of the new king, Louis XII, he became chief minister. Subsequently he was appointed cardinal and papal legate in France. He devoted himself primarily to the furtherance of Louis's ambitions in Italy and was lieutenant general in Italy at the conquest of Milan (1500). His ambitions for the papal crown were disappointed by the election of Pius III (1503), but Julius II designated him (1503) papal legate in France for life. He negotiated the abortive treaties of Blois (1504) and helped form the League of Cambrai (1508; see CAMBRAI, LEAGUE OF). His domestic administration was beneficent. By his patronage of artists and writers, he contributed, more than any other figure of his time, to the promotion of the Renaissance in France.

Amboise (äbwäz'), town (estimated pop. 6,736), Indre-et-Loire dept., N central France, in Touraine, on the Loire. Although it trades in wine and woolens, the town is chiefly famous for its château built in late Gothic style, with Renaissance additions. It was a royal residence from the reign of Charles VIII (who was born and died here) to that of Francis II. Leonardo da Vinci, who probably worked on it, is said to be buried in its chapel. Amboise was the scene (1560) of a Huguenot plot against the GUISE family. In 1563, the Edict of Amboise was signed here.

Amboise, conspiracy of, also known as the **Tumult of Amboise,** 1560, plot of the Huguenots and other enemies of Charles and François de GUISE, in France. It was possibly supported by Elizabeth I of England and by Calvin in Geneva. The plan, presumably worked out by Louis I de CONDÉ, provided for a march, led by Godefroi de la Renaudie, a nobleman from Limousin, on the castle of Amboise, the abduction of King FRANCIS II, and the arrest of the duke and the cardinal. Cardinal de

Woodcut of the execution of the conspirators of Amboise.

Guise was forewarned, and the rebels, beaten before they had united their forces, were ruthlessly massacred. For weeks the bodies of hundreds of conspirators were hanging from the castle and from every tree in the vicinity. The Huguenots were enraged; to appease them Catherine de' Medici used her power to appoint the moderate Michel de l'Hôpital chancellor. His first act was to bring about the Edict of Romorantin (1560), which halted Protestant persecution until the outbreak (1562) of the Wars of Religion.

Ambon: see AMBOINA.

Amboy (ăm′boi), city (pop. 2,067), N Ill., SSW of Rockford, in a farm area; inc. 1857.

Ambracia (ămbrā′shù), modern Arta, city of ancient Greece, in Epirus, on the Arachus river and near the Ambracian Gulf, an inlet of the Ionian Sea. Founded (7th cent. B.C.) by Corinthian colonists, it was ceded (294 B.C.) by Macedon to Pyrrhus, who made it the capital of Epirus. It was conquered by Rome in 189 B.C. It is the modern Greek town of Arta (pop. 9,441), an agricultural trading center.

Ambridge, borough (pop. 13,865), W Pa., on the Ohio and NW of Pittsburgh; inc. 1905. It has steel plants and manufactures metal products and electrical machinery. The site was originally an Indian village. Members of the HARMONY SOCIETY established here the communistic settlement Economy (1825–1906). Some of the old buildings remain.

Ambrogio Stefani da Fossano: see BERGOGNONE.

Ambrose, Saint (ăm′brōz), 340?–397, bishop of Milan, doctor of the Church, b. Trier, of Christian parents. Educated at Rome, he became (c.372) governor of Liguria and Aemilia—with the capital at Milan. He was much loved for his justice. Popular demand caused his appointment (374) as bishop, though he was reluctant and lacked religious training. After much study he became the chief Catholic opponent of Arianism in the West. He was adviser to Emperor GRATIAN, whom he persuaded to outlaw (379) all heresy in the West. He firmly refused the demands of Justina and the young Emperor VALENTINIAN II to surrender a church of his diocese to the Arians. "The Emperor," he preached, "is in the Church, not above

Saint Ambrose (detail from mosaic).

it." He imposed a heavy public penance upon THEODOSIUS I for the massacre at Salonica (390). Ambrose's eloquent preaching spurred the conversion of St. Augustine. His writings, mostly homilies based on Scripture, have come down to us largely from his hearers. They reveal wide classical learning, knowledge of patristic literature, and a

Roman bent toward the ethical and practical. Of his formal works, *On the Duties of the Clergy* (*De officiis ministrorum*) shows the influence of Cicero; *On the Christian Faith* (*De fide*) was written at Gratian's request. Ambrose's method of biblical interpretation was allegorical, following Philo and Origen. About 386 he arranged hymns and psalms for the congregation to sing antiphonally. A PLAIN SONG called Ambrosian chant is attached to his name. His hymns, written in the iambic dimeter that became standard in Western hymnody, were widely imitated. Only a few are extant. The Ambrosian Rite used in Milan today is probably a development of a liturgy Ambrose introduced. Feast: Dec. 7. See biography by F. H. Dudden (1935).

ambrosia (ămbrō′zhù), in Greek religion, food with which the Olympian gods preserved their immortality. It was accompanied by nectar, wine of the gods.

Ambrosian Library, founded c.1605 in Milan by Cardinal Federigo Borromeo. It became one of the earliest libraries to be opened to the public. The collection is rich in classical manuscripts, notably Homer and Vergil, in incunabula, and in Oriental texts. The library also has a good collection of paintings and sculpture.

Amchitka (ămchĭt′kù), island, 40 mi. long, off W Alaska, one of the ALEUTIAN ISLANDS.

Amecameca (ämä″kämä′kä), town (pop. c.10,000), SE of Mexico city. It is the starting point for ascents of Popocatépetl and Ixtacíhuatl. The sanctuary of El Sacro Monte, the most venerated spot in Mexico next to the shrine of Guadalupe, is on a hill above the town.

Amen: see AMON.

amendment, in law, alteration of the provisions of a legal document. The term usually refers to the alteration of a STATUTE or a CONSTITUTION, but it is also applied in PARLIAMENTARY LAW to proposed changes of a bill or motion under consideration and in judicial PROCEDURE to the correction of errors. A statute may be amended by the passage of an act which is identified specifically as an amendment or which renders some previous statutory provision nugatory. Written constitutions, however, for the most part must be amended by an exactly prescribed procedure. The CONSTITUTION OF THE UNITED STATES, according to provision in Article 5, may be amended when two thirds of each house of Congress approves a proposed amendment and three fourths of the states thereafter ratify it. Congress decides whether state ratification shall be by vote of the legislatures or by popularly elected conventions. Only in the case of the Twenty-first Amendment (the repeal of prohibition) was the convention system used. The constitutions of many states (e.g., New York) require that a proposed constitutional amendment be submitted to a referendum.

Amenemhet I (ä″měněm′hět, ä″–), d. 1970 B.C., founder of the XII dynasty of ancient EGYPT. He came of a powerful family of Thebes and seized (c.2000 B.C.) the kingship. The XII dynasty ushered in the Middle Kingdom of Egypt. Amenemhet centralized the government and subjected the long-powerful nobles to a virtually feudal state. His son and successor, SESOSTRIS I was coregent from 1980. **Amenemhet II,** d. 1903 B.C., son and successor of Sesostris I, was coregent with his father (1938–1935 B.C.), then sole ruler (1935–1906), finally coregent with his son and successor, SESOSTRIS II. He reopened the mines of Sinai. **Amenemhet III,** d. 1801 B.C., was the son and successor of SESOSTRIS III, with whom he had been coregent. He extended the irrigation system. Thousands of acres in the Fayum were reclaimed. Under his successor, **Amenemhet IV,** d. 1792 B.C., the power of the dynasty declined, and his successor, a woman, Sebenekfrure, was last of her family. The dynasty of Pharaohs named Amenemhet or Sesostris maintained peace throughout their hegemony, thus enabling the arts and sciences to flourish as they never would again.

Amenhotep I (ä″měnhō′těp, ä″–) or **Amenophis I** (ä″měnō′fĭs), fl. 1570 B.C., king of the XVIII dynasty of ancient Egypt, successor to his father, Amasis I. His chief exploits were military. He pushed southward into Nubia and reestablished Egypt's boundary at the second cataract, as previously fixed by Sesostris III. He invaded Syria as far as the Euphrates. His successor, THUTMOSE I, was not his son. **Amenhotep II** or **Amenophis II,** son and successor of THUTMOSE III, succeeded (1448 B.C.) as coregent and later ruled alone for 26 years. There are records of his prowess in hunting and horsemanship. He put down a revolt in Syria and maintained his father's conquests. His tomb is at Thebes; he had also built extensively at Karnak. On his death (c.1420 B.C.) he was succeeded by his son THUTMOSE IV. **Amenhotep III** or **Amenophis III** succeeded his father, Thutmose IV, c.1411 B.C. His reign (until c.1372 B.C.) marks the

Amenhotep III (detail from Egyptian stone statue).

start of the decline of the XVIII dynasty. It was the age of Egypt's greatest splendor; there was peace in his Asiatic empire (in spite of incursions by Bedouins and Hittites) and he invaded Nubia only once. This is the period of extreme elaboration in Egyptian architecture and sculpture. Amenhotep III built extensively at Thebes, Luxor, and Karnak. His wife TIY was given an unprecedented position as queen consort and exerted much influence over her husband and his son and successor, IKHNATON. During Amenhotep III's reign the first traces appeared of the "solar monotheism" of the god Aton, elaborated by Ikhnaton. Tablets found at Tel-el-Amarna shed light on the sociopolitical conditions in Egypt and Asia Minor in the 14th cent. B.C.

Amenia (ùmē′nèù), uninc. town (pop. 7,546), SE N.Y., NE of Poughkeepsie near the Conn. line, in a farm and dairy region; founded 1788. Thomas Lake Harris had (1863–67) his Brotherhood of the New Life settlement in Amenia.

Amenophis: see AMENHOTEP.

America [for Amerigo VESPUCCI], the lands of the Western Hemisphere—North America, Central America (sometimes Middle America), and South America. In English, America and American are frequently used to refer only to the United States. Martin WALDSEEMÜLLER was the first to use the name.

America, patriotic hymn of the United States beginning, "My country 'tis of thee." The words were written in 1831 by Samuel Francis Smith while he was a theological student in Andover, Mass. According to his own account he was asked by Lowell Mason to examine a book of German songs with the idea of either translating some of them or of writing English words to them. There he found the tune (possibly to the words *Heil dir im Siegerkranz*) which inspired his poem, and only later did he discover that he had used the tune of God Save the King, which was known in America as early as 1761. The tune has been—almost certainly incorrectly—attributed to Henry Carey or the *Harmonica Anglica*.

American, river rising in three forks in N central California, in the Sierra Nevada near Lake Tahoe, and flowing W and SW into the Sacramento river at Sacramento. Gold discoveries in 1848 along the river and its forks played an important part in the history of California.

Americana (ùmĕrĭkā′nù, –kă′nù, –kä′nù), defined as all that has been printed about the Americas, printed in the Americas, or written by Americans, but usually restricted to the formative period in the history of the two continents. The Columbus letter (1493), a two-leaf newssheet announcing to the Spanish court the discovery of the islands of the Indies, is the earliest known printing about America. Richard Hakluyt's *Divers Voyages touching the Discovery of America* was published in London in 1582. Early American books were printed by Juan PABLOS, Stephen DAYE, and William BRADFORD (1722–91). The John Carter Brown Library, Providence; the New York Public Library; the Newberry Library, Chicago; and the Huntington Library, San Marino, Calif., all have fine collections of Americana. See John C. Oswald, *Printing in the Americas* (1937); Joseph Sabin, Wilberforce Eames, and R. W. G. Vail, *Bibliotheca*

Americana: a Dictionary of Books Relating to America (29 vols., 1868–1937); Charles Evans, *American Bibliography, 1639–1800* (13 vols., 1903–55).

American Academy in Rome, founded in 1894 as the American School of Architecture in Rome by Charles F. McKim and enlarged in 1897 with the founding of the American Academy in Rome for students of architecture, sculpture, and painting. It was incorporated by act of Congress in 1905. In 1913 its charter was amended to include the American School of Classical Studies in Rome. It awards annually to U.S. citizens competitive fellowships bearing a yearly stipend, a travel allowance, and residence in Rome. Fellowships are awarded in architecture, painting, sculpture, music, landscape architecture, and art history.

American architecture. Each group of settlers in North America brought with it the building techniques and the prevailing forms of its home country and thus gave rise to different types of colonial building. But in all areas the differences between American and European conditions and climates, the fact that available building materials were not those of the home country, the frequent lack of trained architects and craftsmen, and often the poverty of the settlers produced rapid and profound change. Thus in French America stone building was rare and was often replaced by a sort of stucco over half timber or, in the St. Lawrence valley, by wood; a characteristic low, rectangular plan with high hipped roofs, however, persisted. Only in New Orleans, where the government sent skilled architects and engineers, was anything produced which approached the sophistication of the home country. The comparatively short Spanish reign in Florida also produced highly complex structures, such as the forts at St. Augustine and Matanzas, the St. Augustine cathedral, and various houses; but this beginning had little enduring influence. In the Southwest, however, the Spanish impress was more permanent; there the settlers borrowed widely the Indian techniques of construction in small-stone masonry and in adobe and produced work admirably fitted to its surroundings. In it the Mexican baroque details and church forms appeared in a new and simpler guise, as in the Texas, New Mexico, Arizona, and California missions. The Dutch settling in New Amsterdam were essentially traders and, well backed from Holland, rapidly developed a typical 17th-century Dutch village. But outside the large centers they modified their building types. The English settlements were of two basic types: one, in the South, based on the large mansion house and plantation system; the other, in the North, based on small-scale individual activities in farming, fishing, lumbering, and commerce. In both cases the settlers tried first to build as they had at home—many-gabled half-timber houses of late Gothic inspiration. In the South brick rapidly superseded wood as the chief building material, and the growing classicism of English architecture was almost immediately reflected, as in the official buildings of Williamsburg. In the North the climate rapidly forced the covering of half-timber houses, the lowering of roof slopes, and the simplification of plans; poverty (except in space and natural resources) prompted simplicity of detail. A type of residence which became popular in the wilderness and on the Western frontier by the mid-18th cent. was the LOG CABIN. During this time a growing prosperity and widening commerce brought a new influx of well-trained craftsmen, and English architectural books became increasingly available. There was a flowering of native craftsmen and designers who adapted the English precedent to American conditions with great skill. The result can be seen especially well in Charleston (S.C.), Annapolis, Philadelphia, Portsmouth (N.H.), Newburyport, Marblehead, and the earlier buildings of Salem (Mass.). The same period produced many churches in which the current English types by Christopher Wren and James Gibbs received simple, but elegant, American interpretations (e.g., St. Paul's Chapel, New York). Toward the end of the colonial period, styles based on a more direct study of ancient Roman and Greek structures were beginning to appear in Europe. The Adam trend (see ADAM, ROBERT) rapidly appeared in America, especially in interior detail. In a more monumental way the Adam style is typical of the work of Charles BULFINCH in Boston and of Samuel McINTIRE in Salem, both among the growing number of native-born designers. Architectural books began to be published in America, and American simplifications of Adam work were spread widely by means of the earlier books of Asher BENJAMIN. Both Washington and Jefferson gave serious thought to architecture and were deeply involved in the building of WASH-INGTON, D.C. Both looked to the ancient classic world as the truest source of inspiration. Jefferson's ideals were perfectly expressed in his own house at Monticello and in the Virginia capitol and the Univ. of Virginia. The eventual result was the CLASSIC REVIVAL in America. This was introduced largely by European architects who came to the New World in search of commissions and honor. The Greek revival appeared first in the work of Benjamin Henry LATROBE in Philadelphia and Washington and was spread widely by the architects who followed him. The later books of Asher Benjamin and those of Minard Lafever spread the new type of detail over the country, and examples of the style can be found in Louisiana and Maine, in the Carolinas and Wisconsin. Yet certain regional constants persisted beneath this uniformity of style. The plantation regions still built great mansions, often with two-story colonnades, and farmhouses of basically 18th-century type still dominated much of New England; it was in the port cities that the uniformity was greatest. Temple-type porticoes decorated churches, banks, and public buildings. Meanwhile, prior to the Mexican War, in the Southwest the Spanish tradition remained supreme, although in California it was becoming more and more modified by the environment and was borrowing occasionally also from the Eastern states. The houses of Monterey are typical of this mixture. As early as the end of the 18th cent. the "castellated Gothic" of the English dilettanti began to have American imitators and became increasingly popular in the United States from 1835 on, especially for churches and cottages; the Gothic work of A. J. Davis, Richard Upjohn, and Minard Lafever won instant acclaim, and the widely distributed books of A. J. DOWNING on domestic architecture and landscape gardening helped spread the new gospel. Many of the cottages and mansions were well planned, original, and charming. Local designers often interpreted the Gothic stone detail in wood. Just before and during the Civil War, the writings of Ruskin began to influence American architects profoundly. An epidemic of American versions of the Victorian Gothic followed but was generally short-lived. It left, however, a valuable residue in the forcing of a new, more logical, and deeper questioning of the bases of

New Orleans street, St. Louis Cathedral in the background.

City gates of St. Augustine, Fla.

San Luis Rey, one of the many early California missions.

Boston's Old State House shows Dutch influence.

Old log building

Colonial Governor's Palace, Williamsburg, Va.

design. The two decades following the Civil War were confused, in architecture as in politics. Great strides in industrialization changed building methods and techniques. A new study of the functional basis of house design brought many experimental forms into being. Westward expansion and growing urbanization made an extraordinary amount of building necessary, but they promoted crude speculation in land and often resulted in jerry-building. At the same time new wealth sought expression in unbridled ostentation, and increasing foreign travel brought acquaintance with all types of European building, overwhelming existing local traditions of taste and technique. Under such conditions eclecticism in taste was inevitable, and in the United States eclecticism dominated architecture from the late 1880s to the great economic debacle of the 1930s. Many architects went to Paris, if possible to the École des Beaux-Arts, to receive the traditional doctrines. In the earlier periods, almost up to the Civil War, the architect and the engineer had often been identical or at least had worked for the same ends. Eclecticism put an end to this unity. The engineer designed the structural ele-

Boston State House, designed by Charles Bulfinch.

Monticello, Thomas Jefferson's home.

St. John's Church, Washington D.C., from the original drawing and design by Benjamin H. Latrobe.

ments which the architect decorated; in the process both forgot the great principle of the oneness of visible form and structure. Yet throughout this chaotic period certain creative efforts continued. One was the development of a high technical ability in planning, i.e., in arranging spaces within a building so that they would function efficiently. Another was the extraordinary development of the techniques of industrialized building in steel and in reinforced concrete, together with the organization of the building industry to make possible the swift and economical erection of projects of almost any size. In both planning and the techniques of building the United States was far in advance of most European centers. Thus the basic search for an expressive and functional architecture never entirely died. The old colonial and classic revival tradition of direct construction continued long to dominate in many of the simpler buildings. The later Ruskinian influence made many designers rebel against the senseless details of the ruling taste. The work of Henry Hobson RICHARDSON expressed this rebellion. The William Morris movement toward realizing the importance of craftsmanship also had tremendous influence. These protests were climaxed by the work of the so-called Chicago school and in the designs and writings of its arch-prophet, Louis Henry SULLIVAN. Of his many followers, Frank Lloyd WRIGHT, one of the acknowledged founders of the modern movement, was the most famous. Hints of new and different kinds of architecture being built abroad were becoming known. The new work that came gradually into being had four chief roots. First, new economic conditions which forced attention on new problems—mass housing and community planning, great power developments, and new types of factory. From these problems flowed others, such as recreational developments and shopping centers; from power developments came the inspiration of social purpose and great scale; from factory design (as emphasized by the industrial demands of the Second World War) came new approaches to planning, a study of the use of new materials, and a new realization of the importance of the human element in industrial buildings. Second, the work in Europe of the International school, especially of

Christopher Wren's spire on the Old Church, Sandwich, Mass.

Le Corbusier and Gropius, and that of other, freer modern European architects, such as Oud and Mendelsohn and Aalto and other Scandinavian designers (see MODERN ARCHITECTURE). Third, the work of Frank Lloyd Wright and the inspiration derived from the continually changing products of his superb creative imagination. This proved a valuable counterinfluence against the more rigid and formal doctrines of the International school. Frequently local and traditional materials—stone and wood, for instance—were used in close combination with newer materials such as large sheets of plate glass and metal posts or frames. Fourth, and perhaps most important, the result of the coupling of applied science and industrial production. This produced a great number of new materials—metal alloys, plastics, adhesives—and rendered cheaper and more available many older materials such as glass and wood veneers. It led also to increased perfection in mechanical equipment, especially in heating (as in panel or radiant heating) and ventilation (as in air conditioning). The new architecture of the United States is increasingly flexible. It produces different results in different regions, as climate and materials suggest; it adapts itself to buildings of all types—schools, churches, factories, government buildings, houses. It is growing visually richer as its techniques and materials are increasingly mastered; little by little it is becoming as satisfactory emotionally as it has been physically. See S. F. Kimball, *Domestic Architecture of the American Colonies and Early Republic* (1922) and *American Architecture* (1928); Talbot Hamlin, *American Spirit in Architecture* (1926) and *Greek Revival Architecture in America* (1944); J. M. Fitch, *American Building* (1948) and *Architecture and the Esthetics of Plenty* (1961); Louis Henry Sullivan, *Autobiography of an Idea* (1926); Frank Lloyd Wright, *Autobiography* (1943); the writings of Lewis Mumford; J. E. Burchard and Albert Bush-Brown, *The Architecture of America: a Social and Cultural History* (1961).

American art. The North American colonies in the 17th cent. enjoyed neither the wealth nor the leisure to cultivate the fine arts extensively. The colonial craftsman in pewter, silver, glass, or textiles followed closely the European model. The 17th-century "limners," generally unknown by name, turned out crude but often charming portraits in the Elizabethan style, the Dutch baroque manner, or the English baroque court style, with the preferred style depending upon the European background of both the artist and his patron. The portrait painters alternated "limning" with coach and sign painting or other types of craftsmanship, and even in the 18th cent. it was seldom possible to earn a living by art alone. The silversmith Paul Revere turned his talents to commercial engraving and the manufacture of false teeth. The crafts in general followed English, Dutch, and Bavarian models, though in furniture some variations appeared in the work of talented craftsmen such as Samuel McIntire and Duncan Phyfe. In the first half of the 18th cent. a growing demand for portrait painting attracted such artists as John Smibert, Peter Pelham, and Joseph Blackburn from England, Gustavus Hesselius from Sweden, Jeremiah Theus from Switzerland,

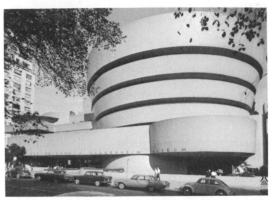
Frank Lloyd Wright's Guggenheim Museum, New York City.

American Pavilion, Expo 67, Quebec, Canada.

United Nations Building, New York City.

Furnishings of 17th-century household in New England.

Eighteenth - century American glass mug.

Clark Mills' equestrian statue of General Andrew Jackson.

mecca of American painters who for half a century came to study under him. His training in historical painting did not stand them in good stead on their return to America, where no demand existed for such work. Gilbert Stuart, however, emerged from his tutelage a superb portrait painter and after gaining success in England returned to America, where he executed a long series of famous and charming portraits and set a standard rarely surpassed in this country. Of all the arts sculpture was, perhaps, the least cultivated in the colonies. Apart from the anonymous carvers of tombstones and ships' figureheads, William Rush is almost the only known native sculptor to have practiced in pre-Revolutionary and early Federalist times. The period from the birth of the republic to the Civil War did not see much increased demand for the fine arts. Such early painters as Washington Allston, Samuel F. B. Morse, John Vanderlyn, and John Trumbull, who sought a market in America for historical painting in the classical manner of Jacques Louis David, were quickly disillusioned. Portrait painting alone could provide the patronage enjoyed by such men as Mather Brown, Henry Benbridge, Edward Savage, Thomas Sully, John Neagle, Chester Harding, and the miniaturists Edward G. Malbone and John Wesley Jarvis. None of these men equaled Stuart or Copley, but all of them produced work of real interest. Perhaps even more interesting, however, was the gradual rise of a number of excellent genre painters—Henry Inman, William Sidney Mount, Eastman Johnson, and George Caleb Bingham. These were the earliest painters of the American scene. Meanwhile J. J. Audubon achieved fame as the painter of American birds. It is significant that he had to go to England for recognition and publication of his work. The first half of the 19th cent. saw the first school of American landscape painting.

and Pieter Vanderlyn from Holland. Joseph Badger, Robert Feke, Ralph Earl, John Trumbull, and Charles Willson Peale did not depart widely from the tradition of 18th-century English portraiture, but while their work is harder and cruder, it is often more vigorous. In the early work of John Singleton COPLEY this vigor is combined with a great native talent. Another 18th-century American painter, Benjamin WEST, set up shop in London and became painter to the king and president of the Royal Academy. Although his training and practice were European, his studio became the

Thomas Doughty and Thomas Cole started the HUDSON RIVER SCHOOL, which was continued by Asher Durand, John Frederick Kensett, and Frederick Edwin Church. Despite a tendency toward the panoramic, the better work of these men showed a direct inspiration by nature which has never ceased to be an important factor in American art. In sculpture, portraiture provided the main source of patronage. John Frazee and Hezekiah Augur with little training produced forceful and original work in marble and wood. Horatio Greenough began the long tradition of the American sculptor in Italy, where he was soon followed by Thomas Crawford, Hiram Powers, and Harriet Hosmer. The atmosphere and aesthetic taste of the American artists' colony in Rome is described in detail by Hawthorne in *The Marble Faun* (1860). The American sculptors in Italy were greatly influenced by the neoclassicist Thorvaldsen. More authentic talents, perhaps, were Clark Mills, whose figure of Gen. Andrew Jackson was the first equestrian statue cast in America, and Thomas Ball and William Rimmer, whose untutored work had originality and power. In painting, the post-Civil War period produced works of enduring worth and striking individuality. It is probable that in no period has art enjoyed more ardent patronage in America. Not only the newly wealthy industrialists but also the state and Federal governments showed an unprece-

dented readiness to support the arts. Much of the more popular work of the period, such as the historical and mural paintings of Leutze and the panoramas of Bierstadt, have relatively little aesthetic interest today. But Whistler, Ryder, Eakins, and Winslow Homer have seldom been equaled in our history. The four are strikingly dissimilar. Whistler, an expatriate, cultivated a delicate art of suggestion in his oils and etchings alike. Ryder, a hermit, produced a visionary art of deep significance. Eakins painted with uncompromising honesty the everyday world about him. And Homer's water colors are among the strongest realistic interpretations of pure landscape. This was also the period of the fine romantic landscape painters George Inness, Alexander H. Wyant, Homer D. Martin, and Ralph Blakelock. In Inness, and perhaps even more in William Morris Hunt, the influence of the Barbizon school was brought to America. Although French influence had begun to supplant German, the portrait painters William M. Chase and Frank Duveneck reflect the art practiced in Munich, as the earlier genre painters had reflected the influence of artists in Düsseldorf. John La Farge, who studied in Paris, did much to widen the cultural horizon. His religious murals and stained glass set a new standard for these arts in America. John Singer Sargent excelled rather in society portraiture, and Elihu Vedder and Edwin Abbey in illustration. At

Thomas Eakins' Signora Gomez d'Arza.

George Wesley Bellows' Portrait of a Boy.

John Singleton Copley's Portrait of John Adams.

Winslow Homer's The Northeaster.

the close of the century John Twachtman, Childe Hassam, Ernest Lawson, and Mary Cassat worked under the direct influence of French impressionism. Under the same influence Maurice Prendergast created original, boldly colorful images of passing scenes. In sculpture after the Civil War there was an increased demand for commemorative work. In the late 19th cent. John Quincy Adams Ward introduced a strong note of realism into a tradition suffering from the somewhat vapid classicism of the Italianates. His heroic Washington in bronze at the New York Subtreasury Building is an American masterpiece. His student Daniel Chester French also devoted his talents to monumental sculpture. William Rimmer's *Dying Centaur* showed realistic strength, and his extensively illustrated *Art Anatomy* (1877) was admired by artists and physicians alike. In addition to portraits and monumental work, an illustrative sculpture of small figures and genre groups became popular. The workshop of John Rogers was most successful in this, and later Frederick Remington's small bronzes extended the scope of native realism westward to include the cowboy. Neoclassic tendencies dominated in the work of Olin Warner and Augustus Saint-Gaudens, both of whom studied in Paris. Daniel Chester French's early training was with Ward in America, but his *Minute Man* was modeled on a classic ideal, as were most of his later works. Saint-Gaudens became the leading sculptor of the period, setting standards of excellence with his New York Farragut monument and the Shaw Memorial in Boston. In the early 20th cent. sculptors such as Paul Bartlett, Karl Bitter, Frederick MacMonnies, George Barnard, and Lorado Taft exhibited a continuing conflict between naturalistic and idealized modes of representation. A significant cultural development of the era was the founding and expansion of American museums, whose collections were important to the art student and public alike. Museums, together with the rapid growth of art galleries, private collections, and art schools, widened the understanding of the European past and lessened the naiveté of earlier periods. Under the impetus of new techniques of reproduction the art of illustration flourished. The work of Edwin Abbey, Arthur Frost, and Howard Pyle was outstanding, appearing in *Harper's* and numerous other illustrated magazines and books. American art turned in the 20th cent. to exploitation of new techniques and new expression. The functional precision of the machine strongly influenced all the arts. The development of photography forced a reevaluation of the representational nature of painting, while the formal and expressive capacities of modern European art opened fresh fields for the artist. In reflecting the radical European tendencies, American art in general maintained a more constant interest in local color and subject matter. Early in the century a vigorous movement toward realism in subject and freedom in technique was headed by such men as Robert Henri, John Sloan, and George Luks. With others they formed the Eight, a group that sought the founding of art on a broader social basis. Photographer Alfred Stieg-

John Quincy Adams Ward's bronze monument of George Washington at the Subtreasury Building, downtown New York City.

Gutzon Borglum's Mount Rushmore monument.

litz's 291 Gallery offered America early glimpses of fauve and cubist work and in addition exhibited abstract paintings by such Americans as Max Weber, Marsden Hartley, and John Marin. The full force of European modern art was presented to shocked Americans in the famous Armory Show of 1913, organized by Arthur Davies and other artists. Under the influence of this exhibition, the early work of such Americans as Joseph Stella, Charles Demuth, and Stuart Davis revealed new abstract tendencies. George Bellows and Rockwell Kent remained popular realists, and Edward Hopper and Charles Burchfield developed a more poignant personal realism. John Marin caught the imposing breadth of nature in his water colors, while Georgia O'Keeffe, Charles Sheeler, and Peter Blume combined realism with varying degrees of precise formal design. A chauvinistic espousal of the American scene flourished under Thomas Benton and Grant Wood in the early '30s, while the same decade and the '40s saw the rise of more personally meaningful, socially conscious art in the work of Ben Shahn, Philip Evergood, Jacob Lawrence, and Raphael and Moses Soyer. Government sponsorship of the arts during the depression years was the chief means by which many artists were able to continue work. Two independent programs, the Dept. of the Treasury's Section of Fine Arts and the Federal Art Project of the Works Progress Administration, were responsible for the embellishment of many public buildings with murals and the creation of smaller works for display in public institutions. In painting since 1945 the work of all but the most intensive realists,

Daniel Chester French's statue of Abraham Lincoln.

211

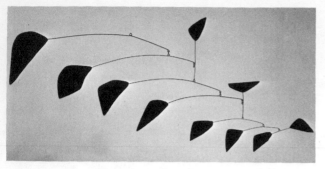

Alexander Calder's mobile Ten Black.

such as Andrew Wyeth, has tended increasingly toward abstraction. Such artists as Arshile Gorky, Irene Pereira, Morris Graves, and Mark Tobey have developed and employed abstraction in works of highly personal symbolic content, whereas painters such as Jackson Pollock, Willem de Kooning, Adolph Gottlieb, and Franz Kline have created a bold and unique imagery that has made American painting a dominant influence in world art (see ABSTRACT EXPRESSIONISM). American sculpture in the 20th cent. produced both monumental and life-sized works in the traditional styles, including French's statue of Lincoln in the Lincoln Memorial, Washington, and Gutzon Borglum's Mt. Rushmore monument, the classicizing figures of Paul Manship, and Mahonri Young's naturalistic athletes and laborers. However, the dominant tendency has been toward abstract design and expressive form, a trend to which William Zorach and Gaston Lachaise contributed early figurative work. Alexander Calder pioneered in the use of mobile welded metal forms, adding motion as a new dimension in sculpture. In the '40s and '50s the free play of abstract forms in light and space, plus the use of new materials, have been vigorously exploited by David Smith, Theodore Roszak, Herbert Ferber, Isamu Noguchi, and Richard Lippold. By mid-century most museums had come to play important roles in promoting artists, exhibiting new work, and educating the public about art. In addition many businesses and corporations have acquired significant collections and become important factors in art patronage. See articles under individual artists, e.g., Thomas EAKINS. See Lorado Taft, *The History of American Sculpture* (rev. ed., 1930); Holger Cahill and A. H. Barr, *Art in America* (1935); A. T. Gardner, *Yankee Stonecutters* (1945); Virgil Barker, *American Painting* (1950); John Baur, *Revolution and Tradition in Modern American Art* (1958); Oliver Larkin, *Art and Life in America* (rev. ed., 1960); J. C. T. Flexner, *That Wilder Image: the Painting of America's Native School from Thomas Cole to Winslow Homer* (1962).

American Colonization Society, organized Dec., 1816–Jan., 1817, at Washington, D.C., to transport free Negroes from the United States and settle them in Africa. The freeing of many slaves, principally by idealists, created a serious problem, since no sound provisions were made for establishing them in society on an equality with white Americans anywhere in the United States. Robert FINLEY, principal founder of the colonization society, found much support among prominent men, notably Henry Clay. Money was raised—with some indirect help from the Federal government when (1819) Congress appropriated $100,000 for returning to Africa Negroes illegally brought to the United States. In 1821 an agent, Eli Ayres, and Lt. R. F. Stockton of the U.S. navy purchased land in Africa, where subsequently Jehudi ASHMUN and Ralph R. Gurley laid the foundations of LIBERIA. The colonization movement came under the bitter attack of the abolitionists, who charged that in the South it strengthened slavery by removing the free Negroes. The Negroes themselves were not enthusiastic about abandoning their native land for the African coast. The colonization society, with its associated state organizations, declined after 1840. More than 11,000 Negroes were transported to Liberia before 1860. From 1865 until its dissolution in 1912, the society was a sort of trustee for Liberia. See E. L. Fox, *The American Colonization Society, 1817–1840* (1919); P. J. Staudenraus, *The African Colonization Movement* (1961).

American Falls, city (pop. 2,123), co. seat of Power co., SE Idaho, on the Snake and WSW of Pocatello. The American Falls themselves were well known to travelers on the Oregon Trail. The town grew after the arrival of the railroad in 1892. American Falls Dam (94 ft. high; 5,227 ft. long; completed 1927) created a reservoir which covered most of the city. The new city, a half mile removed, has a hydroelectric plant and is the center of an irrigated farm section producing chiefly potatoes, sugar beets, and grains. The reservoir, 36 mi. long, is a part of the MINIDOKA PROJECT. A state trout hatchery is nearby.

American Federation of Labor and Congress of Industrial Organizations (AFL–CIO), a federation of autonomous labor unions in the United States, Canada, and U.S. dependencies, formed in Dec., 1955, by the merger of the American Federation of Labor (AFL) and the Congress of Industrial Organizations (CIO).

American Federation of Labor. In 1881 parts of workingmen's trade organizations, meeting in Pittsburgh, formed the Federation of Organized Trade and Labor Unions in the United States and Canada. In 1886 at another conference in Columbus, Ohio, this group reorganized as the American Federation of Labor. The new federation was opposed to the broad socialistic and political ideals of the KNIGHTS OF LABOR; it was, instead, a loose, decentralized organization recognizing the trade autonomy of each of its member national craft unions. It operated through national labor and trade locals that formed into city central bodies and state and national federations. Individual workers were not members of the AFL but only of the affiliated local or national union, and from its inception it emphasized organization of skilled workers on a craft ("horizontal") basis, as opposed to an industrial ("vertical") basis. The AFL's object was to define and protect separate craft jurisdictions, to encourage legislation favorable to wage earners, and to provide assistance to its affiliates in organizing workers. The AFL was against the entry of organized labor into politics, and operating under the precepts laid down by Samuel Gompers, it was relatively static as a social force, though it did secure higher wages, shorter hours, workmen's compensation, and laws against child labor. It also helped to secure the 8-hour day for government employees and the exemption of labor from anti-trust legislation (see CLAYTON ANTI-TRUST ACT). Under the leadership of Gompers, and after his death in 1924, that of William GREEN and then George MEANY, the AFL became the largest labor federation in the United States, with a membership of over 10,000,-000 at the time of its merger with the CIO. Divorced throughout most of its history from the radical element in American labor, the AFL was split in 1935 when dissident elements within the federation protested its conservative organization policies in regard to the mass-production industries. The formation of the Committee for Industrial Organization (later the Congress of Industrial Organizations) by the dissidents resulted in the suspension (Sept., 1936) and then expulsion (Oct. 1937) from the AFL of 10 affiliates. Two of these unions were later readmitted—the INTERNATIONAL LADIES GARMENT WORKERS UNION (June, 1940) and the UNITED MINE WORKERS OF AMERICA (Jan., 1946). The UMW stalked out again in Dec., 1947, because of a difference with the AFL leadership over the filing of non-Communist affidavits as required by the Taft-Hartley Labor Act. The federation maintained its prevailing craft-union philosophy, even in the face of the growth of mass-production industries that made the organization of workers along craft lines difficult.

Congress of Industrial Organizations. Within the AFL there grew up in the early 1930s a strong minority faction that advocated organizing the unorganized workers in the basic mass-production industries (such as steel, auto, and rubber) on an industry-wide basis. John L. LEWIS of the United Mine Workers led this faction in forming a Committee for Industrial Organization in late 1935. This group (changing its name in 1938 to Congress of Industrial Organizations) immediately launched organizing drives in the basic industries. The spectacular success of these drives, particularly in auto and steel, enhanced the CIO's prestige to the point where it seriously challenged the AFL's former hegemony within U.S. organized labor. After fruitless negotiation the parent body revoked the charters of 10 international unions, all members of the dissident minority. The CIO, under the presidency of Lewis until 1940, and of Philip MURRAY thereafter until his death in 1952, followed more militant policies than the AFL. The CIO's Political Action Committee, headed by Sidney HILLMAN of the Amalgamated Clothing Workers Union, played an active role in the CIO's attempt to enlist the support of its membership behind candidates whose election was considered important to labor's interests. The CIO grew rapidly until its affiliated international unions numbered 32 at the time of the 1955 merger, with an estimated membership of c.5,000,000. Its growth, however, was marked by internal dissension; one such dispute led to the withdrawal in 1938 of one of its original constituent unions, the International Ladies

Garment Workers Union (ILGWU) and its reaffiliation with the AFL. Another dispute, this time over Lewis's support of Wendell Willkie in the 1940 presidential election, led Lewis to resign the CIO presidency. Coolness developed between Lewis and Murray and culminated in the withdrawal of the UMW from the CIO (1942) and its subsequent short-termed reaffiliation (1946–47) with the AFL. In the same period that the AFL was more or less successfully grappling with the problem of racketeers and gangster-dominated affiliates, the CIO was faced with a similar problem in ridding itself of Communist influence. In 1948 after a bitter struggle the CIO barred Communists from holding offices in the organization, and in 1949–50 the CIO expelled 11 of its affiliated unions, which were Communist-dominated, for slavishly following the Communist line. During the Second World War the CIO (like the AFL) pledged a no-strike policy. The CIO joined (1945) the World Federation of Trade Unions (WFTU), exacerbating its relations with the AFL since the latter had refused to participate in the WFTU because of possible Communist trade-union domination of that body. This obstacle to U.S. labor unity was removed by the CIO's withdrawal from the WFTU in 1949; and relations were further improved by subsequent AFL and CIO cooperation in helping to form the International Confederation of Free Trade Unions.

Merger. During the entire period of the alienation of the CIO from the AFL the idea of merger was considered by elements in both federations. It was not until the early 1950s, however, that such merger ideas gained headway. By that time both federations had proved their sustaining power as labor organizations; it had become evident that craft and industrial unions could exist side by side within the labor movement. Furthermore labor's concern over the apparent antiunion policies of President Dwight D. Eisenhower's administration gave new meaning to the movement for labor unity. The death in 1952 of the presidents of both organizations paved the way for the appointment of leaders more amenable to unity. The AFL chose George Meany and the CIO picked Walter P. REUTHER, of the United Auto Workers. An indication of the possibility of a merger occurred in 1954 with the announcement that a no-raiding agreement had been negotiated between the two organizations. This was soon followed in Dec., 1955, by a merger agreement. At its first convention in 1955 the merged organizations, now called the American Federation of Labor and Congress of Industrial Organizations (AFL–CIO), elected Meany as its president. The new organization has five operating levels. The first is the biennial convention in which, under the organization's constitution, ultimate authority is vested. The second level is the executive council, which governs the AFL–CIO between conventions and is composed of the executive officers (president and secretary-treasurer) and the 27 vice-presidents (17 from former AFL and 10 from former CIO unions). A general board (the convention in microcosm) acts on the third level as an advisory body to the council. On the fourth level the executive officers handle the day-to-day operations of the organization; they are advised on the fifth level by an executive committee consisting of the officers and 6 vice presidents (3 each from former AFL and CIO organizations). In addition to these levels of operating authority, the AFL–CIO carried over autonomous departments from the AFL (such as the Building Trades Department) and added an Industrial Union Department to handle the common problems of the former CIO unions. The AFL–CIO also created a series of standing committees to handle problems in specific spheres of the federation's interests; the most notable of these is the Committee on Political Education (COPE). The AFL–CIO supported the Democratic presidential candidates in 1956 and 1960. Committed to advancing the welfare of its members, the AFL–CIO has lobbied actively against "right to work laws" (by which no worker could be barred from a job because he refused to join a union) and other legislation deemed inimical to organized labor's interests. The organization, under severe pressure from public opinion (heightened by congressional investigative activity) has moved to eliminate undesirable elements from its ranks. In 1957 under the leadership of David Dubinsky the AFL–CIO adopted anti-racket codes, and the convention expelled the INTERNATIONAL BROTHERHOOD OF TEAMSTERS (which under Dave BECK and James R. HOFFA had gained a notorious reputation) for alleged failure to meet the parent organization's ethical standards. The AFL–CIO took a major step in 1961 in the direction of settling internal disputes by setting up a mandatory arbitration procedure. AFL–CIO membership in 1962 exceeded 14,000,000. See Samuel Gompers, *Seventy Years of Life and Labor* (1925); Arthur Goldberg, *AFL–CIO; Labor United* (1956); Philip Taft, *The A.F. of L. from the Death of Gompers to the Merger* (1959); Walter Galenson, *The CIO Challenge to the AFL* (1960).

American Fork, city (pop. 6,373), N central Utah, on American Fork Creek in the valley of Utah Lake, S of Salt Lake City; settled 1850 by Mormons, inc. 1853. A poultry-raising center in an irrigated area, it is served by the Provo river project. Mt. Timpanogos (12,008 ft.) is nearby.

American Fur Company, chartered by John Jacob ASTOR (1763–1848) in 1808 to compete with the great fur-trading companies in Canada—the North West Company and the Hudson's Bay Company. Astor's most ambitious venture, establishment of a post at ASTORIA, Oregon, to control the Columbia river valley fur trade, was made under a subsidiary, the Pacific Fur Company. His early operations around the Great Lakes were under another subsidiary, the South West Company, in which Canadian merchants had a part. The War of 1812 destroyed both companies. In 1817, after an act of Congress excluded foreign traders from U.S. territory, the American Fur Company commanded the trade in the Lakes region. An alliance made in 1821 with the Chouteau interests of St. Louis gave the company a monopoly of the trade in the Missouri river region and later in the Rocky Mts. (see MOUNTAIN MEN). The company was one of the first great American trusts. It maintained its monopoly by the customary early practice of buying out or crushing any small company that threatened opposition. When Astor withdrew in 1834, the company split and the name became the property of the former northern branch under Ramsey Crooks, but popular usage still applied it to succeeding companies. The American Fur Company strongly influenced the history of the frontier, not only by preparing the way for permanent settlement but by opening Great Lakes commercial fishing, steamboat transportation, and trade in lead. See H. M. Chittenden, *The American Fur Trade of the Far West* (3 vols., 1902); Bernard De Voto, *Across the Wide Missouri* (1948); P. C. Phillips, *The Fur Trade* (1961).

Americanization, term used to describe the cultural process by which the immigrant to the United States gradually assimilates American speech, ideals, traditions, and ways of life. The name has also been given to the movement fostering assimilation, which grew to crusading proportions in the first quarter of the 20th cent. as a result of the great immigration from the eastern and southern countries of Europe from 1880 to the outbreak of the First World War (see IMMIGRATION). Fear and suspicion of the newcomers and of their possible failure to become assimilated gave impetus to the movement. Joined by social workers interested in improving the slum conditions surrounding the immigrants and by representatives of the business and industrial world some of whom feared the source of cheap labor might be subverted by spread of radical social doctrines, organizations were formed to propagandize and to agitate for municipal, state, and Federal aid to educate the immigrants and teach them American ways. Spearheading the drive were the North American Civic League for Immigrants (a New England group), the Committee for Immigrants in America, and the National Americanization Committee (both with headquarters in New York city). The coming of the First World War with the resultant heightening of American nationalism strengthened the movement. The Federal bureaus of education and of naturalization joined in the crusade and aided the private Americanization groups. Giant rallies, patriotic naturalization proceedings, and Fourth of July celebrations featured the campaign. With America's entry into the struggle, Americanization was made an official part of the war effort. State after state passed legislation providing for night-school classes and other facilities for the education and Americanization of the foreign-born. The anti-Red drive conducted by the Dept. of Justice in 1919–20 stimulated the movement and led to even greater legislative action on behalf of Americanization. Virtually every state which had a substantial foreign-born population had provided educational facilities for the immigrant by 1921. The passage of this legislation plus the return of "normalcy" and, more especially, the coming of the quota system of immigration caused the Americanization movement to subside; private groups disbanded. See E. G. Hartmann, *The Movement to Americanize the Immigrant* (1948).

American Labor party, organized in New York by labor leaders and liberals in 1936, primarily to support Franklin D. Roosevelt's New Deal and the men favoring it in national and local elections. It gathered strength in New York state and particularly in New York city and had considerable weight there in tipping the scales toward chosen Democratic or Republican candidates. After 1939 it was much torn by strife between left-wing and right-wing factions, chiefly concerning policy toward the USSR. In 1944 an anti-Communist group led by David DUBINSKY, defeated in the primaries, withdrew to form the Liberal party. In 1948 the party polled over 500,000 votes for Henry A. Wallace for president, but many members withdrew in opposition to his candidacy. Failing to poll 50,000 votes in the 1954 New York state election, it lost its place on the New York ballot. In 1956 the party was voted out of existence by its New York state committee.

American Legion, national association of the veterans of the First and Second World Wars, founded in Paris in 1919. The preamble to the constitution, adopted at the convention in St. Louis that same year, expresses its purposes in part as, "to uphold and defend the Constitution of the United States; to maintain law and order; to foster and perpetuate a one hundred percent Americanism; . . . to safeguard and transmit to posterity the principles of justice, freedom, and democracy; to consecrate and sanctify our comradeship by our devotion to mutual helpfulness." To achieve these ends the American Legion has done much work in social welfare, particularly child care. It is by far the largest of the veterans' associations and, with its system of state departments and local posts centered in headquarters at Indianapolis, exerts considerable influence on the national life. The annual convention, at which policies are formulated, gains much attention, and the political force of the organization is considerable. The efforts of the American Legion have been bent not only to obtaining benefits for the veterans but also to building up the military strength of the United States and to attacking "subversive" or "anti-American" teachings and organizations. Its policies have been criticized by opponents as reactionary, as in William Gellermann's book, *The American Legion as Educator* (1938). It is organized on a nonpartisan, nonpolitical basis. There is also a woman's auxiliary for the wives, mothers, sisters, and daughters of veterans. Veterans of the women's corps of the armed services in the Second World War are members of regular posts. See Richard Seelye Jones, *A History of the American Legion* (1947).

American literature in English began with the writings of English adventurers and colonists in the New World chiefly for the benefit of readers in the mother country. Matter-of-fact relations and descriptions, reports, and highly argumentative accounts of scenes and events in America were welcomed in England. Some reached the level of literature, as in the robust and perhaps truthful account of his adventures by Captain John Smith and the sober but tendentious journalistic histories of John Winthrop and William Bradford in New England. From the start, however, the literature of New England was also directed to the edification and instruction of the colonists themselves, intended to direct them in the ways of the godly. The first work published in the Puritan colonies was the *Bay Psalm Book* (1640), and the whole effort of the divines who wrote furiously to set forth their views —among them men so opposite as Roger Williams and Cotton Mather—was to defend and to pro-

mote visions of the religious state. A few literate men and women spoke loudly on the edge of the wilderness. Even their poetry was offered uniformly to the service of God. Michael Wigglesworth's *Day of Doom* (1662) was uncompromisingly theological, and Anne Bradstreet's poems, issued as *The Tenth Muse Lately Sprung Up in America* (1650), were pious. The best of the Puritan poets, Edward Taylor, whose work was not to be published until two centuries after his death, wrote metaphysical verse worthy of comparison with that of George Herbert. Sermons and tracts poured forth until austere Calvinism found its last utterance in the words of Jonathan Edwards. In the other colonies writing was usually more mundane and on the whole less notable, though the journal of the Quaker John Woolman is highly esteemed, and some critics maintain that the best writing of the colonial period was that in the witty and urbane observations of William Byrd of Westover, gentleman planter of Virginia, whose works, like those of Taylor, were published many years after his death.

A New Nation and a New Literature. The approach of the American Revolution and the achievement of the actual independence of the United States was a time of intellectual activity as well as social and economic change. The men who were the chief molders of the new state included excellent writers, among them Thomas Jefferson and Alexander Hamilton. They were well supported by others such as Philip Freneau, first American lyric poet of distinction and able journalist; Thomas Paine, pamphleteer and later attacker of conventional religion; and Francis Hopkinson, polemicist and first American musical composer. The variously gifted Benjamin Franklin forwarded American literature not only by his own writing but also by founding and promoting newspapers and periodicals. Small literary groups sprang up in Boston, New York, Philadelphia, Charleston, and other cities, all intended to develop a truly American literature. Many of the literary aspirants, such as John Trumbull, Timothy Dwight, Joel Barlow, and the other Connecticut Wits, used English models. The infant American theater was somewhat nationalistic in character, with its first comedy by Royall Tyler, *The Contrast* (1787), as also with the dramas of William Dunlap. The first American novel, *The Power of Sympathy* (1789) by William Hill Brown, only shortly preceded the Gothic romance of the first professional American novelist, Charles Brockden Brown. All the American writers in the small literary clubs and outside them hoped for recognition from England. All of them traveled abroad when they could to absorb the older culture. Two men from New York were the first to win the coveted international recognition: Washington Irving, who first won attention by presenting American folk stories, and James Fenimore Cooper, who wrote enduring tales of adventure on the frontier and at sea. William Cullen Bryant had by 1825 made himself the leading poet of America with his delicate lyrics extolling nature and his smooth philosophic poems in the best mode of romanticism. Even more distinctly a part of the romantic movement were such poets as Joseph Rodman Drake and Fitz-Greene Halleck. The younger Henry

Wadsworth Longfellow also belonged to the romantic movement. He won the hearts of Americans with glib, moralizing verse and also commanded international respect. A New Englander, he yet stood somewhat outside what Van Wyck Brooks called *The Flowering of New England*. Ralph Waldo Emerson and Henry David Thoreau stood at the center of that intellectual movement (partly expressed in Transcendentalism), which made a deep impression upon their native land and upon Europe. High-mindedness, moral earnestness, the desire to reform society and education, the assertion of a philosophy of the individual as superior to tradition and society—all these were strongly American. Emerson, Thoreau, and others such as Margaret Fuller and Bronson Alcott insisted upon such principles. Men so diverse as James Russell Lowell, Boston "Brahmin," poet, and critic, and John Greenleaf Whittier, bucolic poet, joined in support of the abolitionist cause, while the more worldly and correct Oliver Wendell Holmes reflected the vigorous intellectual spirit of the time, as did the historians William Hickling Prescott, George Bancroft, Francis Parkman, and John Lothrop Motley. The solemn histories were as distinctly American as the broadly humorous writing that became popular early in the 19th cent. This was usually set forth as the sayings of a semiliterate, often raffish, and always shrewd American character. Among these characters were Major Jack Downing (Seba Smith), Hosea Biglow (James Russell Lowell), Artemus Ward (Charles Farrar Browne), Petroleum Vesuvius Nasby (David Ross Locke), Josh Billings (Henry Walker Shaw), and Sut Lovingood (G. W. Harris). Far apart from these was Edgar Allan Poe, whose skilled and deeply emotional poetry, clearly expressed aesthetic theories, and tales of mystery and horror won for him a more respectful audience in Europe than —originally, at least—in America. In the 1850s came Nathaniel Hawthorne's novel *The Scarlet Letter* (1850), depicting the gloomy atmosphere of early Puritanism; Herman Melville's *Moby Dick* (1851), which infused into a rousing adventure tale of whaling days an overwhelmingly dark and enigmatic allegory; and the rolling measures of Walt Whitman's *Leaves of Grass* (1st ed., 1855), which employed a new kind of poetry and proclaimed the optimistic principles of American democracy. All were important events in the history of literature written in English.

The Literature of a Reunited Nation. The rising conflict between the North and the South that ended in the Civil War was reflected in regional literature. The crusading spirit against Southern slavery in Harriet Beecher Stowe's overwhelmingly successful novel *Uncle Tom's Cabin* was matched by the violent anti-Northern diatribes of William Gilmore Simms, who had earlier gained his reputation by his vigorous historical adventure stories of the Carolinas. While the Civil War was taking its inexorable course, the case for reunion was set forth in the purest and most exact statement of American thought, the Gettysburg Address of President Abraham Lincoln. Once the war was over, literature gradually took on a national aspect, for writings though regional in origin became national in audience. The stories of the California gold fields by Bret Harte, the romantic California poems of Joaquin Miller, the rustic novel of Edward Eggleston, *The Hoosier Schoolmaster* (1871), the rhymes of James Whitcomb Riley, the New England genre stories by Sarah Orne Jewett and Mary E. Wilkins Freeman, the rueful sketches of Louisiana by George W. Cable, even the romance of the Old South woven by the poetry of Henry Timrod and Sidney Lanier and the fiction of Thomas Nelson Page—all were seized eagerly by the readers of a nation. The classic juvenile by Louisa May Alcott, *Little Women* (1868–69), was laid in New England but lasted to give pleasure to generations of young readers everywhere. Perhaps the outstanding example of genius overcoming any regionalism in scene can be found in the stories of Tom Sawyer and Huckleberry Finn by Mark Twain. In his humorous books Mark Twain also transcended the localism of the early 19-century humorists, such as Augustus Baldwin Longstreet. The connection of American literature with writing in England and Europe was again stressed by William Dean Howells, who was not only an able novelist but an instructor in literary realism to other American writers. Though he himself had leanings to social reform, he did encourage what has come to be called "genteel" writing, long dominant in American fiction. The mold for this sort of writing was broken by the American turned Englishman, Henry James, who wrote of people of the upper classes but with such psychological penetration, subtlety of narrative, and complex technical skill that he is recognized as one of the great masters of fiction. His influence was quickly reflected in the novels of Edith Wharton and others and continued to grow in strength in the 20th cent. The realism preached by Howells was turned by some writers away from any bourgeois levels, particularly by Stephen Crane in his poetry and in his fiction—*Maggie: a Girl of the Streets* and the Civil War story, *The Red Badge of Courage* (1895); these were forerunners of naturalism, which reached heights in the hands of Theodore Dreiser and of Jack London, who was a fiery social reformer as well as a writer of Klondike stories. Ever since the Civil War voices of protest and doubt have been heard. Mark Twain (with Charles Dudley Warner) had in *The Gilded Age* held the post-war get-rich-quick era up to scorn. By the early 20th cent. Henry Adams was musing upon the effects of the dynamo's triumph over man, and Ambrose Bierce literally abandoned a civilization he could not abide. Poetry, meanwhile, had tended to the pretty-pretty—with the startling exception of the Amherst recluse, Emily Dickinson, whose terse, precise, and enigmatic poems, published in 1890, after her death, put her immediately into the ranks of major American poets. The post-romantic poetry of Richard Hovey, Bliss Carman, and William Vaughn Moody was well constructed but minor. Drama after the Civil War into the 20th cent. continued to rely, as it had before, on spectacles, on the plays of Shakespeare, and on some of the works of English and Continental playwrights. A few popular plays such as *Uncle Tom's Cabin* and *Rip Van Winkle* were based on American fiction, others were crude melodrama. Realism, however, came to the theater with some of the plays of Bronson Howard, James A. Herne, and

William Vaughn Moody, and even some of the later plays of the popular Clyde Fitch. A revolution in poetry was announced with the founding in 1912 of *Poetry: a Magazine of Verse*, edited by Harriet Monroe. It published the work of Ezra Pound and the imagists—Amy Lowell, H. D. (Hilda Doolittle), John Gould Fletcher, and their English associates, all declaring against romantic poetry and in favor of the exact word after the manner of Greek and Latin classic writers, the French Symbolists, and Chinese and Japanese poets. Apart from movements and groups, other poets moved along their individual paths: Edwin Arlington Robinson, who wrote dark, brooding lines on man in the universe; Edgar Lee Masters, who used free verse for realistic biographies in *A Spoon River Anthology* (1915); his friend Vachel Lindsay; Carl Sandburg, who tried to capture the speech, life, and dreams of America; and Robert Frost, who wrote with evocative simplicity and won universal admiration.

The Lost Generation and After. The years immediately after the First World War brought a highly vocal rebellion against established social, sexual, and aesthetic conventions and a vigorous attempt to establish new values. Young artists flocked to Greenwich Village, to Chicago, and to San Francisco, determined to protest and intent on making a new art. Others went to Europe, living mostly in Paris as expatriates. They willingly accepted the name given them by Gertrude Stein: the lost generation. Out of their disillusion and rejection, the writers built a new literature, impressive in the glittering 1920s and the years that followed. Romantic clichés were abandoned for extreme realism or for complex symbolism and created myth. Language grew so frank that there were bitter quarrels over censorship, as in the troubles about James Branch Cabell's *Jurgen* (1919) and—much more notably—Henry Miller's *Tropic of Cancer* (1931). The influence of new psychology and of Marxian social theory was strong. Out of this highly active boiling of new ideas and new forms came writers of recognizable stature in the world: Ernest Hemingway, F. Scott Fitzgerald, William Faulkner, Thomas Wolfe, John Dos Passos, John Steinbeck, e. e. cummings. The man who came to be dominant as a dramatist was Eugene O'Neill, the greatest by far of the dramatists the United States has produced. Other writers also enriched the theater with comedies, social reform plays, and historical tragedies. Among them were Maxwell Anderson, Philip Barry, Elmer Rice, S. N. Behrman, Marc Connelly, Lillian Hellman, Clifford Odets, and Thornton Wilder. The social drama and the symbolic play were further developed by Arthur Miller, William Inge, and Tennessee Williams. By the 1960s the influence of foreign movements was much felt with the development of "off-Broadway" theater. One of the new playwrights who gained especial notice was Edward Albee. The naturalism that governed the novels of Dreiser and the stories of Sherwood Anderson was intensified by the stories of the Chicago slums by James T. Farrell and later Nelson Algren. Violence in language and in action was extreme in some of the novels of the Second World War, notably those of James Jones and Norman Mailer. Not unexpect-

edly after the First World War Negro writers came forward, casting off the sweet melodies of Paul Lawrence Dunbar and speaking of social oppression. Countee Cullen, James Weldon Johnson, Claude McKay, and Langston Hughes were succeeded by Richard Wright and James Baldwin. Poetry after the First World War was largely dominated by T. S. Eliot and his followers, who imposed intellectuality and a new sort of classical form that had been urged by Ezra Pound. Eliot was also highly influential as a literary critic and contributed to making the period 1920–60 one that was to some extent dominated by literary analysts and promoters of various warring schools. Among those critics were Henry L. Mencken, Edmund Wilson, Lewis Mumford, Malcolm Cowley, Van Wyck Brooks, John Crowe Ransom, Yvor Winters, Allen Tate, R. P. Blackmur, Robert Penn Warren, and Cleanth Brooks. The victories of the new over the old in the 1920s did not mean the disappearance of the older ideals of form even among lovers of the new. Much that was traditional lived on in the lyrics of Conrad Aiken, Sara Teasdale, Edna St. Vincent Millay, and Elinor Wylie. In the later years of the period two poets gained world recognition though they had been quietly writing before: Wallace Stevens and William Carlos Williams. The admirable novels of Willa Cather did not resort to new devices; the essays of E. B. White were models of pure style, as were the stories of Katherine Anne Porter. Humor left the broadness of George Ade's *Fables* for the acrid satire of Ring Lardner and the highly polished writing of Robert Benchley and James Thurber. Historical novels continued to deal in romance, with new realistic trappings as in Margaret Mitchell's phenomenally successful *Gone with the Wind* (1936), Hervey Allen's *Anthony Adverse* (1933), and the novels of Kenneth Roberts, but such historical writing as that of Stephen Vincent Benet (in prose and poetry) and MacKinlay Kantor had simplicity without romance. Some of the younger writers of the young 1960s such as John Updike and Philip Roth were highly praised for style, while the products of the BEAT GENERATION were notable primarily for vividness and deep-going naturalism. See *Literary History of the United States* (ed. by Robert E. Spiller and others; rev. ed., 1955); D. E. Scherman and Rosemarie Redlech, *Literary America: a Chronicle of American Writers from 1607–1952* (1952); Van Wyck Brooks, "Makers and Finders" series; Alfred Kazin, *On Native Grounds* (1942; new ed., 1956).

American Museum of Natural History, incorporated in New York city in 1869 to promote the study of natural science and related subjects. Buildings on its present site were opened in 1877. Among the buildings since added are the Hayden Planetarium (opened 1935) and the Roosevelt Memorial building (completed 1936). It maintains exhibitions in all branches of natural history, including anthropology and ecology. As a result of its wide explorations and its program of research the museum has acquired specimens and data of great value. Resources are derived from endowment, grants from the city, and a membership fund. Among the facilities for study are an extension library; illustrated lectures; publications; a special school service whereby the museum cooperates with city schools; circulating exhibits; habitat groups of animals and plants; a mineral and gem collection; an unrivaled assemblage of skeletons of extinct animals, especially dinosaurs; and replicas of invertebrates in glass. The Indians of North and South America are admirably portrayed, with exhibits of their basketry, pottery, and porcelain.

The American Museum of Natural History, New York City.

American party: see KNOW-NOTHING MOVEMENT.

American Philosophical Society, first scientific society in America, founded in 1743 in Philadelphia. It was an outgrowth of the junto formed by Benjamin Franklin in 1727. Franklin was the first secretary of the society, and Thomas Hopkinson the first president. In 1769 the Philosophical Society merged with the American Society for Promoting Useful Knowledge. This combined organization elected Franklin its first president, an office which he held until his death. David Rittenhouse and Thomas Jefferson were his immediate successors. The society, which has a notable library, takes its members from all fields of intellectual and scientific study. Its transactions date from 1771 and records of its proceedings from 1838.

American Red Cross: see RED CROSS.

American Revolution, 1775–83, struggle by which the THIRTEEN COLONIES on the Atlantic seaboard of North America won independence from Great Britain and became the United States. It is also called the American War of Independence. By the middle of the 18th cent., differences in life, thought, and interests had developed between the mother country and the little colonies expanding between the sea and the mountains. Local institutions took

shape in the colonies, and though there was little feeling of intercolonial unity (as shown by the failure of the plan of union in the ALBANY CONGRESS), there was a general appreciation of divergence from English attitudes and interests. The British government, like other imperial powers in the 18th cent., favored a policy of MERCANTILISM, and many colonials felt that their commercial activities were unfairly limited. The NAVIGATION ACTS, intended to regulate commerce in the British interest, could not be well enforced on the long American coast, and smuggling, though officially a crime, was generally regarded in the colonies as an open and honorable profession. There had been brushes between officials and colonials, some quite serious (e.g., BACON'S REBELLION), but the underlying causes of trouble emerged only after 1763. The Treaty of Paris in that year ended the FRENCH AND INDIAN WARS and removed a long-standing threat to the colonies. At the same time the ministry (1763–65) of George GRENVILLE in Great Britain undertook a new colonial policy intended to make the colonies pay for their defense and return revenue to the mother country. The tax levied on molasses and sugar in 1764 caused some consternation among New England merchants and makers of rum; the tax itself was smaller than the one already on the books, but the promise of stringent enforcement was novel and ominous. It was the STAMP ACT (1765) with its direct demand for revenue that roused among the colonial people a violent outcry which was spearheaded by the Northern merchants, lawyers, and newspaper publishers who were directly affected. Everywhere leaders such as James Otis, Samuel Adams, and Patrick Henry denounced the act with eloquence, societies called the SONS OF LIBERTY were formed, and the STAMP ACT CONGRESS was called to protest that Parliament was violating the rights of true-born Englishmen in taxing the colonials, who were not directly represented in the supreme legislature. The threat of boycott and refusal to import English goods supported the colonial clamor. Parliament repealed (1766) the Stamp Act but passed an act formally declaring its right to tax the colonies. The incident was closed, but a barb remained to wound American feelings. Colonial political theorists—not only hotheads such as Samuel Adams, Patrick Henry, Josiah QUINCY (1744–75), and Alexander MacDougall but also moderates such as John DICKINSON, John ADAMS, and Benjamin FRANKLIN—asserted that taxation without representation was tyranny. The teachings of 18th-century French philosophers and continental writers on law, such as Emmerich de Vattel, as well as the theories of John LOCKE, were implicit in the colonial arguments based on the theory of NATURAL RIGHTS. The colonials claimed that they were subject only to the king, not to a parliament in which they had no representation; but George III, by the actions of his ministers, had shown himself to be a tyrant. Trouble flared when the Chatham ministry adopted (1767) the TOWNSHEND ACTS, which taxed numerous imports; care was taken to levy only an "external" or indirect tax, since direct taxes had been hotly challenged by the colonials. The indirect taxes were challenged too, and though the duties were not heavy, the principle was at-

The Boston Massacre, engraving by Paul Revere.

Mountain Boys, together with a force under Benedict Arnold, took Fort Ticonderoga from the British, and two days later Seth WARNER captured Crown Point. Boston was under British siege, and before that siege was climaxed by the costly British victory usually called the battle of Bunker Hill (June 17, 1775) the Congress had chosen (June 15, 1775) George WASHINGTON as commander in chief of the Continental armed forces. The war was on in earnest. Some delegates had come to the Congress already committed to declaring the colonies independent of Great Britain, but even many stalwart upholders of the patriot cause were not ready to take such a step. The lines were being more clearly drawn between the pro-British LOYALISTS and the colonial patriots. The time was one of indecision, and the division of the people was symbolized by the split between Benjamin Franklin and his Loyalist son, William FRANKLIN. The Loyalists were numerous, especially among the holders of large properties (although the landed proprietors of Virginia produced more than their share of patriot leaders). A large part of the population was more or less neutral, swaying to this side or that or else remaining inert in the struggle, which was to some extent a civil war. So it was to remain to the end. Civil government and administration had fallen apart and had to be patched together locally. In some places the result was bloody strife, as in the partisan raids in the Carolinas and Georgia and the Mohawk valley massacre in New York; elsewhere hostility did not produce open struggles. In January, 1776, Thomas Paine wrote a pamphlet, *Common Sense*, which urged the patriot cause. Its influence was tremendous, and

Committee of Congress drafting the Declaration of Independence. Left to right: Thomas Jefferson, John Adams, Benjamin Franklin, Robert Livingston, Roger Sherman.

tacked. Incidents came in interrupted sequence to make feeling run higher and higher—the seizure of a ship belonging to John HANCOCK in 1768, the bloodshed of the BOSTON MASSACRE in 1770, the burning of H.M.S. GASPEE in 1772. Even repeal of the Townshend Acts in 1770 did no more than temporarily quiet the turmoil, for the tax on tea was kept as a sort of token of Parliament's supremacy. Indignation in New England at the monopoly granted to the East India Company led to the BOSTON TEA PARTY in 1773. Despite the earnest pleas of William Pitt the elder (see CHATHAM, WILLIAM PITT, 1ST EARL OF) and Edmund BURKE, Parliament replied with coercive measures. These (and the QUEBEC ACT) the patriotic colonials called the INTOLERABLE ACTS, and resistance was prompt. The Sons of Liberty and individual patriots were already spreading statements of the colonial cause to win over merchant and farmer, workingman and sailor. Committees of correspondence had been formed by the patriots to exchange information and ideas (frequently with more regard for passion and rhetoric than for accuracy) and to build colonial unity, and in 1774 these committees prepared the way for the CONTINENTAL CONGRESS. The representatives at this First Continental Congress, except for a few radicals, had not met to consider independence, but wished only to persuade the British government to recognize their rights. A plan of reconciliation offered by Joseph GALLOWAY was rejected. It was agreed that the colonies would refuse to import British goods until colonial grievances were righted; those grievances were listed in petitions to the king; and the congress adjourned. Before it met again the situation had changed. On the morning of April 19, 1775, shots had been exchanged by patriots and British soldiers, men had been killed, and a revolution of violence had begun (see LEXINGTON AND CONCORD, BATTLES OF). On the very day (May 10, 1775) that the Second Continental Congress met, Ethan ALLEN and his Green

it was read everywhere with enthusiastic acclaim. In arms, however, the cause did not prosper greatly. Delegations to the Canadians had been unsuccessful, and the QUEBEC CAMPAIGN (1775–76) ended in disaster. The British gave up Boston in March, 1776, but the prospects were still not good for the ill-trained, poorly armed volunteer soldiers of the Continental army when the Congress decided finally to declare the independence of the Thirteen Colonies. The DECLARATION OF INDEPENDENCE is conventionally dated July 4, 1776. Drawn up by Thomas Jefferson (with slight emendations), it was to be one of the great historical documents of all time. It did not, however, have any immediate good effect. The British under Gen. William HOWE and his brother, Admiral Richard Howe, came to New York harbor. After vain attempts to negotiate a peace, the British forces struck. Washington lost Brooklyn Heights (see LONG ISLAND, BATTLE OF), retreated northward, was defeated at Harlem Heights in Manhattan and at White Plains, and took part of his dwindling army into New Jersey. Thomas Paine in a new pamphlet, *The Crisis*, exhorted the patriots to courage in desperate days, and Washington showed his increasing military skill and helped to restore patriot spirits in the winter of 1776–77 by crossing the ice-ridden Delaware and winning small victories over forces made up mostly of Hessian mercenaries at Trenton (Dec. 26) and Princeton (Jan. 3). In 1777 the British attempted to wipe out the flickering revolt by a concerted plan to split the colonies with converging expeditions concentrated upon the Hudson valley. Gen. William Howe, instead of taking part in it, moved into Pennsylvania, defeated Washington in the battle of Brandywine (Sept. 11), took Philadelphia, and beat off (Oct. 4) Washington's attack on Germantown. Meanwhile the British columns under Gen. John BURGOYNE and Gen. Barry ST. LEGER had failed (see SARATOGA CAMPAIGN), and Burgoyne on Oct. 17, 1777, ended the battle of Saratoga by surrender to Gen. Horatio GATES.

The victory is commonly regarded as the decisive battle of the war, but its good effects again were not immediate. The patriot army still had to endure the hardships of the cruel winter at VALLEY FORGE, when only loyalty to Washington and the cause of liberty held the half-frozen, half-starved men together. Among them were three of the foreign idealists who had come to aid the colonials in their struggle—KALB, STEUBEN, and LAFAYETTE. At Valley Forge, Steuben trained the still-raw troops, who came away a disciplined fighting force giving a good account of themselves in 1778. Sir Henry CLINTON, who had succeeded Howe in command, decided to abandon Philadelphia for New York, and Washington's attack upon the British in the battle of Monmouth (see MONMOUTH, BATTLE OF) was cheated of success mainly by the equivocal actions of Gen. Charles LEE. The warfare in the Middle Atlantic region settled almost to stagnation, but foreign aid was finally arriving. Agents of the new nation—notably Benjamin Franklin,

The Battle of Saratoga, October 17th, 1777.

Washington Crossing the Delaware, by Emanuel Leutze.

Arthur Lee, Silas Deane, and later John Adams—were striving to get help, and in 1777 Beaumarchais had succeeded in getting arms and supplies sent to the patriots in time to help win the battle of Saratoga. That victory made it easier for France to enter upon an alliance with the United States, for which Franklin and Vergennes signed (1778) a treaty. Spain entered the war against Great Britain in 1779, but Spanish help did little for the United States, while French soldiers and sailors and French supplies and money were of crucial importance. The warfare had meanwhile shifted from the quiescent North to other theaters. George Rogers Clark by his daring exploits (1778–79) in the West, climaxed by the second capture of Vincennes, established patriot prestige on the frontier. Gen. John Sullivan led an expedition (1779) against the British and Indians in upper New York. The chief fighting, however, was in the South. The British had taken Savannah in 1778. In 1780 Sir Henry Clinton attacked and took Charleston (which had resisted attacks in 1776 and 1779) and sent Gen. Cornwallis off on the Carolina campaign. Cornwallis swept forward to beat Horatio Gates soundly at Camden (Aug., 1780), and only guerrilla bands under Francis Marion, Andrew Pickens, and Thomas Sumter continued to oppose the British S of Virginia. Another low point had been reached in American fortunes. Bitter complaints of the inefficiency of the Congress, political conniving, lack of funds and food, and the strains of long-continued war had increased widespread apathy and disaffection, and the British tried to take advantage of the division among the people. In 1780 occurred the most celebrated of the disaffections, the treason of Benedict Arnold. Lack of pay and shortages of clothing and food drove some Continental regiments into a mutiny of protest in Jan., 1781. The dark, however, was already lifting. A crowd of frontiersmen with their rifles defeated a British force at Kings Mt. in Oct., 1780, and Nathanael Greene, who had replaced Gates as commander in the Carolina campaign, and his able assistant, Daniel Morgan, together with Thaddeus Kosciusko and others, ultimately forced Cornwallis into Virginia. The stage was set for the Yorktown campaign. Now the French aid counted greatly, for Lafayette with patriot troops held the British in check, and it was a Franco-American force which Washington and the comte de Rochambeau led from New York S to Virginia. The French fleet under Admiral de Grasse played the decisive part. Previously naval forces had been of little consequence in the Revolution. State navies and a somewhat irregular national navy had been of less importance than Revolutionary privateers. Esek Hopkins had led a raid in the Bahamas in 1776, John Barry won a name as a gallant commander, and John Paul Jones was one of the most celebrated commanders in all U.S. naval history, but their exploits were single incidents. It was the French fleet—ironically the same one defeated by the British under Admiral Rodney the next year in the West Indies—which bottled up Cornwallis at Yorktown. Outnumbered and surrounded, the British commander surrendered (Oct. 17–19, 1781), and the fighting was over. The rebels had won the American Revolution. The Treaty of Paris (see Paris, Treaty of) formally recognized the new nation in 1783, though many questions were left unsettled. The United States was floundering through a post-war depression and seeking not too successfully to meet its administrative problems under the Articles of Confederation (see Confederation, Articles of). The leaders in the new country were those prominent either in the council halls or on the fields of the Revolution, and the first three Presidents after the Constitution of the United States was adopted were Washington, Adams, and Jefferson. Some of the more radical Revolutionary leaders were disappointed in the turn toward conservatism when the Revolution was over, but liberty and democracy had been fixed as the highest ideals of the United States. The Amer-

John Trumbull's painting Surrender of Cornwallis at Yorktown, *in the Capitol, Washington, D.C.*

ican Revolution had a great influence on liberal thought throughout Europe. The struggles and successes of this youthful democracy were much in the minds of those who brought about the French Revolution, and most assuredly later helped to inspire revolutionists in Spain's American colonies. Naturally the stirring events of the birth of the country have been often represented in U.S. literature. It has given dramatic material to playwrights

July 4, 1776. Citizens outside Independence Hall in Philadelphia, Pa., in anticipation of the decision by Congress.

from William Dunlap to Maxwell Anderson, to novelists from James Fenimore Cooper and William G. Simms to S. Weir Mitchell, Paul Leicester Ford, and Kenneth Roberts. Older histories, still read for their literary value, are those of George Bancroft, John Fiske, and G. O. Trevelyan. Countless excellent studies have been made of particular aspects and incidents; some examples are H. E. Wildes, *Valley Forge* (1938); R. B. Morris, ed., *The Era of the American Revolution* (1939); Carl Van Doren, *Secret History of the American Revolution* (1941) and *Mutiny in January* (1943); Lynn Montross, *Rag, Tag and Bobtail: the Story of the Continental Army* (1952); Carl Berger, *Broadsides and Bayonets: the Propaganda War of the American Revolution* (1961). For works of more general interest, see C. H. McIlwain, *The American Revolution: a Constitutional Interpretation* (1923, new ed., 1958); J. F. Jameson, *The American Revolution Considered as a Social Movement* (1926, new ed., 1961); J. C. Miller, *Origins of the American Revolution* (1943, new ed., 1959); C. R. Ritcheson, *British Politics and the American Revolution* (1954); L. H. Gipson, *The Coming of the Revolution* ("New American Nation" series, 1954); Henry Steele Commager and R. B. Morris, eds., *Spirit of 'Seventy-Six* (1958); Samuel Flagg Bemis, *The Diplomacy of the American Revolution* (rev. ed., 1957); Howard Peckham, *The War for Independence* (1958); R. R.

Palmer, *The Age of the Democratic Revolution* (1959); J. B. Mitchell, *Decisive Battles of the American Revolution* (1962).

American Samoa: see SAMOA.

American Society for the Prevention of Cruelty to Animals (A.S.P.C.A.), founded (1866) in America by Henry BERGH to shelter homeless animals, to assist farmers in caring for their livestock, and to cooperate with law enforcement agencies in the prosecution of game-law violators. The A.S.P.C.A. is patterned on the English organization, the Royal Society for the Prevention of Cruelty to Animals, founded in 1824 through the efforts of Richard Martin (1754–1834), an Irish member of Parliament. See *How the A.S.P.C.A. Operates* (1961).

American University, at Washington D.C.; Methodist; founded by Bishop J. F. Hurst, chartered 1893, opened in 1914. It was at first a graduate school; an undergraduate college was opened in 1925. Programs provide for student research at many government institutions.

American Veterans Committee, founded in Jan., 1943, as an organization of veterans of the Second World War and designated the American Veterans Committee in Oct., 1944. It had over 25,000 members in 1961. The AVC differs from other veterans' groups in its opposition to benefits for veterans beyond those based on service-incurred disabilities or the needs of readjustment to civilian life ("Citizens first, veterans second"). The AVC's interest is not limited to veterans affairs; its 1960 platform supported the UN and collective-security agreements in the field of foreign policy, and domestically urged the extension of civil rights and increased government activity to maintain economic prosperity and expand social-welfare programs.

American Veterans of World War II and Korea (Amvets), organization of veterans of the Second World War and Korean campaign, founded in Dec., 1944. The Amvets had posts in every state by 1947, when Congress granted a national charter to the organization. It is mainly concerned with veterans' benefits and rights, and in 1960 its membership exceeded 125,000.

americium (ămûri′shēŭm), radioactive element of the ACTINIDE SERIES (symbol=Am; in group III B of the PERIODIC TABLE; for physical constants, see ELEMENT, table). It is produced in the nuclear reactor from isotopes of plutonium. A series of reactions involving neutron capture yields Pu^{241}, which emits gamma rays and becomes Am^{241} with a half life of c.500 yrs. Americium was discovered in 1945 by G. T. SEABORG, R. A. James, L. O. Morgan, and Albert Ghiorso, as a fission product. Besides other isotopes, metallic americium and various compounds of it have been produced.

Americus (ŭmĕr′ĭkŭs), city (pop. 13,472), co. seat of Sumter co., SW Ga., SE of Columbus; inc. 1832. It is an industrial center in a farm and timber area and the seat of a junior college. Charles Lindbergh made his first solo flight from Souther Field here. ANDERSONVILLE is nearby.

Amersfoort (ä′mûrsfōrt), city (estimated pop. 70,170), in Utrecht prov., central Netherlands. An old town with medieval houses, a 14th-century water gate, and the 15th-century Gate of Our Lady, it is now a manufacturing center. Johan van Oldenbarneveldt was born here.

Amery (ā'mûrē), city (pop. 1,769), NW Wis., NW of Eau Claire; settled 1884, inc. 1919.

Ames, Ezra, 1768–1836, American painter, b. Framingham, Mass. Early in his life he worked as a carriage painter, miniaturist, engraver, and practical decorator, first in Worcester, Mass., and later in Albany, N.Y., where he settled. His portrait of Governor De Witt Clinton of New York (1818; Albany Inst. of History and Art) established his renown as a vigorously realistic portraitist. Among his many skillful likenesses are those of Gouverneur Morris (New-York Historical Society) and Stephen van Rensselaer (New York State Historical Association). See monograph by Theodore Bolton and I. F. Cortelyou (1955).

Ames, Fisher, 1758–1808, American political leader, b. Dedham, Mass., grad. Harvard, 1774; son of Nathaniel Ames. Admitted to the bar in 1781, he began political pamphleteering and by a speech in the Massachusetts convention that ratified the Federal Constitution started on the road to becoming a leading Federalist. As a Congressman (1789–97) and after his retirement he was high in party councils, a staunch follower of Hamilton, and a vicious opponent of Jefferson. Of Ames's able speeches perhaps the best known was that made in 1796 when the House was disposed to nullify Jay's Treaty by withholding appropriations; he spoke for the treaty. He was the archetype of the New England conservative of his period, a strong proponent of order and of the rights of property.

Ames, James Barr, 1846–1910, American jurist, b. Boston, grad. Harvard Law School, 1873. At Harvard he became associate professor (1873), professor (1877), and dean (1895). A disciple of LANGDELL, Ames insisted that legal education should require the study of actual cases instead of abstract principles of law. He was instrumental in introducing the case method in the teaching of law, a method in general use by American law schools at the time of his death. Ames's careful historical and legal scholarship is displayed in his *Lectures on Legal History* (1913).

Ames, Joseph, 1689–1759, English bibliographer. He compiled *Typographical Antiquities* (1749), a valuable list of English books printed before 1600.

Ames, Joseph Sweetman, 1864–1943, American physicist, b. Manchester, Vt., grad. Johns Hopkins (B.A., 1886; Ph.D., 1890). He was associated with Johns Hopkins throughout his career, serving successively as professor of physics and director of the physical laboratory, as provost, as president (1929–35), and as president emeritus. An authority on aerodynamics, he was a member of the National Advisory Committee for Aeronautics from 1917 to 1939 (chairman from 1927). He wrote several books in the field of physics.

Ames, Nathaniel, 1708–64, American almanac maker, b. Bridgewater, Mass. His *Astronomical Diary and Almanack*, begun in 1725 and issued after c.1732 from Dedham, Mass., was highly popular and served as a model for Franklin's *Poor Richard's Almanack* and later almanacs. After Ames's death it was continued to 1795 by his son Nathaniel, Jr. The elder Ames was a physician and also after 1750 landlord of the Sun Tavern at Dedham. He was the father of Fisher Ames. See Samuel Briggs, ed., *The Essays, Humor, and Poems*

of *Nathaniel Ames* (1891); G. L. Kittredge, *The Old Farmer and His Almanack* (1904).

Ames, Oakes, 1804–73, American manufacturer, railroad promoter, and politician, b. Easton, Mass. With his brother Oliver (1807–77) he managed the family's well-known shovel factory at Easton. The business expanded under demands from the expanding Midwest frontier and the Western gold diggings. Active in founding the Republican party in Massachusetts, Ames served in Congress from 1863 to 1873. Interested in the construction of the Union Pacific Railroad, Ames secured control of the CRÉDIT MOBILIER OF AMERICA after ousting T. C. DURANT, its founder. The financial scandals of that company brought upon Ames in 1872 public disgrace and the censure of Congress.

Ames, Oakes, 1874–1950, American botanist, b. North Easton, near Brockton, Mass., grad. Harvard (B.A., 1898; M.A., 1899). He was associated with Harvard from 1899, becoming professor of botany in 1926, Arnold professor of botany in 1932, and research professor of botany in 1935 (emeritus from 1941). An authority on orchids, he is the author of many articles and of *Orchidaceae* (7 fascicles, 1905–22) and *Enumeration of the Orchids of the United States and Canada* (1924). He also wrote *Economic Annuals and Human Cultures* (1939).

Ames, city (pop. 27,003), central Iowa, on the Skunk river N of Des Moines; platted 1865, inc. 1869. Its chief product is electronic equipment. IOWA STATE UNIVERSITY OF SCIENCE AND TECHNOLOGY and many Federal and state institutes, including the National Animal Disease Laboratory, are here.

Amesbury, rural district (pop. 22,594), Wiltshire, S England. There are British remains predating the Roman occupation. In 980 the widow of King Edgar founded Amesbury Abbey, where Queen Guinevere of Arthurian legend is believed to have died. A popular retreat for women of nobility for several centuries, the abbey was completely rebuilt in 1661. STONEHENGE, the chief megalithic monument in Britain, is nearby.

Amesbury, town (pop. 10,787), NE Mass., on the Merrimack river and NE of Lawrence; settled 1654, inc. 1668. Transportation equipment, leather and felt goods, and electrical machinery are produced. John Greenleaf Whittier lived here most of his life, and his house is preserved. Josiah Bartlett was born in Amesbury.

amethyst (ăm'ûthĭst) [Gr.,=non-drunkenness], variety of QUARTZ, violet to purple in color, used as a gem. It is the most highly valued of the semiprecious quartzes. It is associated with a number of superstitions, being regarded as a love charm, as a potent influence in improving sleep, and as a protection against thieves and drunkenness. Brazil, Uruguay, Ceylon, Siberia, and parts of North America are important sources of supply. The so-called Oriental amethyst or purple sapphire is not a variety of quartz, but a very much harder and rarer stone—a variety of corundum.

Amharic (ămhä'rĭk), standard language of Ethiopia. It belongs to the Ethiopic group of Hamito-Semitic languages. See LANGUAGE (table).

Amherst, Jeffrey Amherst, Baron (ăm'ûrst), 1717–97, British army officer. He served in the War of the Austrian Succession and in the early part of the Seven Years War. In 1758 he was sent to America as a major general to lead the Louisburg campaign in the last of the French and Indian Wars. The capture (1758) of the French fortress gave Britain her first important victory in the war, and Amherst replaced James Abercromby as supreme commander in America. The next year (1759), pushing northward from Albany, he took Crown Point and Ticonderoga, but he arrived too late to help General Wolfe take Quebec. He directed (1760) the capture of Montreal and returned (1763) to England. In the American Revolution, Amherst refused to command British troops in New England, but in 1778 he became commander in chief of home defenses. Amherst, for whom Amherst College is named, was created baron in 1776 and made a field marshal in 1796. See his journal (ed. by J. C. Webster, 1931); biography by J. C. Long (1933).

Amherst, town (pop. 10,788), N N.S., Canada. It is a manufacturing and lumbering town in a region noted for scenic beauty. Nearby are the ruins of Fort Lawrence and Fort Beauséjour, built in 1750–51 on the English-French boundary.

Amherst. 1 Uninc. town (pop. 10,306), W Mass., NE of Northampton; settled 1703, inc. 1759. Emily Dickinson was born and lived here all her life, and Noah Webster lived here, 1812–22. The town, named for Lord Jeffrey Amherst, includes the unincorporated village of North Amherst (pop. 1,009). Amherst is the seat of the Univ. of Massachusetts (see MASSACHUSETTS, UNIVERSITY OF) and of **Amherst College,** (for men), which was

Kirby Memorial Theater at Amherst College.

opened in 1821 as a development of Amherst Academy (chartered 1816) and chartered in 1825 by Congregationalists. A leading and well-endowed small college with noted alumni, it has fostered the missionary spirit, emphasized liberal arts education, and pioneered in organizing survey courses, student-health programs, and student government. The trustees administer the Folger Shakespeare Memorial Library, Washington, D.C.,

and the Merrill Center for Economics at Southampton, N.Y. The college maintains a cooperative library and study program with Mount Holyoke and Smith colleges and the Univ. of Massachusetts. **2** Town (pop. 2,051), S N.H., SW of Manchester. It was granted by Massachusetts in 1728 to soldiers of King Philip's War and their heirs, settled c.1733, and incorporated in 1760. Horace Greeley and G. W. Kendall were born here. Franklin Pierce was married in the Robert Means House (built 1785). **3** City (pop. 6,750), N Ohio, near Lake Erie NW of Elyria; settled c.1810. It is a fruitgrowing area and is noted for its sandstone quarries. **4** Town (pop. 1,200), co. seat of Amherst co., central Va., NNE of Lynchburg, in a fruit and tobacco area.

Amherstburg, town (pop. 4,452), S Ont., Canada, on the Detroit river S of Detroit. Fort Malden was built here in 1796. When the War of 1812 began, it was a British naval station as well as a garrison town. At the close of the war Amhertsburg was held by the Americans. It is now a summer resort.

Amherst College: see AMHERST, Mass.

Amherstdale, uninc. village (pop. 1,716 including Robinette), SW W.Va., W of Beckley.

Ami (ā′mī) [Heb.,=architect], servant of Solomon whose descendants came out of exile. Ezra 2.57. Amon: Neh. 7.59.

Amici, Giovanni Battista (jōvän′nē bät-tēs′tä ämē′-chē), 1786–1863, Italian astronomer, mathematician, and naturalist. He became director of the observatory and professor of anatomy at Florence and published papers on various scientific subjects. His most important work was in designing and improving physical and astronomical apparatus, especially the microscope and reflecting telescope.

Amicis, Edmondo de: see DE AMICIS, EDMONDO.

Amida (ă′mĭdù, ùmĭ′dù), ancient city, E Asia Minor. Located on the Tigris, it was a Roman colony from A.D. 230 and was captured (4th cent.) by Shapur II of Persia. It is the modern DIYARBAKIR, Turkey.

Amidas, Philip: see AMADAS, PHILIP.

amide: see AMMONIA.

Amiel, Henri Frédéric (ärē′ frādārēk′ ämyĕl′), 1821–81, Swiss critic. He was unsuccessful and unnoticed during his life, but the posthumous publication of his *Journal intime* (1883; Eng. tr., of augmented ed., 1936) aroused great interest. It is a document of scrupulous self-observation. See Van Wyck Brooks, *Malady of the Ideal* (1913).

Amiens (ă′mēùnz, -ĕnz″, Fr. ämyē′), city (estimated pop. 92,506), capital of Somme dept., N France, in Picardy, on the Somme. An important communications and textile center, it also trades in grain, sugar, wool, and leather. Originally a Gallo-Roman town, it was an episcopal see from the 4th cent. The historical capital of PICARDY, it was overrun and occupied by many invaders. It was conquered by HENRY IV in 1597. Here, in 1802, the treaty of Amiens was signed. The Cathedral of Notre Dame (begun 1220) is the largest and one of the finest French Gothic cathedrals. It is 470 ft. long and has a nave 140 ft. high; the transept dates from the 14th cent.; the spire (370 ft. high) and the large rose window were added in the 16th cent. Near the cathedral stands a statue of Peter the Hermit, who

Cathedral of Notre Dame in Amiens, France.

carbon atom of the peptide linkage has an oxygen atom attached to it. Amino acids are released in the small intestine by digestion of food proteins and are then carried in the blood stream to the body cells, where they are used for growth, maintenance, and repair. In the cells, during METABOLISM, peptide linkages are formed and broken by EN-ZYMES. The amino acids may be used as structural units or they may be broken down into fragments. Many of the amino acids necessary in metabolism can be synthesized in the human or animal body when needed; these are called nonessential. How-ever, certain amino acids cannot be synthesized in the body; these are termed essential and must be provided in the protein diet. Every amino acid except glycine can occur as either of two optically active isomers (composed of the same atoms but in a different spatial arrangement); the more com-mon isomer in nature is the L- form. Some ANTI-BIOTICS contain the D- form. NUCLEIC ACIDS are involved in determining which amino acids are present in a protein. The actual sequence of amino acids is known for very few proteins, INSULIN being one of them. Frederick SANGER received the 1958 Nobel Prize in Chemistry for his determina-tion of the structure of insulin.

Amiot, Joseph: see AMYOT, JOSEPH.

Amis, Kingsley, 1922–, English novelist, b. London, grad. Oxford, 1947. His first and best-known novel, *Lucky Jim* (1954), a brilliant comic satire on the academic life, classified him as one of England's ANGRY YOUNG MEN. The sense of cultural and social disillusionment is more fully explored in his *That Uncertain Feeling* (1955), *I Like It Here* (1958), and *Take a Girl Like You* (1960). A collection of his poetry, *A Case of Samples: Poems 1946–1956*, appeared in 1956. Amis is also the author of *New Maps of Hell* (1960), a survey of science fiction.

Amish Church: see MENNONITES.

Amisus: see SAMSUN.

Amite (ùmēt′), town (pop. 3,316), parish seat of Tangipahoa (tăn′jĭpùhō″) parish, SE La., NE of Baton Rouge; settled 1836, inc. 1861. The town is in an area producing strawberries, cotton, corn, timber, and dairy goods. Concrete products and machinery are made.

Amittai (ămĭt′āī) [Heb.,=loyal], father of Jonah. Jonah 1.1.

Amityville (ăm′ĭtēvĭl), residential village (pop. 8,318), SE N.Y., on the south shore of Long Island, E of New York city; settled 1780, inc. 1894. It is a summer resort with some industry.

Ammah (ăm′ù), hill near Gibeon. 2 Sam. 2.24.

Amman (ämän′), city (pop. 108,304), capital of Jor-dan, on the Jabbok (or Wadi Zerka) and NE of the Dead Sea. On a site occupied since prehistoric times, it is the biblical Rabbah (răb′ù) or Rabbath-Ammon, capital of the Ammonites. It was con-quered (11th cent. B.C.) by King David, but re-gained its independence under Solomon. Deut. 3.11; Joshua 13.25; 15.60; 2 Sam. 11.1; 12.26–29; 17.27; 1 Chron. 20.1; Jer. 49.2,3; Ezek. 21.20; 25.5; Amos 1.14. It was taken by Assyria (8th cent. B.C.) and by Antiochus III (c.218 B.C.). Ptolemy II renamed it Philadelphia. It was a member of the Decapolis. After 30 B.C. the city was rebuilt by the Romans. Later it was conquered (A.D. 635) by the Arabs. In 1921 Amman became

was born at Amiens. Lamarck, Delambre, and Choderlos de Laclos were also born here.

Amiens, Treaty of, 1802, peace treaty signed by France, Spain, and the BATAVIAN REPUBLIC on the one hand and Great Britain on the other. England was to give up most conquests made in the FRENCH REVOLUTIONARY WARS, and France was to evacu-ate Naples and restore Egypt to the Ottoman Em-pire. The peace, though much acclaimed, lasted barely a year (see NAPOLEON I).

Aminadab (ùmĭn′ù–), variant of AMMINADAB.

amine: see AMMONIA.

amino acid, any one of a class of simple organic compounds containing carbon, hydrogen, oxygen, nitrogen, and in certain cases sulfur. These com-pounds are distinguished by the presence of char-acteristic groups of atoms known as the carboxyl (1 carbon atom, 2 oxygen atoms, and 1 hydrogen atom) and the amino group (1 nitrogen atom and 2 hydrogen atoms). There are about 20 different amino acids commonly found in nature, and they are linked together in chains (peptide linkages) to form the proteins comprising living matter (see PROTEINS). The characteristic protein is deter-mined by several factors, among which are the nature of the individual amino acids present (not all 20 are always present in the thousands of proteins in living matter), the amount of the individual amino acid per molecule of protein, and the mode of linkage between amino acids (e.g., peptide and sulfur-to-sulfur linkages). The pep-tide linkage is the most important in protein structure. It consists of a carboxyl carbon atom of one amino acid connected to the nitrogen atom of the amino group of another amino acid. The

Bartolomeo Ammanati built the court façade of Pitti Palace in Florence, Italy.

the capital of Trans-Jordan, and after the Second World War it grew rapidly, absorbing refugees from Palestine. It is a transportation hub, especially for pilgrims to Mecca, and is a commercial center noted for its colored marble. There is a Moslem college (opened 1948) and a large airport (completed 1956).

Ammanati, Bartolomeo (bärtōlōmä′ō äm-mänä′tē), 1511–92, Italian sculptor and architect. He studied under Bandinelli in Florence and assisted Jacopo Sansovino in his work on the Library of St. Mark's, Venice. Ammanati, whose style was much influenced by Michelangelo's Medici tombs, made a colossal statue of Hercules, at Padua. In Rome he collaborated with Vignola and Vasari in their work at the villa of Pope Julius III. His best work here was in the Ruspoli Palace and in the court of the Collegio Romano. Returning to Florence in 1557, he became architect to Cosimo de' Medici. He made the Santa Trinità bridge over the Arno and a number of fountains, among them the Neptune fountain for the Piazza della Signoria. He built the court façade of Pitti Palace, the Guigni Palace, and a cloister of Santo Spirito. The poet Laura Battiferri was his wife.

Ammann, Othmar Hermann (ôt′mär, ŏ′mŏn), 1879–, American civil engineer, b. Switzerland, grad. Federal Polytechnic Institute, Zurich, 1902. He came to the United States in 1904 and was naturalized in 1924. He served (1925–39) with the Port of New York Authority and was its director of engineers (1937–39). An authority on bridges, he participated in either the designing or the construction of Hell Gate, George Washington, Triborough, and Bronx-Whitestone bridges in New York city and of San Francisco's Golden Gate Bridge.

ammeter: see GALVANOMETER.

Ammi (ăm′ī) [Heb.,=my people], figurative name of Israel after reconciliation with God. Hosea 2.1. Cf. LOAMMI.

Ammianus Marcellinus (ămēā′nŭs märsĭlī′nŭs), c.330–c.400, Latin historian, b. Antioch. After retiring from a successful military career, he wrote a history of the Roman Empire as a sequel to that of Tacitus, his model. The history, in 31 books, covered the years from A.D. 96 to 378; only Books XIV–XXXI, covering the years A.D. 353–78, sur-

vive. Though written in an extremely rhetorical style, his work is reliable and impartial, and his literary ability has been highly esteemed by modern scholars. A pagan and an admirer of Julian the Apostate, Ammianus was not prejudiced against Christianity. See E. A. Thompson, *Historical Work of Ammianus Marcellinus* (1947).

Ammiel (ăm′ēĕl) [Heb.,=people of God]. **1** Spy. Num. 13.12. **2** Father of MACHIR **2**. **3** Porter of the Temple. 1 Chron. 26.5. **4** See ELIAM **1**.

Ammihud (ăm′ĭhŭd, ŭmī′hŭd) [Heb.,=people of Judah]. **1** Ancestor of Joshua. Num. 1.10; 2.18; 7.48,53; 10.22; 1 Chron. 7.26. **2** Simeonite. Num. 34.20. **3** Naphtalite. Num. 34.28. **4** Judahite. 1 Chron. 9.4. **5** Father of a king of Geshur. 2 Sam. 13.37.

Amminadab (ŭmĭn′ŭ–) [Heb.,=my tribe is princely]. **1** Aaron's father-in-law. Ex. 6.23; Num. 1.7; 2.3; 7.12; 10.14; Ruth 4.19,20; 1 Chron. 2.10. Aminadab: Mat. 1.4; Luke 3.33. **2** Head of a Levitical family. 1 Chron. 15.10–12. **3** The same as IZEHAR.

Amminadib (ăm″ĭnā′dĭb, ŭmĭn′ŭdĭb), word of uncertain significance. Cant. 6.12.

Ammishaddai (ăm″ĭshăd′āī), [Heb.,=people of the Almighty], Danite, father of AHIEZER **1**. Num. 1.12; 2.25; 7.66,71; 10.25.

Ammizabad (ŭmĭz′ŭbăd) [Heb.,=my people have given], son of BENAIAH **1**. 1 Chron. 27.6.

Ammon (ăm′ŭn), in the Bible, people living E of the Dead Sea. Their capital was Rabbath-Ammon, the present Amman (Jordan). Their god was Milcom, to whom Solomon built an altar. 1 Kings 11.5; 2 Kings 23.13. A Semitic people, they flourished from the 13th to the 8th cent. B.C. and were then absorbed by the Arabs. Excavations in Jordan show that they had a highly developed kingdom. They were hostile to the Hebrews, to whom they were related. Their eponymous ancestor was Lot's son. Gen. 19.38; Deut. 2.19,20,37; 23.3,4; Judges 3.13; 1 Sam. 11; 2 Sam. 10–12; 2 Chron. 20; Neh. 2.10; 4.7; Jer. 49.1–6.

Ammon, Egyptian god: see AMON.

Ammon, village (pop. 1,882), SE Idaho, ESE of Idaho Falls, in an irrigated farm area.

ammonia [from SAL AMMONIAC, said to have been made first near the temple of Jupiter Ammon in Egypt], compound (boiling point −33.5°C; melting point −77.7°C.), each molecule comprising three atoms of nitrogen to one atom of hydrogen. A colorless gas at ordinary temperatures, it has a characteristic penetrating odor and is slightly more than one half as heavy as air. The "ammonia" sold for household use is an aqueous solution; the gas is extremely soluble in water, one volume of water dissolving about 1,200 volumes of ammonia at 0°C. The solution exhibits basic properties, since only a part of the gas goes into solution and the rest reacts with the water to form ammonium hydroxide, the active cleansing agent. Because it is easily liquefied by pressure and absorbs a relatively large amount of heat when the liquid reverts under reduced pressure to the gas, ammonia is used extensively in REFRIGERATION. It reacts with acids to form salts: e.g., with nitric acid it yields ammonium nitrate, used in making explosives; with hydrochloric acid, ammonium chloride, or SAL AMMONIAC; and with sulfuric acid, ammonium sulfate, used in fertilizers. It is employed also in the preparation of nitric acid in the OSTWALD PROCESS and in the preparation of soda by the SOLVAY PROCESS. Ammonia is prepared in several ways: as a by-product in the destructive distillation of coal; synthetically, by the HABER PROCESS; and by the cyanamide process, in which calcium carbide is heated with nitrogen, the resulting calcium cyanamide being treated with steam under pressure to form ammonia and calcium carbonate. Ammonia is prepared in the laboratory by heating an ammonium salt with a strong base. Originally it was obtained by the destructive distillation of the horns and hoofs of animals, and the resulting solution of the gas was known consequently as spirits of hartshorn. The compound occurs in nature as a minor constituent of the air, in volcanic gases, and among the decomposition products of animal and vegetable matter. When an atom of hydrogen is added to the ammonia molecule, the ammonium radical is formed, comprising one atom of nitrogen and four of hydrogen. The radical does not occur free, but only in compounds; in solution it forms a positively charged ion. It behaves chemically as a monovalent metal, its compounds resembling those of the more active monovalent metals, such as potassium and sodium. Among the compounds considered derivatives of ammonia are amides, amines, and AMINO ACIDS. Acetamide, benzamide, and formamide are examples of amides. Amides are formed by the replacement of one or more of the hydrogen atoms of the ammonia molecule by an equal number of the characteristic RADICAL of an organic acid, such as the acetyl radical of acetic acid, to make acetamide, or the benzoyl radical of benzoic acid, to make benzamide. Amines can be derived from ammonia by replacing one or more of the hydrogen atoms in the ammonia molecule with a corresponding number of alkyl radicals (each a chain of carbon and hydrogen atoms) or of aryl radicals (each a ring of carbon and hydrogen atoms). Both amides and amines are classified as primary, secondary, or tertiary according to the number of hydrogen atoms replaced in the ammonia molecule.

ammoniac or **gum ammoniac** (ŭmō′nĕăk″), yellowish substance with a sickening, bitter taste, obtained in the milky exudence from the injured stem of a plant (*Dorema ammoniacum*) found in Persia, India, and S Siberia. It is a gum resin soluble in alcohol, benzol, carbon disulphide, and ether. In industry it is used in the manufacture of porcelain cements, and in medicine as an expectorant. When gum ammoniac is distilled it yields a liquid, oil of ammoniac.

ammonite (ăm′ŭnīt), one of a type of extinct marine mollusks, related to the nautilus and resembling it in having an elaborately coiled and chambered

Ammonite

shell. The type included numerous species, which were widely distributed during the Mesozoic era.

ammonium, RADICAL (chemical formula=NH_4), having one nitrogen atom linked to each of four hydrogen atoms. It has a positive valence of one.

amnesia [Gr.,=forgetfulness], condition characterized by loss of memory for long or short intervals of time. It may be caused by injury, shock, senility, severe illness, or mental disease. In some cases, memory of events prior to the illness is lost; in others, events following the illness are forgotten. One form of the condition known as tropic amnesia or coast memory affects white men on the west coast of Africa; this condition is thought to be hysteric in origin. APHASIA of the amnesic variety is caused by an organic brain condition and is not to be confused with other forms of amnesia. To cure amnesia, attempts are made to establish associations with the past by suggestion, and HYPNOTISM is sometimes employed.

amnesty (ăm′nŭstē), in law, exemption from prosecution for crime. Amnesties are usually extended to a group of persons during a period of prolonged disorder or insurrection. The criminals are offered a promise of immunity from prosecution if they will abandon their unlawful activities. After a revolution or civil war the victorious side will often extend amnesty to the losers; e.g., the United States granted a qualified amnesty to the Confederate forces after the Civil War. An amnesty is distinguished from a PARDON, which is an act of forgiveness after the criminal has already been convicted.

Amnon [Heb.,=faithful]. **1** David's eldest son. He ravished his half sister Tamar and was killed for it by her brother Absalom. 2 Sam. 3.2; 13. **2** Judahite. 1 Chron. 4.20.

amoeba or **ameba** (both: ŭmē′bŭ) [Gr.,=change],

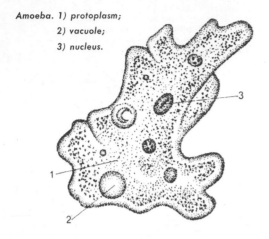

Amoeba. 1) protoplasm;
2) vacuole;
3) nucleus.

unicellular animal of the genus *Amoeba* of the class Sarcodina of the phylum PROTOZOA. The amoeba consists of a single CELL in which the cytoplasm is differentiated into fluid, granular endoplasm in the interior, and clear, comparatively firm ectoplasm on the outside. Amoebae move and capture their food by means of pseudopods [Gr.,=false feet], temporary extensions formed by flowing cytoplasm. The mechanism of amoeboid movement is not clearly understood; various theories account for it by changes in surface tension and viscosity. Provided the pseudopod does not encounter an obstacle, an injurious chemical, bright light, or heat, the bulk of the animal flows in the same direction until another pseudopod forms and the flow is changed, the animal thus moving in a slow, irregular course. Amoebae can distinguish food (e.g., algae, diatoms, bacteria, and other protozoans) from other material and use different tactics in approaching plant and animal food. When captured and ingested, the food is surrounded by a bubble-like vacuole and digested by enzymes. Solid wastes are egested—in effect simply left behind—through any point in the surface membrane. A contractile vacuole regulates the water content. Respiration is by diffusion of gases through the membrane. Reproduction is by binary fission (splitting), the nucleus dividing by mitosis; when an amoeba is divided artificially the portion containing the nucleus forms a new membrane and continues as a whole animal, while the other portion lives on whatever food material is present but is unable to digest or reproduce and soon dies. In the absence of food or water the cell contracts and forms a hard-walled cyst, from which it emerges when conditions are again favorable. Amoebae are found in fresh and salt water and in damp soil; many live in or on other animals. Of the latter, *Endamoeba histolytica*, the cause of amoebic dysentery, inhabits man's alimentary tract and produces ulceration of the intestinal wall. *A. proteus*, a common fresh-water species, averages 1/100 in. in length. Members of the closely related genus *Pelomyxa* (or *Chaos*) are

multinucleated protozoans reaching a diameter of 8 mm, visible to the naked eye. Other amoeboid protozoans of the class Sarcodina are the marine radiolarians, which form silicate skeletons; their fresh-water counterparts, the heliozoans; and the shell-bearing FORAMINIFERA.

Amok (ā'–) [Heb.,=deep], postexilic Jewish family. Neh. 12.7,20.

amole: see SOAP PLANT.

Amon (ā'mŏn) **1** Died c.640 B.C., king of Judah (c.642–c.640 B.C.), son and successor of Manasseh. He was inattentive to the worship of God, and the biblical accounts denounce him strongly. Jeremiah was his contemporary. Amon was murdered, and Josiah succeeded him. 2 Kings 21.19–26; 2 Chron. 33.20–25. **2** Ahab's governor of Samaria. 1 Kings 22.26; 2 Chron. 18.25. **3** See AMI.

Amon (ā'mŭn, ä'–) or **Ammon** (ā'mŭn) or **Amen** (ā'mĕn), Egyptian deity. He was originally the chief god of Thebes, and he with his wife Mut and their son Khensu were the divine Theban triad of deities. Amon grew increasingly important in Egypt, and eventually he (identified as Amon Ra; see RA), became the supreme deity. He was identified with the Greek Zeus, the Roman Jupiter. Amon's most celebrated shrine was at Siwa in the Libyan desert; the oracle of Siwa later rivaled those of Delphi and Dodona. He is frequently represented as a ram or as a human with a ram's head.

amontillado (ùmŏn"tĭlä'dō), dry SHERRY noted for its delicate bouquet, resembling the wine of Montilla, from which it derives its name. A blend of pale, dry sherries of the *palma* type, it assumes in aging a darker tint.

Amontons, Guillaume (gēyŏm' ämōtō'), 1663–1705, French physicist. He is known for his work on friction and on the relationship of temperature and pressure and also as an inventor of instruments such as the hygrometer.

Amor: see EROS.

Amoraim: see SCRIBE.

Amorites (ăm'ûrīts), a people of Canaan. There is evidence of them also in Babylonia, where in the 18th cent. B.C. they established a dynasty at Babylon; their most powerful king was Hammurabi. At the time of Joshua the Amorites were living both E and W of the Dead Sea. They were subdued and gradually absorbed by the Israelites. Gen. 10.16; 14.7; 15.16; Num. 13.29; 21.13,21–32; Deut. 1.4–7; 4.47,48; Joshua 5.1; 10.6.

amortization, the reduction, liquidation, or satisfaction of a debt. Amortization may also mean the sum used for this purpose. The term is commonly used in ascertaining the investment value of securities. Thus, if a security is bought at more than its face value, a part of the premium is periodically charged off in order to bring the value of the security to par at maturity; if the security is bought at less than its face value, the discount is similarly charged off. Another application of amortization is to treat dividends of investments having limited duration, such as mine stocks, as both interest on capital and as return of capital by designating part of the dividends as return of capital and reinvesting this part at a set rate. The term necessary for the stock to return its original cost can then be calculated. Paying off a mortgage by installments or paying off this or any other debt by a SINKING FUND is amortization. Amortization by paying off a certain number of bonds each year is practiced by public corporations. National governments of limited credit and private companies commonly amortize by sinking funds. Governments with stronger credit usually refund debts by the issuance of new bonds. The satisfying of a debt by a single payment may also be termed amortization. See H. A. Finney, *Principles of Accounting* (4th ed., 1952).

Amory (ā′mŭrē), city (pop. 6,474), NE Miss., N of Columbus and near the Tombigbee; founded 1887. It is a railroad, shipping, and trade center for a cotton and livestock area.

Amos (ā′mŭs), book of the Old Testament, third of the books of the Minor Prophets. The prophet was a shepherd of Tekoa in S Palestine, who preached in the mid-8th cent. B.C. in the northern kingdom of Israel under Jeroboam II, especially against hypocritical worship, oppression of the poor, and immorality. Israel was at the peak of her political might, but was ridden with social injustices. The book falls into three parts: God's judgment on various Gentile nations, finally on Israel (1–2); three sermons on the doom of Israel (3–6); and five visions of destruction (7–9), of which the last promises redemption. The book contains powerful passages. The name of another Amos occurs in the genealogy of Luke 3.25. For bibliography, see OLD TESTAMENT.

Amos, town (pop. 6,080), W Que., Canada, NE of Rouyn. It is in a mining region.

Amoy (ùmoi′), Mandarin *Hsia-men*, city (pop. c.224,300), S Fukien prov., China, on Amoy island, at the mouth of the Lung river. It is a port and a leading manufacturing center, producing noodles, paper, and wine. Amoy has an excellent natural harbor, whose growth was limited by the lack of hinterland transportation until the construction (1957) of the Yingtan-Amoy RR. Opposite Amoy proper, across the inner harbor, is the island of Kulangsu or Kulanghsu, the former foreign settlement and a fine residential section. Amoy was one of the earliest seats of European commerce in China, with Portuguese (16th cent.) and Dutch (17th cent.) establishments. It was captured (1841) by the British in the OPIUM WAR and became a TREATY PORT in 1842. Long a Chinese port of emigration, mainly to SE Asia, Amoy receives money sent back from emigrants abroad to their relatives. The city has the Univ. of Amoy (1921).

Amoz (ā′mŏz), father of the prophet Isaiah. Isa. 1.1.

ampelopsis (ăm″pĭlŏp′–) [from Gr.,=looking like a vine], botanically, name for woody ornamental vines of the genus *Ampelopsis*, but from long association also used in horticultural practice for the VIRGINIA CREEPER, BOSTON IVY, and others of related genera of the GRAPE family. Species of *Ampelopsis* native to Asia and North America have showy berries of various colors. The pepper-vine (*A. arborea*) is indigenous to the S United States.

Ampère, André Marie (ăm′pēr; Fr. ädrā′ märē′ äpĕr′), 1775–1836, French physicist, mathematician, and natural philosopher. He was professor of mathematics at the École polytechnique, Paris, and later at the Collège de France. Known for his contributions to electrodynamics, including the formulation of Ampère's law, he confirmed and amplified the work of OERSTED on the relationship of electricity and magnetism, and he invented the astatic needle. The ampere was named for him. His writings include *Observations électro-dynamiques* (1822) and *Essai sur la philosophie des sciences* (1838–43).

André Marie Ampère

ampere [for A. M. Ampère], electrical unit of current strength and unit of measurement of rate of flow of electricity. The intensity of a current (in amperes) is equal to (according to OHM'S LAW) the electromotive force (volts) divided by the resistance (ohms). Thus, if a conductor of one ohm resistance

Ampelopsis

has a potential difference of one volt between its ends, a one-ampere current will flow through it. The coulomb [for C. A. de Coulomb] is defined as the quantity of electricity carried past a given section of a conductor in one second by a current of one ampere; the ampere thus equals one coulomb per second. The ampere is defined more exactly as that amount of current flowing through each of two long, parallel wires one meter apart, which causes a magnetic force of 2×10^{-7} newton on each meter of each wire. The international ampere, formerly the legal standard, equals .99985 ampere.

Amphiaraüs (ăm″fēŭrā′ŭs), in Greek legend, a prophet, one of the ill-fated SEVEN AGAINST THEBES. He foresaw the disaster of the expedition, but his wife, Eriphyle, bribed by Polynices with the magic necklace of Harmonia, compelled him to go. Before setting out he commanded his sons, Alcmaeon and Amphilochus, to avenge his death on their mother and to make a second expedition against Thebes. Amphiaraüs also was one of the Argonauts.

amphibian (ămfĭ′bēŭn), in zoology, cold-blooded vertebrate animal of the class Amphibia, which is intermediate between the fish and the reptiles. Animals of this group characteristically undergo a metamorphosis from an aquatic (see TADPOLE) to a terrestrial or partly terrestrial form. See FROG; NEWT; SALAMANDER; TOAD.

amphibious warfare (ămfĭ′bēŭs), the combination of land and sea forces to take or defend a military objective. The general strategy is very ancient and was extensively employed by the Greeks in their warfare, e.g., in the Athenian attack on Sicily in 415 B.C. The term is, however, of recent coinage. It is sometimes applied to the joint operations of the Allied army and naval forces in the disastrous Gallipoli campaign (1915) of the First World War. In the Second World War amphibious warfare was widely employed. When Japan entered the Second World War on a large scale in Dec., 1941, combined air, land, and naval operations were used by the Japanese to capture their objectives, particularly islands such as the Philippines, Java, and Sumatra. These operations were not, however, typical of the problems of amphibious warfare, since in the Japanese landings there was little opposition. The same was true of the Allied landing in North Africa in Nov., 1942. The problem faced by the Allies in the reconquest of Europe and the Pacific islands was how to land their forces on a heavily defended coast line. This problem was solved by the construction of special vessels called landing craft that were seaworthy and yet capable of allowing tanks and infantry to emerge without difficulty into shallow water for landing. The typical pattern of an Allied amphibious operation was heavy and continued air and naval bombardment of the enemy defenses, followed by a landing of troops with complete equipment from landing craft; the landing forces were supported in the early stages by naval guns until land artillery could come into action. By use of this method the Allies were able to invade heavily defended Pacific Islands such as Tarawa (1943), Saipan (1944), Iwo Jima (1945), Okinawa (1945).

Amphibious warfare was widely used by the U.S. in the Second World War.

Coast Guard landing craft dashes in over the surf with troops and supplies during invasion in the Hollandia area of Dutch New Guinea.

In Europe the Allies made landings on Sicily (1943) and Italy (1943–44). The most spectacular example of amphibious warefare was the invasion of Normandy by the Allies from England on June 6, 1944. This action was a prime example of combined movements of naval craft, land forces, and aircraft (used for offense, protection of other forces, and transport). Although the American invasion of Inchon (1950) during the Korean war and the British and French invasion of Egypt during the Sinai crisis (1957) are notable examples of amphibious operations there are many who argue that the classic age of this particular type of amphibious warfare came and went in the Second World War. The effects, however, of nuclear weapons and guided missiles have not yet been actually demonstrated. See J. A. Isely and P. A. Crowl, *The U.S. Marines and Amphibious War* (1951); Bernard Fergusson, *The Watery Maze: the Story of Combined Operations* (1961).

amphictyony (ămfĭk′tēō″nē, –ŏ″nē, –ûnē″), in ancient Greece, a league connected with maintaining a temple or shrine. There were a number of these, but by far the most important was the Great Amphictyony or Delphic Amphictyony, a league originally of 12 tribes, which had meetings in the spring at the temple of Demeter at Anthela near Thermopylae and in the autumn at Delphi. The Amphictyonic Council passed legislation regarding religious matters and had power to declare a sacred war against an offender. Each tribe had two votes. By the 6th cent. the religious organization had begun to have political influence. The greater city-states, by using pressure on the lesser, got control of more tribal votes and were able to control laws and policy. The significance of the Amphictyonic Council was shown by Philip II of Macedon, who, after managing to get on the council by securing the votes of the Phocians, used sacred wars as a pretext for furthering his con-

quests in Greece. This one large unifying organization, therefore, in the end had no real unifying power in divided Greece. The Great Amphictyony continued in existence (but with no power) until late in the Roman Empire.

Amphilochus (ămfĭ′lŭkŭs), in Greek legend, son of Amphiaraüs and ERIPHYLE and brother of Alcmaeon. He was one of the EPIGONI, and with his brother slew Eriphyle for her treachery in bringing about their father's death.

Amphion: see ANTIOPE 1.

Amphipolis (amfĭ′pŭlĭs), ancient city of Macedonia, on the Strymon (Struma) river near the sea and NE of later Salonica. The place was known as Ennea Hodoi [nine ways] before it was settled and was of interest because of the gold and silver and timber of Mt. Pangaeus (Pangaion), to which it gave access. Athenian colonists were driven out (c.464 B.C.) by Thracians, but a colony was established in 437 B.C. Amphipolis became one of the major Greek cities on the N Aegean. This colony was captured by Sparta, and Brasidas and Cleon were both killed in a battle here in 422. After it was returned to Athens in 421, it actually had virtual independence until captured (357) by Philip II of Macedon. He had promised to restore it to Athens, and his retention of Amphipolis was a major cause of the war with Athens. It was the capital (168–148 B.C.) of Macedonia Prima, one of the Roman republics. Paul, Silas, and Timothy passed through Amphipolis. Acts 17.1. Nearby is the modern Greek village of Amphipolis.

amphitheater [Gr.], open structure serving for the exhibition of gladiatorial contests, struggles of wild beasts, sham sea battles, and similar spectacles. There is no Greek prototype of amphitheaters, which were primarily Roman and were built in many cities throughout the empire. More or less well-preserved examples are in Rome (see COLOSSEUM), Verona, and Capua in Italy; at

The Colosseum in Rome, Italy, is one of the most impressive ancient amphitheaters.

Nîmes and Arles in France; at Cirencester in England; and at sites in Sicily, Greece, and North Africa. The typical amphitheater was elliptical in shape, with seats, supported on vaults of masonry, rising in many tiers around an arena at the center; corridors and stairs facilitated the circulation of great throngs. The arena itself was usually built over the quarters for gladiators, wild animals, and storage. Until the erection of the Colosseum (A.D. 80), practically all amphitheaters were of wood, the notable exception being that of stone built at Pompeii c.70 B.C. The word *amphitheater* is now applied to modern structures which may bear little resemblance to their ancient prototypes.

Amphitrite (ămfītrī′tē), in Greek mythology, queen of the sea; daughter of Nereus. She was the wife of Poseidon and mother of Triton.

Amphitryon (ămfī′trĕun, –ŏn″), in Greek mythology, son of Alcaeus. While betrothed to Alcmene he accidentally killed her father, Electryon. Together they fled to Thebes, but she demanded that he defeat Pterelaos, her father's enemy. This Amphitryon did, but on the night of his return Zeus took Amphitryon's form and came into Alcmene's bed. That night she conceived children by both Zeus and Amphitryon. Hercules was the son of Zeus, Iphicles the son of Amphitryon.

Amplias (ămp′lēus) or **Ampliatus** (ămplēā′tùs), Christian in Rome to whom Paul sent greetings. Rom. 16.8.

amplification, radio: see TUBE, VACUUM.

Amram [Heb.,=my people is exalted]. **1** Moses' father; ancestor of a Levitical family. Ex. 6.18,20; Num. 3.19,27; 26.58,59; 1 Chron. 6.2,3,18; 23.12, 13; 24.20; 26.23. **2** See HEMDAN. **3** Jew who had married a foreign wife. Ezra 10.34.

Amram ben Scheschna (shĕsh′nä) or **Amram Gaon** (gä′ōn), d. 874, Hebrew scholar. He is chiefly known as the author of the *Seder Rab Amram* (prayer book), a compilation of the order of prayers, with their context for the whole year and the liturgical laws governing the ceremonial observ-ances of all the holidays. This book is the basis for the modern orthodox Jewish religious rites.

Amraphel (ăm′rùfĕl, ămrā′fùl): see CHEDORLAOMER and HAMMURABI.

Amritsar (ŭmrĭt′sùr), city (pop. 325,747), Punjab state, NW India, near the border of Pakistan. It is a trade center and makes carpets, fabrics of goat hair, and handicrafts. The center of the Sikh religion, Amritsar was founded in 1577 by Ram Das, the fourth guru [Hindustani,=teacher], on land given by Akbar. The Golden Temple (refurbished 1802), set in the center of a lake, is especially

The Golden Temple in Amritsar, India.

Amphitrite and Poseidon, *mural from Herculaneum, Italy.*

sacred to Sikhs. The city was the center of a Sikh empire in the early 19th cent., and modern Sikh nationalism was founded here. It has Khalsa College and a branch of the provincial university. Here, in April, 1919, in the Jalianwala Bagh, an enclosed park, occurred the Amritsar massacre; hundreds of Indian nationalists were killed and thousands wounded when they were fired upon by troops under British control.

Amru-l-Kais (äm'rōōl-kīs'), 6th cent., Arabian poet. His verse is, like all the poetry of the pre-Islamic period, intensely subjective and formally perfect. He was esteemed by Arabs as the great model for erotic poetry. He probably went to Constantinople and lived for many years in high favor with the imperial court. He is represented in the MUALLAQAT. His name is also spelled Imru-l-Kais.

Amsdorf, Nikolaus von (nē'kōlous fŭn äms'dôrf) 1483–1565, German Protestant reformer. He became a devoted supporter of Martin Luther. Elector John Frederick I of Saxony appointed Amsdorf bishop of Naumberg in 1541, but after the elector was captured by Emperor Charles V, the office was withdrawn (1547). A zealous defender of Luther's doctrines, Amsdorf attacked all who deviated from them in the slightest, including Melanchthon. He took part in the founding of a new university at Jena and superintended the Jena edition of the works of Luther.

Amsterdam (ăm'stûrdăm″, Dutch ämstûrdäm'), city (estimated pop. 869,602), constitutional capital and largest city of the Netherlands, in North Holland prov., W Netherlands. A major port, it is also the seat of one of the world's chief stock exchanges, a center of the diamond-cutting industry, and one of the great commercial, intellectual, and artistic capitals of Europe. It is mainly on the south bank of the Ij—the Ij being the mouth of the short Amstel river (for which Amsterdam is named) on the Zuider Zee. Amsterdam is connected with the North Sea by the North Sea Canal (opened in 1876), which accommodates the largest ocean-going vessels, and by the older North Holland Canal. The Merwede Canal connects with the Rhine delta and thus with industrial NW Germany, with which there is considerable transit trade. A transportation center, the city has Schiphol airport, one of the finest in Europe. Because of the soft ground, Amsterdam is built on wooden piles and is cut by about 40 concentric and radial canals flanked by streets and crossed by some 400 bridges. The many old and picturesque houses along the canals, once patrician dwellings, are now mostly offices and warehouses. The main streets are the Dam, on which stand the Nieuwe Kerk (15th–17th cent.) and the 17th-century Dam Palace (formerly the city hall, since 1808 a royal palace); the Damrak, with the stock exchange; and the Kalvertstraat and Leidenschestraat, which are the chief shopping centers. Outstanding buildings are the Oude Kerk [old church], consecrated in 1306; the weighhouse (15th cent.); the city hall (16th cent.);

Amsterdam, Netherlands. Railroad station at left, Church of St. Nicolas at right.

and the Beguinage (Dutch *Begijnenhof*), or almshouses, of the 17th cent. Chartered in 1300, Amsterdam joined the Hanseatic League in 1369. Having accepted the Reformation, the people of Amsterdam in 1578 expelled their pro-Spanish magistrates and joined the rebellious Netherland provinces. The commercial ruin of Antwerp and Ghent and a large influx of refugees from all nations (notably of Flemish merchants, of Jewish diamond cutters from Portugal and Spain, and of French Huguenots) contributed to the rapid growth of Amsterdam after the late 16th cent. The Peace of Westphalia (1648), by closing the Scheldt (Escaut) to navigation, further stimulated the prosperity of Amsterdam at the expense of the Spanish Netherlands. Taken (1795) by the French, Amsterdam became the capital of the kingdom of the Netherlands under Louis Bonaparte. The constitution of 1814 made it the capital of the Netherlands. However, The Hague remains the seat of the government and of the sovereigns, who are merely sworn in at Amsterdam. Occupied in the Second World War by German troops from 1940 to 1945, Amsterdam suffered severe hardship and (after the premature Dutch rising late in 1944) even famine. Of the Jews (about 10 percent of the pre-war population) only a few survived. The birthplace of Spinoza and Hobbema and the residence (1632–69) of Rembrandt, Amsterdam reached its apex as a center of thought and art in the 17th cent.; it has since then maintained its high reputation. Rembrandt and the other Dutch masters are best represented in the world-famous Rijks Museum, or National Museum, founded in 1808 by Louis Bonaparte. Among the many other notable museums are the municipal museum, with a magnificent Van Gogh collection, and Rembrandt's house. Amsterdam is also famous for the Concertgebouw Orchestra. The Univ. of Amsterdam, the largest center of learning in the Netherlands, was founded as an academy in 1632 and became a university in 1876. Near the city is the Bosplan, an enormous man-made national park.

Amsterdam, industrial city (pop. 28,772), E central N.Y., on the Mohawk and NW of Albany; inc. 1885. Carpets and rugs have been made here since the mid-19th cent. Other manufactures include clothing and novelties. Fort Johnson, home of Sir William Johnson, is nearby.

Amu Darya (ä′mŏō där′yŭ, ämŏō′ däryä′), river, c.1,550 mi. long, rising in central Asia in the Pamir mountains. It flows generally northwest, marking much of the boundary between the USSR and Afghanistan and between the Turkmen SSR and the Uzbek SSR. It enters the Aral Sea through a delta 90 mi. long. The Amu Darya is rich in fish, and it provides much water for irrigation in arid regions of the USSR and portions of Afghanistan. In ancient times it was called the Oxus and figured importantly in the history of Persia and in the campaigns of Alexander the Great.

amulet (ă′myŏōlĭt), object or formula that credulity and superstition have endowed with the power of warding off harmful influences. The use of the amulet to avert danger and to dispel evil has been known in different religions and among diverse peoples. Like the talisman and the charm, the amulet is believed to be the source of an impersonal

Amulet from the Solomon Islands.

force that is an inherent property of the object rather than the manifestation of a deity working through that object (see FETISH and TABOO). Although amulets are most often worn on the body, hanging from the neck or strapped to the arm or leg, they may also serve as protective emblems on walls and doorways. Sometimes the amulet consists of a spoken, written, or drawn magic formula, such as ABRACADABRA and the MAGIC SQUARE, or of a symbolic figure, such as the wheel of the sun-god and the Aryan swastika. In many cultures the teeth, claws, and other parts of an animal are supposed to communicate their properties to the wearer. Although belief in amulets is most widespread in primitive societies, it has survived in modern civilization. Saints' relics are still considered to be efficacious in warding off illnesses, and common superstition has endowed such things as the rabbit's foot with the property of being able to bring good luck. In some of the higher religions the use of amulets, such as the Jewish phylactery and the Roman Catholic cross, are more strictly related to ritual and serve as personal reminders to the wearers of their relationship to God.

Amundsen, Roald (rō'äl ä'mŏŏnsún), 1872–1928, Norwegian polar explorer. He served (1897–99) as

Roald Amundsen

first mate on the *Belgica* (under the Belgian Adrien de Gerlache) in an expedition to the Antarctic, and he commanded the *Gjöa* in the arctic regions in the first negotiation of the NORTHWEST PASSAGE (1903–6); the *Gjöa* was the first single ship to complete the route through the Northwest Passage. His account appeared in English as *Amundsen's North West Passage* (1908). He then purchased Fridtjof Nansen's *Fram* and prepared to drift toward the North Pole and then finish the journey by sledge. The news that Robert E. Peary had anticipated him in reaching the North Pole caused Amundsen to turn his eyes south. In striving for the South Pole he was successful, reaching it on Dec. 14, 1911, after a dash by dog team and skis from the Bay of Whales (an inlet of Ross Sea). He arrived there just 35 days before Robert F. SCOTT. This story he told in *The South Pole* (Eng. tr., 1913). He had added much valuable scientific and geological information to the knowledge of Antarctica. In 1918, back in the arctic regions, he set out to negotiate the Northeast Passage in the *Maud*. After two winters he arrived at Nome, the first after N. A. E. Nordenskjöld to sail along the whole northern coast of Europe and Asia. Amundsen then turned to air exploration. He and Lincoln ELLSWORTH in 1925 failed to complete a flight across the North Pole, but the next year in the *Norge*, built and piloted by Umberto NOBILE, they succeeded in flying over the pole and the hitherto unexplored regions of the Arctic Ocean N of Alaska. A bitter controversy followed with Nobile as to the credit for the success. Yet in 1928 when Nobile crashed in the *Italia*, Amundsen set out on a rescue attempt which cost him his life. The story of the ventures with Ellsworth written by the two of them appear in *Our Polar Flight* (1925) and *The First Crossing of the Polar Sea* (1927). See the autobiographical *My Life as an Explorer* (Eng. tr., 1927); biographies by Bellamy Partridge (1929) and Charles Turley (1935).

Amur (ämŏŏr'), Chinese *Hei-lung-kiang* (hä-lŏŏng'-jëäng'), river, formed by the confluence of the SHILKA and ARGUN in NE Asia. One of the major Asiatic rivers, it is c.2,700 mi. long. It flows parallel to the Soviet-Manchurian border and then courses NE through the Maritime Territory into the Tatar Strait opposite the island of Sakhalin. Its estuary is 10 mi. wide. The Amur, which is navigable for its entire length during the ice-free months (May–Nov.), is an important artery for the transport of grain and lumber and is rich in fish. The chief tributaries originating in Siberia are the Zeya, Bureya, and Amgun; those originating in Manchuria are the Sungari and Ussuri.

Amurath. For Ottoman sultans thus named, see MURAD.

Amvets: see AMERICAN VETERANS OF WORLD WAR II AND KOREA.

amylase: see DIASTASE.

Amyot, Jacques (zhäk' ämyō'), 1513–93, French humanist, translator of Heliodorus' *Aethiopica* (1547), of Longus' *Daphnis and Chloë* (1559), and particularly of Plutarch's *Lives* (1559).

Amyot or **Amiot, Joseph** (zhôzĕf' ämyō'), 1718–1794?, French Roman Catholic missionary in China, a Jesuit. He wrote *Mémoires concernant l'histoire, les sciences . . . et les usages . . . des chinois* (15 vols., 1776–89) and was one of the first Europeans to make Chinese literature, antiquities, and customs known to Europe. He was an early authority on the Manchu language.

Amyraut, Moïse (môēz' ämērō'), or **Moses Amyraldus** (ămǐräl'dús), 1596–1664, French Protestant theologian. As pastor of Saumur he won a reputation as theologian and orator, and he was appointed (1631) to present to Louis XIII the protest of the synod against infractions of the Edict of Nantes. He became professor of theology at Saumur and wrote extensively on theological subjects.

Amzi (ăm'zĭ) [Heb.,=strong]. **1** Levite. 1 Chron. 6.46. **2** One of a priestly family. Neh. 11.12.

Anab (ā'năb) [Heb.,=grape tower], hill town, SW Palestine, the modern Khirbet Anab (Jordan), SSW of Hebron. Joshua 11.21; 15.50.

Anabaptists (ăn"úbăp'–) [from Gr.,=rebaptizers], name applied in scorn to certain Christian sects holding that infant baptism is not authorized in Scripture and that baptism should be administered to believers only. A convert if baptized in infancy must be rebaptized. Anabaptists were prominent in Europe during the 16th cent., forming part of the radical wing of the Reformation. Their principal centers were in Germany, Switzerland, Moravia, and the Netherlands. They are to be distinguished from the BAPTISTS, primarily an English group. The religious ideas of the Anabaptists antedate the Reformation. Though they were never united either politically or doctrinally, they held certain views in common for which they were persecuted everywhere. Among these were their desire for radical religious, social, and economic reform and their advocacy of the separation of Church and state. In their beliefs great stress was placed upon individual conscience and private inspiration. Perhaps their most characteristic and most influential belief was their conception of the church as a voluntary association of believers. Martin Luther regarded them as enemies of the Reformation and added to their persecution. Most of the Anabaptists were peace loving and moderate, but extremists led by Thomas MÜNZER, a Saxon pastor, helped to incite the Peasants' War. Leaders like Melchoir Hoffman, a Swabian farmer, spread doctrines of an imminent return of Christ and the "reign of God," without church or dogma. In Münster c.1533 some of the Anabaptists set up a theocracy, first under the direction of Bernard Rothmann, a preacher, and Jan Matthys, a fanatical Dutch baker, then under Bernhard Knipperdollinck. In 1534 JOHN OF LEIDEN proclaimed himself King David and ruled this theocracy in which communal ownership of property and polygamy were practiced. This extreme form of Anabaptism ended with the execution of the leaders in 1535. Another group of Anabaptists, under the leadership of MENNO SIMONS, became MENNONITES. Others, descendants of the followers of Jacob Hutter, moved in 1874 from Russia to South Dakota (see HUTTERISCHE COMMUNITY). See studies by E. B. Bax (1903) and R. J. Smithson (1935).

Anabasis (ǔnǎ′bǔsǐs) [Gr.,=going up, i.e., to the sea from the interior], celebrated Greek prose history of the campaign of CYRUS THE YOUNGER, by XENOPHON. It tells the story of the retreat of the Ten Thousand after the battle of CUNAXA (401 B.C.). Xenophon was himself a member of the Ten Thousand, a mercenary band collected by Clearchus; they went up the Tigris, into Armenia in December, going due northward through the mountains, finally down to the sea at Trapezus (Trebizond) and thence back home to Greece. This retreat, through rugged country, in bitter weather, by a band of men who had practically no supplies and were much harassed by the Persians, is testimony to Greek courage. The Ten Thousand marched some 1,300 mi. from Sardis to Cunaxa and more than 900 from there to Trapezus.

Anacharsis (ǎnǔkär′sǐs), fl. c.600 B.C., Scythian philosopher. He is supposed to have toured Greece and Asia Minor. Many maxims are attributed to him by classical writers.

Anacletus, Saint: see CLETUS, SAINT.

Anaconda (ǎnǔkŏn′dǔ), city (pop. 12,054; alt. c.5,280 ft.), co. seat of Deer Lodge co., SW Mont., NW of Butte; laid out 1883, inc. 1888. Marcus DALY chose this place for the smelter of the Anaconda Copper Mining Company and in the 1890s tried unsuccessfully to make it the state capital. The present high-stacked smelter, one of the largest in the world, dominates the life of the city and produces copper, zinc, and manganese. There are foundries, machine shops, and plants manufacturing arsenic, sulphuric acid, and phosphate fertilizer.

anaconda, nonvenomous constrictor snake of South America, largely aquatic but partially arboreal. It is related to the boa constrictor and the PYTHON. The anaconda, largest of the true boas, has been known to reach a length of 37 ft. and to have a wide girth. It is olive green with black spots and rings. It eats birds, small mammals, and fish, which it squeezes to death before swallowing.

Anacortes (ǎnǔkôr′těz), city (pop. 8,414), NW Wash., on Fidalgo Island, on the Strait of Georgia

S of Bellingham; settled 1860, platted 1876, inc. 1890. It is a port of entry and a shipping and processing center for a lumbering, farming, and fishing region.

Anacostia (ǎnǔkŏs′tēǔ), river rising near Bladensburg, Md., and flowing c.24 mi. before entering the Potomac at Washington, D.C.

Anacreon (ǔnǎk′rēǔn, –ŏn), fl. c.521 B.C., Greek lyric poet, b. Teos in Ionia. He lived at Samos and at Athens, where Hipparchus patronized him. His poetry, graceful and elegant, celebrates the joys of wine and love. Little of his verse survives. The Anacreontics (–ŏn′tǐks) are poems after the manner of Anacreon written from Hellenistic to late Byzantine times.

Anadarko (ǎnǔdär′kō), city (pop. 6,299), co. seat of Caddo co., SW Okla., on the Washita river and SW of Oklahoma City; founded 1901. It is the center of a rich area producing cotton, grains, alfalfa, livestock, and oil. Among the many Indians in the section are some of the few remaining of the once great Delaware tribe. An Indian exposition is held annually. The Southern Plains Indian Arts and Crafts Museum is here. Just southeast of Anadarko is "Indian City," containing authentic replicas of different types of Indian villages.

Anadyr (ǔnǔdǐr′), river, extreme NE Asiatic RSFSR, rising in the Anadyr plateau. It flows c.695 mi. generally S below the Anadyr range and E past the Kamchatka peninsula into Anadyr Bay, an inlet of the Bering Sea. There are coal and gold deposits near its mouth. The town of Anadyr (pop. c.5,600), capital of the CHUKCHI NATIONAL OKRUG, Khabarovsk Territory, is a port on the Anadyr estuary.

anae-, for words beginning thus: see ANE-.

anagram [Gr.,=something read backward], rearrangement of the letters of a word or words to make another word or other words. A famous Latin anagram was an answer made out of the question that Pilate asked. The question was *Quid est veritas?* [What is truth?], and the answer *Est vir qui adest* [it is the man who is here]. An anagram that reads the same backward as forward is a palindrome, e.g., "Able was I ere I saw Elba."

Anah (ā′nǔ), name appearing several times in the genealogy of Esau's family. Three persons may be distinguished, but if the genealogy refers to tribes rather than to persons, Anah may be a single tribal name. Gen. 36; 1 Chron. 1.

Anaharath (ǎn″ǔhā′rǎth), unidentified town, E central Palestine. Joshua 19.19.

Anaconda

Anaheim (ăn'ŭhīm), city (pop. 104,184), S Calif., SE of Los Angeles; founded by Germans in 1857 as an experiment in communal living, inc. 1870. An important industrial center in a citrus-fruit and walnut area, Anaheim has chemical plants, electronic firms, and canneries. Since the opening in 1955 of the amusement park Disneyland, perhaps the most expensive tourist attraction ever built, the city has become a popular tourist center. Designed to please adults and children alike, Disneyland is composed principally of Tomorrowland, Frontierland, Fantasyland, and Adventureland. Unique transportation facilities, ranging from mule rides to simulated space flights, are offered. Some of Walt Disney's most famous characters are represented in Fantasyland.

Anahuac (ănŭwăk'), resort and fishing city (pop. 1,985), co. seat of Chambers co., SE Texas, at the mouth of the Trinity and E of Houston, in a rice, cattle, and oil area. A prominent port of early Texas, it was the scene of two clashes (1832, 1835) in which Anglo-American settlers successfully opposed officials of the Mexican government.

Anáhuac (änä'wäk) [Aztec,=near the water], geographical term used variously in Mexico before the Spanish Conquest. Today it commonly refers to that part of the central plateau of Mexico comprising the Pánuco and Lerma river systems and the lake basin of the Valley of Mexico.

Anaiah (ăn"āī'ŭ, änä'yŭ), the name of two who returned from the Exile. Neh. 8.4; 10.22.

Anak (ā'năk), in the Bible, ancestor of the Anakim (ăn'ŭkĭm) or Anakims, a race of giants inhabiting Hebron and its vicinity at the time of the conquest of Canaan. Arba is given as Anak's father, and his sons are given as Ahiman, Sheshai, and Talmai. Joshua and Caleb practically extirpated the race. Num. 13.22,28,33; Deut. 1.28; 9.2; Joshua 11.21; 14.15; 15.13,14; 21.11; Judges 1.20.

analysis, chemical: see CHEMISTRY and ASSAYING.

Anamim (ăn'ŭmĭm), unidentified tribe of Egypt. Gen. 10.13; 1 Chron. 1.11.

Anammelech (ŭnăm'ŭlĕk), god of an otherwise unknown Samaritan cult. 2 Kings 17.31.

Anamosa (ănŭmō'sŭ), city (pop. 4,616), co. seat of Jones co., E central Iowa, NE of Cedar Rapids and on the Wapsipinicon river, in a limestone area; inc. 1856. Electronic equipment is produced. Grant Wood was born near Anamosa. A state park is nearby.

Anan (ā'nŭn) [Heb.,=cloud], sealer of the covenant. Neh. 10.26.

Ananda: see PALI LITERATURE.

Anandale (ăn'ŭndāl), uninc. town (pop. 2,827), central La., SSW of Alexandria.

Anani (änä'nī) [Heb.,=God protects], descendant of David. 1 Chron. 3.24.

Ananiah (ā"nŭnī'ŭ) [Heb.,=God protects]. **1** Ancestor of AZARIAH **20**. **2** Benjamite town, probably just N of Jerusalem. Neh. 11.32.

Ananias (ăn"ŭnī'ŭs) [Gr.,=Heb. ANANIAH and HANANIAH]. **1** Man who, with his wife Sapphira, held back part of a gift to the church and lied

The Enchanted Castle in Disneyland, Anaheim, Calif.

about it. They were rebuked by Peter and fell dead. Acts 5.1–11. The name has become a term for liar. **2** High priest at Jerusalem, a Roman sympathizer, hated by most of the Jews for his oppression and his alliance with the Roman interest. He was assassinated between A.D. 60 and 67. Acts 23.2–5; 24. **3** Christian at Damascus who took charge of Paul after his conversion. Acts 9.10–22. **4** One of the THREE HOLY CHILDREN.

Ananites: see KARAITES.

anaphylaxis, hypersensitive state that may develop after introduction of a foreign protein (or other antigen) into the body tissues. When an anaphylactic state exists, a second dose of this same protein will cause a violent allergic reaction. Anaphylaxis results from the production of specific antibodies in the tissues; the violent reaction is produced by the neutralization of antigens by antibodies in the tissues. Anaphylaxis differs from immunity; in immunity, antibodies circulate in the blood and neutralize antigens without producing a violent reaction. See also ALLERGY.

Anarajapura: see ANURADHAPURA.

anarchism (ăn′ŭrkĭzŭm) [Gr.,=having no government], theory that equality and justice are to be sought through the abolition of the state and the substitution of free agreements between functional and territorial groups. Capitalism and private property, considered limitations on the freedom of personality, would be abolished. Necessary production would be carried on by decentralized, freely associating groups. Anarchism differs from SOCIALISM in considering the state an intrinsic evil. Zeno of Citium, founder of Stoic philosophy, is regarded as the forefather of anarchism. It is important to distinguish the philosophic and literary school of anarchism from that which has a political tendency and even a program. The philosophy of modern political anarchism was outlined in the 18th and 19th cent. by William GODWIN, P. J. PROUDHON, and others. BAKUNIN attempted to orient the First INTERNATIONAL towards anarchism but was defeated by Marx. Bakunin gave modern anarchism a collectivist and violent tone that has persisted despite the revisionary efforts of KROPOTKIN and Leo TOLSTOY. Political anarchism in Russia was suppressed by the Bolsheviks after the Russian Revolution. Anarchism's only real mass following was in Latin countries, where its doctrines were often combined with those of SYNDICALISM, especially in Spain. In the United States early anarchists such as Josiah WARREN were associated with cooperatives and with utopian colonies. Violent doctrines were introduced from Europe, and after the Haymarket riot in Chicago in 1886 and the assassination of President McKinley in 1901 a law was passed forbidding anarchists to enter the country. The execution of Sacco and Vanzetti in 1927 attests the fear of anarchism in America. As an organized movement anarchism is well-nigh dead, but it retains importance as a philosophical attitude and a political tendency. See Paul Eltzbacher, *Anarchism* (1900; new American ed., 1960); C. E. M. Joad, *Introduction to Modern Political Theory* (1924); Herbert Read, *Poetry and Anarchism* (1938); J. J. Martin, *Men against the State* (1953); George Woodcock, *Anarchism* (1962).

Anastasia, Saint (ănŭstā′shŭ), 4th cent., Roman

noblewoman, kind to the poor, martyred under Diocletian. She is mentioned in the Canon of the Mass. In the Roman Church, her feast is Dec. 25 and is commemorated in the Christmas Mass at dawn. In the Orthodox Eastern Church her feast is Dec. 22.

Anastasia (Anastasia Nikolayevna) (ănŭstā′shŭ nyĭkŭlī′ŭfnă), 1901–1918?, youngest daughter of Tsar Nicholas II, last of the Russian tsars. It is generally believed that she was killed with the rest of her immediate family after the Russian Revolution, though several women later claimed to be Anastasia.

Anastasius I (ănŭstā′shŭs, –zhŭs), c.430–518, Roman emperor of the East (491–518); successor of Zeno, whose widow he married. He broke the power which the Isaurians had enjoyed since Leo I, made peace with Persia, maintained friendly relations with Theodoric the Great, and made Clovis I an ally. His reign saw the revision of tax collection and the abolition of gladiatorial contests. He built a wall to protect Constantinople against the Slavs and Bulgars. His Monophysite inclinations stirred religious unrest throughout the empire. He was succeeded by Justin I.

Anath (ā′–), father of SHAMGAR.

anathema (ŭnă′thĭmŭ) [Gr.,=set aside, as a devoted object], traditional Christian decree of EXCOMMUNICATION in its severest form. The usual form of a canon of a council is, "If anyone does so-and-so, let him be anathema." In 1 Cor. 16.22 the expression Anathema Maranatha (mă′rŭnă′thŭ) includes an Aramaic word; the whole probably means "anathema—may the Lord come!"

Anathoth (ăn′ŭthŏth, –thōth). **1** Town, NE of Jerusalem, the modern Ras el-Kharrubeh, near Anata (Jordan). It was the home of Jeremiah. Jer. 1.1; 1 Chron. 12.3; 1 Kings 2.26; Neh. 7.27. Its adjective is Antothite, Anetothite, Anathotite. 1 Chron. 27.12; 12.3. **2** Chief of the people. Neh. 10.19. **3** Benjamite. 1 Chron. 7.8.

Anatolia (ănŭtō′lēŭ) [Gr.,=sunrise], Asiatic part (287,117 sq. mi.; pop. 25,516,249) of TURKEY. It

Ruins at Nicaea in Anatolia.

comprises 97 percent of all Turkey. Anatolia, the westernmost part of Asia, is a plateau crossed by mountains and is a peninsula between the Black Sea on the north, the Aegean Sea on the west, and the Mediterranean on the south. It is almost identical with, and is sometimes used to mean, ASIA MINOR.

anatomy [Gr., =to cut apart], study of body structure and structural relationships, upon which all phases of medicine and surgery are dependent. Little was known about human anatomy in ancient times because dissection, even of corpses, was forbidden. In the 2d cent., GALEN, largely on the basis of animal dissection, made valuable contributions to the field that remained authoritative until the 14th and 15th cent., when a limited number of cadavers were made available to the medical schools. A better understanding of the science was soon reflected in the discoveries of VESALIUS, William HARVEY, and John HUNTER. Modern anatomy includes the study of living tissue as well. Embryology treats of prenatal life; histology and cytology deal with cellular life. Comparative anatomy is concerned with the structural differences of various animal forms. An international anatomic nomenclature was established in 1895 in Basel, Switzerland.

Anau: see ANNAU.

Anawalt (ăn'ǔwôlt), town (pop. 1,062), S W.Va., WNW of Bluefield and near the Va. line.

Anaxagoras (ăn"ŭksăg'ŭrus), c.500–c.428 B.C., Greek philosopher of Clazomenae. He is credited with having transferred the seat of philosophy to Athens. He was closely associated with many famous Athenians and is believed to have been the teacher of Socrates. His belief that the sun was a white-hot stone and that the moon was made of earth that reflected the sun's rays resulted in a charge of atheism and blasphemy, forcing him to flee to Lampsacus, where he died. Rejecting Empedocles' four elements (earth, air, fire, and water), Anaxagoras posits an infinity of particles, or "seeds," each unique in its qualities. All natural objects are composed of particles having all sorts of qualities; a preponderance of similar though not identical particles creates the difference between wood and stone. Anaxagoras' universe, before separation, was an infinite, undifferentiated mass. The formation of the world was due to a rotary motion produced in this mass by an all-pervading mind (*nous*). This led to the separating out of the "seeds" and the formation of things. Although Anaxagoras was the first to give mind a place in the universe, he was criticized by both Plato and Aristotle for only conceiving of it as a mechanical cause rather than the originator of order. See F. M. Cleve, *The Philosophy of Anaxagoras* (1949).

Anaximander (ùnăk"sĭmăn'dùr), c.611–c.547 B.C., Greek philosopher, b. Miletus; pupil of THALES. He made the first attempt to offer a detailed explanation of all aspects of nature. Anaximander argued that since there are so many different sorts of things, they must all have originated from something less differentiated than water, and this primary source, the boundless or the indefinite (*apeiron*), had always existed, filled all space, and by its constant motion separated out from itself opposites, e.g., hot and cold, moist and dry. These opposites interact by encroaching on one another and thus repay one another's "injustice." The result is a plurality of worlds which successively decay and return to the indefinite. The notion of the indefinite and its processes prefigured the later conception of the indestructibility of matter. Anaximander also had a theory of the relation of earth to the heavenly bodies, important in the history of astronomy. His view that man achieved his physical state by adaptation to environment, that life had evolved from moisture, and that man developed from fish, anticipates the theory of evolution. See C. H. Kahn, *Anaximander and the Origins of Greek Cosmology* (1960).

Anaximenes (ăn"ŭksĭm'ĭnēz), Greek philosopher, 6th cent. B.C., last of the Milesian school founded by Thales. With THALES he held that a single element lay behind the diversity of nature, and with ANAXIMANDER he sought a principle to account for diversity. That single element he believed to be air. The principle of diversification he taught was rarefaction and condensation. Different objects hence were merely different degrees of density of the one basic element. Anaximenes anticipates the spirit of modern scientific practice which seeks to explain qualitative differences quantitatively.

Ancenis, Peace of, 1468, treaty of peace between LOUIS XI of France and Francis II of Brittany, made at Ancenis near Nantes, France.

ancestor worship, ritualized propitiation and invocation of dead kin. Closely related to the primitive concept of ANIMISM, ancestor worship is based on the belief that the spirits of the dead continue to dwell in the natural world and have the power to influence the fortune and fate of the living. It probably evolves from the fear that the death of an individual, especially if he is a king, hero, or renowned man, could constitute a major threat to the solidarity of a community. Ancestor worship has been found in various parts of the world and in diverse cultures. It was a minor cult among the Romans (see MANES). The practice reached its highest elaboration in W Africa and in the ancient Chinese veneration of ancestors. It is also well developed in the Japanese SHINTO cult and among the peoples of Melanesia. See also APOTHEOSIS.

Anchieta, José de (zhōōzě' dù ānshēä'tä), 1530–97. Brazilian missionary, a Jesuit, b. Canary Islands of Spanish parents. A tireless traveler and pioneer, he spread Portuguese control and settlement and was a founder of the city of São Paulo. He wrote in Spanish, Latin, Portuguese, and Tupi and wrote poetry as well as prose tracts on history, philosophy, and religion. He is usually regarded as the first Brazilian writer. See H. G. Dominian, *Apostle of Brazil* (1958).

Anchises (ănkī'sēz), in Greek mythology, Trojan shepherd. He was seduced by Aphrodite, and from this union Aeneas was born. When Anchises boasted of the goddess's love, Zeus crippled him.

anchor, device cast overboard to secure a ship, boat, buoy, or some other floating object by means of weight, friction, or hooks called flukes. The anchor normally rests firmly on the bottom of the sea or stream. In ancient times an anchor was merely a large stone or a bag or basket of stones; a bag of sand; or, as with the Egyptians, a lead-weighted log. The Greeks are credited with the first use of iron anchors. The Romans had metal devices with arms like modern anchors. Changes and improvements over the centuries have resulted in two types of modern anchor. The ordinary anchor consists of the shank (the stem, at the top of which is the anchor ring), the stock (the crosspiece at the top of the shank, either fixed or removable), the crown (the bottom portion), and the arms, attached near the base of the shank at a right angle to the stock and curving upward to end in the flat, triangular flukes, or palms. The patent anchor, unlike the ordinary one, has either no stock at all or a stock lying in the same plane as the arms, which are not rigidly fixed but can pivot on either side of the shank. Modern ships have several anchors; usually there are two forward and two aft (the sheet anchors). A stream anchor is lighter than the regular anchor and is used in narrow or congested waters. A grapnel is a simple shank from which radiate four or five upturned hooks. A sea anchor is a wooden or metal framework covered with canvas and weighted at the bottom; it is a temporary device used by disabled ships. Formerly made of wrought iron, anchors are now usually of forged steel.

Anchorage (ăng'kŭrĭj). **1** City (pop. 44,237), S central Alaska, at the head of Cook Inlet. Founded (1914) as a town for the headquarters and shops of the Alaska RR then being constructed, it grew as a railroad town, but also became a center of fishing, a market and supply point for gold-mining regions to the north, the metropolis for the coal mining and farming of Matanuska Valley, and the air-traffic capital of Alaska. Glenn Highway connects it with the Alaska Highway. The Second World War saw the establishment of the largest U.S. army post in Alaska and a large U.S. air force base nearby. Air and rail traffic grew enormously. After the war it remained a defense center and continued to grow as Alaska's largest city. See Evangeline Atwood, *Anchorage* (1957). **2** Town (pop. 1,170), N Ky., a suburb E of Louisville; inc. 1876.

Anchor Bay Gardens, uninc. village (1,830), SE Mich., on Lake St. Clair and NNE of Detroit. Selfridge Air Force Base is nearby.

anchoret or **anchorite:** see HERMIT.

anchovy: see HERRING.

anchovy pear: see BRAZIL NUT.

ancien régime (äsyẽ' räzhẽm') [Fr.,=old regime], expression used specifically to designate the order of things in France before the social and political changes of the French Revolution (1789). See FRANCE and FRENCH REVOLUTION.

Ancona, Alessandro d': see D'ANCONA, ALESSANDRO.

Ancona (ăngkō'nů, Ital. ängkō'nä), city (estimated pop. 94,840), capital of Ancona prov., chief city of Marches, central Italy, on the Adriatic. A leading Adriatic port, it is also an industrial center, with shipyards. Late in the 4th cent. B.C., Greeks from Syracuse took refuge in Ancona. It prospered under the Romans, and Trajan enlarged its harbor. In the 9th cent. A.D. it became a semi-independent maritime republic under the nominal rule of the popes, under whose direct control it passed in 1532. The city suffered great damage in the Second World War, and although the white marble Arch of Trajan was undamaged, the Byzantine Romanesque Cathedral of San Ciriaco (11th–13th cent.) was partly destroyed.

Ancre, Concino Concini, marquis d': see CONCINI.

Ancren Riwle (ăng'krŭn rē'ōōlů, rōōl', äng'krŭn) [Mid. Eng.,=anchoresses' rule], English tract written c.1200 by an anonymous cultivated English churchman for the instruction of three young ladies

Cathedral of San Ciriaco, Ancona, Italy.

The fertile basin of the Guadalquivir in Andalusia, Spain.

The alcazar of Seville, Andalusia, Spain.

who were about to settle in a hermitage in the West Midlands. The work, important as a sample of early Middle English prose, depicts the manners and customs of the time. See edition by M. B. Salu (1956).

Ancus Martius (ăng′kŭs mär′shŭs), fourth king of ancient Rome (640?–616? B.C.). This semilegendary king is supposed to have enlarged the area of Rome.

ancylostomiasis: see HOOKWORM.

Ancyra: see ANKARA.

Andalsnes or **Aandalsnes** (both: ôn′däls-näs″), town (pop. 1,346), More and Romsdal prov., W Norway. It is a popular and beautiful tourist resort with salmon fishing in the Rauma river. It was heavily damaged by German bombardments in 1940.

Andalusia (ăndŭlōō′zhŭ, –shŭ), Span. *Andalucía* (än″dälōōthē′ä), region (33,675 sq. mi.; pop. 5,893,396), S Spain, on the Mediterranean, the Strait of Gibraltar, and the Atlantic. Spain's largest and most populous region, it comprises the provinces of Almería, Cádiz, Córdoba, Granada, Huelva, Jaén, Málaga, and Seville, all named for their chief cities. Andalusia covers all S Spain. It is crossed in the north by the Sierra Morena and in the south by mountain ranges which rise in the snow-capped Sierra Nevada to the highest peak in Spain, Mulhacén (11,411 ft.). Between the ranges lies the fertile basin of the Guadalquivir. With a subtropical climate, Andalusia has many affinities with Africa, which it faces. Barren lands contrast with richly fertile regions, where cereals, grapes, olives, sugar cane, and citrus and other fruits are produced. Cattle, bulls for the ring, and fine horses are bred. Industries, based generally on local agricultural produce, include wine making, flour milling, and olive oil extracting. The rich mineral resources, exploited since Phoenician and Roman times, include copper, iron, zinc, and lead. Mediterranean peoples have been attracted to this region since ancient times, and because of this Andalusia is one of Europe's most strikingly colorful regions. In the 11th cent. B.C., the Phoenicians settled here and founded several coastal colonies, notably Gadir (now CÁDIZ) and, supposedly, the inland town of Tartessus, which became the capital of a flourishing kingdom (sometimes identified with the biblical TARSHISH). Greeks and Carthaginians came in the 6th cent. B.C.; the Carthaginians were expelled (3d cent. B.C.) by the Romans, who included S Spain in the province of Baetica. In A.D. 711 the MOORS, crossing the Strait of Gibraltar, established here the center of their western emirate (see CÓRDOBA). Andalusia remained under Moorish rule until in the 13th cent. most of it was reconquered by the kings of Castile; only the Moorish kingdom of GRANADA survived; it, too, fell to the Catholic kings in 1492. The Moorish period was the golden age of Andalusia. Agriculture, mining, trade, and industries (textiles, pottery, and leather working) were fostered and brought tremendous prosperity; the Andalusian cities of Córdoba, SEVILLE, and Granada, embellished by the greatest Moorish monuments in Spain, were celebrated as centers of culture, science, and the arts. From the 16th cent. Andalusia, except the flourishing ports of Seville and Cádiz, through which passed the wealth of the New World, generally suffered in the decline of Spain. Gibraltar was ceded to Britain in 1713. With Catalonia, Andalusia was a stronghold of anarchism during the Spanish republic (est. 1931); it fell early, however, to the Insurgents in the Spanish civil war of 1936–39. Despite the natural wealth of the region, poverty is widespread; Andalusian farm laborers are among the poorest in Europe. The region has seen recurrent demonstrations against the Franco regime. Moorish influence is still strong in the character, language, and customs of the people. Andalusian songs, dances, and festivals enjoy great popularity; these are also influenced by the large groups of gypsies who live in the region.

Andalusia (ăndŭlōō'shŭ, –zhŭ), city (pop. 10,263), co. seat of Covington co., S Ala., near the Fla. line S of Montgomery, in a farm and pine area; settled c.1830, inc. 1876. Manufactures include lumber and textile products.

Andaman and Nicobar Islands (ăn'dŭmŭn, nĭk'-ōbär), territory (3,215 sq. mi.; pop. c.63,500), India, in the Bay of Bengal. Port Blair, in the Andamans, is the capital. Comprising the Andaman Islands (2,508 sq. mi.) in the south and the Nicobar Islands (707 sq. mi.) in the north, the territory chiefly exports tropical products and lumber. Known since the 7th cent. A.D., the Andamans, consisting of over 200 islands, were famous in modern times for the penal colony established here in 1858 but abolished in 1945. The population is made up of native Negritos and settlers from the Indian mainland. The Nicobars, which constitute some 19 small islands, are separated from the Andamans by a 90-mile-wide channel. The native population is of Mongoloid stock. The Nicobars passed to the British in 1869.

Andelys, Les (läzädŭlē'), town, (estimated pop. 5,648), in Eure dept., N France, Normandy, on the Seine. On the border between Normandy proper and the Norman VEXIN, it was of considerable strategic importance in the Middle Ages. Today it is a commercial center, with metal and glass works. Richard I of England built (1197) the impressive CHÂTEAU GAILLARD nearby. Nicolas Poussin was born here.

Anderlecht (än'dŭrlĕkht), town (estimated pop. 93,734), in Brabant prov., central Belgium, on the Charleroi-Brussels Canal. It is a residential and industrial suburb of Brussels. Erasmus lived (1517–21) here.

Andermatt (än'dŭrmät), village, Uri canton, S central Switzerland, near the Reuss. It is a health resort and sports center. The St. Gotthard Tunnel runs beneath the village. Nearby the Russians under SUVAROV defeated (1799) the French during the French Revolutionary Wars. The village has a 12th-century church.

Andernach (än'dŭrnäkh), town (pop. 19,025), Federal Republic of Germany, in Rhineland-Palatinate, W Germany, on the Rhine. A busy port, it has manufactures of chemicals, millstones, and pottery. Drusus founded a garrison here. In 939 at Andernach Emperor Otto I defeated the rebellious dukes of Franconia and Lotharingia. From 1167 until 1801 it belonged to the archbishopric of Cologne. In 1815 it was ceded to Prussia and was placed in the Rhine Prov. Andernach has a 15th-century tower and a 16th-century town hall.

Andersen, Hans Christian, 1805–75, Danish poet, novelist, and writer of fairy tales. Reared in poverty, he left Odense at 14 to seek his fortune in Copenhagen. He proved unsuccessful as an actor, but his poetic promise won him generous patrons and finally interested King Frederick VI, who educated him at public expense. In 1829 the fantasy *A Journey on Foot from the Holmen Canal to the Eastern Point of Amager* was published, and in 1830 a collection of poems followed. Granted a

traveling pension by the king, Andersen wrote sketches of the European countries he visited. His first novel, *Improvisatoren* (1835), marked the turning point in his career. The critics, who had derided him as temperamental, egotistical, and ineffectual, now granted him some favor. His novels, factual and sentimental, were for a time considered his forte. However, with his first book of fairy tales, *Eventyr* (1835), he found the medium of expression that was to immortalize his genius. More volumes followed—about one a year—until he was recognized as Denmark's greatest author and as a storyteller without peer. His sense of fantasy, power of description, and acute sensitivity contributed to his mastery of the fairy tale. Among his many widely beloved stories are "The Fir-Tree," "The Ugly Duckling," "The Snow Queen," "The Little Mermaid," and "The Red Shoes." See his autobiography (1855; Eng. tr., 1871); biographies by Signe Toksvig (1934), Rumer Godden (1955), and Fredrik Book (Eng. tr., 1962).

Hans Christian Andersen

Andersen Nexo, Martin (mär'tēn än'dŭrsĕn nĕksû'), Dan. *Nexø*, 1869–1954, Danish novelist. Born in a Copenhagen slum, he spent his impoverished childhood largely on the island of Bornholm. Both locales appear centrally in his novels. His famous proletarian novels *Pelle the Conqueror* (4 vols., 1906–10; Eng. tr., in one volume, 1930) and *Ditte, Daughter of Mankind* (5 vols., 1917–21; Eng. tr., in one volume, 1931) relate the struggles of the poor and did much to improve social conditions in Denmark. Though admittedly a propagandist for social reform, he transcended this role and created a memorable group of tender human portraits. He also wrote on Russia, where he spent many of his later years. The first two volumes of his four-volume autobiography have been translated as *Under the Open Sky* (1938). See Harry Slochower, *Three Ways of Modern Man* (1937).

Anderson, Carl David, 1905–, American physicist, b. New York city, grad. California Institute of Technology (B.S., 1927; Ph.D., 1930). Associated with the institute's physics department from 1930, he became professor in 1939. For his discovery (1932) of the positron, he shared with V. F. Hess the 1936 Nobel Prize in Physics. The MESON (or mesotron) was discovered in cosmic rays in 1936 by Anderson and his associate S. H. Neddermeyer and almost simultaneously by J. C. Street and E. C. Stevenson at Harvard.

Anderson, Elizabeth Garrett, 1836–1917, English physician. A sister of Millicent Garrett Fawcett, Elizabeth also worked for woman suffrage. With difficulty she obtained a private medical education under accredited physicians and in London hospitals; in 1865 she was licensed to practice by the Scottish Society of Apothecaries. In London in 1866 she opened a dispensary, later a small hospital, for women and children, the first in England to be staffed by women physicians; it was known after 1918 as the Elizabeth Garrett Anderson Hospital. Largely as a result of her efforts, British examining bodies opened their examinations to women.

Anderson, Elizabeth Milbank, 1850–1921, American philanthropist, b. New York city. From 1884 she used her large fortune to advance higher education of women and in behalf of enlightened charity. In memory of her parents she established (1905) the Memorial Fund Association, later called the Milbank Memorial Fund, the income from which was to be used "to improve the physical, mental, and moral condition of humanity, and generally to advance charitable and benevolent objects."

Anderson, Dame Judith, 1898–, Australian actress, originally named Frances Margaret Anderson. She made her debut in Sydney in 1915; in 1918 she came to the United States and by 1924 was recognized as an actress of tragedy. In 1936 she played the queen to Gielgud's Hamlet and in 1937 she made her London debut in *Macbeth* with Laurence Olivier, later (1941) creating the same role opposite Maurice Evans. The title role in *Medea* by Robinson Jeffers, which she first created in 1947, was hailed as a triumph of acting. She was made a Dame of the British Empire in 1960.

Anderson, Marian, 1902–, American Negro contralto, b. Philadelphia, where she received most of her musical education. She began her concert career in 1924 and achieved her first great successes in Europe. After her return to the United States in 1935, she soon became known to Americans as a great singer and musician; her voice, rich and full, with a wide range, displayed much vocal color. In 1955 she was the first Negro singer to be engaged by the Metropolitan Opera Company. She was appointed alternate delegate to the United Nations in 1958. See her autobiography, *My Lord, What a Morning* (1956).

Anderson, Mary, 1872–, American labor expert, chief (1919–44) of the Women's Bureau, U.S. Dept. of Labor, b. Sweden. She came to the United States in 1888. After some years as an industrial worker in garment and shoe factories, she became an organizer for the National Boot and Shoe Workers' Union and one of the founders of the National Women's Trade Union League. In 1918 she

Mount Fitz Roy, 10,958-ft. peak in the Andes on the Argentina-Chile boundary near Lake Viedma.

was appointed assistant to the chief of the Women's Bureau, becoming its chief in 1919. On her retirement (1944) she was succeeded by Frieda S. Miller. See her autobiography, *Woman at Work* (1951).

Anderson, Maxwell, 1888–1959, American dramatist, b. Atlantic, Pa., grad. Univ. of North Dakota, 1911, M.A. Stanford, 1914. He was a journalist until 1924, when *What Price Glory?*, written in collaboration with Laurence Stallings, was produced with great success. Anderson's plays, many of which are written in blank verse, are concerned with social and moral problems, either in contemporary settings, as in *Winterset* (produced 1935), or in romantic historical scenes, as in *Elizabeth the Queen* (produced 1930) and *Mary of Scotland* (produced 1933). Among other works are *Saturday's Children* (produced 1927), *Gods of the Lightning* (written with Harold Hickerson; produced 1928), *Valley Forge* (produced 1934), *High Tor* (produced 1936), *Key Largo* (produced 1939), and *Joan of Lorraine* (produced 1946). Anderson also wrote the libretto for Kurt Weill's *Lost in the Stars* (produced 1949; based on Alan Paton's *Cry the Beloved Country*). See study by M. D. Bailey (1957).

Anderson, Robert, 1750–1830, English editor, b. Scotland. He is known for his *Complete Edition of the Poets of Great Britain* (14 vols., 1792–1807).

Anderson, Robert, 1805–71, American army officer, defender of FORT SUMTER, b. near Louisville, Ky., grad. West Point, 1825. He fought in the Black Hawk, Seminole, and Mexican wars and was promoted major in 1857. In Nov., 1860, he took command of the U.S. force in the harbor of Charleston, S.C., where he distinguished himself in the Fort Sumter controversy. Anderson, made a brigadier general in the regular army (May, 1861), commanded the Dept. of Kentucky (June–Oct.). He retired from active service in Oct., 1863. In Feb., 1865, he was brevetted major general for his gallant service in the defense of Fort Sumter.

Anderson, Sherwood, 1876–1941, American novelist and short-story writer, b. Camden, Ohio. Starting work at the age of 14 with little formal education behind him, Anderson came to be recognized as one of the most significant writers of his day. After serving briefly in the Spanish-American War, he became a successful advertising man and later a manager of a paint factory in Elyria, Ohio. Anderson, however, abandoned both his job and his family and went to Chicago to become a writer. His first novel, *Windy McPherson's Son* (1916), concerning a boy's life in Iowa, was followed by *Marching Men* (1917), a chronicle about the plight of the working man in an industrial society. The latter work established the theme that was to become the primary concern of his later novels and short stories—the conflict between organized society and the subsconscious instincts of the individual. In *Winesburg, Ohio* (1919), Anderson's best-known and perhaps greatest novel, he explores the loneliness and frustration of small-town lives. In his later novels—*Poor White* (1920), *Many Marriages* (1923), and *Dark Laughter* (1925)—he continues to explore, but generally with less skill, the spiritual and emotional sterility of a success-oriented machine age. Anderson's unique talent, however, found its best expression in his short stories. Such collections as, *The Triumph of the*

Egg (1921), *Horses and Men* (1923), and *Death in the Woods* (1933) contain some of his most compassionate and penetrating writing. See his autobiographical *Story Teller's Story* (1924) and *Tar: A Midwest Childhood* (1926); memoirs (1942); letters (ed. by H. M. Jones and W. B. Rideout, 1953).

Anderson. 1 City (pop. 4,492), N central Calif., SSE of Redding, in a timber and dairy area; founded 1872, inc. 1956. Lumber products are made. **2** Industrial city (pop. 49,061), co. seat of Madison co., E central Ind., on the White River and NE of Indianapolis; platted 1823, inc. as a town 1838, as a city 1865. Its manufactures include automotive and recreational equipment. Anderson College (Church of God; coeducational; 1917) is here. Nearby Mounds State Park has numerous prehistoric mounds. The Moravians had an Indian mission nearby in 1801–6. The unincorporated village of Anderson East Side (pop. 3,778) is adjacent. **3** City (pop. 41,316), co. seat of Anderson co., NW S.C., between the Saluda and the Savannah rivers, SW of Greenville, in a farm, cotton, and livestock region; founded 1826, laid out 1827, inc. 1833. Textiles, fiber glass, and sewing machines are made. It is the seat of a junior college.

Anderson, river of the Mackenzie dist., Northwest Territories, Canada, flowing into the Arctic Ocean at Liverpool Bay. It is c.465 mi. long.

Andersonville, village (pop. 263), SW Ga., NNE of Americus; inc. 1881. In **Andersonville Prison** (now a state park) here, tens of thousands of Union soldiers were confined (1864–65) in the Civil War under conditions so bad that over 12,000 of them died. Andersonville National Cemetery, nearby, contains more than 13,000 soldiers' graves. See W. B. Hesseltine, *Civil War Prisons* (1930); MacKinlay Kantor, *Andersonville* (1955); and John McElroy, *This Was Andersonville* (ed. by Roy Meredith, 1957).

Andersson, Karl Johan (yōō′hän än′dùrsōn″), 1827–67, Swedish explorer in Africa. In 1850 he and Francis Galton set out from Walvis Bay (in South-West Africa) to explore Damaraland and Ovamboland, but they were able only to reach the Etosha Pan. On a second trip Andersson reached Lake Ngami (long the goal of explorers) and penetrated for 60 mi. beyond it. A subsequent journey (1859) took him to the Kubango river in Bechuanaland. He died while seeking out the upper reaches of the Kunene river. He wrote *Lake Ngami* (1855) and *The Okavango River* (1861). *Notes of Travel in South Africa* is a posthumous account of his last trip.

Andes (ăn′dēz), mountain system, over 4,000 mi. long, South America. The ranges run generally parallel to the Pacific coast and extend from Tierra del Fuego northward as the backbone of the entire continent. The Falkland Islands are a continuation of the Andes, and evidence shows that the system is continued in Antarctica. The Andes go through seven South American countries— ARGENTINA, CHILE, BOLIVIA, PERU, ECUADOR, COLOMBIA, and VENEZUELA. The ranges are continuous and make one of the world's most important mountain masses, loftier than any other except the Himalayas; there are many peaks higher than Mt. McKinley, the highest in North America. Far south in Tierra del Fuego, the mountains run east and west, then turn north between Argentina and Chile. The westernmost of the mountains run into the sea, lining the coast of S Chile with islands. In the mountains of the Patagonian border are high glacier-fed lakes in both Argentina and Chile. The highest range of the Andes is on the central and northern Argentine-Chilean border. Here are lofty ACONCAGUA (highest mountain of the Western Hemisphere) and TUPUNGATO; between them is USPALLATA PASS, with the Transandine Railway and the Christ of the Andes. Other major peaks such as LLULLAILLACO flank the main range, and in northern Chile subandean ranges enclose the high, cold Desert of ATACAMA. The central Andes broaden out in Bolivia and Peru in multiple ranges with high plateau country and many high intermontane valleys, where the great civilization of the Inca had its home. High in the mountains on the Peru-Bolivian border is Lake Titicaca. In Bolivia are the notable volcanoes, ILLIMANÍ and ILLAMPÚ, and in S Peru is El MISTI. The western or coastal range in Peru has lofty peaks (notably HUASCARÁN) and is crossed by the highest railroad of the Andes (from La Oroya to Lima). The ranges approach each other again in Ecuador, where the N Andes begin. Between two volcanic cordilleras (including the cloud-capped CHIMBORAZO and COTOPAXI) are rich intermontane basins. In Colombia the Andes divide again, the western range running between the coast and the Cauca river, the central between the Cauca and the Magdalena, and the eastern running north parallel to the Magdalena, then stretching out on the coast into Venezuela. The Andes continue in some of the islands of the West Indies, and in Panama northern Andean spurs connect with the mountains of Central America and thus with the Sierra Madre and the Rockies. Obviously the Andes do much to determine the whole pattern of communication, climate, weather, and life in South America. Andean waters reach the

Orinoco, the Amazon, and the Río de la Plata. The plateaus and valleys of Bolivia, Peru, Ecuador, and Colombia have been peopled since remote times and saw the rise not only of the Inca and the Chibcha but some of the earliest Indian civilizations in the Western Hemisphere. Agriculture was the basis of these cultures (the native llama and alpaca were domesticated later), and the lands there are still tilled mainly for subsistence crops. Commercially the Andes have always been important for great mineral wealth, especially copper, silver, and tin. Recently certain Andean areas have developed a tourist trade. See A. G. Ogilvie, *Geography of the Central Andes* (1922); Claude Arthaud and F. Hébert-Stevens, *The Andes: Roof of America* (Eng. tr., 1956); P. E. James, *Latin America* (1959).

Andhra Pradesh (än'drŭ prä'dãsh), state (106,052 sq. mi.; pop. c.35,980,000), SE India. The capital is Hyderabad. It was created in 1956 from the Telugu-speaking portions of Madras and Hyderabad states. It includes the northern portion of the Coromandel Coast of the Bay of Bengal, and although mountainous in the Eastern Ghats, it is largely a plain drained by the Penner, the Kistna, and the Godavari rivers. Rice, sugar cane, peanuts, and cotton are raised, and there are deposits of coal, chrome, and manganese. For the history of the state, see MADRAS, HYDERABAD, and COROMANDEL COAST.

Andizhan (ăndĭzhăn', Rus. ŭndyēzhän'), city (pop.c. 130,000), capital of Andizhan oblast, E central Uzbek SSR, in the Fergana Valley, on the Andizhan-Say river. An industrial center, it is in an irrigated area producing cotton and silk. Andizhan has been known since the 9th cent.

Andocides (ăndŏs'ĭdēz), c.440–390 B.C., one of the Ten Attic Orators (see ORATORY). In 415 B.C. he was accused of mutilating the hermae and, in association with ALCIBIADES, of other sacrilege. He went into exile, and one of his speeches was a plea to be restored to citizenship. After he returned in 403, he was again accused (399) of sacrilege and again defended himself.

Andorra (ăndô'rŭ), Fr. *Andorre* (ädôr'), small state (191 sq. mi.; pop. c.6,500), high in the E Pyrenees between France and Spain, under the joint suzerainty of the president of France and the bishop of Urgel (Spain). Drained by the Valira river, Andorra comprises several high mountain valleys generally poor in soil but supporting large flocks of sheep. Smuggling is an important occupation. Andorra has iron and lead deposits, marble quarries, and extensive pine forests. It has two radio stations, one of them French-controlled. The people, Catalan in speech and Catholic in religion, live in six villages; Andorra la Vella (Span. *Andorra la Vieja*) is the most important. In 843 Emperor Charles II made the count of Urgel overlord of Andorra; in 1278 the bishop of Urgel was made joint suzerain. The rights of the count passed by inheritance through the counts of Foix and the house of Albret to Henry IV of France, and from the French kings to the French presidents. Actually, Andorra has always maintained virtual independence, paying homage to France and Spain only through nominal yearly gifts—960 francs and 460 pesetas, respectively. Andorra is governed by a council of 24, elected by the heads of families and

One of the many glacier-fed lakes of the Chilean Andes.

Andorra location map

Andorra la Vella, the most important village of the tiny state.

led by a syndic. A semi-feudal state, Andorra is an ancient communal agrarian organization.

Andover (ăn′dō̄vûr). **1** Town (pop. 15,878), NE Mass., near the Merrimack river and SSE of Lawrence; settled 1643, inc. 1646. Woolen and rubber goods are produced. PHILLIPS ACADEMY and Abbot Academy (preparatory; for girls; 1829) are here. The former Andover Theological Seminary is now at Newton Center. Samuel Francis Smith wrote the words for *America* while a student at the seminary. The town has art galleries and several old buildings. Harriet Beecher Stowe lived in Andover and is buried here. **2** Village (pop. 1,247), SW N.Y., SSW of Hornell, in an oil region; inc. 1892. **3** Village (pop. 1,116), NE Ohio, SSE of Ashtabula, in a rich farm area; inc. 1883.

Andrada e Silva, José Bonifácio de: see BONIFÁCIO, JOSÉ.

Andrade, Olegario Víctor (ōlāgä′ryō vĕk′tōr ändrä′dhä), 1839?–1882, Argentine poet, journalist, and patriot, sometimes called the national poet of Argentina. Although he supported himself by writing for provincial newspapers and in 1880 was made editor in chief of the government newspaper in Buenos Aires, *Tribuna nacional*, his fame was won through his poems. These, strongly influenced by Victor Hugo, have a grandiloquent and sonorous tone and are marked by fervent praise for the fatherland and for the progress of the Latin race. Among his best-known poems is "El nido de cóndores" (written 1877), which describes San Martín's crossing of the Andes.

Andrassy, Julius, Count (ŏn′dräsh-shē), Hung. *Andrássy Gyula* (dyōō′lŏ), 1823–90, Hungarian statesman. One of the leading figures in the revolution and the war of independence of 1848–49, he supported the liberal program of Louis KOSSUTH and after the Hungarian defeat went into exile, mostly in Paris and London, until 1858. With Francis DEAK he then rose to prominence in the negotiations leading to the compromise (*Ausgleich*)

of 1867, which created the AUSTRO-HUNGARIAN MONARCHY. Andrassy was (1867–71) the first constitutional premier of Hungary. He opposed Austrian interference, attained the creation of a separate Hungarian defense force, put down the opposition led by Kossuth's partisans, and established Magyar supremacy at the expense of the Slavic and other minorities of the kingdom. In 1870 his influence was largely responsible for keeping Austria-Hungary neutral in the Franco-Prussian War. As foreign minister of the Dual Monarchy (1871–79) he reversed the anti-Prussian policy of his predecessor, Beust, held Austria-Hungary to the THREE EMPERORS' LEAGUE, and signed (1879) the Dual Alliance with Germany (see TRIPLE ALLIANCE AND TRIPLE ENTENTE). His chief program was to limit Russian expansion in the Balkans and to maintain the *status quo* among the Slavic peoples. At the Congress of Berlin (see BERLIN, CONGRESS OF) in 1878, he obtained for the Dual Monarchy the right to occupy BOSNIA AND HERCEGOVINA. This step provoked much opposition in Hungary because it

Count Julius Andrassy

further increased the Slavic element in the empire, and Andrassy resigned.

Andrassy, Julius, Count, Hung. *Andrássy Gyula,* 1860–1929, Hungarian statesman; son of the elder Count Andrassy. He occupied several cabinet posts before becoming (1900) minister of the interior of Hungary in the coalition cabinet under WEKERLE. He opposed the Austrian diplomacy of 1914, and as foreign minister (late in 1918) he severed all connections with Germany in the hope of obtaining a separate peace for Austria-Hungary. In 1921 he was involved in the attempt of King Charles (Emperor CHARLES I) to regain the Hungarian throne, and he later led the royalist opposition to Admiral Horthy and Count Stephen Bethlen. He wrote a number of political and historical studies, notably *Bismarck, Andrassy, and Their Successors* (1927, in English).

André, Brother (ä′drä, än′drä, Fr. ãdrä′), 1845–1937, Canadian Roman Catholic mystic, b. St. Grégoire d'Iberville, Que. His secular name was Alfred Bissette, Bassette, or Bessette. For some 40 years he was a porter at a school in Montreal. His simple, devout life began, after c.1900, to attract attention. Many miraculous cures were attributed to him. Through his efforts the Oratory of St. Joseph was built in Montreal. See biographies by H. P. Bergeron (Eng. tr., 1938), K. K. Burton (1952), and Alden Hatch (1959).

André, John (ändrä′, än′dre), 1751–80, British spy in the American Revolution. He was captured (1775) by Gen. Richard Montgomery in the Quebec campaign but was exchanged and became adjutant general under Sir Henry Clinton. Major André negotiated with Benedict ARNOLD for the betrayal of West Point and was captured (Sept. 23, 1780), when returning to New York, by John Paulding, David Williams, and Isaac Van Wart, near Tarrytown, N.Y. He was tried, condemned, and hanged at Washington's headquarters at Tappan, despite protests from Clinton. Major André's charming personality and his talents in the arts had won him many American friends, who mourned him as a romantically tragic young man. See J. T. Flexner, *The Traitor and the Spy* (1953).

Andrea del Sarto: see SARTO, ANDREA DEL.

Andreanof Islands: see ALEUTIAN ISLANDS.

Andree, Karl Theodor (tä′ōdōr än′drä), 1808–75, German journalist and geographer. His works include geographies of North America and Argentina. He founded and edited *Globus,* an ethnographic and geographic publication continued by his son **Richard Andree** (rĭkh′ärt), 1835–1912, who was an ethnographer of central Europe.

Andree, Salomon August (sä′lōōmôn ou′gŭst ändrä′), Swed. *Andrée,* 1854–97, Swedish polar explorer. An aeronautical engineer, he was the first to attempt arctic exploration by air. His first attempt by balloon in 1896 was unsuccessful, owing largely to bad weather. In 1897, however, he set out again in a balloon called the *Eagle.* Beset by mishaps from the start, Andree and his party reached as far as 82° 56′ N, where insufficient food and clothing halted their progress. All died of exposure. Search expeditions failed, and it was not until 1930 that a Norwegian scientific expedition accidentally found the remains and diaries of Andree and his

two companions. These diaries are included in *Andrée's Story* (Eng. tr., 1930). See G. P. Putnam, *Andrée: the Record of a Tragic Adventure* (1930).

Andreev, Leonid Nikolayevich: see ANDREYEV.

Andreini (ändrāē′nē), family of Italian actors celebrated in the COMMEDIA DELL'ARTE of the 16th and 17th cent. **Francesco Andreini** (fränchäs′kō), 1548–1624, joined the Gelosi troupe of players, excelled as the Capitano, and composed scenarios such as *Le bravure del capitán Spavento* (1607). More celebrated was his wife, **Isabella Andreini** (ē″zäbäl′lä), 1562–1604, whose maiden name was Canali. Beautiful, virtuous, and well educated, she was perhaps the most famous actress of her time. After joining the Gelosi troupe, she became a leading player when it was managed by Francesco Andreini, whom she married in 1578. The heroines which she portrayed were later given the name Isabella. She wrote the pastoral *Mirtilla* (1588); her letters appeared in 1607 (new ed., 1647). She was lauded by the poets Tasso and Marini, and after her death a medal was struck in her honor. See Rosamond Gilder, *Enter the Actress* (1931). Her son **Giovanni Battista** or **Giambattista Andreini** (jōvän′nē bät-tēs′tä; jämbät-tēs′tä), 1579?–1654, was an actor, a writer, and a director. He probably had early training in the Gelosi and c.1604 managed the Fedeli troupe. He gained fame for his portrayal of Lelio, an inamorato, and for his poems, comedies, and religious plays. His play *L'Adamo* (1614) is said to have been a source for Milton's *Paradise Lost.* Giovanni's wife, **Virginia Andreini** (vērjē′nyä), 1583–c.1628, whose maiden name was Ramponi, was an actress of repute, noted for her portrayal of Florinda, an inamorata. See Allardyce Nicoll, *Masks, Mimes, and Miracles* (1931).

Andrew, Saint [Gr.,=manly], one of the Twelve Disciples, brother of Peter. Mat. 4.18; 10.2; Mark 3.18; 13.3; Luke 6.14; John 1.40–42; 6.8,9; 12.22;

Saint Andrew Led to the Cross, *painting by Guido Reni.*

Acts 1.13. Tradition calls him a missionary in Asia Minor, Macedonia, and S Russia, with his martyrdom in Greece. He is said to have died on an Xshaped cross (St. Andrew's cross). He is patron saint of Russia and Scotland. Feast: Nov. 30.

Andrew II, d. 1235, king of Hungary (1205–35), son of Bela III. He invited the Teutonic Knights into S Transylvania in 1211, but expelled them in 1225. In 1224, however, he gave to the other Germans settled there the right to establish an autonomous administration. He continued his predecessors' policy of alienating crownlands to the magnates, and the lesser nobles forced him to issue a Golden Bull (1222), which strengthened the royal power and the liberties of the majority of the nation. This "Magna Carta," expanded in 1231, extended the old nobility's privileges (immunities from local courts, taxes, and military service abroad) to the lesser nobles, most of whom were freemen in the king's service. It made royal ministers responsible to the diet, which was to meet annually, and gave the right of resistance to the nobles if any of the bull's provisions were violated. Foreigners were not to receive office without consent of the diet, and offices were not to be hereditary. Nobles were also protected against arbitrary arrest or punishment. Andrew took part (1217) in the Fifth Crusade. He was the father of St. Elizabeth of Hungary and of Bela IV, his successor.

Andrew, John Albion, 1818–67, Civil War governor of Massachusetts (1861–66), b. Windham, Maine, grad. Bowdoin, 1837. He practiced law in Boston, but his antislavery sympathies drew him into politics. He was one of the organizers of the Free-Soil party and later of the Republican party. Soon after taking office as governor, he secured special legislation placing the militia in readiness and an appropriation for transporting it to Washington. When Lincoln's call came, the 6th Massachusetts was the first regiment to reach the capital. The same spirit characterized Andrew's actions throughout the war, and his zeal was imparted to the people. When peace came, he advocated a policy of friendship and leniency toward the South. See biography by H. G. Pearson (1904); W. B. Hesseltine, *Lincoln and the War Governors* (1948).

Andrewes, Lancelot (ăn'drōōz), 1555–1626, Anglican divine, bishop of Chichester (1605), of Ely (1609), and of Winchester (1619). One of the most learned men of his time, he was among the first to be selected to create a new English version of the Bible, the Authorized Version. He had a royal chaplaincy to Elizabeth, James I, and Charles I. His preaching gained him great favor with King James, who was keenly interested in theology. The great theologian of the High Church party of the 17th cent., Andrewes was opposed to Puritanism, his position being somewhat similar to that of LAUD. His outstanding characteristics were his goodness and piety. His contributions to charity were also noteworthy. His *XCVI Sermons* were edited (1629) by Bishops Laud and Buckeridge; his *Private Devotions,* translated (1647) from his noble prayers in Greek and Latin, passed through a number of editions. Richard Crashaw, the poet, paid him a beautiful tribute in "Upon Bishop Andrewes' Picture before His Sermons," and Milton, a Puritan, wrote a Latin elegy on his death. See biographies by R. L. Ottley (1894), Alexander Whyte (1896), M. F. Reidy (1955), and P. A.

Welsby (1958); T. S. Eliot, *For Lancelot Andrewes* (1928).

Andrew Johnson National Monument: see NATIONAL PARKS AND MONUMENTS (table).

Andrews, Charles McLean, 1863–1943, American historian, b. Wethersfield, Conn. A graduate of Trinity College, Hartford (B.A., 1884), and of Johns Hopkins (Ph.D., 1889), he was associate professor at Bryn Mawr (1889–1907) and professor at Johns Hopkins (1907–10) and Yale (1910–31). Andrews, a leader in the reinterpretation of British colonial policy in America, studied the colonies in the light of the larger imperial problem, and his seminar in colonial institutions at Yale stimulated much able research in this field. He himself capped his long, distinguished career with *The Colonial Period of American History* (4 vols., 1934–38; Vols. I–III, *The Settlements*; Vol. IV, *England's Commercial and Colonial Policy*). This excellent work won him the 1935 Pulitzer Prize for history and, in 1937, the gold medal for history and biography awarded only every 10th year by the National Institute of Arts and Letters. His other books include *Colonial Self-Government, 1652–1689* (1904, in the "American Nation" series), *The Fathers of New England* (1919) and *Colonial Folkways* (1919; both in the "Chronicles of America" series), and *The Colonial Background of the American Revolution* (1924). He also compiled manuscript and bibliographical guides and wrote works on various historical subjects. See biography by A. S. Eisenstadt (1956).

Andrews, Elisha Benjamin, 1844–1917, American educator and administrator, b. Hinsdale, Vt. He served in the Civil War, afterwards graduating from Brown in 1870 and from Newton Theological Seminary in 1874. He became successively president of Denison Univ., president of Brown Univ., superintendent of schools in Chicago, and chancellor of the Univ. of Nebraska, from which he retired in 1908. He is probably best known for his work at Brown; under his direction the university experienced a period of rapid expansion, in which a women's college, now known as Pembroke College, was created. Andrews's numerous works include *Wealth and Moral Laws* (1894) and *The History of the United States* (6 vols., 1913).

Andrews, Lorrin, 1795–1868, American missionary to the Hawaiian Islands, b. present Vernon, Conn., grad. Princeton Theological Seminary, 1825. He founded (1831) on Maui a training school for teachers, offered courses in printing (which he had himself learned from a book), and began (1834) publishing the first Hawaiian newspaper. After 1841 he had posts in the royal Hawaiian government, becoming (1852) an associate justice of the supreme court. His great cultural contribution was his *Dictionary of the Hawaiian Language* (1865; revised by H. H. Parker, 1922).

Andrews, Roy Chapman, 1884–1960, American naturalist and explorer, b. Beloit, Wis., B.A. Beloit College, 1906, M.A. Columbia Univ., 1913. Connected with the American Museum of Natural History, New York, from 1906, he was its director from 1935 to 1942. Between 1908 and 1914 he made several trips to Alaska, along the coast of Asia, and in Malayan seas to study aquatic mammals. He later conducted (1917–30) several expeditions into central Asia to study both fossil and living plants and animals; he discovered some of the world's great fossil fields, which have yielded the remains of many ancient animals and plants previously unknown to science. He described these expeditions in several books and discussed them all in *The New Conquest of Central Asia* (1932). His writings also include *Meet Your Ancestors* (1945), *In the Days of the Dinosaur* (1959), and the autobiographical works *Under a Lucky Star* (1943) and *An Explorer Comes Home* (1947).

Andrews, Stephen Pearl, 1812–86, American reformer and author, b. Templeton, Mass. He was a fervent abolitionist, an accomplished linguist and the inventor of a universal language, and a proponent of the Pitman shorthand system which he did much to introduce into America. In *The Science of Society* (1851–53) he elaborated upon the anarchistic ideas of Josiah WARREN. His other writings include *The Basic Outline of Universology* (1872).

Andrews, Thomas, 1813–85, Irish chemist and physicist. He discovered and named the phenomenon of critical temperature, the temperature above which a gas cannot be liquefied, no matter how great the amount of pressure.

Andrews, William Loring, 1837–1920, American bibliophile, b. New York city. He was a founder of the library of the Metropolitan Museum of Art and of the Grolier Society and the Society of Iconophiles. He wrote on New York city and on early books and printers.

Andrews. 1 Town (pop. 1,132), N Ind., N of Marion and near the Wabash river, in a farm area. **2** Town (pop. 1,404), extreme SW N.C., SW of Asheville, in the Nantahala National Forest near the Ga. line. It has lumber mills and a large hosiery mill. **3** Town (pop. 2,995), E S.C., NNE of Charleston; inc. 1909. It makes textiles and wood products and processes minerals. **4** City (pop. 11,135), W Texas, in the Llano Estacado and NW of Midland. Originally a prairie cow town, it grew rapidly in the 1950s when great quantities of oil began to be produced. Ranching and truck farming are still important.

Andreyev, Leonid Nikolayevich (lyǐûnyēt′ nyǐkûlǐ′ûvǐch ǔndrã′ûf), 1871–1919, Russian writer. His early stories were realistic studies of everyday life. Gorki was attracted by the note of social protest in his work and used his influence to obtain publication of Andreyev's first volume of short stories. After 1902 Andreyev turned to more metaphysical themes, using allegory and symbol to achieve his sometimes startling effects. This trend alienated Gorki and by 1912 their friendship ended. Among Andreyev's works are *The Red Laugh* (1905; Eng. tr., 1905), a drama inspired by the Russo-Japanese War, and *When the King Loses His Head* (1906; Eng. tr., 1920), suggested by the Revolution of 1905. Besides the popular drama of a circus clown, *He Who Gets Slapped* (1916; Eng. tr., 1921), his best-known plays are *Anathema* (1904; Eng. tr., 1910), an allegory on the futility of goodness; *The Seven Who Were Hanged* (1908; Eng. tr., 1909); and *The Pretty Sabine Women* (1912; Eng. tr., 1914), a political satire. *Judas Iscariot* (1910; Eng. tr., 1947) is a collection of short stories. The pessimism

of his later writings cost Andreyev his popularity. An anti-Bolshevik, he died in Finland. His name also appears as Andreev. See *Letters of Gorky and Andreev, 1899–1912* (1958); biography by Alexander Kaun (1924).

Andreyevsky, Sergei Arkadyevich (syǐrgã′ ûrkä′dyǐvǐch ǔndrã′ûfskē), 1847–1918, Russian lawyer and literary critic. He recognized early the importance of Dostoyevsky (in an essay on *The Brothers Karamazov*, 1888). His masterpiece is the autobiographical and psychoanalytical *Book of Death* (1922).

Andria (än′drēä), city (estimated pop. 70,050), in Apulia, S Italy. It is an agricultural market. Nearby Emperor Frederick II built the imposing Castel del Monte with eight round towers. There is also a restored 12th-century cathedral with an 8th-century crypt.

Andric, Ivo, Serbo-Croatian *Andrić* (ē′vō än′drǐch), 1892–. Yugoslav novelist, b. Bosnia. As a student

Ivo Andric

he worked for the independence and unity of the South Slavic peoples, and after the formation (1918) of the Kingdom of the Serbs, Croats, and Slovenes (later Yugoslavia) he served in diplomatic posts. His best-known work is a historical trilogy (1945) on Bosnia: *The Bridge on the Drina* (Eng. tr., 1959), *Bosnian Story* (Eng. tr., 1959), and *Young Miss*. Other works include poems and novellas. In his writings Andric explores the misery of man's struggle for existence and his link with the universe; he finds meaning in the enduring past. Andric was awarded the 1961 Nobel Prize in Literature.

Androgeus: see MINOS.

Andromache (ăndrŏ′mŭkē), in Greek legend, Trojan woman; wife of Hector and mother of Astyanax. After the Trojan War, she was carried away by

Hector takes leave of Andromache (Roman fresco).

Neoptolemus, whose father, Achilles, had slain her husband. Neoptolemus died, and she married Hector's brother Helenus. She is mentioned in the *Iliad*. The plays of Euripides and Racine which bear her name tell of her captivity by Neoptolemus.

Andromeda (ăndrŏ′mŭdŭ), in Greek mythology, princess of Ethiopia; daughter of Cepheus (sē′fŭs) and Cassiopeia (kăsēŏpē′ŭ). According to most legends Cassiopeia angered Poseidon by saying that Andromeda (or possibly Cassiopeia herself) was more beautiful than the nereids. Poseidon sent a sea monster to prey upon the country; he could be appeased only by the sacrifice of the king's daughter. Andromeda in sacrifice was chained to a rock by the sea; but she was rescued by PERSEUS, who killed the monster and later married her. Cassiopeia, Cepheus, and Andromeda were all set among the stars as constellations.

Andromeda, in astronomy, a northern constellation lying south of Cassiopeia and merging on the west with Pegasus. The brightest of the spiral nebulae is in Andromeda. To the naked eye the NEBULA looks like a faint star with a hazy outline; its distance from the earth has been estimated to be from c.750,000 to c.1,500,000 light years, and its size is believed to be about that of our Milky Way galaxy. The Soviet astronomer I. S. SHKLOVSKY speculated in 1962 that in outer space the most likely place for intelligent life is the great spiral nebula of Andromeda.

Andronicus I (Andronicus Comnenus) (ăndrŭnĭ′kŭs; kŏmnē′nŭs), 1120?–1185, Byzantine emperor (1183–85), nephew of John II. He acceded to the throne by strangling his cousin ALEXIUS II. Though notorious in his younger years for his scandalous morals, he was a competent, if cruel, ruler. He took strict measures to protect the peasants against the great landowners, enforced honesty on the tax collectors, and was the terror of corrupt officials. His severity and his failure to stop the rapid advance of WILLIAM II of Sicily against the capital led to his overthrow and the elevation of ISAAC II. Andronicus was tortured to death by the rabble. He was the last of the Comneni on the throne of Constantinople.

Andronicus II (Andronicus Palaeologus) (pălēŏ′-lŭgŭs), 1258–1332, Byzantine emperor (1282–1328), son and successor of Michael VIII. He devoted himself chiefly to church affairs, renewing the schism by renouncing (1282) the union established at the Second Council of Lyons. He made a treaty with the rising kingdom of Serbia. Against the Ottoman menace he allied himself with Roger de FLOR, with little success. His reign, shared from 1295 to 1320 with his son Michael IX, was cut short by his grandson, who forced him into a monastery and became emperor as Andronicus III.

Andronicus III (Andronicus Palaeologus), c.1296–1341, Byzantine emperor (1328–41), grandson of Andronicus II, whom he deposed. His chief minister was John Cantacuzene (later Emperor John VI). During his reign the Ottoman Turks gained almost complete control of Asia Minor, while STEPHEN DUSHAN of Serbia conquered part of Macedonia and Albania. He was succeeded by his son, John V.

Andronicus [Gr.,=conqueror of men], apostle at Rome. Rom. 16.7.

Andronicus, Livius: see LIVIUS ANDRONICUS.

Andros, Sir Edmund, 1637–1714, British colonial governor in America, b. Guernsey. As governor of New York (1674–81) he was bitterly criticized for his high-handed methods, and he was embroiled in disputes over boundaries and duties (see NEW JERSEY), going so far as to arrest Philip CARTERET. When James II, partly influenced by Edward RANDOLPH, consolidated all the New England colonies into the Dominion of New England, he named (1686) Andros governor. In 1688 New York and the Jerseys were also put under his control. The suppression of charters and colonial assemblies, interference with local customs and rights, and Andros's overbearing ways caused intense friction. After news of the overthrow of James II in 1688 reached the colonies, the colonials in Boston rebelled (1689), seized Andros and other officials, and sent them to England as prisoners. He was soon released and later was governor of Virginia (1692–97) and governor of Guernsey, England (1704–6). See V. F. Barnes, *Dominion of New England* (1923)

Andros (ăn′drŏs), island (146 sq. mi.; pop. 12,928), in the Aegean Sea, the northernmost and second largest of the CYCLADES. The port of Andros is the capital and chief town. This island produces silk, wine, and lemons. It also has manganese deposits. Colonized by Athens in the 5th cent. B.C., Andros rebelled in 410 B.C., became a free state, and later passed successively to Macedon, Pergamum, and Rome. Seized (1204) from the Byzantines by Venice and made a principality, it remained almost entirely under Venetian rule until its conquest (1514) by the Turks. In 1829 it passed to Greece.

Androscoggin (ăndrŭskŏg′ĭn), river, c.171 mi. long, formed in NE New Hampshire and flowing south, then east, to enter W Maine. Later turning south again, it joins the Kennebec near Bath. Long important for logging, it now also furnishes power for Rumford, Auburn, Lewiston, and other towns.

Andros Island: see BAHAMA ISLANDS.

Androuet du Cerceau (ãdrōō-ā′dü sĕrsō′), family of French architects active in the 16th and 17th cent. It was founded by **Jacques Androuet** (zhäk′), c.1520–c.1584, surnamed du Cerceau [Fr.,=circle] from the emblem of a circle marking his workshop. He is best known for his writings and his fanciful engravings of decorative architectural elements. Attributed to him are designs for two châteaux, Verneuil and Charleval. Of his two sons, who both worked on the Louvre, **Baptiste Androuet du Cerceau** (bätēst′), c.1545–90, designed the Pont Neuf spanning the Seine at Paris and became supervisor of royal construction in Paris, while **Jacques Androuet du Cerceau** the younger, c.1556–1614, worked on the Tuileries. Baptiste's son **Jean Androuet du Cerceau** (zhã′), c.1585–1650, is known for his mansions in Paris, of which an example is the Hôtel de Sully.

Andrusov, Treaty of (ăn′drōōsŏf″, Rus. ŭndrōō′sŭf), 1667, signed by Poland and Russia at the village of Androsovo (ŭndrŏ′sŭvŭ) (formerly Andrusov), RSFSR, SW of Smolensk. It ended the war of Tsar ALEXIS of Russia against JOHN II of Poland. Russia gained the Smolensk and Seversk provinces and Ukraine E of the Dnieper (left-bank Ukraine), including Kiev.

Andújar (ändōō′här), city (pop. 35,900), Jaén prov., S Spain, in Andalusia, on the Guadalquivir river. Its pottery and its water-cooling jars made of porous stone are famous. A painting by El Greco hangs in the Gothic Church of Santa María.

Anegada: see VIRGIN ISLANDS, BRITISH.

Aneirin: see ANEURIN.

Anem (ā′nĕm), the same as EN-GANNIM **2**.

anemia, condition in which the number of circulating red blood cells is insufficient or the cells are deficient in hemoglobin content. It has many causes:

Anemones

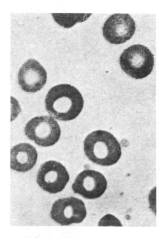

Hypochromic anemia. Pale red blood cells showing central depressions.

excessive loss of blood as in hemorrhage; destruction of blood components as by bacterial toxins or chemical agents; familial or hereditary factors as in sickle-cell anemia; a decrease in blood formation as in pernicious anemia; iron deficiency because of low iron intake or poor absorption; and abnormalities in the bone marrow. Regardless of the cause of the anemia, certain signs and symptoms are characteristic of its presence because of a reduction in the oxygen-carrying capacity of the blood or a decrease in total blood volume. These are pallor of the skin and mucous membranes, weakness, dizziness, easy fatigability, drowsiness, ringing in the ears, and spots before the eyes. Severe cases show difficulty in breathing, heart abnormalities, and digestive complaints, and the nerves are affected. Each type of anemia requires specific treatment. Transfusions are indicated after severe hemorrhage. Iron-deficiency anemia will respond to treatment with iron and iron-rich foods. Other substances helpful in various types of anemia are liver extract, vitamin B_{12}, folic acid, and cortisone.

anemometer: see WIND.

anemone (ùnĕm′ùnē) or **windflower,** any of the perennial herbs, wild or cultivated, of the genus *Anemone* of the BUTTERCUP family. A rich legendary history has gained the anemone many names and attributes. It is said to have sprung from the blood of Adonis; Romans held it valuable in preventing fever; it has been applied for bruises and freckles; for some it is tainted with evil and by the Chinese has been associated with death. The name windflower is accounted for in several ways,

one of which is Pliny's statement that anemone blossoms are opened by the wind. Anemones contain an acrid principle—anemonin—poisonous, but formerly used medicinally. Best known of the wild kinds are the white- or purplish-flowered wood anemone (*A. quinquefolia*), sometimes known specifically as windflower, and the greenish-white-flowered tall anemone or thimbleweed (*A. virginia*) with thimble-shaped fruit. The most common cultivated kinds include the tall, autumn-flowering Japanese anemone (*A. japonica*) for gardens and the florists' poppy anemones (*A. coronaria*), native to the Mediterranean area. Similar to the anemone is the wild rue anemone of another buttercup family genus (*Anemonella* or *Syndesmon*). The PASQUEFLOWER is sometimes included in *Anemone*.

Aner (ā′nùr). **1** Ally of Abraham. Gen. 14.13,24. **2** Levitical town, E of the Jordan. 1 Chron. 6.70.

aneroid barometer: see BAROMETER.

anesthesia (ănĭsthē′zhù) [Gr.,=insensibility], loss of sensation, especially of touch, induced by drugs. General anesthetics, usually employed in surgical operations of long duration, cause unconsciousness and are usually inhalation anesthetics. These gases include ether, nitrous oxide, and cyclopropane). Avertin, given rectally, is sometimes used to initiate general anesthesia and is later supplemented by an inhalant anesthetic. Local anesthetics (e.g., novocaine and ethyl chloride) are used in dentistry and in minor surgery and affect sensation only in the region of application. Anesthesia of short duration may be induced by intravenous injection of sodium pentothal. Spinal anesthesia is produced by injecting the anesthetic beneath the membrane of the spinal cord. This method is often used in surgery of the abdomen and legs. Caudal anesthesia, used in obstetrics, is produced by injecting the anesthetic into the sacral canal. Muscle relaxants, such as curare and its derivatives, are used to reduce the amount of conventional anesthetic required. Body temperature may be lowered in conjunction with the use of anesthetics. Extensive heart and brain surgery can be carried out at body temperatures which are 10 or more degrees Fahrenheit below normal. The metabolic rate is so much reduced that cells are not damaged by the lack of circulating blood. The various forms of anesthesia are frequently used in combination; in the United States, a skilled anesthetist is present at all major operations. Anesthetics are also used in the treatment of certain types of mental illness. Early experimenters with nitrous oxide (laughing gas) were Sir Humphry DAVY of England and Horace WELLS of the United States. Ether was used as a general anesthetic in the United States by Crawford W. LONG in 1842, but more general use of ether came after a demonstration at the Massachusetts General Hospital in Boston by William T. G. MORTON in 1846. Sir James Y. SIMPSON in 1847 was the first to employ a general anesthetic in obstetrics. See R. F. Woolmer, *The Conquest of Pain* (1961).

Aneto, Pico de (pē′kō dä änä′tō), Fr. *Pic de Néthou* or *Pic d'Anethou*, peak, 11,168 ft. high, NE Spain, in the Maladetta group near the French border; highest of the Pyrenees.

Anetothite (ăn′ĭtōthĭt): see ANATHOTH.

Aneurin (ă′nyōōrĭn, ä′–) or **Aneirin** (ä′nīrēn), fl. c.600, Welsh bard whose reputed writings are contained in a 13th-century manuscript *Book of Aneirin*. Included in this manuscript is *Gododin*, a 900-line elegiac poem on a defeat of the Welsh by the Saxons. The poem is one of the oldest extant works of Welsh literature and contains probably the earliest explicit allusion to King Arthur.

aneurysm (ăn′yōōrĭzŭm), localized dilatation of a blood vessel, particularly an artery. Dilatation of an artery, and therefore weakness of that portion of the arterial wall, may be congenital, or it may

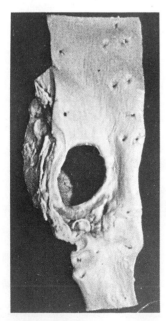

Pocket-like aneurysm of the wall of the aorta.

be caused by syphilis, high blood pressure, arteriosclerosis, bacterial and fungus infections, or penetrating injury as from a bullet or knife. An aneurysm may be asymptomatic or it may cause varying symptoms depending upon its location and whether the expanding mass is pressing on adjacent nerves or vital organs. The weakened arterial walls of an aneurysm are always in danger of sudden rupture with resulting hemorrhage and death. Aneurysms occur most commonly in the large arteries; the aorta, the largest vessel in the body, is the one most often affected. They also occur in the arteries within the skull and in other areas of the body. The only treatment is surgical where feasible, i.e., excision of the dilated saclike portion of the affected artery. This may require replacement by an arterial graft, a portion of vessel similar in length and calibre taken from the body of a dead person. There has also been successful replacement with tubes made of synthetic material such as nylon or Dacron.

Angara (äng″gürä′, Rus. ŭn-gürä′), river, S central Asiatic RSFSR, the outlet of Lake Baikal and a right tributary of the Yenisei. The Upper Angara (Rus. *Verkhnyaya Angara*)$_n$ c.400 mi. long, rises NE of Lake Baikal, into which it empties, forming a delta; it is partly navigable. It flows within the Buryat-Mongol Autonomous SSR. The Angara proper, more than 1,150 mi. long, leaves Lake Baikal at its southwestern end, flows N past Irkutsk, turns west after receiving the Ilim river, and joins the Yenisei above Strelka; it is navigable between Irkutsk and Bratsk. Below its junction with the Ilim it is also known as the Upper Tunguska (Rus. *Verkhnyaya Tunguska*). There are iron, coal, and gold deposits in its basin. A hydroelectric station is at Irkutsk, and a larger hydroelectric project was begun in 1959 at Bratsk.

Angara or **Angaran shield,** large, geologically stable area of Precambrian rocks comprising much of the eastern Soviet Union, including Siberia. It is named for the Angara river. Parts of the shield are thinly covered by strata of lower Paleozoic sediments. It is thought to have remained since the early Paleozoic era, above the level of invading seas that flooded most continental land masses. It is bounded, in general, on the west by the Yenisei river, on the east by the Lena river, on the north by the Arctic Ocean, and on the south by the general latitude of Lake Baikal.

angel [Gr.,=messenger], bodiless, immortal spirit, limited in knowledge and power, accepted in the traditional belief of Judaism, Christianity, and Islam. Angels appear frequently in the Bible, often in critical roles, e.g. visiting Abraham and Lot (Gen. 18; 19), wrestling with Jacob (Gen. 32.24–32), and guiding Tobit (Tobit 5). In the Gospels an angel announced the Incarnation to the Virgin Mary (Luke 1), and an angel at the empty tomb revealed the Resurrection (Mat. 28.3). The Bible also speaks of guardian angels, protecting individuals or nations. Dan. 10.13,20; Mat. 18.10. The "angels of the churches" are perhaps their bishops. Rev. 2–3. The hierarchy of angels in three choirs appears early in the Christian era; the classes are, from the highest: seraphim, cherubim, thrones; dominations, virtues, powers; principalities, archangels, angels. Eph. 1.21; Col. 1.16. From these two passages Dionysius the Areopagite fixed the number and order of angels in *The Celestial Hierarchy*. Roman Catholics and Orthodox venerate angels, and the cult of guardian angels is especially extensive in the West (feast of Guardian Angels: Oct. 2). Protestants generally abandoned the cult of angels. The angels of Hell, or dark angels, or devils, are the evil counterpart of the heavenly host; the chief of them, Satan (or Lucifer), was cast out of heaven for leading a revolt. They are often viewed as the initiators of evil temptations. Job 1–2; Isa. 14.4–23; Mat. 25.41; Luke 10.18; Eph. 6.12; Jude 9. Famous literary treatment of angels are those of Milton's *Paradise Lost* and Dante's *Divine Comedy*. See ARCHANGEL; CHERUB; SERAPH; GABRIEL; MICHAEL; RAPHAEL; SATAN.

Angela dei Merici, Saint (än'jälä dā'ē mārē'chē), 1470–1540, Italian nun of the third order of St. Francis. She was the founder of the Ursulines, a teaching order. Feast: May 31.

Saint Angela dei Merici

Angel Falls, waterfall, SE Venezuela, in the Guiana Highlands. One of the highest uninterrupted waterfalls in the world, it is said to be between 3,300 and 5,000 ft. high.

angelfish: see BUTTERFLY FISH.

Angelholm (ĕng"ŭlhôlm'), city (pop. 12,922), Kristianstad prov., S Sweden, on the Kattegat, N of Halsingborg. It has tanneries. Tourists are attracted to its fine beaches on Skalderviken Bay. The city, first chartered in 1516, is also known as Engelholm.

angelica (ănjĕl'ĭkù), any species of the genus *Angelica*, plants of the CARROT family native to the Northern Hemisphere and New Zealand, valued for their potency as a medicament and protection against evil spirits and the plague, which probably accounts for the name. Angelica is a poetic symbol for inspiration. The roots and fruits yield angelica oil, used in perfume, confectionery, medicine, and for flavoring liqueurs (such as angelica). The species most often used for these purposes is *A. archangelica*, a subarctic and alpine plant of the Old World once widely grown but now little cultivated outside Germany. This and a few other species are sometimes used as ornamentals.

Angelico, Fra (frä änjĕl'ĭkō), c.1400–1455, Florentine painter, b. Vicchio, Tuscany. He was variously named Guido (his baptismal name), or Guidolino, di Pietro; and Giovanni da Fiesole. After his death he was called Il Beato Fra Giovanni Angelico, although he was never officially beatified. Little is known of his family or early training. He took his vows c.1425 in the Dominican order. The first picture of certain date (1433) by Angelico is his *Madonna of the Linen Guild* (St. Mark's convent, Florence). It is supposed that his activity began at least 10 years earlier, and that he first painted small pictures, such as *St. Jerome Penitent* (Princeton Univ.) and miniatures. Other works suggested for this period (1423–33) are *Virgin and Child Enthroned with Twelve Angels* (Staedel Inst., Frankfurt); *Virgin and Child with Angels* (National Gall., London); *Madonna of the Star* and *Naming of the Baptist* (both: St. Mark's convent, Florence). It is thought that Angelico was first influenced by Gentile da Fabriano, and that he soon adopted Masaccio's advances in spatial conception. Critics have assigned to the 1430s such works as the *Annunciation* (Cortona); *Coronation of the Virgin* (Louvre); *Deposition* and *Last Judgment* (both: St. Mark's convent, Florence). In 1436, under the protection of Cosimo de' Medici, the Dominicans of Fiesole moved to the convent of San Marco in Florence. Fra Angelico supervised the fresco decoration of the building. Among the works considered to be by his hand are the *Crucifixion with St. Dominic* (cloisters) and the great *Crucifixion* (chapter house). In the convent also are frescoed *Noli mi Tangere, Annunciation, Transfiguration, Mocking of Christ, Presentation in the Temple, Virgin and Child with Saints*, and others. In 1445 he was summoned to Rome by Pope Eugenius IV to decorate the Cappella del Sacramento in the Vatican. In 1447 he visited Orvieto, where, assisted by his pupil Benozzo Gozzoli, he painted *Christ as Judge* and the *Prophets* in the Cappella Nuova of

Angelica

The Annunciation, by Fra Angelico.

the cathedral. Returning to Rome, he designed in the following year his greatest and most unified scenes—episodes from the lives of St. Stephen and St. Lawrence. However, the execution of this project was probably carried out mainly by pupils. Fra Angelico treated none but religious subjects, and his works are pervaded by a remarkable purity. Adapting the artistic innovations of his time (e.g., volumetric clarity and spatial depth), he interpreted them in terms of the greatest spirituality. Angelico endowed the new forms with his own incomparable sense of coloring and unity. In the United States he is represented by the *Crucifixion* (Fogg Mus., Cambridge); *Assumption and Dormition of the Virgin* (Gardner Mus., Boston); *Temptation of St. Anthony Abbot* (Mus. of Fine Arts, Houston, Texas); *Crucifixion* and *Nativity* (both: Metropolitan Mus.). See monographs by John Pope-Hennessy (1952) and G. C. Argan (1955).

Angel Island, W Calif., N of San Francisco in San Francisco Bay. It was discovered in 1775. The U.S. army used it as a base from 1863 to 1946 and in 1952 established a radar and missile site. A section of the island is a state park.

Angell, James Burrill, 1829–1916, American educator, editor, and diplomat, b. Scituate, R.I., grad. Brown, 1849, and studied abroad. He became professor of modern languages at Brown. Resigning in 1860, he served as editor of the Providence *Journal.* Later, as president of the Univ. of Vermont (1866–71) and of the Univ. of Michigan (1871–1909), Angell became known as an administrator. In this period he served also as minister to China (1880–81) and to Turkey (1897–98). See his *Reminiscences and Selected Addresses* (1912); biography by S. W. Smith (1954).

Angell, James Rowland, 1869–1949, American educator and psychologist, b. Burlington, Vt., grad. Univ. of Michigan (B.A., 1890; M.A., 1891), M.A. Harvard, 1892; son of James B. Angell. After study abroad, he taught at the Univ. of Minnesota, then at the Univ. of Chicago (1894–1920), where he became professor and head of the psychology department (1905), dean of the university faculties (1911), and acting president (1918–19). He served as president of Yale from 1921 until his retirement in 1937; in his administration the physical facilities of Yale were greatly expanded. In 1937 he became educational counselor of the National Broadcasting Company. His writings include several standard psychology textbooks, *Chapters from Modern Psychology* (1912), *American Education* (1937), and articles on psychology and education.

Angell, Sir Norman, 1872?–, British internationalist and economist, whose name originally was Ralph Norman Angell Lane. He came to fame with *The Great Illusion* (1910), in which he posited that the common economic interests of nations make war futile. At the close of the First World War he

255

worked for a generous peace and international co-operation. In *Peace with the Dictators?* (1938) he attacked the British Conservative policy of condoning Japanese and Italian aggressions. After the Second World War he urged unity among the Western democracies in such works as *Defence and the English-speaking Role* (1958). Knighted in 1931, Norman Angell was awarded the 1933 Nobel Peace Prize. See his autobiography (1951).

Angels Camp, city (pop. 1,121), central Calif., E of Stockton; founded 1848 after the discovery of gold in the Mother Lode; inc. 1912. It is said that this site is the locale of Mark Twain's story of the jumping frog. A state park is nearby.

Angelus (ăn′jŭlŭs), family name of three Byzantine emperors (1185–1204): see ISAAC II; ALEXIUS III; ALEXIUS IV.

Angelus (ăn′jŭlŭs) [Latin,=angel], daily prayer of the Roman Catholic Church, said usually three times daily, as announced by a bell, traditionally at six in the morning, at noon, and at six in the evening. It is said in honor of the Incarnation and consists of three repetitions of the Hail Mary together with verses and a prayer. It takes its name from the opening word of the Latin version: *Angelus Domini nuntiavit Mariae* [the angel of the Lord declared unto Mary].

Angelus Silesius (ăn′jŭlŭs sĭlē′zhŭs), pseud. of **Johannes Scheffler** (yōhän′ŭs shĕf′lŭr), 1624–77, German poet. He is best known for his pastoral lyric cycles *Heilige Seelenlust* (1657–68) and *Cherubinischer Wandersmann* (1674–75), which can be interpreted as Christian as well as pantheistic. Scheffler's mysticism strongly influenced 18th-century PIETISM.

Angerman, Swed. *Ångermanälven* (ông′ŭrmänĕl″vŭn), river, 280 mi. long, rising in N central Sweden and flowing into the Gulf of Bothnia at Harnosand. It is one of the main arteries for the floating of logs from the forests to the coast for processing.

Angermanland, Swed. *Ångermanland* (ông′ŭrmän-länd″), historic province, NE Sweden. It is now administratively divided between VASTERNORRLAND and VASTERBOTTEN provinces.

Angers (äzhä′), city (estimated pop. 102,142), capital of Maine-et-Loire dept., W France, in Anjou, on the Maine. A commercial and industrial center, it is also known for its wine. The largest slate quarries in France are located here. Of pre-Roman origin, it became the seat (870–1204) of the powerful counts of ANJOU and the historical capital of the province. There is a fine cathedral (12th–13th cent.) and a museum containing remarkable 14th-century tapestries and a large collection of the sculpture of DAVID D'ANGERS. The 13th-century castle and the 15th-century house of Olivier Barrault were among the buildings damaged in the Second World War.

Angevin (ăn′jŭvĭn) [Fr.,=of Anjou], name of two medieval dynasties originating in France. The first ruled over parts of France and over Jerusalem and England; the second ruled over parts of France and over Naples, Hungary, and Poland, with a claim to Jerusalem. The older house issued from one Fulk, who became count of Anjou in the 10th cent. Among his descendants was FULK (1092–1143), king of Jerusalem (Fulk V of Anjou). A younger son inherited the kingship of Jerusalem as

Baldwin III and was succeeded by Amalric I, Baldwin IV, and Baldwin V, with whom the branch ended (1186). Fulk's elder son, GEOFFREY IV (Geoffrey Plantagenet), inherited Anjou, conquered Normandy, and married Matilda of England, daughter of Henry I of England. Their son became (1154) the first Angevin (or Plantagenet) king of England as HENRY II. His successors were Richard I, John, Henry III, Edward I, Edward II, Edward III, and Richard II, after whom the English branch split into the houses of Lancaster and of York. A nephew of Richard I and John became (1196) duke of Brittany as Arthur I. From his sister and her Capetian husband, PETER I (Pierre Mauclerc), the subsequent rulers of Brittany issued. The Breton line of the Angevins came to an end with the marriages of ANNE OF BRITTANY and her daughter to the kings of France. The second house of Anjou was a cadet branch of the Capetians and originated with Charles, a younger brother of King Louis IX of France. Charles was made count of Anjou, acquired Provence by marriage, and in 1266 was invested by the pope with Naples as Charles I of Naples. His successors were Charles II, Robert, and JOANNA I of Naples and Provence. On the death (1382) of Joanna I the succession to Naples was contested by two cadet branches, both descended from Charles II of Naples. The first was represented by Charles of Durazzo (CHARLES III of Naples), a great-grandson through the male line, and by his children, Lancelot and Joanna II. They retained, for the most part, actual possession of the kingdom, despite the efforts of the rival line, issued from Margaret, a daughter of Charles II. Margaret married Charles of Valois, whose son and grand-

Castle of Angers, France.

son were Philip VI and John II of France. John made his younger son, Louis, duke of Anjou; Joanna I of Naples adopted Louis as heir; Louis thus became LOUIS I of Naples and Provence. His successors were Louis II, Louis III, and René. Though the last two were successively designated as heirs by Joanna II, Naples was seized by Alfonso V of Aragon and eventually remained in Spanish hands. René became duke of Lorraine by marriage. His heir, Charles of Maine, died in 1486 without issue, and Anjou, Maine, Provence, and the Angevin claim to Naples all passed to the French crown. The theoretical claim to Jerusalem stemmed from Charles I of Naples, whom Pope John XXI invested (c.1276) with the title. René's claim to the title was transmitted to the house of Lorraine. The Hungarian branch of Anjou began (1308) with Charles Robert (CHARLES I of Hungary), a grandson of Charles II of Naples. Charles I's son became king of Hungary and Poland as Louis I. Hungary passed to Louis's daughter Mary and to her husband, Emperor Sigismund, and Poland to Ladislaus II of Poland, husband of Louis's daughter Jadwiga.

Anghiera, Pietro Martire d' (pyä′trō märtē′rä däng-gyä′rä), 1457?–1526, Italian geographer and historian. In 1487 he removed to Spain. Knowing Columbus, Vespucci, Magellan, and other explorers and navigators, he was in regular receipt of information about the explorations in his time. His chief work is *De orbe novo decades octo* (1530).

Angier (ăn′jŭr), town (pop. 1,249), central N.C., SSW of Raleigh, in a farm area.

Angilbert, Saint (ăng′gĭlbûrt), d. 814, Frankish statesman and courtier under Charlemagne, abbot of Centula (now Saint-Riquier), near Amiens. He was highly regarded in the Carolingian revival as a writer of Latin poetry. Feast: Feb. 18.

angina pectoris (ănjī′nŭ pĕk′tŭrĭs) [Latin,=tightening of the heart], condition characterized by chest pain and caused by occlusion (closure) of the coronary arteries, resulting in insufficient supply of oxygen to the heart muscle. The pain is usually experienced under or to the left of the sternum (breast bone) and extends down the left arm or right arm or both. Angina pectoris occurs usually after the age of 50, more often in men than in women, and frequently follows exertion, excitement, overeating, or exposure to cold. Associated symptoms are faintness and difficulty in breathing. Drugs (e.g., amyl nitrite or nitroglycerine) which dilate the blood vessels of the heart are used in treatment. In all cases, physical activity and emotional strain must be avoided. The basic treatment, however, depends on the cause.

Angkor (ăng′kôr), site of several capitals (now in ruins) N of Tonle Sap, NW Cambodia, for five and a half centuries the heart of the KHMER EMPIRE. Extending over an area of 40 sq. mi., the ruins contain some of the most imposing monuments in the world. The first capital was founded by Yasovarman I (889–900) and was centered around the pyramidal temple of Phnom Bakheng. To the southeast of the original capital, a new temple complex, **Angkor Wat** (wät, vät) [Angkor temple], was created under Suryavarman II (1113–50). Planned as a sepulcher and a monument to the divinity of the monarch, it is probably the most

Relief of a nymph on a wall of Angkor Wat.

One of the more than 50 towers of Angkor Thom.

gigantic religious structure in the world. Surrounded by a vast moat, the temple is approached by means of an extensive causeway bordered on either side by balustrades in the form of giant nagas (divine serpents). This avenue leads to a magnificent entrance gate. Through a network of galleries and courts and atop a step-pyramid on two immense set-back platforms is the temple proper. It consists of five lofty acorn-shaped towers, four corner towers joined by galleries to the central sanctuary. The architecture of Angkor Wat, derived from the stupa form, is enormously impressive, but the most remarkable feature of the temple compound is its sculptural ornament, covering thousands of feet of wall space. The decoration is in the form of low relief of impeccable craftsmanship, illustrating scenes from the legends of Vishnu and Krishna, with some historical events from the life of the king. More delicate in proportions than their Indian prototypes, many of the figures, in their elegance of gesture and stateliness of pose, bear a resemblance to Cambodian dancers of today. In 1177 Angkor was sacked by the Chams, and Angkor Wat fell into ruins. Jayavarman VII (1181–c.1218) established a new capital, **Angkor Thom** (tōm′) [the great Angkor], N of Bakheng. The buildings of an already existing city were used as residential palaces and governmental buildings; an excellent system of moats and canals was constructed. At the entrances of the capital, four gates face the four cardinal points. They open onto four avenues which meet at the Bayon, the temple erected in the center of the city. Above the four entrance gates to the capital are carved imposing stone faces, generally thought to symbolize the bodhisattva Lokesvara. The avenues are lined with balustrades, consisting of 27 mammoth figures on each side holding a naga. Under Jayavarman VII the Bayon was used as a Buddhist sanctuary but suffered alterations at a later Hindu period. The central tower bears a giant image of Buddha, which has been interpreted as the incarnation of Jayavarman VII. Surrounding the main structure is a forest of more than 50 smaller towers covered with multiple heads that are thought to have been a reflection of the ubiquitous power of the divinity. The buildings are covered with elaborate decoration, more spontaneously and realistically rendered than that at Angkor Wat, and again illustrating historical episodes from the life of the king. Angkor was raided in the 14th and 15th cent. by the Thai. It was abandoned c.1432 for Phnom Penh. Overgrown by the jungle, the ruins were discovered by the French in 1861. Since then many of the monuments have been restored to their former glory. See Bernard Groslier and Jacques Arthaud, *The Arts and Civilization of Angkor* (Eng. tr., 1957).

angler, member of a family of European and American bottom-dwelling predacious fishes. The angler lies on the bottom and lures its prey with a long, wormlike appendage that extends forward and dangles over its mouth. When the lure is touched the huge mouth opens automatically. The deep-sea anglers are fantastic fishes, many with luminescent lures, that live at depths of 200 to 600 fathoms. The various species grow from 6 to 40 in. long. The parasitic males attach themselves to the females and do not develop eyes and digestive organs. The small (under 6 in.) sargassum fishes, with armlike pectoral fins and mottled coloration adapted to merge with the kelp in which they live, are found in warm Atlantic waters, as are the 8- to 12-inch batfishes, named for their jointed pec-

Angler fish

torals. The goosefish, the largest angler (up to 4 ft. and 50 lb.), is capable of swallowing fish as big as itself.

Angles: see ANGLO-SAXONS.

Anglesey or **Anglesea** (both: ăng′gŭlsē), county (pop. 51,700) 275 sq. mi., an island off the northwest coast of Wales. It is a region of low, rolling hills. The principal industries are agriculture and stock raising. HOLYHEAD, on nearby Holyhead Island, is the eastern terminus of the mail service to Dublin. Two bridges over the MENAI STRAIT connect the island to the mainland. The town of Menai Bridge has long been a stock-trading center for NW Wales. Anglesey is said to have been the last refuge of the druids in Britain. Penmynydd, at the center of the island, was the home of Owen Tudor, founder of the house of Tudor.

anglesite (ăng′glŭsīt), pale green, blue, yellow to white, or colorless mineral, a sulphate of lead that is formed by oxidation of GALENA, crystallizing in the orthorhombic system and occurring also in granular or massive form. It is widely distributed and commonly associated with galena and other lead minerals. It is a minor lead ore.

Angleton, city (pop. 7,312), co. seat of Brazoria co., S Texas, SSW of Houston; settled 1896, inc. 1912. It grew as a rail center in a region that once boasted large plantations, but now depends on industrial production in the county.

Anglican Communion, the body of churches in all parts of the world that are in communion with the Church of England (see ENGLAND, CHURCH OF). The Communion is composed of regional churches, provinces, and separate dioceses bound together by mutual loyalty as expressed in the Lambeth Conference. National member churches include the Protestant Episcopal Church of America (see EPISCOPAL CHURCH, PROTESTANT), the Scottish

Episcopal Church, the Church in Wales, the Church of Ireland (see IRELAND, CHURCH OF), and the Nippon Sei Ko Kwai (Japan). There are separate dioceses in Jerusalem and Egypt. The dioceses and missionary districts total 331, and there are over 34 million baptized members. Worship is liturgical and is regulated by the BOOK OF COMMON PRAYER. A world-wide Anglican Congress met at Minneapolis, Minn., in 1954. See G. F. S. Gray, *The Anglican Communion* (1958); J. W. C. Wand, *Anglicanism in History and Today* (1961).

angling: see FISHING.

Anglo-Catholic movement: see OXFORD MOVEMENT.

Anglo-Egyptian Sudan: see SUDAN.

Anglo-Saxon Chronicle, collective name given several English monastic chronicles in Anglo-Saxon, all stemming from a compilation made from old annals and other sources c.891, probably under the direction of King Alfred. This original chronicle was later edited by monks in various monasteries with additions, omissions, and continuations. The account begins with the start of the Christian era, but most of the very early material is drawn from Bede's history. From the period of the wars between Saxons and Danes onward, most of the annals are original and are the sole source for much of our knowledge of events. The writing is generally in sparse prose, but some poems are inserted, notably the stirring "Battle of Brunanburh" (see BRUNANBURH). Of the four chronicles recognized as distinct and called the Winchester Chronicle, the Abingdon Chronicle, the Worcester Chronicle, and the Peterborough Chronicle, one (the Peterborough) extends to 1154. See Charles Plummer, ed., *Two of the Saxon Chronicles Parallel* (1892–99); *The Peterborough Chronicle* (tr. by Harry A. Rositzke, 1951); *The Anglo-Saxon Chronicle* (tr. by Dorothy Whitelock and others, 1962).

Anglo-Saxon literature, the literary writings in Old English (see ENGLISH LANGUAGE). Much of the early literature of England was in Latin. The earliest Anglo-Saxon poems, although recorded after the conversion of the English to Christianity, reveal a strong current of old Germanic paganism. The great example of this half-pagan poetry is the epic BEOWULF. A dignified, often sad, tone pervades *Beowulf* and many of the shorter poems of the period, which include WIDSITH, of great interest to students of Anglo-Saxon culture, and *Deor*, a lament of stern beauty. Religious poetry in Anglo-Saxon begins with the hymn of CÆDMON, recorded by Bede; poets of Cædmon's school and others paraphased the Bible and achieved some stirring poetry, especially in the epic fragment JUDITH. The work of CYNEWULF and his followers reflects the growing interest in saints' lives and legends and in homilies. For vividness and religious intensity, "The Dream of the Rood" is notable; "The Battle of Maldon" and "The Battle of Brunanburh" (see MALDON and BRUNANBURH) breathe the heroic spirit of the Anglo-Saxons in war. The usual form of early Anglo-Saxon poetry is an alliterative, four-stress line, broken by a caesura into two half lines and end-stopped. Rhyme was only an ornament until the later period, which was marked by increasing use of run-on line and rhyme. Stylistic features include "kennings"— e.g., "whale's road" for "sea"—and repetition

with variations. Literary prose began to be written in Anglo-Saxon instead of Latin when King Alfred made his extensive and excellent translations from Latin to educate his people. The ANGLO-SAXON CHRONICLE may have been undertaken at his order. The final original prose is to be found in the homilies of ÆLFRIC and of Wulfstan, bishop of Worcester and archbishop of York. See G. P. Krapp and E. V. K. Dobbie, ed., *The Anglo-Saxon Poetic Records* (6 vols., 1932–53); C. W. Kennedy, *The Earliest English Poetry* (1943); Kemp Malone, "The Old English Period," in A. C. Baugh, ed. *A Literary History of England* (1948); G. K. Anderson, *The Literature of the Anglo-Saxons* (1949).

Anglo-Saxons, name given to the Germanic-speaking peoples who settled in England after the decline of Roman rule there. The Angles (Latin *Angli*) mentioned by Tacitus are probably the same people, who seem to have come from what is now Schleswig in the later decades of the 5th cent. Their settlements in the eastern central and northern portions of the country were the foundations for the later kingdoms known as EAST ANGLIA, MERCIA, and NORTHUMBRIA. The SAXONS, a Germanic tribe who had been continental neighbors of the Angles, also settled in England in the late 5th cent. after earlier marauding forays there. The later kingdoms of SUSSEX, WESSEX, and ESSEX were the outgrowths of their settlements. The Jutes, a tribe about whom very little is known except that they probably came from the area around the mouths of the Rhine, settled in Kent (see KENT, KINGDOM OF) and the Isle of Wight. The use of the term "Anglo-Saxons" to denote the non-Celtic settlers of England dates from the 16th cent. In more modern times it has been loosely used to denote any of the people (or their descendants) of the British Isles, including the Danes and the Normans. See F. M. Stenton, *Anglo-Saxon England* (2d ed., 1947); R. H. Hodgkin, *History of the Anglo-Saxons* (3d ed., 1953).

Angmagssalik (ängmäg'sälĭk), trading post, on E Greenland, on the coast just S of the Arctic Circle. The radio meteorological station, established here in 1925, has great strategic importance.

Angola (ăng-gō'lù) or **Portuguese West Africa,** overseas province (with CABINDA 481,351 sq. mi.; pop. c.4,605,000) of Portugal, SW Africa, on the Atlantic Ocean. The capital is Luanda. Angola extends c.1,000 mi. along the coast between the Congo on the north and the Cunene river on the south. It is otherwise bordered by the Republic of the Congo

Angola location map

Luanda, capital of Angola.

Bantu family in front of their primitive hut.

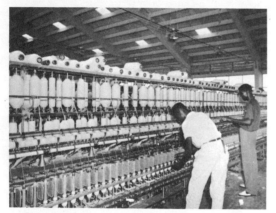

Cotton textile manufacturing in a suburb of Luanda.

on the north and east, by Northern Rhodesia on the east, and by South-West Africa on the south. Angola consists of a coastal lowland and of a vast dissected tableland (average alt. 6,000 ft.) rising abruptly from the coastal strip, then sloping gently E toward the Congo and Zambesi basins. This central plateau (called Bié Plateau in the high section near Nova Lisboa) is one of Africa's major watersheds. Rainfall is generally low, and nearly all the land is desert or savanna. In the northeast, however, there are densely forested valleys which yield hardwoods, and along the coast there is a narrow strip where rainfall is heavy and palm trees are cultivated. Much of the savanna region is suitable for raising livestock, especially goats and sheep. The crops of Angola include coffee, cotton, sisal, rubber, cacao, and palm oil. Along the coast there is fishing and fish canning and processing. Diamonds are mined and petroleum resources are exploited, but large deposits of copper, iron, and manganese ores remain mostly undeveloped. Industry, formerly of minor importance, has expanded into the manufacturing of jute, cotton textiles, paper, and a variety of plastic and rubber products. An important source of revenue is the Benguela railway, which carries metals from the mines of Katanga and those of the Copperbelt of Northern

Rhodesia. The railroad extends from Beira in Mozambique W across Africa to the port of Lobito in Angola. The country has, besides, several shorter rail lines and a fair road net. The population is overwhelmingly Bantu, but the number of Europeans has greatly increased since 1951, when immigration was officially encouraged; there is also a sizable colored (mixed) population. The Portuguese first explored Angola in the late 15th cent., and except for a short occupation (1641–48) by the Dutch it has always been under Portugal's control. A permanent Portuguese colony was founded at Luanda in 1575 and another at Benguela in 1617. From the 17th cent. until 1836, when slaving was abolished, Angola supplied most of the slaves exported to Brazil. In the years 1905–20 Portugal was engaged in pacifying bellicose tribes in Angola. The modern development of Angola began only after the Second World War. In 1951 the colony of Angola became an overseas province, and government-sponsored plans to develop hydroelectric power, transportation, and industrial expansion were initiated. At the same time the government promised constitutional equality for all. Many native Africans, nevertheless, still suffered repression, and inspired by nationalist movements elsewhere they rose (1961) in revolt. The Portuguese army quickly quelled the uprising and many native Angolans fled to neighboring countries, especially to the Republic of the Congo. In 1962 a group of refugees in the Congo, led by Holden Roberto (b. 1925), an Angolan political leader, organized to overthrow the Portuguese regime in Angola. See C. C. Egerton, *Angola in Perspective* (1957); James Duffy, *Portuguese Africa* (1959); T. M. Okunia, *Angola in Ferment* (1962).

Angola (ăng″gō′lù). **1** Resort city (pop. 4,746), co. seat of Steuben co., extreme NE Ind., NNE of

Fort Wayne; platted 1838, inc. as a town 1886, as a city 1906. In an area of hills and lakes near Pokagon State Park, it has some manufacturing. **2** Village (pop. 2,499), W N.Y., near Lake Erie and SW of Buffalo, in a farm area; inc. 1873. A state park is nearby.

Angora: see ANKARA.

Angostura: see CIUDAD BOLÍVAR.

angostura bark (ăng″gŭstū′rù, –stōōr′ù), bitter bark of a South American tree (*Cusparia febrifuga*) of the RUE family. Formerly valued as a tonic and quinine substitute, it is now used in **angostura bitters,** an aromatic appetizer often added to cocktails.

Angoulême, Charles de Valois, comte d'Auvergne, duc d' (shärl′ dù välwä′ kŏt′ dōvĕrn′yù dük′ dägōōlĕm′), 1573–1650, natural son of Charles IX of France. He turned against Henry IV, conspired with Henriette d'ENTRAGUES, his half sister, and was imprisoned until 1616. After his release he held high military rank. He left memoirs.

Angoulême, Margaret of or Marguerite d': see MARGARET OF NAVARRE.

Angoulême, Marie Thérèse Charlotte, duchesse d' (märē′ tārĕz shärlŏt′ düshĕs′). 1778–1851. wife of Louis Antoine d'Angoulême; daughter of Louis XVI. She was imprisoned (1792–95) by the revolutionists. Energetic and ambitious, she exerted considerable political influence in the reigns of Louis XVIII and Charles X. She died in exile at Frohsdorf, Austria.

Angoulême (ägōōlĕm′), city (estimated pop. 43,170), capital of Charente dept., W France, on the Charente. An important communications center, it also has paper mills and liquor distilleries. Of pre-Roman origin, it was an early episcopal see and became (9th cent.) the seat of the counts of ANGOUMOIS as vassals of the dukes of AQUITAINE. Ceded (1360) to England, it was recovered (1373) by Charles V and became an appanage of Orléans-Angoulême, a branch of the house of Valois.

Angoumois (ägōōmwä′), region and former province, W France, surrounding Angoulême, its chief city, and occupying most of Charente dept. In the Charente valley there are excellent vineyards. The brandy made from their grapes is called cognac, after Cognac, the chief distillery center. The region was ruled by the counts of ANGOULÊME, the last of whom became king of France in 1515 as Francis I and definitively incorporated Angoumois into the royal domain.

Angra do Heroísmo (äng′grù dōō ĕrōēzh′mō), town (pop. c.10,300), capital of Angra do Heroísmo dist., in the Azores, a port on Terceira island. It has the 17th-century castle of St. John the Baptist.

Angren (ŭn-gryĕn′), city (pop. c.56,000), E Uzbek SSR, E of Tashkent. The largest lignite-mining center in central Asia, it was developed during and after the Second World War.

angry young men, term applied to a group of English writers of the 1950s whose heroes share certain rebellious and critical attitudes toward society. This phrase, which was originally taken from the title of Leslie Allen Paul's autobiography, *Angry Young Man* (1951), became current with the production of John Osborne's play *Look Back in Anger* (1956). The word *angry* is probably inappropriate; *dissentient* or *disgruntled* perhaps is more accurate. For this group not only expresses discontent with the staid, hypocritical institutions of English society—the so-called Establishment—but betrays disillusionment with itself and with its own achievements. Included among these writers are the playwrights Osborne and Arnold Wesker and the novelists Kingsley Amis, John Braine, John Wain, and Alan Sillitoe.

Anders Jons Angstrom

Angstrom, Anders Jons, Swed. *Anders Jöns Angström* (än′dùrs yûns′ ōng′strûm), 1814–74, Swedish physicist. He was educated at the Univ. of Uppsala and in 1839 became a member of its faculty. He is particularly remembered for his study of light, especially spectrum analysis. He mapped the solar spectrum, discovered hydrogen in the solar atmosphere, and was the first to examine the spectrum of aurora borealis. See ANGSTROM UNIT. His son **Knut Johan Angstrom** (knüt′ yōō′hän), 1857–1910, is known for his work on solar radiation.

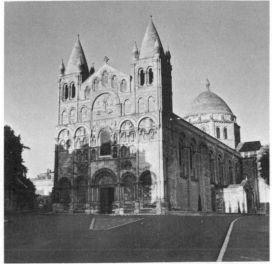

St. Peter's Cathedral in Angoulême, France.

angstrom unit (ăng′strŭm) [for A. J. Angstrom], unit of length, 1/100,000,000 of a centimeter, used to measure wave lengths of light or electromagnetic radiation. Visible light, ultraviolet light, and X rays are measured in angstroms.

Anguier, François (frăswä′ ägyä′), 1604–69, French sculptor. He is noted for the monuments of the Longuevilles and of Jacques Souvré (Louvre). His most ambitious work is probably the mausoleum of Henri II, duc de Montmorency, in Moulins. His brother **Michel Anguier** (mēshĕl′), 1614–86, collaborated in this project. The work of both brothers reflects the classical baroque influence of Algardi, with whom they studied in Rome. In Paris, Michel executed the marble group *The Nativity*, now in the Church of Saint-Roch. He also made decorations for the apartments of Anne of Austria in the Louvre and worked on reliefs for the triumphal arch at Porte Saint-Denis. A third brother, **Guillaume Anguier** (gēyŏm′), 1628–1708, a painter, was director of the Gobelin factory.

Anguilla, British West Indies: see SAINT KITTS.

Anguille, Cape (ăng-gĭl′), most westerly point of Newfoundland, Canada.

Anguille Range, W N.F., Canada, running NE from Cape Anguille into the highlands of St. George Bay.

Angus, earls of: see DOUGLAS, ARCHIBALD.

Angus, county (pop. 278,370), 874 sq. mi., E Scotland; formerly called Forfarshire. FORFAR is the county town. The terrain varies from wild rugged mountains (the Sidlaw Hills and part of the Grampians) to the fertile valleys of the North and South Esk and the Isla. Oats, barley, and root crops are grown; cattle, sheep, and horses are raised. The coastal towns engage in fishing and boat building. Angus is a center of the Scottish textile industry, processing jute at DUNDEE, ARBROATH, BRECHIN, and MONTROSE. There are numerous relics of early Pictish and Roman occupation, and the famous GLAMIS Castle.

Anhalt (än′hält), former state, central Germany, surrounded by the former Prussian provinces of Saxony and Brandenburg. It was included in 1947 in the state of SAXONY-ANHALT. Dessau, the capital, and Köthen were the chief cities. A level area except for the outliers of the lower Harz mts. in the west, the region of Anhalt is drained by the Elbe. Sugar beets are the main crop; grain and cattle are produced in the western section. The land has some mineral resources (salt, lignite, copper, and zinc). Industry is mainly limited to manufactures of chemicals and textiles. Anhalt until 1918 was ruled by one of the most ancient houses of Germany, issued from a son of Albert the Bear. It was divided, at most times, into several principalities held by various branches of the family. Reunited into a single duchy in 1863, it joined the German Empire in 1871, became a republic in 1918, and joined the Weimar Republic. Celebrated members of the house of Anhalt were Leopold I, prince of Anhalt-Dessau, and Sophie of Anhalt-Zerbst, empress of Russia as Catherine II.

Anhwei or **An-hui** (both: än′hwā′), province (c. 56,000 sq. mi.; pop. c.31,500,000), E central China. Hofei is the capital. Anhwei may be divided into two climatic areas. The northern half, within the N China plain and watered by the Hwai river, is cold in winter and dry throughout the year. It has a single harvest annually, the chief crops being wheat, kaoliang, soybeans, sweet potatoes, and cotton. The southern half, through which the Yangtze river flows, enjoys a relatively moist, warm climate. Often two crops a year are grown there, mainly rice, barley, and sugar cane, and mulberry trees are raised for silk culture. Tea is grown in the southeast. Coal and iron ore are abundant throughout the province; Hwainan is a large coal-mining center. Communications in Anhwei are fairly good. The Yangtze is open to oceangoing vessels, the Hwai and its affluents are navigable by junk, and an intricate canal system connects the two rivers. A railroad connecting Nanking and Shanghai crosses the province, and there are many motor roads. Part of N Anhwei was transferred to Kiangsu in 1955.

anhydride (ănhī′drĭd, –drĭd) [Gr.,=without water], any nonmetallic oxide (acid anhydride or acidic oxide) that reacts with water to form an ACID. An anhydride is also any metallic oxide (basic anhydride or basic oxide) that reacts with water to form a base. For example, sulfur trioxide is an acid anhydride, since it reacts with water to form sulfuric acid. Calcium oxide is a basic anhydride since it reacts with water to form calcium hydroxide.

Ani (ä′nē), ancient ruined city of Asia Minor, now in NE Turkey, SE of Kars. An ancient settlement, the city became the capital of Armenia in the 10th cent. It was often besieged by invaders and was finally destroyed by an earthquake in the 14th cent. There are notable ruins of a cathedral (built 989–1001) and several churches (11th–13th cent.) and remnants of a double wall.

ani, bird: see CUCKOO.

Aniakchak (ănēăk′chăk), volcano, W Alaska, in the Aleutian Range, on the Alaska Peninsula. It erupted in 1931. Aniakchak has a crater more than 6 mi. in diameter.

Aniam (ünī′ŭm) [Heb.,=the people's lament], Manassite. 1 Chron. 7.19.

Aniene (änyā′nā), Latin *Anio*, river, in Latium, central Italy. Some 60 mi. long, it empties into the Tiber just above Rome. Two aqueducts have carried water from the Aniene to Rome since ancient times, and now the river also supplies several hydroelectric plants. Below Tivoli, where it forms a celebrated waterfall, it is also called the Teverone.

aniline (ăn′ŭlēn) [New Latin,=belonging to anil, from Arab.,=indigo, from Sanskrit,=blue], colorless, oily liquid compound of carbon, hydrogen, and nitrogen; an amine, basic in character, boiling at 184° C. and solidifying at –6° C. It is of great importance in the dye industry, being used as the starting substance in the manufacture of many dyes—e.g., indigo—and as an aid in the manufacture of others. For this reason many dyes have the word *aniline* in their common name, such as aniline black (one of the best black dyes known), aniline red, yellow, blue, purple, orange, green, and others. Today these synthetic dyes have largely replaced the natural ones. Aniline is prepared commercially by the reduction of nitrobenzene, a product of coal tar. It was obtained originally from three sources, from indigo, from coal tar, and from the reduction of nitrobenzene. It was some time, however, before these products were shown to be identical by A. W. von HOFMANN, a German chemist, who gave aniline its name.

Anim (ā'–) [Heb.,=fountains], town, Palestine, SW of Hebron. Joshua 15.50. It is referred to as Hawini in the Tel-el-Amarna letters.

animal, any member of the animal kingdom as distinguished from the plant kingdom. Demarcation between animals and plants is usually based on a fundamental difference in their method of obtaining food. Plants (see PLANT) characteristically manufacture their food from inorganic substances (usually by photosynthesis). Animals, on the other hand, must secure food already organized into organic substances. In addition, most animals have specialized means of locomotion, possess nervous systems and sense organs, and are adapted for securing, ingesting, and digesting their food. In all but the simpler forms there is a distinct alimentary canal or digestive system. Almost all animals, unlike most plants, possess a limited scheme of growth; i.e., the adults of a given species are nearly identical in their maximum size and characteristic form. It is easy to distinguish between plants and animals of the higher groups, but among the simpler and microscopic forms it is often difficult. Some single-celled organisms, e.g., *Euglena,* possess chlorophyll and carry on photosynthesis but have a flexible cell membrane rather than the cellulose wall characteristic of plant cells. *Euglena* can swim freely by lashing the water with its flagellum. Classification of such forms is controversial; however, they may have evolved from the common ancestors of plants and animals that most scientists believe to have existed in the very early stages of organic evolution. Animals and plants are interdependent—green plants provide oxygen and are the ultimate source of all food for animals. Animals provide carbon dioxide through their respiration and minerals through the decomposition of their dead bodies. In zoological CLASSIFICATION the animal kingdom is divided into the two subkingdoms of PROTOZOA (one-celled animals) and metazoa (many-celled animals). The metazoa comprise numerous INVERTEBRATE phyla and the phylum Chordata. The distinguishing characteristics of the chordates are a notochord (a dorsal stiffening rod) in the embryo, a dorsal hollow SPINAL CORD and GILL slits (sometimes present only during embryonic stages, e.g., in the frog and man). The chordates include three primitive subphyla of a few species in which these features are present only at certain stages of the life cycle. The fourth and major chordate subphylum is the Vertebrata (see VERTEBRATE), in which the embryonic notochord develops into the SPINAL COLUMN of the adult. The word animal is sometimes incorrectly limited to the class Mammalia (see MAMMAL). The scientific study of animals is called ZOOLOGY; the study of their relation to their environment and of their distribution is animal ECOLOGY. For specific approaches to the study of animals and plants, see BIOLOGY.

animated cartoon: see CINEMA.

animism, belief that within every object dwells an individual spirit or force which governs its existence. It has been said that upon this concept rests the historic structure of religion. Since primitive man did not distinguish between animate and inanimate objects or between physical and mental processes, everything in the universe was thought to have its own individuality. Men, animals, plants, stones, as well as emotions, dreams, and ideas alike, were regarded as having indwelling spirits. More generalized are the ideas of manito among American Indians and of mana which originated among Melanesians of the South Seas. A kind of transcendental force, mana is thought to be the spirit that pervades all objects and things and is responsible for the good and evil in the universe. In philosphy, the term animism is applied to a doctrine which holds that the principle of life, called the vital force, cannot be reduced to the mechanistic laws of physics and chemistry, but is separate and distinct from matter. See FETISH, TABOO, TOTEM, IDOL, SHAMAN, ANCESTOR WORSHIP, and AMULET.

Anio, river: see ANIENE.

anise (ăn'ĭs), annual plant (*Pimpinella anisum*) of the carrot family, native to the Mediterranean region but long cultivated elsewhere for its aromatic and medicinal qualities. It has flat-topped clusters of small yellow or white flowers followed by seedlike fruits—the aniseed of commerce, used in food flavoring. From the seeds and sometimes from the leaves is derived anise oil (obtained also from the star anise, an unrelated woody plant). The oil, composed chiefly of anethole, is used in medicinals, dentifrices, perfumery, beverages, and, in drag hunting, to scent a trail for the dogs in the absence of a fox. The anise of the Bible (Mat. 23.23) is dill, a plant of the same family. Anisette is an anise-flavored liqueur.

Anita (ùnē'tù), town (pop. 1,233), SW Iowa, WSW of Des Moines; platted 1869, inc. 1875.

Anjou (ăn'jōō, Fr. äzhōō'), region and former province, W France, on both sides of the Loire and E of Brittany. Its chief towns are Angers, the capital, and Saumur. It occupies, roughly, Maine-et-Loire dept. A fertile lowland, it is well watered by the Loire, Mayenne, Sarthe, Loir, and Maine rivers. Chiefly an agricultural area, it has excellent vineyards which produce the renowned Vouvray and Saumur sparkling wines. Conquered first by Caesar, it fell (5th cent.) under the Franks, and became (9th cent.) a countship under Charlemagne. By the 10th cent. it was in the hands of the first line of the counts of Anjou (see ANGEVIN dynasty), who expanded their holdings vigorously. FULK NERRA acquired Saumur from the counts of BLOIS. His successor, Geoffrey Martel, won TOURAINE from Blois (1044) and Maine from Normandy (1051). FULK (d. 1143), after protracted wars with HENRY I of England over the possession of Maine, married his son GEOFFREY (Geoffrey Plantagenet) to Henry's daughter Matilda. Geoffrey ruled Anjou (1129–51) and conquered Normandy, of which he was crowned duke in 1144. His son, later HENRY II of England, married ELEANOR OF AQUITAINE and brought most of W France to England. When Henry II's grandson, ARTHUR I, duke of Brittany, rebelled against his uncle, JOHN of England, he won the support of PHILIP II of France, to whom he paid homage (1199) for Anjou, Maine, and Touraine. After Arthur's premature death, Philip II seized (1204) all Anjou; John's attempt at reconquest failed. In 1246 Louis IX of France gave Anjou in appanage to his brother Charles, count of Provence, who later also became king of Sicily and Naples (see CHARLES I). Charles II of Naples gave Anjou as dowry to his daughter Margaret when she married Charles of Valois, son of Philip III of France. When their son became (1328) King PHILIP VI of France, Anjou was again reunited to the French crown. John II of France, however, made Anjou a duchy (1360) and gave it to his son Louis (later LOUIS I of Naples). Louis XI of France inherited Anjou after the death (1480) of RENÉ, grandson of Louis I, and the death (1481) of Charles of Maine, René's brother, the last of the Angevin line. Anjou was definitively annexed to France in 1487. In the 16th cent. Anjou was held as appanage at various times; the last duke was FRANCIS of Alençon and Anjou.

Ankara (ăng′kŭrŭ, äng′kärä), city (pop. 646,151), capital of Turkey, central Anatolia. It is a completely modern city with impressive public buildings, wide streets, universities, theaters, and an opera. Known in ancient days as Ancyra and later as Angora, it was an important commercial center from Hittite times; in the 1st cent. A.D. it became the capital of a Roman province. It flourished under Augustus; in the ruins of a marble temple dating from his reign was found the *Monumentum Ancyranum*, a set of inscribed tablets valuable as a record of Augustan history. Here Tamerlane defeated and captured (1402) Sultan Bajazet I. Ankara soon after began to decline and in the early years of the 20th cent. was a small town known only for the production of mohair. In 1920 Kemal Ataturk made it the seat of his Turkish Nationalist government. In 1923 it replaced Istanbul as the capital of all Turkey, partly to break with past tradition, partly to take advantage of the central situation of Ankara. The city grew with amazing speed and is now the second largest in Turkey. Except for several mosques and the ancient citadel atop a high hill, it has few historic remains. The mausoleum of Ataturk, completed in 1935, is the outstanding modern monument.

Ankeny (ăng′kŭnē), town (pop. 2,964), central Iowa, N of Des Moines, in a farm area.

Anking (än′chǐng′), city (pop. c.105,300), SW Anhwei prov., China. The city is a port and trading center on the Yangtze river. It was formerly called Hwaining.

Anklesvar (ŭngklä′svŭr), town (pop. 77,843), Gujarat state, W India. It is the center of an oil-rich region. Ankaleshwar is another spelling.

Anmoore, town (pop. 1,050), N central W.Va., just SE of Clarksburg.

Ann, Cape, NE Mass., N of Massachusetts Bay. It is noted for its old fishing villages, resorts, and artists' colonies, especially GLOUCESTER and ROCKPORT. See Roger W. Babson and F. H. Saville, *Cape Ann* (1936).

Anna (Anna Ivanovna), 1693–1740, empress and tsarina of Russia (1730–40), daughter of Ivan V and niece of Peter I (Peter the Great). On the death of her distant cousin, Peter II, she was chosen empress by the supreme privy council, which thus hoped to gain power for itself. Anna signed articles limiting her power but she soon

Anna Ivanovna

restored autocratic rule, with support from the lesser nobility and the imperial guards. She made minor concessions to the nobles, but restored the security police and terrorized opponents. Distrusting the nobility, she excluded Russians from high positions and surrounded herself with Baltic Germans. Her favorite, BIRON, had the most influence. Allied with Emperor CHARLES VI, Anna intervened in the War of the POLISH SUCCESSION, in-

The old section of Ankara, capital of Turkey.

Countryside in Annam.

stalled Augustus III as king of Poland, and attacked Turkey in 1736. Charles's separate peace with the Turks at Belgrade forced Russia to make peace in turn, at the price of all recent conquests save Azov. During Anna's reign began the great Russian push into central Asia. Anna was succeeded by her grandnephew, Ivan VI.

Anna [Gr.,=Heb. HANNAH]. **1** Aged prophetess who hailed Jesus' presentation at the Temple. Luke 2.36–38. **2** In Tobit, the mother of young Tobias.

Anna, city (pop. 4,280), S Ill., S of Carbondale; inc. 1865. A shipping and processing center in an orchard and farm area, it also produces shoes. A state mental hospital is here.

Anna Amalia, duchess of Saxe-Weimar (ämä′lyä, zäk′sü-vī′mär), 1739–1807, German patron of letters and science; niece of Frederick II of Prussia and mother of Charles Augustus. Her court at Weimar attracted such authors as Herder, Wieland, Goethe, and Schiller. She wrote the music for Goethe's *Erwin und Elmire.*

Anna Comnena (kŏmnē′nü), b. 1083, d. after 1148, Byzantine princess and historian; daughter of Emperor Alexius I. She plotted, during and after her father's reign, against her brother, JOHN II, in favor of her husband, Nicephorus Bryennius, whom she wished to have on the throne. She failed and retired to a convent. There she wrote the *Alexiad* (finished in 1148), one of the outstanding Greek historical works of the Middle Ages. Covering the reign of Alexius I and the First Crusade, it tends to glorify her father and his family; however, Anna's familiarity with public affairs and her access to the imperial archives give her work great value. There is an English translation by Elizabeth A. S. Dawes (1928). See Georgina Buckler, *Anna Comnena* (1929).

Anna Ivanovna: see ANNA, empress of Russia.

Anna Leopoldovna (lyä″üpôl′ düvnü) or **Anna Karlovna** (kär′lüvnu), 1718–46, duchess of Brunswick-Wolfenbüttel, regent of Russia (1740–41); daughter of Charles Leopold, duke of Mecklenburg-Schwer-in, and of Catherine, sister of Empress Anna of Russia. She married the prince of Brunswick-Wolfenbüttel, and their son, IVAN VI, succeeded (1740) Anna as emperor. After the deposition of Ivan by Empress ELIZABETH, Anna Leopoldovna and her husband were imprisoned. She died in childbirth.

Annam (ŭnăm′, ă′năm″), historic region (c.58,000 sq. mi.) and former state, in central Viet Nam. In 1954, when Viet Nam was divided on a line approximately following the 17th parallel, Annam went largely to South Viet Nam. Between Tonkin on the north and Cochin China on the south, the region of Annam extends nearly 800 mi. along the South China Sea. The ridge of the Annamese cordillera separates N and central Annam from Laos on the west, then swings southeastward and runs along the coast of S Annam, which includes the plateaus that stretch to the borders of Cambodia and Cochin China. In N and central Annam there are narrow coastal plains, interrupted by spurs of mountains that almost reach the sea as at Porte d'Annam, a pass important in Annamese history. The short, often torrential rivers, flowing west to east, form deltas given over to the growing of rice, but the crop is too small to feed the population. Sugar, tea, cinnamon, and cocoa are other agricultural products; raw silk, cotton, and rubber are the chief industrial crops. There is little industry, aside from the weaving of silk and cotton and the preparation of various fish products. Annam has deposits of iron, manganese, chrome, tin, phosphates, and bauxite. The principal cities are HUÉ (the former capital), BINH DINH (the largest city), TOURANE (the chief seaport), Quangtri, and Vinh. The cities are served by a good railroad and highway system. The inhabitants of Annam are mostly fishermen and farmers. Of the various peoples, most important are the Annamese (the vast majority); others are the Chinese, the Thai, the Muong, and remnants of the Chams. The Annamese have been strongly influenced by Chinese culture. Confucian principles permeate their social structure; and although they are nominally Mahayana Buddhists, Confucian, Buddhist, and Taoist elements have been combined into a popular religion that is basically a blend of animism and ancestor worship. The origins of the Annamese state may be traced to the peoples of the Red River valley in Tonkin. After more than 2,000 years of contact with the Chinese, they fell under Chinese rule as the result of a Chin invasion c.214 B.C. and remained subject (with some interruptions after A.D. 923) until 1428, when the Annamese rose and established an independent kingdom. The region to which the Chinese gave the name Annam comprised, besides Tonkin, all of N Annam. The kingdom of the Chams, or CHAMPA, occupied S Annam from late in the 2d cent. A.D. Against the incursions of the Chams, the Chinese and later the Annamese of Tonkin fought a long series of wars, indecisive until 1472, when the Chams were defeated and the Annamese kingdom was extended southward to the vicinity of Tourane. The native Annamese dynasty, the Le line, that had overthrown the Chinese fell into decadence. In 1542, after several rebellions, the Le dynasty was defeated and by 1558 the kingdom was in effect divided between two great families, the Le line, ruling from modern Hanoi over Tonkin and Annam as far south as Porte d'Annam, and the Nguyens, ruling from Hué over Annam from Porte d'Annam to the

Annamese in a marketplace in Hué.

vicinity of Quinhon. It was to these two domains that Europeans, whose first extensive contacts with Indo-China came in the 16th cent., gave the names of Tonkin and Cochin China. In the 17th cent. the lords of Hué pushed southward, taking from the Chams the remainder of present-day Annam and penetrating the Cambodian provinces on the lower Mekong. The early 18th cent. saw their control extended into parts of Laos and, at the expense of Cambodia, to the shores of the Gulf of Siam. The dynasties of Hué and Tonkin were overthrown in the last decades of the 18th cent., but Nguyen-Anh, a Hué general, made a treaty with the French in 1787 whereby he ceded Tourane and Poulo Condore in exchange for military aid. By 1802 Nguyen-Anh had reunited all Annamese lands as the empire of Annam. He was proclaimed emperor in 1806 after the Chinese had recognized his claim. In 1807 the Annamese extended a protectorate over Cambodia, which led in succeeding years to frequent wars against Siam. After the death of Nguyen-Anh, his successor, attempting to withdraw into isolation, mistreated French nationals and Annamese Christian converts. The way was thus opened for French military operations, beginning in 1858, which resulted in the seizure of Cochin China and of Tonkin. A French protectorate over Annam was established in 1884, as well as a separate protectorate over Tonkin, both protectorates being recognized by the Chinese emperor. In 1887 Annam became part of the Union of Indo-China. In the Second World War Indo-China was occupied by the Japanese, who set up the autonomous state of Viet Nam, comprising Tonkin, Annam, and Cochin China; Bao Dai, the last emperor of Annam, was established as ruler. After the war, Annamese and Tonkinese nationalists demanded independence for the new state of Viet Nam, and Annam (like Tonkin and Cochin China) was plunged into a long series of bloody disorders (see VIET NAM).

Annandale-on-Hudson (ăn'ŭndăl–), uninc. village, SE N.Y., on the east bank of the Hudson and S of Hudson. It is the seat of BARD COLLEGE.

Annapolis (ŭnăp'ŭlĭs). **1** City (pop. 23,385), state capital, and co. seat of Anne Arundel co., central Md., on the south bank of the Severn river near its mouth on Chesapeake Bay SSE of Baltimore. The city, which contains many Colonial buildings, is a port of entry and the business and shipping center for the fruit and vegetable farmers of S Maryland. Sea food is packed, and small sea craft are built here. It was settled c.1648 as Providence by Puritans from Virginia, who successfully revolted against the Catholic governor in 1655 only to lose control after the Restoration in England. Later it was called Anne Arundel after the wife of the 2d Lord Baltimore, and in 1694, when it became the provincial capital, it was named Annapolis for Anno of England. It rapidly became an important colonial social and commercial center. The first newspaper in Maryland was published here in 1745. The town was the scene of the Annapolis convention (1786), which led to the FEDERAL CONSTITUTIONAL CONVENTION. Points of interest include the statehouse (1772), meeting place of Congress (1783) where Washington resigned as commander in chief of the Continental army; the Old Treasury (c.1695); the library (1737); SAINT

U.S. Naval Academy at Annapolis, Md.

ruins of the fort. The officers' quarters (built 1797–98) have been restored as a museum.

Annapurna (ŭn-nŭpoōr'nù), massif of the Himalayas, N central Nepal. It rises in the west to Annapurna I (26,502 ft.) and in the east to Annapurna II (26,041 ft.). Annapurna I was first climbed in 1950 by the French expedition led by Maurice Herzog. Herzog's book, *Annapurna* (Eng. tr., 1953), gives the altitude as 26,493 ft., but the figure 26,502 is based on the use of a more exact metrical conversion factor.

A member of the Herzog party during the climbing of Annapurna I in 1950.

JOHN'S COLLEGE; and the UNITED STATES NAVAL ACADEMY. **2** Uninc. village (pop. 1,472), W Wash., on an arm of Puget Sound W of Seattle.

Annapolis, river of W Nova Scotia, Canada, rising NE of Annapolis Royal and flowing into Annapolis Basin. Its valley is noted for apple orchards.

Annapolis Basin, tidal arm of the Bay of Fundy, c.25 mi. long and 3 to 5 mi. wide, W N.S., Canada. Its entrance, about a half mile wide and bordered by 500-foot cliffs, is known as Digby Gut.

Annapolis Convention, 1786, interstate convention called by Virginia to discuss a uniform regulation of commerce. It met at Annapolis, Md. With only five of the thirteen states—Delaware, New Jersey, New York, Pennsylvania, and Virginia—represented, there could be no full-scale discussion of the commercial problems the nation faced as a result of the weak central government under the Articles of Confederation. The main achievement of the convention was the decision to summon a new meeting for the express purpose of considering changes in the constitution of the Federal union to make the union more powerful. An address was drawn up by Alexander Hamilton and was sent to all the states, asking them to send delegates to Philadelphia in May, 1787. The move was extraconstitutional, but Congress passed a resolution urging attendance. The call from Annapolis was heeded and delegates from twelve states met. From this Federal Constitutional Convention was to emerge the Constitution of the United States.

Annapolis Royal, town (pop. 800), W N.S., Canada, on the Annapolis river 6 mi. above the Annapolis Basin. Founded as Port Royal by the sieur de MONTS in 1605 (see SAINT CROIX **1**), it was destroyed (1614) by the British under Samuel ARGALL but was rebuilt by the French. The fort changed hands between French and English five times from 1605 to 1710, when it finally capitulated to a force of New Englanders under Francis Nicholson. The name was then changed in honor of Queen Anne. The fort resisted attacks by French and Indians in 1744 and 1745. Fort Anne National Park (c.30 acres; est. 1917) includes the

Ann Arbor, city (pop. 67,340), co. seat of Washtenaw co., S Mich., on the Huron river and W of Detroit, in a rich fruitgrowing area; laid out 1824, inc. as a village 1833, as a city 1851. Ann Arbor grew as a farm trade center; it now makes machine tools, ball bearings, automobile parts, and cameras. The city is the seat of the Univ. of Michigan (see MICHIGAN, UNIVERSITY OF) and several museums. Indian trails crossed here, and there are several Indian mounds in the region.

Annas [Gr. for Heb. HANANIAH], Jewish high priest who examined Jesus. Nonbiblical sources say that he was retired high priest. His son-in-law was Caiaphas. John 18.13,24; Acts 4.6–22.

Annau or **Anau** (ŭnou'), village, S central Turkmen SSR, 5 mi. SE of Ashkhabad, near the Iranian border. It has a 15th-century mosque, a citadel, ancient burial mounds, and other remains. Here Raphael Pumpelly discovered (1903) traces of habitation dating back to c.3000 B.C. There are indications of ancient cultivation of grain, and beautifully designed pottery has been found. The discovery has been related to other excavations throughout central Asia. See Raphael Pompelly, *The Prehistoric Civilization of Anau* (1908).

Saint Anne, Madonna, and Child, *painting by Pinturicchio.*

Anne, Saint [ultimately from Heb. HANNAH], in tradition, mother of the Virgin and wife of St. Joa-
chim. She is not mentioned in Scripture, but her
cult is very old. In the West she has been especially
popular since the Middle Ages. She is patroness of
Quebec prov., and Ste Anne de Beaupré is one of
the most visited of New World shrines. Brittany,
also under her patronage, has the renowned shrine
of Ste d'Auray, with its pilgrimage (the pardon
of Auray). St. Anne is invoked by women in childbirth. In art, she is usually an elderly veiled
woman and often appears teaching her daughter to
read. Her name also appears as Anna. Feast:
July 26.

Anne, 1665–1714, queen of England, Scotland, and
Ireland (1702–7), later queen of Great Britain and
Ireland (1707–14), daughter of James II and Anne
Hyde; successor to William III. Reared as a Prot-
estant and married (1683) to Prince George of
Denmark (d. 1708), she was not close to her
Catholic father and acquiesced in the GLORIOUS
REVOLUTION (1688) which put William III and her
sister, Mary II, on the throne. With them she was
soon on bad terms because of private animosities,
partially caused by Anne's favorite. This woman
was her attendant and intimate friend from girl-
hood, Sarah Jennings, who had married John
Churchill (later 1st duke of MARLBOROUGH) and

who was to exercise great influence in Anne's private and public life. They addressed each other as
Mrs. Morley (Anne) and Mrs. Freeman (Sarah) to
avoid obligations of rank. Of Anne's many children
the only one to live much beyond babyhood—the
duke of Gloucester—died at the age of 11 in 1700.
Since neither she nor William had surviving children
and support for her exiled Catholic half brother
rose and fell in Great Britain (see STUART, JAMES
FRANCIS EDWARD, and JACOBITES), the question of
succession continued vexed after the Act of SET-
TLEMENT (1701) and after Anne's accession. The
last Stuart ruler, she was the first to rule over Great
Britain, which was created when the Act of Union
joined Scotland and England in 1707. Her reign,
like that of William III, was one of transition to
parliamentary government; Anne was, for example, the last English monarch to exercise (1707) the
royal veto. Domestic and foreign affairs alike
were dominated by the War of the SPANISH SUC-
CESSION, called Queen Anne's War in America (see
FRENCH AND INDIAN WARS). On the Continent the
duke of Marlborough won glory for English arms.
At home the costs of the fighting were an issue
between the Tories, who were cool to the war, and
the Whigs, who favored it. Party lines were slowly
hardening, but party government and ministerial
responsibility were not yet established; intrigues
and the favor of the queen still made and unmade
cabinets, though public opinion and elections did
have increasing influence. Thus it was at least
partly through the pressure of the Marlboroughs
that Anne was induced, despite her Tory sympathies, to oust Tory ministers in favor of Whigs.
The Marlboroughs forced the dismissal of Robert
HARLEY in 1708, though the scolding duchess had
already lost much of her power to Anne's new
favorite, the quiet Abigail MASHAM, kinswoman
and friend of Harley. When the unpopularity of
the war and the furor over the prosecution of Henry
SACHEVERELL showed the power of the Tories (who
won the elections of 1710) and made the move
feasible, Anne recalled Harley to power, and the
Marlboroughs were dismissed. Harley, created
earl of Oxford, was political leader until 1714, when
he was replaced by his Tory colleague and rival,

Queene Anne of England

Viscount Bolingbroke (see ST. JOHN, HENRY). Soon afterward the queen died, and, Jacobite plans having failed, she was succeeded by GEORGE I of the house of Hanover. Queen Anne was a dull, stubborn, but conscientious woman devoted to the Church of England and within it to the High Church party. She supported the act (1711) against "occasional conformity" and the Schism Act (1714), both directed against dissenters and both repealed in 1718. She also created a trust fund called Queen Anne's Bounty for poor clerical livings. Her reign also saw developments in the intellectual awakening that produced such thinkers as George Berkeley and Sir Isaac Newton and such scholars and writers as Richard Bentley, Swift, Pope, Addison, Steele, and Defoe. The British press grew rapidly as a political instrument. Sir Christopher Wren and Sir John Vanbrugh were at the same time setting in stone and brick the rich elegance that was perhaps the most attractive aspect of life and society under Queen Anne. See biography by M. R. Hopkinson (1934); G. M. Trevelyan, *England under Queen Anne* (3 vols., 1930–34); G. N. Clark, *The Later Stuarts* (1934).

annealing, process in which glass, metals, and other materials are treated in order to render them less brittle and make them more workable. It consists in heating and then cooling very slowly and uniformly; the time and temperatures are controlled and are set according to the properties desired. Annealing increases ductility and lessens the possibility of a failure in service by relieving internal strains. No quenching is done, as in TEMPERING.

Anne Boleyn, queen of England: see BOLEYN, ANNE.

Annecy (änsē′), town (estimated pop. 33,114), capital of Haute-Savoie dept., SE France, in Savoie, on Lake Annecy. A popular tourist resort, it also has metal and textile industries. In 1535 the bishop of GENEVA, driven out by the Reformation, made it his residence. St. FRANCIS OF SALES, who was born here, was bishop from 1602 to 1622; his memory still fills the city, which has many fine churches, monasteries, and seminaries. Annecy is now a diocese in its own right. The center of the city, traversed by narrow canals, is medieval in character. The castle of the counts of Geneva (12th–14th cent.) dominates Annecy from a hill.

Anne de Beaujeu (dù bōzhü′), c.1460–1522, regent of France. With her husband, Pierre de Beaujeu, duc de Bourbon, she acted as regent for her brother, Charles VIII, after the death (1483) of Louis XI. Preserving the royal authority, she put down the rebellious great nobles and subdued Brittany. In 1491 she and her husband arranged the marriage of Charles VIII to ANNE OF BRITTANY, and soon afterward their influence declined.

annelid: see EARTHWORM and WORM.

Annensky, Innokenty Feodorovich (ēnŭkĕn′tyē fyô′dŭrŭvĭch ŭnyĕn′skē), 1856–1909, Russian symbolist poet. A classical scholar, he translated Euripides before he began to publish verse in 1904. His highly metrical lyrics sing death, suffering, and beauty. His scant output is collected in *Quiet Songs* (1904) and *The Cypress Chest* (1910).

Anne of Austria, 1601–66, queen of France, daughter of Philip III of Spain. Married to Louis XIII (1615), she was neglected by her husband and sought the society of Mme de CHEVREUSE. She injured her reputation by unwise frivolities, especially by her flirtation with the duke of Buckingham; she was accused by Cardinal Richelieu of treasonable correspondence with Spain but was pardoned (1637). In spite of the express wish of her husband, she assumed (1643) full powers as regent for her son LOUIS XIV. She entrusted the government to MAZARIN, and her administration

Anne of Austria

was disturbed by the wars of the FRONDE. After Mazarin's death (1661), her son excluded her from participation in affairs of state. Anne of Austria is a central figure of Dumas's *Three Musketeers*.

Anne of Bohemia, 1366–94, queen consort of Richard II of England, daughter of Emperor Charles IV. She was married to Richard early in 1382 and quickly gained popularity in England. It was probably through her entourage that the writings of John Wyclif were introduced into Bohemia, where they gained much prominence through the teachings of John HUSS.

Anne of Brittany, 1477–1514, queen of France as consort of CHARLES VIII (1491–98) and of LOUIS XII (1499–1514). The daughter of Duke FRANCIS II of Brittany, she inherited the duchy in 1488. Her hand and her duchy were eagerly sought by a number of suitors. A French army under Louis de La Trémoille invaded (1488) Brittany, while Jean d'Albret, Archduke Maximilian (later Emperor MAXIMILIAN I), Louis d'Orléans (later Louis XII of France), and HENRY VII of England sent small forces to young Anne's assistance. La Trémoille was victorious, and Anne was forced to promise to marry only with the consent of the French crown. Warfare was resumed in 1489, and Anne appealed to Maximilian for protection. In 1490 Maximilian married Anne by proxy but failed to assist her with armed strength. Besieged at Rennes, Anne was forced by the French to annul her marriage, and in 1491 she was married to Charles VIII. It was agreed that if Charles died before Anne without issue, she was to marry his successor. Accordingly, in 1499, she married Louis XII, who had previously obtained a divorce from his first wife. Brittany remained theoretically separate, but the marriage (1514) of Claude, Anne's daughter by Louis XII, to

Francis of Angoulême (later Francis I of France) led to the eventual incorporation (1532) of Brittany into France. See biography by H. J. Sanborn (1917).

Anne of Cleves (klĕvz), 1515–57, queen of England, fourth wife of Henry VIII. She was the sister of William, duke of Cleves, one of the most powerful of the Protestant princes. After the death of Jane Seymour, Henry was free to marry again, and a marriage with Anne for political purposes was considered advisable and was especially forwarded by Thomas CROMWELL. The marriage was agreed upon in 1539. Although Henry tried to break the contract after seeing his bride, they were married in Jan., 1540. Henry found Anne dull and unattractive, and a turn in policy destroyed the political utility of the marriage. In July, Henry had the marriage declared null and void. Anne gave her consent and, by agreement, lived the rest of her life in England.

Anne of Denmark, 1574–1619, queen consort of James I of England, daughter of Frederick II of Denmark and Norway. She married James in 1589 and was crowned with him at Windsor in 1603. Court entertainments and the embellishment of buildings interested her more than affairs of state. Although not openly a Catholic, Anne attended Mass privately and refused communion in the Church of England. Of her six children, the three who survived infancy were Henry, prince of Wales (d. 1612); Charles (later Charles I); and Elizabeth (later electress palatine and queen of Bohemia).

annexation, formal act by which a state asserts its sovereignty over a territory newly incorporated within its dominions. Many varieties of territories have been subject to annexation, chief among them those uninhabited by civilized peoples, those inhabited by settlers of the annexing power, those which already have the status of protectorates of the annexing state, and those conquered by the force of arms. The governing body of the annexing power must ratify the act of annexation, and the consent of other interested powers must be obtained in order that the annexation be generally recognized in international law. The full exercise of the annexing power's sovereignty is the final objective test of the validity of annexation. Objections of philosophers such as Kant and efforts to establish the self-determination of inhabitants as the only grounds for the transfer of territory have been realized in the Charter of the United Nations which does not recognize annexation as an instrument of national policy. In America, the annexation of Texas by the United States in 1845 led to war with Mexico.

Anniston, city (pop. 33,657), co. seat of Calhoun co., NE Ala., ENE of Birmingham, in a mining region of the Appalachian foothills. Founded in 1872 as an iron-manufacturing "company town," it was opened for settlement in 1883. It manufactures iron, steel, wood, textile, chemical, and concrete products. The town of West End Anniston (pop. 5,485) is adjacent to Anniston. Nearby are a fish hatchery and U.S. Fort McClellan.

annual, plant that germinates, blossoms, and dies within one growing season. Annuals propagate themselves by seed only, as distinguished from biennials and perennials. They are thus especially suited to environments that have a short growing season. Cultivated annuals are usually considered to be of three general types: tender, half-hardy, and hardy. Tender and half-hardy annuals do not mature and blossom in one ordinary temperate growing season unless they are started early under glass and are set outdoors as young plants. Hardy annuals are usually sown where they are expected to bloom. Quite often they reseed themselves year after year and in effect become perennials. Blooming is prolonged by cutting the flowers before the seeds can form. Typical annual flowers are species of cosmos, larkspur, petunia, and zinnia; annual vegetables include corn, tomatoes, and wheat. See F. F. Rockwell and E. C. Grayson, *The Complete Book of Annuals* (1955).

annuity: see INSURANCE.

annulment of marriage: see NULLITY OF MARRIAGE.

Annunciation of the Virgin: see MARY.

Annunzio, Gabriele D': see D'ANNUNZIO, GABRIELE.

anode: see ELECTRODE and ELECTROLYSIS.

anodyne: see SEDATIVE.

Anoka (ùnō′kù), city (pop. 10,562), co. seat of Anoka co., E Minn., on the Mississippi at the confluence of the Rum, NNW of Minneapolis; settled 1844, laid out 1853, inc. 1878. Originally a trading post and lumber town, it grew as a farm trade center and resort. Ammunition and metal products are made. A state mental hospital is here.

Anopheles: see MOSQUITO.

Anouilh, Jean (zhä′ änōō̃ē′yù), 1910–, French dramatist. His various plays have contemporary,

Jean Anouilh

historical, or classical settings. A favorite theme is the bitter contrast between the world of romantic dreams and that of grotesquely harsh reality; however, while disclosing the indignity of the human situation Anouilh still maintains the dignity of man. Among his works are *Antigone* (1944; New York, 1946), *The Waltz of the Toreadors* (1952; New York, 1957), *The Lark* (1953; New York, 1955); and *Becket* (1959; New York, 1960). See study by L. C. Pronko (1961).

Anquetil Duperron, Abraham Hyacinthe (äbrä-äm′ yäsĕt′ äkùtĕl′ düpĕrō̃′), 1731–1805, French Orientalist. While studying for the priesthood (which he did not enter), he became deeply interested in Eastern languages. After study (1755–61) in India, chiefly with the Parsis, he returned to Europe with 180 manuscripts and a knowledge of Sanskrit, Avestan, Pahlavi, and Persian. His three-volume translation of the *Zend-Avesta* (1771) introduced Zoroastrian texts to Europe. It was bitterly criticized by Sir William Jones and other scholars in England. Anquetil Duperron also translated the *Upanishads* into Latin and wrote works on India.

Ansbach (äns'bäkh), city (pop. 33,237), Federal Republic of Germany, W Bavaria, on the Rezat river. It manufactures cars, motors, chemicals, and plastics. Now the capital of Middle Franconia, the city developed around an 8th-century Benedictine abbey. It became the residence of the Franconian branch of the Hohenzollern in 1331. It passed to Prussia in 1791 and to Bavaria in 1806. The 12th-century Romanesque Church of St. Gumbertus was rebuilt in the 15th cent. Formerly the name appeared as Anspach.

Anschar or **Anscharius, Saint:** see ANSGAR, SAINT.

Anschluss: see AUSTRIA.

Anselm, Saint (än'sĕlm), 1033?–1109, Italian prelate, archbishop of Canterbury, Doctor of the Church (1720), b. Aosta, Piedmont. After a carefree youth of travel and schooling in Burgundy he became disciple and companion of LANFRANC, famed theologian and prior of the monastery at BEC which Anselm soon joined (1060). Anselm became prior (1063) and abbot (1078) and brought widespread fame to the school there. Monastic holdings in England threw him into English public life, and he won the esteem of William the Conqueror. He was a frequent visitor to Lanfranc at Canterbury, and when the latter died, Anselm succeeded him as archbishop (1093). He disputed the right of WILLIAM II to invest him, reserving this for the pope, URBAN II, whom William refused to recognize. With the support of loyal barons, Anselm momentarily overcame the king's intransigence and took the pallium from Urban's legate. Anselm's further reform-minded efforts to free the Church from secular control met stiff resistance. When he went to Rome for support, William banished him and confiscated the diocesan properties. At the Council of Bari (1098) Anselm ably defended the *Filioque* of the CREED in the East-West controversy on the Procession of the Holy Spirit. The new king, HENRY I, recalled Anselm, who proved valuable in arranging Henry's marriage to Matilda of Scotland and in gaining the support of the barons for the king in his dispute with Robert of Normandy. Conflict over lay INVESTITURE broke out afresh, however, and Anselm refused to consecrate bishops and abbots nominated by the king. He was again banished while appealing in Rome. Anselm eventually (1107) won Henry's agreement to surrender the right of investiture in exchange for homages from Church revenues—a compromise that in effect established papal supremacy in the English Church. Many consider this Anselm's greatest achievement. His writings mark him as the founder of scholasticism. A strict Augustinian, operating from the formula *fides quaerens intellectum* (faith seeking understanding), he believed in an essential harmony between revelation and reason. He was the first to incorporate successfully the rationalism of Aristotelian dialectics into theology. Though he wrote no great Summa, his precision together with his mystical insight give permanent value to such works as *Cur Deus Homo?* (1094–98), on the ATONEMENT. He constructed rational proofs for God's existence in *Monologium* (c.1070), and in the sequel *Proslogium* he advanced his famous ontological proof which deduces God's existence from man's notion of a perfect being in whom nothing is lacking. In *De Fide Trinitatis* he defended universals against the nominalist ROSCELIN. He taught the immaculate conception of Mary in *De Conceptu Virginali* and is said to have instituted that feast in England. Feast: April 21. See biography by Joseph Clayton (1933).

Ansgar, Saint (äns'gär), 801–65, Frankish missionary to Scandinavia, called the Apostle of the North. He was the first archbishop of Hamburg (from 831). Other forms of the name are Anskar, Anschar, and Anscharius. Feast: Feb. 3. See C. H. Robinson, *Anskar, the Apostle of the North* (1921).

Anshan (än'shän'), city (pop. c.600,000), central Liaoning prov., China, on a branch of the South Manchurian RR. An iron and steel center, it has China's largest steel mill and several plants. It was developed as a metallurgical center largely by the Japanese, who occupied the region. The Russians dismantled much of the mill between 1944 and 1946, but by 1956 the mill and plants had been rebuilt.

Anshun (än'shoon'), town (pop. c.805,000), W central Kweichow prov., SW China. It is noted for its coal deposits.

Anskar, Saint: see ANSGAR, SAINT.

Ansley, Clarke Fisher, 1869–1939, American teacher and editor, b. Swedona, near Springfield, Ill., grad. Univ. of Nebraska, 1890. After teaching English at Nebraska, he was professor of English at the State Univ. of Iowa (1899–1917) and dean of its College of Fine Arts (1911–15). Having turned to editing, he conceived the idea of a one-volume general encyclopedia, compact enough and simply enough written to serve as a guide to the "young Abraham Lincoln." This work was started in 1928 as *The Columbia Encyclopedia* with Ansley as its editor in chief. Both the first edition (1935) and the first supplement (1938) were completed under his direction.

Anson, Adrian Constantine, 1851–1922, American baseball player-manager, known usually as "Cap" or "Pop" Anson, b. Marshalltown, Iowa. For most of his career he played with the Chicago club of the National League and was four times league batting champion. As manager (1879–97), he led the team to five pennants. In 1939 he was elected to the National Baseball Hall of Fame; his lifetime batting average was .339.

Anson, George Anson, Baron, 1697–1762, British admiral. In his famous voyage (1740–44) around the world, Anson, in spite of shipwrecks and scurvy, inflicted great damage on Spanish shipping and returned to England with a rich prize. He was raised to the peerage after his popular naval victory (1747) off Cape Finisterre. Appointed then as first lord of the admiralty, he assisted William Pitt, Lord Chatham, in reorganizing naval administration. See *A Voyage round the World* (comp. by Richard Walter, rev. ed., 1911); biographies by M. V. Anson (1912) and S. W. C. Pack (1960).

Anson, Sir William Reynell, 1843–1914, English jurist. He was a founder of the school of law at Oxford Univ. From 1899 to his death he sat in Parliament as a member for Oxford. His *Principles of the English Law of Contract* (1879) and *The Law and Custom of the Constitution* (1886–92) are frequently consulted standard works. See memoir ed. by H. H. Henson (1920).

Anson. 1 Town (pop. 2,252), central Maine, on the Kennebec W of Skowhegan; inc. 1798. Wood products are made. **2** City (pop. 2,890), co. seat of Jones co., W central Texas, NNW of Abilene; settled c.1880, inc. 1904. Formerly a cow town, today it is primarily a shipping point for cotton and other crops, with cotton gins and some small industries. Oil wells and a refinery are in the area. To the southeast are the ruins of Fort Phantom Hill, a frontier outpost built in 1851.

Ansonia. 1 City (pop. 19,819), SW Conn., on the Naugatuck and NW of New Haven; settled from Derby 1651, inc. 1893. It is coextensive with Ansonia town, which was incorporated in 1889. It has manufactures of copper, brass, and other metals. **2** Village (pop. 1,002), W Ohio, N of Greenville, in a rich farm area; inc. 1885.

Ansted, town (pop. 1,511), S W.Va., SE of Charleston; settled 1790. It is the trade center for a mining region. Hawks Nest State Park is near.

Anstey, F., pseud. of **Thomas Anstey Guthrie,** 1856–1934, English author, b. London. He relinquished his law practice to write humorous fiction. His best and most successful works were marked by an atmosphere of fantasy and include *Vice Versa* (1882), *The Tinted Venus* (1885), and *The Brass Bottle* (1900). Besides translating several comedies of Molière, he wrote the play *The Man from Blankley's*, successfully produced in 1901. See his autobiography, *A Long Retrospect* (1936).

ant, any of the 2,500 species of insects constituting the family Formicidae of the order Hymenoptera, to which the bee and the wasp also belong. Ants are cosmopolitan in distribution. All species show some degree of social organization. The body is divided into three distinct regions; the narrow front part of the abdomen, called the waist or pedicel, is characteristic. Ants are usually black or various shades of brown, red, or yellow. North American species nest in a system of galleries in the soil, often under a dome of excavated earth, sand, or debris; in cavities in dead wood or in living plant tissue; in papery nests attached to twigs and rocks; and in buildings and sometimes in ships. Colonies range from a few dozen to half a million or more individuals, consisting of fertile females or queens, winged males, and wingless, infertile females that may be workers, soldiers, or members of other specialized castes. Those ordinarily seen are worker ants. Shortly after the annual mating flight the male dies, and the fertilized queen, now capable of laying continuously for the rest of her life (up to 15 years), returns to earth to establish a colony. She bites or scrapes off her wings, excavates a chamber, and rears her brood, feeding the innumerable curved, legless white larvae from her own mouth. These offspring are workers, which enlarge the nest and care for the queen and the following generations. The life span of a worker ant is from 4 to 7 years. In some species the queen cannot establish the colony herself and is adopted by workers of her own or another species. Slave-making ants, which are unable to feed themselves, raid the nests of other species and carry off larvae

The ponerine ant, a carnivore, is indigenous to the southern United States and Central America.

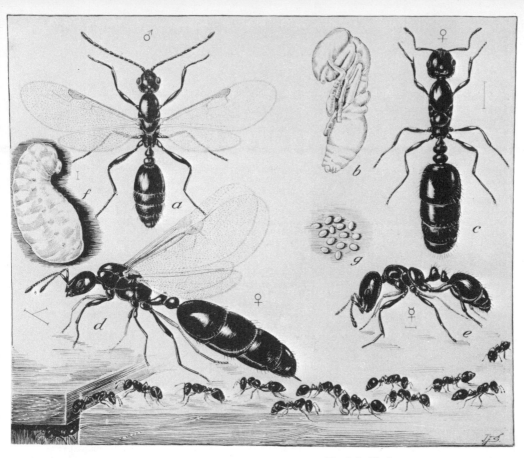

The little black ant. a. male; b. pupa; c. female; d. female with wings; e. worker; f. larva; g. eggs; (all greatly enlarged). Below, a group of workers in line of march (about three times actual size).

or pupae to serve as workers. Adult ants may be herbivorous, carnivorous, or omnivorous. They are fond of the honeydew excreted by the APHID and other small insects, which they feed and protect. House pests among the ants include Pharaoh's ant, a common, small, yellowish species; the odorous house ant; the Argentine ant, found in warmer climates; the little black ant; and the black carpenter ant, a biting species that damages timbers. The black pavement ant gnaws at roots and steals seeds. The mound-building ant makes large anthills. The agricultural ants, some of which are called leaf cutters, parasol ants, fungus growers, and harvester ants, are widely distributed pests numerous in the warmer regions. The Texas leafcutting ant, a serious crop pest, feeds on a fungus cultivated on macerated leaf tissue in its underground nest. In tropical America and Africa are found the carnivorous, nomadic army or driver ants, which travel like armies in long columns, overrunning anything in their path. The sting of the red ant and others is due to the presence of FORMIC ACID. The TERMITE is miscalled white ant. See publications of the U.S. Dept. of Agriculture; W. M. Wheeler, *Ants* (1910); J. S. Huxley, *Ants* (1930); C. P. Haskins, *Of Ants and Men* (1939); Wilhelm Goetsch, *The Ants* (Eng. tr., 1957).

Antaeus (ăntē'ùs), in Greek mythology, giant; son of Poseidon. He became stronger whenever he touched the earth, his mother, GAEA. He killed everyone with whom he wrestled until Hercules overcame him by lifting him in the air.

Diagram of an anthill and tunnels built by ants that feed on honeydew produced by corn root aphids.

Antakya: see ANTIOCH, Turkey.

Antalcidas (ăntăl'sĭdùs), d. after 371 B.C., Spartan diplomat. The agent of Sparta in Persia, he managed to undermine Athenian influence there and persuaded Artaxerxes II to agree to the so-called Peace of Antalcidas or King's Peace (386 B.C.), but the terms were those of the Persian king. Cyprus and the Greek cities in Asia Minor were returned to Persia; other Greek city-states were to be independent. Although Athens was allowed to retain the islands of Imbros, Lembros, and Scyros, Athens suffered from the terms of the peace. The treaty was much criticized as ignominious for Greece. Sparta used the terms to justify arrogant action against other city-states, thus bringing on the Spartan defeat at LEUCTRA in 371 B.C.

Antalya (äntälyä'), city (pop. 50,963), capital of Antalya prov., SW Turkey, on the Mediterranean Sea. It is a seaport and textile center and has a small shipbuilding industry. Nearby are chrome and manganese deposits. Founded in the 2d cent. B.C. by Attalus II, king of Pergamum, it was known as Attaleia or Attalia, and later as Adalia. It is mentioned in Acts 14.25 as the port whence Paul and Barnabas sailed to Antioch. It passed under Seljuk control in the 13th cent. and in the 15th cent. was attached to the Ottoman Empire. Situated on a steep cliff, Antalya is a picturesque town surrounded by an ancient wall. Nearby are the ruins of many ancient cities.

Antar (äntär'), fl. 600, Arabian warrior and poet, celebrated in his own day as a hero, for he rose from

Glacier of Mt. Erebus on Ross Island in Ross Sea, Antarctica.

slave birth to be a tribal chief. His poetry is represented by one poem in the MUALLAQAT. He is the hero of the popular Arabic *Antar*, a romance which has developed over centuries. He has become in it the ideal of a Bedouin chief, rich, generous, brave, and kind. His name also appears as Antara.

Antarctica (ănt″ärk′tĭkù), continent, area between 5,000,000 and 6,000,000 sq. mi., surrounding the South Pole. The waters about the continent are sometimes called the Antarctic Ocean but actually are only the southernmost parts of the Atlantic, Pacific, and Indian oceans. The seas, whipped by cold, violent winds and clogged with drifting ice, ice packs, and mountainous icebergs, also show extreme and rapid variability that makes them doubly dangerous to navigation. The continent was therefore completely unknown until modern times and is still imperfectly known although rapid strides have been made in acquiring knowledge of this region. Its roughly circular outline is broken by two deeply indenting seas, Ross Sea on the Pacific side and Weddell Sea on the Atlantic side, and by a long narrow land projection, the Palmer Peninsula, which stretches toward South America, some 600 mi. away. The other southernmost lands, Africa and Australia and New Zealand, are much farther away, and the great southern continent is isolated by distance as well as difficulty of access. The coasts are protected from intruders by belts of pack ice, sometimes hundreds of miles wide, and by hanging ice shelves, which end in sheer ice cliffs 50 to 200 ft. high. These ice barriers and the glaciers that come from the mountains and thrust tongues of ice into the sea "calve," making enormous icebergs (many 30 mi. or more long). Beneath the ice shelves there are some small islands, but Antarctica has only a few large islands, and those are near the Palmer Peninsula. Off the tip of the peninsula are the South Shetlands. The South Orkneys in the Atlantic and Macquarie in the Pacific are farther away. The Falklands, which show antarctic conditions, lie closer to South America. The term "Antarctic Archipelago" was originally a misnomer given to the Palmer Peninsula (and the adjacent land) under the impression that it was an island; part of the string of islands off the peninsula is still sometimes called the Antarctic Archipelago but is now more usually called the Palmer Archipelago. Antarctica itself is upheaved in giant mountain ranges, some with peaks rising over 15,000 ft. high. The central area is a high plateau hidden under a perpetual ice cap. Almost all of the continent (with an estimated average altitude of 6,000 ft., almost twice that of any other continent) is, indeed, covered by a vast ice sheet. In recent years glaciologists have reported that this ice mass is becoming larger in contrast to the ice mass in the arctic regions. It has unassailably the severest climate on earth, with winter temperatures dropping to −70°F. and even −80°F. and in the brief, unthawing antarctic summers temperatures remain an average of 15°F. lower than those of the ARCTIC REGIONS. In broad general plan the two ends of the earth are in truly antipodal contrast—in the north a circumpolar landlocked sea; in the south a circumpolar ocean-surrounded land mass. From this difference comes the much more intense cold in the

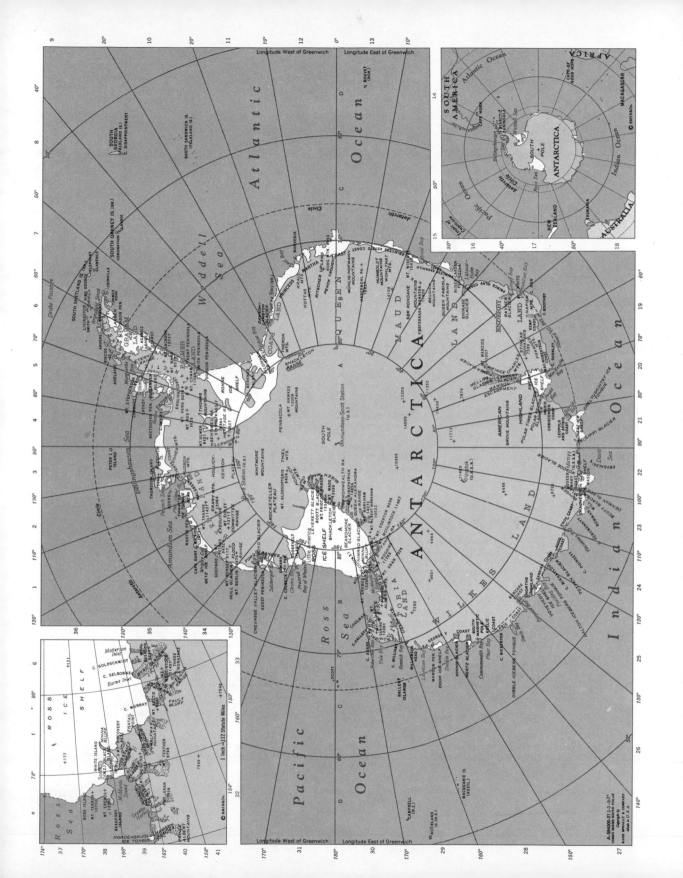

Coast of Macquarie Island in the South Pacific Ocean, the base of the Mawson polar expedition.

south and the graver dangers and difficulties of exploration.

History of Exploration. Although there was for centuries a tradition that another land lay south of the known world, attempts to find it were defeated by the ice. Navigators—notably Capt. James Cook in 1774—made their way into antarctic waters, and the British mariner William Smith discovered the South Shetlands in Feb., 1819, and confirmed his discovery the following autumn. The discovery of Antarctica itself came as a by-product of the search by whalers for new whaling grounds, or sealers for seal rookeries, although the question as to who made it is still in some dispute. An American, Capt. Nathaniel PALMER, in Nov., 1820, sighted an unknown coast. He told the Russian voyager, Admiral Bellingshausen, who, speaking of it to others, called it Palmer's Land. An Englishman, Capt. Edward Bransfield, sailed between the South Shetlands and the continent in Jan., 1821, and probably saw the continent. In 1830 another Englishman, John BISCOE, sighted high mountains; two years later he landed on an island and, thinking it part of the mainland, called it and the nearby peninsula Graham Land. Hence the double name for the peninsula which Americans call Palmer Peninsula and the British call Graham Land. The British also question Palmer's log and consider either Bransfield or Biscoe the discoverer. The voyages of James Weddell, John Balleny, Dumont d'Urville, Charles Wilkes, and James C. Ross followed in the first half of the 19th cent. That of Ross was important in opening the Ross Sea approach. For nearly a half century then interest in polar exploration concentrated on the arctic region. A renewed turn to the south was marked by the explorations of the Belgian, Adrien de Gerlache, in 1897–99; his expedition was the first to winter in the area of Antarctica. As the 20th cent. began, scientific interest quickened and led to a number of well-equipped expeditions, notably those of C. E. BORCHGREVINK, William BRUCE, Erich von DRYGALSKI, Otto Nordenskjold, Robert F. SCOTT, Jean

B. CHARCOT, and Sir Douglas MAWSON; all these wintered in the Antarctic. Extensive scientific surveys were made. Several expeditions were fired by the desire to reach the South Pole; E. H. SHACKLETON failed (1908–9), but Roald AMUNDSEN succeeded (Dec. 14, 1911), to be followed almost immediately (Jan. 18, 1912) by Robert F. Scott. Considerable knowledge of the interior of Antarctica was gained, but the First World War interrupted the search. When interest was resumed, the airplane provided a new method of exploration, with George Hubert WILKINS and Richard E. BYRD as the pioneers. The years just before and after 1937 were highly productive, with the British expedition (1934–37) under John Rymill, the Norwegian expedition (1936–37) of Lars Christensen, the fourth antarctic journey (1938–39) of Lincoln ELLSWORTH, and the voyage (1937–39) of the British *Discovery II*, on the fifth of her two-year commissions to investigate the distribution and the feeding grounds of whales. In 1939–40 the U.S. Antarctic Service, with Richard E. Byrd in command, pursued research from two bases 2,000 mi. apart, one (see LITTLE AMERICA) on the Bay of Whales (an inlet of Ross Sea), the other on Palmer Peninsula. A British expedition under J. W. S. Moor in 1944 evolved plans for systematic study of the peninsula and the mainland coast, including the establishment of meteorological stations. In the years 1946–48 knowledge of Antarctica was tremendously increased by three U.S. expeditions. The U.S. navy's "Operation Highjump," led by Byrd, was by far the largest, most completely organized, and most thoroughly mechanized expedition ever sent to Antarctica. It involved 12 navy vessels, airplanes, a submarine, and many scientists and experts, as well as some 4,000 navy officers and men. Achievements were commensurate with its size. Topographical knowledge was greatly broadened by exploratory flights, recorded by moving pictures. Unfrozen areas were found, especially a warm-lake region in the quadrant toward Australia; a bay or inland sea some 20,000 sq. mi. in area was discovered; many new lofty peaks were noted; and islands under the Ross ice shelf were indicated by the magnetometer. Photomapping clarified old knowledge and added new. Photographs, specimens, and data were brought back to the United States for analysis. A smaller naval expedition in 1947–48 supplemented the work by further photomapping, by more investigation of the warm-lake region, and by obtaining tons of mineral specimens. The expedition (1946–48) led by Finn Ronne centered at the

Dog team near Little America base camp on Ross ice shelf.

Admiral Byrd in camp during "Operation Highjump."

base of the Palmer Peninsula and cooperated with the British Falkland Islands Dependencies Survey. Many discoveries were made, including a mountain range running SE from the Palmer Peninsula to the high, snow-covered central plateau, which was shown to be a continuation of the Andes. Ronne also discovered a new island in the area of the Weddell Sea. It was demonstrated that the theory that a strait between Ross Sea and Weddell Sea cuts Antarctica is almost certainly false. In 1947 Australia sent an official expedition into the antarctic regions. Chile and Argentina, the USSR, Norway (cooperating with Britain and Sweden), and Japan all showed interest in Antarctica in the years after the Second World War. The wide range of national interest reflects a similarly wide range of conflicting claims to antarctic territory. The latent strife of opposing national interests was demonstrated by the tension caused in 1939 when German aviators dropped flags at various points on the coast. The various claims on Antarctica cut the continent and its surrounding waters like pieces of a pie that has as its circumference the circle of lat. 69° S. Beginning at long. 20° W and reading clockwise, the claims are: Norway, long. 20° W–45° E (Queen Maud Land); Australia, long. 45° E–

160° E (Australian Antarctic Territory), except for the Adélie Coast (French) between long. 136° E and 142° E; New Zealand, long. 160° E–150° W (Ross Dependency); officially unclaimed but explored by U.S. expeditions, long. 150° W–90° W; and the area of overlapping claims—Chile, long. 90° W–53° W, Argentina, long. 74° W–25° W, and Great Britain, long. 80° W–50° W south of lat. 58° S and long. 50° W–20° W south of lat. 50° S. The USSR, while making no specific claims, insists upon Russian rights by reason of Bellingshausen's work. The United States recognizes no claims in Antarctica and makes no official claims, although U.S. explorers have dropped flags on areas they have explored.

Developments in the '50s and '60s. In the 1950s there was intensified study and exploration of Antarctica. In 1956 occurred the first known airplane landing and the first parachute jump at the South Pole, as well as the first U.S.–Antarctica telephone call. During the International Geophysical Year (1957–58), some 30 countries participated in antarctic studies, and great knowledge was gained. As part of the IGY program the United States established a number of stations and observation sites here ("Operation Deepfreeze"); Admiral Richard E. Byrd was placed in command. Great Britain sponsored (1955–58) the Trans-Antarctic Expedition, led by Sir Edmund Hillary and Sir Vivian Fuchs; both Hillary and Fuchs reached the South Pole. Accomplishments during the IGY included the delineation of the physical features of Antarctica; the discovery of a huge mountain range, the Pensacola Mts., which rise 5,000 ft. above the ice sheet; and explorations of over 14,000 mi. of previously unexplored land. In 1961 the United States undertook the largest scientific research program ever conducted in the antarctic. In 1959 a treaty, proposed by the United States, was accepted by 12 nations (including the United States and the USSR) whereby each country agreed to keep any possible warfare out of Antarctica and to preserve the area for scientific research. This treaty, which was ratified by the United States in 1960, recognized no existing national claims to any sectors of Antarctica. One of the usual requisites for establishing claims to a territory—that of settlement—had, heretofore, proved impossible. In 1951, however, the French established the first permanent human settlement in Antarctica by establishing a base at Adélie Land. The **antarctic regions** are definitely not friendly to man. Though the Antarctic Circle is drawn the same distance (23° 30′ of latitude) from the South Pole that the Arctic Circle is from the North Pole, the area of antarctic weather conditions is much greater than that of arctic weather conditions. The cold is intensified by the incredibly strong winds that blow mainly outward from the central plateau of Antarctica and drive the melting shore ice and the great icebergs to sea and extend the area of cold to lat. 50° S. While the arctic regions have a rapid and varied summer vegetation, some year-round and abundant summer animal life, and human inhabitants, the antarctic regions have only mosses, lichens, and algae as vegetation, no year-round land animal life except a wingless insect about ½ in. long and microscopic organisms, and no native human inhabitants. What other animal life there is relies on the sea and is found only in the sea and directly on the coast. There are, however, a surprising number of birds: the emperor penguin is the only year-round resident, but Adélie penguins and smaller birds are summer visitors. In that season whales and seals also arrive. Many scientists say, however, that Antarctica may have been tropical or temperate millions of years ago and may again be habitable millions of years from now. A Norwegian-English expedition, based in Queen Maud Land, found (1950–52) evidence of primitive forms of animal life. Various regions of Antarctica have been found to contain deposits of valuable minerals. A vast coal field was discovered in the area of the South Polar Plateau, and in 1959 the USSR discovered and explored a mountain

wilderness in Queen Maud Land which was found to be rich in iron, mica, and graphite. Classic narratives of antarctic exploration include Robert F. Scott, *The Voyage of the "Discovery"* (1905) and *Scott's Last Expedition* (1913); E. H. Shackleton, *The Heart of the Antarctic* (1909); Roald Amundsen, *The South Pole* (Eng. tr., 1913); Sir Douglas Mawson, *The Home of the Blizzard* (1915); Richard E. Byrd, *Little America* (1930) and *Discovery* (1935); Sir Vivian Fuchs and Sir Edmund Hillary, *The Crossing of Antarctica* (1958); Finn Ronne, *Antarctic Conquest* (1949) and *Antarctic Command* (1961). For more general studies, see Otto Nordenskjold and Ludwig Mecking, *The Geography of the Polar Regions* (Eng. tr., 1928); J. Gordon Hayes, *Antarctica* (1928) and *Conquest of the South* (1932); Andrew Croft, *Polar Exploration* (rev. ed., 1947); U.S. Board on Geographical Names, *The Geographical Names of Antarctica* (1947); Thomas Henry, *The White Continent* (1951); John Giaever, *The White Desert* (1955); Lord Mountevans, *The Antarctic Challenged* (1956); Walter Sullivan, *Quest for a Continent* (1957); Paul Siple, *90° South* (1960); Laurence Kirwan, *A History of Polar Exploration* (1960); Emil Schulthess, *Antarctica* (1960); Frank Debenham, *Antarctica* (1961).

Antares (ăntâr′ēz) [Gr.,=similar to Mars, i.e., in color], red STAR in the constellation Scorpio. A rare supergiant, Antares is one of the brightest and largest stars known. It is c.220 light years from the earth and is c.250,000,000 mi. in diameter.

anteater, name applied to various animals which feed on ants, termites, and other insects, but more properly restricted to a completely toothless group of the order Edentata. There are three genera, all found in tropical Central and South America. The great anteater or ant bear (*Myrmecophaga*) has an elongated, almost cylindrical head and snout, a sticky tongue about 12 in. long, a coarse-haired body about 4 ft. long, and a long, broad tail. The large, sharp claws on the forefeet are weapons of defense and are used to open the hard earth mounds of termites. The collared or lesser anteater (*Tamandua*), less than half the size of the great

One of the ships of the U.S. Task Force 68 heads home from the Bay of Whales.

anteater, is a short-haired yellowish and black arboreal creature. The arboreal two-toed anteater (*Cyclopes*) is the size of a squirrel and has a prehensile tail and silky yellow fur. The banded anteater of Australia is a marsupial; the spiny anteater, also of Australia, is related to the platypus. For the scaly anteater, see PANGOLIN.

antelope, name applied to a large group of hoofed ruminant mammals of the order Artiodactyla. They are usually included in the family Bovidae but are in some classifications considered a separate family, Antilopidae. The true antelopes are confined to Africa and Asia. Their unbranched horns, unlike the antlers of the deer, are not shed and consist of a hollow chitinous shell with a bony core. Africa is the home of most antelopes, including the bushbuck, waterbuck, lechwe, marshbuck, impala or palla, kudu, nyala, springbuck, bongo, dik-dik, klipspringer, ELAND, and GNU. The GAZELLE is a small delicate antelope. Native to India are the nilgai or blue bull, the four-horned antelope, and the black buck; the saiga lives on the steppes of S Russia and in central and W Asia, and the chiru in Tibet. The hunting of antelopes for their flesh, hide, and horns has greatly reduced their numbers, some to the verge of extinction. Many are protected in Kruger National Park, Transvaal, and in other reserves. See also PRONGHORN and ROCKY MOUNTAIN GOAT.

antelope brush, low, deciduous shrub (*Purshia tridentata*) of the ROSE family, widely distributed in the W United States, where it is a characteristic constituent of the vegetation on arid slopes and desert ranges. One of the most important Western browsing plants, it provides abundant forage throughout the year for both cattle and deer.

antenna (ăntĕn′ù) or **aerial** (âr′ēŭl), in radio, a system of wires or metal bars used to project or intercept radio waves. The idea of using an antenna was developed by Guglielmo Marconi (c.1897). The antenna has a frequency characteristic based on the relationship between its physical dimensions and the wave length of the signal, i.e., a wire of a given length is inherently tuned to a radio wave that is a simple fraction of that length. While any straight vertical conductor will serve as an antenna, a horizontal antenna will radiate and intercept the greatest amount of energy at right angles to itself. This quality enables transmitters to concentrate their signals into desired areas. In receivers this same quality enables selection of one of several signals having the same frequency but arriving from different directions. Vacuum-tube and receiving-circuit improvements and the introduction of the loop antenna have eliminated the need for an external antenna in most locations. For high frequencies, however, such as television, frequency modulation, and radar, antennas designed to meet specific circuit requirements are still necessary.

Antenor (–tē′nŭr), in Greek mythology, wise elder of Troy who urged that Helen be returned to Menelaus. The Greeks spared him and his family when they sacked Troy. A later myth portrays Antenor as a traitorous spy who opened the door of the wooden horse. Agenor was his son.

Antenor, fl. last half of 6th cent. B.C., Greek sculptor, who executed the bronze statues of Harmodius and Aristogiton. In 480 B.C. Xerxes carried these

South American anteater

Large male sable antelope from Africa.

statues away from Athens, but they were discovered later at Susa by Alexander and sent back. A marble figure of a woman, signed on the base by this artist, was found in the ruins of the Acropolis at Athens.

Antequera (äntäkä′rä), city (pop. 43,576), Málaga prov., S Spain, in Andalusia. At the foot of the Sierra de los Torcales, it is the center of a fertile agricultural region. The Cueva de Menga, a large prehistoric burial chamber, was discovered in the vicinity in 1842.

Antequera y Castro, José de (hōsā′ dā äntäkä′rä ē kä′strō), 1690–1731, leader of a revolt in Paraguay. A Peruvian lawyer and prosecutor of the *audiencia* of Charcas, he was sent to Asunción to probe charges against the governor of Paraguay, Diego de los Reyes. Antequera sided with the opposition, became governor himself, and upheld the celebrated doctrine that "the authority of the people is superior to that of the king." He led the uprising of the COMUNEROS in a war against the authority of the viceroy and was finally captured and beheaded in 1731. This first struggle for freedom was the forerunner of the Spanish American revolts against Spain.

Anteros: see EROS.

anthem [ultimately from ANTIPHON], short nonliturgical choral composition used in Protestant services, usually accompanied and having an English text. The term is used in a broader sense for "national anthems" and the Latin motets still used occasionally in Anglican services. A full anthem is entirely choral, while a verse anthem includes parts for solo singers. It arose in the Anglican Church, as the English counterpart of the Latin motet, at the hands of Christopher Tye (c.1500–1573), Thomas TALLIS, and William BYRD (c.1543–1623). Early anthems were often in the style of Latin motets, sometimes being merely an English text set to well-known motets. In the late 17th cent. composers such as Henry Purcell and John Blow, under Italian influences, wrote verse anthems with several movements, as in cantatas. G. F. Handel's anthems, in the tradition of the full anthem, are, like those of Purcell and Blow, too elaborate for ordinary church use. Since the 19th cent. extracts from oratorios, masses, Passions, etc., are commonly used as anthems, but these pieces are no longer anthems in the original sense of the term. See M. B. Foster, *Anthems and Anthem Composers* (1901); Ernest Walker, *A History of Music in England* (3d rev. ed. by J. A. Westrup, 1952).

anthemion (ănthē'mĕŭn), commonly called a palmette, a radiating, fan-shaped motive or ornament suggestive of a palm leaf or of honeysuckle and found in Egyptian, Assyrian, and Aegean art. It was profusely used by the Greeks and Romans on their buildings and on all sorts of decorative objects.

Anthemius of Tralles (ănthē'mēŭs, trăl'ĕz), 6th cent., Greek architect, engineer, and mathematician. By order of Emperor Justinian and with the aid of Isidorus of Miletus, he built (532–37) the Church of HAGIA SOPHIA in Constantinople.

anthology, collection of selected literary pieces of varied authorship. The name literally means "gathered flowers" and was first given to the GREEK ANTHOLOGY. Although it usually contained short, choice poems or epigrams, in modern times an anthology has come to include all forms of literary composition.

Anthon, Charles, 1797–1867, American classical scholar, b. New York city, grad. Columbia, 1815. He taught at Columbia College from 1820 to his death and was also rector (1830–64) of Columbia Grammar School. His editions of classical texts were among the first American editions to have notes and explanations for study. He issued editions of Sir William Smith's classical dictionaries and also compiled one of his own, based on a French original.

Anthony, Saint (ăn'tŭnē, ăn'thŭnē), 251?–c.350, Egyptian hermit, called St. Anthony of Egypt and St. Anthony the Abbot. At 20 he became a hermit, and at 35 he went into seclusion. At this time he experienced, says tradition, every temptation the devil could devise, but he repelled them. A colony of hermits grew up about him, and after 20 years he emerged to rule them in a community, the monks being in solitude except for worship and meals. After a few years he went away to the desert near Thebes, where he lived most of the rest of his long life. St. Anthony was the father of Christian MONASTICISM; his community became a model, particularly in the East, but he did not write the rule ascribed to him. His type of community is seen in the West among the Carthusians. He is a patron of herdsmen. St. ATHANASIUS wrote his life. The temptation of St. Anthony has inspired works of literature, particularly a novel by Flaubert, and early became a popular theme in Western art. Feast: Jan. 17.

Anthony, Marc: see ANTONY.

Anthony, Susan Brownell (ăn'thŭnē), 1820–1906, American reformer and leader of the woman-suffrage movement, b. Adams, Mass.; daughter of Daniel Anthony, Quaker abolitionist. From the age of 17, when she was a teacher in rural New York, she agitated for equal pay for women teachers, for coeducation, and for college training for girls. When the Sons of Temperance refused to admit women into their movement, she organized the first women's temperance association, the Daughters of Temperance. At a temperance meeting in 1851 she met Elizabeth Cady Stanton, and from that time until Mrs. Stanton's death in 1902 they were associated as the leaders of the woman's movement in the United States and were bound by a warm personal friendship. Susan B. Anthony lectured (1851–60) on women's rights and on abolition, and, with Mrs. Stanton, secured the first laws in the New York state legislature guaranteeing to women rights over their children and control of property and wages. In 1863 she was a coorganizer of the Women's Loyal League to support Lincoln's government, especially his emancipation policy. After the Civil War she opposed granting suffrage to freedmen without also giving it to women, and many woman-suffrage sympathizers broke with her on this issue. She and Mrs. Stanton organized the National Woman Suffrage Association. In 1890 this group united with the American Woman Suffrage Association to form the National American Woman Suffrage Association, of which Miss Anthony was president from 1892 to 1900. In 1872 she led a group of women to the polls in Rochester, N.Y., to test the right of women to the franchise under the terms of the Fourteenth Amendment. Her arrest, trial, and sentence to a fine (which she refused to pay) were a *cause célèbre;* other women followed her example until the case was decided against them by the Supreme Court. From 1869 she traveled and lectured throughout the United States and Europe, seeing the feminist movement gradually advance to respectability and political importance. The secret of her power, aside from her superior intellect and strong personality, was her unswerving singleness of purpose. With Elizabeth Cady Stanton and Matilda Joslyn Gage, she compiled Volumes I to III of the *History of Woman Suffrage* (1881–86), using a personal legacy to buy most of the first edition and present the volumes to colleges and universities in the United States and Europe. The *History* was completed by Ida Husted Harper (Vols. IV–VI, 1900–1922; Susan B. Anthony contributed to Vol. IV). See biographies by R. C. Dorr (1928), Katharine Anthony (1954), and Alma Lutz (1959).

Anthony (ăn'thŭnē). **1** City (pop. 2,744), co. seat of Harper co., S Kansas, SW of Wichita near the Okla. line; laid out 1878, inc. 1879. **2** Town (pop. 1,082), extreme W Texas, NNW of El Paso, on the N.Mex. line.

Anthony of Padua, Saint, 1195–1231, Portuguese Franciscan, b. Lisbon. He was renowned for his eloquence. In a vision he received the child Jesus in his arms, and he is usually represented thus in art. He was known as a preacher and for his holy life and was canonized the year after he died in Padua. He has a reputation as a miracle worker and is popularly invoked by Roman Catholics to find lost articles. Pope Pius in 1946 declared him a Doctor of the Church. Feast: June 13. See biography by Mary Purcell (1960).

anthracene (ăn'thrŭsēn), solid organic compound derived from coal tar. The molecule of anthracene is composed of 14 carbon atoms and 10 hydrogen atoms. When pure, it is colorless and has a violet fluorescence. Its melting point is 218°C. and its boiling point at normal barometric pressure is 342°C. It is insoluble in water, but quite soluble in carbon disulfide and and less soluble in alcohol, methyl alcohol, benzene, chloroform, and other solvents. Anthracene darkens in sunlight. The molecular structure is composed of three BENZENE rings fused together side by side. Anthracene is an important source for manufacturing such substances as anthraquinone and ALIZARIN dyes. It is the first member of the **anthracene series** of aromatic hydrocarbons, which are related structurally and include naphthacene. In the molecule of each member of the series the number of hydrogen atoms is always 18 less than twice the number of carbon atoms.

anthracite: see COAL.

anthrax, acute infectious disease caused by the anthrax bacillus. The bacilli affect animals primarily (anthrax has been epidemic among cattle); they may be transmitted secondarily to man. Transmission normally occurs through contact but also through breathing of germ-laden air. Individuals who handle hides of animals (e.g., farmers, butchers, and veterinarians) or sort wool are particularly susceptible; anthrax is therefore included among the occupational diseases. Pustules occur commonly on the hands, face, and neck; the bacilli may also cause lesions in the lungs and the brain. To prevent contagion, hides and wool which may carry the anthrax spores are disinfected. Pure cultures of the anthrax bacillus were obtained in 1876 by Robert KOCH, who demonstrated the relationship of the microbe to the disease; confirmation of the bacillus as the cause of anthrax was provided by PASTEUR, who also developed a method of vaccinating sheep and cattle against anthrax. A cell-free vaccine has been produced for treating anthrax in man. Sulfonamides and antibiotics have also proved effective.

anthropology (ănthrŭpŏl'ŭjē) [from Gr. *anthropos* = man], classification and analysis of man and society, descriptively, historically, and physically. Its unique contribution to studying the bonds of man's social relations has been the distinctive concept of CULTURE. It has also differed from other sciences concerned with man and his behavior (especially sociology) in its emphasis on data from nonliterate peoples and archaeological exploration. Emerging as an independent science in the late 18th and early 19th cent., anthropology was associated from the beginning with various other emergent sciences, notably biology, geology, linguistics, psychology, and archaeology. Its rise is also linked with the philosophical speculations of the Enlightenment about the origins of human society and the sources of myth. A unifying science, anthropology has not lost its connections with any of these branches, but has incorporated all or part of them and often employs their techniques and conclusions. It is divided primarily into physical anthropology and cultural anthropology. Physical anthropology deals basically with the problems of human evolution, including human paleontology and the study of RACE and of body build or constitution (somatology). It uses the methods of ANTHROPOMETRY, as well as those of genetics, physiology, and ecology. Cultural anthropology includes ARCHAEOLOGY, which studies the material remains of prehistoric and extinct cultures; ethnography, the descriptive study of living cultures; ETHNOLOGY, which utilizes the data furnished by ethnography, the recording of living cultures, and archaeology, to analyze and compare the various cultures of mankind; social anthropology, which evolves broader generalizations based partly on the findings of the other social sciences; and LINGUISTICS, the science of language. Applied anthropology is the practical application of anthropological techniques to areas such as colonial administration, industrial relations, and minority-group problems. In Europe the term anthropology usually refers to physical anthropology alone. See A. L. Kroeber, *Anthropology* (1948); Clyde Kluckhohn, *Mirror for Man* (1949); R. L. Beals and Harry Hoijer, *Introduction to Anthropology* (1953); Melville J. Herskovits, *Cultural Anthropology* (1955); Ralph Linton, *The Tree of Culture* (1955); Felix M. Keesing, *Cultural Anthropology* (1958); John J. Honigmann, *The World of Man* (1959); Mischa Titiev, *Introduction to Cultural Anthropology* (1959); Morton H. Fried, ed., *Readings in Anthropology* (2 vols., 1959); Margaret Mead and R. L. Bunzel, ed., *The Golden Age of American Anthropology* (1960); J. B. Hoyt, *Man and the Earth* (1962).

anthropometry (ănthrŭpŏm'ŭtrē), technique of measuring the human body in terms of dimensions, proportions, and ratios such as those provided by the cephalic index. Once the standard approach to racial classification, it has been replaced by genetic interpretations and the study of environmental influences (see ECOLOGY). The anthropometrical method contributed to the development of statistical analysis. It is now applied to studies of growth and constitution. See Ashley Montagu, *A Handbook of Anthropometry* (1960).

anthropomorphism (ăn"thrŭpomôr'fĭzŭm) [Gr.,= having human form], in religion, conception of divinity as being in human form. The ascription of human forms to gods as well as to the divine spirits of things such as the winds and the rivers, events such as war and death, and abstractions such as love, beauty, strife, and hate is widespread in time and place. As used by students of religion and anthropology the term is applied to certain systems of religious belief, inevitably polytheistic. Although some degree of anthropomorphism is characteristic of nearly all polytheistic religions, it is perhaps most widely associated with the Homeric gods and later Greek religion. Anthropomorphic thought is said to have developed from three primary sources: animism, legend, and the need for visual presentation of the gods. In Christianity the term *anthropomorphic* is derogatory, used in accusing some sects of naïve and nonspiritual views of God.

Antibes (ăntēb'), town (estimated pop. 27,064), in Alpes-Maritimes dept., SE France, on the RIVIERA. A seaport, it exports oranges and olives and is the center of a great flower-growing region. It was founded as a Greek colony (Antipolis) in the 4th cent. B.C. A fortified port, it still has the 16th-century Fort Carré. There are Roman ruins south of the port. Antibes is popular with tourists, and nearby is the fashionable resort Cap d'Antibes.

antibiotic (ăn″tēbīŏ′tĭk), chemical substance usually obtained from microorganisms that tends to inhibit the growth of or destroy certain other microorganisms. That a microorganism is capable of destroying one of another species was first observed by Pasteur, who pointed out that this action might be put to therapeutic use. The phenomenon of microbial antibiotic action was observed by other scientists later, notably by Metchnikoff, but it had no practical application until René J. DuBOS demonstrated at the Rockefeller Institute in New York city that a soil bacterium was capable of decomposing the starchlike capsule of the pneumococcus, without which the pneumococcus is harmless and does not cause pneumonia. Dubos then found in the soil (1939) a microbe, *Bacillus brevis*, from which he obtained a substance (tyrothricin) that was highly effective against a wide range of bacteria. Tyrothricin was found to be toxic to red blood and reproductive cells but could be used to good effect when applied externally. Although Sir Alexander Fleming first observed in 1928 that *Penicillium notatum*, a common mold, had destroyed staphylococcus in culture, no practical method of extracting the active agent, penicillin, was found until 1938. Even by 1942, with large-scale research taking place on both sides of the Atlantic, there was only enough of the drug to treat 15 wounded men in the British army. The U.S. War Production Board took over the task of manufacturing penicillin in realization of the fact that its role in the war effort could be of utmost importance. Soon the supply became ample, first as a natural extraction and later in synthetic form. Although penicillin was effective against many bacteria and many diseases, there were also many on which it had no action. A search for other antibiotic substances was begun. In 1943 Selman A. Waksman discovered streptomycin (derived from a moldlike bacterium, *Streptomyces griseus*), used to treat tularemia, forms of tuberculosis, and other diseases. Chloromycetin, produced from *Streptomyces venezuelae*, is used in typhoid fever, typhus, and other infections. Aureomycin (*Streptomyces aureofaciens*) is successful in the treatment of undulant fever, amebic dysentery, pneumonia, Rocky Mountain spotted fever, and typhus fever. Antibiotic drugs include terramycin, chloramphenicol, and many others, and the search for still others continues. The antagonistic action of an antibiotic need not depend on its ability to destroy completely its adversary; any action that interferes with the life processes of a microorganism is just as effective therapeutically as total destruction. The indiscriminate use of antibiotics, preva-

Culture of Penicillium chrysogenum yields the antibiotic penicillin.

Each lot of antibiotics is laboratory-tested before being shipped to market.

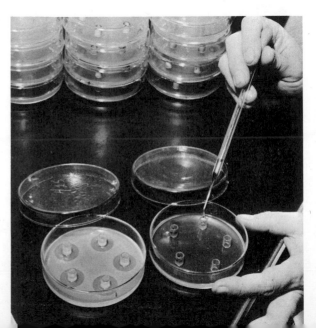

lent at first, then waned. Almost all antibiotics may cause reactions in some persons that it is undesirable to risk except in the face of a serious infection. Furthermore, resistant strains of organisms emerge when these drugs are used for trivial causes so that they become ineffective when a greater need for them arises. Used wisely and cautiously, their benefits to mankind are immeasurable. See S. A. Waksman, *Microbial Antagonisms and Antibiotic Substances* (1945); Samuel Epstein and Beryl Williams, *Miracles from Microbes* (1946).

antibody, specific substance elaborated by the tissues when the body is invaded by a foreign agent. These foreign agents, or antigens, may be bacteria, bacterial toxins, viruses, or foreign proteins. Antibodies are designed to perform specific duties so that one type of antibody will not be effective against any antigen except the one that stimulated its formation. Antibodies may be agglutinins, antitoxins, or bacteriolysins, but whatever their mode of action, if present in sufficient quantity, they combat the agents of disease or confer IMMUNITY before the disease can establish itself. See also ANTITOXIN.

Antichrist (ăn′tĭkrīst), in Christian belief, a person who will represent on earth the powers of evil by opposing Christ, glorifying himself, and causing many to leave the faith. He will be destroyed by Christ at the time of the Second Coming. Similar ideas are expressed in Zoroastrianism. Christians have often identified enemies of their faith with the Antichrist; e.g., with early Christians it was Nero, with some Protestants the pope. 1 John 2.18–22; 4.3; 2 John 7; Rev. 13.

Anti-Comintern Pact: see COMINTERN and AXIS.

Anti-Corn-Law League, organization formed in 1839 to work for the repeal of the English CORN LAWS. It was an affiliation of groups in various cities and districts with headquarters at Manchester and was an outgrowth of the smaller Manchester Anti-Corn-Law Association. Richard COBDEN and John BRIGHT were its leading figures. See Norman McCord, *The Anti-Corn-Law League, 1838–1846* (1958).

Anticosti (ăntĭkŏs′tē), low, flat island (pop. 532), 135 mi. long and 10 to 30 mi. wide, E Que., Canada, at the head of the Gulf of St. Lawrence NE of the Gaspé Peninsula. The island was discovered by Cartier in 1534. Louis XIV granted it to Jolliet as a reward for his discovery of the Mississippi, and his heirs held it until 1763, when it was annexed to Newfoundland. It was returned to Canada in 1774 and has been privately owned since 1895. Lumbering for pulpwood is the chief occupation on the island.

anticyclone [opposite of a cyclone], area of high barometric pressure from which the air moves spirally outward into areas of lower pressure. The air is deflected by the earth's rotation according to Ferrel's law (clockwise in the Northern Hemisphere, counterclockwise in the Southern Hemisphere). The atmosphere in an anticyclone is characterized by clear skies, low humidity, and lack of precipitation. In the United States, anticyclones, or "highs," move in a general easterly direction.

antidote: see POISON.

"Soldiers" monument, Antietam Battlefield Site, Sharpsburg.

Antietam campaign (ăntē′tŭm), Sept., 1862, of the Civil War. After the second battle of BULL RUN, Gen. R. E. LEE crossed the Potomac to invade Maryland and Pennsylvania. At Frederick, Md., he divided (Sept. 10) his army, sending Stonewall Jackson to capture the large Union garrison at Harpers Ferry and thus clear his communications through the Shenandoah Valley. With the remainder, Lee marched NW toward Hagerstown. Gen. G. B. McCLELLAN learned of this division of forces and moved to attack. In the battle on South Mt. (the Blue Ridge N of the Potomac, 12 mi. W of Frederick) on Sept. 14, 1862, McClellan defeated Lee's rear guard and took the passes of that range. Lee then fell back to Sharpsburg (c.9 mi. W of South Mt.), where his position lay behind Antietam Creek. On Sept. 15 the Harpers Ferry garrison capitulated to Jackson, who, with part of his command, joined Lee before McClellan attacked. The battle of Antietam (or Sharpsburg) opened on the morning of Sept. 17. Early assaults on Lee's left were bloody but indecisive, and McClellan failed to press the slight Union advantage with his available reserves. In the afternoon Burnside's corps crossed the Antietam over the bridge on Lee's right and drove the Confederates back, but A. P. Hill's division arrived from Harpers Ferry and repulsed the attack. The battle was not renewed. On Sept. 18–19 Lee recrossed the Potomac into Virginia unmolested. The fighting at Antietam was so fierce that Sept. 17, 1862, is said to have been the bloodiest single day of the war with some 23,000 dead and wounded, evenly divided between the sides. It was a Union victory only in the sense that Lee's invasion was stopped. McClellan has been blamed for not pursuing Lee with his superior forces. The scene of the battle of Antietam has been set aside as a national battlefield site (183.63 acres; est. 1890). See K. P. Williams, *Lincoln Finds a General* (Vol. II, 1950).

Anti-Federalists, in American history, opponents of the adoption of the Federal Constitution. Leading Anti-Federalists included George Mason, Elbridge Gerry, Patrick Henry, and George Clinton. Later, many of the Anti-Federalists opposed the policies of the FEDERALIST PARTY and of Alexander HAMILTON. See J. T. Main, *The Anti-Federalists: Critics of the Constitution* (1961).

antifreezing solution, nonfreezing solution commonly used in the cooling systems of internal-combustion engines expected to operate in temperatures below the freezing point of water. Such solutions include ethanol (ethyl alcohol), methanol (methyl alcohol), and ethylene glycol. A desirable antifreezing solution should not corrode metal parts, attack rubber, or become viscous at low temperatures. Rather, it should remain freely liquid at below freezing yet show little evaporation at ordinary temperatures. Most commercial antifreezing solutions contain an inhibitor to prevent rust—a necessary measure if the cooling system is to operate efficiently.

antifriction metal, ALLOY used in BEARINGS when ball or roller bearings are not used. Tin, antimony, lead, zinc, and copper in various combinations and proportions are used to make antifriction metals such as BABBITT METAL and white metal.

antigen: see ANTIBODY.

Antigo (ăn'tĭgō), city (pop. 9,691), co. seat of Langlade co., NE Wis., NE of Wausau; settled 1876, inc. 1885. Dairy and wood products are made.

Antigone (ăntĭ'gùnē), in Greek legend, daughter of Oedipus. She followed her father in his banishment and disgrace. When her brothers Eteocles and Polynices killed each other in the war of the SEVEN AGAINST THEBES, Creon, King of Thebes, forbade the burial of the rebel Polynices. Antigone disobeyed his command and performed the funeral service. In Sophocles' *Antigone* she hangs herself in the tomb where Creon ordered her buried alive. In a later version of the story, she is rescued by Creon's son and sent to live among the shepherds.

Antigonish (ăn″tĭgōnĭsh'), town (pop. 4,344), NE N.S., Canada, on the West River near its mouth and NE of Truro. It was settled by the French in 1763, by the English in 1784. The town is known for its cooperative movement, promoted by SAINT FRANCIS XAVIER UNIVERSITY.

Antigonus I (Antigonus Cyclops) (ăntĭ'gùnùs sī'-klŏps), 382?–301 B.C., general of ALEXANDER THE GREAT and ruler in Asia. He was made (333 B.C.) governor of Phrygia, and after the death of Alexander he was advanced by the friendship of ANTIPATER, who with PTOLEMY I and CRATERUS, supported Antigonus in 321 against PERDICCAS and EUMENES. In the wars of the DIADOCHI, Antigonus was the leading figure because he seems to have had the best chance to re-create Alexander's empire. He had control of Asia Minor, Syria, and Mesopotamia at the time (316) when Eumenes was murdered. His great power, however, ultimately

caused LYSIMACHUS, SELEUCUS I, and Ptolemy I to unite against him. Antigonus' son, Demetrius Poliorcretes (later DEMETRIUS I of Macedon), was an able agent in the bid to build the empire by invading Greece, and Antigonus defeated (306) Ptolemy, but both Antigonus and Ptolemy were conquered at the battle at Ipsus (301). Antigonus was killed.

Antigonus II (Antigonus Gonatas) (gōnā'tùs), c.320–239 B.C., king of Macedon, son of Demetrius I. He took the title king on his father's death but made good his claim only by defeating the Gauls in Thrace and by taking Macedon in 276. His rule was very troubled; PYRRHUS attacked him, and so did Ptolemy II. A confederation of Greek cities headed by Athens waged (c.266–c.262 B.C.) the so-called Chremonidean War against him. Antigonus won the war, captured Athens, and restored the Macedonian state. However, the Achaean League, under Aratus, gained power c.251. Nevertheless Antigonus maintained himself and for a brief period united Greece. He was himself a philosopher and a patron of philosophy and poetry. Upon his death he was succeeded by his son, DEMETRIUS II.

Antigonus III (Antigonus Doson) (dō'sŏn,–sùn), d. 221 B.C., king of Macedon. On the death of Demetrius II he became regent for Demetrius' son Philip (PHILIP V). He married the widow of Demetrius, and in 227 he proclaimed himself king. The attacks of CLEOMENES III on the ACHAEAN LEAGUE caused its leader, Aratus, to request help from Antigonus, and he led his troops south in 224. In 222 he crushed Cleomenes at Sellasia in Laconea and took Corinth as his reward. Meanwhile he had reconstituted the Hellenic League, and when he died he left power in Greece as well as Macedon to Philip.

Antigua (ăntē'gwù, Span. äntē'gwä) or **Antigua Guatemala** (gwätùmä'lù, Span. gwätämä'lä) [Span.,=Old Guatemala], town (pop. 16,500), S central Guatemala. Founded in 1542 by survivors from nearby CIUDAD VIEJA, which had been destroyed by flood and earthquake, Antigua became the capital of Spanish Guatemala. In the 17th cent. it flourished as one of the richest capitals of the New World, rivaling Lima and Mexico city; by the 18th cent. its population had increased to c.100,000. Its university was a center of the arts and learning, and its churches, convents, monasteries, public buildings, and residences were characterized by massive luxury. Antigua, dominated by the volcanoes AGUA, (12,310 ft. high), Acatenango (12,982 ft. high), and Fuego (12,854 ft. high), was continually subject to disaster from volcanic eruptions, flood, and earthquake. In 1773 two earthquakes leveled the city. The Spanish captain general ordered (1776) the removal of the capital to a plain supposedly free from earthquakes and there founded GUATEMALA city. Antigua is now a major tourist center with many fine Spanish colonial buildings. It is also the commercial center of a rich coffee-growing region.

Antigua (ăntē'gù, ăntē'gwù), island, area 108 sq. mi., British West Indies. In the LEEWARD ISLANDS, it is the principal island of the Antigua presidency (pop. c.57,000), with SAINT JOHN'S as the capital. It is hilly with a much-indented coast.

Antigua, island in the British West Indies.

Island dependencies of the presidency are Barbuda (62 sq. mi.) and Redonda (1 sq. mi.). The climate is equable, and the islands are a popular resort for hunters and fishermen. Chief products are sugar, molasses, and cotton. Discovered by Columbus in 1493, Antigua was ignored until the British established a settlement in 1632. For a short time in 1666 the French occupied it, but it was almost immediately returned to the British. The island joined (1958) the short-lived Federation of the West Indies, and was a member of the Leeward Islands colony until the colony was dissolved in 1959. In 1940 the United States was granted the right to operate defense bases under a 99-year lease.

Antigua Guatemala: see ANTIGUA OR ANTIGUA GUATEMALA.

antihistamine, any substance that reduces the physiological effect of HISTAMINE in tissues excepting those substances that act by producing a physiological effect opposite to and independent of the histamine.

Anti-Lebanon, anc. *Anti-Libanus,* Arabic *Jebel esh-Sharqi,* mountain range between Syria and Lebanon, rising to Mt. HERMON. It is noted for its forests of oak, pine, cypress, and juniper. The name also appears as Anti-Liban.

Antilles: see WEST INDIES.

Antilochus (ăntĭ′lŭkŭs), in Greek mythology, young hero of the Trojan War, a favorite of Achilles. While protecting his father, Nestor, he was killed by Memnon. He was buried with Achilles and Patroclus.

Anti-Masonic party, American political organization which rose after the disappearance in W New York in 1826 of William Morgan. A former Mason, he had written a book purporting to reveal Masonic secrets. The Masons were said, without proof, to have murdered him, and in reaction local organizations arose to refuse support to Masons for public office. In New York state Thurlow WEED and William H. SEWARD attempted unsuccessfully to use the movement, which appealed strongly to the poorer classes, to overthrow Martin VAN BUREN and the ALBANY REGENCY. Anti-Masonry spread from New York to neighboring states and influenced many local and state elections. At Baltimore, in 1831, the Anti-Masons held the first national nominating convention of any party and issued the first written party platform—innovations followed by the older parties. The vote for their presidential candidate, William WIRT, mostly hurt Henry Clay. Usually the Anti-Masons in national politics acted with the NATIONAL REPUBLICAN PARTY in opposition to Jacksonian democracy, and in 1834 they helped to form the WHIG PARTY. See W. B. Hesseltine, *The Rise and Fall of Third Parties* (1948).

antimatter, matter comprising the antiparticles that are counterparts of the elementary particles of ordinary matter. For example, the antiparticle of the ELECTRON, the positron, has the same mass but an equal and opposite electrical charge. Antimatter is extremely rare in the vicinity of the earth, but antiparticles have been found among the decay products of cosmic rays, and they also are produced artificially. Most antiparticles are extremely short-lived, since they react with ordinary particles to annihilate each other. The positron, the positively charged antiparticle of the negative electron and the first antiparticle to be discovered, was predicted by QUANTUM THEORY (Dirac's relativistic theory of the electron, 1928) and found in cloud-chamber photographs of cosmic-ray action by Carl D. ANDERSON in 1932. Pair production, the conversion of a photon into a positron and an electron, and induced radioactive disintegration of light nuclei, e.g., by boron and aluminum, are sources of positrons. The annihilation of a positron and an electron produces two or three photons. Such annihilation may be preceded by the formation of a neutral "atom": a positronium. Because of the difference in electrical charge, the magnetic moment of the positron is opposite to that of the electron. Similarly, the positively-charged PROTON has an antiparticle of almost equal mass but opposite charge and magnetic moment, the antiproton. The NEUTRON and antineutron have no charge, but equal and opposite magnetic moments. An antiproton or antineutron and a proton or neutron annihilate to produce several pi mesons. So far as is known, the NEUTRINO has no mass, charge, or magnetic moment, but it does have an antiparticle, the antineutrino, which plays a different but symmetrical part in beta decay and the decay of pi mesons. The antineutrino is long-lived, since both it and the neutrino have only a very small tendency to react with anything, including each other. It is believed that every elementary particle has a corresponding antiparticle, and it is possible that there exists a universe, or even a part of the known universe, in which antimatter predominates over ordinary matter and forms atoms and molecules.

antimetabolite: see METABOLITE.

antimony (ăn'tĭmō"nē), metallic element (symbol= Sb [Latin *stibium*]; in group V A of the PERIODIC TABLE; for physical constants, see ELEMENT, table). The common allotropic form (see ALLOTROPY) is metallic in appearance but displays properties of both a metal and a nonmetal. It unites with hydrogen to form stibine, a poisonous gas. With oxygen it forms several compounds, a trioxide, a tetroxide, and a pentoxide. The trioxide when heated with the bitartrate of potassium yields tartar emetic. Antimony unites directly with the halogens and combines with sulfur. It is employed in making alloys including BRITANNIA METAL, TYPE METAL, BABBITT METAL, and sometimes PEWTER. Because it expands upon solidification, it makes good castings. It is employed also in the preparation of battery plates, in the vulcanizing of special rubber, and in paints and explosives. Its compounds have long been used in medicine, e.g., TARTAR EMETIC. It is mixed with soot to make kohl, used by Eastern women as an eye cosmetic. Antimony rarely occurs free in nature, but its ores are widely distributed. The chief commercial source of the element is STIBNITE, a sulfur compound known since early times. A method for the extraction of antimony from it was first described in the works of BASILIUS VALENTINUS. Although known to the ancients, the element itself was not adequately described until the beginning of the 18th cent.

Stibnite, the black mineral sulfide ore of antimony.

by LÉMERY. Antimony may be detected in compounds by the MARSH TEST.

Antin, Mary, 1881–1949, American author, b. Polotsk, Russia, educated at Columbia Univ. She emigrated to the United States in 1894 and married Amadeus Grabau in 1901. She is known for her writings on the immigrant, notably *The Promised Land* (1912).

antineutrino and **antineutron:** see ANTIMATTER.

antinomianism (ăntĭnō'mēŭnĭzŭm) [Gr.,=against law], the belief that Christians are not bound by the moral law, particularly that of the Old Testament. The idea was strong among the Gnostics, especially MARCION. Certain heretical sects in the Middle Ages practiced sexual license as an expression of Christian freedom. In the Protestant Reformation theoretical antinomian views were maintained by the Anabaptists and Johann Agricola. Anne Hutchinson was persecuted for supposed antinomianism. The sixth chapter of Romans is the usual refutation for antinomianism.

Antinoüs (ăntĭ'nōŭs), c.110–130, favorite of Em-

Antinoüs

peror Hadrian, b. Bithynia. He was with the emperor constantly until on a journey in Egypt he was drowned in the Nile—some say in saving Hadrian's life. His beauty was legendary, and Hadrian mourned him greatly, had him deified, founded the city of Antinoöpolis in Egypt in his honor, and seems to have renamed the youth's birthplace Antinoöpolis. A cult was inaugurated in his honor, coins were struck with Antinoüs' head on them, and many busts and statues were made.

Antioch (ăn'tēŏk), town of ancient Phrygia, near the Pisidian border. The site is north of the present Antalya, Turkey. It was founded by Seleucus I and became a center of Hellenistic influence. It was visited by St. Paul. Acts 13.14; 14.21; 2 Tim. 3.11.

Antioch or **Antakya** (äntäkyä'), Turk. *Antakya*, city (pop. 45,848), capital of Hatay prov., S Turkey, on the Orontes river, at the foot of Mt. Silpius and near the sea. It was founded c.300 B.C. by Seleucus I near two already existing Greek colonies and was named for his father; the population was largely Macedonian. Lying at the crossing of routes from the Euphrates to the sea and from El BIKA to Asia Minor, it soon grew into one of the largest commercial centers and most sumptuous cities of the world. It was occupied by Pompey in 64 B.C., and soon became the largest and most important Roman city in the region. Various emperors built great temples, a forum, a theater, baths, aqueducts, and many other public buildings. The two main streets, at right angles to each other, were lined with marble colonnades and adorned with temples, palaces, and statues. Except for the remains of a thick wall, there is little of the old city visible today. It was here that the followers of Jesus were first called Christians after having severed themselves from the synagogue (see Acts 11.26; 13.1). Antioch is one of the three original patriarchates (see PATRIARCH). Aurelian, who recovered it from Shapur I of Persia, erected more magnificent buildings and churches. It was a great center of Christian learning and played a significant role in the theological controversies of the early Christian church (see CHRISTIANITY). St. John Chrysostom estimated the population (4th cent.) at 200,000. In 540 Antioch fell to the Persians, and in 637 to the Arabs. Nicephorus II reconquered it (969) for the Byzantine Empire, but in 1085 it fell, through treason, to the Seljuk Turks. The army of the First Crusade (see CRUSADES) laid siege to Antioch in 1097 and conquered it in 1098. BOHEMOND I was made prince of Antioch. His principality, which extended from Iskenderun southward beyond Latakia, was one of the most powerful of the Crusaders' states. In 1108 Bohemond was forced to recognize Emperor Alexius I of Byzantium as his suzerain, but the Byzantines could not long enforce

their claims and Bohemond's successors held Antioch as a virtually independent fief from the Latin Kingdom of Jerusalem. After its fall (1268) to the Mamelukes of Egypt, Antioch declined; in 1516 it was conquered by the Ottoman Turks. The city was occupied by French troops in 1919, and attached to the French-mandated territory of Syria. In 1939 it was restored to Turkey with the sanjak of ALEXANDRETTA. The city has suffered many severe earthquakes; the most destructive in recent times was in 1872. Modern Antioch occupies but a fraction of the ancient city. Excavations begun in 1935 at Antioch and at its ancient suburban resort, Daphne, have yielded splendid mosaics (1st–6th cent. A.D.)—mostly copies of lost paintings—and many other important remains. An earlier find was the Great Chalice of Antioch (see CHALICE), held by many to be the Holy Grail. Many of the archaeological finds are housed in a modern museum.

Antioch. 1 City (pop. 17,305), W Calif., on the San Joaquin and NE of Oakland; founded 1849–50, inc. 1872. It is a processing center in a farm region. **2** Summer resort village (pop. 2,268), NE Ill., near the Wis. line NNW of Chicago, in a lake region; settled 1836, inc. 1857. Chinaware and metal furniture are made.

Antioch College, at Yellow Springs, Ohio; coeducational; chartered 1852, opened 1853. Horace Mann, Antioch's first president, envisioned a program stressing not merely the development of the intellect, but of the whole personality, especially the individual's social conscience and competence.

Outskirts of Antioch, Turkey.

Great Chalice of Antioch, excavated in 1910.

This goal was not realized until the presidency of Arthur E. Morgan in 1921. Through the cooperative work-study program the college years are divided between off-campus work and on-campus study, both full time. This system usually requires five years. Students are given an important voice in community government, college policy formulation, and other administrative affairs. Also, Antioch maintains its own foreign study program. In conjunction with the Universities of Guanajuato (Mexico), Besançon (France), and Tübingen (Germany), Antioch Centers for University Education have been established. Antioch students in different programs, however, attend other foreign schools. On campus the Fels Research Institution for studying human development, the Charles F. Kettering Foundation for studying solar energy, and other experimental and research centers employ noncollege scientists, students, and teachers.

Antiochia Margiana: see MERV.

Antiochus I (Antiochus Soter) (ăntĭ′ŭkŭs sō′tŭr), b. c.324 B.C., d. c.262 or 261 B.C., king of Syria (280–261? B.C.), son of SELEUCUS I. He did not, like his father, seek to expand in Europe. The Seleucid holdings were much reduced, particularly

Antiochus I

by the Egyptians under Ptolemy II. He was a great founder of cities.

Antiochus II (Antiochus Theos) (thē′ŏs), d. 247 B.C., king of Syria (261?–247 B.C.), son of Antiochus I. In warfare with Ptolemy II he had varied fortune, but his marriage to Ptolemy's daughter Berenice sealed the peace, and Antiochus was confirmed in most of the Syrian possessions his father

had lost. On the death of Antiochus, his son by an earlier marriage, SELEUCUS II, and Berenice in behalf of her infant son struggled for the throne; a war with Ptolemy III ensued.

Antiochus III (Antiochus the Great), d. 187 B.C., king of Syria (223–187 B.C.), son of Seleucus II. At his accession the Seleucid empire was dissolving.

Antiochus III

He could not restore it completely, but he did much to revive the glory of the Seleucid dynasty. He led an expedition (212–205 B.C.) to the eastern provinces and went as far as India. Though he was earlier defeated by the Egyptians at Raphia (modern Rafa), he and Philip V of Macedon undertook in 202 B.C. to wrest Egyptian territories from the boy king, Ptolemy V. Antiochus did not properly appreciate the growing power of Rome. While Philip V was engaged by the Roman armies, Antiochus recovered S Syria and Asia Minor. In 199 he won a decisive victory over the Egyptians; Palestine then reverted to Syria, having been under Egyptian rule for almost a century. In 196 he seized the Thracian Chersonese and thus alarmed the Greeks. They as well as the Egyptians sought the aid of the Romans. Antiochus, who disregarded the advice of Hannibal in 193, waited and then challenged Rome by accepting the invitation of the Aetolian League to interfere in Greece in 192. The Romans crushed him (191) at Thermopylae and again at Magnesia (190). He also lost naval engagements, and in 188 he was forced to give up all his territory W of the Taurus. Thus the Seleucid empire became a purely inland Asiatic state, and dreams of reviving Alexander's empire died.

Antiochus IV (Antiochus Epiphanes) (ēpĭ′fŭnēz), d. 163 B.C., king of Syria (175–163 B.C.), son of Antiochus III; successor of his brother Seleucus IV. His nephew (later Demetrius I) was held as a hostage in Rome, though still claiming the throne. Antiochus is best known for his attempt to Hellenize Judaea and extirpate Judaism—a policy that instigated the rebellion of the MACCABEES. Antiochus invaded Egypt, which was torn by strife between Ptolemy VI and his brother (later Ptolemy VII), and would probably have conquered that land if the Romans had not intervened in his siege of Alexandria (168). Antiochus was briefly succeeded by his son, Antiochus V, a boy king who was overthrown by Demetrius I.

Antiope (ăntī'ủpē), in Greek mythology. **1** Theban princess, daughter of Nycteus. She was seduced by Zeus and bore him twin sons, Zethus (zē'thủs) and Amphion (ăm'fēủn). Fleeing to Sicyon to escape the wrath of her father, she was forced to abandon her infants on Mt. Cithaeron, where they were raised by shepherds. After Nycteus committed suicide, Antiope was pursued and captured by her uncle Lycus and his wife Dirce, who treated her with great cruelty. Later the sons of Antiope revenged their mother; they dethroned Lycus and punished Dirce by tying her to the horns of a bull. They then put a wall around the city with stones which were placed together by the music of Amphion's lyre. Zethus married the nymph

Antiope between Zethus and Amphion (marble relief).

Thebe, and after she died he married AËDON. Amphion married Niobe. **2** A queen of the Amazons, sister of Hippolyte. According to one legend she was abducted by THESEUS and became the mother of Hippolytus.

antiparticle: see ANTIMATTER.

Antipas (ăn'tĭpăs). **1** See HEROD. **2** Martyr at Pergamum, traditionally its first bishop. Rev. 2.13.

Antipater (ăntī'pủtủr), d. 319 B.C., Macedonian general. He was one of the ablest and most trusted lieutenants of PHILIP II and was a friend and supporter of ALEXANDER THE GREAT. When Alexander went on his Asiatic campaign, Antipater was left as regent (334–323 B.C.) in Macedon. He resisted the attempt of Olympias to gain the regency and governed ably except that his policy of supporting tyrants and oligarchs made him unpopular in Greece. After the death of Alexander he put down a rebellion of many of the Greek cities in the Lamian War and punished Athens. By imposing a more oligarchic form of government on Athens, he drove Demosthenes to commit suicide. Antipater was a leading opponent of the regent, Perdiccas, and after Perdiccas was defeated in 321 by Ptolemy I, Antigonus I, and Craterus, it was Antipater who held the kingdom together. After his death it fell violently apart in the wars of the DIADOCHI.

Antipater, in the Bible: see HEROD.

Antipatris (ăntĭp'ủtrĭs), city, Roman Palestine, founded by Herod the Great and named after his father. It was some 10 mi. NE of Joppa, on the north-south road. Paul was taken there on the way to Caesarea. Acts 23.31.

Antiphilus (ăntĭf'ĭlủs), fl. 4th cent. B.C., Greek painter, of Alexandrian origin. He invented a grotesque caricature called gryllos, a creature part man, part animal or bird. He painted portraits of Philip of Macedon and Alexander the Great.

Antiphon (ăn'tĭfŏn, –fủn), c.479–411 B.C., Athenian orator. He rarely spoke in public but wrote defenses for others to speak. Of his 15 extant orations three were for use in court, the rest for the instruction of his pupils. A few fragments of other speeches survive, but some may be the work of Antiphon the Sophist, who also lived in Athens in the 5th cent. B.C. Antiphon did much to advance Attic prose writing. His position in politics was with the conservative aristocrats, and he was instrumental in setting up the Four Hundred in 411 B.C. When they fell, Antiphon was executed among the first, before ALCIBIADES returned.

antiphon (ăn'tĭfủn), in liturgical music, generally a short text sung before and after a psalm or canticle. The main use is in group singing of the office in a monastery. However, introit, offertory, and communion of the Mass were originally antiphons which later were used independently. Certain festival chants, sung preparatory to the Mass itself, are called antiphons. There are also the four antiphons of the Blessed Virgin Mary, which are in the nature of office hymns and are sung by alternating choirs (i.e., antiphonally), each one belonging to a certain portion of the year. The best known of these is *Salve Regina*, of whose text there are many polyphonic settings.

Antipodes (ăntĭp'ủdēz), rocky uninhabited islands, (area c.24 sq. mi.), S Pacific, c.450 mi. SE of New Zealand, to which they belong. The Antipodes are so named because of their location in relation to Greenwich, England.

antipodes [Gr.,=having feet opposite], people or places diametrically opposite on the globe. Thus antipodes must be separated by half the circumference of the earth (180°), and one must be as far north as the other is south of the equator; midnight at one is noonday at the other. New Amsterdam and St. Paul, small islands nearly midway between South Africa and Australia, are more nearly antipodal to Washington, D.C., than is any other land.

antipope [Latin,=against the pope], ecclesiastic elected by a group in the Roman Catholic Church whose election was later declared uncanonical and illegitimate as opposed to another ecclesiastic declared legitimate supreme pontiff. Important antipopes were NOVATIAN; Clement III (see GUIBERT OF RAVENNA); Nicholas V (see RAINAL-DUCCI, Pietro); Clement VII (see ROBERT OF GENEVA); Benedict III (see LUNA, PEDRO DE); John XXIII (or by a different count, John XXII; see COSSA, BALDASSARRE); and Felix V (see Amadeus VIII), who was the last antipope.

antiproton: see ANTIMATTER.

antique. The term is used collectively to designate classic Greek and Roman works of art, particularly sculptures; as an adjective to indicate an object, a period, or a style of ancient or early times; and as a noun, for objects of art, furniture, rugs, pottery, metalwork, costumes, jewelry, and household goods of early production. The demand and prices paid for antiques have led to the widespread making of reproductions and reconstructions, some with spurious marks of age.

Anti-Saloon League, U.S. organization working for prohibition of the sale of alcoholic liquors. Founded in 1893 as the Ohio Anti-Saloon League at Oberlin, Ohio, by representatives of temperance societies and evangelical Protestant churches, it came to wield great political influence. Vigorously led by James Cannon, Jr. (1864–1944), a Methodist bishop, the League played an important role in securing the passage of the Eighteenth Amendment. See P. H. Odegard, *Pressure Politics: Story of the Anti-Saloon League* (1928); biography of Bishop Cannon by Virginius Dabney (1949).

anti-Semitism, sentiment, ranging from antipathy to violent hatred, against the JEWS. Before the 19th cent., anti-Semitism was largely religious, based on dislike for the "perfidious" Jews who crucified Christ, and was expressed in the later Middle Ages by sporadic persecutions and expulsions—notably the expulsion from Spain under Ferdinand and Isabella—in severe economic and personal restriction (see GHETTO), and in fantastic legends such as those of ritual murder by Jews of Christian children. However, the Jews being generally restricted to the profession of unpopular trades (notably usury), the sentiment was also economic in nature. After the emancipation of the Jews, brought about by the Enlightenment of the 18th cent. and by the French Revolution, religious and economic motives were gradually replaced by "race" feeling. This development was due not only to the rising nationalism of the 19th cent. but also to the conscious preservation, among Orthodox Jews, of cultural and religious barriers that isolated the Jewish minorities from their fellow citizens. Jewish reaction to this phenomenon found political expression in ZIONISM. The unpopularity of the Jews, on whom all evils could be blamed with impunity, was exploited either by demagogues, such as Édouard DRUMONT in France, to stir the masses against an existing government, or by reactionary governments, as in Russia, to find an outlet for popular discontent. The millions of Russian and Polish Jews who, after the assassination (1881) of Alexander II, fled the pogroms (see POGROM) and found refuge in other countries contributed to the popular feeling that Jews were aliens and intruders. In addition, a spurious document, the "Protocols of the Wise Men of Zion," purporting to outline a Jewish plan for world domination, emerged in Russia early in the 20th cent. and has circulated throughout the world ever since. After the Russian Revolution of 1917, the Jews were accused of plotting to dominate the world by their international financial power or by a Bolshevik revolution. Pseudoscientific theories of "Aryan" superiority directed against the Jews emerged in the 19th cent. with the writings of Count GOBINEAU and Houston Stewart CHAMBERLAIN and found their climax in those of Alfred ROSENBERG. These theories were incorporated in the official doctrine of German NATIONAL SOCIALISM by Adolf Hitler. Hitler's persecution of the Jews during the Second World War is unparalleled in history. It is estimated that between 5 and 6 million European Jews were exterminated between 1939 and 1945 (see CONCENTRATION CAMP). The end of persecution has not meant the end of anti-Semitism as the sporadic attacks on synagogues in many countries since the end of the Second World War indicate. In the USSR and the Soviet-bloc nations of Eastern Europe, where anti-Semitism is officially outlawed, it has reappeared in new forms. See Emil J. Long, *Two Thousand Years: a History of Anti-Semitism* (1953); Adolf Leschnitzer, *The Magic Background of Modern Anti-Semitism* (1956).

antiseptic, an agent that inhibits the growth of microorganisms without necessarily destroying them. Examples of antiseptics are alcohol, iodine, carbolic acid in dilute solution, sunlight, and water at high temperature. Powders of the sulfanilamide drug group are used in surgical wounds as an antiseptic. LISTER was the first to employ an antiseptic (carbolic acid) in surgery, following the discovery by PASTEUR that microorganisms are the cause of infection. Modern surgical techniques for avoiding infection are founded on asepsis, the absence of pathogenic organisms. Sterilization is the chief means of achieving asepsis.

antislavery movement: see SLAVERY and ABOLITIONISTS.

Antisthenes (ăntĭs'thŭnēz), b. 444? B.C., d. after 371 B.C., Greek philosopher, founder of the

Antisthenes

CYNICS. Most of his paradoxical views stemmed from his early Sophist orientation, even though he became one of Socrates' most ardent followers. He believed that man's happiness lay in cultivating virtue for its own sake. To attain virtue, man must reduce to a minimum his dependence on the external world, disregard social convention, shun pleasure, and live in poverty. Antisthenes, like Xenophanes, repudiated polytheism, substituting one god, whom he described as unlike anything known to man. His view that each individual is unique had implications for ethics and for a theory of knowledge.

Anti-Taurus: see TAURUS.

antitoxin, substance formed in the body to neutralize the poisonous products (toxins) of bacteria. By introducing small amounts of a specific toxin into the healthy body, it is possible to stimulate the production of antitoxin (see ANTIBODY) so that the body's defenses are already established against invasion by specific bacteria. Antitoxins may also be produced in the bodies of animals and then transferred to humans for the purpose of bolstering IMMUNITY.

Anti-Trust Act: see CLAYTON ANTI-TRUST ACT and SHERMAN ANTI-TRUST ACT.

Antium: see ANZIO.

Antlers, town (pop. 2,085), co. seat of Pushmataha co., SE Okla., near the Kiamichi river and S of McAlester; inc. 1903. Its chief industry is lumbering, although dairying and truck farming are also important.

Antofagasta (äntōfägä'stä), city (pop. c.100,000), N Chile. A port on the Pacific, it is the most important of the republic's northern cities. Antofagasta was founded by Chileans in 1870 to exploit nitrates in the Desert of Atacama, then under Bolivian administration. Its occupation by Chilean troops in 1879 began the War of the Pacific (see PACIFIC, WAR OF THE), and after the war it was, with the province, ceded to Chile. Antofagasta has depended primarily on nitrates and copper exports, often threatened by sharp fluctuations in world demands. The open harbor is partially protected by a breakwater. With highway and rail connections to N Chile, Bolivia, Argentina, and S Chile, the city has become an international commercial center. It is also a major industrial hub with large foundries and ore refineries. Backed by desert hills, Antofagasta enjoys a fine climate but hardly ever receives rain. Water is piped in from the San Pedro river, 280 mi. away.

Antoine, André (ädrä' ätwän'), 1858–1943, French theatrical director, manager, critic. In opposition to the teachings of the Paris Conservatory, he formed (1887) his own company, the THÉÂTRE LIBRE, and presented, by means of private subscriptions, the foremost works of the naturalistic school. Financial failure forced him to relinquish the theater in 1894. In 1897 he founded the Théâtre Antoine, where he continued the tradition of his Théâtre Libre for 10 years. From 1906 to 1914 he was director of the Odéon in Paris, and after the First World War he became a drama critic and the dean of French theatrical writers.

Antoine, Père (pâr' ăntwän') [Fr.,=Father Anthony], 1748–1829, Spanish priest in New Orleans, a Capuchin friar. His Spanish name in religion was

Antofagasta, Chile's port on the Pacific.

Antonio de Sedella; his family name was Mareno. Through many years of service at St. Louis Cathedral under Spanish, briefly French, and then U.S. rule, he won his French congregation from distaste for his harshness to great love and respect. He was almost constantly at war with the authorities. The Spanish colonial rulers once sent him back as a prisoner to Spain, and U.S. officials were later highly incensed at his secret dealings with the Spanish. The legend that he was empowered to introduce the Inquisition to Louisiana but refrained from doing so is apparently based on fact. He is the chief figure in the historical novel *Père Antoine* (1947) by E. F. Murphy.

Anton, city (pop. 1,068), NW Texas, in the Llano Estacado NW of Lubbock, in a cotton, grain, and dairy region; est. 1924.

Antonelli, Giacomo (jä'kōmō äntōněl'lē), 1806–76, Italian statesman, cardinal of the Roman Church, adviser to Pope PIUS IX. He received the red hat in 1847, presided over the council drafting the constitution for the Papal States, and became the premier of the pope's first constitutional cabinet. After returning (1849) from his exile in Gaeta, Pius IX made him secretary of state. His vigorous diplomacy was directed against Italian national unification.

Antonello da Messina (äntōněl'lō dä mäs-sē'nä), c.1430–1479, Italian painter, b. Messina. Antonello appears to have had early contact with Flemish art. In his deft handling of the oil medium, his rendering of transparent surfaces and minute landscape details, a strong northern influence can be seen. About 1475 he went to Venice. There he painted the *San Cassiano Altarpiece,* of which only fragments now exist (Vienna). His style affected the art of Bellini and other Venetians. He was also an excellent portrait painter; examples of his por-

Crucifixion, *painting by Antonello da Messina.*

traiture are in the Metropolitan Museum, the Philadelphia Museum, the Louvre, and in Berlin. Other paintings by him are *Ecce Homo* (Metropolitan Mus.); *Madonna and Child* (National Gall. of Art, Washington, D.C.); *Pietà* (Venice); *Crucifixion* (Antwerp).

Antonescu, Ion (yôn äntônĕ′skŏŏ), 1882–1946, Rumanian marshal and dictator. He served in the First World War, later became chief of staff, but fell into disfavor with King Carol II because of his suspected intrigues with the IRON GUARD. In the Second World War, on Sept. 2, 1940, Carol, threatened with revolution and German intervention, appointed Antonescu premier with dictatorial powers. Two days later Antonescu forced the king to abdicate in favor of Carol's son, MICHAEL. In Nov., 1940, Rumania joined the Axis Powers, and Antonescu gave Hitler virtual control over Rumanian economy and foreign policy, tolerated violent pogroms against the Jews, and declared (June 22, 1941) a "holy war" on Russia. With two Russian armies deep in Rumania, King Michael in Aug., 1944, had Antonescu and his cabinet arrested in a theatrical coup. Antonescu was tried (1946) for war crimes, sentenced, and executed.

Antonines (ăn′tŭnīnz), collective name of certain Roman emperors of the 2d cent., usually listed as ANTONINUS PIUS; his adopted sons, MARCUS AURELIUS and Verus; and COMMODUS.

Antoninus, Saint (ăntōnĭ′nŭs), 1389–1459, Italian churchman, named Antoninus Pierozzi. He was a Dominican and became archbishop of Florence. He ruled well and was renowned for his charitable work in the city. His *Summa moralis* is a pioneering work in moral theology, of interest for its treatment of commercial ethics and the morality of banking. It is a valuable record of the effect the new economic changes were having on everyday life. Feast: May 10. See Bede Jarrett, *St. Antonino and Medieval Economics* (1914).

Antoninus, Wall of, ancient Roman wall built across N Britain from the Firth of Forth to the Firth of Clyde by the prefect Lollius Urbicus in the reign of Antoninus Pius—probably A.D. 140–42. Built as a defense against the peoples to the north, it had a ditch on the north, 19 forts along its southern side, and was 37 mi. long. Its construction was similar to that of Hadrian's Wall. It was abandoned c.185. See Sir George Macdonald, *The Roman Wall in Scotland* (2d ed., 1934).

Antoninus Pius (Titus Aurelius Fulvus Boionius Arrius Antoninus) (pī′ŭs), A.D. 86–A.D. 161, Roman emperor (138–161). After a term as consul (120) he went as proconsul to Asia, where he governed with distinction. He was adopted by the emperor Hadrian and, on succeeding him, administered the empire with marked ability and integrity. Italy was embellished with fine buildings, and the provinces were eased of much of their financial burden. During his reign the Wall of Antoninus was built in Britain. His wife was Faustina, aunt of his successor, MARCUS AURELIUS.

Antonito (ăn′tùnē′tō), town (pop. 1,045; alt. c.7,900 ft.), S Colo., S of Alamosa near the N.Mex. line; inc. 1889. It is a railroad center for a large farm and livestock area.

Antony or **Marc Antony,** Latin *Marcus Antonius,* c.83 B.C.-30 B.C., Roman politician and soldier. He was of a distinguished family; his mother was a relative of Julius CAESAR. Antony was notorious from his youth for riotous living, but even his enemies admitted his courage. Between 58 B.C. and 56 B.C. he campaigned in Syria with Aulus Gabinius and then in Gaul with Caesar, who made a protégé of him. In 52 B.C. he became quaestor and in 49 B.C. tribune. When the situation between POMPEY and Caesar became critical, Antony and Q. CASSIUS Longinus, another tribune, vetoed the bill to deprive Caesar of his army and fled to him. Caesar crossed the Rubicon, and the civil war began. At the battle of Pharsala, Caesar took the right wing, and Antony gave distinguished service as the leader of the left. After Caesar's assassination (44 B.C.), Antony, then consul, aroused the mob against the conspirators and drove them from the city. When Octavian (later AUGUSTUS), Caesar's adopted son and heir, arrived in Rome, Antony joined forces with him, but they soon fell out. Antony went to take Cisalpine Gaul as his assigned proconsular province, but Decimus BRUTUS would not give it up, and Antony besieged him (43 B.C.) at Mutina (modern Modena). The senate, urged by CICERO, who had excoriated Antony in the *Philippics,* sent the consuls Aulus HIRTIUS and C. Vibius Pansa to attack Antony. The consuls fell in battle, but Antony retired into Transalpine Gaul. Octavian now decided for peace and arranged with Antony and M. Aemilius LEPIDUS the Second Triumvirate, with Antony receiving Asia as his command. In the proscription following this treaty Antony had Cicero killed. Antony and Octavian crushed the republicans at Philippi, and the triumvirate ruled the empire for five years. In 42 B.C. Antony met CLEOPATRA, and their love affair began. While Antony was in Egypt, his wife, Fulvia, became so alienated from Octavian that civil war broke out in Italy. At about the time Antony arrived in Italy, Fulvia died (40 B.C.) and peace was restored between Octavian and Antony, who married Octavian's sister Octavia; she became, thereafter, Antony's devoted partisan and the strongest force for peace between the two. In 36 B.C., Antony undertook an invasion of Parthia. The war was costly and useless, and Antony succeeded only in adding some of Armenia to the Roman possessions. In 37 B.C., Antony settled in Alexandria as the acknowledged lover of Cleopatra. He gave himself up to pleasure, caring neither for the growing ill will in Rome nor for the increasing impatience of Octavian. In 32 B.C. the senate deprived Antony of his powers, and civil war became inevitable. In 31 B.C., Antony and his fleet met M. Vipsanius Agrippa with Octavian's fleet off Actium, and Antony found his great galleys were no match for the swift small craft that Octavian had built. In the middle of the battle Cleopatra retired with her boats, and Antony followed her. His navy surrendered to Octavian. The situation of the two lovers was desperate. Returning to Alexandria, they set about fortifying Egypt

Banquet of Antony and Cleopatra, painting by Tiepolo.

against Octavian's arrival. When at length Octavian did come (30 B.C.), Antony committed suicide, under the impression, it is said, that Cleopatra had died already. She killed herself soon afterward. Of the many dramas on the tragedy the best known by far is Shakespeare's *Antony and Cleopatra*. The name also appears as Marc Anthony.

Antothijah (ăntŭthī′jŭ), descendant of Benjamin. 1 Chron. 8.24.

Antothite (ăn′tōthĭt): see ANATHOTH.

Antrim (ăn′trĭm), county (pop. 273,923), 1,098 sq. mi., NE Northern Ireland. BELFAST is the county town. The eastern and seaward area of the county is a picturesque region of mountains and glens; to the west, where Antrim borders on Lough Neagh, there are the fertile valleys of the Bann and the Lagan. On the northern coast, near Portrush, is the extraordinary basaltic formation known as the GIANT'S CAUSEWAY. The region is chiefly agricultural (oats, flax, potatoes), with fishing and cattle breeding important occupations. Belfast is a major British port and the chief industrial center of Northern Ireland. There are no other large urban areas. Larne, Lisburn, Ballymena, Carrickfergus, and Antrim are important local centers.

Antrim, town (pop. 1,448), Co. Antrim, E Northern Ireland, on Lough Neagh. An agricultural market in a flax-growing region, it has linen mills. The round tower here dates from c.900.

Antrim, town (pop. 1,121), S N.H., on the Contoocook and SW of Concord; settled 1741, inc. 1777. Cutlery and wood products are made.

Antung (än′tŏong′), former province (c.24,000 sq. mi.), NE China. The capital was Tunghwa. It was bordered on the southeast by the Yalu river, which separated it from Korea, and by the Bay of Korea. A part of Manchuria, it was included in Manchukuo and was created a province in 1945. In 1954 Antung became part of Liaoning prov.

Antung, city (pop. c.360,000), SE Liaoning prov., China, at the mouth of the Yalu river. It is a port, connected by rail with Mukden and with Sinuiji in North Korea. The Supung Dam on the Yalu supplies power for the city's sawmills, match factories, and food-processing plants. Antung was opened as a treaty port in 1907.

Antwerp (ăn′twûrp), Flemish *Antwerpen* (änt′-věrpŭn), Fr. *Anvers* (ävĕr′), province (1,104 sq. mi.; estimated pop. 1,416,441), N Belgium. It is a flat cultivated plain drained by the Scheldt river and the Albert Canal. Antwerp (the capital) and Malines are the chief cities. The province, which is mostly Flemish-speaking, was part of the duchy of BRABANT.

Antwerp, Flemish *Antwerpen*, Fr. *Anvers*, city (estimated pop. 259,658; with suburbs, 856,845), capital of Antwerp prov., N Belgium, on the Scheldt river. Rivaled only by Rotterdam as the largest seaport of continental Europe, Antwerp is also one of the great historic and artistic cities of Europe. It is a world center of the diamond trade and industry, the seat of the oldest stock exchange (founded 1460), and an industrial center (oil refineries, a petrochemical industry, automobile assembly plants, shipyards, and flour mills). Its industrial suburbs manufacture metal goods, electronic equipment, chemicals and dyes, leather, and photographic supplies. The city is connected with the

Guildhalls line the Groote Markt in Antwerp, Belgium.

industrial regions of SE Belgium by the ALBERT CANAL and has an active transit trade to and from W Germany, notably the Ruhr district. An early seat of the counts of Flanders and one of the old communes of Brabant, Antwerp rose to prominence with the decline (15th cent.) of Bruges and Ghent. In 1446 the English Merchant Adventurers gave the port great impetus by moving their factory from Bruges to Antwerp. By the middle of the 16th cent. Antwerp was the commercial and financial hub of Europe. The diamond industry, established in the 15th cent., expanded greatly after the arrival of Jewish craftsmen expelled from Portugal. Antwerp's prosperity suffered in 1576 when the city was sacked by mutinous Spanish troops (the "Spanish Fury") and again in 1584–85 when the city battled a 14-month siege by the Spanish under Alexander Farnese. The Peace of Westphalia (1648) closed the Scheldt to navigation, and Antwerp declined rapidly. Napoleon I revived its trade, but the Dutch-Belgian treaty of separation (1839) gave the Netherlands the right to collect tolls on Scheldt shipping. The expansion of Antwerp as a major modern port dates only from 1863, when Belgium redeemed this right by a cash payment. Antwerp suffered great hardship in the First World War when it was besieged by the Germans and in the Second World War when it was heavily attacked (after 1944) as a major Allied supply base. The artistic fame of Antwerp dates from the rule (15th cent.) of Philip the Good of Burgundy, who founded an academy of painting here. Quentin MASSYS and RUBENS made Antwerp their home, and Sir Anthony VAN DYCK was born here. Many of their works are in the museums and churches of Antwerp. Christophe PLANTIN (16th cent.) made the city a printing center. Among the many splendid buildings of Antwerp are the Cathedral of Notre Dame (14th–15th cent.), one of the finest of Gothic cathedrals, with a spire 400 ft.

high; the Church of St. Paul and the town hall (both 16th cent.); and the old guildhalls that line the Groote Markt [market place]. The city also has a world-famous zoological garden.

Antwerp, rural village (pop. 1,465), NW Ohio, on the Maumee near the Ind. line, NW of Lima; inc. 1864. Cheese is made here.

Anu (ā′nōō), ancient sky-god of Sumerian origin, worshiped in Babylonian religion. The son of Apsu (the underworld ocean) and Tiamat (primeval chaos), Anu was king of the great triad of gods, which included the earth-god Enlil and the water-god Ea.

An Uaimh: see NAVAN.

Anub (ā′nŭb), Judahite. 1 Chron. 4.8.

Anubis (ȧnū′bĭs), Egyptian god of the dead. He presided over the embalming of the dead, and is represented as a jackal-headed man.

Anubis

Anuradhapura (ŭnōō'rädŭpōō'rŭ), or **Anarajapura** (ŭnä'räjŭ-), town (pop. c.22,500), N central Ceylon. It has rice plantations and vegetable gardens but is chiefly famous for its vast Buddhist ruins and as a center of pilgrimage. The site of an ancient city, it was from the 4th cent. B.C. to the late 8th cent. A.D. the capital of Ceylon and one of the leading Buddhist centers of the world. After a Tamil invasion it was abandoned in favor of POLLONARRUA. Ruins include several colossal stupas (some larger than the pyramids of Egypt), a temple hewn from rock, and the Brazen Palace (so called from its metal roof). It also has a sacred BO TREE grown from a slip of the tree at BUDDH GAYA under which Buddha is believed to have attained enlightenment.

Anvers: see ANTWERP.

Anville, Jean Baptiste Bourguignon d' (zhä' bäptēst' bōōrgēnyō' dävēl'), 1697–1782, French geographer and cartographer. His maps of ancient geography, characterized by careful, accurate work and based largely on original research, are especially valuable. He became cartographer to the king, who purchased his maps, atlases, and other geographical material (the largest collection in France); Anville himself made more than 200 maps.

Anyang (än'yäng'), city (pop. c.135,000), N Honan prov., China. This coal-mining center was once a capital of the SHANG dynasty and one of the earliest centers of Chinese civilization. Excavations, begun here in 1928, have revealed a rich Bronze Age culture.

Anza, Juan Bautista de (hwän' boutēs'tä dä än'sä), 1735–88, Spanish explorer and official in the Southwest and the Far West, founder of San Francisco, b. Mexico. Accompanied by Father F. T. H. Garcés and a small expedition, he opened (1774) an overland road from Sonora through present Arizona to California, reaching San Gabriel and Monterey. Viceroy A. M. Bucareli, alarmed by the threatened encroachments of the Russians and the British on the Pacific coast, sent (1775) Anza on a new expedition to establish a colony. In 1776 he chose the site of San Francisco, where a presidio was founded by one of his lieutenants and a mission was founded by Father Francisco Palóu under the direction of Father Junípero Serra. Later, as governor of New Mexico (1777–88), Anza built up Spanish frontier defenses and established order. Journals of men on his California journey are in *Anza's California Expeditions* (ed. by H. E. Bolton, 5 vols., 1930). For his diaries and a study of his administration, see A. B. Thomas, *Forgotten Frontiers* (1932).

Anzengruber, Ludwig (lōōt'vĭkh än'tsŭngrōō"bŭr), 1839–89, Austrian writer. An actor and a clerk in the imperial police, Anzengruber had little financial success as a writer until the production (1870) of the anticlerical play *Der Pfarrer von Kirchfeld* [the parish priest of Kirchfeld]. An immediate success, it was the first of a series of folk plays and was followed by *Der Meineidbauer* (1871; Eng. tr., *The Farmer Forsworn*, 1913–15) and *Die Kreuzelschreiber* (1872; Eng. tr., *The Crossmakers*, 1958). *Das vierte Gebot* (1878; Eng. tr., *The Fourth Commandment*, 1912) is an early example of NATURALISM. Anzengruber also wrote short stories and two novels.

Anzhero-Sudzhensk (ŭnzhĕ"rŭ-sōōjĕnsk'), city (pop. c.116,000), SW Asiatic RSFSR. On the Trans-Siberian RR, it manufactures mining equipment and pharmaceuticals. One of the oldest and, since the end of the 19th cent., one of the largest coal-mining centers of the Kuznetsk Basin, the city was formed in 1928 out of the towns of Anzherka and Sudzhenka.

Anzio (än'zēō, Ital. än'tsyō), Latin *Antium*, town (estimated pop. 15,217), Latium, central Italy, on the Tyrrhenian Sea. A Volscian town, it later became a favorite resort of the Romans. Nero was

Ruins of Nero's villa in Anzio, Italy.

born here; among the ruins of his villa two famous statues, the Apollo Belvedere and the *Girl of Anzio*, were found. Anzio declined in the Middle Ages, was later a residence of the popes, and is now a flourishing beach resort. In Jan., 1944, Allied troops landed here to draw German forces from CASSINO and thus effected a breakthrough (May, 1944) to Rome.

Anzus Treaty, agreement signed Sept., 1951, under which all members will "act to meet the common danger" in case of attack in the Pacific area against any one member. At the end of 1962 the members were Australia, New Zealand, and the United States.

Aomori (äōmô'rē), city (pop. 202,211), capital of Aomori prefecture, extreme N Honshu, Japan, on Aomori Bay. First opened to foreign trade in 1906, Aomori is now the chief port of N Honshu. Rice, textiles, and tobacco are among its exports, many of which are shipped to Hokkaido. A modern city, it was rebuilt after a disastrous fire in 1910 and again after severe air raids in 1945. **Aomori** prefecture (3,719 sq. mi.; pop. 1,426,606) has rich timber lands and famous apple orchards. Aomori, Hachinoke, and Hirosake are the major cities.

aorist: see TENSE.

Aosta, Emmanuel Philibert of Savoy, duke of (äô'-stú, –stä), Ital. *Emanuele Filiberto di Savoia, duca d'Aosta*, 1869–1931, Italian general; son of King Amadeus of Spain and cousin of Victor Emmanuel III of Italy. In the First World War he held the Piave front after the Italian defeat at Caporetto and later occupied Friuli. He became a marshal in 1926. His son Amadeus (1898–1942), who succeeded to his title, was viceroy of Ethiopia (1937–41). He surrendered to the British in 1941 after a valiant defense.

Aosta (äô'stú, –stä, Ital. äô'stä), town (estimated pop. 28,446), chief city of Val d'Aosta, NW Italy, near the junction of the Great and Little St. Bernard roads. Aosta is mainly industrial, with chemical and textile manufactures. Emperor Augustus founded (c.25 B.C.) a colony here on the site of an older settlement. In the 11th cent. Aosta was given as a fief to Humbert, the founder of the Savoy dynasty; the cadet line of the house bore the titles of the dukes of Aosta. Roman remains include walls and gates, a triumphal arch, a theater, and an amphitheater. There are medieval towers and a fine cathedral (9th–15th cent.).

Aosta, Val d' (väldäô'stä), autonomous region (1,260 sq. mi.; estimated pop. 100,276), NW Italy, bordering on France in the west and Switzerland in the north. Aosta is the capital. Until 1945 the region was Aosta prov., in Piedmont. The Italian constitution of 1947 made it a free zone outside the Italian customs barrier. A high Alpine country, the Val d'Aosta includes the Italian slopes of Mont Blanc, the Matterhorn, and Monte Rosa; its highest peak is the GRAN PARADISO. The population is concentrated in the picturesque valleys of the DORA BALTEA and its tributaries. The Great and the Little SAINT BERNARD roads join in the upper Aosta valley. Cereals, grapes, and livestock are produced, and there are many fashionable winter resorts. After passing (11th cent.) to the counts of Savoy, the region shared the history of PIEDMONT. The feudal system long prevailed here; more than 70 castles are still standing. A French dialect is spoken.

Apache (ùpăch'ē), town (pop. 1,455), SW Okla., N of Lawton, in a farm region; settled and inc. 1901.

Apache Indians, North American Indian tribes of the Southwest. They speak Nadene languages, the southernmost branch of which is called Apachean (see LANGUAGE, table). The NAVAHO INDIANS also speak an Apachean language. Since some of the names of different Apache tribes are synonymous or nearly so, the resulting confusion has made them hard to identify in early literature. There were many groups—E of the Rio Grande along the mountains were the Jicarilla, the Lipan, and the Mescalero groups. In W New Mexico and Arizona were the Western Apache, including the Chiricahua and the Coyotero. The Kiowa Apache in the early southward migration attached themselves to the Kiowa, whose history they have since shared. The Apache as known in historic times were dependent upon hunting game and gathering roots and berries. The women were expert at making basketry, but the arts of pottery and weaving were not highly developed. Social organization was simple, but the Apache mother-in-law taboo—a man could not speak to, or look directly at, his mother-in-law—was remarkably rigorous. The Apache are known principally for their fierce fighting qualities. They successfully resisted the advance of Spanish colonization, but the acquisition of horses and new weapons, taken from the Spanish, led to increased intertribal warfare. The Eastern Apache were driven from their traditional plains area when (after 1720) they suffered defeat at the hands of the advancing COMANCHE INDIANS. Relations between the Apache and white men gradually worsened with the passing of Spanish rule in Mexico and with the increasing number of white men in the Southwest. By mid-19th cent. when the United States acquired the region from Mexico, Apache lands were in the path of the American westward movement. The futile but strong resistance which lasted until the beginning of the 20th cent. brought national fame to several of the Apache leaders—COCHISE, GERONIMO, MANGAS COLORADAS, and VICTORIO. Remnants

The village of Antignano with Monte Rosa in the distance in Val d'Aosta, Italy.

of the Apache tribes now live in reservations in Arizona. See C. R. Kant, *The Western Apache Clan System* (1957); C. L. Sonnichsen, *The Mescalero Apaches* (1958); J. D. Forbes, *Apache, Navaho, and Spaniard* (1960).

Apalachee Bay (ăpůlăch′ē), arm of the Gulf of Mexico, NW Fla., S of Tallahassee.

Apalachee Indians, tribe of North American Indians once centered about Apalachee Bay, NW Florida. Prosperous agriculturalists, they fought off the raids of the Creek Indians until early in the 18th cent. Combined Indian and British forces then conquered them, wiping out their villages along with Spanish missions and garrisons. Many of the Apalachee were sold into slavery, and a remnant who fled to Louisiana were extinct a century later.

Apalachicola (ăp″ůlăchĭkō′lů), city (pop. 3,099), co. seat of Franklin co., NW Fla., SW of Tallahassee; founded c.1820, inc. 1838. On Apalachicola Bay (a fine landlocked harbor) at the mouth of the Apalachicola river, it is a port of entry and an important center for oyster, shrimp, and other fisheries. Its position as one of the country's largest cotton-shipping ports after 1830 was ruined by the Civil War blockade. A bridge (1935) spans the bay from east to west. The spelling Appalachicola is incorrect.

Apalachicola, river, NW Fla., formed by the junction of the CHATTAHOOCHEE and the FLINT rivers at the Ga. line in Lake Seminole, which in turn is formed by the Jim Woodruff Dam (67 ft. high; 6,500 ft. long; completed 1957). The river flows c.90 mi. S to Apalachicola Bay and is navigable throughout its length.

Aparri (äpär′rē), city (pop. 33,500), on N Luzon, the Philippines. It is the port for a large tobacco-producing area.

apartheid (ůpärt′hīt) [Afrikaans=apartness], system of racial segregation peculiar to the Republic of South Africa. Racial segregation and the supremacy of the white man have long been accepted as natural and logical in South Africa, and until 1948, when D. F. Malan included the policy of apartheid in the Nationalist party platform, racial discrimination was never a political issue. Since then there has been bitter, and sometimes bloody, strife over apartheid. As officially stated, the purpose of apartheid is to perpetuate the domination of the country by its white minority in the face of rising nationalism throughout Africa. To accomplish this, the nonwhite populations—the Bantu (African Negroes), the Asiatic (Indian), and the Coloureds (mulattoes)—are to be set apart on reserved lands, their movements restricted, and their national political and economic rights severely curtailed. Most of the land, including the major mineral areas and the cities, is reserved for the whites. The Bantu, by far the largest segment of the population (about 70 percent) are to have about 12 percent of the land. The major target of apartheid legislation, the Bantu are not permitted to vote or hold property or to work outside of designated areas; in urban centers they are subject to curfew regulations, and passbook requirements. Despite public demonstrations against apartheid, UN resolutions, and church opposition, the policy has been applied with increased vigor, particularly under H. F. VER-

Mescalero Apache Indian crown dancer performs in annual intertribal Indian ceremonial at Gallup, N.M.

WOERD; in 1961 South Africa withdrew from the Commonwealth rather than yield to pressure over its racial policies and in the same year the three South African denominations of the Dutch Reformed Church left the World Council of Churches rather than abandon their advocacy of apartheid. In 1962 the South African government announced that it intended to establish the first self-governing Bantu reservation to be called the Transkei. There will be a native parliament in the Transkei, but the more serious aspects of rule will remain in the hands of the central government. See N, C. Phillips, *The Tragedy of Apartheid* (1960); Patrick Von Rensburg, *Guilty Hand: the History of Apartheid* (1962).

apartment house, building having three or more dwelling units. Though this form of dwelling has existed since early times and we find numerous examples in Roman and medieval cities, its most important development came with the Industrial Revolution. After 1850 crowded slums began to develop in the cities of Europe and the United States. Few good low-cost multiple dwellings were built before the First World War, but great progress was made in the development of more luxurious apartment buildings, particularly in Paris and Vienna. In the 1880s fireproof steel-frame construction, the improvement of the elevator, and the introduction of electric lighting made possible the rapid evolution of the apartment building. In 1901

New York put into effect a tenement-house law; its purpose was to protect occupants against fire hazards and unsanitary and unsafe conditions. Between 1919 and 1934 there appeared in Europe many commendable low-cost housing developments. Important examples are the project by Gropius at the Siemensstadt in Berlin, J. J. P. Oud's group at the Hook in Holland, and H. P. Berlage's apartments in Amsterdam. There has been subsidized public housing in the United States since 1937. A phenomenal increase in the building of apartments has taken place since 1921 in all the larger cities, reaching its peak in New York. There the private house was largely replaced. The city has buildings that shelter only a few families and others that domicile thousands. They run a full economic range from the cheapest walk-up apartments without elevator service to the extremely luxurious duplex and triplex suites of the very rich. The cooperative apartment is a building in which the tenants belong to a corporation which owns the building. The apartment hotel combines the accommodations of an apartment, including cooking space, with the services characteristic of a hotel. Apartment houses have now spread to the suburbs of the larger cities, where they often include gardens, tennis courts, and children's playgrounds. See Talbot Hamlin, *Forms and Functions of Twentieth Century Architecture* (1952).

apatite (ăp'ŭtīt), mineral, compound of calcium and phosphorus containing chlorine, fluorine, or both (sp. gr. 3.17–3.23; hardness 4½–5). It is transparent to opaque in shades of green, brown, yellow, white, red, and purple. The yellow-green variety, called asparagus stone, and the blue-green manganapatite are used to a limited extent in jewelry. Large deposits of apatite are mined for use in making phosphatic fertilizers. Apatite is a minor constituent in many types of rock and is found extensively in the E United States and Canada, in Europe and in Africa.

Apaturia (ăpŭchōō'rēŭ, –tyōō'rēŭ), in Greek religion, annual festival celebrated by the Ionians and the Athenians. It was held in October or November, in the season when various phratries (clans) met to induct new members and pay homage to the gods.

ape, name for certain primates. It is now usually limited to those which most closely resemble man—the GORILLA, the CHIMPANZEE, the ORANGUTAN, and the GIBBON. Formerly ape was used as a synonym for monkey or applied to certain tailless monkeys. The anthropoid apes differ from the typical Old World monkeys in having no external tail and no cheek pouches. The arms are longer than the legs. Apes are chiefly arboreal, but they can stand in a semierect position. They have 32 teeth, a vermiform appendix, a flattened breastbone, and a brain which is similar in structure to that of man but smaller. See R. M. Yerkes and A. W. Yerkes, *The Great Apes* (1929).

Apeldoorn (ä'pŭldōrn), city (estimated pop. 103,126), in Gelderland prov., E central Netherlands. A rail junction, it has varied manufactures. Nearby are the royal summer palace of Het Loo and several sanatoriums.

Apelles (ŭpĕl'ēz), fl. 330 B.C., Greek painter, the most celebrated of antiquity, but now known only through descriptions of his works. He is supposed to have studied under Ephorus of Ephesus and under Pamphilus of Amphipolis at Sicyon. He was court painter to Philip II of Macedon and to Alexander the Great. Among portraits of Alexander was one in the Temple of Diana at Ephesus which showed him wielding the thunderbolts of Zeus. Apelles excelled in painting horses, and according to Pliny the portrait of Antigonus Cyclops on horseback was his masterpiece. Most famous, perhaps, was the picture of Aphrodite rising from the sea. A painting made by Botticelli from Lucian's description of Apelles' *Calumny* is in the Uffizi. Apelles is said to have been the first to recognize the talents of PROTOGENES.

Apelles, Christian at Rome. Rom. 16.10.

Apennines (ă'pŭnīnz), Ital. *Appennino* (ăp-pān-nē'nō), mountain system, traversing the entire length of the Italian peninsula. From the Cadibona Pass in Liguria, where it joins the Ligurian Alps, to the Strait of Messina, it is c.840 mi. long; the mountains of Sicily are a continuation. The greatest width is c.80 mi. The highest peak, in the GRAN SASSO D'ITALIA group, rises to c.9,560 ft.; but generally the peaks are much lower. There are several volcanic lakes and volcanoes (two, VESUVIUS and ETNA, are still active) and many mineral springs. The few important rivers (Arno, Tiber, and Volturno) all flow W into the Tyrrhenian Sea. The Apennines are pierced by many railroad tunnels and highway passes, and by the Appian, Cassian, Flaminian, and Salarian ways (see ROMAN

Gran Sasso d'Italia range of the Apennines.

ROADS). The peaks mostly have a bare, savage aspect, and settlers have preferred the valleys and the fertile basins. Pastures are very extensive, and the lower hills are covered with olive groves and vineyards. The forests of the Apennines (chestnut, birch, oak, and pine) have been greatly reduced by man through the centuries; attempts at reforestation are being made. In the mountains there are many hydroelectric plants.

Apex (ā'pĕks), town (pop. 1,368), central N.C., WSW of Raleigh. Lumber is processed here.

Apharsachites (ùfär'sùkīts) or **Apharsathchites** (ùfär'săthkīts), Assyrian colonists settled in Samaria. Ezra 4.9; 5.6; 6.6. The **Apharsites** (ùfär'sīts) apparently were another group of colonists. Ezra 4.9.

aphasia (ùfā'zhù) [Gr.,=speechlessness], condition caused by a lesion of the brain, in which an individual is unable to express himself in speech or in writing or to comprehend the written or spoken word. Treatment consists of reeducation; the oral and lip-reading methods employed in the education of deaf and mute children have been found to be of assistance in therapy.

Aphek (ā'fĕk). **1** Canaanite royal town, the modern Ras el-Ain or Rosh Hayim (Israel). Its wells are still in use. Herod called it Antipatris. It is mentioned in Egyptian documents dating from the 19th cent. B.C. Joshua 12.18. See APHEKAH. **2** Canaanite city in Asher. Joshua 13.4; 19.30. Aphik: Judges 1.31. **3** Place where Ahab defeated Benhadad. 1 Kings 20.26–30; 2 Kings 13.17. **4, 5** Two places, where the Philistines encamped, perhaps the same as **1**. 1 Sam. 4.1; 29.1.

Aphekah (ùfē'kù), unidentified place, probably the same as APHEK **4**. Joshua 15.53.

Aphiah (ùfī'ù) ancestor of King Saul. 1 Sam. 9.1.

aphid (ā'fĭd, ăf'ĭd) or **plant louse,** tiny, usually green, pear-shaped insect injurious to crops and other vegetation; also called green fly and blight. Aphids damage plants by inserting their beaks into the stems and leaves and sucking the juices. They also transmit virus diseases and form and live in galls. Some are wingless; others have transparent or colored wings. The life cycle is complex and varies in different species; there is also much variation in form among individuals of the same species. In many species wingless females hatch in the spring and produce, by PARTHENOGENESIS and viviparously, up to 12 successive generations of wingless females. Winged females develop in the fall and migrate to another host plant, where a sexual generation is produced. The fertilized eggs, deposited in crevices of the plant, hatch the following spring and the cycle repeats itself. Insect enemies, fungi, and damp weather help to check the vast numbers of aphids. Many species exerete a sweet substance called honeydew, prized as food by ants, flies, and bees. Certain species of ants tend aphids as man does cattle, hence the name "ant cows." Among the aphids causing serious damage to food crops are the grain, cabbage, cornroot, apple, woolly apple, and hickory aphids and the alder and beech-tree blights. The PHYLLOXERA is closely related.

Aphik (ā'fĭk): see APHEK **2**.

Aphrah (ăf'rù), in the punning passage of Micah 1.10, apparently the name of a town. The name meant "dust" in Hebrew or sounded like a word meaning "dust," hence probably the use of the name.

Aphrodite (ăphrùdī'tē), in Greek religion, goddess of love and of beauty. In some myths she was the child of Zeus and Dione. In most myths she rose from the foam of the sea, and she is called Aphrodite Anadyomene (ănùdĭō'mùnē). She rose where Uranus' sex organ had fallen after he had been

Aphrodite

mutilated by Cronus. Worshiped throughout Greece, she differed in representation according to her various attributes. As Aphrodite Urania (ūrā'nēù), she was a celestial goddess, the embodiment of pure or spiritual love; as Aphrodite Pandemos (păndē'mùs), she was a goddess of marriage and family life, the essence of earthly or sensual love. She was also worshiped as a war goddess, as at Sparta, and as a sea goddess and patroness of sailors. Aphrodite had important cults at Cythera on Crete, at Paphos and Amathas on Cyprus, at Corinth, and at Mt. Eryx in Sicily. Probably of Eastern origin, she was similar in many of her attributes to the Oriental goddesses Astarte and Ishtar. Although Zeus gave her in marriage to Hephaestus, Aphrodite gave her love to others. She loved Ares, by whom she bore not only Harmonia but, in some myths, Eros and Anteros. She was the mother both of Hermaphroditus by Hermes and of Priapus by Dionysus. Zeus caused her to love the shepherd Anchises, by whom she bore Aeneas. ADONIS, in whose legend Aphrodite appears as a goddess of fertility, also won her favors. It was to Aphrodite that Paris awarded the apple of discord, which caused the dispute leading ultimately to the Trojan War. By the Romans, Aphrodite was identified with Venus.

Aphses (ăf'sēz) [Heb.,=dispersion], head of a priestly course. 1 Chron. 25.15.

Apia (ăpē'ù), town (pop. 19,023), capital of Western Samoa, on the northern coast of UPOLU island. The chief port of Western Samoa, it has been since 1923 the port of entry for TOKELAU.

Apianus, Petrus (pē'trùs āpēā'nùs), Latinized from **Peter Bienewitz** or **Bennewitz** (pā'tùr bē'nùvĭts, bĕn'ùvĭts), 1495–1552, German cosmographer and mathematician. He was professor of mathematics at Ingolstadt and was noted for his knowledge of astronomy and his general learning. Best known among his writings is the *Cosmographia* (1524), which has some of the earliest maps of America.

Apicius, Marcus Gabius (ŭpĭsh'ŭs), 1st cent. A.D., Roman gourmet. He squandered most of his large fortune on feasts and then, anticipating a need to economize, committed suicide. The cookbook called *Apicius* probably dates from a century later.

Apis (ā'pĭs), in Egyptian religion, sacred bull of Memphis, said to be the incarnation of Osiris or of Ptah. His worship spread throughout the Mediterranean world and was particularly important during the Roman Empire. See also SERAPIS.

Apo, Mount (ä'pō), active volcano, 9,690 ft. high, on S Mindanao, the Philippines. It is the highest peak of the islands.

apocalypse (ŭpŏk'ŭlĭps) [Gr.,=uncovering], type of ancient Hebrew and Christian literature dealing with the end of the world. The writing, mostly in the form of visions, is characterized by rich imagery and obscure symbols. In the New Testament the book of REVELATION is often called the Apocalypse. In the Old Testament apocalyptic elements appear extensively in Isaiah, Ezekiel, Daniel, Joel, and Zechariah. The book called 4 ESDRAS is one of the chief Jewish apocalypses; other PSEUDEPIGRAPHA are also apocalyptic. Modern books of this sort are seen among the works

Archangel Michael Battling the Dragon; 15th-century woodcut from Albrecht Dürer's Apocalypse.

of SWEDENBORG. See also FOUR HORSEMEN OF THE APOCALYPSE.

Apocrypha (ŭpŏk'rĭfů) [Gr.,=hidden things], appendix to the Authorized (or King James) Version of the Old Testament containing the following books and parts of books: 1 and 2 ESDRAS; TOBIT; JUDITH; ESTHER 10.4–16.24; WISDOM; ECCLESIASTICUS; BARUCH; Dan. 3.24–90 (see DANIEL and THREE HOLY CHILDREN); Dan. 13 (see SUSANNA 1); Dan. 14 (see BEL AND THE DRAGON); the Prayer of Manasses (see MANASSEH **2**); 1 and 2 MACCABEES. The Western canon includes all these except 1 and 2 Esdras and the Prayer of Manasses, which are often given in an appendix to editions of the Vulgate (where the 1 and 2 Esdras of the Apocrypha are called 3 and 4 Esdras). For Protestants the Apocrypha is not an ultimate norm of doctrine, discipline, and worship (see OLD TESTAMENT). For Jewish and Christian works resembling biblical books but not included in the Western or the Hebrew canon—sometimes called apocryphal—see PSEUDEPIGRAPHA. See B. M. Metzger, *An Introduction to the Apocrypha* (1957).

Apodaca, Juan Ruiz de (hwän' rōōēth' dä äpōdhä'-kä), 1754–1835, Spanish viceroy and military leader. He was sent to London by the Central Junta of Seville to gain English support against Napoleon. After service as governor of Cuba (1812–15), Apodaca, as viceroy of New Spain (1816–21), devoted himself to repressing revolutionary movements. The royalist cause was at first successful, but with the defection of Iturbide it failed. Feeling that Apodaca was not making sufficient effort to put down the revolution, a group in Mexico city, headed by the Masons, forced him to surrender his authority. He returned (1821) to Spain where he held various offices. He had the title visconde de Venadito.

Apollinaire, Guillaume (gēyōm' äpōlēnâr'), 1880–1918, French poet. An illegitimate child, he was christened Wilhelm Apollinaris de Kostrowitzky. Apollinaire, a leader in the restless period of technical innovation and experiment in the arts in the early 20th cent., wrote Gothic short stories (as in *L'Hérésiarche et Cie*, 1910) and bizarre, lyrical poems (collected especially in *Alcools*, 1913, and *Calligrammes*, 1918), which contributed to the formation of a new school of French poetry. His book *Les Peintres cubistes* (1913; Eng. tr., *The Cubist Painters*, 1949) explained the new painting (see CUBISM). *Les Mamelles de Tirésias* (1918), a play, was one of the earliest examples of SURREALISM, and he called the technique the rational arrangement of the improbable.

Apollinarianism (ŭpŏlĭnâ'rēŭnĭzŭm), heretical doctrine taught by Apollinaris or Apollinarius (c.315–c.390), bishop of Laodicea, near Antioch. A celebrated scholar and teacher, author of scriptural commentary, philosophy, and controversial treatises, he propounded the theory that Christ possessed the Logos in place of a human mind, and hence, while perfectly divine, he was not fully human. Apollinarianism was popular in spite of its repeated condemnation, particularly by the First Council of Constantinople. It anticipated MONOPHYSITISM.

Apollinaris Sidonius (Caius Sollius Apollinaris Sidonius) (ŭpŏlĭnâ'rĭs sĭdō'nēŭs, sĭdō'–), fl. 455–75, Latin writer, b. Lyons. He had a minor part in imperial politics and was bishop of Clermont. He wrote inconsequential panegyric poetry and letters that are an interesting historical source. Canonized by the Roman Catholic Church, he is called St. Sidonius.

Apollo (ùpŏ′lō), in Greek religion, one of the most important OLYMPIAN gods, concerned especially with prophecy, medicine, music and poetry,

Apollo Belvedere

archery, and various bucolic arts, particularly the care of flocks and herds. His cult was Panhellenic, and his prophecies bore great authority. His chief oracular shrine was at DELPHI, which he was said to have seized, while still an infant, by killing its guardian, the serpent Python. This event was celebrated every eight years in the festival of the Stepteria, in which a youth impersonating Apollo set fire to a hut (called the palace of Python) and then went into exile to Tempe, where he was purified of his deed. At Delphi, Apollo was primarily a god of purification. He had other notable shrines at Branchidae, Claros, Patara, and on the island of Delos, where it was said he and his twin sister, Artemis, were born to LETO and Zeus. Apollo was a highly moral god, frequently associated with the higher developments of civilization, such as law, philosophy, and the arts. As patron of music and poetry, he was often connected with the MUSES and was said to be the father of Orpheus by Calliope. Apollo may have been first worshiped by primitive shepherds as a god of pastures and flocks; but it was as a god of light, Phoebus or Phoebus Apollo (fē′bùs), that he was most widely known. After the 5th cent. B.C. he was frequently identified with Helios, the sun-god. Apollo was the father of Aristaeus and of Asclepius. His amorous affairs, however, were not particularly successful. Daphne turned into a laurel rather than submit to him, and Marpessa refused him in favor of a mortal. In Roman religion he was worshiped in various forms, most significantly as a god of healing and of prophecy. In art he was portrayed as the perfection of youth and beauty. The most celebrated statue of him is the **Apollo Belvedere** (bĕl″vĭdēr′), a marble statue in the Belvedere of the Vatican,

Rome, a Roman copy, dating from the early empire, of a Greek original in bronze. The right forearm and the left hand were restored by a pupil of Michelangelo. The statue represents the god as a vigorous and triumphant youth, naked except for the chlamys draped over his extended left arm.

Apollo, borough (pop. 2,694), W Pa., NE of Pittsburgh; laid out 1815, inc. 1848. Steel is made.

Apollo Belvedere: see APOLLO, in Greek religion.

Apollodorus (ùpŏl″ōdôr′ùs), fl. 430–400 B.C., Athenian painter, called the Shadower, said to have introduced the use of light and shade to model form. Among his few known works are *Ajax Struck by Lightning* and *Priest in the Act of Devotion;* both were at Pergamum in the time of Pliny the Elder.

Apollonia (ăpŭlō′nĕù) [Gr.,=of Apollo], name of several ancient Greek towns. The most important was a port in Illyricum on the Adriatic. It was founded by Corinthians and was later a Greek and a Roman intellectual center. Julius Caesar used it as a base. Octavian (later AUGUSTUS) was here when he received news of Julius Caesar's death. Among the other towns of this name, there was one in Thrace on the Aegean (a town famous for a large statue of Apollo), one in N Sicily, and another in the Chalcidice (visited by Paul on his way to Salonica. Acts 17.1).

Apollonius (ăp″ùlō′nēùs) [Latin,=of Apollo]. **1** Governor of Coele-Syria and Phoenicia for Seleucus IV. He oppressed the Jews and was killed by Judas Maccabaeus. 1 Mac. 3.10–24; 2 Mac. 4.4; 5.24. **2** Governor of Coele-Syria under Alexander Balas. 1 Mac. 10.69.

Apollonius of Perga, fl. 247–205 B.C., Greek mathematician of the Alexandrian school. He produced a treatise on conic sections which included, as well as his own work, much of the work of his predecessors, among whom was Euclid. In the works of Apollonius of Perga Greek mathematics reached its culmination.

Apollonius of Tralles: see FARNESE BULL.

Apollonius of Tyana (tīä′nù), fl. A.D. 100?, Greek philosopher, leading exponent of Neo-Pythagorean-

Apollonius of Tyana

ism (see PYTHAGORAS). Inasmuch as his biographer, Philostratus, is considered unreliable, nothing is certainly known of Apollonius' life. Of his works, only fragments of a biography of Pythagoras and a treatise on sacrifice are extant.

Christ and the Apostles; The Tribute Money, fresco by Masaccio.

Apollonius Rhodius (rō'dē-us), 3d cent. B.C., epic poet of Alexandria and Rhodes. He became librarian at Alexandria. His extant work, the *Argonautica*, is a Homeric imitation in four books on the story of the Argonaut heroes; he and Callimachus carried on a famous literary quarrel.

Apollos (ù-pŏl'ùs) [Gr.,=belonging to Apollo], Alexandrian Jew who became a Christian missionary. Acts 18.24–19.1; 1 Cor. 1.12; 3.4–6; 4.6.

Apollyon (ù-pŏl'yùn), Greek name of the destroying angel. Rev. 9.11. See SATAN and HELL.

Apopka (ù-pŏp'kù), city (pop. 3,578), central Fla., NW of Orlando; settled 1856. It is a growing center for house plants. Sanlando Springs and Rock Springs are nearby.

Apopka, Lake, central Fla., popular fishing lake. Winter Garden is on its south shore.

apoplexy or **stroke,** destruction of brain tissue as a result of intracerebral hemorrhage, THROMBOSIS (clotting), or embolism (obstruction in a blood vessel caused by clotted blood or other matter foreign to the blood stream). Cerebral hemorrhage or thrombosis usually occurs in elderly persons with constricted arteries (see ARTERIOSCLEROSIS) although either may also be caused by inflammatory or toxic damage to the cerebral blood vessels. Cerebral embolism may occur at any age, even in children. Symptoms of stroke develop suddenly. In severe brain damage there may be deep coma, paralysis of one side of the body, and loss of speech, followed by death or by permanent neurological disturbances after recovery. If the brain damage sustained has been slight, there is usually complete recovery. When the stroke has been caused by thrombosis or by an EMBOLUS, anticoagulants are administered to prevent further attacks. The injection of procaine hydrochloride,

a local anesthetic, into nerve cells at the base of the neck is reported to bring patients out of coma almost immediately, and the administration of cortisone has been found to accelerate recovery of victims of strokes from blood clots.

apostle (ù-pŏs'ùl) [Gr.,=envoy], one of the prime missionaries of Christendom. The apostles par excellence are SS. PETER, ANDREW, JAMES (the Greater), JOHN, THOMAS, JAMES (the Less), JUDE (or Thaddaeus), PHILIP, BARTHOLOMEW, MATTHEW, SIMON, and MATTHIAS (replacing JUDAS ISCARIOT). Traditionally the list of the Twelve Disciples includes Judas and not Matthias, and the list of the Twelve Apostles includes Matthias and not Judas. St. PAUL is always classed as an apostle, and so are sometimes a few others, such as St. BARNABAS. The principal missionary to any country is often called its apostle, e.g., St. Patrick is the apostle of Ireland, St. Augustine the apostle of England. For the Apostles' Creed, see CREED; for the *Teaching of the Apostles,* see DIDACHE; for the earliest account of their activities, see ACTS OF THE APOSTLES. See E. J. Goodspeed, *The Twelve: the Story of Christ's Apostles* (1957).

Apostle Islands, group of over 20 islands, off N Wisconsin, in SW Lake Superior. Their wave-eroded cliffs are noted. Madeline, the largest, is reached by ferry from Bayfield and includes the town of La Pointe (pop. 130). A French trading post was built here in 1693, evacuated in 1698, and reoccupied from 1718 to 1759. Later (early 19th cent.) the American Fur Company had a post here.

Apostolic Constitutions: see CONSTITUTIONS, APOSTOLIC.

apostolic delegate: see LEGATE.

apostolic succession, in Christian theology, the doctrine asserting that the chosen successors of the apostles enjoyed through God's grace the same authority, power, and responsibility as the apostles. Therefore the bishops of today, as the successors of previous bishops, going back to the apostles, have this power by virtue of this unbroken chain. For the Orthodox, Roman Catholic, and Anglican churches, this link with the apostles is what guarantees for them their authority in matters of faith, morals, and the valid administration of sacraments. Essential to maintaining the apostolic succession is the right consecration of bishops. Apostolic succession is to be distinguished from the Petrine supremacy (see PAPACY). Protestants see the authority given to the apostles as unique, proper to them alone, and hence reject any doctrine of a succession of their power. The Protestant view of ecclesiastical authority differs accordingly. See ORDERS, HOLY; CHURCH.

apostrophe: see PUNCTUATION and ABBREVIATION.

apotheosis (ŭpŏ″thēō′sĭs, ă″pŭthē′ŭsĭs), the act of raising a person who has died to the rank of a god. Historically, it was most important during the later Roman Empire. In an emperor's lifetime his genius was worshiped, but after he died he was often solemnly enrolled as one of the gods to be publicly adored. It is difficult to say where ANCESTOR WORSHIP ends and apotheosis begins, at least so far as a royal family is concerned.

Apoxyomenus (ŭpŏk″sēŏm′ĭn ŭs) [Gr.,=scraping one's self], a Roman copy in marble of a bronze statue (c.325–300 B.C.) by LYSIPPUS. It represents an athlete scraping the sand and oil from his body with a strigil after a contest in the palaestra. It was found in Rome in 1849 and is preserved in the Vatican.

Appaim (ăp′āĭm) [Heb.,=the nostrils], Jerahmeelite. 1 Chron. 2.30,31.

Appalachia (ăpŭlăch′ŭ), town (pop. 2,456), extreme SW Va., in the Cumberland Plateau near the Ky. line, NW of Bristol; settled 1890, inc. 1906. It is a railroad junction in a coal region.

Appalachian Mountains (ăpŭlā′chŭn, —chĕŭn, —lăch′–), general name for the numerous groups of elevations in E North America, extending SW from the St. Lawrence valley in Quebec prov., Canada, to the Gulf Coast plain in Alabama. They include the WHITE MOUNTAINS, GREEN MOUNTAINS, CATSKILL MOUNTAINS, ALLEGHENY MOUNTAINS, BLUE RIDGE, BLACK MOUNTAINS, GREAT SMOKY MOUNTAINS, CUMBERLAND PLATEAU, and other ranges. The Appalachians, mainly formed by folding (see MOUNTAIN), consist largely of sedimentary rocks and are for the most part much worn down. In general, the eastern portions are more rugged than the western, which are largely plateau formations of horizontal rock structure. Mt. Mitchell, 6,684 ft. high, in the Black Mts., is the highest elevation in the system. Valuable coal deposits, iron, petroleum, and gas are found in parts of the Appalachians. Comprising some of the most beautiful scenery in the U.S., the mountains abound in resorts. Crossed by few passes, the system especially in the central sections was a barrier against early westward expansion and played an important part in the history of the United States. See Douglas W. Johnson, *Stream Sculpture on the Atlantic Slope* (1931); N. M. Fenneman, *Physiography of Eastern United States* (1938).

Appalachian Trail, for hikers, extending 2,050 mi. along the ridges of the Appalachian Mt. system from Mt. Katahdin, Maine, to Mt. Oglethorpe, N Ga. It owes its inception to Benton MACKAYE. See guides published by the Appalachian Trail Conference.

Appalachicola: see APALACHICOLA.

apparition, spiritualistic manifestation of a person or object in which a form not actually present is seen with such intensity that belief in its reality is created. The ancient and widespread belief in apparitions and ghosts (specters of dead persons) is based on the idea that the spirit of a man, or of

The Blue Ridge Parkway joins Great Smoky Mountains National Park in western North Carolina. The Great Smokies are part of the Appalachian range.

any object, is endowed with volition and motion of its own. Apparitions, especially particular shapes attached to certain legends or superstitions, are often considered as premonitions or warnings. They may appear in any form and may manifest themselves to any or all the senses. The most malignant apparitions are said to be those of persons who have died violent or unnatural deaths, those with guilty secrets, and those who were unburied or not buried with proper rites. However, not all apparitions are believed to be dangerous; many, especially those associated with a particular religion, are thought to be signs of divine intervention. Summoning apparitions by means of incantations, crystal gazing, polished stones, hypnotic suggestion, and various other ways is one of the oldest practices of DIVINATION. See also SPIRITISM.

appeal, in law, hearing by a superior court to consider correcting or reversing the judgment of an inferior court, because of errors allegedly committed by the inferior court. The party appealing the decision is known as the appellant, the party who has won the case in the lower court as the appellee. The term is also sometimes used to describe the review by a court of the action of a government board or administrative officer. There are two types of errors, of fact and of law. An error of fact is drawing a false inference from evidence presented at the trial. An error of law is an erroneous determination of the legal rules governing PROCEDURE, EVIDENCE, or the matters at issue between the parties. Ordinarily, only errors of law may be reviewed in appeal. In an appeal from an action tried in equity, however, the appellate court passes on the entire record, both as to facts and law. Should the appeals court conclude that no error was committed, it will affirm the decision of the lower court. If it finds that there was error, it may direct a retrial or grant a JUDGMENT OR DECREE in favor of the party who lost in the lower court. The determinations of appeals courts are usually printed, often with an opinion indicating the basis for the court's decisions. Such opinions are of great utility in guiding the inferior courts and are often cited as precedents in future cases.

appendix, a small tubular structure, 3 to 4 in. long and ¼ to 1 in. thick, projecting from the caecum (large intestine) on the right side of the lower abdominal cavity. The structure has no function in man and is considered a vestigial remnant of some previous organ or structure that was unnecessary to man in his evolutionary progress. Infection of an accumulation and hardening of waste matter in the appendix may give rise to **appendicitis,** the symptoms of which are severe pain in the abdomen, nausea, vomiting, fever, abdominal tenderness, and muscle spasm. A blood count usually shows a rise in the number of white corpuscles. Appendicitis may occur at any age, although it is more prevalent in persons under 40 years of age. The danger in appendicitis is that the appendix can rupture, either spontaneously or because the patient has injudiciously been given laxatives or an enema, and that the infection can spread to the peritoneum (see PERITONITIS). Surgery is indicated in appendicitis, preceded and followed by antibiotic therapy.

Appenzell (ä'pûntsĕl), canton, NE Switzerland. A rural and sparsely populated region, it is mainly a meadowland dotted with small farms. Appenzell retains many ancient customs and is famous as a centuries-old embroidery center. It was ruled after the 11th cent. by the abbots of St. Gall, against whom it revolted in 1403. In 1411 Appenzell allied itself with the Swiss Confederation, which had helped defeat the abbots. It became a Swiss canton in 1513, and in 1597 it split into two independent half-cantons. Ausser-Rhoden or Outer Rhodes (94 sq. mi.; pop. 48,920), with its capital at HERISAU, accepted the Reformation. Inner-Rhoden or Inner Rhodes (67 sq. mi.; pop. 12,943), with its capital at the town of Appenzell (estimated pop. 5,001), remained Catholic.

Appert, Nicolas (nēkôlä' äpâr'), sometimes known as **François Appert** (fräswä'), 1750–1841?, French originator of a method of CANNING. This process, based on his theory that heat destroys or neutralizes the ferments which cause food spoilage, consisted in heating foods for varying periods in corked bottles. After years of experimentation he opened in 1806 a factory (destroyed 1814) at Massy, near Paris, and in 1810 published his results (Eng. tr., *The Art of Preserving,* 1920), winning a prize of 12,000 francs which had been offered by the French government for a method of preserving foods for army and navy stores. He lost public confidence after an investigation by Gay-Lussac, who, although supporting Appert's method, opposed his theory. However, through the influence of Berthollet, Appert was able in 1817 to establish a factory in Paris.

Apphia (ăf'ēù), Christian woman associated with Philemon. Philemon 2.

Appia, Adolphe (à'dôlf' äp'pyä), 1862–1928, Swiss theorist of modern stage lighting and décor. In interpreting the ideas of Wagner in scenic designs for his operas, Appia rejected painted scenery for the three-dimensional set; he felt that shade was as necessary as light to link the actor to this setting in time and space. His use of light, through intensity, color, and mobility, to set the atmosphere and mood of a play created a new perspective in SCENE DESIGN. See his *Work of Living Art* and *Man Is the Measure of All Things* (Eng. tr., 1960).

Appian (ă'pēun), fl. 2d cent., Roman historian. He was a Greek, born in Alexandria. His history of the Roman conquests from the founding of Rome to the reign of Trajan is strongly biased in favor of Roman imperialism, but it reproduces many documents and sources which otherwise would have been lost. Of the 24 books, written in Greek, only Books VI–VII and Books XI–XVII have been fully preserved.

Appiani, Andrea (ändrä'ä äp-pyä'nē), 1754–1817, Italian neoclassical painter and Napoleon's Italian court painter, active in Lombardy. His frescoes include work in churches and palaces of Milan. A portrait of Canova is among his oils.

Appian Way (ă'pēun), Latin *Via Appia,* most famous of the ROMAN ROADS, built (312 B.C.) under Appius Claudius Caecus. It connected Rome with Capua and was later extended to Beneventum (now Benevento), Tarentum (Taranto), and Brundisium (Brindisi). It was the chief highway to Greece and the East. Its total length was more

The ancient Appian Way near Rome, Italy.

to several insect and fungus pests, for which the orchards are sprayed. The hardwood is used for cabinetmaking and fuel. The crab apples are wild North American and Asiatic species of *Malus* now cultivated as ornamentals for their fragrant white to deep pink blossoms—e.g., the American sweet or garland crab apple (*M. coronaria*), the prairie crab apple (*M. ioensis*), and the Siberian crab-apple (*M. baccata*). The small, hard, sour crab-

Red Delicious apples on branch.

than 350 mi. The substantial construction of cemented stone blocks has preserved it to the present. Branch roads led to Neapolis (Naples), Barium (Bari), and other ports. On the first stretch of road out of Rome are interesting tombs and the Church of St. Sebastian with its catacombs. In 1784 Pope Pius VI built the new Appian Way from Rome to Albano, parallel with the old.

Appii forum (ăp′ēī) [Latin,=Appius′ market], important stop on the Appian Way, c.40 mi. E of Rome. It was at the head of a canal through the Pontine Marshes. When Paul arrived here on his way to Rome, he was met by Christians from the city. Acts 28.15. The modern Italian successor is Foro Appio.

Appius Claudius: see CLAUDIUS, Roman gens.

apple, any tree of the genus *Malus* of the ROSE family. Apples were formerly considered species of the pear genus *Pyrus*, with which they share the characteristic pome fruit. The common apple (*M. sylvestris*) is the best known and is commercially the most important temperate fruit. Apparently native to the Caucasus mountains of W Asia, it has been under cultivation since prehistoric times. According to ancient tradition the forbidden fruit of the Garden of Eden was the apple (Gen. 3). In religious painting, the apple represents the fruit of the tree of knowledge of good and evil, as do occasionally the pear and the quince. It was sacred to Aphrodite in classical mythology. The apple is now widely grown in thousands of varieties, e.g., the Golden Delicious, Winesap, Jonathan, and McIntosh. The tree is hardy in cold climates and the firm fruit is easy to handle and store. Most apples are consumed fresh, but some are canned or used for juice. Apple juice (sweet cider) is partly fermented to produce hard cider and fully fermented to make vinegar. Wastes from fermenting processes are a major source of PECTIN. APPLEJACK is a liquor made from hard cider. Western Europe, especially France, is the chief apple-producing region; in North America, also with an enormous total output, Washington is the leading apple-growing state, but very many areas grow crops at least for local consumption. The tree is subject

apple fruits are used for preserves, pickles, and jelly; in growth and culture these trees are similar to the common apple.

Appleby, John Francis, 1840–1917, American farmer, b. Oneida co., N.Y. He was the inventor of the Appleby knotter, patented in 1878 after long experimenting. It was first manufactured on a large scale after its value was recognized by William Deering and it was soon adopted on harvesters generally. It is still commonly used on grain binders.

Appleby, municipal borough (pop. 1,751), county town of Westmorland, N England, in the Eden valley. A market center, it has a 16th-century grammar school.

Applegarth, Robert, 1834–1924, English trade-union leader, a carpenter by trade, b. Kingston-on-Hull. A charter member of the Amalgamated Society of Carpenters and Joiners, he became in 1862 its general secretary; under his leadership the society, with other unions, pressed the fight for legalization of unions and for protection of their funds. This fight was successfully concluded in 1871. See biography by A. W. Humphrey (1913); John Bowditch and Clement Ramsland, *Voices of the Industrial Revolution* (1961).

Applegate, Jesse, 1811–88, American pioneer in Oregon, b. Kentucky. With his family he moved (1821) to Missouri, and there in 1843 he joined the "great emigration" of more than 900 people over the Oregon Trail—a trek pictured in his *Day with the Cow Column in 1843* (ed. by Joseph Schafer, 1934, pub. with *Recollections of My Boyhood* by Applegate's nephew). A leader on the westward journey, he was elected (1845) a member of the legislative committee of the provisional government which ruled Oregon until it became (1849) a U.S. territory. Later he helped organize the new government and, as surveyor general, did much exploring and opened a wagon route to California.

applejack, brandy made by partly freezing hard cider and removing the ice or by distilling hard cider or fermented apple pomace. It is said to have been made in this country as early as 1698. Approximately half of the volume produced each year is distilled in New Jersey.

apple of discord: see PARIS, in Greek mythology.

Appleseed, Johnny: see CHAPMAN, JOHN.

Appleton, Daniel, 1785–1849, American publisher, b. Haverhill, Mass. He built up in New York one of the largest publishing houses in the country. The firm was continued by his sons under the name D. Appleton & Company. See G. M. Overton, *Portrait of a Publisher* (1925).

Appleton, Sir Edward Victor, 1892–, English physicist, grad. St. John's College, Cambridge. After returning from active service in the First World War he became assistant demonstrator in experimental physics at the Cavendish Laboratory in 1920. He was professor of physics at the Univ. of London (1924–36) and professor of natural philosophy at Cambridge Univ. (1936–39). From 1939

to 1949 he was secretary of the Dept. of Scientific and Industrial Research. Knighted in 1941, he received the 1947 Nobel Prize in Physics for his contributions to the knowledge of the ionosphere which led to the development of radar.

Appleton. 1 Village (pop. 2,172), W Minn., on the Pomme de Terre and NW of Montevideo; settled 1869, laid out 1870, inc. 1871. It is a farm trade center. All streets in the village are named after its citizens who were killed in the Second World War. **2** City (pop. 48,411), co. seat of Outagamie co., E Wis., on the Fox near its exit from the north end of Lake Winnebago, in a dairying and stock-raising region; settled in the 1830s, inc. 1857. Falls provide power for the city's industries. Appleton makes paper and wood products, woolen goods, and machinery. It had the nation's first hydroelectric plant (1882) and the state's first electric streetcar (1886). The city is the seat of LAWRENCE COLLEGE OF WISCONSIN. Harry Houdini was born in Appleton.

Appleton City, city (pop. 1,075), W Mo., SE of Kansas City, in a farm and timber area; founded 1868, inc. 1870.

apple worm: see CODLING MOTH.

appliqué: see EMBROIDERY and NEEDLEWORK.

Appomattox (ăpŭmă′tŭks), town (pop. 1,184), co. seat of Appomattox co., central Va., E of Lynchburg, near the source of the Appomattox river; inc. 1925. R. E. Lee surrendered to U. S. Grant at nearby **Appomattox Courthouse,** April 9, 1865. After P. H. Sheridan's victory at Five Forks on April 1, 1865, Lee abandoned PETERSBURG and Richmond and retreated west, planning to unite at Danville, Va., with the army of J. E. Johnston, who was still holding out against W. T. Sherman in North Carolina. But Grant pursued vigorously. Part of the Union army pressed hard on Lee's flank and rear, while Sheridan cut off further retreat at Appomattox Courthouse. Realizing the futility of carrying on the struggle, Lee surrendered the remnants of the Army of Northern Virginia on April 9. The surrender marked the virtual end of the war, as the remaining Confederate armies, on hearing of Lee's capitulation, followed suit. The site of the

Appomatox courthouse

General Robert E. Lee (left) signs the document surrendering the Army of Northern Virginia to General Ulysses S. Grant (center, seated).

surrender has been made a national historical park (937.34 acres; est. 1954). See Burke Davis, *To Appomattox: 9 April Days, 1865* (1959).

Apponaug, R.I.: see WARWICK.

Apponyi, Albert, Count (ŏp'pônyē), 1846–1933, Hungarian statesman. The son of the conservative chancellor, George Apponyi, he entered the house of deputies in 1872. Though a royalist, he favored liberal electoral reforms and, as minister of education (1907), free education in elementary schools. However, the rigid state control which accompanied his program roused bitter opposition. In 1920, as chief Hungarian delegate to the Paris Peace Conference, Apponyi signed, under protest, the Treaty of Trianon (see TRIANON, TREATY OF). He represented his country in the League of Nations until his death.

apprenticeship, system of learning a trade from one who is engaged in it and of paying for the instruction by a given number of years of work. Apprenticeship flourishes wherever there is handicraft production. It was known in ancient Babylon, Egypt, Greece, and Rome, as well as in Europe and to some extent in the United States. Typically, a master of a trade agrees to instruct a young man, to give him shelter, food, and clothing, and to care for him during illness. The young man binds himself to work for the master for a given time. After that he may become a journeyman, working for a master for wages; then—sometimes without service as a journeyman—he may set up as a master himself. The medieval guilds supervised to some extent the relation of master and apprentice and decided the number of apprentices in a given guild. The Industrial Revolution, with its introduction of machinery, put an end to most of these guilds, but apprenticeship continues in highly skilled trades, competing with technical schools. The terms of apprenticeship are regulated by many trade unions, as well as by law. It is sometimes arranged for orphans and other wards of the state. In recent years trainee programs, providing for work at reduced pay levels while in training, have been instituted by many corporations.

appropriation, in constitutional law, the allotment by a legislature of money for a particular purpose. The Constitution of the United States provides that no money may be drawn from the Treasury except under appropriations made by law and that no appropriations shall be made for more than two years. In the United States a general appropriation bill is passed at the beginning of each session of Congress; in England, at the end of sessions of Parliament. Legislative appropriation is always required in democratic governments. See also BUDGET.

APRA (ä'prä), or the *Alianza Popular Revolucionaria Americana,* now officially called the Partido Aprista, a radical political party generally confined to Peru. Members are called Apristas. Founded (1924) by Víctor Raúl HAYA DE LA TORRE while in exile, the party advocates radical reform, particularly the emancipation of the Indian, the betterment of agrarian conditions, and some socialization of industry. During Haya de la Torre's exile, José Carlos MARIÁTEGUI was its leading spokesman in Peru. In the early years of the party Latin American nationalism was also an important fea-

ture of its program. Though originally influenced by Marxism, it is expressly anti-Communist. Characterized as rabble rousers and implicated in acts of political terror, the Apristas were outlawed from 1931 to 1945, when the party virtually took control of Peru. In 1948, following an abortive Aprista-led revolt in the port city of Callao, and with the country on the verge of civil war, a military junta headed by General Manuel ODRÍA took power, and the party was again outlawed. The APRA party was legalized in 1956 when Manuel Prado, a conservative, was elected president with its support. In the 1962 presidential election, later invalidated by another military coup, the party obtained a majority of the votes.

Apra Harbor (ä'prä) or **Port Apra,** on the west coast of Guam, WSW of Agana. The only good harbor on the island, it is a port of entry closed to foreign vessels except by permit. There is a large U.S. naval base here.

Apraksin, Feodor Matveyevich (fyô'dŭr mŭtvyä'ŭvĭch ŭpräk'syĭn), 1671–1728, Russian admiral. He helped Peter the Great create the Russian navy and won several naval battles in Peter's wars against Sweden. He was made count in 1709.

apricot [Arabic from Latin, =early ripe], tree, *Prunus armeniaca,* and its fruit, of the plum genus of the ROSE family, native to temperate Asia and long

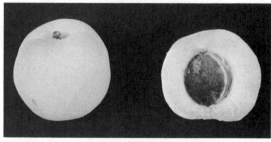

Apricot

cultivated in Armenia. The fruit is used raw, canned, preserved, and dried. California is the chief place of cultivation in the United States, although by selecting suitable varieties the apricot can be grown in most regions where the peach is hardy. Apricots are used in the making of a cordial and also for apricot brandy.

Apries (ā'prē-ēz), king of ancient Egypt (588–569 B.C.), of the XXVI dynasty. Successor of Psamtik II, Apries sought to recover Syria and Palestine. He attacked Tyre and Sidon but failed (586 B.C.) to relieve the siege of Jerusalem by NEBUCHADNEZZAR. A revolt in Egypt caused him to seek the assistance of AMASIS II, who killed him and took the throne. Apries is called Pharaoh-Hophra (fā'rōhŏf'rŭ) in the Bible (Jer. 44).

April: see MONTH.

apse [Gr., =round vault, loop], the termination at the sanctuary end of a church, generally semicircular in plan but sometimes square or polygonal. The apse appeared early in Roman temples and basilicas; it was originally a semicircular recess with a half

Apse of the Basilica di San Vitale in Ravenna, Italy.

dome as ceiling and contained the monumental statue of the deity. The motive was adopted in the early Christian churches; in these the apse occupied the eastern end of the building where the altar, the bishop's throne, and the seats of the clergy were placed. A fine example of this early form is in the cathedral of Torcello near Venice. Because of its location and function in the church services, the apse became the architectural climax of the church interior and was richly ornamented. In the early churches, the half-dome ceiling was incrusted with handsome mosaics, the walls were veneered with fine marbles, and the altar and pulpits were also richly decorated. The apse steadily increased in liturgical and architectural emphasis, chapels were added to it. In English Gothic architecture the apse was in most cases a square termination, and in Italy its form remained a simple semicircle, as the chapels were in another part of the church. In France the entire choir—composed of apse, ambulatory, and radiating chapels (the whole termed a *chevet*)—attained, in the 12th and 13th cent., its great splendor.

Apsheron (ŭpshĭrôn′), peninsula, E Azerbaijan SSR. Extending c.40 mi. into the Caspian Sea, it is a hilly area at the eastern end of the Greater Caucasus mountain range. One of the USSR's major oil reserves, it has fields at Balakhany, Sabunchi, and Surakhany. There are also natural gas wells, salt lakes, mineral springs, and mud volcanoes. The peninsula is considered part of Greater BAKU.

apteryx: see KIWI.

Apuleius, Lucius (ă″pyoōlē′ŭs), fl. 2d cent., Latin writer, b. Hippo (now Bône, Algeria). His *Golden Ass* or *Metamorphoses*, a romance, is the only Latin novel to survive in entirety. It has been tremendously popular, influencing strongly the later novel, e.g., the works of Boccaccio, Cervantes, Fielding, and Smollett. Other works by Apuleius include *The Apology* or *On Magic*, his defense in a suit brought by his wife's family for gaining her affections by magic; *Florida*, an anthology from his own works; and *On the God of Socrates*, *On the Philosophy of Plato*, and *On the World*, philosophical treatises.

Offshore oil wells on the Apsheron peninsula.

308